SECULAR CHORAL MUSIC IN PRINT

1991 SUPPLEMENT

Edited by

F. Mark Daugherty

and

Susan H. Simon

Music-In-Print Series, Vol. 2s

MUSICDATA, INC.
Philadelphia, 1991

The Music-In-Print Series to date:

Vols. 1a,b. Sacred Choral Music In Print, Second Edition (1985)
Vol. 1c. Sacred Choral Music In Print, Second Edition: Arranger Index (1987)
Vol. 1s. Sacred Choral Music In Print: 1988 Supplement
Vols. 2a,b. Secular Choral Music In Print, Second Edition (1987)
Vol. 2c. Secular Choral Music In Print, Second Edition: Arranger Index (1987)
Vol. 2s. Secular Choral Music In Print: 1991 Supplement
Vol. 3. Organ Music In Print, Second Edition (1984)
Vol. 3s. Organ Music In Print: 1990 Supplement
Vol. 4. Classical Vocal Music In Print (1976) (out of print)
Vol. 4s. Classical Vocal Music In Print: 1985 Supplement
Vol. 5. Orchestral Music In Print (1979)
Educational Section of Orchestral Music In Print (1978)
Orchestral Music In Print: 1983 Supplement
Vol. 6. String Music In Print, Second Edition (1973) (out of print)
String Music In Print: 1984 Supplement
Vol. 7. Classical Guitar Music In Print (1989)
Music-In-Print Master Composer Index 1988
Music-In-Print Master Title Index 1988

Music-In-Print Series: ISSN 0146-7883

Copyright © 1991 by Musicdata, Inc.

All rights reserved under International and Pan-American Copyright Conventions by Musicdata, Inc.

Printed by Port City Press, Baltimore, Maryland

Musicdata, Inc.
P.O. Box 48010
Philadelphia, Pennsylvania 19144-8010

Library of Congress Cataloging-in-Publication Data

Daugherty, F. Mark, 1951-
    Secular choral music in print. 1991 supplement / edited by F.
Mark Daugherty and Susan H. Simon.
        p.   cm. — (Music-in-print series, ISSN 0146-7883 ; vol. 2s)
    Includes index.
    ISBN 0-88478-027-9
    1. Choral music—Bibliography. I. Simon, Susan H. 1943-
II. Title. III. Series: Music-in-print series ; v. 2s.
ML128.V7D3   1987 Suppl.
016.7825′4′0263—dc20
                                                    91-15287
                                                    CIP
                                                    MN

Contents

Preface.. v

Guide to Use.. vii

List of Abbreviations xi

Secular Choral Music In Print: 1991 Supplement 1

Arranger Index....................................... 131

Publisher Directory 147

Advertisements 177

　　　Index to Advertisers............................... 177

Preface

Present day choruses and choirs have ready access to a larger and more varied repertoire than was available to the most knowledgeable and sophisticated musicians of earlier periods. The thousands of publications listed in the present volume, along with those contained in *Secular Choral Music In Print, 2nd Edition,* offer a choice of music from more than six centuries. Although many of the publications listed in these volumes are new editions of old works, it is also true that contemporary composers have not neglected the choral medium either. Conductors wishing to present varied and unusual programs can certainly find the musical materials listed within these pages.

Musicdata has endeavored to provide as complete a list as possible of secular choral music in print throughout the world. *Secular Choral Music In Print: 1991 Supplement* is designed to be used in conjunction with *Secular Choral Music In Print, 2nd Edition* and contains listings of music published since 1986.

The scope of *Secular Choral Music In Print: 1991 Supplement* includes all published secular music intended for performance by choral ensembles with and without accompaniment. However, the issue of whether a piece is secular or sacred remains a problem and we must often rely on a publisher's indications to resolve the matter. In the absence of any guidance from the publisher we have chosen to include pieces that straddle the line and may also be suitable for religious worship services.

The distinction between composer and arranger is often blurred and inconsistent in publishers' catalogs. Since this editorial question is impossible to resolve, we have once again included an Arranger Index enabling the user to look up a piece under both composer and arranger.

We have attempted to rotate initial articles in titles to aid alphabetizing and this practice is followed with German, French, Danish, Dutch, Italian, Spanish, Norwegian, and Swedish articles.

Music publishers have actively participated in the preparation of this volume by submitting catalogs marked with their new listings published since the revised edition of the base volume appeared in 1987. Obviously, our work is very dependent on the cooperation of music publishers and we wish to offer our thanks to those publishers who have generously assisted us by providing accurate, up-to-date listings.

We wish to thank Margaret Farish for her invaluable assistance with the Publisher Directory, and thanks again to Mark Resnick whose tireless efforts and vision have made the Music-In-Print Series a reality.

Philadelphia, Pennsylvania
March 1991

F. Mark Daugherty
Susan H. Simon

Guide to Use

THE MUSIC-IN-PRINT SERIES

The Music-In-Print series is an ongoing effort to locate and catalog all music in print throughout the world. The intention is to cover all areas of music as rapidly as resources permit, as well as to provide a mechanism for keeping the information up to date.

Since 1973, Musicdata, Inc. has solicited catalogs and listings from music publishers throughout the world. Using the information supplied by co-operating publishers, the series lists specific editions which are available from a publisher either for sale or on a rental basis in appropriate categories. The volumes in the series are basically organized by the primary performing force, instrument or instrumental family, such as Sacred Choral Music, Organ Music or String Music.

It is often difficult to define the boundaries between the various broad areas of music covered by the volumes in the series. The definition of sacred and secular choral music varies from publisher to publisher; some major choral works are no longer listed in Orchestral Music, reflecting changing editorial practice; some solo vocal music is in Orchestral Music; etc. The user is advised to consult the preface to individual volumes for greater definition of scope. Use of more than one volume may well be necessary to locate an edition or all editions of a work.

Editorial policy is to include as much information as the publisher supplies, within the limits of practicality. An important goal of the series is to try to bring together different editions of a composition under a single title.

VOLUME FORMAT

The volumes of the Music-In-Print series have two basic formats: unified or structured. Reference to the editor's preface and the table of contents will assist in determining how a given volume is organized.

The unified volumes (e.g., Organ Music, Orchestral Music) are arranged in a single alphabetical interfiling of composers' names, titles of works and cross references. The title under a composer's name serves as the focus for major information on each composition. In the absence of a composer, the title in the main alphabet becomes the focal point for this information.

The structured volumes (e.g., String Music) are arranged by an imposed framework: instrumentation, time period, type of work or other categorization. Within each section, entries are alphabetized by composer name or, in the absence of a composer, by title. Entries will be repeated in all appropriate sections. A structured volume also contains a Composer/Title Index and, in some cases, other specialized indexes. The Composer/Title Index is a single alphabetical list of composers' names, composition titles and cross references, with a reference to the section(s) of the volume in which complete edition information will be found. The running heads on each page of the catalog enable the user to quickly find the proper section.

ENTRY TYPES

Two basic types of entries appear in the Music-In-Print series: normal and collection. A normal entry describes a single piece of music. A collection consists of any two or more associated pieces.

NORMAL ENTRY CONTENT

In order to bring together all different editions of a composition under a uniform and/or structured title, many musical form titles are translated into English (so, Konzert becomes Concerto, Fantaisie becomes Fantasy, etc.).

For each title there are two types of information: a) generic information about the composition and b) specific information pertaining to the editions which are in print. Included in the generic information category are the uniform title of the composition, a structured title for the work (e.g., Concerto No. 2 In D Minor; Cantata No. 140), a thematic catalog number or opus and number designation, the larger source from which the work was taken, and remarks.

Following the generic information about the piece is the information about the individual editions. This information includes the arranger, the published title of the edition if different from the uniform title, the language of the text (for vocal works), instrumentation required for performance, the duration of the work in minutes (') and seconds ("), a difficulty rating assigned to the edition by the publisher or editor, the format of the publication, publisher, publisher's number, and price or rental information concerning the edition.

Following is an example of a typical entry under a composer:

MOZART, WOLFGANG AMADEUS (1756-1791)
Nozze Di Figaro, Le: Overture
[4']
2.2.2.2. 2.2.0.0. timp,strings
sc,parts RICORDI-IT rental   (M1)
"Marriage of Figaro, The: Overture"
sc,parts BREITKOPF-W f.s.   (M2)

In this entry under the composer, Wolfgang Amadeus Mozart, the title of an excerpt, "Overture", follows the original title of the complete work, "Nozze Di Figaro, Le". It is scored for 2 flutes, 2 oboes, 2 clarinets, 2 bassoons, 2 horns, 2 trumpets, timpani and strings. Duration is approximately 4 minutes. The code RICORDI-IT indicates the publisher of the first listed edition; score and parts are offered by this publisher on rental. The sequence number (M1) marks the end of the information on this edition. The English title "Marriage Of Figaro, The: Overture" is given for the next edition which is published by BREITKOPF-W; score and parts for this edition are for sale.

The full names and addresses of all publishers or U.S. agents are given in the publisher list which follows the list of editions at the end of the book.

Following is an example of an entry with a structured title:

MOZART, WOLFGANG AMADEUS (1756-1791)
Symphony No. 25, [excerpt]
(Gordon, Philip) 2.1.2.1.al-
sax. ten-sax. 2.2.1.1.timp,perc,
strings [3'] (Menuetto, [arr.])
PRESSER sets $7.50, and up, sc
$1.50   (M3)

Here a structured title "Symphony No. 25," requires a different form of listing. The excerpt, "Menuetto", has been arranged by Philip Gordon for 2 flutes, oboe, 2 clarinets, bassoon, alto saxophone, tenor saxophone, 2 horns, 2 trumpets, trombone, tuba, timpani, percussion and strings. Du-

ration is three minutes. The publisher, PRESSER, offers sets of parts priced at $7.50 and up. A separate score is available for $1.50.

INSTRUMENTATION

Instrumentation is given in the customary order. When a work is scored for full orchestra, the number of wind players required is indicated by two groups of numbers—four for woodwinds (flute, oboe, clarinet, bassoon) and four for brass (horn, trumpet, trombone, tuba). Other instruments are listed by name, or abbreviated name. A number placed before a named instrument indicates the number of players. A slash is used for alternate instrumentation.

The common auxiliary wind instruments are not mentioned by most publishers. For example, 2.2.3.3. for woodwinds indicates the work is scored for two flutes, but it *may* include a piccolo part which can be played by one of the flutists. Similarly, it is possible that parts for English horn, bass clarinet and contrabassoon are provided but no additional players will be required. If the publisher does specify the auxiliary instruments required, this information is given either in parentheses (the number of players is not affected) or after a plus sign (an additional player is needed).

Example:

2(pic).2+opt ob.3(opt bass-clar).2+contrabsn.
4.2.3.0+opt tuba.timp,2-3perc,harp,cel/pno,
strings

This example is scored for 2 flutes and piccolo (played by one of the flutists), 2 oboes plus an optional third oboe, 3 clarinets (one may play the optional bass clarinet part), 2 bassoons plus contrabassoon (additional player required), 4 horns, 2 trumpets, 3 trombones, optional tuba, timpani, percussion (2 or 3 players), harp, celeste or piano, and strings.

The term "orch" may be substituted for a detailed listing if the publisher has not provided the instrumentation for orchestral works.

Solo instrumental parts are listed following the complete orchestration of a work.

Choral parts are given as a list of voices (e.g., SATB, TTBB, etc.). The term "cor" (and similar terms) may be substituted when the publisher has not listed the specific voices.

Solo vocal parts are given as a list of voices followed by the term "solo" or "soli." The term "solo voice(s)" is used when the publisher does not specify the voice(s). (No attempt has been made to give equivalents for scale ranges listed by publishers.)

REMARKS

The remarks are a series of codes or abbreviations giving information on the seasonal or other usage of the piece, the type of music, and the national origin and century for folk or anonymous pieces. (These codes also make it possible to retrieve, from the data base developed for the Music-In-Print series, specialized listings of music for particular seasons, types, etc.) Following this Guide to Use will be found a complete List of Abbreviations.

PRICES

Only U.S. dollar prices are given, and we can give no assurance of their accuracy. They are best used for making rough comparisons. The publishers should be consulted directly for current prices.

SEQUENCE NUMBERS

An alphanumeric number, appearing on the right margin, has been assigned to each edition represented in this catalog. These are for the purpose of easing identification and location of specific entries.

COLLECTION ENTRY CONTENT

An attempt has been made to provide the user with access to pieces contained within collections, while still keeping the work within reasonable bounds of time and space. Accordingly, the following practices have been adopted:

If the members of a collection are published separately, they are listed individually, regardless of the number of pieces involved. If the collection is only published as a whole, the members are listed only if they do not exceed six in number. For larger collections, a code is given indicating the number of pieces and whether or not the contents are listed in the publisher's catalog. For example,

CC18L indicates a collection of 18 pieces which are *listed* in the publisher's catalog

CC101U indicates a collection of 101 pieces which are *unlisted* in the publisher's catalog

CCU indicates a collection of an unknown number of pieces

Whenever the members are listed, they are also cross-referenced to the collection. For example, consider the following entry:

FIVE VOLUNTARIES, [ARR.]
(Davies, Peter Maxwell) 3.3.2.1, 3.3.0.0.
timp,perc,strings,cont sc,parts
SCHOTT 10994 f.s.
contains: Attaignant, Pierre,
Magnificat; Clarke, Jeremiah,
King William's March; Clarke,
Jeremiah, Serenade; Couperin,
Louis, Sarabande; Croft, William,
March Tune   (F1)

Published by Schott, edition number 10994, this collection edited by Peter Maxwell Davies contains five members, which are not published separately. Under each of the members there is a cross reference saying 'see FIVE VOLUNTARIES, [ARR.]'.

Collection entries also contain many of the elements of information found in normal entries. For example, the entry shown above contains arranger, instrumentation, format of publication, publisher and publisher number.

Collections of several pieces published as a whole, but having no overall title, create another problem. In this case the complete publication information is given under the composer or title of the first piece listed, together with the comment 'contains also,' followed by titles of the other collection members.

CROSS REFERENCES

In order to provide the user with as many points of access as possible, the Music-In-Print series has been heavily cross referenced. In the unified volumes, the cross references are interfiled with the composers' names and the titles. In the structured volumes, cross references only appear in the Composer/Title Index.

Works may be located by title, with or without knowing the name of the composer. Using the first example by Mozart above, this composition may be located under either its Italian or English title in the main alphabet, as well as under the composer.

To make this possible the following cross references would exist in the main alphabet:

NOZZE DI FIGARO, LE: OVERTURE
see Mozart, Wolfgang Amadeus

and

MARRIAGE OF FIGARO, THE: OVERTURE see
Mozart, Wolfgang Amadeus, Nozze Di
Figaro, Le: Overture

and in addition, the following cross reference would be found under the composer's name:

Marriage of Figaro, The: Overture
*see Nozze Di Figaro, Le: Overture

Cross references are employed also to assist in the search for works frequently identified by popular names or subtitles, such as the "Surprise" Symphony of Haydn and the "Jupiter" Symphony of Mozart.

Numerous cross references have been made from unused and variant forms of composer names to assist the user in finding the form of name chosen for the series.

COLLECTION CROSS REFERENCES

Whenever the members of a collection are listed, they are cross referenced to the collection. In unified volumes, these are interfiled with composers' names and titles. In structured volumes, these cross references only occur in the Composer/Title Index.

Using the above example, FIVE VOLUNTARIES, [ARR.], there is a cross reference under each of the composers saying 'see FIVE VOLUNTARIES, [Arr.]'. (If a collection member lacks a composer, the cross reference will occur at the title.)

When collections are also published separately, the cross references in both directions read 'see also'. If the members are only published separately (i.e., the collection were not published as a whole) then the cross reference under the collection would read 'see' and under the members, 'see from'. Thus, 'see' and 'see also' direct the user to information concerning publication, while 'see from' provides access to the collection of which a given publication is a part.

With untitled collections, which are listed under the first composer and/or title, the cross reference 'see' under each of the other collection members directs the user to the full entry under the first member, at which point complete edition information will be found.

COMPOSER/TITLE INDEX

The Composer/Title Index is a single alphabetical listing of composer names, composition titles and cross references. This index is used to identify the location of a specific entry in a structured volume.

The actual reference is usually under the composer name, and only under a title when a work is not attributable to a person. The reference is to the chapter and/or section of the volume which contains the entry for the music sought.

For example, in String Music, IV.1 refers the user to Chapter IV, Section 1: String Quartets. Similarly, VIII refers to Chapter VIII: Music for Eight Instruments. Reference to the table of contents and the head of each page of the volume will assist the user in finding the appropriate section containing the information sought.

ARRANGER INDEX

The Arranger Index lists in alphabetical order all arrangers and editors cited in a specific volume. The arranger's or editor's name is listed in all capital letters. In the case of multiple arrangers, the arranger names appear together, separated by semi-colons. The listing under each arranger name gives the composer and title of each arranged (edited) work, in alphabetical order. If a work has no composer, it is listed by title. In the case of uniform and translated titles, the uniform titles are the ones appearing in the index.

This arrangement allows the user to look up any desired arranger or editor and then scan for the composers and titles of desired works. Once the composer and title have been determined, the work may then be looked up in the catalog itself to obtain complete bibliographic and ordering information.

MASTER INDEX

The Music-In-Print Master Index provides a single place to look in order to locate any composer or title listed in the Music-In-Print series. The Master Index eliminates all problems of knowing whether a specific piece of music is listed in a base volume, supplementary volumes, or not at all.

The Master Composer Index lists all composers found within the Music-In-Print series. Under each composer's name is a complete alphabetical listing of the titles of works by that composer to be found in the series. Next to each title is a number or series of numbers referring the user to the volume or volumes containing the specific piece. A key explaining these numbers and the volumes to which they correspond is to be found on the reverse side of the title page. Once the user has located the correct volume, it is easy to find the specific piece in the volume's alphabetical sequence. In the case of structured volumes, reference should be made to the Composer/Title Index in each volume.

The Master Title Index lists in a single alphabetical listing all titles of works within the Music-In-Print series. Each title is followed by a reference number or series of numbers, directing the user to the volume or volumes containing the specific title as explained above.

Additionally, as more supplementary volumes are added to the Music-In-Print series, certain volumes may update the Master Index in a specific area from time to time, through the publication of a specialized Master Index. In this way, the user can easily locate a piece of music within the volumes dealing with a specific area.

List of Abbreviations

The following is a general list of abbreviations developed for the Music-In-Print series. Therefore, all of the abbreviations do not necessarily occur in the present volume. Also, it should be noted that terms spelled out in full in the catalog, e.g. woodwinds, tuba, Easter, Passover, folk, Swiss, do not appear in this list.

A	alto
acap	a cappella
accomp	accompaniment
acord	accordion
Adv	Advent
Afr	African
Agnus	Agnus Dei
al-clar	alto clarinet
al-fl	alto flute
al-sax	alto saxophone
Allelu	Alleluia
AmInd	American Indian
ampl	amplified
Anh.	Anhang (supplement)
anti	antiphonal
app	appendix, appendices
arr.	arranged
Asc	Ascension
ASD	All Saints' Day
aud	audience
Austral	Australian
B	bass
Bald	Baldwin organ
Bar	baritone
bar horn	baritone horn
bar-sax	baritone saxophone
bass-clar	bass clarinet
bass-fl	bass flute
bass-sax	bass saxophone
bass-trom	bass trombone
bass-trp	bass trumpet
bds	boards
Belg	Belgian
Benton	thematic catalog of the works of Ignace Pleyel by Rita Benton
Bibl	Biblical
bk	book
Boh	Bohemian
boy cor	boys' chorus
Braz	Brazilian
Bryan	thematic catalog of the symphonies of Johann Wanhal by Paul Bryan
bsn	bassoon
BVM	Blessed Virgin Mary
BWV	Bach-Werke-Verzeichnis; thematic catalog of the works of J.S. Bach by Wolfgang Schmieder
BuxWV	Buxtehude-Werke-Verzeichnis; thematic catalog of the works of Dietrich Buxtehude by G. Kärstadt (Wiesbaden, 1974)

C&W	Country & Western
C.Landon	numbering of the keyboard sonatas of Joseph Haydn by Christa Landon
camb	cambiata
Can	Canadian
cant	cantata
Carib	Caribbean
CC	collection
CCU	collection, unlisted
CCUL	collection, partially listed
cel	celesta
Cen Am	Central American
cent	century
cf.	compare
Chin	Chinese
chord	chord organ
Circum	Circumcision
clar	clarinet
cloth	clothbound
cmplt ed	complete edition
Cnfrm	Confirmation
Commun	Communion
cong	congregation
Conn	Conn organ
cont	continuo
contrabsn	contrabassoon
copy	ed produced to order by a copy process
cor	chorus
cor pts	choral parts
cor-resp	choral response
Corpus	Corpus Christi
cradle	cradle song
cym	cymbals
D.	thematic catalog of the works of Franz Schubert by Otto Erich Deutsch
Dan	Danish
db	double bass
db-tuba	double-bass tuba
dbl cor	double chorus
Ded	Dedication
degr.	degree, 1-9 (difficulty), assigned by editor
desc	descant
diag	diagram(s)
diff	difficult

Dounias	thematic catalog of the violin concertos of Giuseppe Tartini by Minous Dounias
Doxol	Doxology
ea.	each
ECY	End of Church Year
ed	edition
educ	educational material
elec	electric
Ember	Ember Days
Eng	English
enl	enlarged
Epiph	Epiphany
eq voices	equal voices
Eur	European
evang	evangelistic
Eve	Evening
F.	thematic catalog of the instrumental works of Antonio Vivaldi by Antonio Fanna
f(f)	following
f.s.	for sale
fac ed	facsimile edition
facsim	facsimile(s)
Fest	festivals
film	music from film score
Finn	Finnish
fl	flute
Fr	French
Gd.Fri.	Good Friday
Ge.	thematic catalog of the works of Luigi Boccherini by Yves Gerard
Gen	general
Ger	German
Giegling	thematic catalog of the works of Giuseppe Torelli by Franz Giegling
girl cor	girls' chorus
glock	glockenspiel
gr. I-V	grades I-V, assigned by publisher
Greg	Gregorian chant
gtr	guitar
Gulbransen	Gulbransen organ

Hamm	Hammond organ	L	listed	Paymer	thematic catalog of the
Harv	Harvest	Landon	numbering of the keyboard		works of G.B. Pergolesi
Heb	Hebrew		trios of Joseph Haydn by		by Marvin Paymer
Helm	thematic catalog of the works		H.C.R. Landon	pce, pcs	piece, pieces
	of C.P.E. Bach by	Lat	Latin	Pent	Pentecost
	Eugene Helm	liturg	liturgical	perc	percussion
Hill	thematic catalog of the	Longo	thematic catalog of the	perf mat	performance material
	works of F.L. Gassmann		sonatas of Domenico	perf sc	performance score
	by George Hill		Scarlatti by Alessandro	Perger	thematic catalog of the
Hob.	thematic catalog of the		Longo		instrumental works of
	works of Joseph Haydn	Lowery	Lowery organ		Michael Haydn by Lothar
	by Anthony van Hoboken				Perger
Holywk	Holy Week			pic	piccolo
horn	French horn	Magnif	Magnificat	pic-trp	piccolo trumpet
hpsd	harpsichord	maj	major	pipe	pipe organ
Hung	Hungarian	man	manualiter; on the manuals	pno	piano
HWC	Healey Willan Catalogue		alone	pno-cond sc	piano-conducting score
		mand	mandolin	pno red	piano reduction
		manuscript	manuscript (handwritten)	Pol	Polish
		med	medium	Polynes	Polynesian
ill	illustrated, illustrations	mel	melody	pop	popular
Ind	Indian	men cor	mens' chorus	Port	Portuguese
inst	instruments	Mex	Mexican	pos	position
intro	introduction	Mez	mezzo-soprano	PreClass	Pre-Classical
ipa	instrumental parts available	MIN	Musicdata Identification	pref	preface
ipr	instrumental parts for rent		Number	Proces	processional
Ir	Irish	min	minor	Psntd	Passiontide
Isr	Israeli	min sc	miniature score	pt, pts	part, parts
It	Italian	mix cor	mixed chorus		
		Morav	Moravian		
		Morn	Morning		
		mot	motet	quar	quartet
				quin	quintet
J-C	thematic catalog of the			Quinqua	Quinquagesima
	works of G.B. Sammartini	Neth	Netherlands		
	by Newell Jenkins and	NJ	Name of Jesus		
	Bathia Churgin	No.	number		
Jap	Japanese	Nor Am	North American	rec	recorder
Jew	Jewish	Norw	Norwegian	Reces	recessional
jr cor	junior chorus	Nos.	numbers	Refm	Reformation
Jubil	Jubilate Deo	Nunc	Nunc Dimittis	rent	for rent
				repr	reprint
				Req	Requiem
		ob	oboe	rev	revised, revision
K.	thematic catalog of the	oct	octavo	Royal	royal occasion
	works of W.A. Mozart by	offer	offertory	Rum	Rumanian
	Ludwig, Ritter von	Op.	Opus	Russ	Russian
	Köchel; thematic catalog	Op. Posth.	Opus Posthumous	RV	Ryom-Verzeichnis; thematic
	of the works of J.J. Fux	opt	optional, ad lib		catalog of the works of
	by the same author	ora	oratorio		Antonio Vivaldi by Peter
Kaul	thematic catalog of the	orch	orchestra		Ryom
	instrumental works of	org	organ		
	F.A. Rosetti by Oskar	org man	organ, manuals only		
	Kaul	orig	original		
kbd	keyboard				
Kirkpatrick	thematic catalog of the			S	soprano
	sonatas of Domenico			s.p.	separately published
	Scarlatti by Ralph	P., P.S.	thematic catalogs of the	Sab	Sabbath
	Kirkpatrick		orchestral works of	sac	sacred
Kor	Korean		Antonio Vivaldi by Marc	sax	saxophone
Krebs	thematic catalog of the		Pincherle	sc	score
	works of Karl Ditters	p(p)	page(s)	Scot	Scottish
	von Dittersdorf by Karl	Palm	Palm Sunday	sec	secular
	Krebs	pap	paperbound		

Septua	Septuagesima	trom	trombone	Wolf	thematic catalog of the symphonies of Johann Stamitz by Eugene Wolf
Sexa	Sexagesima	trp	trumpet		
show	music from musical show score	TV	music from television score	wom cor	womens' chorus
		TWV	Telemann-Werke-Verzeichnis; thematic catalog of the works of G.P. Telemann by Mencke and Ruhncke	WoO.	work without opus number; used in thematic catalogs of the works of Beethoven by Kinsky and Halm and of the works of J.N. Hummel by Dieter Zimmerscheid
So Am	South American				
sop-clar	soprano clarinet				
sop-sax	soprano saxophone				
Span	Spanish				
speak cor	speaking chorus				
spir	spiritual	U	unlisted		
sr cor	senior chorus	UL	partially listed	Wq.	thematic catalog of the works of C.P.E. Bach by Alfred Wotquenne
study sc	study score	unis	unison		
suppl	supplement	US	United States		
Swed	Swedish			Wurlitzer	Wurlitzer organ
SWV	Schütz-Werke-Verzeichnis; thematic catalog of the works of Heinrich Schütz by W. Bittinger (Kassel, 1960)			WV	Wagenseil-Verzeichnis; thematic catalog of the works of G.C. Wagenseil by Helga Scholz-Michelitsch
		vcl	violoncello		
		vibra	vibraphone		
		vla	viola		
T	tenor	vln	violin		
tamb	tambourine	voc pt	vocal part		
temp blks	temple blocks	voc sc	vocal score		
ten-sax	tenor saxophone	VOCG	Robert de Visée, Oeuvres Completes pour Guitare edited by Robert Strizich	Xmas	Christmas
Thanks	Thanksgiving			xylo	xylophone
Thomas	Thomas organ	vol(s)	volume(s)		
TI	Tárrega Index; thematic catalog of the Preludes, Studies, and Exercises of Francisco Tárrega by Mijndert Jape				
		Whitsun	Whitsuntide		
		WO	without opus number; used in thematic catalog of the works of Muzio Clementi by Alan Tyson	Z.	thematic catalog of the works of Henry Purcell by Franklin Zimmerman
timp	timpani				
transl	translation				
treb	treble				
Trin	Trinity				

A

A BORDEAUX
(Rollin, J.) 2-4pt cor HEUGEL
HE 32347   (A1)

A BUG FOR ALL SEASONS see Berger, Jean

A CAPPELLA FOR DOUBLE CHORUS see Gould,
Morton

A CHASA!-RENTRONS
(Barblan, Emmanuel) SATB,acap
HUGUENIN EB 228   (A2)

A CHE TORMI IL BEN MIO see Monteverdi,
Claudio

A DIOS MI CHAPARITA °folk song,Mex
(Scherer, E.) SATB,kbd/acord,opt gtr
MULLER 2748   (A3)

A DYP AV RIKDOM see Ugland, Johan Varen

A.E.I.O.U. see Level, Pierre Yves

A HVOR SALIG see Ostern, Per Hroar

A LA CLAIRE FONTAINE
(Mermoud, Robert) 3pt cor HUGUENIN
EB 337 see from Trois Chansons
Populaires   (A4)
(Seckinger) TTBB MULLER 938 see from
Zwei Franzosische Volkslieder   (A5)

A LA MONTAGNE see Schumann, Robert
(Alexander)

A LA MUSIQUE see Handel, George
Frideric

A LA RURRU NINO see Neaum, Michael

A LA SAINT-MEDARD see Revil, Rudi

A LA SUISSE see Kelterborn, Louis

A LA VOLETTE
see J'ai Vu Le Loup, Le R'nard, Le
Lievre

A L'AMOUR JE DECLARE LA GUERRE see
Debousset, Jean-Baptiste

A L'AMOUR RENDONS LES ARMES see Rameau,
Jean-Philippe

A L'AUBERGE see Bron, Patrick

A L'ENSEIGNE DE LA FILLE SANS COEUR see
Villard, Jean (Gilles)

A L'HEURE SOLENNELLE see Huguenin,
Charles

A.M.D.G see Britten

A MIDI: EN SOUVENIR D'AIX see Kremer,
Clemens

A PARIS see Loupias, H.P.

A PEINE DEFIGUREE see Eluard, P.

A ROVIN'
(Jeffers) TB EARTHSNG EM-9 $.50   (A6)

A-ROVING
(Shaw, Robert; Parker, Alice) TTBB,T
solo LAWSON LG 51054 $.75   (A7)

A UN AUBESPIN see Piguet, R.

A VUESTROS PIES, MADRE
(Fourcaud, G.) mix cor (latin
american) HEUGEL HE 32517   (A8)

AAN DE KUNST: O HEIL'GE KUNST see
Schubert, Franz (Peter)

AAN SILVESTRE REVUELTAS, VAN MEXICO,
BIJ ZIJN DOOD see Pluister, Simon

AAS, ESLE BERNTSEN
Forste Sne, Den
SATB NORSK   (A9)

AB LA DOLCHOR see Berl, Christine

ABANDONNEE, L'
(Gevaert, Francois-Auguste) SATB,acap
HUGUENIN EB 417   (A10)

ABDUL THE MAGICIAN see Crawley,
Clifford

ABECEDAIRE see Dimey, B.

ABELYAN, L.
School Of Choral Singing, A: Vol. 2
*see Sokolov, Nikolai
Alexandrovich

ABEND BEI ROBERT STOLZ, EIN see Stolz,
Robert

ABENDHIMMEL, DER see Bruckner, Anton

ABENDLIED see Mendelssohn-Bartholdy,
Felix

ABENDLIED see Reger, Max

ABENDMUSIK see Hollfelder, Waldram

ABENDSTANDCHEN see Brahms, Johannes

ABRAHAM
Honved Banda
(Grieshaber) men cor,pno LEUCKART
LSB 113 f.s.   (A11)

Reich' Mir Zum Abschied Noch Einmal
Die Hande
(Hess) men cor,opt pno LEUCKART
LSB 114 f.s.   (A12)
(Hess) mix cor,opt pno LEUCKART
LSB 514   (A13)

ABRAHAM, DIANA
Minor Bird, A
unis cor,pno BOSTON 14043 $.55
(A14)

ABSCHIED VOM WALDE see Mendelssohn-
Bartholdy, Felix

ABSCHIEDSLIED see Kratochwil, Heinz

ABSCHIEDSLIED: ICH WUNSCHE DIR GLUCK
see Deutschmann, Gerhard

ABSENCE see Berkeley, Michael

ABSENT DE VOUS JE LANGUIS DE TRISTESSE
see Dumont, Henri

ABT, FRANZ (1819-1885)
Keinen Tropfen Im Becher Mehr
men cor BOHM   (A15)

Nacht, De: Door Heel De Omtrek Melden
4 eq voices,acap ZENGERINK 35 (A16)

Vagues Chantent, Les
3pt cor,pno/strings HUGUENIN EB 338
(A17)
Woudconcert: Mejuffrouw Lente Geeft
Concert
(Regenzki, N.) [Dutch] 3 eq voices,
acap ZENGERINK V-G 273   (A18)

ABT, DER REIT, DER see Poos, Heinrich

ACCEPTANCE see Brunner

ACH BAUMCHEN, DU STEHST GRUNE see
Reger, Max

ACH BLUMLEIN BLAU see Strauss-Konig,
Richard

ACH BLUMLEIN BLAU VERDORRE NICHT see
Kracke, Hans

ACH, DIESES SCHWARZE AUGENPAAR
(Karpowitsch) men cor ZIMMER. 609
(A19)

ACH ELSLEIN, LIEBES ELSELEIN see
Hollfelder, Waldram

ACH, ELSLEIN, LIEBES ELSELEIN see
Senfl, Ludwig

ACH, WENN ES NUN DIE MUTTER WUSST see
Zoll, Paul

ACHT KLANKSTUDIES see Lijnschooten,
H.V.

ACHTER DE SCHUTTING WORDT GEBOUWD see
Zelm, Jan van

ACHTERBERGLIEDEREN see Pieper, Rene

ACIS AND GALATEA see Handel, George
Frideric

ACRE FOR A BIRD, AN see Silsbee, Ann

ACTUALITES see Vidalie

ADAMS
Three Epitaphs
SA/unis cor SOUTHERN $1.25   (A20)

ADAMS, LESLIE (1932-   )
Madrigal
SATBB,acap NEW MUSIC NMA-137 $.60
(A21)
Under The Greenwood Tree
SATB [3'] sc AM.COMP.AL. $4.25 (A22)

ADE ZUR GUTEN NACHT see Zahner, Bruno

ADELAIDE see Debronckart, J.

ADIEU AU PAYS see Brunner, M.

ADIEU FOULARD see Turellier, Jean

ADIEU, MEIN KLEINER GARDEOFFIZIER see
Stolz, Robert

ADIEU, MONSIEUR LE PROFESSEUR see
Bourtayre

ADIEU SWEET AMARILLIS see Wilbye, John

ADIEU, SWEET AMARYLLIS see Wilbye, John

ADIEUX A LA JEUNESSE °folk song,Fr
(Wagner) 4pt mix cor LAWSON 703 (A23)

ADIOS, CATEDRAL DE BURGOS °folk song,
Span
(Shaw, Robert; Parker, Alice) TTBB,A
solo LAWSON 658   (A24)

ADLE SINE MENNE
(Eielsen, Steinar) SATB MUSIKK
MH 2466 see from Tre Folkeviser Fra
Rogaland   (A25)

ADLER, RICHARD (1921-   )
Hernando's Hideaway
(Shaw) SATB CPP-BEL T3850HC1 $1.25,
accomp tape available   (A26)
(Shaw) SAB CPP-BEL T3850HC3 $1.25,
accomp tape available   (A27)

ADLER, SAMUEL HANS (1928-   )
Allen
SATB,acap LAWSON 52430 $.80   (A28)

Archibald
SATB,acap LAWSON 52427 $.80   (A29)

Betsy
SATB,acap LAWSON 52429 $.80   (A30)

Choose Life
mix cor,MezT soli,orch [35']
SCHIRM.G   (A31)

Cynthia
SATB,acap LAWSON 52426 $.80   (A32)

High Flight
SATB,opt pno,chamber orch SCHIRM.G
50480297 $.95, ipr   (A33)

I Think Continually Of Those
SATB,acap LAWSON 52403 $.90   (A34)

Lucille-Anne; Jeff
SATB,acap LAWSON 52428 $1.00   (A35)

Rededication
TTBB LUDWIG L-5221 $3.00   (A36)

Sue
SATB,acap LAWSON 52431 $.80   (A37)

Timothy
SATB,acap LAWSON 52432 $.80   (A38)

Wisdom Cometh With The Years
SATB,1.1.1.1. 0.3.1.0. timp,strings
PEER   (A39)

ADOLPHE, BRUCE
Canticum Arcanum
SATB,vln,pno [17'] AM.COMP.AL.
$16.40   (A40)

ADVENT LEGEND, AN see Lee

ADVICE FROM "POOR RICHARD": COURTSHIP
AND MARRIAGE see Johnson, Albert R.

AESCHBACHER, WALTHER (1901-1969)
Bauern, Die °see Paysans, Les

Cantate De Fete °CCU
men cor, solo voices,orch/pno
HUGUENIN EB 217   (A41)

Coupeuse De Joncs, Le
eq voices,pno HUGUENIN EB 130 (A42)

Forgerons, Les °cant
"Schmiede, Die" [Fr/Ger] TTBB
HUGUENIN EB 217   (A43)

Gottin Der Freude, Die °Fest,cant
"Joie, La" [Fr/Ger] TTBB HUGUENIN
EB 217C   (A44)

Joie, La °see Gottin Der Freude, Die

Laud Al Pur E Meister Grischun
TTBB HUGUENIN EB 410   (A45)

Lune Blanche, La
TTBB HUGUENIN EB 208   (A46)

AESCHBACHER, WALTHER (cont'd.)

Notre Vie Est Un Passage
TTBB HUGUENIN EB 234   (A47)

Oiseau Bleu, L'
eq voices,pno HUGUENIN EB 128 (A48)

Paysans, Les °Fest,cant
"Bauern, Die" [Fr/Ger] TTBB
HUGUENIN EB 217B   (A49)

Schmiede, Die °see Forgerons, Les

AESOP'S FABLES see Smith, Gregg

AFORISMEJA SEKAKUOROLLE JA ORKESTERILLE
see Englund, Einar

AFRICAN JIGSAW see Rose, Peter

AFTENVIND see Killengreen, Christian

AFTER ALL see Pitchford, Dean

AGADA see Karachevsky

AGAIN THE LEAVES ARE FALLING °Swed
SCHIRM.G 322800 $.70   (A50)

AGAINST ALL ODDS
(Strommen) SATB CPP-BEL 2004AC1X
$1.25   (A51)
(Strommen) SSA CPP-BEL 2004AC2X $1.25
(A52)
(Strommen) TTB CPP-BEL 2004AC4X $1.25
(A53)

AGAY, DENES (1911-   )
Remembrance
SATB BOURNE B238667 $.70   (A54)

AGINCOURT SONG see Willan, Healey

AGNEAU BLANC, L' see Lauber, Emile

AGNESTIG, CARL-BERTIL
Sol
2pt jr cor,pno MUSIKK MH 2472 (A55)

AGO LONA (AFRO-BRAZILIAN) see Nobre,
Marlos

AH, DOLENTE PARTITA see Monteverdi,
Claudio

AH, IN SADNESS I NOW LEAVE see
Monteverdi, Claudio, Ah, Dolente
Partita

AH, LEAVE ME NOT TO PINE see Sullivan

AH! SI J'AVAIS UN SOU
(Blanc, H.) "P'tit Bonnet Carre" 2pt
cor HEUGEL HE 32400   (A56)

AH, SUMMER! (THE DRAGONFLY) see Berger,
Jean

AHLIN, SVEN (1951-   )
Drom Om Elysium
16pt mix cor STIM   (A57)

Genom Vasensdjupet °Op.9
mix cor,acap STIM   (A58)

Sanslose, Den
mix cor STIM   (A59)

AHNUNG DES ENDES see Meijering, Chiel

AHROLD, FRANK A. (1931-   )
Merry Mountain Raindrops
4pt mix cor,fl,pno LAWSON 52020
(A60)

AIGLE NOIR, L' see Barbara

AIMABLE PASTOURELLE see Blanchard

AIME! see Haydn, [Franz] Joseph

AIME-MOI BERGERE
(Will, M.) SATB,acap HUGUENIN CH 973
(A61)

AIME-MOI, BERGERE see Le Febvre,
Jacques

AIN'T GOT TIME TO DIE see Burger, David
Mark

AIN'T TOO TIRED TO DANCE see Kweller,
Lee

AIR DE LA BETISE, L' see Brel, Jacques

AIRD, DONALD (1924-   )
Night Voyages
SATB,SATB soli,pno [28'] (texts
from Elizabethan lyrics) sc
FALLEN LEAF $25.00, perf mat rent
(A62)

AL IS DEN TIJT NU DOLOREUS see
Wintelroy, Johan

AL OLIVO °folk song,Span
(Shaw, Robert; Parker, Alice) TTBB
LAWSON 670   (A63)

AL PAR DEL RUSTELLETTO see Schubert,
Franz (Peter)

ALABIEFF, A.
Nachtigall, Die
SATB MOLENAAR 15020505   (A64)

ALAIN, JEHAN (1911-1940)
Chanson A Bouche Fermee
(Alain, Marie-Claire) 4pt mix cor,
acap HUGUENIN S 8610 P   (A65)

Fantaisie Pour Choeur A Bouche Fermee
(Alain, Marie-Claire) 3-4pt mix
cor,acap HUGUENIN S 8611 P   (A66)

ALBERT, PRINCE CONSORT OF QUEEN
VICTORIA (1819-1861)
Love's Plea, A
(Mccarthy) 4pt mix cor,pno LAWSON
52028   (A67)

ALBERTA HOMESTEAD; UP THE YCLETAW see
Cable, Howard

ALBERTSEN, PER HJORT (1919-   )
Geitosten
SSA NORSK NMO 10040   (A68)

ALBRECHT
Come And See!
SATB SHAWNEE 1812 $.80   (A69)

Last Shopping Day Until Christmas,
The
2pt cor SHAWNEE 0322 $.95   (A70)

Lights!
SAB SHAWNEE 0366 $.95   (A71)
2pt cor SHAWNEE 0086 $.95   (A72)

What Do I Want In My Christmas
Stocking?
SA SHAWNEE 0312   (A73)

ALCESTE: INCIDENTAL MUSIC see Handel,
George Frideric

ALCHIMISTE, L' see Morin, M.

ALDEMA, GIL
Story Of Garoo, The
jr cor ISRAELI IMP 1708   (A74)

ALEGORIA BUFFA see Prado, Jose-Antonio
(Almeida)

ALEXANDER, HAIM (1915-   )
Three Bird Songs °CC3U
jr cor ISRAELI IMP 1700   (A75)

ALEXANDER BALUS see Handel, George
Frideric

ALEXANDER GRAHAM BELL, TEACHER OF THE
DEAF see Roberts, Ruth

ALEXANDER'S FEAST see Handel, George
Frideric

ALEXANDER'S RAGTIME BAND see Berlin,
Irving

ALEXANDRINA see Bojarsky

ALEXANDROV, A.
Selected Choruses °CCU
(Semenovsky, D.) [Russ] cor,acap/
pno MEZ KNIGA 175   (A76)

ALFARERO see Kyllonen, Timo-Juhani

ALGRA, JOH. (1894-1973)
Feestzang: Hij Leve Lang
4 eq voices,acap ZENGERINK 473
(A77)

ALICE IN WONDERLAND see Bailey, Maurice

ALIN, PIERRE
Noel, Noel Est Venu
1-4pt cor HUGUENIN see from
CHANSONS POUR LA JEUNESSE,
SEPTIEME CAHIER   (A78)

ALINDER, HAKAN (1941-   )
Se! Krouthen
mix cor&jr cor,T solo,orch STIM
(A79)

ALIVE AND WELL AND ROLLING DOWN THE
VALLEY see Clarke, Henry Leland

ALL ALONG THE VALLEY see Getty, Gordon

ALL-AMERICAN (CHORAL REVIEW) see Brymer

ALL- AMERICAN SONGBOOK °CCU
cor CPP-BEL TMF0113 $5.95   (A80)

ALL AT ONCE
(Buchholz) SATB CPP-BEL 3905AC1X
$1.25, accomp tape available (A81)
(Buchholz) SSA CPP-BEL 3905AC2X
$1.25, accomp tape available (A82)
(Buchholz) SAB CPP-BEL 3905AC3X
$1.25, accomp tape available (A83)

ALL DAY I HEAR see Fetler

ALL FANCIES FROM YOUR MIND DEPORTING
see Episcopius, L., Laet Varen Alle
Fantasie

ALL FOR ONE WORLD see Collins

ALL I NEED
(Strommen) SATB CPP-BEL 3890AC1X
$1.25   (A84)
(Strommen) SSA CPP-BEL 3890AC2X $1.25
(A85)
(Strommen) SA CPP-BEL 3890AC5X $1.25
(A86)

ALL IN GREEN WENT MY LOVE RIDING see
George, Earl Robert

ALL IN THE MORNING see Coombes, Douglas

ALL MEIN GEDANKEN see Gebhard, Hans

ALL MEIN GEDANKEN see Philipp, Franz

ALL MY TOMORROWS see Besig

ALL MY TRIALS °spir
(Cooper, Kenneth) SB&camb,SA soli
CAMBIATA S980145 $.70   (A87)
(McNeil, Albert) SATB,med solo (med)
GENTRY JG2026 $.65   (A88)

ALL OUT OF LOVE
(Nowak) SATB CPP-BEL 3825AC1X $1.25
(A89)

ALL OVER THE WORLD see Donnelly

ALL THAT I LOVE IS HOME see Parkinson,
Rebecca

ALL THE PRETTY LITTLE HORSES °folk
song
(Frackenpohl, Arthur) SSA LEONARD-US
08602415 $.85   (A90)
(Vance) SATB SCHIRM.G 322760 $.80
(A91)

ALL THE PRETTY LITTLE HORSES see
Artman, Ruth Eleanor

ALL THE WORLD'S A STAGE see Tate,
Phyllis

ALL THINGS JOYFUL
(Valentine) SATB CPP-BEL SV8520 $.95
(A92)

ALL THINGS OF WONDER AND LOVE see
Culver

ALL THROUGH THE NIGHT
(Lallement, Bernard) "Au Coeur De La
Nuit" SATB A COEUR JOIE 282   (A93)
(Morgan) TTBB,acap CPP-BEL FEC 09396
$.95   (A94)

ALL-TID see Kleiberg, Stale

ALL UNDER THE WILLOW TREES see Carr

ALL YE WHO MUSIC LOVE
(Burger, Dave) SSAB CPP-BEL SV8510
$.95   (A95)

ALL YE WHO MUSIC LOVE see Oliphant

ALL YOU NEED IS LOVE see Lennon, John

ALLA PRIMAVERA see Cacioppo, Curt

ALLDAHL, PER-GUNNAR (1943-   )
Har Ar Stunden, Det
mix cor,pno STIM   (A96)

Och Det Vart Morgon
mix cor,pno 4-hands STIM   (A97)

ALLE FANGT AN °Xmas
(Deutschmann, Gerhard) mix cor BOHM
(A98)

ALLE LEUT' SIND AUSGEGANGEN see Seiber,
Matyas Gyorgy

ALLEGRO, IL PENSEROSO AND IL MODERATO,
L' see Handel, George Frideric

ALLEGRO, IL PENSEROSO ED IL MODERATO,
L' see Handel, George Frideric

ALLELUIA see Biggs, Richard Keys

ALLELUIA see Huguenin, Charles

ALLELUIA see Kunz

ALLELUIA! SING WITH JOY see Perry

ALLEN
Home For The Holidays
(Ringwald) TTBB SHAWNEE 0243 $.75
(A99)

ALLEN see Adler, Samuel Hans

ALLEN, DAVID LEN
Gifts That Are Mine To Give
SAB UNIVERSE 392-00575   (A100)

ALLEN, DAVID LEN (cont'd.)

Little Lamb
SATB UNIVERSE 392-00530   (A101)

My Christmas Wish
SATB UNIVERSE 392-00646   (A102)

What Makes A Dad?
SAB,pno UNIVERSE 392-00556 f.s.
(A103)

ALLEWEIL EIN WENIG LUSTIG see
Gunsenheimer, Gustav

ALLONS, ALLONS GAI see Willaert, Adrian

ALLONS AU VERT BOCAGE see Costeley,
Guillaume

ALLONS DANS LES GRANDS BOIS: FEUILLES
D'AUTOMNE see Missa

ALLONS DANSER AUSSI see Morley, Thomas

ALLONS DANSER AUSSI (CHANT DE MAI) see
Morley, Thomas

ALLONS DANSER MA BELLE see Pantillon,
G.L.

ALLONS VIVRE A LA CAMPAGNE see
Schubert, Franz (Peter)

ALOEETTE, VOGHEL CLEIN see Geraedts,
Jaap

ALOETTE, MY THRUSH, MY SWEET see
Geraedts, Jaap, Aloeette, Voghel
Clein

ALONE IN THE NORTH see Rimsky-Korsakov,
Nikolai

ALONG COMES A WOMAN
(Strommen) SATB CPP-BEL 3871AC1X
$1.25   (A104)
(Strommen) SAB CPP-BEL 3871AC3X $1.25
(A105)
(Strommen) TTB CPP-BEL 3871AC4X $1.25
(A106)

ALONG THE FIELD AS WE CAME BY see
Getty, Gordon

ALONG THE ROAD OF VICTORIES °CCU
[Russ] cor,acap MEZ KNIGA 165 (A107)

ALONG THE WAY see Weigl, [Mrs.] Vally

ALORS QUE MON COEUR S'ENGAGE see
Bonnet, Pierre

ALS DE ZIELE LUISTERT see Maassen,
Johannes Ant.

ALS DONKERE DAGEN HENENGAAN see Stenz,
Herman, Lenteliedje

ALS GE IN BLIJDSCHAP see Kaaij, Willem
Hendrik V. D., Ode Aan De Muziek

ALS IK BIJ UW WIEGSKEN STA see Stenz,
Herman, Moederliedje

ALS IN ONS HART see Laetantius, Br.

ALS JE BIDT see Warnaar, D.J.

ALS WIR JUNGST IN REGENSBURG WAREN see
Kanetscheider, Artur

ALT I UNIVERSET see Kleiberg, Stale

ALTDEUTSCHE LIEBESLIEDER see Kocher-
Klein, Hilda

ALTDEUTSCHES SCHLACHTLIED see Strauss,
Richard

ALTE IST VERGANGEN, DAS see Bauer,
Gluck Zum Neuen Jahr

ALTE LIEBESLIEDER, BOOK 1 see
Hodkinson, Sydney P.

ALTE LIEBESLIEDER, BOOK 2 see
Hodkinson, Sydney P.

ALTE LIEBESLIEDER, BOOK 3 see
Hodkinson, Sydney P.

ALTE LIED, DAS
(Biebl) men cor ZIMMER. 606   (A108)

ALTENA, MAARTEN (1943-   )
Dance
chamber choir [12'] DONEMUS   (A109)

ALTER, DAS see Poos, Heinrich

ALTER JOE see Foster, Stephen Collins

ALTERHAUG, BJORN
Som Blomsten
[Norw] SATB&men cor&wom cor,fl,pic,
3trp,3trom,tuba NORGE   (A110)

ALTHOUGH WHEN I DEPART see Rore,
Cipriano de

ALTHOUSE
And We Sing Gloria
SATB SHAWNEE 1866 $.95   (A111)

Don't Count Your Chickens
SATB SHAWNEE 1843 $.90   (A112)
SAB SHAWNEE 0386 $.90   (A113)
2pt cor SHAWNEE 0096 $.90   (A114)

Gee, It's A Wonderful Day
2pt cor CPP-BEL SV8517 $.95   (A115)

Gloria!
SATB SHAWNEE 1806 $.85   (A116)

Headin' West (Three Cowboy Songs)
°CCU
2pt cor SHAWNEE 0072 $1.25   (A117)

I Just Can't Say Goodbye To You
SATB SHAWNEE 1852 $.95   (A118)

It All Begins With Me
SATB SHAWNEE 1863 $.95   (A119)

It's Time To Go
SATB SHAWNEE 1808 $.85   (A120)
SSA SHAWNEE 0528 $.85   (A121)
SAB SHAWNEE 0368 $.85   (A122)
2pt cor SHAWNEE 0087 $.85   (A123)

Shout Amen!
SATB SHAWNEE 1860 $.95   (A124)
SAB SHAWNEE 0321 $.85   (A125)
2pt cor SHAWNEE 0291 $.85   (A126)

Soar Like An Eagle
SATB SHAWNEE 6478 $.95   (A127)

Train Bound For Glory
SATB SHAWNEE 1867 $.95   (A128)
SAB SHAWNEE 0401 $.95   (A129)
2pt cor SHAWNEE 0010 $.95   (A130)

What A Team! °see Brownsey

ALTHOUSE, JAY
Can't Help Singing
SATB ALFRED 7442   (A131)
SAB ALFRED 7443   (A132)
SSA ALFRED 7444   (A133)

From Sea To Shining Sea
cor ALFRED   (A134)

Hold On To Your Dream
cor ALFRED   (A135)

'Liza Jane
cor ALFRED   (A136)

My Home Town
SATB ALFRED 7589 $.95   (A137)
SAB ALFRED 7590 $.95   (A138)
SSA ALFRED 7591 $.95   (A139)

Sing, Sing Of Christmas
ALFRED   (A140)

Wake Up, It's Springtime °see
Kupferschmid, Steven

ALTIJT SO MOET IC TRUEREN see Van Der
Muelen, Servaes

ALTINK, H.
Avondster
SSA MOLENAAR 15014602   (A141)
SATB MOLENAAR 15000602   (A142)

In 'T Voorjaar
SATB MOLENAAR 15005002   (A143)

ALTO RHAPSODY see Brahms, Johannes

ALTRO NON E'L MIO AMOR see Festa,
Costanzo

ALTSTEIRISCHES LICHTMESSLIED
cor HIEBER MH 5034   (A144)

ALWAYS
(Snyder, Audrey) SATB CPP-BEL
3917AC1X f.s., accomp tape
available   (A145)
(Snyder, Audrey) SAB CPP-BEL 3917AC3X
$1.10, accomp tape available   (A146)

ALWES
Ask And It Shall Be Given
SATB oct DEAN HRD 138 $.95   (A147)

ALWES, CHESTER
Psalms Of Ascent (from Bay Psalm
Book) CC3U
TTBB,pno OXFORD 19 3857537   (A148)

AM, MAGNAR (1952-   )
Cage Birds Dream, A
mix cor,vln,2perc,pno NORSK
NMO 10029 A   (A149)

AM, MAGNAR (cont'd.)

Gjev Meg Jorda
[Norw] men cor,T solo NORGE   (A150)

Miracle And A Tear, A
[Norw] SATB NORGE   (A151)

Sit Ein Liten Einsam Fugl, Det
SSA NORSK NMO 10041   (A152)

To Plantar For Ljose Royster
[Norw] jr cor [2'] NORGE   (A153)

Veinje
[Norw] SATB&wom cor&men cor,3clar,
bass clar,vcl NORGE   (A154)

AM ABEND see Genzmer, Harald

AM BRUNNEN VOR DEM TORE see Schubert,
Franz (Peter)

AM HERBSTABEND see Naegeli, Hans Georg

AM, STRAM, GRAM see Level, Pierre Yves

AMADE, L.
Important, C'est La Rose, L' °see
Becaud, Gilbert

AMANDA see Galay, Daniel

AMANECER see Sojo, Vincente E.

AMARILLI, MIA BELLA see Caccini

AMARILLI, MY FAIR ONE see Caccini,
Amarilli, Mia Bella

AMATEUR CHORUS SINGS, AN, VOL. 8 °CCU
[Russ] cor MEZ KNIGA 177   (A155)

AMATEUR CHORUS SINGS, AN, VOL.9 °CCU
[Russ] MEZ KNIGA 176   (A156)

AME DES POETES, L' see Trenet, Charles

AMEN see Crawford

AMERICA IS (OFFICIAL STATUE OF LIBERTY
SONG) see Raposo, Joseph G.

AMERICA (MY COUNTRY, TIS OF THEE) see
Carey, Henry

AMERICA, MY FRIEND see Bourque, Richard

AMERICA - MY HOME see Blevins, Patsy
Ford

AMERICA, MY HOME see Brown, Raymond

AMERICA SINGS- COMMUNITY SONGBOOK
°CC200U
cor CPP-BEL TMF0114 $5.50   (A157)

AMERICA STANDS FREE see Erickson, Frank
William

AMERICA THE BEAUTIFUL see Jordan

AMERICA, THE BEAUTIFUL see Ward, Samuel
Augustus

AMERICA, WHICH WAY ARE YOU GOING? see
Stilman

AMERICAN CREED, THE see Moore

AMERICAN EARTH, THE see Duson, Dede

AMERICAN ESSAY, AN see Van de Vate,
Nancy Hayes

AMERICAN HERITAGE TRIBUTE, AN
(Chinn) SATB,acap CPP-BEL SV8562
$1.25   (A158)

AMERICAN NAMES see Bialosky, Marshall
H.

AMERICAN NEBULA, THE see Moore, Carman

AMERICAN PORTRAIT, AN
(Lojeski, Ed) SATB LEONARD-US
08401201 f.s., accomp tape
available, ipa   (A159)
(Lojeski, Ed) SAB LEONARD-US 08401202
f.s., accomp tape available, ipa
(A160)
(Lojeski, Ed) 2pt cor LEONARD-US
08401203 f.s., accomp tape
available, ipa   (A161)

AMERICANA see Erickson, Frank William

AMI, UN see Ducarroz, M.

AMI QUE J'AVAIS AU LOGIS, L' see
Touati, Raymond

AMIE, NE VOUS SOIT ETRANGE see Patry,
Andre J.

AMITIE, L' see Bourgeois, Gerard

AMITIE ET PATRIE see Anonymous

AMMANN, BENNO (1904-   )
   Madchen Von Misox, Das
   men cor,acap ZIMMER. 558   (A162)

   Schone Aus Dem Maggia-Tal, Die
   men cor,acap ZIMMER. 559   (A163)

   Schone Von Onsernone, Die
   men cor,acap ZIMMER. 557   (A164)

AMON see Edler, Robert

AMONG THE APPLE TREES see Spencer,
   Williametta

AMOR CHE DEGGIO FAR see Monteverdi,
   Claudio

AMOR IN HET BOOTJE see Gastoldi,
   Giovanni Giacomo, Amor Nel Battello

AMOR, IO SENTO L'ALMA see Lauridsen,
   Morten Johannes

AMOR-LAMENTO DELLA NINFA see
   Monteverdi, Claudio

AMOR NEL BATTELLO see Gastoldi,
   Giovanni Giacomo

AMOR VITTORIOSO see Gastoldi, Giovanni
   Giacomo

AMORE TRADITORE see Bach, Johann
   Sebastian

AMOUR' DE MOI, L' see Jacotin, Jacques

AMOUR DE MOY, L'
   (Scherer, Ernst) 4pt wom cor MULLER
   SM 2406   (A165)

AMOUR EN DIX-NEUF PONTS see Provins, J.

AMOUR ME POINT see Jacotin, Jacques

AMOUR, QUAND FUS-TU NE? see Le Jeune,
   Claude

AMOUR SANS AMOUR, L' see Daniel,
   Etienne

AMOUR T'APPELLE, L' see Curti, F.

AMOUR TRIOMPHE, L' see Gluck, Christoph
   Willibald, Ritter von

AMOUR VOYANT L'ENNUI see Certon, Pierre

AMOUREUX, UN see Bruhier, Antoine

AMOURS, PARTES see De Sermisy

AMSTERDAM see Brel, Jacques

AMUSING SONG see Kopelent, Marek

AMYNTAS WITH HIS PHYLLIS FAIR see
   Pilkington, Francis

AN DEN AETHER see Medek, Tilo

AN DEN MOND see Badings, Henk

AN DEN VETTER see Haydn, [Franz] Joseph

AN DER DONAU, WENN DER WEIN BLUHT see
   Grothe

AN DER KIRCHE WOHNT DER PRIESTER see
   Hauptmann, Moritz

AN DIE FRAUEN see Haydn, [Franz] Joseph

AN DIE HEIMAT see Brahms, Johannes

AN DIE MUSIK see Fischbach, Klaus

AN DIE MUSIK see Spohr, Ludwig (Louis)

AN DIE MUSIK: DU HOLDE KUNST see
   Schubert, Franz (Peter)

AN DIE MUSIK: FESTIVAL HYMNE see Brugk,
   Hans Melchior

AN DIE MUSIKANTEN see Seckinger, Konrad

AN DIE SONNE see Schubert, Franz
   (Peter)

AN DIE STERNE see Schumann, Robert
   (Alexander)

AN IHREN GENIUS see Genzmer, Harald

AND I CAME ALIVE see Perry

AND MILES TO GO BEFORE I SLEEP see
   Kitzke, Jerome P.

AND THE EAGLES see Lindenfeld, Harris
   Nelson

AND WE SING GLORIA see Althouse

AND WITH AH! BRIGHT WINGS see Zallman,
   Arlene (Proctor)

ANDALUSIAN LOVE SONG see Walters,
   Edmund

ANDANTE
   (Roosli, Joseph) men cor,acap PELIKAN
   PE 1203   (A166)

ANDENKEN see Mendelssohn-Bartholdy,
   Felix

ANDERE JACHT, DE see Dekker, J.

ANDERSON
   Christmas Time (More Than Just A Day)
   2pt treb cor CPP-BEL SV8202 $.95
                                   (A167)
   School Is Out *see Barge

   Softly, Softly Fell The Snow
   SSA KJOS C8902 $.80   (A168)

ANDERSON, BETH
   If You Had A Thought In Your Head
   SATB [1'] AM.COMP.AL. $.40   (A169)

ANDERSON, GAYLENE
   Safe And Warm
   SATB,kbd UNIVERSE 392-00501 $.75
                                   (A170)

ANDERSON, LEROY (1908-1975)
   Sleigh Ride
   SSA CPP-BEL 69008 $1.25   (A171)
   (Edwards) SA CPP-BEL 60503 $1.25
                                   (A172)
   (Edwards) SSA CPP-BEL 60328 $1.25
                                   (A173)
   (Edwards) SAB CPP-BEL 60527 $1.25
                                   (A174)
   (Edwards) SATB CPP-BEL 60060 $1.25
                                   (A175)
   Syncopated Clock, The
   SA CPP-BEL 60506 $1.25   (A176)
   SSA CPP-BEL 60331 $.95   (A177)
   SATB CPP-BEL 60062 $.95   (A178)

ANDERSON, T.J.
   What Time Is It?
   boy cor,fl,2clar,2alto sax,tenor
     sax,baritone sax,4trp,3trom,
     drums,pno,synthesizer,db [16']
   AM.COMP.AL. sc $24.45, pts $49.40
                                   (A179)

ANDERSON, WILLIAM H.
   April
   see Omens Of Spring

   Omens Of Spring
   unis cor,pno LESLIE 1128 f.s.
     contains: April; Omens Of Spring;
     See The Cherry Blossoms Swing
                                   (A180)
   Omens Of Spring
   see Omens Of Spring

   See The Cherry Blossoms Swing
   see Omens Of Spring

ANDERSSON, MAGNUS F. (1953-   )
   Tre Dikter Av Lars Gustaf Andersson
     *CCU
   mix cor STIM   (A181)

ANDERSSON, TOMMY B. (1964-   )
   Du Som Ar...
   wom cor,vla,org STIM   (A182)

   Hjartstilla
   mix cor STIM   (A183)

ANDREAE, VOLKMAR (1879-1962)
   Chasseron, Le
   (Favez, Daniel) SATB,acap HUGUENIN
   CH 1184   (A184)

ANDRIESSEN, HENDRIK (1892-1981)
   Dormeur Du Val, Le
   unis cor,pno ZENGERINK R 282 see
     from Trois Pastorales   (A185)

   Sensation
   unis cor,pno ZENGERINK R 282 see
     from Trois Pastorales   (A186)

   Tete De Faune
   unis cor,pno ZENGERINK R 282 see
     from Trois Pastorales   (A187)

   Trois Pastorales *see Dormeur Du
     Val, Le; Sensation; Tete De Faune
                                   (A188)

ANDRIESSEN, JURRIAAN (1925-   )
   Crossing The Bar
   SATB,acap HARMONIA 3684   (A189)

   Du Hast Diamanten Und Perlen
   SATB,acap HARMONIA 3685 see from
     Vier Heine-Lieder   (A190)

ANDRIESSEN, JURRIAAN (cont'd.)
   Jungling Liebt Ein Madchen, Ein
   SATB,acap HARMONIA 3685 see from
     Vier Heine-Lieder   (A191)

   Sie Haben Mich Gequalet
   SATB,acap HARMONIA 3685 see from
     Vier Heine-Lieder   (A192)

   Vier Heine-Lieder *see Du Hast
     Diamanten Und Perlen; Jungling
     Liebt Ein Madchen, Ein; Sie Haben
     Mich Gequalet; Wenn Zwei Von
     Einander Scheiden   (A193)

   Wenn Zwei Von Einander Scheiden
   SATB,acap HARMONIA 3685 see from
     Vier Heine-Lieder   (A194)

ANGLORUM FERIAE see Johnson, Robert
   Sherlaw

ANGULO, MANUEL (1930-   )
   Once Canciones Populares Espanolas
     *CC11L
   SATB,acap ALPUERTO 1031   (A195)

ANIMAL SONGS THAT TICKLE YOUR FUNNY
   BONE! see Roberts, Ruth

ANIMULA see Zender, Hans

ANNABEL LEE see Getty, Gordon

ANNABEL LEE see Hobbs, James

ANNCHEN VON THARAU
   (Silcher, Friedrich) TTBB HARMONIA
   3822   (A196)

ANNIE LAURIE
   (Gates, C.) SATB,pno (med diff)
   THOMAS 1C137726 $.90   (A197)

ANNIVERSARY CHORUSES see Diemer, Emma
   Lou

ANONYMOUS
   Amitie Et Patrie
   2pt cor HUGUENIN EB   (A198)

   Beggar's Song, The: 0, Here We Come
     Awandring
   (Lagas, R.) "Wij Comen Hier
     Gheloopen" SATB,acap (diff)
   ZENGERINK G 522   (A199)

   Bergere Legere
   (Smeets, Leo) [Fr] 3 eq voices,acap
   ZENGERINK V 157   (A200)

   Blauwe Lucht
   (Kort, Jacobus) mix cor ZENGERINK
   123   (A201)

   C'est Grand Erreur *16th cent
   (Guentner, Francis J.) SATB,acap
   BOURNE B239335-357 $.65   (A202)

   C'est Grande Erreur
   (Maitre, M.M.) mix cor,rec HEUGEL
   HE 32132 contains also: Je Ne
     Sais Pas Comment   (A203)

   Chanson De Goliard
   (Turellier, Jean) 2 eq voices,inst
   HEUGEL HE 32409   (A204)

   Coeur De Vous, Le
   (Agnel, A) 2-3pt mix cor HEUGEL
   HE 31884   (A205)

   Daar Was Een Sneeuwwit Vogeltje
   5pt mix cor,acap ZENGERINK 447
                                   (A206)

   Daer Was E Wuf Die Spon
   (Hermans, Petra) mix cor ZENGERINK
   411   (A207)
   (Schmitz, Jan) [Dutch] 3 eq voices,
     acap ZENGERINK V-G 411   (A208)

   Dale Si Le Das
   (Agnel, A.) 3pt mix cor HEUGEL
   HE 32233 contains also: En Avila
                                   (A209)

   Den Uyl Die Op Den Peerboom Zat
   (Hermans, Petra) [Dutch] 3 eq
     voices,acap ZENGERINK V-G 412
                                   (A210)

   Des Winters Als Het Regent
   (Hermans, Petra) [Dutch] 3 eq
     voices,acap ZENGERINK V-G 414
                                   (A211)

   Du Coeur Le Don
   (Agnel, A.) 2pt mix cor HEUGEL
   HE 31881   (A212)

   En Als De Boer Een Paar Blokskens
     Heeft
   mix cor ZENGERINK 93   (A213)

   En Avila
   see Anonymous, Dale Si Le Das

ANONYMOUS (cont'd.)

Faute D'argent, C'est Douleur Non
  Pareille
  see Richafort, Joannes, Trut Avant,
  Il Faut Boire

Geluckig Is Het Land
  (Hermans, Petra) [Dutch] 3 eq
  voices,acap ZENGERINK V-G 401
                                    (A214)
  (Zwaan, Jacobus) 4 eq voices,acap
  ZENGERINK M.401   (A215)

Gildebroeders, Maakt Plezieren
  [Dutch] 3 eq voices,acap ZENGERINK
  V-G 415   (A216)

Guillaume Se Va Chaufer
  [Fr/Eng] SSATB,opt inst BROUDE BR.
  CR 32   (A217)

Holland Is Een Heerlijk Land
  [Dutch] 3 eq voices,acap ZENGERINK
  V 408   (A218)

I Went To The Market
  (Shaw, P.) unis men cor&4pt mix
  cor,opt gtr HEUGEL HE 32407
                                    (A219)

Ik Zeg Adieu, Wij Moeten Scheiden
  (Steen, Hendrik) mix cor ZENGERINK
  106   (A220)

Ik Zeg Adieu, Wij Twee Wij Moeten
  Scheiden
  (Schmitz, Jan) 4 eq voices,acap
  ZENGERINK 80   (A221)

In Kommer Far
  SSAATB STIM 8511-061   (A222)

Incessament, Je M'y Tourmente
  (Maitre, M.M.) 3pt mix cor HEUGEL
  HE 32310   (A223)

I've Been To Harlem
  (Shaw, P.) 4pt mix cor,gtr HEUGEL
  HE 32408   (A224)

J'ai Mis Mon Coeur
  (Agnel, A.) 3 eq voices HEUGEL
  HE 31891   (A225)

J'aurais Grand Tort
  (Maitre, M.M.) 3pt mix cor HEUGEL
  HE 32459   (A226)

Je Demeure Seule Egaree
  (Agnel, A.) 3 eq voices/3pt mix cor
  HEUGEL HE 32403   (A227)

Je Ne Sais Pas Comment
  see Anonymous, C'est Grande Erreur

'K Heb Mijn Wagen Volgeladen
  (Scheren, Frans) 4 eq voices,acap
  ZENGERINK 180   (A228)

Komt Vrienden In Het Ronde
  4 eq voices,acap ZENGERINK 418
                                    (A229)
  (Schmitz, Jan) 3 eq voices,acap
  ZENGERINK V 84   (A230)

Lieblich Hat Sich Gesellet
  see MADRIGALE FUR GEMISCHTEN CHOR A
  CAPPELLA: BLATT VII

M'amie Un Jour
  (Agnel, A.) 2-3pt mix cor HEUGEL
  HE 32017   (A231)

Men Roept Van Groenlands Bergen
  (Zwager, Piet) 4 eq voices,acap
  ZENGERINK 12   (A232)

Merk Toch Hoe Sterk
  (Buurman, H.H.) 4 eq voices,acap
  ZENGERINK 247   (A233)

Mon Cher Troupeau
  SATB,acap HUGUENIN EB 37   (A234)

Naar Oostland Willen Wij Rijden
  (Geraedts, Henri) SSATB,acap
  ZENGERINK 125   (A235)

O Nederland, Let Op U Saeck
  (Kerper, Willem) 4 eq voices,acap
  ZENGERINK 213   (A236)
  (Smeets, Leo) [Dutch] 3 eq voices,
  acap ZENGERINK V 107   (A237)

Patriotjes, De: Wat Zullen Ons
  Patriotjes Eten
  (Geraedts, Henri) 4 eq voices,acap
  ZENGERINK 419   (A238)

Pensez De Faire Garnison
  (Dottin, G.) 3pt mix cor HEUGEL
  HE 31842   (A239)

Quand Je Bois Du Vin Claret
  (Agnel, A.) 3pt mix cor HEUGEL
  HE 32234   (A240)

ANONYMOUS (cont'd.)

Rondo °15th cent
  (Corpataux, Michel) SATB,acap
  HUGUENIN CH 1185   (A241)

Si J'ai Eu Du Mal Ou Du Bien
  (Agnel, A.) 2-3 eq voices HEUGEL
  HE 32047   (A242)

Vier Weverkens Zag Men Ter Botermarkt
  Gaan
  (Hermans, Petra) mix cor ZENGERINK
  416   (A243)

Wie Gaat Mee Over Zee
  (Zwaan, Jacobus) 4 eq voices,acap
  ZENGERINK 187   (A244)

Wij Comen Hier Ghelooepen
  mix cor ZENGERINK 522   (A245)

Wij Comen Hier Ghelooepen °see
  Beggar's Song, The: O, Here We
  Come Awandring

Wij Zangers: Wij Trekken De Voren
  mix cor ZENGERINK 432   (A246)

Wilhelmus Van Nassauen: Tiemen Ottink
  4 eq voices,acap ZENGERINK 51
                                    (A247)

Winter Is Vergangen, Die
  (Bogert, Hans Van Den) [Dutch] 3 eq
  voices,acap ZENGERINK V 24 (A248)

ANOTHER BRIDGE TO CROSS see Strommen,
  Carl

ANS FENSTER KOMMT UND SEHT see Thurm,
  Joachim

ANSINK, CAROLINE (1959-   )
  Water Zal De Stenen Breken, Het
  SATB,ob,clar,2sax,2trom,2perc,pno
  DONEMUS   (A249)

ANTHEM FOR PEACE see Davidson, Charles
  Stuart

ANTHOLOGIE PRO-ARTE: PREMIER CAHIER
  °CC7L
  cor HUGUENIN EB 181 contains works by
  Bach, Barblan, de Lassus and others
                                    (A250)
ANTHOLOGIE PRO-ARTE: DEUXIEME CAHIER
  °CC6L
  cor HUGUENIN EB 193 contains works by
  Barblan, Huber, Morley, and others
                                    (A251)
ANTHOLOGIE PRO-ARTE: TROISIEME CAHIER
  °CC6L
  cor HUGUENIN EB 199 contains works by
  Weber, Mozart, Morley and others
                                    (A252)
ANTHOLOGY FOR CONDUCTING, AN: VOL. 6
  °CCU
  [Russ] cor,pno MEZ KNIGA 171 contains
  opera choruses by non-Russian
  composers   (A253)
ANTHOLOGY OF SOVIET CHILDREN'S SONGS,
  AN: VOL. 3 °CCU
  [Russ] jr cor,pno MEZ KNIGA 517
                                    (A254)
ANTHOLOGY OF SOVIET CHILDREN'S SONGS,
  AN: VOL. 4 °CCU
  [Russ] jr cor,pno MEZ KNIGA 220
                                    (A255)
ANTHOLOGY OF SOVIET CHILDREN'S SONGS,
  VOL. 2 °CCUL
  [Russ] jr cor,pno MEZ KNIGA 488
                                    (A256)
ANTHONY
  Poetry In Motion (composed with
  Kaufman)
  (Strommen) SATB SHAWNEE 1875 $1.00
                                    (A257)
  (Strommen) 2pt cor SHAWNEE 0405
  $1.00   (A258)
  (Strommen) 2pt cor SHAWNEE 0111
  $1.00   (A259)

ANTIGONE see Mendelssohn-Bartholdy,
  Felix

ANTIPHON see Vaughan Williams, Ralph

ANTSEV, M.
  Selected Choruses °CCUL
  (Lebedeva, N.) [Russ] cor,acap/pno
  MEZ KNIGA 171   (A260)

ANYONE LIVED IN A PRETTY HOW TOWN see
  Jeffers

ANYTHING YOU WANT TO BE see Reese

APAGE, SATANAS! see Pinos, Alois

APHORISM see Perder, Kjell

APHORISM 1: CONCERNING THE
  INTERPRETATION OF NATURE AND THE
  KINGDOM OF MAN see Fongaard, Bjorn

APHORISM 23: CONCERNING THE
  INTERPRETATION OF NATURE AND THE
  KINGDOM OF MAN see Fongaard, Bjorn

APOKALYPSE see Thiele, Siegfried

APOTHELOZ, JEAN (1900-1965)
  Chanson De La Belle
  SATB,acap HUGUENIN EB 165   (A261)

  Chanson De La Marine
  TTBB HUGUENIN EB 163   (A262)

  Chanson Du Printemps
  SATB,acap HUGUENIN EB 166   (A263)

  Ermite, L'
  TTBB HUGUENIN EB 169 see from
  Quatre Ballades Francaises (A264)

  Et You, You, You
  TTBB HUGUENIN EB 169 see from
  Quatre Ballades Francaises (A265)

  Fille Morte Dans Ses Amours, La
  TTBB HUGUENIN EB 169 see from
  Quatre Ballades Francaises (A266)

  Paroles Que Tu M'as Dites, Les
  TTBB HUGUENIN EB 169 see from
  Quatre Ballades Francaises (A267)

  Quatre Ballades Francaises °see
  Ermite, L'; Et You, You, You;
  Fille Morte Dans Ses Amours, La;
  Paroles Que Tu M'as Dites, Les
                                    (A268)
  Renouveau
  3pt cor,pno/orch HUGUENIN EB 236
                                    (A269)
  Sur La Tombe D'une Sauterelle
  3pt cor HUGUENIN EB 470   (A270)

APPELDOORN, DINA (1884-1938)
  Molen, De: Zie Den Molen Draaien
  mix cor ZENGERINK 384   (A271)

  T'avont Sullen Wi Vrolic Sijn
  TTBB ZENGERINK 14   (A272)

  Wijd Is 'T Land En Wijd De Zee
  mix cor ZENGERINK 213   (A273)

  Wijde Rust: Wijde Rust Ligt Overal
  4 eq voices,acap ZENGERINK 169
                                    (A274)
  Zomeravond: Op Gindse Stoppelvelden
  mix cor ZENGERINK 384   (A275)

  Zwerverslied: Ik Heb Geen Vrouw
  4 eq voices,acap ZENGERINK 175
                                    (A276)
APPENZELLER, BENEDICTUS
  Chansons °CCU
  (Thompson, Glenda) cor VER.NED.MUS.
  MMN 14   (A277)

APPLAUSE see Strouse, Charles Louis

APPLAUSE, APPLAUSE (MEDLEY OF BROADWAY
  RHYTHM- APPLAUSE) see Strouse,
  Charles Louis

APPLE-TREE MADRIGALS, THE see Warren,
  B.

APPLES see Honigman, Saul

APPROACHING WINTER see Forbes,
  Sebastian

APRIL see Anderson, William H.

APRIL see Fetler

APRIL see Sagvik, Stellan

APRIL IS IN MY MISTRESS' FACE see
  Maslanka, David Henry

APRIL IS IN MY MISTRESS' FACE see
  Morley, Thomas

APRIL IS IN MY MISTRESS' FACE see
  Vance, M.

APRIL'S RAIN see Cooper, Steve

ARAGON, L.
  Nous Dormirons Ensemble (composed
  with Ferrat, Jean)
  (Grindel, J.) 4pt mix cor HEUGEL
  HE 32257   (A278)

ARBEAU, THOINOT (JEHAN TABOUROT)
  (1520-1595)
  Pavane: "Bella, Qui Tiens Ma Vie"
  see MADRIGALE FUR GEMISCHTEN CHOR A
  CAPPELLA: BLATT VII

  Pavane: Belle Qui Tiens Ma Vie
  see Bonnet, Pierre, Francion Vint
  L'autre Jour
  SATB,acap HUGUENIN EB 284   (A279)
  TTBB HUGUENIN CH 634   (A280)

ARBRE, L'
  (Geoffray, Cesar) 4pt mix cor HEUGEL
    HE 32156   (A281)

ARC EN CIEL see Gauffriau, Jean

ARCADELT, JACOB (ca. 1505-1568)
  Chanson: Nous Voyons Que Les Hommes
    mix cor ZENGERINK 264   (A282)

  Dormendo Un Giorno A Baia
    (Agnel, A.) 3pt mix cor HEUGEL
      HE 32314 see from Trois Madrigaux
      A 3 Voix Mixtes   (A283)

  Gravi Pene In Amor
    (Agnel, A.) 3pt mix cor HEUGEL
      HE 32314 see from Trois Madrigaux
      A 3 Voix Mixtes   (A284)

  Je Ne Me Confesserai Point
    (Agnel, A.) 3pt mix cor HEUGEL
      HE 32070   (A285)

  Margot
    (Erb) 4pt mix cor LAWSON 897   (A286)

  Now Spring In All Her Glory
    (Greyson) SATB BOURNE B238683 $.80
                                          (A287)

  Trois Madrigaux A 3 Voix Mixtes *see
    Dormendo Un Giorno A Baia; Gravi
    Pene In Amor; Voi Mi Ponesti Un
    Foco   (A288)

  Voi Mi Ponesti Un Foco
    (Agnel, A.) 3pt mix cor HEUGEL
      HE 32314 see from Trois Madrigaux
      A 3 Voix Mixtes   (A289)

ARCH, GWYN
  Sospan Fach
    TTBB,pno [2'45"] ROBERTON 53111
                                          (A290)

ARCHER DU ROI, L' see Ducarroz, M.

ARCHIBALD see Adler, Samuel Hans

ARE YOU LONESOME TONIGHT
  (Jamison) SSAA (women's barbershop)
    BOURNE B238766 $.50   (A291)

ARE YOU READY FOR CHRISTMAS? see Clapp

ARES EN IRENE see Verbesselt, Auguste

ARIA (FROM SUITE IN D MAJOR) see Bach,
  Johann Sebastian

ARISE AND SING see Halferty

ARKANSAS TRAVELER, THE *folk song
  (Porter) SATB SCHIRM.G 234000 $.80
                                          (A292)

ARMATO
  I Still Believe (composed with
    Cantorelli, Beppe)
    (Ray, Jerry) SATB ALFRED 7614
      $1.25, accomp tape available
                                          (A293)
    (Ray, Jerry) SAB ALFRED 7615 $1.25,
      accomp tape available   (A294)
    (Ray, Jerry) SSA ALFRED 7616 $1.25,
      accomp tape available   (A295)
    (Ray, Jerry) 1-2pt cor ALFRED 7617
      $1.25, accomp tape available
                                          (A296)

ARMER, ELINOR
  Spin, Earth
    4pt mix cor,pno/org LAWSON 51859
                                          (A297)

ARMONIE IN CONCORSO *CC15L
  cor A COEUR JOIE   (A298)

ARNE, THOMAS AUGUSTINE (1710-1778)
  Hush To Peace
    (Hunter) 3pt men cor LAWSON 775
                                          (A299)

  Rule Britannia
    SATB,pno/brass NOVELLO rent   (A300)

ARNESTAD, FINN (1916-   )
  Ave Caecilia
    [Lat] treb cor,opt T solo,opt vcl
      (based on Prelude in D minor by
      J.S. Bach) NORGE   (A301)

  Motto - Sommer Og Regn
    [Norw] 3 eq voices NORGE   (A302)

  Svarterabben
    [Norw] men cor,acap NORGE   (A303)

ARNETH-KANTATE see Bruckner, Anton

ARODIN, SIDNEY
  Lazy River *see Carmichael, Hoagy

AROUND FRYDEK see Zamecnik, Evzen

AROUNDABOUT CHRISTMAS see Crawley,
  Clifford

ARRANGEMENTS AND TRANSPOSITIONS FOR
  CHORUS BY K. LEBEDEV *CCU
    [Russ] cor,acap/pno MEZ KNIGA 170

                                          (A304)
ARRIVEE DE LA NOCE see Cossetto, Emil

ARS LONGA VITA BREVIS see Malmlof-
  Forssling, Carin

ARTHUR MURRAY TAUGHT ME DANCING IN A
  HURRY
  (Huff) SATB CPP-BEL 5725AC1X $1.25,
    accomp tape available   (A305)
  (Huff) SSA CPP-BEL 5725AC2X $1.25,
    accomp tape available   (A306)
  (Huff) SAB CPP-BEL 5725AC3X $1.25,
    accomp tape available   (A307)

ARTMAN
  Happy Music In The Air
    2pt cor LEONARD-US 08583465 $.85
                                          (A308)
  Isn't It Strange?
    SATB LEONARD-US 08594658 $.85
                                          (A309)
  Nutcracker (Youth Musical) (composed
    with Beall)
    cor sc LEONARD-US 09970760 $20.00,
      accomp tape available   (A310)

  Snowy Clouds On A Summer Day
    SSA SHAWNEE 0535 $.95   (A311)

  Song Of The Littlest Angel
    SSA CPP-BEL SV7813 $.95   (A312)
    SA CPP-BEL SV7710 $.95   (A313)

ARTMAN, RUTH ELEANOR (1919-   )
  All The Pretty Little Horses
    unis cor CPP-BEL SV8550 $1.10
                                          (A314)
  Let's Hear It For America!
    1-2pt cor CPP-BEL SV8702 $1.20,
      accomp tape available   (A315)

ARVOLA, TAPANI
  Koulukuoro 9 *CC6U
    SA FAZER F.M. 07860-0   (A316)

AS A BROOKLET see Schubert, Franz
  (Peter), Al Par Del Rustelletto

AS FAST AS THOU SHALT WANE see Ehrlich,
  Abel, Sonnet 11 By Shakespeare

AS I RODE OUT THIS ENDERS NIGHT see
  Spencer, Williametta

AS I SAT UNDER A SYCAMORE TREE see
  Spencer, Williametta

AS LATELY WE WATCHED see Barnes

AS LONG AS I HAVE MUSIC see Price

AS MARIDER-LE MARIAGE
  (Barblan, Emmanuel) SATB,acap
    HUGUENIN EB 227   (A317)

AS SOON AS THE MOON LIFTS OUT OF THE
  SEA see Frank, Marcel [Gustave]

AS SPRING BREAKS FORTH see Baker

AS THE LEAVES FALL see Liebergen

AS THE WIND COLORS see Udow, Michael
  William

AS THE WIND DOTH BLOW see Berkeley,
  Michael

AS TORRENTS IN SUMMER see Elgar, [Sir]
  Edward (William)

ASGEIRSSON, JON (1928-   )
  Bragging Song, A
    men cor ICELAND 010-13   (A318)

  Four Traditional Songs
    mix cor [13'] ICELAND 010-5   (A319)

  Humoresque
    mix cor [2'] ICELAND 010-10   (A320)

  In These Times...
    jr cor [12'] ICELAND 010-1   (A321)

  There Will Be Sun
    mix cor [9'] ICELAND 010-22   (A322)

  Time And Water
    mix cor [30'] ICELAND 010-3   (A323)

ASH GROVE, THE
  (Willeiegger, H.R.) mix cor,acap
    PELIKAN PE 1181   (A324)

ASHEIM, NILS HENRIK (1960-   )
  Kor Uten Ord
    SATB,2trom [9'] NORGE   (A325)

ASHFORD, NICKOLAS (1942-   )
  Reach Out And Touch (Somebody's Hand)
    (composed with Simpson, Valerie
    R.)
    (Snyder, Audrey) SATB CPP-BEL
      SV8490 $1.40   (A326)
    (Snyder, Audrey) SAB CPP-BEL SV8491

ASHFORD, NICKOLAS (cont'd.)

    $1.40   (A327)
    (Snyder, Audrey) 2pt cor CPP-BEL
      SV8492 $1.40   (A328)

ASHTON
  Christmas Cha Cha, A
    SS&camb,SA soli CAMBIATA A485190
      $.80   (A329)

ASHTON, BOB BRUCE (1921-   )
  Two Christmas Partner Songs *CC2U,
    Xmas
    S&camb,SA soli CAMBIATA T483172
      $.75   (A330)

  Where Are The Flowers?
    SSB&camb CAMBIATA A485186 $.80
                                          (A331)

ASK AND IT SHALL BE GIVEN see Alwes

ASPLUND, DAVID
  Mister Music Man
    2pt cor LEONARD-US 08599440 $.85
                                          (A332)

ASS, LION AND COCK, THE see Smith,
  Gregg

ASSALINDE
  Proestants Fugitifs
    1-4pt cor HUGUENIN see from
    CHANSONS POUR LA JEUNESSE,
    SEPTIEME CAHIER   (A333)

ASSO
  Comme Un P'it Coqu'licot (composed
    with Valery)
    (Passaquet, R.) 4pt mix cor HEUGEL
      HE 32001   (A334)

ASSOZIATIONEN see Domhardt, Gerd

ASTLEY, RICK
  She Wants To Dance With Me
    (Hanson, Mark) SATB CPP-BEL
      2694SC1X $1.40, accomp tape
      available   (A335)
    (Hanson, Mark) SSA CPP-BEL 2694SC2X
      $1.40, accomp tape available
                                          (A336)
    (Hanson, Mark) SAB CPP-BEL 2694SC3X
      $1.40, accomp tape available
                                          (A337)

AT THE ROUND EARTH'S IMAGIN'D CORNERS
  see Berkeley, Michael

AT THE SPINNING WHEEL see Orlov

ATKINSON
  Say "No" To Drugs
    SA/SAB KJOS C8707 $.80   (A338)

ATKINSON, CONDIT ROBERT (1928-   )
  Turn That Water Off!
    2pt treb cor,pno,opt gtr GALAXY
      1.2932 $.85   (A339)

ATLANTIS see Kvam, Oddvar S.

ATSEY ZEYTIM OMDIN *folk song
  (Adler) "Olive Trees Stand" SATB
    SCHIRM.G 455130 $.70   (A340)

ATT BLI GAMMAL UNDER DISKUSSION see
  Jeverud, Johan

ATT LIKNA DIG see Lindgren, Olof

AU BOIS QUI CHANTE see Morley, Thomas

AU BON VIEUX TEMPS
  (Barblan, Emmanuel) SATB,acap
    HUGUENIN EB 93 see from Trois
    Chansons D'autrefois   (A341)

AU BORD D'UNE TOMBE see Lauber, Emile

AU BRUIT DES BROCS see Schumann, Robert
  (Alexander)

AU CARREFOUR DES TROIS BROUILLARDS see
  Daniel, Etienne

AU CHANT DU MERLE see Schmidt-Wunstorf,
  Rudolf

AU CHATEAU see Naty, Jean

AU CLAIRE DE LA LUNE
  (Hunter) 4pt mix cor,pno LAWSON 649
                                          (A342)

AU COEUR DE LA NUIT see All Through The
  Night

AU DETOUR DE LA COLLINE see Bovet,
  Joseph

AU FLANC DU COTEAU see Jean P'tit Jean

AU FLANC DU COTEAU (CHANSONS DU
  VIGNERON) see Barblan, Emmanuel

AU GRENIER see Ducarroz, M.

AU JOLI BOIS see Tessier, Charles

AU JOLI JEU DU POUSSE AVANT see Janequin, Clement

AU JOLI SON DU SANSONNET see Contentez-Vous

AU JOLI SON DU SANSONNET see Gero, Ihan

AU JOLY BOIS see Penet, Hilaire

AU JOLY JEU see Janequin, Clement

AU LARGE see Huguenin, Charles

AU MARCHE DE YANOCHIDA
(Langree, Alain) 2-3 eq voices A COEUR JOIE 9 016 see from Quartre Chansons Populaires Hongroises (A343)

AU MOIS DE MAI see Rietz, Julius

AU PAYS see Landry, Fredy

AU PORT DE DIEPPE see Blanchard

AU PRESSOIR see Lauber, Emile

AU VILLAGE see Schubert, Franz (Peter)

AUBADE see Schubert, Franz (Peter)

AUBADE see Schubert, Franz (Peter), Standchen

AUBADES see Schmidt-Wunstorf, Rudolf

AUBE, L' see Lauber, Emile

AUCTIONEER, THE
(Shaw, Kirby) TBB LEONARD-US 08655581 $.95 (A344)

AUDREY SNYDER COLLECTION, THE see Snyder, Audrey

AUF, AUF ZUM FROHLICHEN JAGEN see Kelling, Hajo

AUF DE SCHWABSCHE EISEBAHNE see Deutschmann, Gerhard

AUF DE SCHWABSCHE EISEBAHNE see Weiss-Steinberg, Hans

AUF DEM SEE see Mendelssohn-Bartholdy, Felix

AUF DEM SEE see Naegeli, Hans Georg

AUF DER HEIDE BLUHN DIE LETZTEN ROSEN see Stolz, Robert

AUF DES GALERIES see Steuermann, Edward

AUF DIE PFERDE, KOSAKEN see Pappert, Robert

AUF, DU JUNGER WANDERSMANN see Lemacher, Heinrich

AUF WIEDERSEHEN see Pappert, Robert

AUFBRUCH AUS DEM WIRTSHAUSE see Sertorius

AUFRAY, H.
Jour Ou Le Bateau Viendra, Le (composed with Dylan, Robert (Bob)) (Terral, F.) 4pt mix cor HEUGEL HE 32510 (A345)

Pipeau, Le (composed with Delanoe) (Lavoisy- Drouot, Ch.) 4 eq voices, rec,gtr HEUGEL HE 32290 (A346)

AUGURIES OF INNOCENCE see Yavelow, Christopher Johnson

AUGUST see Johnsen, Hallvard

AULD LANG SYNE
(Liebergen, Patrick M.) "Song For Parting, A" SATB CPP-BEL SCHCH77108 $1.10 (A347)
(Lonna, Kjell) SATB, solo voices PROPRIUS 7969 contains also: Blow The Wind Southerly; Sang Til Deg, En (A348)
(Shaw, Robert; Parker, Alice) TTBB LAWSON 51018 (A349)

AULD LANG SYNE see Kaspersma, G.

AULD LANG SYNE (BONNIE'S MEDLEY 2) see Beekum, Jan Van

AULO NOVIS GAUDET see Strategier, Herman

AUS DEM JAHRESLAUF see Lampart, Karl

AUS DER TRAUBE IN DIE TONNE see Lissmann, Kurt

AUS GRAUER STADTE MAUERN see Lang, H.

AUS "MIRZA SCHAFFY" see Hauptmann, Moritz

AUS NOWGOROD ZOGEN BOJAREN see Jechali Bojare

AUS UNSEREM SINGSCHULGARTEN, HEFT 1: IM REIGEN DES JAHRES see Jochum, Otto

AUS UNSEREM SINGSCHULGARTEN, HEFT 2: HEITERE MUSE see Jochum, Otto

AUS UNSEREM SINGSCHULGARTEN, HEFT 3: UM LIEBE UND WIEGE see Jochum, Otto

AUS UNSEREM SINGSCHULGARTEN, HEFT 4: STANDELIEDER see Jochum, Otto

AUSBUND SCHOENER TEUTSCHER LIEDLEIN, EIN
(Forster, G.) 4pt mix cor SCHROTH 101 (A350)

AUSSERLICH UND INNERLICH see Miller, Franz R.

AUSSI BIEN QUE DE PLUIE see Holstein, Jean-Paul

AUSTIN, JOHN
Chamber Music: Seven Songs
SSA,strings,winds,harp [12'] AM.COMP.AL. $12.10 (A351)

Four Love Songs
SATB,strings,winds,harp,pno [20'] AM.COMP.AL. sc $28.95, pt $41.20, pno red $18.30 (A352)

Four Madrigals (Blake)
SATB [10'] AM.COMP.AL. $6.90 (A353)

AUSTIN, LARRY (1930-)
Triptych
SATB,string quar [10'] AM.COMP.AL. $10.70 (A354)

AUSTRALIAN SEA SHANTIES see Finnissy, Michael

AUTOMNE see Delarue-Mardrus, Lucie

AUTOMOBILE, THE see Weidberg, Ron, Hamechonit

AUTRE JOUR J'ETAIS EN ROUTE, L'
see Moi, Gardais Les Chevres
(Brasseur, M.A.; Teniere, C.) 2pt jr cor,Orff inst HEUGEL HE 32367 contains also: Moi Je Gardais Les Chevres (A355)

AUTUM see Kalabis, Viktor

AUTUMN see Copeland, Carol

AUTUMN see Forbes, Sebastian

AUTUMN see Paull

AUTUMN see Tchaikovsky, Piotr Ilyich

AUTUMN AND THE RAINDROP'S ADVENTURE see Franco, Johan

AUTUMN PICTURES see Sveinsson, Atli Heimir

AUTUMN RAIN see Joubert, John

AUTUMN SONG see Mendelssohn-Bartholdy, Felix

AUTUMN SONG see Sculthorpe, Peter [Joshua]

AUTUMN SONG, AN see Melton, William E.

AUTUMN STORM see Falik, Yuri

AUTUMN TUNE see Haxton, Kenneth

AUX ACCENTS DE NOTRE HARMONIE see Mehul, Etienne-Nicolas

AUX AIEUX see Cornaz, Emmanuel

AUX JOURS DE LONGUE FAIM see Daniel, Etienne

AUX MARCHES DU PALAIS see Turellier, Jean

AVALOS
It's A Happy Day
TTB,pno,perc CPP-BEL PROCH 02856 $1.10 (A356)

AVE CAECILIA see Arnestad, Finn

AVECQUES VOUS MON AMOUR FINIRA see Le Blanc, Didier

AVERKAMP, ANTON (1861-1934)
Wilgen, De: Daar Waren Eens Zeven Wilgen
SSA/TTB ZENGERINK 175 (A357)

AVERRE
Hand 'N Hand °see Ross

AVEUGLE see Huguenin, Charles

AVNI, TZVI (1927-)
City Plays Hide And Seek, The °see Ha'ir Mesaheket Mahboyim

Ha'ir Mesaheket Mahboyim
"City Plays Hide And Seek, The" [Heb] 3pt treb cor,acap [5'] ISR.MUS.INST. 6587 (A358)

Praises Of The Day
[Heb] mix cor,acap ISR.MUS.INST. 6285 see from Three Madrigals (A359)

Praises Of The Night [1]
[Heb] mix cor,acap ISR.MUS.INST. 6285 see from Three Madrigals (A360)

Praises Of The Night [2]
[Heb] mix cor,acap ISR.MUS.INST. 6285 see from Three Madrigals (A361)

Three Madrigals °see Praises Of The Day; Praises Of The Night [1]; Praises Of The Night [2] (A362)

Wind In The West
jr cor ISRAELI IMP 1705 (A363)

AVONDGEBET: DE NACHT, DE MOEDER VAN DE RUST see Smeets, Leo

AVONDKLOKKEN: HOOR, DE GOLVEN DRAGEN...JUBILATE see Bortnjanski'j, Dimitri

AVONDLIED see Evertse, J.

AVONDLIED: O PLECHTIG UUR, GIJ DOET ONS ZIELRUST SMAKEN see Hol, Richard

AVONDROOD: NOG NAUWLIJKS IS HET GROEN DER BOOMEN see Zwager, Piet

AVONDSTER see Altink, H.

AVONDSTILTE: HOE ZACHT DAALT D'AVOND NEDER see Coljee, Jan

AVRIL see Reymond, Herny

AVSHALOMOV, JACOB (1919-)
Raptures
5pt cor,winds,brass,strings [22'] AM.COMP.AL. $18.30 (A364)

AVSKED see Welin, Karl-Erik

AWAKE! ARISE! GO FORTH see Price

AWARE see Borishansky, Elliot

AWAY WITH THESE SELF-LOVING LADS see Dowland, John

AXION ESTI see Theodorakis, Mikis

AYER
Oh! You Beautiful Doll °see Brown

AYERES OR PHANTASTICKE SPIRITES FOR THREE VOICES see Weelkes, Thomas

"AYES" HAVE IT, THE see Mitchell, Bob

AYEZ PITIE DU GRAND MAL QUE J'ENDURE see Sermisy, Claude de (Claudin)

AZ DER REBBE GEHT see Binder, Abraham Wolfe

B

BABYLON'S FALLING °spir
  (Baeriswyl, Henri) SATB,acap HUGUENIN
    CH 2023   (B1)
  (Baeriswyl, Henri) TTBB HUGUENIN CH
                                         (B2)

BACAK, JOYCE EILERS (1941-   )
  Bound For Jubilee
    SATB CPP-BEL SV7903 $.95, accomp
      tape available   (B3)
    TTBB CPP-BEL SV7904 $.95, accomp
      tape available   (B4)

  I Love Christmas
    SSA/unis cor CPP-BEL SCHCH 07732
      $1.10   (B5)

  Lady Of The Harbor
    SAB CPP-BEL SV7829 $.95   (B6)

  Voice From A Dream, A
    SA CPP-BEL SCHCH 02130 $.95   (B7)

BACCHANALIAN SONG see Rimsky-Korsakov,
  Nikolai

BACH
  It's So Easy
    cor ALFRED   (B8)

BACH, JOHANN CHRISTOPH (1642-1703)
  Meine Freundin Ist Schon
    SATB,SATB soli,vln,3vla,cont
      HANSSLER 30.503   (B9)

BACH, JOHANN SEBASTIAN (1685-1750)
  Amore Traditore (Cantata No. 203)
    see Bach, Johann Sebastian, Weichet
    Nur

  Aria (From Suite In D Major)
    (Swingle, Ward) SATB,db,perc CPP-
      BEL 64334 f.s.   (B10)

  Bouree (From The English Suite, No.2)
    (Swingle, Ward) SATB,db,perc CPP-
      BEL 64335 f.s.   (B11)

  Cantata No. 201 °see Phoebus Und Pan

  Cantata No. 202 °see Weichet Nur

  Cantata No. 203 °see Amore Traditore

  Cantata No. 204 °see Ich Bin In Mir
    Vergnugt

  Choruses From Cantatas, Vol. 2 °CCU
    [Ger/Russ] cor,pno MEZ KNIGA 170
                                         (B12)

  Freut Euch Alle °BWV 207a,No.9
    mix cor,cont,opt brass BAREN. 6905
                                         (B13)

  Fugue In C Minor
    (Swingle, Ward) SATB,db,perc CPP-
      BEL 64337 $1.10   (B14)

  Fugue In D Major (From The Well
    Tempered Clavier)
    (Swingle, Ward) SATB,db,perc CPP-BEL
      64383 $1.25   (B15)

  Geschwinde, Ihr Wirbelnden Winde
    (from Cantata 201, Phoebus And
    Pan)
    [Ger] SATTBB,orch KALMUS K 06637
      $3.50   (B16)

  Give Ear Unto My Words
    (Wagner) SATB oct DEAN HRD 199 $.75
                                         (B17)

  Ich Bin In Mir Vergnugt (Cantata No.
    204)
    see Bach, Johann Sebastian, Weichet
    Nur

  Phoebus Und Pan (Cantata No. 201)
    cor min sc LEA 84   (B18)

  Preise Dein Glucke, Gesegnetes
    Sachsen °BWV 215
    SSAATTBB,STB soli,orch BAREN.
      BA 5195   (B19)

  Scat Bourree
    (Averre) SAB,kbd PRESSER 392-41538
      $.90   (B20)

  Selected Chorales, Vol. 2 °CCU
    [Russ] mix cor,acap MEZ KNIGA 168
                                         (B21)

  Sleepers Wake: Chorale-Prelude
    (Swingle, Ward) SATB,db,perc CPP-
      BEL 64343 $1.25   (B22)

  Weichet Nur (Cantata No. 202)
    cor min sc LEA 85 contains also:
      Amore Traditore (Cantata No.
      203); Ich Bin In Mir Vergnugt
      (Cantata No. 204)   (B23)

BACH, JOHANN SEBASTIAN (cont'd.)

  Zerreisset, Zersprenget, Zertrumment
    Die Gruft (from Cantata 205)
    [Ger] SATB,hpsd,org,orch KALMUS
      K 06641 $5.25   (B24)

"BACH, P.D.Q." (PETER SCHICKELE)
  see also SCHICKELE, PETER

BACH, WILHELM FRIEDEMANN (1710-1784)
  Kein Halmlein Wachst Auf Erden
    (Biebl, F.) mix cor,acap BOHM (B25)

BACHARACH, BURT F. (1928-   )
  Back To Bacharach: A Medley °medley
    (Kern) SATB CPP-BEL CO113C1X $2.25,
      accomp tape available   (B26)
    (Kern) SSA CPP-BEL CO113C2X $2.25,
      accomp tape available   (B27)
    (Kern) SAB CPP-BEL CO113C3X $2.25,
      accomp tape available   (B28)

  I'd Like To Teach The World To Sing
    TTBB MOLENAAR 13003404   (B29)

  Walk On By
    (Finetti) SATB CPP-BEL 0198WC1X
      $1.25, accomp tape available
                                         (B30)

BACHOREK, MILAN (1939-   )
  Barrier, The
    men cor,acap [5'] CESKY HUD.   (B31)

  Blue One, The
    jr cor,pno [10'] PANTON   (B32)

  Chorus For Mixed Choir
    mix cor/jr cor [7'] CESKY HUD.
                                         (B33)

  Lidice
    men cor&wom cor, solo voices&
    narrator,perc,orch [30'] PANTON
                                         (B34)

  Little Evening Music °CC3U
    jr cor,fl CESKY HUD.   (B35)

  Lost Sweetheart And Sweet Jack
    mix cor [8'] CESKY HUD.   (B36)

  Poem Of Hukvaldy, The
    jr cor&wom cor,STBar soli,orch
    [28'] CZECH   (B37)

  Song Of The Home, The
    mix cor,Bar solo,clar,vln,vcl,pno
    [12'] CESKY HUD.   (B38)

  Sorry-Cards For Kept-In Pupils
    jr cor,cel,pno 4-hands, children's
    toys [12'] CESKY HUD.   (B39)

BACK IN NINETEEN TWENTY-NINE
  (Hicks, Val) TTBB NATIONAL WHC-162
    $.70   (B40)

BACK TO BACHARACH: A MEDLEY see
  Bacharach, Burt F.

BACK TO THE FUTURE: A MEDLEY
  (Brymer, Mark) SATB LEONARD-US
    08637161 f.s., ipa   (B41)
  (Brymer, Mark) SAB LEONARD-US
    08637162 f.s., ipa   (B42)
  (Brymer, Mark) 2pt cor LEONARD-US
    08637164 f.s., ipa   (B43)

BACKER, HANS (1908-   )
  Bitt Dich Gar Schon °see Spielmann
    Und Das Madchen, Der

  Es War Einmal Ein Kleiner Mann
    men cor BOHM   (B44)

  Kommt Mit, Wohin Die Freude Zieht!
    °song cycle
    wom cor/jr cor,S solo,chamber orch/
    pno 4-hands BOHM   (B45)

  Lob Der Meister: Frohliche
    Handwerkskantate
    3pt jr cor,solo voice,orch/pno 4-
    hands,Orff inst BOHM   (B46)

  Neues Kleid Zur Lust Und Freud, Ein
    3pt wom cor, solo voices&narrator,
    orch BOHM   (B47)

  Nur Ein Wenig Geduld
    3pt wom cor,acap BOHM   (B48)

  Spielmann Und Das Madchen, Der
    "Bitt Dich Gar Schon" mix cor BOHM
                                         (B49)

  Tiritomba
    men cor BOHM   (B50)

  Wahre Freundschaft Soll Nicht Wanken
    mix cor,acap BOHM   (B51)

  Wenn Alle Brunnlein Fliessen
    men cor BOHM   (B52)

  Wer Der Musik Ergeben °cant
    wom cor/jr cor,SBar soli,orch BOHM
                                         (B53)

BACON, BOYD
  Child Of Christmas Morn, The
    SATB,kbd,opt trp THOMAS 1C588835
      $1.35   (B54)

  Family At Christmas, The
    SATB BECKEN 117   (B55)

  From My Window
    SA NEW MUSIC NMA-180 $.75   (B56)

  Like The Flight Of An Eagle
    SATB (med) THOMAS 1C588906 $.95
                                         (B57)

  Music, You Gave Me Music
    ALFRED   (B58)

  Old Ironsides
    SATB,pno SOMERSET SP-797 $1.00
                                         (B59)

  Rock And Roll Drummer
    1-2pt cor ALFRED 7636 $.95   (B60)

BACON, ERNST L. (1898-   )
  Colorado Trail, The
    SATB,pno LAWSON 519   (B61)

  Cradle Song, A
    2pt wom cor,pno LAWSON 708 f.s. see
    from Four Innocent Airs   (B62)

  Four Innocent Airs °see Cradle Song,
    A; Return Of Spring; Schoolboy,
    The; Where Go The Boats   (B63)

  John Hardy
    SATB,pno LAWSON 518   (B64)

  Return Of Spring
    2pt wom cor,pno LAWSON 705 f.s. see
    from Four Innocent Airs   (B65)

  Schoolboy, The
    2pt wom cor,pno LAWSON 707 f.s. see
    from Four Innocent Airs   (B66)

  Shouting Pilgrim
    SATB,pno 4-hands LAWSON 520   (B67)

  Where Go The Boats
    2pt wom cor,pno LAWSON 706 f.s. see
    from Four Innocent Airs   (B68)

BADA REGNEN, DE see Lindgren, Olof

BADEN, CONRAD (1908-   )
  Hoyr Kor Kyrkjeklokka Lokkar °Op.57
    [Norw] SATB,org [13'] NORGE   (B69)

  Vaarkjenning °Op.92,No.1
    [Norw] SA NORGE   (B70)

BADER, K.
  Komm Zum Tanz
    men cor,pno BOHM   (B71)

BADINGS, HENK (1907-1987)
  An Den Mond
    SATB,A solo,acap HARMONIA 3784
                                         (B72)

  Cantiones Sacrae Et Profanae, Vol. 7
    °CC1OL
    SATB HARMONIA HU 3788   (B73)

  Daar Was Een Wuf Die Spon
    SATB MOLENAAR 15021802   (B74)

  Missa Antiphonica
    dbl cor,acap [17'] DONEMUS   (B75)

  Nachtgesang
    [Ger/Dutch] SSA HARMONIA 3734 (B76)

  Ode: La Terre De Java
    [Fr] SATB,acap HARMONIA 3691   (B77)

BAERISWYL, HENRI
  Saltimbanques
    SATB,acap HUGUENIN CH   (B78)

BAILEY
  Jason And The Argonauts
    1-2pt cor KJOS V79A pno-cond sc
      $3.95, cor pts $1.25   (B79)

  Space Shuttle, The
    1-2pt cor KJOS 6194 $.70   (B80)

BAILEY, MAURICE
  Alice In Wonderland °CC7L
    SSA,pno/instrumental ensemble,opt
    string quar OXFORD 19 335249 4
    f.s., ipr   (B81)

BAINTON, EDGAR LESLIE (1880-1956)
  Go, Lovely Rose
    TTBB,acap NOVELLO 16 0203   (B82)

BAIR
  This Is Your Day
    SATB CPP-BEL SV8454 $.95   (B83)

BAJECZKA O CHORYM KOTKU see Wallek-
  Walewski, Boleslaw

BAK DEI SISTE BLANAR see Brevik, Tor

BAKER
As Spring Breaks Forth
SATB HARRIS HC-4073 $.75   (B84)

BAKER'S DOZEN, A see Frazee, J.

BAKFARK, BALINT (VALENTIN) (1507-1576)
Vache Noire, La
(Opienski, Henryk) SATB,acap
HUGUENIN EB 61   (B85)

BAKKE, RUTH (1947-   )
Brudeslatt Fra Sogn
SATB NORSK   (B86)

Utvikling?
[Norw] SSAA NORGE   (B87)

BAKSA, ROBERT FRANK (1938-   )
Song To A Doll
SA,pno PRESSER 392-00663 $.75 (B88)

BALAIO
(Leleu, Francoise) 3 eq voices,gtr,
perc,opt vcl HEUGEL HE 32603   (B89)

BALALIN see Loupias, H.P.

BALANCEMENTS see Reibel, Guy

BALAZS, FREDERIC (1920-   )
Concerto For Orchestra And Voices
wom cor,winds,brass,strings,5perc,
harp [28'] AM.COMP.AL.   (B90)

Pueblo Bonito
cor,fl,English horn,bass clar,horn,
trp,harp,pno,perc,strings [30']
AM.COMP.AL.   (B91)

BALKIN, ALFRED (1931-   )
Little Love Goes A Long Way, A
(Jackman, Jerry) SAB BUGZY BGZ-1011
(B92)

BALL, M.
Pageant *Op.26
mix cor,winds,brass NOVELLO rent
(B93)

BALLAD DE BON CONSEYL see Taylor

BALLAD OF MAGNA CARTA, THE see Weill,
Kurt

BALLAD OF MY FATHER, THE see Weigl,
[Mrs.] Vally

BALLAD OF THE LION AND THE LAMB, THE
see Cohen

BALLADE see Massis

BALLADE AU HAMEAU: CETTE FILLE, ELLE
EST MORTE see Bordewijk-Roepman,
Johanna

BALLADE DES DAMES DE PARIS see Calmel,
Roger

BALLADE DES TROIS COMPAGNONS see Patry,
Andre J.

BALLADE EN NOVEMBRE see Vanderlove,
Anne

BALLADE FINALE see Calmel, Roger

BALLADE OM FREDEN see Kvandal, Johan

BALLADE POUR PRIER NOTRE DAME see
Calmel, Roger

BALLADE SUR LA PAIX see Jaubert,
Maurice

BALLADE VAN DE FIETS see Bruyns, M.

BALLADE VAN DE FIETS see Vermulst, Jan

BALLADE VAN HET ZOUT see Vermulst, Jan

BALLADE VAN HET ZOUT, DE see Vermulst,
Jan

BALLADEN see Schroeder, Hermann

BALLADEN OM NARKIS OCH EKO see Hvoslef,
Ketil

BALLERINA GIRL see Richie, Lionel

BALLET DES OMBRES, LE see Berlioz,
Hector (Louis)

BALLETTI A CINQUE VOCI see Gastoldi,
Giovanni Giacomo

BALLIF, CLAUDE (1924-   )
Coup De Des, Un *Op.53
cor,4perc,2timp,2db TRANSAT.
TR001595   (B94)

BALLOU, PHILIP
Fable
SATB [6'0"] APNM sc $4.75, cor pts
rent   (B95)

BALLY, PAUL
T'en Souvient-Il Encore?
TTBB HUGUENIN CH 885   (B96)

BALMER, LUC (1898-   )
Ode De Ronsard
SATB,acap HUGUENIN EB 207   (B97)

BALOO, BALOO *Scot
(Rhein) 2pt treb cor/2pt mix cor
SCHIRM.G 323390 $.80   (B98)

BALZONELLI, ALBERTO
Con Alas En Los Ojos
"With Wings He'll Touch Your
Eyelids" SATB LAWSON 52202 (B99)

Jugaba La Nina Aquella
"That Girl Playing" 3pt mix cor
LAWSON 52201   (B100)

That Girl Playing *see Jugaba La
Nina Aquella

With Wings He'll Touch Your Eyelids
*see Con Alas En Los Ojos

BANCHIERI, ADRIANO (1568-1634)
Contrepoint Des Animaux
see Banchieri, Adriano, Festin Du
Jeudi Gras

Festin Du Jeudi Gras
SSATB CAILLARD PC 67 contains also:
Contrepoint Des Animaux   (B101)

BANDIETENKOOR see Verdi, Giuseppe

BANDURA
(Karpowitsch) men cor ZIMMER. 619
(B102)

BANGE LIEBE *see Zoll, Paul,
Madchenlied; Zoll, Paul, Mein Herz,
Ich Will Dich Fragen   (B103)

BANGE LIEBE see Zoll, Paul

BANK, JACQUES (1943-   )
Proloog En Tussenstuk 1 (from Een
Tanthologie)
cor,T solo [8'30"] DONEMUS   (B104)

Requiem Voor Een Levende
SATB,speaking voice,3db,4sax,
9acord,3perc [50'] DONEMUS (B105)

BANKS O'DOON, THE *Scot
(Rhein) SATB SCHIRM.G 322560 $.70
(B106)

BANUWA *folk song
see Sonthonay, F., Fete Des Ours, La
(Mason, R.) 3 eq voices,gtr,rec
HEUGEL HE 31979 contains also: Fete
Des Ours, La   (B107)

BAR-AM, BENJAMIN
Little Songs For Big Children *CC8U
[Heb/Eng] mix cor,acap
ISR.MUS.INST. 152   (B108)

BAR YOHAI see Davidowitz

BARBARA
Aigle Noir, L'
(Turellier, J.) 2pt mix cor,gtr
HEUGEL HE 32259   (B109)

Petit Bois De Saint-Amand, Le
(Humbert, G.) 3 eq voices HEUGEL
HE 32482   (B110)

BARBARA ALLEN *folk song,Eng
(Terri, Salli) "Barb'ry Ellen" SATB
LAWSON 855   (B111)

BARBARA ALLEN see Willcocks, David
Valentine

BARBERINE see Levinas, M.

BARBER'S TALE, A see Bennett

BARBLAN, EMMANUEL
Au Flanc Du Coteau (Chansons Du
Vigneron) *see J'ai Plante Une
Arbalete; Jean P'tit Jean;
Plantons La Vigne   (B112)

Dors Mon Enfant Sage
3pt cor HUGUENIN EB 272   (B113)

J'ai Plante Une Arbalete
SATB,acap HUGUENIN EB 69 see from
Au Flanc Du Coteau (Chansons Du
Vigneron)   (B114)

Jean P'tit Jean
SATB,acap HUGUENIN EB 69 see from
Au Flanc Du Coteau (Chansons Du
Vigneron)   (B115)

BARBLAN, EMMANUEL (cont'd.)

Mariette
3pt cor HUGUENIN EB 273   (B116)

Patrie
TTBB HUGUENIN EB 193C   (B117)

Plantons La Vigne
SATB,acap HUGUENIN EB 69 see from
Au Flanc Du Coteau (Chansons Du
Vigneron)   (B118)

Sulla Barchetta-Dans Mon Bateau
SATB,acap HUGUENIN EB 229 (B119)

BARBLAN-OPIENSKA, LYDIA
Roses De Saadi, Les
eq voices,pno HUGUENIN EB 117
(B120)

BARBRA ELLEN
(Oxley, Harrison) [3'30"] ROBERTON
392-00505 $1.00   (B121)

BARB'RY ELLEN see Barbara Allen

BARGE
School Is Out (composed with Guida;
Anderson)
(Althouse) 2pt cor SHAWNEE 0103
$1.00   (B122)
(Althouse) SAB SHAWNEE 0395 $1.00
(B123)
(Althouse) SATB SHAWNEE 1858 $1.00
(B124)

BARJA, ANGEL
Canciones Populares Del Reino De Leon
*CC17L
mix cor ALPUERTO 1301   (B125)

Caro Mea
mix cor PILES 417   (B126)

BARKIN, ELAINE R. (1932-   )
Two Emily Dickinson Choruses
SATB [5'0"] APNM sc $4.75, cor pts
rent   (B127)

BARLEY
Gull And I, The
(Bagan) 2pt mix cor,pno LAWSON
52233   (B128)

BARLOW, BETTY
Happy Birthday, U.S.A. (composed with
Merman, Joyce)
SA,pno WIDE WORLD $.75   (B129)

BARNES
As Lately We Watched *Xmas
SATB,kbd,opt strings oct DEAN
HRD 177 $1.10   (B130)

Round Robin
SATB LAWSON LG 52355 $.70   (B131)

Walking Home From School
SATB LAWSON LG 52356 $.70   (B132)

BARNETT, STEVE
Mi Y'maleil (from Arise And Be Free)
SATB,acap TRANSCON. 991294 $.85
(B133)

Mi Zeh Hidlik (from Arise And Be
Free)
SATB,acap TRANSCON. 991295 $1.35
(B134)

S'vivon (from Arise And Be Free)
SATB,acap TRANSCON. 991293 $.75
(B135)

Y'mei Chanukah (from Arise And Be
Free)
SATB,acap TRANSCON. 991292 $1.20
(B136)

BAROQUE SUITE see Davidson, Charles
Stuart

BARQUE D'AZENOR, LA see Blanchard

BARQUE OF CLANRONALD, THE see Roberton,
Hugh Stevenson

BARRIER, THE see Bachorek, Milan

BARRON
Canadien Errant, Un
SATB HARRIS HC-5023 $1.25   (B137)

BASHMAKOV, LEONID (1927-   )
Muutamat Kevaan Paivat
men cor,acap FAZER F 07762-8 (B138)

BASTIANNSE, F.
Lied Van De Dorschers, De
(Wolff, H.W.D.) SATB MOLENAAR
15006503   (B139)

BATEAU IVRE, LE see Packer, Randall

BATELIERE, LA
(Huguenin, Charles) 1-4pt cor
HUGUENIN see from Chansons Pour La
Jeunesse, Troisieme Cahier   (B140)

BATESON, THOMAS (ca. 1570-1630)
  Your Shining Eyes And Golden Hair
    (Greyson) BOURNE B238808 $.65
                                    (B141)

BATTAGLIA see Gabrieli, Andrea

BAUER
  Alte Ist Vergangen, Das *see Gluck
    Zum Neuen Jahr

  Es Flog Ein Klein's Waldvogelein
    mix cor BOHM   (B142)

  Gluck Zum Neuen Jahr
    "Alte Ist Vergangen, Das" mix cor
    BOHM   (B143)

BAUER VON ESELSKIRCHEN, DER see Lassus,
  Roland de (Orlandus)

BAUERN, DIE see Aeschbacher, Walther,
  Paysans, Les

BAUERNWERK see Kutzer, Ernst

BAUM
  Music! Music! Music! *see Weiss

BAUMANN, LUDWIG (1866-1944)
  Ihr Berge Lebt Wohl
    TTBB MULLER 152   (B144)

BAUMGARTL, MICHAEL
  Zwei Gesange *CC2U
    5pt mix cor,perc sc BREITKOPF-L
    7946   (B145)

BAUTA see Bergh, Sverre

BAVICCHI, JOHN ALEXANDER (1922-   )
  Three Score Reflections
    2pt mix cor&unis cor,pno/org,opt
    brass,opt woodwinds,opt perc
    OXFORD 385732-4 f.s.   (B146)

BAYEZA KUSASA: BANTU-LIEDER AUS SUD-
  UND SUDWESTAFRIKA *CCU
    SATB, solo voices,perc MULLER 2750
                             (B147)

BE A CHAMPION! see Brymer, Mark

BE CAREFUL WHAT YOU SAY see Pfautsch,
  Lloyd Alvin

BE JOYFUL AND SING see Harlan

BE LIFE A BUTTERFLY see Strid

BE MERRY ALL THAT BE PRESENT see
  Wuorinen, Charles

BE SMART, DON'T START see Hawthorne,
  Grace

BE STILL, MY SOUL see Sibelius, Jean

BEACH BOYS MEDLEY, A *medley
  (Fry) SATB CPP-BEL 1529BC1X $2.25
                             (B148)
  (Fry) SSA CPP-BEL 1529BC2X $2.25
                             (B149)

BEACON, A DOOR, A see Siltman, Bobby L.

BEAL
  Together We'll Make The...
    BB&2camb CAMBIATA L97563 $.80
                             (B150)

BEALE, JAMES (1924-   )
  How Like A Winter *Op.43
    SATB [5'] (Shakespeare) AM.COMP.AL.
    $4.60   (B151)

BEALL
  Nutcracker (Youth Musical) *see
    Artman

BEALL, MARY KAY
  Old Sue's Panda *see Carter, John

BEARD
  I Believe (Quodlibet With Bach-Gounod
    Ave Maria)
    (Tucker) SAB SHAWNEE 0351 $.90
                             (B152)
    (Tucker) 2pt cor SHAWNEE 0066 $.90
                             (B153)

BEARS see Belyea, H.

BEART, GUY
  Souliers, Les
    (Passaquet, R.) 3 eq voices HEUGEL
    HE 32002   (B154)

BEAT GOES ON, THE see Roscoe

BEAU MUSICIEN see Daniel, Etienne

BEAU VOYAGEUR see Vigneault, Gilles

BEAUCARNE, JULOS
  Je Chante Pour Vous
    (Ott, Norbert) 3pt mix cor A COEUR
    JOIE 045   (B155)

BEAUDROT
  Lydia's Carol
    SATB KJOS GC163 $.90, ipa (B156)

  Woodcrest Carol, The
    SATB,opt orch KJOS GC164 $.90, ipa
                             (B157)

BEAUFORT SCALE, THE see Sallinen, Aulis

BEAUSONGE, LUCID
  Oiseau, L'
    (Ott, Norbert) 3pt mix cor A COEUR
    JOIE 1023   (B158)

BEAUTIFUL BUT TRUTHFUL see Pfautsch,
  Lloyd Alvin

BEAUTIFUL DREAMER see Foster, Stephen
  Collins

BEAUTIFUL SOUNDS see Besig, Don

BEAUTY AND THE BEAST see Oliver,
  Stephen

BEAUVERD
  Esquisse Patriotique
    TTBB HUGUENIN CH 1018   (B159)

BECAUD, GILBERT (1927-   )
  Important, C'est La Rose, L'
    (composed with Amade, L.)
    (Dumas, H.) 4pt mix cor HEUGEL
    HE 32333   (B160)

  Nathalie
    (Passaquet, R.) 4pt mix cor HEUGEL
    HE 31853   (B161)

  Orange, L' (composed with Delanoe)
    (Brisset, Ch.) 4pt mix cor,pno
    HEUGEL HE 32578   (B162)

BECK, THOMAS LUDVIGSEN (1899-1963)
  Noregs Vakt
    [Norw] men cor,pno NORGE (B163)

  Under Himmelteiknet
    [Norw] mix cor,acap NORGE (B164)

BECKERATH, ALFRED VON (1901-1978)
  Heinzelmannchen, Die *cant
    unis cor,2rec,2vln,vcl,perc
    SIKORSKI 416 f.s.   (B165)

BECKLER, STANWORTH R. (1923-   )
  "Bust" From Sears Roebuck & Co. *see
    Catalog Cantata Number 2

  Catalog Cantata Number 2
    ""Bust" From Sears Roebuck & Co."
    5pt mix cor,pno LAWSON 52168
                             (B166)

BEDENKLICHKEITEN see Mullich, Hermann

BEDMAR, LUIS (1931-   )
  Canciones A Dos Voces *CCU
    2pt cor ALPUERTO 1032   (B167)

BEE, THE see Shur, Yekutiel

BEEBE
  I'm Makin' My Move!
    SAB SHAWNEE 0363   (B168)

  When I'm A Comedian
    2pt cor SHAWNEE 0065 $.90 (B169)

BEEBE, HANK
  Gloves
    2pt cor LEONARD-US 08602917 $.95
                             (B170)

  Hold It Fast
    2pt cor LEONARD-US 08603267 $.85
                             (B171)

  When I Go A-Christmas-Ing
    2pt cor BECKEN JH506   (B172)

BEEKUM, JAN VAN (1918-   )
  Auld Lang Syne (Bonnie's Medley 2)
    SATB,band MOLENAAR 08 1697 52
                             (B173)

  Bonnie's Medley
    SATB/TTBB,band MOLENAAR 08 1697 07
                             (B174)

  Door De Bossen, Door De Heide (Lente-
    Parade 3)
    SATB,band MOLENAAR 08 1696 53
                             (B175)

  Drei Lustige Lieder
    SATB MOLENAAR 08176007   (B176)

  Fruhlings-Parade *see Lente-Parade

  Good Night Ladies (The Old Timers
    Medley 4)
    SATB,band MOLENAAR 08 1589 54
                             (B177)

  Hoog Op De Gele Wagen (Lente-Parade
    1)
    SATB,band MOLENAAR 08 1696 51
                             (B178)

  It's A Long Way To Tipperary (The Old
    Timers Medley 3)
    SATB,band MOLENAAR 08 1589 53
                             (B179)

BEEKUM, JAN VAN (cont'd.)

  Jingle Bells (The Old Timers Medley
    2)
    SATB,band MOLENAAR 08 1589 52
                             (B180)

  Lente-Parade
    "Fruhlings-Parade" SATB/TTBB
    MOLENAAR 08169608   (B181)

  Massazang, En *see Old Timers
    Medley, The

  My Bonnie Is Over The Ocean (Bonnie's
    Medley 1)
    SATB,band MOLENAAR 08 1697 51
                             (B182)

  Nu Breekt Uit Alle Twijgen (Lente-
    Parade 2)
    SATB,band MOLENAAR 08 1696 52
                             (B183)

  Old Timers Medley, The
    "Massazang, En" SATB MOLENAAR
    08158907   (B184)

  Roept De Plicht (Lente-Parade 4)
    SATB,band MOLENAAR 08 1696 54
                             (B185)

  She'll Be Comin' (The Old Timers
    Medley 1)
    SATB,band MOLENAAR 08 1589 51
                             (B186)

BEERENDS, L. (1895-1972)
  Bekeerd: Al In De Plantage
    4 eq voices,acap ZENGERINK 18 (B187)

BEETHOVEN, LUDWIG VAN (1770-1827)
  Calme De La Mer Et Voyage Heureux
    mix cor HUGUENIN CH 657 (B188)

  Drei Gellert-Lieder *Op.48, CC3U
    TTBB,pno/org HEIDELBERGER 122
                             (B189)

  Ehre Gottes Aus Der Natur, Die
    "Himmel Ruhmen Des Ewigen Ehre,
    Die" 4 eq voices,acap ZENGERINK
    235   (B190)

  Fantasie C-Moll *Op.80
    mix cor,pno,orch cor pts BREITKOPF-
    W CHB 3550 f.s.   (B191)

  Himmel Ruhmen Des Ewigen Ehre, Die
    *see Ehre Gottes Aus Der Natur,
    Die

  Hymne A La Joie
    TTBB HUGUENIN CH 901   (B192)
    (Huguenin, Charles) SATB,acap
    HUGUENIN CH 826   (B193)

  Hymne An Die Nacht
    SATB,acap MULLER SM 132 (B194)

  I Love Thee *see Ich Liebe Dich

  Ich Liebe Dich
    (Goldman) "I Love Thee" 3pt wom cor
    LAWSON 51858   (B195)
    (Goldsmith) "My Love For You" TBB
    KJOS C8612 $.70   (B196)

  Meeresstille Und Gluckliche Fahrt
    *Op.112
    mix cor,orch cor pts BREITKOPF-W
    CHB 3629 f.s.   (B197)

  Music To Goethe's "Egmont"
    [Russ] voc sc MEZ KNIGA 471 (B198)

  My Love For You *see Ich Liebe Dich

  Ninth Symphony: Choral Section (from
    Symphony No. 9)
    [Ger/Eng] SATB,orch KALMUS K 06075
    $5.50   (B199)

  O Swiftly Glides The Bonny Boat
    SATB NATIONAL CMS-126 $.80 (B200)

  Ode To Joy
    (Kuzma; Holcombe) SAB MUSICIANS PUB
    ES-100 $.85   (B201)

  Offrande
    mix cor,solo voice HUGUENIN CH 664
                             (B202)

  Opferlied
    SATB,instrumental ensemble NATIONAL
    NMP-186 $1.00, ipa   (B203)

  Sweet Power Of Song
    SA NATIONAL CMS-131 $.80 (B204)

BEFRUCHTUNG MIT KLAVIERSTUCK see
  Stockhausen, Karlheinz

BEGGAR'S SONG, THE: O, HERE WE COME
  AWANDRING see Anonymous

BEGIN see O'Leary, Jane

BEGINNING see Sigurbjornsson, Thorkell

BEGONE, DULL CARE
(Cobb) 4pt mix cor LAWSON 52086
(B205)

BEGRABNISGESANG see Brahms, Johannes

BEGRABNISLIED see Schubert, Franz
(Peter)

BEGUELIN
Claire Chanson
TTBB HUGUENIN CH 1085   (B206)

Helle Weise
TTBB HUGUENIN CH 1086   (B207)

BEHOLD, YOU ARE CHARMING see Des Prez,
Josquin, Ecce, Tu Pulchra Es

BEI DER FLASCHE see Schumann, Robert
(Alexander)

BEI DES MONDES SCHEINE *folk song
(Desch, Rudolf) 3pt wom cor MULLER
SM 1854   (B208)

BE'IKVOT HEHATUL see Braun, Yeheskiel

BEIL, P.
Schones Hamburg
TTBB,pno SIKORSKI   (B209)

BEIM ABSCHIED ZU SINGEN see Schumann,
Robert (Alexander)

BEKEERD: AL IN DE PLANTAGE see
Beerends, L.

BELAUBRE, LOUIS-NOEL (1932-   )
Six Poems Of Rolland Pierre *CC4U
(Ross) SATB LAWSON 52244 (B210)

BELEN TOCAN A FUEGO, EN see Server,
Juan Pons

BELIEVE ME, IF ALL THOSE ENDEARING
YOUNG CHARMS
(Hunter; Shaw; Parker) TTBB,T solo
LAWSON 528   (B211)
(Willisegger, H.R.) mix cor,acap
PELIKAN PE 1182   (B212)

BELL, LARRY
Prologue And The End Of The World
SATB [7'] (text by Archibald
Macleish) AM.COMP.AL. $8.80
(B213)

BELL NOEL see Frey

BELLA VALMAGGINA see Castelnuovo, V.

BELLE, J.
Int Groene Met U Alderliefste
(Lagas, R.) "Into The Greenwood I
Go, With My Dear Beloved" SATB,
acap (med diff) ZENGERINK G 534
(B214)
Into The Greenwood I Go, With My Dear
Beloved *see Int Groene Met U
Alderliefste

Laet Ons Nu Al Verblijden
(Lagas, R.) "Now Let There Be
Rejoicing This Merry Time Of May"
SATB,acap (diff) ZENGERINK G 520
(B215)
Now Let There Be Rejoicing This Merry
Time Of May *see Laet Ons Nu Al
Verblijden

O Amoureusich Mondeken Root
(Lagas, R.) "Thy Cherry-Red Lips, O
Maiden Meek" SATB,acap (med diff)
ZENGERINK G 525   (B216)

Thy Cherry-Red Lips, O Maiden Meek
*see O Amoureusich Mondeken Root

BELLE AU JARDIN DE MAI see Vuataz,
Roger

BELLE CORINNE see Morin, Jean Baptiste

BELLE EST AU JARDIN D'AMOUR, LA
(Herr, F.) 4pt cor HEUGEL HE 32477
(B217)

BELLE-ILE-EN-MER MARIE-GALANTE see
Voulzy, Laurent

BELLE MARION
see O Caille, Pauvre Caille

BELLES FLEURS, LES see Monin, Claude

BELLS, THE see Rachmaninoff, Sergey
Vassilievich

BELLS AT SPEYER, THE see Senfl, Ludwig

BELLS OF PARADISE, THE
(LaMance) SSA,3rec LAWSON 52166
(B218)

BELLSON, LOUIE
It's The Time Of Year
(Ray, Jerry) 1-2pt cor ALFRED 7682
$.95   (B219)

BELYEA, H.
Bears
unis cor LESLIE 1134 f.s. (B220)

Gnus And Gnats
unis cor LESLIE 1153 f.s. (B221)

Lions
unis cor LESLIE 1142 f.s. (B222)

Monkeys And Ducks
unis cor LESLIE 1135 f.s. (B223)

Rabbits
unis cor LESLIE 1142 f.s. (B224)

Zebras
unis cor LESLIE 1154 f.s. (B225)

BELYEA, W.H.
Slumber Song
unis cor HARRIS HC-1015 $.50 (B226)

BENATZKY
Im "Weissen Rossl" Am Wolfgangsee
(Grieshaber) mix cor,pno LEUCKART
LSB 531   (B227)

BENDER
Old Music For Quiet Hearts
SATB,acap (med diff) THOMAS
1C218401 $.80   (B228)

BENNET, JOHN (ca. 1570-1615)
Weep, O Mine Eyes
SATB A COEUR JOIE 672   (B229)
SATB,acap CAILLARD PC 131 contains
also: Morley, Thomas, Now Is The
Month   (B230)

BENNETT
Barber's Tale, A
2pt cor SHAWNEE 0321 $.95 (B231)

Decorate The Halls!
2pt cor SHAWNEE 0098 $.85 (B232)

Letters To Lindbergh
mix cor NOVELLO 2946 $10.50 (B233)

Santa's Coming
2pt cor SHAWNEE 0079 $.85 (B234)

BENNETT, DAVID (1897-   )
Bye Bye Blues *see Hamm, Fred

BENNETT, JOHN
Coulez, Mes Pleurs!
SATB,acap HUGUENIN EB 383 (B235)

BENNETT, RICHARD RODNEY (1936-   )
Nonsense
mix cor NOVELLO   (B236)

Spell Of Sleep
SATB NOVELLO 16 0194   (B237)

BENNY BUNNY'S BAND see Roberts, Ruth

BENTON
Jason And The Golden Fleece
mix cor NOVELLO 20 0198 (B238)

BERAT, F.
Hameau, Le
2pt cor HUGUENIN CH 287 (B239)
1-4pt cor HUGUENIN see from
CHANSONS POUR LA JEUNESSE,
SIXIEME CAHIER   (B240)

Ma Normandie
1-4pt cor HUGUENIN see from
CHANSONS POUR LA JEUNESSE,
SIXIEME CAHIER   (B241)

Poete, Le
SATB,acap HUGUENIN CH 285 (B242)
1-4pt cor HUGUENIN see from
CHANSONS POUR LA JEUNESSE,
SIXIEME CAHIER   (B243)

BERBEL, MARCELO
Quimey, Neuquen
(Aquilar) 3pt mix cor,pno/gtr
LAWSON 52238   (B244)

BERCEUSE see Cossetto, Emil

BERCEUSE see Distler, Hugo

BERCEUSE see Rossi, Luigi

BERCEUSE BASQUE
(Grimbert, J.) 4pt mix cor,S solo
HEUGEL HE 31897   (B245)

BERCEUSE SAVOYARDE see Ruyssen

BERGE, HAKON (1954-   )
"Vinduer" For Choir And Magnetic Tape
cor,electronic tape NORGE (B246)

BERGE DER HEIMAT see Pappert, Robert

BERGENSIANA see Bergh, Sverre

BERGER
I Am No Longer Who I Was
SATB LAWSON LG 52354 $.85 (B247)

Whene'er You Think Of
SATB LAWSON LG 52352 $.85 (B248)

While I Still Am
SATB LAWSON LG 52353 $.95 (B249)

BERGER, JEAN (1909-   )
A Bug For All Seasons *see Ah,
Summer! (The Dragonfly); Mmm,
Winter (The Cocoon); Oh, Oh, Fall
(The Cricket); Oh, Spring! (The
Caterpillar)   (B250)

Ah, Summer! (The Dragonfly)
2 eq voices KJOS 6197 f.s. see from
A Bug For All Seasons   (B251)

Mmm, Winter (The Cocoon)
2 eq voices KJOS 6199 f.s. see from
A Bug For All Seasons   (B252)

Oh, Oh, Fall (The Cricket)
2 eq voices KJOS 6198 f.s. see from
A Bug For All Seasons   (B253)

Oh, Spring! (The Caterpillar)
2 eq voices KJOS 6196 f.s. see from
A Bug For All Seasons   (B254)

BERGER HE LA!
(Grimbert, J.) 3 eq voices HEUGEL
HE 31902   (B255)

BERGERE AUX CHAMPS, LA see Berthelot,
Rene

BERGERE ET LE MONSIEUR, LA
(Koller, Martin) mix cor BREITKOPF-W
CHB 5181 see from Vier Franzosische
Liebeslieder   (B256)

BERGERE LEGERE see Anonymous

BERGH, SVERRE (1915-1980)
Bauta
[Norw] men cor,acap NORGE (B257)

Bergensiana
[Norw] men cor,acap NORGE (B258)

Kjerringvise Mot Vinter'n
[Norw] men cor,acap NORGE (B259)

Vise Om A Vaera Glad
[Norw] mix cor,acap NORGE (B260)

BERGMAN, ERIK (1911-   )
Forsta Maj *Op.109
men cor,T solo FAZER F.M. 07724-8
(B261)

Four Vocalises Op. 100
men cor,Mez solo FAZER
(CH 76) F 06849-4   (B262)

Hathor-Suite *Op.70
mix cor,SBar soli,instrumental
ensemble FAZER (CH28) F 05203-5
(B263)

Lamento-Burletta
mix cor FAZER (CH 38) F 05429-6
(B264)

Loitsuja *Op.105
men cor,acap FAZER
(CH 78) F 06932-8   (B265)

Regn
cor,acap FAZER CH 82 F 07728-9
(B266)

Sound Of The Bell, The
men cor,solo&narrator,instrumental
ensemble FAZER F 06010-3 (B267)

Tule Armaani *Op.111
men cor,Bar solo FAZER F.M. 07873-3
(B268)

Two Karelian Folk Songs *see Zwei
Karelische Volkslieder

Tyttoset - The Lasses - Three Finnish
Folk Songs *CC3U
mix cor, solo voices FAZER
(CH 41) F 05484-1   (B269)

Ungdomsdrom
men cor,acap FAZER
(CH 84) F 07815-4   (B270)

Zwei Karelische Volkslieder
"Two Karelian Folk Songs" men cor
FAZER F 05375-1   (B271)

BERGSTROME, FLORA
Lullaby
SSA HARRIS HC-6012 $1.25 (B272)

BERGWANDERUNG see Schlerf, L.

BERICHTEN... TOT ONS GEKOMEN IN DE
EERSTE HELFT VAN DE MAAND JANUARI
see Geelen, Mathieu

BERKELEY, MICHAEL
Absence
mix cor,acap OXFORD 19 343543 8 see
from As The Wind Doth Blow (B273)

As The Wind Doth Blow *see Absence;
Women   (B274)

At The Round Earth's Imagin'd Corners
8pt cor,Bar solo,org,opt trp OXFORD
353053-8 $9.75   (B275)

Or Shall We Die?
8pt cor,Bar solo,3.3.3.3. 4.3.3.1.
harp,pno/cel,timp,3-5perc,strings
OXFORD 335401-2 $27.95   (B276)

Women
mix cor,acap OXFORD 19 343543 8 see
from As The Wind Doth Blow (B277)

BERKOVEC, JIRI (1922-   )
Vitej, Maji
jr cor, solo voices,pno SUPRAPHON
H 1222   (B278)

BERKOWITZ, SOL (1922-   )
Cuckoo Bird, The
2pt treb cor,pno LAWSON 52206
      (B279)

Don't Ask Me
2pt treb cor,pno LAWSON 52056
      (B280)

Father William
2pt treb cor,pno LAWSON 52055
      (B281)

I Had A Little Pup
2pt treb cor,pno LAWSON 52057
      (B282)

Passacaglia In Blue
SAB,pno LUDWIG SCS-9198 f.s. (B283)

Petite Lecon, Une *see To Have And
To Be

To Have And To Be
"Petite Lecon, Une" 2pt treb cor,
pno LAWSON 52018   (B284)

BERL, CHRISTINE
Ab La Dolchor
SA,pno [35'] AM.COMP.AL. $21.05
      (B285)

Book Of Sir Tristram, The
SATB [3'] AM.COMP.AL. $6.15 (B286)

Wordsworthian Dream In Blank Verse, A
SSAA,SS soli [10'] AM.COMP.AL.
$10.30   (B287)

BERLIN, IRVING (1888-1989)
Alexander's Ragtime Band
(Hayes) SATB SHAWNEE f.s., accomp
tape available   (B288)
(Wagner, Douglas E.) SAB,kbd
[2'30"] CORONET 392-41461 f.s.
      (B289)

God Bless America
(Ringwald, Roy) SATB SHAWNEE 0275
f.s.   (B290)

God Bless America (Festival Edition)
(Ringwald, Roy) 2pt cor SHAWNEE
0045 $1.00   (B291)
(Ringwald, Roy) SATB SHAWNEE 0978
$.95   (B292)
(Ringwald, Roy) SSA SHAWNEE 0295
$1.00   (B293)
(Ringwald, Roy) TTBB SHAWNEE 0198
$1.00   (B294)
(Ringwald, Roy) SAB SHAWNEE 0094
$1.00   (B295)

Irving Berlin- A Choral Portrait
(Ades) SATB SHAWNEE 1324 $3.50
      (B296)

BERLIOZ, HECTOR (LOUIS) (1803-1869)
Ballet Des Ombres, Le *Op.2
"Dance Of The Ghosts" [Fr/Eng] SATB
SCHIRM.G 321260 $1.25   (B297)

Damnation Of Faust, The
[Eng/Ger] SAATTB,MezTBarB soli,orch
KALMUS K 06096 $17.25   (B298)

Dance Of The Ghosts *see Ballet Des
Ombres, Le

Romeo And Juliet
[Fr/Ger/Eng] 4-8pt cor,ATBar soli,
orch KALMUS K 06090 $17.25 (B299)

BERNSTEIN, ELMER (1922-   )
Step To The Rear
(Billingsley) SATB CPP-BEL T6740SC1
$1.25, accomp tape available
      (B300)
(Billingsley) SAB CPP-BEL T6740SC3
$1.25, accomp tape available
      (B301)
(Billingsley) 2pt cor CPP-BEL
T6740SC5 $1.25, accomp tape
available   (B302)

BERNSTEIN, LEONARD (1918-1990)
Ich Gefall Mir
(Koester, Werner) SSAA,pno SIKORSKI
      (B303)

West-Side Story *medley
(Biersma, P.) SATB (includes
"Tonight", "I Feel Pretty", and
"Maria") MOLENAAR 15010104 (B304)

BERTHELOT, RENE (1903-   )
Bergere Aux Champs, La
(Turellier, Jean) SSA,fl,ob/clar
HEUGEL HE 32101   (B305)

BERTHOMIER, MICHEL
Refuges
SATB A COEUR JOIE MA 3   (B306)

Si
SATB,org A COEUR JOIE CA 6 (B307)

BERTINI, GARY (1927-   )
Shir Katalani Atik (Old Catalan Song)
[Heb] mix cor,acap,S solo [2']
ISR.MUS.INST. 9005   (B308)

BERTRAND, ANTOINE DE (1545-1581)
Ce Ris Plus Doux
SATB,acap CAILLARD PC 123 (B309)

Certes, Mon Oeil
SATB,acap CAILLARD PC 145 (B310)

Mon Dieu, Mon Dieu, Que Ma Maistresse
Est Belle
SATB A COEUR JOIE 677   (B311)

BESIDE THE GOLDEN DOOR see Goldman

BESIG
All My Tomorrows (composed with
Price)
2pt cor CPP-BEL SV8650 $.95, accomp
tape available   (B312)

As Long As I Have Music *see Price

Awake! Arise! Go Forth *see Price

Best Is Yet To Come, The *see Price

Brand New, Glorious Day
SSA CPP-BEL SV8225 $.95   (B313)

Free, And Glad To Be Me! *see Price

Go With A Song In Your Heart *see
Price

If You Try (composed with Price)
2pt cor CPP-BEL SV8412 $1.25 (B314)

It's A Wonderful, Wonderful Feeling
SAB CPP-BEL SV7916 $1.25   (B315)

It's Almost Time For Christmas
(composed with Price)
2pt cor CPP-BEL SV8328 $1.10 (B316)

It's Time For Movin' On
2pt cor SHAWNEE 0064 $.85   (B317)

It's Time To Ring Those Christmas
Bells! *see Price

Let The Tiny Baby Come In *see Price

Little One, Tiny One *see Price

Love Is The Meaning Of Christmas
SATB SHAWNEE 1816 $.95   (B318)

Music Box Carol, A (composed with
Price)
SSA CPP-BEL SV8418 $.95   (B319)

Sing Out The News!
TTBB SHAWNEE 0269 $.85   (B320)

Sleep Little Baby, Sleep
2pt cor SHAWNEE 5250 $.85   (B321)

Walk A Little Slower, My Friend *see
Price

BESIG, DON
Beautiful Sounds (composed with
Breitenstein, Linda)
ALFRED 7445   (B322)

Hi Ho, It's Christmas
cor ALFRED   (B323)

I Think I Need A Friend
cor ALFRED   (B324)

It's Hard To Say Goodbye (composed
with Price, Nancy)
ALFRED 7437   (B325)

Something Special
SAB CPP-BEL SV7926 $.95, accomp
tape available   (B326)

BESIG, DON (cont'd.)

Time For Joy, A
SSA CPP-BEL PROCH 02881 $.95 (B327)
SATB CPP-BEL PROCH 02728 $.95
      (B328)
SAB CPP-BEL PROCH 02883 $.95 (B329)

BESKYDY see Zamecnik, Evzen

BEST FRIENDS see Mitchell, Bob

BEST FROM DIRTY DANCING, THE
(Billingsley, Alan) SATB (contains Do
You Love Me, Hungry Eyes, I've Had
The Time Of My Life) CPP-BEL
C0151C1X $2.50, accomp tape
available   (B330)
(Billingsley, Alan) SSA (contains Do
You Love Me, Hungry Eyes, I've Had
The Time Of My Life) CPP-BEL
C0151C2X $2.50   (B331)
(Billingsley, Alan) SAB (contains Do
You Love Me, Hungry Eyes, I've Had
The Time Of My Life) CPP-BEL
C0151C3X $2.50   (B332)

BEST IS YET TO COME, THE see Price

BEST OF MIAMI SOUND MACHINE, THE
(Hanson, Mark) SATB (contains Conga,
Rhythm Is Gonna Get You, Words Get
In The Way and others) CPP-BEL
C0140C1X $2.50, accomp tape
available   (B333)
(Hanson, Mark) SSA (contains Conga,
Rhythm Is Gonna Get You, Words Get
In The Way and others) CPP-BEL
C0140C2X $2.50   (B334)
(Hanson, Mark) SAB (contains Conga,
Rhythm Is Gonna Get You, Words Get
In The Way and others) CPP-BEL
C0140C3X $2.50   (B335)

BEST OF TIMES, THE
(Nowak) SSA CPP-BEL 1518BC2X $1.25
      (B336)
(Nowak) SAB CPP-BEL 1518BC3X $1.25
      (B337)

BETSY see Adler, Samuel Hans

BETTIS, JOHN
Yesterday Once More *see Carpenter,
Richard Lynn

BEULAH LAND
(Roberts, Howard) SATB LAWSON
LG 51691 $.70   (B338)

BEURDEN, BERNARD VAN (1933-   )
Lente-Wals Voor Lilith
wom cor,2acord,electronic tape
[12'] DONEMUS   (B339)

Lilith Die Is Lief
SATB,acord [6'] DONEMUS   (B340)

BEWARE THE WIND OF SPRING see Leaf

BEWTIES OF THE FLUTE-BALL, THE see
Sims, Ezra

BEYOND THE VILLAGE see Schimmerling,
H.A.

BEZANSON, PHILIP (1916-1975)
Memory
SATB,4horn,strings [7'] AM.COMP.AL.
$6.15   (B341)

BEZENCON, G.
Contrastes (Visages-Mains)
men cor HUGUENIN CH 2074   (B342)

Esperance
mix cor HUGUENIN CH 2067   (B343)

BIALAS, GUNTER (1907-   )
Lamento Di Orlando
SATB,Bar solo,orch BAREN. BA 7136
rent   (B344)

BIALOMIZY, STAN
Music Is Our Heritage
SATB CPP-BEL OCT 02516 $1.20 (B345)

BIALOSKY, MARSHALL H. (1923-   )
American Names
SATB,acap (available in either
printed ed. ($8.00) or xeroxed
ed. ($1.40)) SANJO   (B346)

Eight Riddles From Symphosius And A
Codetta
SAA (available in either printed
ed. ($2.00) or xeroxed ed.
($.75)) SANJO   (B347)

Heart In The Jar, The
SATB,acap (available in either
printed ed. ($6.00) or xeroxed
ed. ($1.00)) SANJO   (B348)

I Wake And Feel The Fell Of Dark
SAA (available in either printed
ed. ($1.00) or xeroxed ed.

BIALOSKY, MARSHALL H. (cont'd.)

($.50)) SANJO   (B349)

Music For Soprano & Choir
SATB,S solo SEESAW   (B350)

No Worst, There Is None
SATB,acap (available in either
printed ed. ($3.00) or xeroxed
ed. ($1.00)) SANJO   (B351)

Roving Gambler, The
SATB,pno (available in either
printed ed. ($6.00) or xeroxed
ed. ($2.00)) SANJO   (B352)

Sight In Camp In The Daybreak Gray
And Dim, A
SATB,acap (available in either
printed ed. ($8.00) or xeroxed
ed. ($1.00)) SANJO   (B353)

Two Poems (In One Song)
SATB,acap (available in either
printed ed. ($4.00) or xeroxed
ed. ($.70)) SANJO   (B354)

BIBUS, LUDWIG
Mal So, Mal So
men cor BRAUN-PER 1056   (B355)

BIDDEN IS NIET ENKEL KNIELEN see
Verboom, Bernard

BIEBL, FRANZ (1906-   )
Buon Giorno Signorina
men cor BOHM see from Canzoni
Italiane   (B356)

Canzoni Italiane °see Buon Giorno
Signorina; Zingarella   (B357)

Durstig Jahr, Das
men cor BRAUN-PER 1013   (B358)

Hei Susu
mix cor BOHM   (B359)

Ich Fahr Dahin
men cor BOHM   (B360)

Im Wald, Im Hellen Sonnenschein
mix cor BOHM   (B361)

In Der Heimat Ist's So Schon
"Was Soll Ich In Der Fremde Tun"
men cor BOHM   (B362)

Kein Schoneres Leben   °see
Schaferlied

Klinge Lieblich Und Sacht
SATB MULLER 517   (B363)

Komm Zu Kolo
men cor,pno ZIMMER. 625   (B364)

Lebensregeln
mix cor BRAUN-PER 1055   (B365)

Letzte Lei, Die
men cor,acap ZIMMER. 616   (B366)

Madchen Vom Lande, Das
men cor,acap ZIMMER. 615   (B367)

Schaferlied
"Kein Schoneres Leben" men cor BOHM
(B368)

Sehnsucht Nach Den Bergen
mix cor BOHM   (B369)

Trara: Frisch Auf Zum Jagen
men cor,horn MULLER SM 1997   (B370)

Vier Verhaltnisse, Die
men cor,pno,opt gtr,opt acord,opt
perc BOHM   (B371)

Was Soll Ich In Der Fremde Tun °see
In Der Heimat Ist's So Schon

Zieh, Schimmel, Zieh!
(Miller, Franz R.) mix cor,4winds
BOHM   (B372)

Zigeunerlager, Das
men cor BRAUN-PER 1011   (B373)
mix cor BRAUN-PER 1012   (B374)

Zingarella
men cor BOHM see from Canzoni
Italiane   (B375)

BIEN QU'A GRAND TORT see Certon, Pierre

BIER, EEN BIER, EEN BIERENBROYKEN, EEN
see Episcopius, L.

BIERSMA, P.
Daarom...
SATB MOLENAAR 15001602   (B376)

BIG BAD JOHN see Dean, Jimmy

BIG GIRLS DON'T CRY
(Shaw, Kirby) SSA LEONARD-US 08655893
$.95, ipa, accomp tape available
(B377)

BIG RIVER: A MEDLEY
(Lojeski) SATB LEONARD-US 08200681
$2.50   (B378)
(Lojeski) SAB LEONARD-US 08200682
$2.50   (B379)
(Lojeski) 2pt cor LEONARD-US 08200683
$2.50, ipa, accomp tape available
(B380)

BIGGS, JOHN (1932-)
Song From Mr. Wilde
SATB,acap CONSORT PR CP 24 $.80
(B381)

Two Russian Folk Songs
SATB,acap CONSORT PR CP 31 $1.10
(B382)

BIGGS, RICHARD KEYS (1886-1962)
Alleluia
SATB,org CONSORT PR CP 401 $.75
(B383)

BIGOT, P.
Fiancee Du Timbalier, La
3 eq voices A COEUR JOIE 9010
(B384)

Paris...
3 eq voices A COEUR JOIE 9014
(B385)

BIGOT, PIERRE
Bottine, La
2 eq voices A COEUR JOIE 9018
contains also: Sur La Route Du
Moulin   (B386)

Sur La Route Du Moulin
see Bigot, Pierre, Bottine, La

Toboggan, Le
2 eq voices A COEUR JOIE 9017
(B387)

BIJTJE, HET: ZOEM-ZOEM-ZOEM, DAAR KWAM
EEN BIJTJE VLIEGEN see Worp,
Johannes

BILL BAILEY, WON'T YOU PLEASE COME
HOME? see Cannon, Hughie

BILLINGS, WILLIAM (1746-1800)
Chester
(Shaw, Robert; Parker, Alice) SATB,
acap LAWSON 501   (B388)

Rosa Of Sharon (from The Sacred Harp)
(Read) SATB,acap LAWSON 820   (B389)

BILLY BOY
see Soldier, Soldier

BIN I NET A PURSCHLE see Strecke,
Gerhard, Obendrauf, Der

BINDER, ABRAHAM WOLFE (1895-1966)
Az Der Rebbe Geht
[Yiddish] SATB,kbd TRANSCON. 990731
$.60   (B390)

BIRD DANCES see Mar-Chaim, Joseph

BIRD YEAR see Slavicky, Klement

BIRDS, THE see Heseltine, Philip
("Peter Warlock")

BIRD'S COURTING SONG °folk song
(Schillio) SATB SCHIRM.G 506890 $.90
(B391)

BIRDS OF PARADISE see Mathews, Peter

BIRTHDAY FRAGMENT see Suben, Joel Eric

BIRTHDAY ODE TO "BIG DADDY" BACH see
Schickele, Peter

BISCARDI, CHESTER (1948-)
Eurydice
SA,winds,brass,pno,4vln,4vcl [12']
AM.COMP.AL. $23.65   (B392)

Hebakes: Five Sapphic Lyrics
SSA/SATB,3perc [5'] AM.COMP.AL.
$9.15   (B393)

Indovinello
12pt cor [5'] AM.COMP.AL. $10.70
(B394)

BIT OF ADVICE, A see Krapf, Gerhard

BIT OF BLISS, A see Krapf, Gerhard

BIT OF WISDOM, A see Krapf, Gerhard

BITT DICH GAR SCHON see Backer, Hans,
Spielmann Und Das Madchen, Der

BITTE AM MORGEN see Medek, Tilo

BLACK FLY SONG, THE see Cable, Howard

BLACK IS see Heilner, Irwin

BLACKBIRD see Lennon, John

BLACKBIRD see Liddell, Claire

BLACKFORD, RICHARD
Through The Eyes Of A Child
SATB&jr cor,2.2.2.2. 2.2.2.0. harp,
strings,timp,perc OXFORD rent (B395)

BLACKSMITH, THE see Brahms, Johannes,
Schmied, Der

BLAIR, DEAN
Lonesome Cowboy: Goodbye Old Paint
SATB,pno (med) THOMAS 1C038416 $.90
(B396)

Piano Student, The
2pt cor,pno THOMAS 1C038922 $.95
(B397)

BLAKE
Three Choruses
SATB NOVELLO 0715 $2.50   (B398)

BLAKE, ALAN
see BALKIN, ALFRED

BLAKE, HOWARD (1938-)
Cultivating The Land (from The New
National Songbook)
SATB,pno LENGNICK 4687   (B399)

I Don't Want To Be A Number (from The
New National Songbook)
SATB,pno LENGNICK 4688   (B400)

BLANC, RENE
Chanson De L'Armailli, La
TTBB HUGUENIN CH   (B401)

Clair Ruisseau, Le
2pt cor,pno HUGUENIN CH 1103 (B402)

BLANCHARD
Aimable Pastourelle
4pt cor,acap JOBERT   (B403)

Au Port De Dieppe
3pt men cor JOBERT   (B404)

Barque D'Azenor, La
4pt cor,acap JOBERT   (B405)

Chanson Du Baleinier
3pt men cor JOBERT   (B406)

Cygne, Le
4pt cor,acap JOBERT   (B407)

Danse, La
4pt cor,acap JOBERT   (B408)

Fialaira, La
3pt wom cor JOBERT   (B409)

Filles De La Rochelle, Les
4pt cor,acap JOBERT   (B410)

Fillettes De Champagne
4pt cor,acap JOBERT   (B411)

Gros Moine, Le
4pt cor,acap JOBERT   (B412)

Hardi Les Gars!
3pt men cor JOBERT   (B413)

J'ai Pris La Clef De Mon Jardin
4pt cor,acap JOBERT   (B414)

J'ai Vu Le Loup
4pt cor,acap JOBERT   (B415)

Menage De La Sainte Famille, Le
4pt cor,acap JOBERT   (B416)

Neveux De Jean Bart, Les
3pt men cor JOBERT   (B417)

Nous Etions Dix Dedans Un Pre
3pt wom cor JOBERT   (B418)

Pique La Baleine
3pt men cor JOBERT   (B419)

Quand J'etais Jeune
4pt cor,acap JOBERT   (B420)

Rosa
4pt cor,acap JOBERT   (B421)

Rose Au Boue, La
3pt wom cor JOBERT   (B422)

Roy A Fait Battre Tambour, Le
4pt cor,acap JOBERT   (B423)

Saint-Gilles
4pt cor,acap JOBERT   (B424)

Tic-Tac Du Moulin, Le
4pt cor,acap JOBERT   (B425)

Trois Belles Princesses
4pt cor,acap JOBERT   (B426)

BLANCHARD (cont'd.)

   Ville De Sarlat
     4pt cor,acap JOBERT   (B427)

   Voici La Pentecote
     4pt cor,acap JOBERT   (B428)

BLANCHE
   Boites A Musique, Les (composed with
     Gab, Marc; Lafarge, Guy)
     (Robin, P.) 4pt mix cor HEUGEL
     HE 32252   (B429)

BLANE, RALPH
   see HUNSECKER, RALPH BLANE

BLANES, G.
   Printemps, Le °see Vidalin, M.

BLANK, ALLAN (1925-   )
   Two Witches, The
     SA,pno [4'] AM.COMP.AL.   (B430)

BLAREAU, LUDOVIC
   Voix Des Naufrages, Les
     SATB,acap HUGUENIN CH   (B431)

BLASFEMI see Thommessen, Olav Anton

BLATT
   Hanukah, Festival Of Lights
     SA CPP-BEL SV8320 $.95   (B432)

BLAUSTEIN, SUSAN
   To Orpheus
     SSATB [6'0"] APNM sc $10.00, cor
     pts rent   (B433)

BLAUWE LUCHT see Anonymous

BLAZING TORCHES OF THE SUN, THE see
   Emmert, Frantisek

BLES MURS, LES see Pantillon, G.L.

BLESSED ARE THOSE WHO WORK FOR PEACE
   see Regner, Hermann

BLESSED DAMOSEL, THE see Debussy,
   Claude, Damoiselle Elue, La

BLEUSE, MARC (1937-   )
   Cortege
     2pt jr cor,tamb,triangle HEUGEL
     HE 32186   (B434)

   Derriere La Montagne
     2pt jr cor,rec/pno HEUGEL HE 32184
     contains also: Holstein, Jean-
     Paul, Dis-Moi, Bon Charbonnier
     (2-6pt jr cor,Orff inst)   (B435)

   Et Pourtant C'est Vrai
     unis jr cor,Orff inst HEUGEL
     HE 32183   (B436)

   Ocean Zero-Zero
     unis jr cor,rec,tamb,gong HEUGEL
     HE 32185   (B437)

   Perruquiers
     7pt mix cor HEUGEL HE 32089 see
     from Trois Chansons De Metiers
                                        (B438)

   Serruriers
     4pt mix cor HEUGEL HE 32090 see
     from Trois Chansons De Metiers
                                        (B439)

   Tonneliers
     4pt mix cor HEUGEL HE 32090 see
     from Trois Chansons De Metiers
                                        (B440)

   Trois Chansons De Metiers °see
     Perruquiers; Serruriers;
     Tonneliers   (B441)

   Trois Comptines Pour Anne °see Guyot

BLEVINS, PATSY FORD
   America - My Home °medley
     SAB (med) GENTRY JG2100 $.95 (B442)

   Christmas Bells Are Ringing
     2pt jr cor,opt handbells oct GENTRY
     JG2068 $.85, pt GENTRY JG0699
     $1.50   (B443)

   It's With You All The Time
     SAB (med easy) GENTRY JG2067 f.s.,
     accomp tape available   (B444)

   Sun Is Shining, The
     2pt cor (easy) GENTRY JG2052 $.85,
     accomp tape available   (B445)

   Tiny Little Baby °Xmas
     2pt cor,pno (med easy) BOCK BG2115
     $.90   (B446)

BLIJDE MARE, EEN see Pelt, R.A. van

BLIJDE MARE KLONK DOOR 'T LAND, EEN see
   Pelt, R.A. van

BLINDE VON HYUGA, DER see De Grandis,
   Renato

BLOMBERG, ERIK (1922-   )
   Ekelundiana XII
     mix cor,pno STIM   (B447)

   Ekelundiana XIV
     mix cor,pno STIM   (B448)

   Fraga
     mix cor STIM   (B449)

   Gladjen
     mix cor STIM   (B450)

   Jamforelse, En
     mix cor STIM   (B451)

   Ros Och Tystnad Doftar Jorden
     4pt mix cor [2'30"] STIM 8511-043
                                        (B452)

   Ursprung
     mix cor STIM   (B453)

   Visa Till En Liten Manniska
     mix cor STIM   (B454)

BLOOM
   What! No Women? °see Meskill

BLOW, JOHN (1649-1708)
   Sing Ye Muses
     SATB,instrumental ensemble NATIONAL
     NMP-187 $.90, ipa   (B455)

BLOW AWAY THE MORNING DEW
   (Leavitt, John) SSA,pno CPP-BEL
     SV8912 $1.10   (B456)

BLOW, BLOW, THOU WINTER WIND see Lane,
   Philip

BLOW, BLOW, THOU WINTER WIND see
   Rutter, John

BLOW, BUGLE, BLOW see Getty, Gordon

BLOW THE CANDLES OUT
   (Smith) SATB SCHIRM.G 312900 $.80
                                        (B457)
   (Wagner, Douglas E.) SATB,kbd CORONET
     392-41481 $.90   (B458)

BLOW THE MAN DOWN see Skolnik, Walter

BLOW THE WIND SOUTHERLY
   see Auld Lang Syne
   (Liebergen, Patrick) 2pt cor,pno
     THOMAS 1C308935 $.95   (B459)

BLOW THY HORN, HUNTER see Cornyshe,
   William (Cornish)

BLOW YE WINDS see Skolnik, Walter

BLUE ONE, THE see Bachorek, Milan

BLUE RONDO A LA CHRISTMAS
   (Strauss) SSAB CPP-BEL SV8625 $1.20,
     accomp tape available   (B460)

BLUE SKY IS LOVELY, THE see Kurz, Ivan

BLUES DU MANGEUR DE CITRON, LE see
   Gauffriau, Jean

BLUES FOR FICKLE FOOLS see Taylor,
   Lemoyne

BLUM, HERBERT
   Vrede (Song Of Olympia)
     (Verheijen, J.) SATB MOLENAAR
     13000904   (B461)
     (Verheijen, J.) TTBB MOLENAAR
     13000903   (B462)

BLYTON, CAREY (1932-   )
   Woman's World, A
     SSA NOVELLO   (B463)

BOARISCHER BAUER see Miller, Franz R.

BOBBY SHAFTO
   (Walters) TTBB,pno ROBERTON 392-00545
     $1.50   (B464)

BOBBY SHAFTOE see Coombes, Douglas

BOBBY SHAFTOE see Willcocks, David
   Valentine

BOCHMANN
   Mit Musik Geht Alles Besser
     (Grieshaber) mix cor,pno LEUCKART
     LSB 515   (B465)
     (Grieshaber) men cor,pno LEUCKART
     LSB 115 f.s.   (B466)

   Wer Ist Hier Jung, Wer Hat Hier
     Schwung
     (Grieshaber) mix cor,pno LEUCKART
     LSB 530   (B467)

BOCK, FRED (1939-   )
   Sandcastles
     SATB (med) GENTRY JG2111 $1.15
                                        (B468)

BOCK, JERRY (1928-   )
   Sunrise, Sunset (from Fiddler On The
     Roof) (composed with Harnick,
     Sheldon)
     3pt mix cor,opt gtr/pno A COEUR
     JOIE 1030   (B469)

BOEDIJN, GERARD H. (1893-1972)
   Liedje
     SATB MOLENAAR 13005203   (B470)

   Ons Lied Van Noord-Holland
     SSA MOLENAAR 13005303   (B471)

BOEKEL, M. (1914-   )
   Nu Daagt Het In Het Oosten
     SATB,band MOLENAAR 03 1122 04
                                        (B472)
     SATB,band MOLENAAR 08 1122 05
                                        (B473)

   Opperste Herder, De
     SATB,band MOLENAAR 08 1118 07   (B474)

BOESCH
   Ceremonial
     eq voices/mix cor,opt inst HEUGEL
     HE 32102   (B475)

BOGERT, HANS VAN DEN
   Lenteliedje: Welkom, Lieve Lenteboden
     [Dutch] 3 eq voices,acap ZENGERINK
     V 323   (B476)

BOITES A MUSIQUE, LES see Blanche

BOITO, ARRIGO (1842-1918)
   Salmodia Finale (from Mefistofele)
     (De Pietto) SATB,pno LAWSON 51910
                                        (B477)

BOJARENLIEDEREN 1 °see Golowalj Moja,
   "Mein Lieber Gatte"; Jechali
   Bojare, "Aus Nowgorod Zogen
   Bojaren"; Nje Boitjessia Djewizy,
   "Madel Habt Keine Angst"; Schto
   Mnje Shit', "Wie Soll Ich Traurig
   Leben"   (B478)

BOJARSKY
   Alexandrina
     SATB SCHIRM.G 232620 $.80   (B479)

BOLD HEART see Weigl, [Mrs.] Vally

BOLERAS SEVILLANAS °folk song,Span
   (Wind) TTBB,S/T solo MULLER 531   (B480)

BOLERAS SEVILLANAS see Neaum, Michael

BOLLER, CARLO
   Coupeuse De Joncs, La
     men cor HUGUENIN   (B481)

   Fanchon
     men cor HUGUENIN   (B482)

BOLLERAS SEVILLANAS see Fabrez, E.

BOLT
   I Want To Be Ready
     SATB SHAWNEE 1864 $.95   (B483)

BOMBARDEMENT: ET DIKT AV PABLO NERUDA
   see Skouen, Synne

BON HOMME! see Kenins, Talivaldis

BON JOUR, BON MOIS see Dukas, Paul

BOND, VICTORIA (1945-   )
   Busted!
     SSAA,pno SEESAW   (B484)

   Canon Of Cans
     SSAA,pno SEESAW   (B485)

   Two Tree-Toads
     SSAA SEESAW   (B486)

BONHEUR, LE see Ninnin, Francois

BONHEUR CRAINTIF see Rietz, R.

BONI, GIOVANNI
   Three Carols °CCU
     SATB SCHIRM.G 501580 $1.25   (B487)

BONITA PINATA see North, Jack King

BONJOUR MADEMOISELLE
   see Gentil Coquelicot

BONJOUR MON COEUR see Castro, Jean de

BONJOUR MON COEUR see Lassus, Roland de
   (Orlandus)

BONN see Kjeldaas, Arnljot

BONNEAU, PAUL (1918-   )
  Buttes Chaumont, Les (from Campagnes
    Parisiennes)
    SAB A COEUR JOIE 1025   (B488)
    2 eq voices A COEUR JOIE 9011 see
      from Campagnes Parisiennes (B489)

  Campagnes Parisiennes *see Buttes
    Chaumont, Les; Jardin Des
    Plantes, Le; Parc Monceau, Le
                                 (B490)

  Jardin Des Plantes, Le (from
    Campagnes Parisiennes)
    SAB A COEUR JOIE 1024   (B491)
    2 eq voices A COEUR JOIE 9011 see
      from Campagnes Parisiennes (B492)

  Parc Monceau, Le (from Campagnes
    Parisiennes)
    3pt mix cor A COEUR JOIE 1026
                                 (B493)
    2 eq voices A COEUR JOIE 9011 see
      from Campagnes Parisiennes (B494)

BONNEN see Roed, Ivar A.

BONNET
  Source, La *see Djian, H.

BONNET, PIERRE (1638-1708)
  Alors Que Mon Coeur S'engage
    SATB,acap HUGUENIN EB 453   (B495)
    SATB A COEUR JOIE 673   (B496)

  Francion Vint L'autre Jour
    SSATB CAILLARD PC 13 contains also:
    Arbeau, Thoinot (Jehan Tabourot),
    Pavane: Belle Qui Tiens Ma Vie;
    Janequin, Clement, Je Ne Connais
    Femme   (B497)

  Je Souffre Un Si Cruel Martyre
    SATB,acap HUGUENIN EB 414   (B498)

BONNIE'S MEDLEY see Beekum, Jan Van

BONSOIR PRINCESSE see Gesseney-Rappo,
  Dominique

BONZORNO, MADONNA BENVEGNUA see
  Scandello, Antonio (Scandellus,
  Scandelli)

BOODLE
  Fugal Carol
    SATB oct DEAN HRD 290 $1.50 (B499)

  Pastoral Carol, A
    SATB oct DEAN HRD 289 $1.10 (B500)

BOOGIE DOWN
  (Chinn) SATB CPP-BEL SV8350 $2.25,
    accomp tape available   (B501)

BOOK OF FOUR-PART MADRIGALS, A *CC12U
  (Arnold, Denis; Harman, Alec; Ledger,
  Philip) 4pt cor OXFORD 343524-1
  f.s.   (B502)

BOOK OF SIR TRISTRAM, THE see Berl,
  Christine

BOOT, SADDLE TO HORSE see Lewis, W.
  Rees

BORDEWIJK-ROEPMAN, JOHANNA (1892-1971)
  Ballade Au Hameau: Cette Fille, Elle
    Est Morte
    mix cor ZENGERINK 338   (B503)

  Dance-Song (from The Dream-Keeper)
    see Bordewijk-Roepman, Johanna,
    Poem

  Poem (from The Dream-Keeper)
    TTBB BANK BOR 250 contains also:
    Dance-Song   (B504)

BORISHANSKY, ELLIOT (1930-   )
  Aware
    SATB [2'] (D. H. Lawrence)
    AM.COMP.AL. $1.95   (B505)

  Eidola
    SATB [4'] AM.COMP.AL. $4.10 (B506)

  House Was Quiet And World Was Calm
    SATB,electronic tape,pno [5']
    AM.COMP.AL. $7.70   (B507)

BORN WITH THE BEAT TO DANCE ON THE
  STREET see McPheeters

BORODIEVYCH, ROMAN
  Kiev And Other Songs *CC12L
    [Ukranian] cor,pno DUMA $9.00
                                 (B508)

BORODIN, ALEXANDER PORFIRIEVICH
  (1833-1887)
  Selected Choruses *CCUL
    [Russ] MEZ KNIGA 160 includes Hymn
    To St. Cyril And St. Methodius,
    choruses from Prince Igor and The
    Valiant Knights (Bogatyri) (B509)

BORTBYTINGARNA see Larsson, Bjorn

BORTNJANSKI'J, DIMITRI
  Avondklokken: Hoor, De Golven
    Dragen...Jubilate
    mix cor ZENGERINK 22   (B510)

BOS, RUUD (1936-   )
  C'etait En Avril
    SATB,acap HARMONIA 3702   (B511)

BOS-MAURER, A. VAN DE
  Mijn Boerenland
    SATB MOLENAAR 13015005   (B512)

  Steppe, Alleen Maar Steppe!
    SATB MOLENAAR 13014905   (B513)

BOSE, HANS-JURGEN VON (1953-   )
  Herbst, Der
    (Holderlin, Fr.) [Ger] mix cor,acap
    SCHOTTS SKR 20015 see from Vier
    Madrigale Aus "Die Leiden Des
    Jungen Werthers"   (B514)

  Ich Leb Ohne Ruh Im Herzen
    (Abschatz, Assmann Von) [Ger] mix
    cor,acap SCHOTTS SKR 20015 see
    from Vier Madrigale Aus "Die
    Leiden Des Jungen Werthers" (B515)

  Ich Will Den Nagenden Beschwerden
    (Lenz, J.M.R.) [Ger] mix cor,acap
    SCHOTTS SKR 20015 see from Vier
    Madrigale Aus "Die Leiden Des
    Jungen Werthers"   (B516)

  Vier Madrigale Aus "Die Leiden Des
    Jungen Werthers" *see Herbst,
    Der; Ich Leb Ohne Ruh Im Herzen;
    Ich Will Den Nagenden
    Beschwerden; Wer War Ich Doch?
                                 (B517)

  Wer War Ich Doch?
    (Lenz, J.M.R.) [Ger] mix cor,acap
    SCHOTTS SKR 20015 see from Vier
    Madrigale Aus "Die Leiden Des
    Jungen Werthers"   (B518)

BOSE SPRUCHE see Schedl, Gerhard

BOSHKOFF, RUTH
  Little Red Riding Hood *CC7U
    jr cor,Orff inst MMB SE-0030 $4.50
                                 (B519)

BOSSLER, KURT (1911-1976)
  Elfenlied
    SSA MULLER 1003   (B520)

  Mond Im Wasser, Der
    SSA MULLER 1002   (B521)

BOTS, J.
  Feestcantate Sint-Cecilia *Op.22
    4 eq voices,acap ZENGERINK 142
                                 (B522)

BOTSCHAFT see Stockhausen, Karlheinz

BOTTCHER, EBERHARD (1934-   )
  To Sanger Om Barn
    [Norw] mix cor,acap NORGE   (B523)

  Venerid
    [Swed] mix cor,acap NORGE   (B524)

BOTTINE, LA see Bigot, Pierre

BOTTJE, WILL GAY (1925-   )
  Diptych
    SSAATTBB,pno [13'] AM.COMP.AL. f.s.
                                 (B525)
  Songs From The Land Between Rivers
    SATB,winds,brass,strings,4perc
    [39'] AM.COMP.AL. $46.35 (B526)

BOUDOIR see Van Wijk, Jan

BOUND FOR JUBILEE see Bacak, Joyce
  Eilers

BOUND FOR THE RIO GRANDE
  (Shaw, Robert; Parker, Alice) TTBB,T
  solo LAWSON 51056   (B527)

BOUNTY OF ATHENA, THE see Clarke, Henry
  Leland

BOUQUET, LE see Prevert, J.

BOUQUET OF ROSES see Nelson

BOUREE (FROM THE ENGLISH SUITE, NO.2)
  see Bach, Johann Sebastian

BOURGEOIS, GERARD
  Amitie, L'
    (Grindel, J.) 4pt mix cor HEUGEL
    HE 31856   (B528)

BOURGEOIS GENTILHOMME, LE see Lully,
  Jean-Baptiste (Lulli)

BOURGUIGNONS, LES see Layolle,
  Francesco

BOURNE BARBERSHOP BLOCKBUSTERS *CC12L
  4pt cor BOURNE B201608 $3.95 (B529)

BOURNE BEST BARBERSHOP *CC12L
  4pt cor BOURNE B201616 $3.95 (B530)

BOURQUE
  Walk Along Beside Me
    SATB SHAWNEE 1801 $.90   (B531)

BOURQUE, RICHARD
  America, My Friend
    SATB ALFRED 7621 $.95   (B532)

BOURREE AUVERGNATE see Langree, Alain

BOURREE DU CELIBATAIRE, LA see Brel,
  Jacques

BOURTAYRE
  Adieu, Monsieur Le Professeur
    (Aufray; Vline) SATB MOLENAAR
    13039804   (B533)

BOUSSET, DE
  O Nuit Plus Belle Que Le Jour
    SATB,acap CAILLARD PC 152   (B534)

BOVET, J.
  Misch-Masch
    men cor HUG FF8813   (B535)

BOVET, JOSEPH (1879-1951)
  Au Detour De La Colline
    TTBB HUGUENIN CH 1088   (B536)

  Cheveux D'or Et D'argent
    eq voices,pno HUGUENIN SP see from
    Trois Chansons Cahier 1   (B537)

  Coucou
    eq voices,pno HUGUENIN SP see from
    Trois Chansons Cahier 3   (B538)

  Fuseau De Ma Grand-Mere, Le
    eq voices,pno HUGUENIN SP see from
    Trois Chansons Cahier 2   (B539)

  Jean Da La "Boilletta"
    eq voices,pno HUGUENIN SP see from
    Trois Chansons Cahier 2   (B540)

  Jonquilles
    eq voices,pno HUGUENIN SP see from
    Trois Chansons Cahier 3   (B541)

  Leneli Du Simmeliberg
    eq voices,pno HUGUENIN SP see from
    Trois Chansons Cahier 2   (B542)

  P'tit Vin D'Lavaux, Le
    SATB,acap HUGUENIN EB 474   (B543)
    (Rochat, J.) TTBB HUGUENIN EB 486
                                 (B544)

  Rever
    eq voices,pno HUGUENIN SP see from
    Trois Chansons Cahier 3   (B545)

  Souvenirs Du Temps Passe, Les
    eq voices,pno HUGUENIN SP see from
    Trois Chansons Cahier 1   (B546)

  Ta Mere
    eq voices,pno HUGUENIN SP see from
    Trois Chansons Cahier 1   (B547)

  Trois Chansons Cahier 1 *see Cheveux
    D'or Et D'argent; Souvenirs Du
    Temps Passe, Les; Ta Mere   (B548)

  Trois Chansons Cahier 2 *see Fuseau
    De Ma Grand-Mere, Le; Jean Da La
    "Boilletta"; Leneli Du
    Simmeliberg   (B549)

  Trois Chansons Cahier 3 *see Coucou;
    Jonquilles; Rever   (B550)

  Vully, Le
    TTBB HUGUENIN CH   (B551)

BOWED DOWN WITH GRIEF AND PAIN see Van
  Der Muelen, Servaes, Altijt So Moet
  Ic Trueren

BOY AND HIS FALSE ALARMS, THE see
  Smith, Gregg

BOY FROM NEW YORK CITY, THE
  (Lapin, Larry) SATB CPP-BEL 4773BC1X
    $1.25   (B552)
  (Lapin, Larry) SSA CPP-BEL 4773BC2X
    $1.25   (B553)
  (Lapin, Larry) SAB CPP-BEL 4773BC3X
    $1.25   (B554)

BOYARINA VERA SHELOGA see Rimsky-
  Korsakov, Nikolai

BOYCE
  Pretty Little Angel Eyes (composed
    with Lee)
    (Althouse) SATB SHAWNEE 1868 $1.00
                                 (B555)
    (Althouse) SAB SHAWNEE 0402 $1.00
                                 (B556)

BOYD, JACK ARTHUR (1932-   )
Deep In The Night
3pt treb cor,acap LAWSON 51946
(B557)
BOYD, ROBERT A.
She Dwelt Among The Untrodden Ways
SATB,acap (med diff) FISCHER,C
CM8237 $.85   (B558)

Sigh No More Ladies
SSAA,acap (med diff) FISCHER,C
CM8238 $.95   (B559)

BRAAL, ANDRIES DE (1909-   )
C'est Le Ton...
SSA,2vln,vla,vcl [11'] DONEMUS
(B560)

BRAFFORD, P.
Menuet Pour La Joconde
(Passaquet, R.) 3 eq voices HEUGEL
HE 32036   (B561)

Petit Atome, Le
(Tritsch, J.) 4 eq voices HEUGEL
HE 32066   (B562)

Polka Des Tortues, La
(Tritsch, J.) 4 eq voices HEUGEL
HE 32067   (B563)

Sirene Et Scaphandrier °see Pottar,
O.

BRAGGING SONG, A see Asgeirsson, Jon

BRAHMS, JOHANNES (1833-1897)
Abendstandchen
(Erb) SAATBB LAWSON LG 52340 $.85
(B564)
Alto Rhapsody (Rhapsody, Op. 53)
[Ger/Eng] TTBB,A solo,orch KALMUS
K 06108 $2.50   (B565)
TTBB cor pts HUGUENIN CH 1153
(B566)
men cor,A solo,orch cor pts
BREITKOPF-W CHB 3428   (B567)

An Die Heimat
SATB NATIONAL NMP-141 $1.00   (B568)

Begrabnisgesang °Op.13
mix cor,winds BREITKOPF-W OB 3225
f.s.   (B569)

Blacksmith, The °see Schmied, Der

Brauner Bursche
SATB CAILLARD PC 186 see from
Zigeunerlieder, Op. 103   (B570)

Darthulas Grabesgesang
(Erb) SAATBB LAWSON LG 52342 $1.25
(B571)
Dauernde Liebe
see Three Songs For Four Voices

Dem Himmel Will Ich Klagen
mix cor,pno BREITKOPF-W CHB 4726
see from Deutsche Volkslieder,
WoO 33   (B572)

Deutsche Volkslieder, WoO 33 °see
Dem Himmel Will Ich Klagen; Es
Ging Sich Unsre Fraue; Es Sass
Ein Schneeweis Vogelein; Es
Stunden Drei Rosen; Es War Einmal
Ein Zimmergesell; Nachtigall,
Sag; Verstohlen Geht Der Mond Auf
(B573)

Drei Gesange °Op.42
6pt mix cor,opt pno sc BREITKOPF-W
CHB 5219 f.s.   (B574)

Drei Quartette °Op.31
4pt cor,pno sc BREITKOPF-W PB 5218
f.s.   (B575)

Entfuhrung, Die
see Three Songs For Four Voices

Erlaube Mir
SATB,acap CAILLARD PC 1005   (B576)

Es Geht Ein Wehen Durch Den Wald
°Op.62,No.6
"I Hear A Sighing In The Trees"
[Ger/Eng] SATB SCHIRM.G 500150
$.80   (B577)

Es Ging Sich Unsre Fraue
mix cor,pno BREITKOPF-W CHB 4729
see from Deutsche Volkslieder,
WoO 33   (B578)

Es Sass Ein Schneeweis Vogelein
mix cor,pno BREITKOPF-W CHB 4727
see from Deutsche Volkslieder,
WoO 33   (B579)

Es Stunden Drei Rosen
mix cor,pno BREITKOPF-W CHB 4725
see from Deutsche Volkslieder,
WoO 33   (B580)

BRAHMS, JOHANNES (cont'd.)

Es Tont Ein Voller Harfenklang
see Vier Gesange

Es War Einmal Ein Zimmergesell
mix cor,pno BREITKOPF-W CHB 4728
see from Deutsche Volkslieder,
WoO 33   (B581)

Fest Und Gedenkspruche °Op.109
mix cor,acap BREITKOPF-W CHB 5188
f.s.
contains: Unsere Vater; Wenn Ein
Starker Gewappneter; Wo Ist Ein
So Herrlich Volk   (B582)

Five Waltzes (from Liebeslieder
Walzer, Op. 52) CC5U
(Shaw, Robert) SATB,pno 4-hands
LAWSON LG 52140 $1.75   (B583)

Four Songs For Three Voices
[Ger/Eng] SSA BROUDE BR. CR 47 f.s.
contains: Gang Zum Liebchen, Der;
Heimliche Liebe; Sehnsucht;
Sonntag   (B584)

Gang Zum Liebchen, Der
see Four Songs For Three Voices

Gang Zur Liebsten
(Sprague, Raymond) SSA,opt pno
LAWSON 52406 $1.00   (B585)

Gartner, Der
see Vier Gesange

German Folk Songs °CCUL
(Shaw, Robert; Parker, Alice) SATB,
acap LAWSON 671   (B586)

Gesang Aus Fingal
see Vier Gesange

Gesang Der Parzen °Op.89
6pt mix cor,orch BREITKOPF-W
CHB 3542 f.s.   (B587)
"Song Of The Fates" [Ger/Eng] 6pt
cor,orch KALMUS K 06051 $3.50 (B588)

Goeden Nacht En Wiegenlied
(Wolff, H.W.De) SATB MOLENAAR
15003403   (B589)

Guten Abend, Gut' Nacht
(Holman, F.) SATB MOLENAAR 15020602
(B590)
Heimliche Liebe
see Four Songs For Three Voices

Horch, Der Wind Klagt
SATB CAILLARD PC 188 see from
Zigeunerlieder, Op. 103   (B591)

I Have A Wish, Dear Mother
(McCullough) 3 eq voices LAWSON
51492   (B592)

I Hear A Sighing In The Trees °see
Es Geht Ein Wehen Durch Den Wald

Ich Fahr Dahin
SATB,acap CAILLARD PC 125 contains
also: Wiegenlied   (B593)

Ich Schell Mein Horn (from Vier
Lieder, Op. 43)
(Van Wely, Max Prick) TTBB BANK
AB 509   (B594)

Im Herbst °Op.104,No.5
SATB,pno BAREN. 19 322   (B595)

In Stiller Nacht
(Neijenrode, H.) SATB MOLENAAR
15018102   (B596)

Jour S'enfuit, Le
SATB,acap HUGUENIN EB 168A   (B597)
HUGUENIN EB 168 contains also:
Brunner, M., Adieu Au Pays;
Parchet, A., Chanson Du Rouet;
Hauptmann, Moritz, Coeurs
Amoureux; Lassus, Roland de
(Orlandus), Las! Voulez-Vous
Qu'une Personne Chante?; Lassus,
Roland de (Orlandus), Quand Mon
Mari Vient De Dehors   (B598)
(Hegar, F.) TTBB HUGUENIN CH 1186
(B599)

Kommt Dir Manchmal
SATB CAILLARD PC 187 see from
Zigeunerlieder, Op. 103   (B600)

Liebeslieder Walzer Suite °Op.52,
Op.65
SATB,2.2.2.2. 2.0.0.0. strings
[17'] KALMUS sc f.s., pts f.s.,
cor pts f.s.   (B601)

Lied Von Shakespeare
see Vier Gesange

BRAHMS, JOHANNES (cont'd.)

Love-Song Waltzes, Op. 52
[Russ/Ger] SATB,pno 4-hands MEZ
KNIGA 167   (B602)

Minnelied
(Sprague, Raymond) SSA,opt pno
LAWSON 52407 $.90   (B603)

Morgen Muss Ich Fort Von Hier
(Sprague, Raymond) LAWSON 52408
$1.00   (B604)

Nachtigall, Sag
mix cor,pno BREITKOPF-W CHB 4730
see from Deutsche Volkslieder,
WoO 33   (B605)

Neue Liebeslieder, Op. 65 °Waltz
4pt cor,pno 4-hands mix cor pts
BREITKOPF-W CHB 3474 f.s.   (B606)
[Russ/Ger] SATB,pno 4-hands MEZ
KNIGA 180   (B607)

Rhapsody, Op. 53 °see Alto Rhapsody

Schicksalslied °Op.54
mix cor,orch cor pts BREITKOPF-W
CHB 3442   (B608)

Schmied, Der
"Blacksmith, The" unis cor,pno
ROBERTON 75336   (B609)

Sehnsucht
see Four Songs For Three Voices

She Walks In Beauty
(Hokanson) SAB&camb CAMBIATA
M117447 $.70   (B610)

Song Of The Fates °see Gesang Der
Parzen

Songs Of Ophelia
(Brisman) 2pt cor BOURNE B238642
$.50   (B611)

Sonntag
see Four Songs For Three Voices

Standchen (from Lieder Und Romanzen,
Op. 14)
(Van Wely, Max Prick) TTBB BANK
AB 511   (B612)

Three Songs For Four Voices
[Ger/Eng] SSAA BROUDE BR. CR 48
f.s.
contains: Dauernde Liebe;
Entfuhrung, Die; Wahrend Der
Trennung   (B613)

Unsere Vater
see Fest Und Gedenkspruche

Verstohlen Geht Der Mond Auf
mix cor,pno BREITKOPF-W CHB 4731
see from Deutsche Volkslieder,
WoO 33   (B614)

Vier Gesange °Op.17
wom cor,2horn,harp BREITKOPF-W
OB 3226 f.s.
contains: Es Tont Ein Voller
Harfenklang; Gartner, Der;
Gesang Aus Fingal; Lied Von
Shakespeare   (B615)

Vineta
(Erb) SAATBB LAWSON LG 52341 $1.25
(B616)
Wahrend Der Trennung
see Three Songs For Four Voices

Waldesnacht
SATB DOBLINGER NR 206   (B617)
SATB,acap CAILLARD PC 135   (B618)

Wenn Ein Starker Gewappneter
see Fest Und Gedenkspruche

Wie Melodien Zieht Es Mir
(Vancil) SATB SOUTHERN f.s.   (B619)

Wiegenlied
see Brahms, Johannes, Ich Fahr
Dahin
SSA MOLENAAR 15026602   (B620)

Wiegenlied: Guten Abend, Gut Nacht
(Poos, Heinrich) TTBB MULLER 1724
(B621)

Wisst Ihr, Wann Mein Kindchen
CAILLARD PC 185 see from
Zigeunerlieder, Op. 103   (B622)

Wo Ist Ein So Herrlich Volk
see Fest Und Gedenkspruche

Zigeunerlieder °Op.103
4pt cor,pno sc BREITKOPF-W PB 5221
f.s., cor pts BREITKOPF-W
CHB 5221 f.s.   (B623)

BRAHMS, JOHANNES (cont'd.)

Zigeunerlieder, Op. 103 °see Wisst
Ihr, Wann Mein Kindchen   (B624)

Zigeunerlieder, Op. 103 °see Brauner
Bursche   (B625)

Zigeunerlieder, Op. 103 °see Kommt
Dir Manchmal   (B626)

Zigeunerlieder, Op. 103 °see Horch,
Der Wind Klagt   (B627)

Zwolf Lieder Und Romanzen °Op.44,
CC12L
wom cor,opt pno BREITKOPF-W
CHB 5199-5200   (B628)

BRAND
When I First Came To This Land
(De Cormier, Robert) SATB LAWSON
LG 51935 $.70   (B629)

BRAND NEW, GLORIOUS DAY see Besig

BRANDON, SEYMOUR (SY) (1945-   )
From The Musician's Yearbook
SATB,pno (3 settings of sayings or
poems from an 1895 pub.) CO OP
$1.00   (B630)

Greeting Card Madrigals °CC3U
SATB CO OP $1.00   (B631)

Of The People
mix cor,SATB soli,3trp,4horn,3trom,
tuba,3perc,org [25'0"] (in 3
mov'ts) CO OP perf mat rent
(B632)

BRANTSCHEN, GREGOR
Geleite Durch Die Wellen
see Brantschen, Gregor,
Rosenkranzkonigin

Rosenkranzkonigin
mix cor,acap CRON contains also:
Geleite Durch Die Wellen (B633)

BRASSENS, GEORGES
Cane De Jeanne, La
(Tritsch, J.) 4 eq voices HEUGEL
HE 32331   (B634)

Chasse Aux Papillons, La
(Holstein) 3pt mix cor,opt pno
CAILLARD PC 176   (B635)
(Passaquet, R.) 4pt mix cor HEUGEL
HE 31848   (B636)

Guerre De 14-18, La
(Passaquet, R.) 4pt mix cor HEUGEL
HE 32037   (B637)

Jeanne
(Passaquet, R.) 4pt mix cor HEUGEL
HE 33616   (B638)

Mauvaise Reputation, La
(Holstein) 3pt mix cor,opt pno
CAILLARD PC 178   (B639)

Pauvre Martin
(Passaquet, R.) 4pt mix cor HEUGEL
HE 31847   (B640)

Petit Joueur De Fluteau, Le
(Passaquet, R.) 4pt mix cor HEUGEL
HE 31853   (B641)

Priere, La
(Bereau, J.S.) 4pt mix cor HEUGEL
HE 31926   (B642)

Sabots D'Helene, Les
(Holstein) 3pt mix cor,opt pno
CAILLARD PC 177   (B643)

BRAUN, YEHESKIEL (1922-   )
Be'ikvot Hehatul
"Follow The Cat" [Heb/Eng] 3pt girl
cor,pno [3'] perf sc
ISR.MUS.INST. 6497   (B644)

Follow The Cat °see Be'ikvot Hehatul

Garland Of Flowers, A °see Zer
Prahim

Hahofesh Hagadol
"Summer Vacation" [Heb/Eng] treb
cor,2mel inst [2'] perf sc
ISR.MUS.INST. 6133   (B645)

Mizmorim Ufizmonot (Vol. 1) °CCU
[Heb/Eng] 3pt girl cor,pno perf sc
ISR.MUS.INST. 6494   (B646)

Mizmorim Ufizmonot (Vol. 2) °CCU
[Heb/Eng] 3pt girl cor,pno perf sc
ISR.MUS.INST. 6495   (B647)

Mizmorim Ufizmonot (Vol. 3) °CCU
[Heb/Eng] 3pt girl cor,pno perf sc
ISR.MUS.INST. 6496   (B648)

BRAUN, YEHESKIEL (cont'd.)
Summer Vacation °see Hahofesh
Hagadol

Three Ancient Songs °CC3U
[Heb/Greek] mix cor,acap
ISR.MUS.INST. 6575   (B649)

Twelve Canons °CC12U
[Heb/Eng] jr cor ISR.MUS.INST. 6132
(B650)

Zer Prahim °song cycle
"Garland Of Flowers, A" [Heb] jr
cor,Mez/T solo,pno [8'] perf sc
ISR.MUS.INST. 6591   (B651)

BRAUNER BURSCHE see Brahms, Johannes

BRAVE AND THE BOLD, THE see Roberts,
Ruth

BRAVNICAR, MATIJA (1897-1977)
Faronika Symphony
cor,orch [15'] DRUSTVO ED.DSS 667
(B652)

BRAY, JO MARIE
Kids Are Special
unis cor,pno (med easy) THOMAS
1C188218 $.60   (B653)

BRAY, KENNETH I.
She's Like The Swallow
SSAA HARRIS f.s.   (B654)

BREAD WILL GROW IN THOSE FIELDS see
Emmert, Frantisek

BREAK, BREAK, BREAK see Flaherty,
Thomas

BREAK FORTH see Retzel, Frank

BREAK FORTH INTO SINGING see Harris

BREAKWAY see Roscoe

BREATHING ROOM: JULY see Eliasson,
Anders

BREDON HILL see Mulholland, James

BREITENSTEIN, LINDA
Beautiful Sounds °see Besig, Don

BREL, JACQUES (1929-1978)
Air De La Betise, L'
(Passaquet, R.) 4pt mix cor HEUGEL
HE 32605   (B655)

Amsterdam
(Meyer, Paul- Philippe) TTBB
HUGUENIN CH 2054   (B656)

Bourree Du Celibataire, La
(Grindel, J.) 4pt mix cor HEUGEL
HE 32256   (B657)

Colombe, La
(Grindel, J.) 4pt mix cor HEUGEL
HE 31998   (B658)

Ne Me Quitte Pas
(Passaquet, R.) 3 eq voices HEUGEL
HE 32606   (B659)

Qu'avons-Nous Fait?
(Grindel, J.) 4pt mix cor HEUGEL
HE 32255   (B660)

BREMER, JETSE (1959-   )
Funf Liederen
chamber choir [16'] DONEMUS (B661)

BRENN SOL see Nystedt, Knut

BRETON, G.
Chanson Du Printemps Retourne °see
Ronsard

BREVIK, TOR (1932-   )
Bak Dei Siste Blanar
[Norw] men cor,acap NORGE (B662)

Etyde
[Norw] men cor,acap NORGE (B663)

Fredens Lys: Et Julespill
[Norw] jr cor,narrator& solo
voices,2vln,vla,vcl NORGE (B664)

Jolekveld
[Norw] mix cor,acap NORGE (B665)

Kattene
[Norw] jr cor NORGE   (B666)

Skalasangen (from Da Kongen Kom Til
Spilliputt)
[Norw] jr cor NORGE   (B667)

Sommerfugl
[Norw] jr cor NORGE   (B668)

BREVIK, TOR (cont'd.)
To Sanger Til Dikt Av Aslaug Vaa
[Norw] wom cor NORGE   (B669)

To Sma
[Norw] SAA NORGE   (B670)

BRIDAL CHORUS see Wagner, Richard

BRIDAL GOWN, THE see Palsson, Pall P.

BRIDGE see Lidl, Vaclav

BRIGANDS' SONGS see Laburda, Jiri,
Rebellenlieder

BRIGHT IS THE RING OF WORDS see Vaughan
Williams, Ralph

BRIGHT LIGHTS °CCU
[Russ] jr cor,pno MEZ KNIGA 530 (B671)

BRIGHT NEW DAY, A see Ross, Brad

BRIGHT NEW DAY WAITING FOR ME, A see
Sprunger, David

BRING A LITTLE JOY see Kirk, Theron
Wilford

BRINGS, ALLEN STEPHEN (1934-   )
Three Holy Sonnets
SATB,2.2.2.2. 4.2.3.1. timp,2perc,
strings [10'] (diff) MIRA voc sc
$7.50, sc $20.00, study sc $8.00
(B672)

BRITAIN, RADIE (1908-   )
Brothers Of The Cloud
TTBB,orch SEESAW   (B673)

BRITISH GRENADIERS, THE see Rutter,
John

BRITTEN
A.M.D.G
mix cor,acap FABER 50816 2 f.s.
(B674)

BROEDERS WILLEN WIJ WORDEN see Kooten,
Gerard Van

BROMFIELD TESTAMENT, THE see Sowash

BRON, PATRICK
A L'Auberge
TTBB HUGUENIN CH 2005   (B675)

Joyeuse Et Edifiante Histoire Du
Galant Vendu Aux Encheres
3pt men cor,pno,perc HUGUENIN
(B676)

Notaire De Cortaillod, Le
SATB,acap HUGUENIN CH 2049 (B677)

BROOKS, RANDY
Grandma Got Run Over By A Reindeer
(Chinn) 2pt cor CPP-BEL 5768GC5X
$1.25, accomp tape available
(B678)
(Chinn) SATB CPP-BEL 5768GC1X
$1.25, accomp tape available
(B679)
(Chinn) SAB CPP-BEL 5768GC3X $1.25,
accomp tape available   (B680)

BROOKS, RICHARD JAMES (1942-   )
I Am He That Aches With Amorous Love
TTBB,pno [4'] AM.COMP.AL. $3.85
(B681)
SATB,pno [4'] AM.COMP.AL. $1.90
(B682)

BROTHERS OF THE CLOUD see Britain,
Radie

BROTONS I SOLER, SALVADOR
Jam Rara Micant Sidera °Op.36
SATB,T solo,brass,perc A COEUR JOIE
177   (B683)

BROUILLARDS DE NOEL, LES
see Machaut, Guillaume de, De Tout
Suis Si Confortee

BROUILLARDS DE NOEL, LES see Caillat,
Stephane

BROWN
Oh! You Beautiful Doll (composed with
Ayer)
(Sterling) SATB SHAWNEE 0000 (B684)

BROWN, CHRISTOPHER (ROLAND) (1943-   )
Strawberry Fair
2pt cor,pno ROBERTON 75339 (B685)

BROWN, GARY
Good News
TTBB CPP-BEL SV7707 $.95   (B686)

BROWN, RAYMOND
America, My Home (composed with
Snyder, Audrey)
2pt cor CPP-BEL SV8205 $.95 (B687)

BROWNSEY
What A Team! (composed with Althouse)
SATB SHAWNEE 1877 $.95   (B688)

BRUCH, MAX (1838-1920)
Frohliche Musicus, Der
(Lemarc, A.) "Vrolijke Zangers, De"
SATB MOLENAAR 15003004   (B689)

Lay Of The Bell, The *see Lied Von
Der Glocke, Das

Lied Von Der Glocke, Das *Op.45
"Lay Of The Bell, The" SATB, solo
voices SCHAUR EE 5173   (B690)

Vrolijke Zangers, De *see Frohliche
Musicus, Der

BRUCKNER, ANTON (1824-1896)
Abendhimmel, Der
TTBB MOLENAAR 15010903   (B691)

Arneth-Kantate
(Nowak, Leopold) SATTBB,TTBB soli,
3horn,2trp,trom MUSIKWISS. see
from Kantaten Und Chorwerke I
                               (B692)
Entsagen
(Nowak, Leopold) SATB,S/T solo,org/
pno MUSIKWISS. see from Kantaten
Und Chorwerke I   (B693)
Fest-Cantate
(Nowak, Leopold) STBB,Bar solo,
winds,timp MUSIKWISS. see from
Kantaten Und Chorwerke II   (B694)
Festgesang (Jodok-Kantate)
(Nowak, Leopold) SATB,STB soli,pno
MUSIKWISS. see from Kantaten Und
Chorwerke I   (B695)
Germanenzug
(Nowak, Leopold) 4pt men cor, solo
voices,brass MUSIKWISS. see from
Kantaten Und Chorwerke II   (B696)
Helgoland
(Nowak, Leopold) 4pt men cor, solo
voices,2.2.2.2. 4.3.3.1. perc,
strings MUSIKWISS. see from
Kantaten Und Chorwerke II   (B697)

Kantaten Und Chorwerke I *see
Arneth-Kantate; Entsagen;
Festgesang (Jodok-Kantate); Mayr-
Kantate; Vergissmeinnicht   (B698)

Kantaten Und Chorwerke II *see Fest-
Cantate; Germanenzug; Helgoland
                               (B699)
Mayr-Kantate
(Nowak, Leopold) TTBB,TTBB soli,
2ob,2bsn,3horn,2trp,3trom
MUSIKWISS. see from Kantaten Und
Chorwerke I   (B700)

Trosterin Musik: Musik! Du
Himmlisches Gebilde
mix cor,acap BOHM   (B701)

Vergissmeinnicht
(Nowak, Leopold) SSAATTBB,SATB
soli,pno MUSIKWISS. see from
Kantaten Und Chorwerke I   (B702)

BRUDER, LASST UNS LUSTIG SEIN see
Siegler, Winfried

BRUDESLATT FRA SOGN see Bakke, Ruth

BRUDIEU, JOAN (? -1591)
Ya Tocan Los Atabales *madrigal
SATB A COEUR JOIE 675   (B703)

BRUGGEN, WILLEM VAN
Voorjaar: De Winter Is Geweken
[Dutch] SSA ZENGERINK V 171   (B704)

BRUGK, HANS MELCHIOR (1909-   )
An Die Musik: Festival Hymne
4-6pt cor,brass/pno BOHM   (B705)

Geburtstagswunsch: Ein Bisschen Mehr
Friede *Op.45,No.2
mix cor BOHM   (B706)

BRUHIER, ANTOINE (fl. ca. 1520)
Amoureux, Un
(Maitre, M. M.) 3 eq voices,opt
3rec HEUGEL HE 32046   (B707)

BRUID, DE see Prins, J.

BRUILOFTSZANGEN I see Schaik, Johan
Ant. Stephanus Van

BRUILOFTSZANGEN I: O LEVENSBRON DER
LIEFDE see Schaik, Johan Ant.
Stephanus Van

BRUK, FRIDRICH
Niin Kuin Pitsia Valoa Vasten...
wom cor,acap FAZER F 07753-7 (B708)

BRUMBASKON I BUMBA: FOLK TUNE FROM
VALDRES see Nystedt, Knut

BRUMEL, ANTOINE (ca. 1475-ca. 1520)
Du Tout Plongiet: Fors Seulement
(Marvin) TTBB oct OXFORD 385727-8
$1.50   (B709)

BRUMES see Veysseyre, Henri

BRUNE, JOSEPH FREDERIK
Lentemorgen: O, Hoe Heerlijk Is 'T Nu
Buiten
mix cor ZENGERINK 108   (B710)

BRUNET
Christmas Love *Xmas
SATB KJOS C8624 $.70   (B711)

Join The World
SATB KJOS C8709 $.60   (B712)

BRUNNER
Acceptance
SATB,acap MUSIC SEV. M70-473 $.85
                               (B713)

BRUNNER, M.
Adieu Au Pays
see Brahms, Johannes, Jour
S'enfuit, Le

BRURELAT FRA VAGA
(Rormark, Joar) mix cor MUSIKK
MH 2434 see from Fire Slatter For
Kor   (B714)

BRUYNEL, TON (1934-   )
Continuation
SATB,electronic tape [10'] DONEMUS
                               (B715)
John's Lullaby
SATB,24strings,electronic tape [9']
DONEMUS   (B716)

BRUYNS, M.
Ballade Van De Fiets
(Vermulst, J.) TTBB MOLENAAR
15011303   (B717)

BRYAN, JOHN
Rip Van Winkle
unis cor,narrator,pno,opt gtr
OXFORD 335426-6 $11.75   (B718)

Selfish Giant, The
unis cor,narrator,pno,opt gtr [28']
OXFORD 19 335448 9   (B719)

BRYMER
All-American (Choral Review)
(composed with Jacobson; Holmes)
SATB,combo/orch cor pts LEONARD-US
08637022 f.s., ipa   (B720)
1-2pt cor,combo/orch cor pts
LEONARD-US 08637026 f.s., ipa
                               (B721)
SAB,combo/orch cor pts LEONARD-US
08637024 f.s., ipa   (B722)

BRYMER, MARK
Be A Champion!
SAB LEONARD-US 08637172 $.95 (B723)
SATB LEONARD-US 08637171 $.95
                               (B724)
SSA LEONARD-US 08637173 $.95, ipa,
accomp tape available   (B725)

God Bless The U.S.A. *see Greenwood

God's Country
SATB LEONARD-US 08637701 $.95
                               (B726)
SAB LEONARD-US 08637702 $.95   (B727)
SSA LEONARD-US 08637703 $.95, ipa,
accomp tape available   (B728)

Have A Merry Merry Merry Merry
Christmas
SATB LEONARD-US 08637771 $.95
                               (B729)
SAB LEONARD-US 08637772 $.95   (B730)
SSA LEONARD-US 08637773 $.95, ipa,
accomp tape available   (B731)

Most Wnderful Time Of The Year, The
SATB LEONARD-US 08638501 $.95
                               (B732)
SAB LEONARD-US 08638502 $.95 (B733)
SSA LEONARD-US 08638503 $.95, ipa,
accomp tape available   (B734)

Rockin' The Paradise
SATB LEONARD-US 08638961 $.95
                               (B735)
SAB LEONARD-US 08638962 $.95 (B736)
SSA LEONARD-US 08638963 $.95, ipa,
accomp tape available   (B737)

When The Going Gets Tough, The Tough
Get Going
SATB LEONARD-US 08639551 $.95
                               (B738)

BRYMER, MARK (cont'd.)
SAB LEONARD-US 08639552 $.95 (B739)
2pt cor LEONARD-US 08639553 $.95,
ipa, accomp tape available   (B740)

BUCCI
Coffee Parfait
see Dinner Anyone? Four Recipes For
Mixed Chorus

Dinner Anyone? Four Recipes For Mixed
Chorus
mix cor MUSICUS f.s.
contains: Coffee Parfait;
Harlequin Salad; Minced Turkey;
Potato- Vegetable Chowder
                               (B741)
Harlequin Salad
see Dinner Anyone? Four Recipes For
Mixed Chorus

Minced Turkey
see Dinner Anyone? Four Recipes For
Mixed Chorus

Potato- Vegetable Chowder
see Dinner Anyone? Four Recipes For
Mixed Chorus

BUCHER, JOHANN
see BUCHNER, JOHANN

BUCHNER, JOHANN (1483- ?)
Tanz Ruber, Tanz Nuber *cant
mix cor,kbd/clar&trp&2vln&db&perc
BOHM   (B742)

BUCK
Ringin' In Christmas Country Style
SA CPP-BEL DMC 08082 F 95   (B743)

BUILD THOU MORE STATELY MANSIONS see
Clarke, Henry Leland

BUILDING A PYRAMID OF MUSICIANSHIP see
Herman

BULLER, JOHN (1929-   )
Finnegan's Floras
SSSSAAATTTTBBB,perc,pno [12']
OXFORD 19 355723 1 f.s.   (B744)

BUNT SIND SCHON DIE WALDER
mix cor BRAUN-PER 1078 see from Drei
Volkslieder   (B745)

BUNT SIND SCHON DIE WALDER see Monter,
Josef

BUON GIORNO SIGNORINA see Biebl, Franz

BURAN
(Karpowitsch) "Schneesturm, Der" men
cor,T solo ZIMMER. 610   (B746)

BURDEN DOWN see Weiss-Steinberg, Hans

BURDET, JACQUES
Tresors De La Chanson Populaire, Les
*CC42U,canon
eq voices,pno HUGUENIN EB   (B747)

BURGER, DAVID MARK (1950-   )
Ain't Got Time To Die
SSAB CPP-BEL SV7949 $.95   (B748)

BURGERS, SIMON (1958-   )
Koning Midas Krijgt Ezelsoren
jr cor,MezAT soli,2.2.2.2. 2.2.0.0.
timp,perc,pno,strings [16']
DONEMUS   (B749)

BURGESS
Gift Of Spring
SAB WILLIS 10839 $.90   (B750)

BURKHARD, WILLY (1900-1955)
Gesicht Jesajas, Das *Op.41
mix cor,STB soli,org,orch HUG
GH 11365   (B751)

BURKHART, F.
Kein Schoner Land
1-3pt wom cor,orch,org/pno BOHM
                               (B752)
Kunst Des Kussens: Nirgends Hin Als
Auf Den Mund
3pt men cor BOHM   (B753)

BURROUGHS
Freedom! Freedom!
unis cor CPP-BEL SV8303 $.95 (B754)

O Come, Modern Man
SATB,narrator,org,opt strings CPP-
BEL OCT 02510 $1.40, ipa   (B755)

BURROUGHS, BOB LLOYD (1937-   )
Star Thoughts
SATB oct DEAN HRD 156 $.75   (B756)

Walk Softly In Springtime
unis cor FISCHER,C SG125 $.70
                               (B757)

BURT, BATES
Christmas Minuet
(Johnson, Paul) SATB GENTRY JG2098
$.85 (B758)

BURTCH, MERVYN (1929-   )
World's End, The
unis cor,pno [1'30"] ROBERTON
392-00486 $.75 (B759)

BURTHEL, JAKOB (1926-   )
Es Fiel Ein Reif
men cor/wom cor BREITKOPF-W
CHB 3621 1 (B760)

Sommer Vergeht, Der
mix cor ZIMMER. 617 (B761)

BURTON
False Sir John
SATB KJOS 8661 $.90 (B762)

I Got Me Flowers °see Herbert

May The Road Rise Up To Meet You
SATB BOURNE B239186 $.65 (B763)

BURTON, MARK
Things Shall Never Die
SATB (text by Charles Dickens)
UNIVERSE 392-00523 (B764)

BURY ME BENEATH THE WILLOW
(Palmer, Anthony) SSA NATIONAL
NMP-170 $.90 (B765)
(Palmer, Anthony) SATB NATIONAL
NMP-176 $.90 (B766)

BUSH, GEOFFREY (1920-   )
Clerk Stephen
SATB,pno/org STAINER W135 (B767)

Joseph Of Arimathea
SATB,pno/org STAINER W136 (B768)

BUSHES AND BRIARS see Vaughan Williams,
Ralph

"BUST" FROM SEARS ROEBUCK & CO. see
Beckler, Stanworth R., Catalog
Cantata Number 2

BUSTED! see Bond, Victoria

BUSY BEN BY THE SEA see Vinson, Harvey

BUTLER
Come, My Light, My Life
SATB SHAWNEE 6475 $.95 (B769)

Lullaby, Gentle Breeze
cor ALFRED (B770)

Morning Serenade
ALFRED (B771)

Today Is Yours And Mine
ALFRED (B772)

BUTLER, EUGENE SANDERS (1935-   )
I Like Music
2pt treb cor,kbd FISCHER,C CM8154
(B773)
Music Is My Life
3 eq voices,kbd FISCHER,C CM8057
(B774)
Music Makes The World Go 'Round
SAB,pno FISCHER,C CM8144 (B775)

Prairie Woman Sings, A
SSA,pno FISCHER,C CM8033 (B776)

Silence Of The Night, The
SATB,pno CPP-BEL OCT 02539 $.95
(B777)
Starry Skies
SAB,kbd FISCHER,C CM8090 (B778)

Three Whimsical Fancies
SATB,acap (med, 3 contemporary
madrigals) GENTRY JG2070 $.90
(B779)

BUTLER, MARTIN (1960-   )
Sirens' Song, The
men cor,SBar soli,1(pic)(alto
fl).1.1(clar in E flat).0.
1.1.1.0. perc,pno,vln,vla,vcl,db,
electronic tape [20'] OXFORD
(B780)

BUTTERFLY see Liddell, Claire

BUTTES CHAUMONT, LES see Bonneau, Paul

BUTTNER, RUDI
Freunde Der Berge °see Herborg,
Dieter

BUTTON UP YOUR OVERCOAT see Puerling,
Gene

BY AN' BY
(Scherer, E.) [Eng] SATB MULLER 2758
(B781)

BY THE POOL see Eben, Petr

BYE BYE BLUES see Hamm, Fred

BYE, BYE LULLY LULLAY see North, Jack
King

BYE, BYE, SLEEP LITTLE ONE see Moore,
Donald

BYRD, WILLIAM (1543-1623)
Nightingale So Pleasant, The
(Agnel, A.) SAT HEUGEL HE 32563
(B782)

Songs Of Sundry Natures
SATB,acap KALMUS K 06834 $4.75
(B783)

C

CABANE, LA see Landry, Fredy

CABLE, HOWARD
Alberta Homestead; Up The Ycletaw
see Sing- Sea To Sea

Black Fly Song, The
see Sing- Sea To Sea

Canadien Errant, Un
see Sing- Sea To Sea

Great Grandma
see Sing- Sea To Sea

I'se The B'y; Bonavist' Harbour
see Sing- Sea To Sea

Red River Valley
see Sing- Sea To Sea

Sing- Sea To Sea
SSA,pno OXFORD 380047-0 $2.75
contains: Alberta Homestead; Up
The Ycletaw; Black Fly Song,
The; Canadien Errant, Un; Great
Grandma; I'se The B'y;
Bonavist' Harbour; Red River
Valley (C1)

CACAVAS
If I Were Santa Claus
SA/unis cor,pno,opt bells CPP-BEL
OCT 02446 $.95 (C2)

CACCINI
Amarilli, Mia Bella °madrigal
(Vree) "Amarilli, My Fair One" 4pt
mix cor LAWSON 927 (C3)

Amarilli, My Fair One °see Amarilli,
Mia Bella

CACIOPPO, CURT
Alla Primavera
SATB, solo voices,fl,clar,bsn,pno,
hpsd,vln,vla,vcl [9'0"] APNM sc
$9.00, pts rent (C4)

Nachtgesang
SATB, solo voices [8'0"] APNM sc
$4.75, cor pts rent (C5)

CACTUS CHRISTMAS TREE, THE see Roberts,
Ruth

CADMUS ET HERMIONE see Lully, Jean-
Baptiste (Lulli)

CADOW, PAUL (1908-   )
Rheinwein Muss Es Sein
men cor,acap ZIMMER. 628 (C6)

Rote Sarafan, Der
wom cor ZIMMER. 629 (C7)

Um Liebe °CC3U
3pt wom cor BOHM (C8)

CAECILIEN-ODE see Handel, George
Frideric

CAGE BIRDS DREAM, A see Am, Magnar

CAHN, SAMMY (1913-   )
Let It Snow! Let It Snow! Let It
Snow!
(Chinn) SATB CPP-BEL SV8715 $.95,
accomp tape available (C9)

CAILLARD, PHILIPPE
J'ai Tant Danse
CAILLARD PC 223 (C10)

Vla L'bon Vent
SSA CAILLARD PC 32 contains also:
Daniel, Chanson A Virer; Daniel,
Minuit Sonne; Ruyssen, Berceuse
Savoyarde (C11)

CAILLAT, STEPHANE
Brouillards De Noel, Les
cor,STB soli HEUGEL HE 31911 (C12)

Fanfarneto
4pt mix cor, solo voices,2rec
HEUGEL HE 31935 (C13)

Filles De Toulon, Les
4pt mix cor,2clar,bsn,tamb HEUGEL
HE 31938 (C14)

CAJKOVSKIJ, PETR ILJIC
see TCHAIKOVSKY, PIOTR ILYICH

CALETTI
Come On! (composed with Kunz)
SATB CPP-BEL SV8308 $.95   (C15)

Daydreamin' Me (composed with Kunz)
SSA CPP-BEL SV8309 $.95   (C16)

CALIFORNIA GIRLS
(Strommen) SATB CPP-BEL 0127CC1X
$1.25   (C17)
(Strommen) SAB CPP-BEL 0127CC3X $1.25
(C18)
(Strommen) TTB CPP-BEL 0127CC4X $1.25
(C19)

CALL OF SONG, THE: VOL. 3 °CCU
[Russ] MEZ KNIGA 184   (C20)

CALM IS THE MORN see Hill, J.

CALM IS THE SEA see Pfeil, Heinrich

CALME DE LA MER ET VOYAGE HEUREUX see
Beethoven, Ludwig van

CALME DU SOIR
(Lauber, Emile) TTBB HUGUENIN SP 4
(C21)

CALMEL, ROGER (1921-   )
Ballade Des Dames De Paris (from
Ballades De Francois Villon)
SATB A COEUR JOIE 180   (C22)

Ballade Finale (from Ballades De
Francois Villon)
SATB A COEUR JOIE 181   (C23)

Ballade Pour Prier Notre Dame (from
Ballades De Francois Villon)
SATB A COEUR JOIE 179   (C24)

CALVISIUS, SETH(US) (1556-1615)
Music Resounds °see Musiken Klang

Musiken Klang
(Malin) "Music Resounds" SSA,acap
CPP-BEL OCT 02375 $1.10   (C25)

CALYPSO MELODY see Swears, Linda

CAMPAGNES PARISIENNES see Bonneau, Paul

CAMPANA, JOSE LUIS (1949-   )
Imago
16pt mix cor,electronic tape
BILLAUDOT   (C26)

CAMPEUR CHANTE, LE see Mahel, Jean

CAMPIAN, THOMAS (CAMPION) (1567-1620)
Never Weather-Beaten Sail °madrigal
(Scott, K. Lee) SATB,acap (med
easy) FISCHER,C CM8222 $.85 (C27)

CAMPION, THOMAS
see CAMPIAN, THOMAS

CAMPRA, ANDRE (1660-1744)
Farfalla, La
"Papillon, Le" 3pt cor HUGUENIN
EB 427   (C28)

Festes Venitiennes, Les
(Lutolf, M.) 4pt mix cor,orch
HEUGEL HE 32470   (C29)

Papillon, Le °see Farfalla, La

CAMPTOWN RACES see Foster, Stephen
Collins

CAMPTOWN RACES see Mabry, John

CAMPTOWN RACES, THE see Foster, Stephen
Collins

CAN Y MELINYDD see Hughes-Jones, Llifon

CANADIEN ERRANT, UN
(Han, Isaac) SATB HARRIS HC-5031 $.95
(C30)

CANADIEN ERRANT, UN see Barron

CANADIEN ERRANT, UN see Cable, Howard

CANAT DE CHIZY, EDITH
Livre D'heures
4pt wom cor,10inst [23'] JOBERT
(C31)

CANCEIRO DE LAMPIAO see Nobre, Marlos

CANCION DE CUNA
(Thayer, Fred) "Sleep Now, My Baby"
SATB,pno BOURNE B239822-357 $.70
(C32)

CANCION DEL RETORNO see Kyllonen, Timo-
Juhani

CANCIONERO GALLEGO see Groba, Rogelio

CANCIONES A DOS VOCES see Bedmar, Luis

CANCIONES ANDALUZAS °CC9L
mix cor ALPUERTO 1033   (C33)

CANCIONES DEL PUEBLO see Carrion,
Alfredo

CANCIONES POPULARES DEL REINO DE LEON
see Barja, Angel

CANCIONES ZAMORANAS, 24 see Manzano
Alonso, Miguel

CANCO DE LA TEMPESTAT see Garvia,
Isabel

CANDLEGLOW see Crocker

CANE DE JEANNE, LA see Brassens,
Georges

CANNON, HUGHIE
Bill Bailey, Won't You Please Come
Home?
(Thygerson) SATB,kbd,opt combo
CORONET 392-41540 $1.10   (C34)

CANON see Pergolesi, Giovanni Battista

CANON see Praetorius, Michael

CANON IN D see Pachelbel, Johann

CANON OF CANS see Bond, Victoria

CANON ON ALLELUIA see Pachelbel, Johann

CANONS TO FOLLOW see Clarke, Henry
Leland

CANONS TO GO BY see Clarke, Henry
Leland

CAN'T HELP SINGING see Althouse, Jay

CAN'T YOU LIVE HUMBLE?
(Christiansen, P.) KJOS C8721 $.80
(C35)

CANTATA FOR THE OPENING OF THE MOSCOW
POLYTECHNIC EXPOSITION see
Tchaikovsky, Piotr Ilyich

CANTATA FOR WOMEN'S VOICES see Van de
Vate, Nancy Hayes

CANTATAS BY SOVIET COMPOSERS, VOL. 2
°CCU
[Russ] MEZ KNIGA 164   (C36)

CANTATAS BY SOVIET COMPOSERS, VOL. 3
°CCU
[Russ] cor,acap MEZ KNIGA 177   (C37)

CANTATE DE FETE see Aeschbacher,
Walther

CANTATE EN FORME DE COLOMBE see Daniel,
Etienne

CANTI PER EUROPA see Grigoriu, Theodor

CANTICLE OF MAN, A see Rawsthorne, Alan

CANTICOS DE AMOR see Prado, Jose-
Antonio (Almeida)

CANTICUM ARCANUM see Adolphe, Bruce

CANTILENA see Koch, Erland von

CANTILENAS PROFANAS see Penders, J.

CANTIONES SACRAE ET PROFANAE, VOL. 7
see Badings, Henk

CANTIQUE PATRIOTIQUE see Zwyssig,
Alberich

CANTO see Ibarrondo, Felix

CANTO see Rossem, Andries van

CANTORELLI, BEPPE
I Still Believe °see Armato

CANTUS EUROPA °CC12L,folk song
(Vermulst, Jan) SAB BANK VER 027
(C38)

CANTUS ROMANTICA °CC12L
(Mierhout, Frank) SSA/SAB EXC.MH
19.009.003 contains works by
Silcher, Schumann, Mozart, and
others   (C39)

CANZONE DELL'AMORE, LA see Filas, Juraj

CANZONI ITALIANE see Biebl, Franz

CAPE ANN see Paynter, John P.

CAPELLE, DIE see Schumann, Robert
(Alexander)

CAPLET, ANDRE (1878-1925)
Trois Chants D'Eglise °CC3U
SSA DURAND   (C40)

CAPRICE see Diemer, Emma Lou

CAPTAIN CORAM'S KIDS see Hurd, Michael

CAR TUNES: MEDLEY OF BEACH BOYS' HITS
(Chinn) SATB CPP-BEL SV8705 $1.25,
accomp tape available   (C41)
(Chinn) TBB CPP-BEL SV8701 $1.25,
accomp tape available   (C42)

CARE LAGRIME MIE see Marenzio, Luca

CARELESS RAMBLES see Hamilton, Iain

CAREY
Jim, Jam, Jump (composed with
Eskelin)
SATB LEONARD-US 08603346 $.95, ipa,
accomp tape available   (C43)

CAREY, HENRY (ca. 1687-1743)
America (My Country, Tis Of Thee)
(Cornwall, J.) SATB,pno UNIVERSE
392-00566 $.85   (C44)

CARL, ROBERT
Sullivan Songs
SATB [9'] AM.COMP.AL. $9.15   (C45)

CARLSEN, PHILIP
Polter Te Creso
14pt cor,1.2+English horn.1+bass
clar.1. 1.1.1.0. strings [8']
AM.COMP.AL. $11.45   (C46)

CARMEL, DOV
Winter Is Past, The
jr cor ISRAELI IMP 1704   (C47)

CARMEN VITALE see Rawsthorne, Alan

CARMICHAEL, HOAGY (1899-1981)
Georgia On My Mind
(Strommen) SATB CPP-BEL SV8337
$1.25   (C48)
(Strommen) SSA CPP-BEL SV8338 $1.25
(C49)

Hoagy Carmichael Choral Festival, A
°medley
SSA,gtr,pno (includes Heart And
Soul, Lazy Bones, and Star Dust)
CPP-BEL SB 01045 $3.95   (C50)

Lazy River (composed with Arodin,
Sidney)
(Shaw, Kirby) SAB CPP-BEL 0073LC3X
$1.10   (C51)
(Shaw, Kirby) SATB,acap CPP-BEL
0073LC1X $1.10   (C52)

Nearness Of You, The
(Chinn, Teena) SATB CPP-BEL
1454NC1X $1.25, accomp tape
available   (C53)
(Chinn, Teena) SSA CPP-BEL 1454NC2X
$1.25, accomp tape available
(C54)
(Chinn, Teena) SAB CPP-BEL 1454NC3X
$1.25, accomp tape available
(C55)

CARMINA see Laburda, Jiri

CARNAVALITO QUEBRADENO
(Maragno, Virtu) 4pt mix cor HEUGEL
HE 32155   (C56)

CARNIVALE DI VENEZIA, IL see Rossini,
Gioacchino

CARO MEA see Barja, Angel

CARO MIO BEN, CREDI MI ALMEN see
Giordani, Tommaso

CAROL, A see Darlow

CAROL, W.
Deck The Hall
(Hicken, K.) SAB,pno/org (med easy)
THOMAS 1C018112 $.60   (C57)

CAROL-NOEL see Wilhousky, Peter J.

CAROL OF THE BELLS see Leontovich,
Mykola

CAROL OF THE RUSSIAN CHILDREN: THE
SLEIGH
(Johnson, Derric) SSAATTBB LEAWOOD
K3002 $.95   (C58)

CAROL OF THE SHEPHERD BOY see Palmer,
Hap

CARP, THE FLEA AND SO ON, THE see
Hurnik, Ilja

CARPENTER, RICHARD LYNN (1946-   )
Merry Christmas, Darling
(Scott, Michael) SATB CPP-BEL
SV8722 $1.25, accomp tape
available   (C59)
(Scott, Michael) SSA CPP-BEL SV8723
$1.25, accomp tape available
(C60)
(Simeone) SATB SHAWNEE 1228 $.95
(C61)
(Simeone) SSA SHAWNEE 0378 $.95

CARPENTER, RICHARD LYNN (cont'd.)

    Op De Top Van Een Wolk °see Top Of
      The World   (C62)

    Something In Your Eyes
      (Buchholz, Buck) SATB CPP-BEL
        6111SC1X $1.25, accomp tape
        available   (C63)
      (Buchholz, Buck) SSA CPP-BEL
        6111SC2X $1.25, accomp tape
        available   (C64)
      (Buchholz, Buck) SAB CPP-BEL
        6111SC3X $1.25, accomp tape
        available   (C65)

    Top Of The World
      (Althouse) SSA SHAWNEE 0504 $.80
                     (C66)
      (Althouse) SAB SHAWNEE 0315 $.80
                     (C67)
      (Althouse) SATB SHAWNEE 1748 $.80
                     (C68)
      (Veltman, B.) "Op De Top Van Een
        Wolk" SATB MOLENAAR 13004304
                     (C69)

    Yesterday Once More (composed with
      Bettis, John)
      (Dijk) TTBB MOLENAAR 13003303 (C70)

CARR
    All Under The Willow Trees
      SATB SCHIRM.G 320270 $.70   (C71)

CARRION, ALFREDO
    Canciones Del Pueblo °CC14L
      mix cor ALPUERTO 1034   (C72)

CARRY ON see Hannisian

CARS see Crawley, Clifford

CARTER
    Starsong
      ALFRED   (C73)

CARTER, ANDREW
    Galloping Godiva °cant
      unis jr cor,3 soli&narrator,pno,opt
        perc OXFORD 19 335506   (C74)

CARTER, DAN
    Shine For Me Again
      SATB JACKMAN JMC7053   (C75)

CARTER, JOHN
    My Wish For You
      SSA,pno SOMERSET SP-791 $.80 (C76)

    Old Sue's Panda (composed with Beall,
      Mary Kay)
      2pt cor LEONARD-US 08603490 $.95
                     (C77)

CASEY, THOMAS
    Drill, Ye Tarriers
      (Casey) SATB SCHIRM.G 232290 $.70
                     (C78)

CASKEN, JOHN
    To Fields We Do Not Know
      mix cor,acap SCHOTT ED 12285 (C79)

CASSEY
    Bouquet Of Roses °see Nelson

    Moonglow °see Hudson, Will

CASSILS, CRAIG
    She's Like The Swallow
      unis cor LESLIE 1156 f.s.   (C80)

CASTELNUOVO, V.
    Bella Valmaggina
      (Frochaux, Jean-Charles) SATB,acap
      HUGUENIN CH 2034   (C81)

    Malcantonesina
      (Frochaux, Jean-Charles) SATB,acap
      HUGUENIN CH 2033   (C82)

    Poschiavina
      (Frochaux, Jean-Charles) SATB,acap
      HUGUENIN CH 2031   (C83)

    Valcolla
      (Frochaux, Jean-Charles) SATB,acap
      HUGUENIN CH 2032   (C84)

CASTRO, JEAN DE (ca. 1540-ca. 1611)
    Bonjour Mon Coeur
      (Agnel, A.) 3 eq voices HEUGEL
      HE 32135   (C85)

    Elle S'en Va De Moi La Mieux Aimee
      (Agnel, A.) 2-3pt mix cor HEUGEL
      HE 32144   (C86)

    Je L'aime Bien
      (Agnel, A.) 3pt mix cor HEUGEL
      HE 32071   (C87)

    Mon Coeur Se Recommande A Vous
      (Agnel, A.) 2-3pt mix cor HEUGEL
      HE 32136   (C88)

CASTRO, JEAN DE (cont'd.)

    Quand Mon Mari Vient De Dehors
      (Agnel, A.) 3pt mix cor HEUGEL
      HE 32308   (C89)

    Tout Ce Qu'on Peult En Elle Veoir
      (Agnel, A.) SAT HEUGEL HE 32557
                     (C90)

    Vous Qui Aimez Les Dames
      (Agnel, A.) 3pt mix cor HEUGEL
      HE 32307   (C91)

CAT AND THE MOON see Putsche, Thomas

CAT CAME BACK, THE °CCU
    (Goetze, M.) 2-3pt jr cor,Orff inst
      MMB SE-0891 $6.00   (C92)

CAT CAME BACK, THE see Miller

CATALOG CANTATA NUMBER 2 see Beckler,
    Stanworth R.

CATCH BOOK [B], THE °CC15OU,round
    (Hillier, Paul) men cor OXFORD
      19 343649 3 f.s. contains works by
      Purcell, Blow, Greene and others
                     (C93)

CATCH THE SPIRIT see Ray, Jerry

CATCHING see Crawley, Clifford

CATEL, CHARLES SIMON (1773-1830)
    Hymne Du 10 Aout (Chute De La
      Royaute)
      SATB,pno A COEUR JOIE CA 21 (C94)

CATHEDRALES, LES see Sylvestre, Anne

CE BEAU PRINTEMPS see Lassus, Roland de
    (Orlandus)

CE MOIS DE MAI see Janequin, Clement

CE MOYS DE MAI see Janequin, Clement

CE MOYS DE MAY see Dufay, Guillaume

CE PETIT VILLAGE see Landry, Fredy

CE QUE J'AIME see Level, Pierre Yves

CE QUI M'ENTRE PAR UNE OREILLE see
    D'Orleans, Ch.

CE RIS PLUS DOUX see Bertrand, Antoine
    de

CEASE SORROWS NOW see Weelkes, Thomas

CEDER? see Haydn, [Franz] Joseph

CEDUNTUR GLADUS see Willaert, Adrian

CEELY, ROBERT PAIGE (1930-   )
    Flee, Floret, Florens
      SATB, SSSSAAAATTTTBBB soli [8'0"]
      APNM sc $11.25, cor pts rent
                     (C95)

CELEBRATE! see Snyder

CELEBRATE TONIGHT! see Gilpin, Greg

CELEBRATIO AMERICAE see Prado, Jose-
    Antonio (Almeida)

CELEBRATIO AMORIS see Prado, Jose-
    Antonio (Almeida)

CELEBRATION NOW! see Ydstie

CENT MILLE CHANSONS see Marnay

CEREMONIAL see Boesch

CEREMONY AFTER A FIRE RAID see Gerber,
    Steven R.

CEREMONY AFTER A FIRE RAID see Mathias,
    William

CERTES, MON OEIL see Bertrand, Antoine
    de

CERTON, PIERRE (ca. 1510-1572)
    Amour Voyant L'ennui
      (Agnel, A.) 2 eq voices HEUGEL
      HE 32499   (C96)

    Bien Qu'a Grand Tort (from
      Polyphonia)
      (Ouvrard, J.P.) 4pt cor HEUGEL 502
                     (C97)

    Dulcis Amica
      (Agnel, A.) 3pt mix cor HEUGEL
      HE 32503   (C98)

    Fortune Helas (from Polyphonia)
      (Ouvrard, J.P.) 4pt cor HEUGEL 503
                     (C99)

    Je Ne Fus Jamais Si Aise
      SSA HARMONIA 3721   (C100)

CERTON, PIERRE (cont'd.)

    Je Ne L'ose Dire
      SATB,acap HUGUENIN EB 12   (C101)

    J'espere Et Crains (from Polyphonia)
      (Ouvrard, J.P.) 4pt cor HEUGEL 501
                     (C102)

CES BELLES MONTAGNES see Cornaz,
    Emmanuel

CESKA PISEN see Smetana, Bedrich

C'EST A L'AUBE see Gerard

C'EST DANS LE MOIS DE MAI
    (Caillard, Philippe) SATB CAILLARD
      PC 119 contains also: Mon Pere
      N'avait Fille Que Moi   (C103)

C'EST GRAND ERREUR see Anonymous

C'EST GRANDE ERREUR see Anonymous

C'EST LA VEILLE ETRAMBIRE
    (Agnel) eq voices HEUGEL HE 32542
      contains also: Trois Canons A Voix
      Egales   (C104)

C'EST L'AMOUR see Gluck, Christoph
    Willibald, Ritter von

C'EST L'AMOUR see Schubert, Franz
    (Peter)

C'EST LE TON... see Braal, Andries de

C'EST MON AMI see Janequin, Clement

C'EST PAR VOUS see Mathey, Paul

C'EST SI BON
    (Weir, Michelle) SATB,combo LEONARD-
      US 08623371 $1.25, ipa, accomp tape
      available   (C105)

C'EST TOI, NEUCHATEL see Huwiler,
    Pierre

C'EST UN VRAI BATEAU, FANTAISIE see
    Vuataz, Roger

C'ETAIT EN AVRIL see Bos, Ruud

C'ETAIT LE BON TEMPS see Gaillard,
    Paul-Andre

CHAGRIN! see Haydn, [Franz] Joseph

CHAGRIN D'AMOUR, UN see Teze, M.

CHAIKOVSKII, PETR IL'ICH
    see TCHAIKOVSKY, PIOTR ILYICH

CHAILLEY, JACQUES (1910-   )
    "De L'information Nulle A Une Espece
      De Poesie" °see Quand Il Neige

    Quand Il Neige
      ""De L'information Nulle A Une
      Espece De Poesie"" 3pt mix cor A
      COEUR JOIE 1028   (C106)

    Rossignol, Mon Mignon
      3 eq voices,pno A COEUR JOIE CA 8
                     (C107)

CHALETS, LES see Pantillon, G.L.

CHALLULAU, PATRICE
    Musique Pour Nicolas Flamel
      mix cor A COEUR JOIE MA 4 (C108)

CHAMBER MUSIC: SEVEN SONGS see Austin,
    John

CHAMBRES DE CRISTAL, LES see Reibel,
    Guy

CHANGE OF MOOD, A: TWO FROST POEMS see
    Kearns, Ann

CHANGEONS PROPOS see Sermisy, Claude de
    (Claudin)

CHANGES see Crosse, Gordon

CHANSON see Jeanquartier, Marianne

CHANSON A BOIRE see Couste, Francis

CHANSON A BOUCHE FERMEE see Alain,
    Jehan

CHANSON A LA MARIEE see Huguenin,
    Charles

CHANSON A VIRER see Daniel

CHANSON A VIRER see Daniel, Etienne

CHANSON D'AUTOMNE see Diepenbrock,
    Alphons

CHANSON DE DOLLY PENTRAETH, LA see
    Daniel, Etienne

CHANSON DE GOLIARD see Anonymous

CHANSON DE GRAND-PERE see Schwartz

CHANSON DE LA BELLE see Apotheloz, Jean

CHANSON DE LA MARINE see Apotheloz, Jean

CHANSON DE LA MARJOLAINE see Schmidt-Wunstorf, Rudolf

CHANSON DE LA PLUS HAUTE TOUR see Roger, Denise

CHANSON DE L'AMOUREUSE see Schmidt-Wunstorf, Rudolf

CHANSON DE L'AMOUREUX see Rochat, Jean

CHANSON DE L'ARMAILLI, LA see Blanc, Rene

CHANSON DE MARINS see Cornaz, Emmanuel, Coup D'riquiqui, Un

CHANSON DE PRINTEMPS see Lauber, Joseph

CHANSON DE QUETE DE CHAMPAGNE see Mon Pere Tot M'a Mariee

CHANSON DE ROSETTE see Vuataz, Roger

CHANSON DE ROUTE see Jacot, Pierre

CHANSON DE TESSA see Giraudoux, J.

CHANSON DE VIRGINIA, LA see Vanderlove, Anne

CHANSON DES TOURBIERS see Pantillon, G.L.

CHANSON DES VIEUX-PRES, LA see Pantillon, G.L.

CHANSON DU BALEINIER see Blanchard

CHANSON DU COUTURIER
(Langree, Alain) SATB CAILLARD PC 51 contains also: Marche Des Soldats De Turenne   (C109)

CHANSON DU PETIT CHIEN see Fevin, Antoine de

CHANSON DU PRINTEMPS see Apotheloz, Jean

CHANSON DU PRINTEMPS RETOURNE see Ronsard

CHANSON DU ROUET see Parchet, A.

CHANSON DU VENT, LA see Torche, Ch.

CHANSON DU VIGNERON, LA
(Landry, Fredy) TTBB HUGUENIN CH 1052   (C110)

CHANSON DU VIGNERON, LA see Landry, Fredy

CHANSON JOYEUSE see Schubert, Franz (Peter)

CHANSON NORVEGIENNE see Turellier, Jean

CHANSON: NOUS VOYONS QUE LES HOMMES see Arcadelt, Jacob

CHANSON TENDRE see Lang, Hermann

CHANSONNIER NIVELLE DE LA CHAUSSEE *CC7OU
fac ed MINKOFF ISBN 2-8266-0752-9 contains works by Busnois, Ockeghem, Dufay, Binchois, Fede and Delahaye   (C111)

CHANSONS see Appenzeller, Benedictus

CHANSONS A 1, 2 ET 3 VOIX, 26 *CC26U
eq voices,pno cor pts HUGUENIN CH 417, sc HUGUENIN CH 299   (C112)

CHANSONS BACHIQUES (REMPLIS TON VERRE VIDE) see Daniel, Etienne

CHANSONS DE ROUTE ET DE BIVOUAC *CCU
(Williamson; Huguenin) cor HUGUENIN CH 401   (C113)

CHANSONS DE TESSA see Giraudoux, J.

CHANSONS JEUNES see Huguenin, Charles

CHANSONS POPULAIRES POITEVINES, 23 see Huguenin, Charles

CHANSONS POPULAIRES POUR LES POILUS ET LES ECOLES, 25 see Gaud, A.

CHANSONS POUR ENFANTS DE TOUT AGE see Vuataz, Roger

CHANSONS POUR LA JEUNESSE, CINQUIEME CAHIER *CC8L
(Huguenin, Charles) 1-4pt cor HUGUENIN   (C114)

CHANSONS POUR LA JEUNESSE, QUATRIEME CAHIER *CC7L
1-4pt cor HUGUENIN   (C115)

CHANSONS POUR LA JEUNESSE, SEPTIEME CAHIER *see Tour De Constance, La; Alin, Pierre, Noel, Noel Est Venu; Assalinde, Proestants Fugitifs; Huguenin, Charles, Laissez Venir A Moi Les Petits Enfants; Zwyssig, Alberich, Cantique Patriotique
                                    (C116)

CHANSONS POUR LA JEUNESSE, SIXIEME CAHIER *see Fanchette, La; Monsieur D'Charette A Dit; Berat, F., Hameau, Le; Berat, F., Ma Normandie; Berat, F., Poete, Le; Schwartz, Chanson De Grand-Pere
                                    (C117)

CHANSONS POUR LA JEUNESSE, TROISIEME CAHIER *see Bateliere, La; Chasseur De Chamois, Le; Filles Du Hameau; Laur, F., Drapeau, Le; Lieb, J.G., Salut! Glaciers Sublimes; Rietz, R., Bonheur Craintif   (C118)

CHANSONS TIREES DE "LA GLOIRE QUI CHANTE" see Lauber, Emile

CHANT D'ADIEU
(Lallement, Bernard) SATB A COEUR JOIE 358   (C119)

CHANT DE LA BERGERE see Sanglard, Abner

CHANT DE LA FORET, LE see Naegeli, Hans Georg

CHANT DE LA ROSE see Cossetto, Emil

CHANT DE LOUANGES see Gounod, Charles Francois

CHANT DE PRINTEMPS see Lauber, Emile

CHANT DES BARDES see Schubert, Franz (Peter)

CHANT DES ESPIRITS AUDESSUS DES EAUX see Schubert, Franz (Peter), Gesang Der Geistern Uber Den Wassern

CHANT DES MOISSONNEURS see Lauber, Emile

CHANT DES MOISSONNEURS D'UKRAINE see Cui, Cesar Antonovich

CHANT DES PAYSANS see Lauber, Emile

CHANT DES SERFS, LE see Vuataz, Roger

CHANT DES SONNEURS, LE see Pantillon, G.L.

CHANT DU BERGER see Lauber, Emile

CHANT DU BUCHERON see Lauber, Emile

CHANT DU DEPART see Mehul

CHANT DU GRILLON see Lanauve, G. De

CHANT DU PREMIER AOUT 1914 see Lauber, Emile

CHANT DU PRINTEMPS see Lauber, Emile

CHANTE, ANTILLES CHANTE see Gamot, Pierre

CHANTE! MON VILLAGE... see Landry, Fredy

CHANTER L'EUROPE 1: MUSIQUES DES PAYS DE L'EST *CC2OU
(Rehak, Jeon) jr cor/eq voices A COEUR JOIE   (C120)

CHANTER L'EUROPE 2: MUSIQUES DES PAYS DE L'OUEST *CC22L
(Rehak, Jeno) 2 eq voices A COEUR JOIE   (C121)

CHANTERIES DU JEUNE AGE, LES see Strimer

CHANTONS, JE VOUS PRIE see Waxman

CHANTONS SUR LA MUSETTE see Rameau, Jean-Philippe

CHANTS D'ALSACE see Huguenin, Charles

CHAPLIN
Smile
SATB BOURNE B240978 $.95   (C122)

CHARLICOU *Belg
(Turellier, J.) 2pt cor,rec,2xylo HEUGEL HE 32508   (C123)

CHARLOTTTOWN
(Terhune) 2pt cor CPP-BEL SV8804 $1.10   (C124)

CHARMANT AMOUR see Morin, Jean Baptiste

CHASALOW, ERIC
Words
SATB [10'0"] APNM sc $3.50, cor pts rent   (C125)

CHASSE, LA
(Lauber, Emile) TTBB HUGUENIN SP 115   (C126)

CHASSE AU CERF see Lauber, Emile

CHASSE AUX PAPILLONS, LA see Brassens, Georges

CHASSERAL see Favez, Daniel

CHASSERON, LE see Andreae, Volkmar

CHASSEUR, LE see Lauber, Emile

CHASSEUR, LE see Moreillon, H.P.

CHASSEUR DE CHAMOIS, LE
(Huguenin, Charles) 1-4pt cor HUGUENIN see from Chansons Pour La Jeunesse, Troisieme Cahier   (C127)

CHATON ET LA SOURIS, LE see Massepin, A.

CHATTANOOGA CHOO CHOO
(Huff) SATB CPP-BEL T3200CC1 $1.25, accomp tape available   (C128)
(Huff) SSA CPP-BEL T3200CC2 $1.25, accomp tape available   (C129)
(Huff) SAB CPP-BEL T3200CC3 $1.25, accomp tape available   (C130)

CHATTON, PIERRE
Printemps Campagnard
SATB,acap HUGUENIN CH 2037   (C131)

Souvenir
SATB,acap HUGUENIN CH 2039   (C132)

CHAUX DE FONDS, LA see Pantillon, G.L.

CHE FASCH QUA TU BEL UTSCHLIN?
see Que Fais-Tu La, Bel Oiseau?

CHECAN IV see Valcarcel, Edgar

CHEERS: A TOAST TO PRIME TIME
(Scott, Michael) SSA (contains Cheers, Who's The Boss, Family Ties and others) CPP-BEL C0143C2X $2.50
                                    (C133)
(Scott, Michael) SAB (contains Cheers, Who's The Boss, Family Ties and others) CPP-BEL C0143C3X $2.50
                                    (C134)
(Scott, Michael) SATB (contains Cheers, Who's The Boss, Family Ties and others) CPP-BEL C0143C1X $2.50, accomp tape available   (C135)

CHEERS: THEME (WHERE EVERYBODY KNOWS YOUR NAME)
(Strommen) SSA CPP-BEL 2695TC2X $1.25
                                    (C136)
(Strommen) SAB CPP-BEL 2695TC3X $1.25
                                    (C137)
(Strommen) SATB CPP-BEL 2695TC1X $1.25   (C138)

CHEMIN DE LA PLAGE, LE see Naty-Boyer, Jean

CHENAUX, B.
Savetier Et Le Financier, Le men cor HUGUENIN CH 2069   (C139)

CHER PAYS see Lauber, Emile

CHERISH
(Strommen) SATB CPP-BEL 2618CC1X $1.25, accomp tape available (C140)
(Strommen) SAB CPP-BEL 2618CC2X $1.25, accomp tape available (C141)
(Strommen) TTB CPP-BEL 2618CC4X $1.25, accomp tape available (C142)

CHERNYHIVS'KI SICHOVYKY
see Chernyhivs'ki Sichovyky And Other Songs

CHERNYHIVS'KI SICHOVYKY AND OTHER SONGS
[Ukranian] DUMA $5.00 contains works by Eremenko, Kytasty and Borodievych
contains: Chernyhivs'ki Sichovyky (SATB,pno); Historic March (3pt cor,pno); Karpats'ki Sichovyky (SATB,pno)   (C143)

CHERRY-RIPE see Silver, S.

CHERUBINI, LUIGI (1760-1842)
Tell Me Truly
(Vancil) SA/unis cor SOUTHERN $.90
(C144)

CHESTER see Billings, William

CHESTER BOOK OF MADRIGALS, THE, BOOK 3:
THE SEASONS °CCU
(Petti, Anthony) mix cor CHESTER
SCHE01255447 f.s. (C145)

CHESTER BOOK OF MADRIGALS, THE, BOOK 4:
DESIRABLE WOMEN °CCU
(Petti, Anthony) mix cor CHESTER
SCHE01255495 f.s. (C146)

CHESTER BOOK OF MADRIGALS, THE, BOOK 7:
WARFARE °CCU
(Petti, Anthony) mix cor CHESTER
SCHE01255709 f.s. (C147)

CHESTER BOOK OF MADRIGALS, THE, BOOK 8:
PLACE NAMES °CCU
(Petti, Anthony) mix cor CHESTER
SCHE01255725 f.s. (C148)

CHEVEUX D'OR ET D'ARGENT see Bovet,
Joseph

CHI SALIRA PER ME see Wert, Giaches de
(Jakob van)

CHIAPANECAS (MEXICAN HAND- CLAPPING)
see Palmer, Hap

CHIARA, JO
Finding My Way °see Schwartz

Let's Take A Christmas Trip (composed
with Schwartz)
2pt cor CPP-BEL SV8553 $.95, accomp
tape available (C149)

CHICHKOV, Y.
Songs For Children °CCU
[Russ] jr cor,pno MEZ KNIGA 537
(C150)

CHILD OF CHRISTMAS MORN, THE see Bacon,
Boyd

CHILD SAID, A see McCray, James

CHILDREN, GO WHERE I SEND THEE
(Moore) SATB CPP-BEL SV8741 $1.25
(C151)

CHILDREN OF THE SEA, THE see Gregor,
Cestmir

CHILDREN OF THE WORLD see Michaels,
David Julian

CHILDREN'S CHOIR see Raichl, Miroslav,
Detske Sbory

CHILDREN'S CHORUS, VOL. 6 °CCU
[Russ] jr cor MEZ KNIGA 514 (C152)

CHILDREN'S CHORUS, VOL. 7 °CCU
[Russ] jr cor MEZ KNIGA 548 (C153)

CHILDREN'S CHORUS, VOL. 8 °CCU
[Russ] jr cor MEZ KNIGA 243 (C154)

CHILDREN'S CHORUSES see Dubravin, Y.

CHILDREN'S SONGS see Liadov, Anatol
Konstantinovich

CHILDREN'S SONGS AND CHORUSES see
Mussorgsky, Modest Petrovich

CHILDREN'S TERZETTOS see Hurnik, Ilja

CHIMES AND BELLS OF CHRISTMAS, THE see
Cobine, Albert Stewart

CHIMNEY SWEEPER, THE see Reed, Everett

CHINN, TEENA
Laughing Matter, A
SATB CPP-BEL SV8740 $.95 (C155)

Snowy Feathers
2pt cor,opt bells CPP-BEL SV8706
$1.10, accomp tape available
(C156)

CHIOME D'ORO see Goldsmith, Owen

CHIPMUNK SONG
(Averre, Dick) 2pt cor LEONARD-US
08643376 $.85 (C157)

CHITTERABOB see Rausch, Carlos

CHIU YEN see Schoen, Victor R.

CHOEUR DES MAGNANERELLES see Gounod,
Charles Francois

CHOEUR DES MESSAGERS DE PAIX see
Wagner, Richard

CHOEUR DES PELERINS see Wagner, Richard

CHOEUR DES SOLDATS see Gounod, Charles
Francois

CHOEUR DES SPARTIATES ET MENUET CHANTE
see Rameau, Jean-Philippe

CHOEUR PATRIOTIQUE see Handel, George
Frideric

CHOICE, A see Owen, John Warren

CHOICE OF HERCULES, THE see Handel,
George Frideric

CHOIR OF CATS, A see Shur, Yekutiel

CHOOSE LIFE see Adler, Samuel Hans

CHOOSE LIFE see Clarke, Henry Leland

CHOPIN, FREDERIC (1810-1849)
Valse
(Cossetto, E.) 4pt mix cor HEUGEL
HE 32591 (C158)

Valse En La Mineur
(Cassetto, E.) SSAATTB HEUGEL
HE 32261 (C159)

CHOR AKTUELL, HEFT 1: SWINGENDE
CHORMUSIK °CCU
(Suttner, Kurt) SATB,opt treb inst
BOSSE 451 f.s. (C160)

CHOR AKTUELL, HEFT 2: VOLKSLIEDER IN
EUROPA °CCU
(Frey, Max) 2-5pt mix cor BOSSE 452
f.s. (C161)

CHOR DER GEFANGENEN see Verdi,
Giuseppe, Teure Heimat

CHOR DER JUNGFRAUEN: SEHT, ER KOMMT IM
SIEGESGLANZ see Handel, George
Frideric, Chorus Of Virgins: See
The Godlike Youth Advance

CHOR DER JUNGLINGE: SEHT DEN SIEGER
RUHMGEKRONT see Handel, George
Frideric, Chorus Of Youths: See,
The Conqu'ring Hero Comes

CHOR DER NACHTLICHTER see Deutschmann,
Gerhard

CHOR DER SELIGE GEISTER see Gluck,
Christoph Willibald, Ritter von

CHOR DER SPINNERINNEN see Wagner,
Richard

CHOR DES LANDVOLKS see Haydn, [Franz]
Joseph, Komm, Holder Lenz!

CHORAL DE PRINTEMPS see Jacquemin, C.

CHORAL D'HIVER see Jacquemin, C.

CHORAL FIGURE see Lijnschooten, H.V.

CHORAL MATINS, A see Weinhorst, Richard

CHORAL MUSIC FOR CHILDREN see Hurnik,
Ilja, Detske Sbory

CHORAL SCENE FROM "THE BACCHAE" OF
EURIPIDES see Tate, Phyllis

CHORAL SONGS see Wiechowicz, Stanislaw,
Z Piesni Choralnych

CHORAL SONGS, VOL. 2 °CCU
[Russ] cor,acap MEZ KNIGA 157 (C162)

CHORAL STUDY see Wigglesworth, Frank

CHORAL TRIBUTE, A see Mechem, Kirke
Lewis

CHORAL WORKS see Glinka, Mikhail
Ivanovich

CHORAL WORKS, VOL. 1 see Sviridov,
Georgy

CHORAL WORKS, VOL. 2 see Sviridov,
Georgy

CHORSINFONIE see Geissler, Fritz,
Sinfonie Nr. 8

CHORUBUNGEN °CC131U
(Wullner; Schwickerath; Stephani) 3-
16pt cor,acap SIKORSKI 250 contains
works by Dufay, Palestrina, Di
Lasso, Vittoria, Eccard, Bach,
Brahms, Distler, Hindemith, Pepping
(C163)

CHORUS FOR MIXED CHOIR see Bachorek,
Milan

CHORUS LINE, A (THE MOVIE): A MEDLEY
(Lojeski) SATB LEONARD-US 08208201
$2.50 (C164)

(Lojeski) SAB LEONARD-US 08208202
$2.50 (C165)
(Lojeski) SSA LEONARD-US 08208203
$2.50, ipa, accomp tape available
(C166)

CHORUS OF THE HEBREW SLAVES see Verdi,
Giuseppe, Va Pensiero

CHORUS OF VIRGINS: SEE THE GODLIKE
YOUTH ADVANCE see Handel, George
Frideric

CHORUS OF YOUTHS: SEE, THE CONQU'RING
HERO COMES see Handel, George
Frideric

CHORUSES see Partzkhaladze, M.

CHORUSES see Schumann, Robert
(Alexander)

CHORUSES BY FRENCH COMPOSERS °CCU
[Russ] cor,acap MEZ KNIGA 169 (C167)

CHORUSES BY RUSSIAN COMPOSERS, VOL. 2
°CCU
[Russ] cor,acap MEZ KNIGA 164 (C168)

CHORUSES BY SOVIET COMPOSERS °CCU
[Russ] cor MEZ KNIGA 169 (C169)

CHORUSES BY SOVIET COMPOSERS °CCU
[Russ] cor,acap/pno MEZ KNIGA 166
(C170)

CHORUSES BY SOVIET COMPOSERS °CCU
(Babichev, I.) [Russ] cor,acap/pno
MEZ KNIGA 167 (C171)

CHORUSES FROM CANTATAS, VOL. 2 see
Bach, Johann Sebastian

CHORUSES FROM COMIC OPERAS BY RUSSIAN
AND SOVIET COMPOSERS, VOL. 2 °CCU
[Russ] wom cor&mix cor,pno MEZ KNIGA
158 (C172)

CHORUSES FROM OPERAS see Verstovsky, A.

CHORUSES FROM OPERAS see Gluck,
Christoph Willibald, Ritter von

CHORUSES FROM OPERAS see Wagner,
Richard

CHORUSES FROM OPERAS see Verdi,
Giuseppe

CHORUSES FROM OPERAS, VOL. 2 see
Rimsky-Korsakov, Nikolai

CHORUSES FROM OPERAS, VOL. 3 see
Rimsky-Korsakov, Nikolai

CHORUSES FROM OPERAS, VOL. 4 see
Rimsky-Korsakov, Nikolai

CHORUSES OF CONCERN see Weigl, [Mrs.]
Vally

CHORUSES TO WORDS BY AFANASY FET °CCU
[Russ] jr cor/wom cor/men cor/mix
cor,acap MEZ KNIGA 159 includes
works by Taneyev, Arensky,
Napravnik, Rebikov, and others
(C173)

CHORUSES TO WORDS BY FYODOR TYUTCHEV
°CCU
[Russ] cor,acap MEZ KNIGA 159 (C174)

CHORUSES TO WORDS BY RUSSIAN POETS see
Yegorov

CHORUSES, VOL. 2 see Taneyev, Sergey
Ivanovich

CHRISTIANSEN
Come Live With Me And Be My Love
SATB SCHIRM.G 320660 $.70 (C175)

Three Choral Songs °CCU
SATB SCHIRM.G 320700 $.70 (C176)

CHRISTMAS, A WONDERFUL TIME OF THE YEAR
see Murray

CHRISTMAS AGAIN see Wade

CHRISTMAS ALLELUIA, A see Snyder

CHRISTMAS BELL WALTZ see Hatch

CHRISTMAS BELLS see Walter, Lana

CHRISTMAS BELLS ARE RINGING see
Blevins, Patsy Ford

CHRISTMAS CANDLELIGHT see Orland, Henry

CHRISTMAS CANON see Hopson

CHRISTMAS CHA CHA, A see Ashton

CHRISTMAS CHEER!
(Leavitt) SATB CPP-BEL C0124C1X
$1.10, accomp tape available (C177)
(Leavitt) SSA CPP-BEL C0124C2X $1.10,

accomp tape available   (C178)
(Leavitt) SAB CPP-BEL CO124C3X $1.10,
accomp tape available   (C179)

CHRISTMAS CHEER see Cooper

CHRISTMAS CHILDREN, THE see Coombes,
Douglas

CHRISTMAS COMES AGAIN see Hopkins

CHRISTMAS COMES ANEW! see Kern

CHRISTMAS COOKIES AND HOLIDAY HEARTS
see Roberts, Ruth

CHRISTMAS DAY see Jefferson

CHRISTMAS FEAST see Madsen

CHRISTMAS IS A TIME FOR JOY see Kirk

CHRISTMAS IS COMIN' ALONG see Ross,
Brad

CHRISTMAS IS COMING
(Hansen) 4pt cor KJOS C8513 $.70
(C180)

CHRISTMAS JOY! see Hayes

CHRISTMAS LEGEND see Orland, Henry

CHRISTMAS LOVE see Brunet

CHRISTMAS LULLABY see Sobaje, Martha

CHRISTMAS LULLABYE, A see Frick

CHRISTMAS MEMORIES see Strommen, Carl

CHRISTMAS MINUET see Burt, Bates

CHRISTMAS MUSIC BY BJORNE ENSTABILE see
London, Edwin

CHRISTMAS NOEL see Ray, Jerry

CHRISTMAS ON THE ISTHMUS OF PANAMA see
Kupferschmid, Steven

CHRISTMAS PAST AND CHRISTMAS PRESENT
see Mechem, Kirke Lewis

CHRISTMAS PICKLE RHAPSODY, A: JOLLY OLD
SAINT PICKLE-LESS see Leavitt, John

CHRISTMAS SECULAR SONGS see Collins

CHRISTMAS SONG see Margolis, Jerome N.

CHRISTMAS SONGS THAT TICKLE YOUR FUNNY
BONE! see Roberts, Ruth

CHRISTMAS STORY, THE see Porter

CHRISTMAS TIME
(Hanson) SATB CPP-BEL 2629CC1X $1.25,
accomp tape available   (C181)
(Hanson) SSA CPP-BEL 2629CC2X $1.25,
accomp tape available   (C182)
(Hanson) SAB CPP-BEL 2629CC3X $1.25,
accomp tape available   (C183)

CHRISTMAS TIME (MORE THAN JUST A DAY)
see Anderson

CHRISTMAS TREE, THE see Coslett, Martin

CHRISTMAS TREE, THE see Dvorak, Antonin

CHRISTMAS TREE, THE see Sangster, D.

CHRISTMAS WALTZ see Thygerson

CHRISTMAS WARMTH see Dossett, Tom

CHRISTMAS! YES, IT'S CHRISTMAS see
Harris, Louis

CHRISTMASTIME! see Harris, Louis

CHRISTMASTIME IS HERE see Pollack, Lisa
Lauren

CHROIETAN BURUZAGI
(Grimbert, J.) 5pt mix cor HEUGEL
HE 32270   (C184)

CHUDOVA, T.
Festive Songs *CCU
[Russ] jr cor,pno MEZ KNIGA 540
(C185)

CHUTE, LA see Lefebvre

CIAIKOVSKI, PIETRO
see TCHAIKOVSKY, PIOTR ILYICH

CICLO see Kyllonen, Timo-Juhani

CIEL EST PUR, LE see Schubert, Franz
(Peter)

CIELITO LINDO
(Fourcaud, G.) mix cor HEUGEL
HE 32520   (C186)

CIELO, EL see Glaser, Werner Wolf

CINDERELLA'S MISFORTUNE see Takemitsu,
Toru

CINDY
(Scott, Michael) 2pt cor CPP-BEL
SV8849 f.s.   (C187)

CINQ CHANTS YOUGOSLAVES see Cossetto,
Emil

CINQ SUITES CANONIQUES see Terral, F.

CIRANDA see Prado, Jose-Antonio
(Almeida)

CIRCLES OF SILENCE see Williams-
Wimberly, Lou

CIRCUS BAND see Crawley, Clifford

CIRCUS SONGS see Crawley, Clifford

CITY PLAYS HIDE AND SEEK, THE see Avni,
Tzvi, Ha'ir Mesaheket Mahboyim

CIVILISATIONS PERDUES see Vanderlove,
Anne

CLAIR DE LUNE see Faure, Gabriel-Urbain

CLAIR RUISSEAU, LE see Blanc, Rene

CLAIRE CHANSON see Beguelin

CLAPP
Are You Ready For Christmas?
2 eq voices KJOS C8602 $.80 (C188)

Put Your Dreams On A Butterfly
2pt cor CPP-BEL SV8420 $.95 (C189)

CLARKE, HENRY LELAND (1907-   )
Alive And Well And Rolling Down The
Valley
unis cor,band/gtr [2'] AM.COMP.AL.
sc $8.45, pts $13.00   (C190)

Bounty Of Athena, The
SSA,pno [10'] AM.COMP.AL. $7.70
(C191)

Build Thou More Stately Mansions
SATB,pno/org [3'] AM.COMP.AL. $3.10
(C192)

Canons To Follow
3-4pt cor,acap [2'] AM.COMP.AL.
$.80   (C193)

Canons To Go By
3-4pt cor,acap [10'] AM.COMP.AL.
$.80   (C194)

Choose Life
SATB,pno/org [3'] AM.COMP.AL. $4.10
(C195)

Difference *canon
3pt cor [1'] AM.COMP.AL. $.45
(C196)

Give All To Love
SATB,pno [3'] AM.COMP.AL. $4.60
(C197)

Hope Of The World, The
SATB,pno [2'] AM.COMP.AL. $3.10
(C198)

I Am Only One
SATB,pno [1'] AM.COMP.AL. $4.10
(C199)

In Praise Of Peace
SA,pno [4'] AM.COMP.AL. $4.60
(C200)

Let Peace Encircle All The World
SATB,pno [1'] AM.COMP.AL. $.45
(C201)

Life
SATB,pno [2'] AM.COMP.AL. $.80
(C202)

Life Has Loveliness To Sell
unis cor,pno [3'] AM.COMP.AL. $1.60
(C203)

Listen To Me
2pt cor,pno [2'] AM.COMP.AL. $1.60
(C204)

Look Up
SAB,pno AM.COMP.AL. $1.60 (C205)

Mountain And The Squirrel, The
SATB,pno [3'] AM.COMP.AL. $4.60
(C206)

No Great, No Small
SATB,pno [3'] AM.COMP.AL. $3.10
(C207)

Out Of The Stars
SATB,pno [5'] AM.COMP.AL. $4.60
(C208)

Patriot Primer
SSA/SAB,pno [10'] AM.COMP.AL. $9.15
(C209)

Peace Means
SA,kbd [4'] AM.COMP.AL. $4.60
(C210)

Plowshares
unis cor,pno [2'] AM.COMP.AL. $.80
(C211)
2pt cor,pno [2'] AM.COMP.AL. f.s.
(C212)

CLARKE, HENRY LELAND (cont'd.)

Pray For Peace
2pt cor,pno [2'] AM.COMP.AL. $1.55
(C213)

Revelation Is Not Sealed
2pt cor,kbd [3'] AM.COMP.AL. $3.10
(C214)

Sleep On, My Friend
SATB,pno [3'] AM.COMP.AL. $4.60
(C215)

To Live To Love
SSA,pno [1'] AM.COMP.AL. $.45
(C216)

Who Is The Patriot
SAB,pno [4'] AM.COMP.AL. $4.60
(C217)

CLASSIC COMPOSERS FOR CHILDREN, VOL. 2
*CCU
[Russ] jr cor MEZ KNIGA 512 (C218)

CLAUSEN
Pretty Saro
TTBB SOUTHERN f.s.   (C219)

CLAUSIER, R.
Dans La Marine Suisse *see Rey, L.

CLEBER, JOSEPH
Postkoets, De
(Biersma, P.) SATB MOLENAAR
13021104   (C220)
(Biersma, P.) TTBB MOLENAAR
15022004   (C221)

CLEMENS, ADOLF (1909-1945)
Es Blies Ein Jager Wohl In Sein Horn
men cor,ST soli,2horn BOHM (C222)

CLEMENS, HENRI
Priere D'un Enfant De Choeur Mourant,
La
unis cor,pno ZENGERINK Z 601 (C223)

CLEMENS, JACOBUS (CLEMENS NON PAPA)
(ca. 1510-ca. 1556)
Like Venus Fair, Beyond Compare *see
Venus Schoon, Een

Lustelijcke Mey, De
(Lagas, R.) "Merry Month Of May,
The" SATB,acap (med diff)
ZENGERINK G 536   (C224)

Merry Month Of May, The *see
Lustelijcke Mey, De

Venus Schoon, Een
(Lagas, R.) "Like Venus Fair,
Beyond Compare" SATB,acap (diff)
ZENGERINK G 537   (C225)

CLEMENS NON PAPA
see CLEMENS, JACOBUS

CLEMENT, JACOBUS
see CLEMENS, JACOBUS

CLEMENTS, JOHN (1910-   )
There Is Sweet Music
SSA CPP-BEL 60383 $1.10 (C226)

CLERK STEPHEN see Bush, Geoffrey

CLOCHE DU SOIR see Lauber, Emile

CLOCHER DE MON VILLAGE, LE see Danks,
Hart Pease, Silver Threads

CLOCHES see Simoncini, Ernest D.

CLOCK WANTS TO SLEEP, THE see
Fleischer, Tzippi

CLOISTER AT KAZBEK, THE see Taneyev

CLOSE OF SPRING see Crawley, Clifford

CLOUD MESSENGERS see Cui, Cesar
Antonovich

CLOWNS see Crawley, Clifford

COBB
Hallelujah, I'm A Bum
SATB LAWSON LG 52277 $.90 (C227)

COBBLER, THE
see Two Irish Songs

COBINE
There's Another Christmas Coming Soon
SATB CPP-BEL SV8219 $.95 (C228)

COBINE, ALBERT STEWART (1929-   )
Chimes And Bells Of Christmas, The
SAB CPP-BEL SV8213 $.95 (C229)

COCKATOO, THE
see Songs Of Papua New Guinea

COCONUT AND BANANA *Carib
(Scherer) SSAA,pno,bongos,gtr MULLER
2754 see from Volkslieder Aus Aller
Welt   (C230)
(Scherer, E.) SATB,pno,bongos,opt gtr

MULLER 2764   (C231)

COENEN, HANS (1911-   )
    Kinder, Heut' Ist Wochenmarkt
    jr cor,pno,Orff inst BOHM   (C232)

COEUR DE LA MATIERE, LE see Jolivet,
    Andre

COEUR DE VOUS, LE see Anonymous

COEUR DE VOUS, LE see Sermisy, Claude
    de (Claudin)

COEUR JOYEUX see Schubert, Franz
    (Peter)

COEURS AMOUREUX see Hauptmann, Moritz

COFFEE GROWS ON WHITE OAK TREES °folk
    song
    (Sanders, V.) 2pt cor,pno (med)
    THOMAS 1C148405 $.60   (C233)

COFFEE PARFAIT see Bucci

COHAN, GEORGE MICHAEL (1878-1942)
    You're A Grand Old Flag
    (Nowak) SATB SHAWNEE 1872 $.95
                                 (C234)
    (Nowak) SAB SHAWNEE 0403 $.95
                                 (C235)
    (Nowak) 2pt cor SHAWNEE 0109 $.95
                                 (C236)
COHEN
    Ballad Of The Lion And The Lamb, The
    SA CPP-BEL DMC 00118 $.95   (C237)

COHEN, EDWARD (1940-   )
    Portrait No. 1
    TB,clar,bass clar,2horn,trp,pno
    [5'0"] APNM sc $7.50, voc sc
    $5.75, pts rent   (C238)

    Serenade For A Summer Evening
    SSATTB,2fl,clar,bass clar,vln,vla
    APNM sc $8.25, voc sc $6.00, pts
    rent   (C239)

COIN BLEU, LE see Renard, Georges

COLD FEET see Mitchell, Bob

COLEMAN, CY (1929-   )
    Colors Of My Life, The
    (Leavitt, John) SATB CPP-BEL SV8716
    $1.10   (C240)

    Colors Of My Life (From Barnum), The
    (Simon, William) SATB CPP-BEL
    T6525CC1 $.95   (C241)
    (Simon, William) SSA CPP-BEL
    T6525CC2 $.95   (C242)

    Hey! Look Me Over: A Medley Of Cy
    Coleman Hits
    (Chinn, Teena) SATB,opt horn CPP-
    BEL C0146C1X $2.50, accomp tape
    available   (C243)
    (Chinn, Teena) SSA CPP-BEL C0146C2X
    $2.50, accomp tape available
                                 (C244)
    (Chinn, Teena) SAB CPP-BEL C1446C3X
    $2.50, accomp tape available
                                 (C245)
    Rhythm Of Life, The
    (Barnes) SATB SHAWNEE 1316 $1.15
                                 (C246)
    (Barnes) SSA SHAWNEE 0420 $1.25
                                 (C247)
    You There In The Back Row
    (Huff) SATB CPP-BEL 5184YC1X $1.25,
    accomp tape available   (C248)

COLERIDGE-TAYLOR, SAMUEL (1875-1912)
    Fall On Me Like A Silent Dew
    SSA,pno [1'30"] ROBERTON 75356
                                 (C249)
    Oh, The Summer
    2pt cor,pno [2'30"] ROBERTON 75357
                                 (C250)
COLINDA: CAJUN FRENCH FOLK SONG
    (Scott, Michael) 2pt cor,triangle,opt
    inst CPP-BEL SV8924 $1.10, accomp
    tape available   (C251)

COLJEE, JAN
    Avondstilte: Hoe Zacht Daalt D'avond
    Neder
    [Dutch] 3 eq voices,acap ZENGERINK
    V 354   (C252)

    Molentje; Hei Molentje, Hoog In De
    Wind
    mix cor ZENGERINK 354   (C253)

COLLINS
    All For One World
    2pt mix cor,SA soli CAMBIATA
    ARS980151 $.65   (C254)

    Christmas Secular Songs
    cor CAMBIATA $2.50   (C255)

COLLINS (cont'd.)
    Hang In There, But Hang Loose
    SS&camb CAMBIATA L117323 $.75
                                 (C256)
    Huckleberry Finn
    (Placek) SSB&camb CAMBIATA $4.95
                                 (C257)
    Huckleberry Finn Album
    cor CAMBIATA $7.95   (C258)

    There Is A Ladye
    S&camb,SA soli CAMBIATA ARS980152
    $.70   (C259)
COLLINS, DAVID
    Crooked Man
    SAT,pno LAWSON 52462 $.90   (C260)

    Humpty Dumpty
    SATB,pno LAWSON 52463 $.90   (C261)

    Mother Goose
    SATB,pno LAWSON 52460 $.80   (C262)

    Old King Cole
    SATB,pno LAWSON 52461 $.80   (C263)

    Old Woman
    SAT,pno LAWSON 52464 $.90   (C264)

COLOMBE, LA see Brel, Jacques

COLORADO TRAIL, THE °folk song
    (Blair, D.) SATB,pno (med) THOMAS
    1C038417 $.70   (C265)
    (Lyle) SSB&camb,SAAB soli CAMBIATA
    U17316 $.70   (C266)

COLORADO TRAIL, THE see Bacon, Ernst L.

COLORS OF MY LIFE, THE see Coleman, Cy

COLORS OF MY LIFE (FROM BARNUM), THE
    see Coleman, Cy

COLOURS OF FRIENDSHIP, THE °CCU,folk
    song
    [Russ] jr cor,pno/acord MEZ KNIGA 521
                                 (C267)
COLUMBUS DAY SONGS THAT TICKLE YOUR
    FUNNY BONE! see Roberts, Ruth

COME AGAIN see Dowland

COME ALONG! see Lentz

COME AND SEE! see Albrecht

COME AWA' DEAR OLD GRANNY see Jones,
    Trevor

COME AWAY, DEATH see Hagemann, Philip

COME AWAY WITH ME see Sprunger, David

COME, DANCE AND SING see McKay

COME FOLLOW ME see Kupferschmid, Steven

COME, FOLLOW THE STAR see Donnelly

COME HERE, BIRDS! °CCU
    [Russ] jr cor,pno MEZ KNIGA 534
                                 (C268)
COME INTO MY LIFE
    (Buchholz, Buck) SATB,opt combo CPP-
    BEL 5050CC1X $1.25, accomp tape
    available   (C269)
    (Buchholz, Buck) SAB,opt combo CPP-
    BEL 5050CC3X $1.25, accomp tape
    available   (C270)

COME, LET US LIGHT THE MENORAH
    (Clarke, Rosemary) 1-2pt cor CPP-BEL
    SV8814 $.95   (C271)

COME LET US SING see Dvorak, Antonin

COME LIVE WITH ME AND BE MY LOVE see
    Christiansen

COME LOVERS FOLLOW ME see Morley,
    Thomas

COME, MY LIGHT, MY LIFE see Butler

COME ON! see Caletti

COME SHEPHERD SWAINS see Wilbye, John

COME, SING A CAROL see Harris, Louis

COME TO US, LITTLE KING see Schram

COMIC DUET FOR TWO CATS see Rossini,
    Gioacchino, Duetto Buffo Di Due
    Gatti

COMME LA TOURTERELLE see Monte,
    Philippe de

COMME UN P'IT COQU'LICOT see Asso

COMMON GROUND see Ray, Jerry

COMPAGNON, LE see Pileur, G.

COMPLAINT see Kreiger, Arthur V.

COMPLAINTE DE FRANCE see Jaubert,
    Maurice

COMPLAINTE DE LA BUTTE see Van Parys,
    Georges

COMPLAINTE DU CORSAIRE, LA see Contet,
    H.

COMPLETE WORKS, VOL. 5: MADRIGALS FOR 4
    AND 5 VOICES see Palestrina,
    Giovanni Pierluigi da

COMPLETE WORKS, VOL. 24: MADRIGALS FOR
    5 VOICES see Palestrina, Giovanni
    Pierluigi da

COMPLETE WORKS, VOL. 74: MADRIGALS FOR
    4 VOICES see Palestrina, Giovanni
    Pierluigi da

COMPOSERS' HUMOUR °CCU
    [Russ] jr cor,acap/pno MEZ KNIGA 239
                                 (C272)
CON ALAS EN LOS OJOS see Balzonelli,
    Alberto

CONCERT MUSIC NO. 2 see Karlins, M.
    William

CONCERTINA-TINA-TINA, VOL. 5 °CCU
    [Russ] jr cor MEZ KNIGA 516 (C273)

CONCERTO FOR ACTIVE FROGS see Le Baron,
    Anne

CONCERTO FOR CHOIR AND CHAMBER
    ORCHESTRA see Hvoslef, Ketil

CONCERTO FOR ORCHESTRA AND VOICES see
    Balazs, Frederic

CONCERTO FOR SINGING CHICKENS AND PIANO
    see Lawrence, Stephen L.

CONCERTS IMAGINAIRES DE LA RENAISSANCE
    °CCU
    (Agnel, A.) 2-6pt cor HEUGEL HE 32391
                                 (C274)
CONFIDENCE MATINALE see Defossez, Rene

CONFITURE DE GENEVRIERS see Lerstad,
    Terje B.

CONGA
    (Chinn) SATB CPP-BEL 5010CC1X $1.25,
    accomp tape available   (C275)
    (Chinn) SAB CPP-BEL 5010CC3X $1.25,
    accomp tape available   (C276)

CONLON, ANNE
    African Jigsaw °see Rose, Peter

    Yanomamo °see Rose, Peter

CONNECTICUT PEDDLER, THE see De
    Cormier, Robert

CONQUERANTS, LES see Huwiler, Pierre

CONQUERORS OF THE PRAIRIES see
    Eremenko, Serhij

CONSOLATION see Haydn, [Franz] Joseph

CONSOLI, MARC-ANTONIO (1941-   )
    Ite
    SATB [6'] (Pound) AM.COMP.AL. $4.60
                                 (C277)
CONSTANTINIDES, DINOS DEMETRIOS
    (1929-   )
    I Never Saw A Moor
    SATB,pno/org SEESAW   (C278)

CONTE, UN see Demierre, Francois

CONTENTEZ-VOUS
    (Agnel, A.) 2 eq voices HEUGEL
    HE 32073 contains also: Au Joli Son
    Du Sansonnet   (C279)

CONTENTEZ-VOUS see Gero, Ihan

CONTET, H.
    Complainte Du Corsaire, La (composed
    with Grassi, A.)
    (Frochet, J.) 4 eq voices HEUGEL
    HE 32192   (C280)

CONTINUATION see Bruynel, Ton

CONTRAPUNCTUS VI see Schnebel, Dieter

CONTRASTES (VISAGES-MAINS) see
    Bezencon, G.

CONTREPOINT DES ANIMAUX see Banchieri,
    Adriano

CONVERGENCE OF THE TWAIN, THE see
    Hamilton, Iain

CONVERSATION HEARTS see Kearns, Ann

CONVERSATIONS BETWEEN MOTHER AND CHILD
    see Hurnik, Ilja

COOK, MELVILLE
    West Sussex Drinking Song
    TTBB,acap [3'] ROBERTON 53141
                                    (C281)

COOMBES, DOUGLAS
    All In The Morning *Xmas,canon
    unis cor,pno LINDSAY   (C282)

    Bobby Shaftoe
    SSA,acap ROBERTON 75211 contains
        also: Ship That Never Returned,
        The   (C283)

    Christmas Children, The
    1-2pt cor,pno LINDSAY   (C284)

    Seven Space Songs *CC7U
    1-2pt jr cor,perc LINDSAY (C285)

    Ship That Never Returned, The
        see Coombes, Douglas, Bobby Shaftoe

    Songs From "Ting Tang The Elephant"
        *CC4U
    unis jr cor,pno,perc LINDSAY (C286)

COOPER
    Christmas Cheer
    SATB KJOS C8820 $.80   (C287)

    Cynic, The
    SATB BOURNE B239962 f.s.   (C288)

    I Sing For You
    SSA SOUTHERN $.50   (C289)

    Scarborough Fair
    SSB&camb HARRIS HCWO-4009 $.75
                                (C290)

COOPER, STEVE
    April's Rain
    SSATB SCHIRM.G 500220 $.95 (C291)

    Light Of Morning
    SSA,acap SOUTHERN SC 195 $.50
                                (C292)
    TTBB,acap SOUTHERN SC-238 $.65
                                (C293)

    Rest For All Eternity
    SSA,acap SOUTHERN SC 194 $.50
                                (C294)
    TTBB,acap SOUTHERN SC 193 $.50
                                (C295)

    Summertime Blues
    SATB,pno SCHIRM.G 50480348 $.85
                                (C296)

    Winter Wild
    SATB,pno SCHIRM.G 50480349 $.95
                                (C297)

COOPERATION see Dossett, Tom

COOTS
    Santa Claus Is Comin' To Town *see
        Gillespie

    Santa Claus Is Comin' To Town: A
        Medley *see Gillespie

COPELAND
    You Can Still Believe In America
    3pt cor CPP-BEL SV8513 $1.25 (C298)

COPELAND, CAROL
    Autumn
    2pt cor CPP-BEL SV8605 f.s. (C299)

COQ ET LE RENARD, LE see Francaix, Jean

COR MIO! MENTRE VI MIRO see Monteverdi,
    Claudio

CORDA NATUS EX PARENTIS (EVIGT FODD UR
    FADERNS HJARTA) see Nilsson,
    Torsten

CORNAZ, EMMANUEL
    Aux Aieux
    TTBB HUGUENIN 268B   (C300)

    Ces Belles Montagnes
    TTBB HUGUENIN EB 195 see from Deux
        Chansons Populaires   (C301)

    Chanson De Marins *see Coup
        D'riquiqui, Un

    Coup D'riquiqui, Un
    "Chanson De Marins" TTBB HUGUENIN
        EB 231   (C302)

    Deux Chansons Populaires *see Ces
        Belles Montagnes; En Revenant De
        La Foire   (C303)

    En Revenant De La Foire
    TTBB HUGUENIN EB 195 see from Deux
        Chansons Populaires   (C304)

CORNAZ, EMMANUEL (cont'd.)
    Enfant De Boheme, L'
    TTBB HUGUENIN EB 198   (C305)

    O Suisse, O Ma Patrie
    TTBB HUGUENIN EB 268A   (C306)

    Roi D'Yvetot, Le
    TTBB HUGUENIN EB 196   (C307)

    Ronde
    TTBB HUGUENIN EB 197   (C308)

    Si Seulement
    TTBB HUGUENIN EB 269   (C309)

    Viatique
    TTBB HUGUENIN EB 230   (C310)

CORNELIUS, PETER (1824-1874)
    Konige, Die *Xmas
    (Ierswoud, Frederik Van) SATB,med
        solo HARMONIA HU 3737 (C311)

CORNYSHE, WILLIAM (CORNISH)
    (? -ca. 1523)
    Blow Thy Horn, Hunter
    (Owen) 3pt mix cor CPP-BEL SV8638
        $1.10   (C312)

CORONATION SCENE see Mussorgsky, Modest
    Petrovich

CORREGGIA, ENRICO
    Death By Water
    SATB,2fl,2horn,2trp,strings,2pno
        SEESAW   (C313)

    Donner La Lumiere
    SATB,strings SEESAW   (C314)

CORTEGE see Bleuse, Marc

CORTEGE NUPTIAL NORVEGIEN see Kjerulf,
    Halfdan

COSLETT, MARTIN
    Christmas Tree, The (composed with
        Johnson, Veronica) *cant
    cor, solo voices,kbd,gtr,rec
        UNIVER. UE 17689 $6.95 (C315)

COSSETTO, EMIL (1908-   )
    Arrivee De La Noce (from Chants De
        Noces)
    4 eq voices HEUGEL HE 32013 (C316)

    Berceuse (from Chants De Noces)
    3 eq voices HEUGEL HE 32087 (C317)

    Chant De La Rose (from Chants De
        Noces)
    4 eq voices,pno HEUGEL HE 32030
                                (C318)

    Cinq Chants Yougoslaves
    3 eq voices HEUGEL HE 32263 (C319)

    Depart De La Jeune Mariee (from
        Chants De Noces)
    3 eq voices HEUGEL HE 32014 (C320)

    Depart Des Convives (from Chants De
        Noces)
    3 eq voices HEUGEL HE 32088 (C321)

    Hora Ali
    4pt mix cor HEUGEL HE 32015 (C322)

    Lamentation (from Chants De Noces)
    4 eq voices,pno HEUGEL HE 32029
                                (C323)

    Mes Verts Paturages (from Chants De
        Noces)
    3 eq voices,pno HEUGEL HE 32085
                                (C324)

    Moja Diridika
    4pt mix cor HEUGEL HE 32162 (C325)

    Pleurez Yeux Noirs (from Chants De
        Noces)
    5 eq voices HEUGEL HE 32031 (C326)

    Quatre Chants Yougoslaves
    4pt mix cor,mand/vln,gtr,vcl HEUGEL
        HE 32262   (C327)

    Vieille Mere (from Chants De Noces)
    3 eq voices HEUGEL HE 32086 (C328)

COSSON, A.
    Voyant Souffrir Celle Qui Me
        Tourmente
    (Agnel, A.) 3 eq voices HEUGEL
        HE 32309   (C329)

COSTELEY, GUILLAUME (1531-1606)
    Allons Au Vert Bocage
    SATB CAILLARD PC 147   (C330)

    J'aime Bien Mieux Souffrir La Mort
    SATB,acap HUGUENIN EB 370 (C331)

    Je Voy Des Glissantes Eaux
    5pt mix cor HEUGEL HE 32351 (C332)

COSTELEY, GUILLAUME (cont'd.)
    Jeu, Le Ris, Le Passetemps, Le
    CAILLARD PC 222   (C333)

    Las, Je N'irai Plus, Je N'irai Pas
    SATB CAILLARD PC 139   (C334)

    Mignonne, Allons Voir Si La Rose
    (Barblan, E.) TTBB HUGUENIN EB 187
                                (C335)

    Prise Du Havre, La
    CAILLARD PC 221   (C336)

    Puisque Ce Beau Mois
    SATB,acap HUGUENIN EB 392 contains
        also: Mauduit, Jacques, Vous Me
        Tuez Si Doucement   (C337)

    Que De Martyre Et De Douleurs
    SATB,acap HUGUENIN EB 371 (C338)

    Que De Passions Et Douleurs
    SATB,acap A COEUR JOIE 679 (C339)

COTTRAU, TEODORO (1827-1879)
    Sancta Lucia
    (Rosting, E.) TTBB MOLENAAR
        15022404   (C340)

COUCOU see Bovet, Joseph

COUCOU, LE see Cucu, Il

COULER DES ROIS, LA see Gesseney-Rappo,
    Dominique

COULEZ, MES PLEURS! see Bennett, John

COUNTRY CORN see Leavitt, John

COUNTRY FAIR, THE (PHILOSOPHICAL
    ANECDOTES) see Sowash

COUNTRY GARDENS see Grainger, Percy
    Aldridge

COUP DE DES, UN see Ballif, Claude

COUP D'RIQUIQUI, UN see Cornaz,
    Emmanuel

COUPEUSE DE JONCS, LA see Boller, Carlo

COUPEUSE DE JONCS, LE see Aeschbacher,
    Walther

COURTIN' SONG, THE see Ritchie, Jean

COURTOIS, JEAN
    Deduc Me Domine
    (Agnel, A.) 3pt mix cor HEUGEL
        HE 32460   (C341)

COUSTE, FRANCIS
    Chanson A Boire (from Quatre
        Chansons)
    (Pagot, Jean) SATB A COEUR JOIE 048
                                (C342)

    Quand Le Guerrier (from Quatre
        Chansons)
    (Pagot, Jean) SATB A COEUR JOIE 049
                                (C343)

    Si J'etais (from Quatre Chansons)
    (Pagot, Jean) SATB A COEUR JOIE 047
                                (C344)

COWLES, DARLEEN
    Fragments Of A Lost Song
    SSA,fl,pno [15'] AM.COMP.AL. $9.95
                                (C345)

COX
    October
    SB&camb,S solo CAMBIATA C485194
        $.80   (C346)

COYNER, LOU (1931-   )
    Softest Things In The World, The
    SSAA,pno [11'] AM.COMP.AL. $3.10
                                (C347)

CRADLE OF FIRE: FIVE SETTINGS OF
    HOLOCAUST SONGS see Isaacson,
    Michael Neil

CRADLE SONG, A see Bacon, Ernst L.

CRAM
    Where'er You Walk
    BB&2camb CAMBIATA C978113 $.70
                                (C348)

CRANBERRIES see Falik, Yuri

CRAWDAD SONG, THE
    (Scherer) SSAA,pno,gtr MULLER 2756
        see from Volkslieder Aus Aller Welt
                                (C349)
CRAWDAD SONG, THE: COME ON, HONEY
    (Scherer, E.) [Eng] SATB,pno,gtr
        MULLER 2761   (C350)

CRAWFORD
    Amen
    (De Cormier, Robert) mix cor LAWSON
        LG 51275 $.70   (C351)

CRAWFORD, JOHN CHARLTON (1931-   )
Little Black Boy, The
SSA,fl,clar,horn,vcl,opt pno GALAXY
1.2977 $1.35   (C352)

CRAWLEY, CLIFFORD
Abdul The Magician
see Magic In The Air

Aroundabout Christmas °Xmas,round
unis cor HARRIS HC-6001 $.95 (C353)

Cars
see Ev'ryday Things

Catching
see Ev'ryday Things

Circus Band
see Circus Songs

Circus Songs
unis cor LESLIE 1157 f.s.
contains: Circus Band; Clowns;
Elephants; Horses; Lions,
(C354)

Close Of Spring
SATB,acap MUSIC SEV. M70-568 $.85
(C355)

Clowns
see Circus Songs

Creatures Great And Small
unis cor,pno/gtr LESLIE 1137 f.s.
contains: Dragons; Gremlins;
Unicorns, The   (C356)

Dawn
unis cor&desc LESLIE 2054 f.s.
(C357)

Dragons
see Creatures Great And Small

Elephants
see Circus Songs

Ev'ryday Things
unis cor,pno/gtr LESLIE 1136 f.s.
contains: Cars; Catching; Food;
Lights   (C358)

Food
see Ev'ryday Things

Grass Is Always Greener
1-2pt cor LESLIE 2058 f.s.   (C359)

Gremlins
see Creatures Great And Small

Horses
see Circus Songs

It's Not Easy
see We Love To Sing

Let Us Remember
unis cor&opt desc,pno/org LESLIE
1131 f.s.   (C360)

Lights
see Ev'ryday Things

Lions,
see Circus Songs

Listen
see Once Upon A Christmas Time

Little Leprechaun
unis cor LESLIE 1148 f.s.   (C361)

Lullaby-Loo
see Once Upon A Christmas Time

Magic Carpet
see Magic In The Air

Magic In The Air
unis cor LESLIE 1143 f.s.
contains: Abdul The Magician;
Magic Carpet; There's Magic In
The Air   (C362)

Northward
see Songs Of The Settlers

Once Upon A Christmas Time
unis cor,pno,gtr,Orff inst LESLIE
1132 f.s.
contains: Listen; Lullaby-Loo;
Once Upon A Christmas Time;
Santa's Pets   (C363)

Once Upon A Christmas Time
see Once Upon A Christmas Time

Our Homestead's On The Flatlands
see Songs Of The Settlers

Pelicans
unis cor LESLIE 1158 f.s.   (C364)

Santa's Pets
see Once Upon A Christmas Time

CRAWLEY, CLIFFORD (cont'd.)

Shadows
2pt cor LESLIE 2053 f.s.   (C365)

Songs Of The Settlers
unis cor LESLIE 1144 f.s.
contains: Northward; Our
Homestead's On The Flatlands;
Songs Of The Settlers; We'll
Blaze A Trail   (C366)

Songs Of The Settlers
see Songs Of The Settlers

Thanksgiving
2pt cor LESLIE 2059 f.s.   (C367)

There's Magic In The Air
see Magic In The Air

Thunder And Lightning
unis cor,pno LESLIE 1130 f.s.
(C368)

Unicorns, The
see Creatures Great And Small

We Love To Sing
unis cor&opt desc,pno LESLIE 1129
f.s.
contains: It's Not Easy; We Love
To Sing; Wishes   (C369)

We Love To Sing
see We Love To Sing

We'll Blaze A Trail
see Songs Of The Settlers

Wishes
see We Love To Sing

CREATORS see Matej, Jozka (Josef)

CREATURES GREAT AND SMALL see Crawley,
Clifford

CRECQUILLON, THOMAS (? -1557)
Oncques Amour (from Polyphonia)
(Ouvrard, J.P.) 4pt cor HEUGEL 508
(C370)

CREED, LINDA
Greatest Love Of All, The °see
Masser, Michael

CRESCENT MOON NOW FLOATING see Larson

CREUX-DU-VAN, LE see Pantillon, G.L.

CRICKET'S WORLD see Grimbert, Jacques

CRIERS see Pinos, Alois

CRISWELL
O Mistress Mine
SATB CPP-BEL OCT 02527 $1.10 (C371)

CROCKER
Candleglow
SATB SHAWNEE 1804 $.90   (C372)

Fond Affection
SSA SOUTHERN $.50   (C373)

CROCKER, EMILY
Now, O Now I Needs Must Part
SATB,acap SOUTHERN SC-229 $.45
(C374)
SAB,acap SOUTHERN SC-230 $.45
(C375)

CROIX EN VALAIS, UNE see Lauber, Emile

CROOKED MAN see Collins, David

CROSS-BEARING CHILD, THE see Kunz

CROSSE, GORDON (1937-   )
Changes
SATB&opt jr cor,SB soli,2.1.2.2.
2.2.2.1. timp,4perc,pno,strings
OXFORD 335620-1 $4.50   (C376)

Dreamcanon I
SATB,A solo,pno,elec pno,perc
OXFORD   (C377)

May Song, A
SSATBB,acap OXFORD 335636-8 $2.20
(C378)
Meet My Folks! (8 Portraits)
treb cor,speaking voice,0.1.1.1.
1.1.0.0. vcl,pno,Orff inst,perc
sc OXFORD 335660-0 $9.10, cor pts
OXFORD 335661-9 f.s.   (C379)

CROSSING THE BAR see Andriessen,
Jurriaan

CROUCH
Molly Malone
TTBB CPP-BEL SV8311 $.95   (C380)

CRUDELE ACERBA see Kerstens, Huub

CRUSH ON YOU
(Buchholz) SATB CPP-BEL 5795CC1X
$1.25, accomp tape available (C381)
(Buchholz) SSA CPP-BEL 5795CC2X
$1.25, accomp tape available (C382)
(Buchholz) SAB CPP-BEL 5795CC3X
$1.25, accomp tape available (C383)

CRYSTAL VOICE see Kweller, Lee

CUATRO MULIEROS, LOS
(Lenoble, J.) 3 eq voices HEUGEL
HE 32163   (C384)

CUCKOO see Liddell, Claire

CUCKOO BIRD, THE see Berkowitz, Sol

CUCU, IL
(Ganter, C.) mix cor,acap PELIKAN
PE1185   (C385)
(Haug, Hans) "Coucou, Le" SATB,acap
HUGUENIN EB 225   (C386)

CUI, CESAR ANTONOVICH (1835-1918)
Chant Des Moissonneurs D'ukraine
(Lallement, Bernard) SATB A COEUR
JOIE 359   (C387)

Cloud Messengers
(Harris, Jerry Weseley) SATB,acap
LAWSON 52417 $.90   (C388)

CULTIVATING THE LAND see Blake, Howard

CULVER
All Things Of Wonder And Love
SATB SHAWNEE 6488 $.95   (C389)

CUNNINGHAM
Sea Song, A
(Swenson) BB&camb CAMBIATA C981158
$.75   (C390)

CURTI, F.
Amour T'appelle, L'
4pt cor,pno/strings HUGUENIN EB 427
(C391)
Mignonne
TTBB HUGUENIN EB 201   (C392)

Saint Jacques
TTBB HUGUENIN EB 278   (C393)

Trop Loin
SATB,acap HUGUENIN EB 202   (C394)

CUSTER, ARTHUR (1923-   )
Dirge In Woods
SATB [3'] AM.COMP.AL. $3.10   (C395)

CUTTER, BILL
My Love Is Like A Red, Red Rose
ALFRED   (C396)

Set My Soul Free
SATB ALFRED 7592 $.95   (C397)

Welcome Spring
ALFRED   (C398)

CYCLE DU VIN, LE
(Helmbacher, Xavier) SAB A COEUR JOIE
281   (C399)

CYGNE, LE see Blanchard

CYGNE D'ARGENT, LE see Gibbons, Orlando

CYNIC, THE see Cooper

CYNTHIA see Adler, Samuel Hans

CZAR FEDOR IVANOVITCH see Sviridov,
Georgy

CZECH SONG see Smetana, Bedrich, Ceska
Pisen

CZECH SONGS see Domazlicky, Frantisek

D

DA DRUNTEN IN JENEM TALE see Forster, Peter

DA VENOSA, GESUALDO
see GESUALDO, [DON] CARLO

DAAR WAS EEN SNEEUWWIT VOGELTJE see Anonymous

DAAR WAS EEN WUF DIE SPON see Badings, Henk

DAAR WAS EEN WUF DIE SPON see Schmitz, J.

DAAROM. . . see Biersma, P.

DACTYLOS PARISIENNES, LES see Schmidt-Wunstorf, Rudolf

DAER WAS A WUF DIE SPON see Schrijvers, Jean

DAER WAS E WUF DIE SPON see Anonymous

DAER WAS EEN KWEZELTJE see Schrijvers, Jean

DAER WAS EEN SNEEUWWIT VOGHELTJE see Schrijvers, Jean

DAG SKA JAG, EN see Lindgren, Olof

DAGEN NA KRUISIGING, DE see Pluister, Simon

DAISY, DAISY see Taylor, Lemoyne

DALE SI LE DAS see Anonymous

DALL'ORIENTE L'ASTRO DEL GIORNO see Rossini, Gioacchino

DAME D'HONNEUR see Jacotin, Jacques

DAME NIGHTINGALE see Schein

DAMMERUNG see Pantillon, G.L.

DAMNATION OF FAUST, THE see Berlioz, Hector (Louis)

DAMOISELLE ELUE, LA see Debussy, Claude

D'AMOUR JE SUIS DESHERITEE see Sermisy, Claude de (Claudin)

D'AMOUR LE BEAU VISAGE see Patry, Andre J.

DANAE, LA
(Grimbert, J.) 3 eq voices HEUGEL
HE 31899   (D1)

DANCE see Altena, Maarten

DANCE AND SECRET see Schnabel, Artur

DANCE AND SING! see MacLeod

DANCE, DANCE, DANCE see Pollack, Bill

DANCE OF THE GHOSTS see Berlioz, Hector (Louis), Ballet Des Ombres, Le

DANCE-SONG see Bordewijk-Roepman, Johanna

DANCIN' AT THE ROCK see Moore, Donald

DANCING IN THE DARK
(Althouse) SAB CPP-BEL 0149DC3X $1.25
(D2)
(Althouse) SATB CPP-BEL 0149DC1X
$1.25   (D3)
(Althouse) SSA CPP-BEL 0149DC2X $1.25
(D4)

DANCING STRING OF JOY, THE see Hallberg, Bengt, Gladjens Dansande Strang

DANIEL
Chanson A Virer
see Caillard, Philippe, Vla L'bon
Vent

Minuit Sonne
see Caillard, Philippe, Vla L'bon
Vent

DANIEL, ETIENNE
Amour Sans Amour, L'
SATB,opt pno CAILLARD PC 156 see
from Neuf Chansons Sur Des Poemes
Contemporains   (D5)

Au Carrefour Des Trois Brouillards
SATB,opt pno CAILLARD PC 160 see
from Neuf Chansons Sur Des Poemes

DANIEL, ETIENNE (cont'd.)

Contemporains   (D6)

Aux Jours De Longue Faim
SATB,opt pno CAILLARD PC 162 see
from Neuf Chansons Sur Des Poemes
Contemporains   (D7)

Beau Musicien
SABar,opt pno CAILLARD PC 157 see
from Neuf Chansons Sur Des Poemes
Contemporains   (D8)

Cantate En Forme De Colombe
4pt mix cor,org,fl A COEUR JOIE
(D9)

Chanson A Virer
SATB CAILLARD PC 32 contains also:
Minuit Sonne   (D10)

Chanson De Dolly Pentraeth, La
SATB,opt pno CAILLARD PC 138 see
from Neuf Chansons Sur Des Poemes
Contemporains   (D11)

Chansons Bachiques (Remplis Ton Verre
Vide) °see Mon Mari Va A La
Taverne; Vive Henri IV   (D12)

Deja Mal Mariee
SATB CAILLARD PC 41 contains also:
Eveille-Toi Renaud   (D13)

Dormir
SATB,opt pno CAILLARD PC 161 see
from Neuf Chansons Sur Des Poemes
Contemporains   (D14)

Eveille-Toi Renaud
see Daniel, Etienne, Deja Mal
Mariee

Gypsie Laddie
SATB CAILLARD PC 132 contains also:
O Arranmore   (D15)

Mon Mari Va A La Taverne
SATB CAILLARD PC 122 see from
Chansons Bachiques (Remplis Ton
Verre Vide)   (D16)

Morbihan
SATB,opt pno CAILLARD PC 159 see
from Neuf Chansons Sur Des Poemes
Contemporains   (D17)

Mots De La Mer
3 eq voices A COEUR JOIE 9013 (D18)

Neuf Chansons Sur Des Poemes
Contemporains °see Amour Sans
Amour, L'; Au Carrefour Des Trois
Brouillards; Aux Jours De Longue
Faim; Beau Musicien; Chanson De
Dolly Pentraeth, La; Dormir;
Morbihan; Si Mes Yeux, Si Mes
Mains; Tournent Les Jours   (D19)

O Arranmore
see Daniel, Etienne, Gypsie Laddie

Ou Vas-Tu?
(Turellier, Jean) SSAB,rec,vcl
HEUGEL HE 32128   (D20)

Si Mes Yeux, Si Mes Mains
SABar,opt pno CAILLARD PC 158 see
from Neuf Chansons Sur Des Poemes
Contemporains   (D21)

Tournent Les Jours
SATB,opt pno CAILLARD PC 155 see
from Neuf Chansons Sur Des Poemes
Contemporains   (D22)

Vive Henri IV
SATB CAILLARD PC 122 see from
Chansons Bachiques (Remplis Ton
Verre Vide)   (D23)

DANK, DER
cor HIEBER MH 5028   (D24)

DANK VOOR UW KOMST see Warnaar, D.J.

DANKS, HART PEASE (1834-1903)
Clocher De Mon Village, Le °see
Silver Threads

Silver Threads
(Volery, Francis) "Clocher De Mon
Village, Le" TTBB,acap HUGUENIN
CH 2083   (D25)

DANNER
Last Invocation, The
SATB WILLIS 10942 $.75   (D26)

Song Of The Universal
SATB WILLIS 10948 $.75   (D27)

DANNY BOY
(Knowles, Julie) SSA ALFRED $.95
(D28)

DANS LA FORET see Lauber, Emile

DANS LA MARINE SUISSE see Rey, L.

DANS LE COEUR DE CHAQUE HOMME see Gauffriau, Jean

DANSE see Moustaki, Georges

DANSE, LA see Blanchard

DANSE DE LOCMINE
see Source Claire, Une

DANSE DES MORTS: MOTET see Distler, Hugo

DANSE MACABRE see Lagger, Oscar

DANSEN EN SPRINGEN see Hassler, Hans Leo, Tanzen Und Springen

DANSEZ see Gagnebin, Henri

DANZIG, EVELYN
Scarlet Ribbons
(Edwards) SA CPP-BEL 60504 f.s.
(D29)

DARION, JOSEPH (1917-   )
Galileo Galilei °see Laderman, Ezra

DARK, THE see White, Gary C.

DARLOW
Carol, A °Xmas
SATB oct DEAN HRD 220 f.s.   (D30)

DARNAL, JEAN CLAUDE
Dites-Moi, M'sieur
(Ziberlin, F.) 3pt mix cor,rec,gtr
HEUGEL HE 31999   (D31)

DARTHULAS GRABESGESANG see Brahms, Johannes

DAS GIBT'S NUR EINMAL see Heymann

DAS IST KINDERSACHE! see Wundrich

DAS MUSS EIN STUCK VOM HIMMEL SEIN see Heymann

DASHING AWAY WITH THE SMOOTHING IRON
(Van Iderstine, A.P.) SATB NEW MUSIC
NMA-176 $.75   (D32)

DASHING AWAY WITH THE SMOOTHING IRON
see Rutter, John

DASHING AWAY WITH THE SMOOTHING IRON
see Webb, Evelyn

DATEMI PACE see Rore, Cipriano de

DAUERNDE LIEBE see Brahms, Johannes

D'AUTRES OISEAUX see Garcin

DAVID OF THE WHITE ROCK see Rollin

DAVIDOWITZ
Bar Yohai
(Coopersmith) [Yiddish/Heb] SATB
SCHIRM.G 455140 $.70   (D33)

DAVIDS NIMM see Rehnqvist, Karin

DAVIDSON
Gladsome Mind, A
SATB oct DEAN HRD 234 $.95   (D34)

DAVIDSON, CHARLES STUART (1929-   )
Anthem For Peace
[Heb/Eng] SATB,solo voice ASHBOURN
$3.00   (D35)

Baroque Suite
[Eng/Heb] SSA,fl,vcl ASHBOURN
$10.00, ipa   (D36)

Freedom's Flame
SAB/SA ASHBOURN $1.00   (D37)

Funny Thing Happened On The Way To
The Seder, A
jr cor ASHBOURN $30.00   (D38)

Hanukkah Nigun
2pt treb cor,pno ASHBOURN $.50
(D39)

I Never Saw Another Butterfly
SSA,orch [30'] voc sc,sc ASHBOURN
f.s., rent   (D40)
SSA,string quar,ob,harp,horn [30']
voc sc,sc ASHBOURN f.s., rent
(D41)

It Happened In Helm
jr cor [15'] ASHBOURN $10.00 (D42)

Saenu
[Heb/Eng] SATB,opt kbd TRANSCON.
990744 $.70   (D43)

Singing Of Angels, A °CC9U
SSA ASHBOURN $15.00   (D44)

DAVIDSON, CHARLES STUART (cont'd.)

Swingin'
SA,pno WIDE WORLD $.75   (D45)

DAVIDSON, ROBERT
see BURROUGHS, BOB LLOYD

DAVIES, BRYAN (1934-   )
Lonely Steppe, The
TTBB,T solo,pno [2'30"] ROBERTON
53096   (D46)

Stenka Razin
TTBB,B solo,pno [3'35"] ROBERTON
53097   (D47)

DAVIES, DAVID
Land Of Song °see Harry, Lyn

DAVIS
Holy Nation
(Marsh) SATB SHAWNEE 6463 $1.00
                               (D48)

Little Drummer Boy (composed with
Onorati; Simeone)
SAB CPP-BEL 60526 $1.20   (D49)
SATB CPP-BEL 60222 f.s.   (D50)

Stand Up And Sing
SAB&camb CAMBIATA C97319 $.70 (D51)

DAVIS, STEPHEN
With Just One Look In Your Eyes
(composed with Morgan, Dennis)
(Althouse) SATB CPP-BEL 2848WC1X
$1.25, accomp tape available
                               (D52)
(Althouse) SSA CPP-BEL 2848WC2X
$1.25, accomp tape available
                               (D53)

DAWN see Crawley, Clifford

DAWN see Emmert, Frantisek

DAWN IN THE FOREST see Dvorak, Antonin

DAWSON
You Got To Reap Just What You Sow
1-3pt cor KJOS T144 $.60   (D54)
TTBB KJOS T143 $.60   (D55)
SATB KJOS T142 $.60   (D56)

DAY AFTER DAY THEY ALL SAY "SING" see
Lassus, Roland de (Orlandus), Tutto
Lo Di Mi Dici

DAY BEFORE CHRISTMAS, THE see Telfer,
Nancy

DAY IN SPRING, A see Woodward, Ralph,
Jr.

DAYBREAK see Kopelent, Marek

DAYDREAMIN' ME see Caletti

DE BERTRAND, A.
see BERTRAND, ANTOINE de

DE CORMIER, ROBERT (1922-   )
Connecticut Peddler, The
(De Cormier, Robert) jr cor LAWSON
LG 52126 $.85   (D57)

Do Not Go Gentle Into That Good Night
mix cor LAWSON LG 52255 $.85 (D58)

Formula, The (from Legacy)
mix cor LAWSON LG 52221 $1.40 (D59)

Harlequinade (from Legacy)
mix cor LAWSON LG 52222 $1.40 (D60)

Legacy (from Legacy)
(De Cormier, Robert) mix cor LAWSON
LG 52223 $.85   (D61)

One And Twenty Pennies
(Okun) men cor,opt gtr,ob,acord
LAWSON LG 51085 $.70   (D62)

Reminder (from Legacy)
mix cor,Bar solo LAWSON LG 52220
$.85   (D63)

DE GRANDIS, RENATO (1927-   )
Blinde Von Hyuga, Der
SATB,SMezTB soli,fl,harp,perc
SEESAW   (D64)

Japanische Jahrenzeiten
SATB SEESAW   (D65)

DE LATTRE, ROLAND
see LASSUS, ROLAND DE

"DE L'INFORMATION NULLE A UNE ESPECE DE
POESIE" see Chailley, Jacques,
Quand Il Neige

DE MARZI, G.
Signore Delle Cime
SATB,acap A COEUR JOIE 354   (D66)

DE MONTE, PHILIPPE
see MONTE, PHILIPPE DE

DE PABLO, LUIS
see PABLO, LUIS DE

DE SERMISY
Amours, Partes
(Harris) "Go Now, My Love" [Fr/Eng]
SATB CPP-BEL OCT 02537 $1.10
                               (D67)
(Harris) "Go Now, My Love" [Fr/Eng]
SSA CPP-BEL OCT 02535 $1.10 (D68)

Go Now, My Love °see Amours, Partes

DE TOUT SUIS SI CONFORTEE see Machaut,
Guillaume de

DE WERT, GIACHES
see WERT, GIACHES DE

DEALE, EDGAR
Drinking Song
SATB,pno ROBERTON 63168   (D69)

Fairest Rose In All The Garden °see
O Du Schoner Rosengarten

Lark In The Clear Air, The
SSA,pno ROBERTON 75344   (D70)

My Lovely Celia
SATB,pno ROBERTON 63164   (D71)

O Du Schoner Rosengarten
"Fairest Rose In All The Garden"
SATB,acap ROBERTON 63170   (D72)

DEAN, JIMMY
Big Bad John
(Lawrence, Stephen L.) unis cor/
TTB,opt combo CPP-BEL SV8745
f.s., accomp tape available   (D73)

DEATH AND THE OLD MAN see Smith, Gregg

DEATH, BE NOT PROUD see Sveinsson, Atli
Heimir

DEATH BY WATER see Correggia, Enrico

DEATH OF CUCHULAIN see Williamson,
Malcolm

DEBOUSSET, JEAN-BAPTISTE (1703-1760)
A L'amour Je Declare La Guerre
SATB,acap HUGUENIN CH 1191   (D74)
(Barblan, E.) TTBB HUGUENIN EB 254
                               (D75)

DEBOUT, FOLLE TROUPE see Schubert,
Franz (Peter)

DEBRONCKART, J.
Adelaide
(Ziberlin, F.) 3-4 eq voices/4pt
mix cor HEUGEL HE 32260   (D76)

DEBUSSY, CLAUDE (1862-1918)
Blessed Damosel, The °see Damoiselle
Elue, La

Damoiselle Elue, La
"Blessed Damosel, The" SSAA,SMez
soli,orch KALMUS K 06886 $2.50
                               (D77)

Dieu! Qu'il La Fait Bon Regarder
SATB CAILLARD PC 214   (D78)

Nuit D'etoiles
SATB,pno CAILLARD PC 213   (D79)

Sirenes (from 3 Nocturnes)
8pt wom cor,pno PETERS 8400 $9.50
                               (D80)

Temps A Laisse Son Manteau, Le
SATB,pno CAILLARD PC 212   (D81)

DECK THE HALL see Carol, W.

DECK THE HALL see Hayes

DECK THE HALLS °Xmas
(Burroughs) SATB CPP-BEL PROCH 03040
$.95   (D82)
(Phelps) SATB KJOS C8609 $.70 (D83)

DECLARATION OF INDEPENDENCE see Mar-
Chaim, Joseph

DECORATE THE HALLS! see Bennett

DEDICATION see Gerschefski, Edwin

DEDRICK
Kites Are Fun
(Andrews) SATB SHAWNEE 1014 $.80
                               (D84)

DEDUC ME DOMINE see Courtois, Jean

DEEP IN THE NIGHT see Boyd, Jack Arthur

DEEP RIVER
(Dessen) CAILLARD PC 1046   (D85)
(Mattson) SATB CPP-BEL SV8526 $.95
                               (D86)

(Terri, Salli) dbl cor,Mez solo
CONSORT PR CP 400 $.70   (D87)

DEEP RIVER WOMAN see Richie, Lionel

DEFOSSEZ, RENE (1905-1988)
Confidence Matinale
mix cor,acap [2'40"] CBDM f.s.
                               (D88)

Etoile Qui Sourit, Une
mix cor,acap [3'55"] CBDM f.s.
                               (D89)

Reflets D'enfance
mix cor,acap [3'30"] CBDM f.s.
                               (D90)

DE'IL'S AWA WI' THE EXISEMAN, THE
°Scot
(Rhein) SATB SCHIRM.G 321580 $.70
                               (D91)

DEIXEU LA TERRA see Salvador, Matilde

DEJA MAL MARIEE see Daniel, Etienne

DEKKER, J.
Andere Jacht, De
SATB MOLENAAR 08168808   (D92)

DELANGE, EDGAR (EDDIE) (1904-1949)
Moonglow °see Hudson, Will

DELANOE
Orange, L' °see Becaud, Gilbert

Pipeau, Le °see Aufray, H.

Tournesol, Le
(Frochot, J.) SATB HEUGEL HE 32551
                               (D93)

DELARUE-MARDRUS, LUCIE
Automne (composed with Passaquet,
Raphael)
3pt cor HEUGEL HE 32285 contains
also: Lanauve, G. De, Chant Du
Grillon (composed with Passaquet,
Raphael) (1-5pt cor)   (D94)

DELFT, MARC VAN (1958-   )
Metamorphosen °Op.4
SSSSSSAAAATTTTBBBBB DONEMUS   (D95)

Music To Move
SATB,band MOLENAAR 03 1610 07 (D96)

DELIUS, FREDERICK (1862-1934)
Sea Drift
SATB,Bar solo,orch KALMUS K 09948
$4.75   (D97)

DELLASANDRO, G.
Mrs. Santa Claus
(Watson, Walter) 2pt jr cor LUDWIG
L-1216 $.95   (D98)

DELLO JOIO, NORMAN (1913-   )
I Dreamed Of A City Invincible
SATB,SBar soli,kbd AMP 50480022
$.95   (D99)

Sing A Song Universal
SATB,pno AMP 50489995 $2.95   (D100)

DELNOOZ, HENRI (1942-   )
Elis
mix cor [28'] DONEMUS   (D101)

DELTA see Dubost

DELUGE, LE see Franken, Wim

DEM DRY BONES
(Smith, Douglas Floyd) TTBB CPP-BEL
PROCH 03045 $1.20   (D102)
(Smith, Douglas Floyd) 3pt mix cor
CPP-BEL PROCH 03042 $1.40   (D103)

DEM HIMMEL WILL ICH KLAGEN see Brahms,
Johannes

DEM VATERLAND see Wolf, Hugo

DEMIERRE, FRANCOIS (1873-1976)
Conte, Un
3pt cor HUGUENIN EB 274   (D104)

DEN ACKERMANN SOLL MAN LOBEN see Zipp,
Friedrich

DEN SOETEN TIJDT see Schrijvers, Jean

DEN UYL DIE OP DEN PEERBOOM ZAT see
Anonymous

DEN UYL DIE OP DEN PEERBOOM ZAT see
Schrijvers, Jean

DENEREAZ, ALEXANDRE (1875-1947)
Rose Sauvage
SATB,acap HUGUENIN EB 231   (D105)

Voyage De Decouvertes
TTBB HUGUENIN EB 50   (D106)

DENHOFF, MICHAEL (1955-   )
Voz Mia, Canta, Canta *song cycle
4-8pt cor,acap,fl MOECK 5306 (D107)

DENK ICH ALLWEIL see Reger, Max,
Vergebens

DENNARD
Hush! Somebody's Callin' My Name
SATB SHAWNEE 1802 $.85   (D108)

DENNE VESLE JENTA see Haugland, Glenn
Erik

DENVER, JOHN
see DEUTSCHENDORF, HENRY JOHN

DEPART DE LA JEUNE MARIEE see Cossetto,
Emil

DEPART DE L'EMIGRANT, LE see Gaugler,
Theodor

DEPART DES CONVIVES see Cossetto, Emil

DEPART DES HIRONDELLES see Lauber,
Emile

DEPASSEL, L.
Soir D'ete
SATB,acap HUGUENIN EB 452   (D109)

DEPUIS LA CITADELLE JUSQU'A see
Pantillon, G.L.

DERE, JEAN (1886-1970)
Jeux Et Chansons *CC11U
unis cor,pno JOBERT   (D110)

DERRIERE LA MONTAGNE see Bleuse, Marc

DERWINGSON, RICHARD
Just Gotta Try
SATB LEONARD-US 08603361 $.95
(D111)
SSA LEONARD-US 08603363 $.95,
accomp tape available, ipa (D112)

DES AILES DE COLOMBE see Divorne, Andre

DES FLEURS EN COURONNE see Schubert,
Franz (Peter)

DES FLEURS EN COURONNES see Schubert,
Franz (Peter)

DES HERRGOTTS WEINKELLER see Pappert,
Robert

DES MULLERS FROLOCHES WANDERN see
Trapp, Willy

DES PREZ, JOSQUIN (ca. 1440-1521)
Behold, You Are Charming *see Ecce,
Tu Pulchra Es

Ecce, Tu Pulchra Es
(Klein) "Behold, You Are Charming"
SATB SCHIRM.G 318610 $.70 (D113)

Je Me Complains
SATTB oct DEAN HRD 137 $.85   (D114)

N'esse Pas Un Grant Desplaisir
[Fr/Eng] SATB DEAN HRD 135 $.75
(D115)
Petite Camusette
(Smijers, A.) SATTBB (diff)
ZENGERINK G 547   (D116)

Secular Works For Three Voices *CCU
(Benthem, Jaap Van; Brown, Howard
Mayer) VER.NED.MUS. NJE 27 (D117)

Works Of Josquin Des Prez, The:
Secular Works, Vol. 1 *CC12L
(Smijers, A.) 5-6pt cor
VER.NED.MUS. J 3   (D118)

Works Of Josquin Des Prez, The:
Secular Works, Vol. 2 *CC12L
(Smijers, A.) 4-6pt cor
VER.NED.MUS. J 5   (D119)

Works Of Josquin Des Prez, The:
Secular Works, Vol. 3 *CC11L
(Smijers, A.) 4-6pt cor
VER.NED.MUS. J 8   (D120)

Works Of Josquin Des Prez, The:
Secular Works, Vol. 4 *CC16L
(Antonowycz, M.; Elders, W.) 3-4pt
cor VER.NED.MUS. J 53   (D121)

Works Of Josquin Des Prez, The:
Secular Works, Vol. 5 *CC16L
(Antonowycz, M.; Elders, W.) 3-4pt
cor VER.NED.MUS. J 54   (D122)

DES SANGERS FLUCH, OP. 139 see
Schumann, Robert (Alexander)

DES WINTERS ALS HET REGENT see
Anonymous

DES WINTERS ALS HET REGENT see
Schrijvers, Jean

DES WINTERS ALS HET REGENT see Velde,
H.v.d.

DES WINTERS ALS HET REGENT see
Vermulst, Jan

DESERT MOON
(Althouse) SATB CPP-BEL 1493DC1X
$1.25   (D123)
(Althouse) SSA CPP-BEL 1493DC2X $1.25
(D124)
(Althouse) SAB CPP-BEL 1493DC3X $1.25
(D125)

DESIR DU PRINTEMPS, LE see Huguenin,
Charles

DESIRE OF ANCIENT THINGS see Eben, Petr

DESPRES, JOSQUIN
see DES PREZ, JOSQUIN

DESSAU, PAUL (1894-1979)
Sieben Und Dreissig Chor- Etuden
*CC37U
mix cor,acap PETERS 10338   (D126)

DETSKE SBORY see Hurnik, Ilja

DETSKE SBORY see Raichl, Miroslav

DEUS QUI BONUM VINUM CREASTI see
Lassus, Roland de (Orlandus)

DEUTSCHE LIEDER see Farkas, Ferenc

DEUTSCHE VOLKSLIEDER, WOO 33 see
Brahms, Johannes

DEUTSCHENDORF, HENRY JOHN (JOHN DENVER)
(1943-   )
Perhaps Love
2pt cor MOLENAAR 13037806   (D127)

DEUTSCHLANDLIED see Haydn, [Franz]
Joseph

DEUTSCHMANN, GERHARD (1933-   )
Abschiedslied: Ich Wunsche Dir Gluck
mix cor BOHM   (D128)

Auf De Schwabsche Eisebahne
mix cor BOHM   (D129)

Chor Der Nachtlichter
(Miller, Franz R.) "Nachtlichter
Sind Wir Allzumal" men cor,2trp,
2trom BOHM   (D130)

Drei Seemannslieder *see Und An
Einen Tag Im Februar; Wer Will
Mit Uns Nach Island Gehn?; Wir
Fahren Ubers Weite Meer   (D131)

Erntelied: Flur Ist Gemaht
mix cor BOHM   (D132)

Fruhmorgens, Wenn Das Jagdhorn
Schallt
men cor BOHM   (D133)

Im Krug Zum Grunen Kranze
men cor BOHM   (D134)

Jetzt Gang I Ans Brunnele
men cor BOHM   (D135)

Kein Feuer, Keine Kohle
mix cor BOHM   (D136)
men cor BOHM see from Zwei
Volksweisen   (D137)

Nachtlichter Sind Wir Allzumal *see
Chor Der Nachtlichter

'S Bussin
mix cor BOHM   (D138)

'S Ist Alles Dunkel
men cor BOHM see from Zwei
Volksweisen   (D139)

Ubers Loaterl
mix cor BOHM   (D140)

Und An Einen Tag Im Februar
men cor BOHM see from Drei
Seemannslieder   (D141)

Wer Will Mit Uns Nach Island Gehn?
men cor BOHM see from Drei
Seemannslieder   (D142)

Wir Fahren Ubers Weite Meer
men cor BOHM see from Drei
Seemannslieder   (D143)

Zwei Volksweisen *see Kein Feuer
Keine Kohle; 'S Ist Alles Dunkel
(D144)

DEUX CANONS see Schumann, Robert
(Alexander)

DEUX CHANSONS DE MAI see Weber, Gustav

DEUX CHANSONS POPULAIRES see Cornaz,
Emmanuel

DEUX CHANTS DE MAI see Schubert, Franz
(Peter)

DEUX CHOEURS see Schubert, Franz
(Peter)

DEUX CHOEURS A 4 VOIX D'HOMMES see
Perrinjaquet, G.

DEUX NEGRO SPIRITUALS *see Little
David; Oh! I Want To Go   (D145)

DEWHURST, ROBIN (1968-   )
Golden Slumbers
TTBB,acap [3'] ROBERTON 53142
(D146)
Will Ye No Come Back Again?
TTBB,pno [2'20"] ROBERTON 53143
(D147)

DI LASSO, ORLANDO
see LASSUS, ROLAND DE

DI RORE, CIPRIANO
see RORE, CIPRIANO DE

DIALOGUE see Le Forestier, Maxime

DICK WHITTINGTON see Holdstock, Jan

DICKAU
Lovers Love The Spring (from Three
From Shakespeare)
SSATB KJOS 8650 $.80   (D148)

O Mistress Mine (from Three From
Shakespeare)
SSATB KJOS 8648 $.70   (D149)

Silvia (from Three From Shakespeare)
SSATB KJOS 8649 $.70   (D150)

DIDN'T IT RAIN see Neaum, Michael

DIDN'T WE
(Chinn) SATB CPP-BEL 2714DC1X $1.25,
accomp tape available   (D151)
(Chinn) SSA CPP-BEL 2714DC2X $1.25,
accomp tape available   (D152)
(Chinn) SAB CPP-BEL 2714DC3X $1.25,
accomp tape available   (D153)

DIDN'T WE ALMOST HAVE IT ALL
(Chinn, Teena) SATB,pno CPP-BEL
2803DC1X $1.25, accomp tape
available   (D154)
(Chinn, Teena) SAB CPP-BEL 2803DC3X
$1.25, accomp tape available (D155)

DIE MIT TRANEN SAEN see Schein, Johann
Hermann

DIEMER, EMMA LOU (1927-   )
Anniversary Choruses
mix cor,pno,opt orch FISCHER,C
04844 f.s., ipr   (D156)

Caprice
SATB,kbd (diff) FISCHER,C CM8261
$1.50   (D157)

I Will Sing Of Mercy And Judgment
(from Anniversary Choruses)
mix cor,pno,opt orch FISCHER,C
CM7804 f.s., ipr   (D158)

O Shenandoah
TTBB,pno FISCHER,C CM7716   (D159)

O To Make The Most Jubilant Song
mix cor,pno FISCHER,C 04880 (D160)

Spring Carol, A
mix cor,pno FISCHER,C CM7279 (D161)

Three Poems By Oscar Wilde
SATB,pno (diff) FISCHER,C CM8313
$1.25   (D162)

DIEPENBROCK, ALPHONS (1862-1921)
Chanson D'Automne
SATB BANK AB 199   (D163)

Tibur
TTBB BANK AB 185   (D164)

DIES HAUS IST MEIN see Seeger, Peter

DIEU D'ISRAEL see Mehul, Etienne-
Nicolas

DIEU! QU'IL LA FAIT BON REGARDER see
Debussy, Claude

DIFFERENCE see Clarke, Henry Leland

DIFFRACTION see Silsbee, Ann

DIGER DAG see Lystrup, Geirr

DIJK, JAN VAN (1918-   )
Nijmegen, Nijmegen *Op.721
SATB,2.2.2.2. 2.2.0.0. timp,2perc,
pno,strings [20'] (pno sc
available) DONEMUS   (D165)

Onbeduidende Polka En Twee
Wiegeliedjes *Op.720
SATB,2.2.2.1. 2.2.2.0. timp,perc,
pno,strings [12'] DONEMUS (D166)

Trek Er Op Uit
unis cor,pno ZENGERINK Z 625 (D167)

DIJKER, MATHIEU (1927-   )
Inviolata
TTBB,org [6'] DONEMUS   (D168)

Inviolata II
4pt men cor,1.1.2.1. 0.0.0.0.
strings,opt org [6'] DONEMUS
(D169)

DIKTEREN OG FLUEN see Simonsen, Melvin

DIMEY, B.
Abecedaire (composed with Popp,
Andre)
4 eq voices HEUGEL HE 32190 (D170)

DINNER ANYONE? FOUR RECIPES FOR MIXED
CHORUS see Bucci

DIPTYCH see Bottje, Will Gay

DIRGE IN WOODS see Custer, Arthur

DIS-MOI, BON CHARBONNIER see Holstein,
Jean-Paul

DIS-MOI JEANNETTE
see Melchior Et Balthazar
unis jr cor,Orff inst HEUGEL HE 32361
contains also: Melchior Et
Balthazar   (D171)

DISCOVER see Petron, Daniel

DISCOVER JOY! see Olson, Lynn Freeman

DISCOVERY see Track, Gerhard, Gefunden

DISNEY SPECTACULAR see Huff, Mac

DISPUTE see Massis

DISTLER, HUGO (1908-1942)
Berceuse (from Morike Chorliederbuch)
(Geoffray, Cesar) SATB A COEUR JOIE
170   (D172)

Danse Des Morts: Motet *Op.12
(Geoffray, Cesar) SATB A COEUR JOIE
176   (D173)

Freude, Holde Freude *Op.16
SATB BAREN. BA 6357 see from Neuen
Chorliederbuch   (D174)

Ich Brech Drei Durre Reiselein
*Op.16
SATB BAREN. BA 6357 see from Neuen
Chorliederbuch   (D175)

Lass, O Lass *Op.16
SATB BAREN. BA 6357 see from Neuen
Chorliederbuch   (D176)

Lob Auf Die Musik *Op.16
SATB BAREN. BA 6357 see from Neuen
Chorliederbuch   (D177)

Neuen Chorliederbuch *see Freude,
Holde Freude, Op.16; Ich Brech
Drei Durre Reiselein, Op.16;
Lass, O Lass, Op.16; Lob Auf Die
Musik, Op.16; Sommerliches
Liebeslied, Op.16   (D178)

Questions *Op.19
SATB A COEUR JOIE 171   (D179)

Sommerliches Liebeslied *Op.16
SATB BAREN. BA 6357 see from Neuen
Chorliederbuch   (D180)

DITES-MOI, M'SIEUR see Darnal, Jean
Claude

DIVORNE, ANDRE
Des Ailes De Colombe
SATB,acap HUGUENIN EB 192 (D181)

DIXIELAND JAMBOREE
(Shaw, Kirby) SATB LEONARD-US
08656791 $.95   (D182)
(Shaw, Kirby) SAB LEONARD-US 08656792
$.95   (D183)
(Shaw, Kirby) 2pt cor LEONARD-US
08656793 $.95, ipa, accomp tape
available   (D184)

DJIAN, H.
Source, La (composed with Faure;
Bonnet)
(Dumas, H.) 4pt mix cor HEUGEL
HE 32329   (D185)

DO MATKI: KOLYSANKA POLSKA, U MOJI
MATUSI see Laprus, Lucjan

DO NOT BE AMAZED see Franck

DO NOT GO GENTLE INTO THAT GOOD NIGHT
see De Cormier, Robert

DO NOT STAND AT MY GRAVE AND WEEP see
Harris, Ronald S.

DO THEY KNOW IT'S CHRISTMAS?
(Nowak) SATB LEONARD-US 08650491 $.85
(D186)
(Nowak) SAB LEONARD-US 08650492 $.85
(D187)
(Nowak) 2pt cor LEONARD-US 08650494
$.85, ipa   (D188)

DO YOU BELIEVE IN MIRACLES? see
Lawrence, Stephen L.

DO YOU HEAR WHAT I HEAR? see Regney,
Noel

DO YOU WANT TO KNOW A SECRET?
(Scott) 3pt mix cor CPP-BEL SV8634
$1.25, accomp tape available (D189)
(Scott) SATB CPP-BEL SV8635 $1.25,
accomp tape available   (D190)

DOBRU NOC
(Plojhar, F.) [Czech/Slovak] TTBB
HARMONIA 3707   (D191)

DOEDELZAK see Wolff, H. de

DOES YOUR CHEWING GUM LOSE ITS FLAVOR
(ON THE BEDPOST OVER NIGHT?)
(Madsen) SATB CPP-BEL 5046DC1X $1.25,
accomp tape available   (D192)
(Madsen) SAB CPP-BEL 5046DC3X $1.25,
accomp tape available   (D193)

DOFTA, DOFTA VIT SYREN see Lilja,
Bernhard

DOLLARHIDE, THEODORE
Lullaby
SAB AM.COMP.AL. $1.60   (D194)

DOLOR see Rivier, Jean

DOMAZLICKY, FRANTISEK (1913-   )
Czech Songs *Op.17
3pt wom cor/jr cor,string quar
[12'] CESKY HUD.   (D195)

DOMHARDT, GERD (1945-   )
Assoziationen *song cycle
mix cor sc BREITKOPF-L 7646 (D196)

Frieden - Halfte Des Lebens, Der
mix cor [8'] sc BREITKOPF-L 7695
(D197)
DOMINE, SALVAM FAC REGINAM NOSTRAM see
Vranken, Petrus Johannes Josephus

DON LEON see Vic, C.H.

DONAHUE
What Is The Key To Happiness
SATB MUSIC SEV. M70-471 $.95 (D198)

DONATI, BALDASSARE (DONATO)
(ca. 1530-1603)
Villotte Napolitaine
(Grimbert, J.) 4pt mix cor HEUGEL
HE 32267   (D199)

DONATO
All Ye Who Music Love *see Oliphant

DONATO, BALDASSARE
see DONATI, BALDASSARE

DONKEY RIDING
(Han, Isaac) SATB HARRIS HC-5030 $.95
(D200)
DONNELLY
All Over The World
(Strid) 2pt cor SHAWNEE 73 $.85
(D201)
(Strid) SAB SHAWNEE 0394 $.95
(D202)
Come, Follow The Star
(Strid) 2pt cor SHAWNEE 0114 $1.25
(D203)
I'm Proud To Call America My Home
(Strid) 2pt cor SHAWNEE 0107 $.95
(D204)
I've Got Music In My Soul
(Strid) 2pt cor SHAWNEE 0101 $.95
(D205)
Spirit Of Christmas, The
(Strid) SA SHAWNEE 0311 $.85 (D206)
We Are The Young
(Strid) SAB SHAWNEE 0397 $.95
(D207)
(Strid) 2pt cor SHAWNEE 0104 $.95
(D208)
Your Imagination (composed with Reed)
(Althouse) 2pt cor SHAWNEE $.85
(D209)

DONNELLY, MARY
I Have A Dream
(Strid, George) SATB ALFRED 7632
$.95, accomp tape available
(D210)
(Strid, George) SAB ALFRED 7633
$.95, accomp tape available
(D211)
(Strid, George) 1-2pt cor ALFRED
7634 $.95, accomp tape available
(D212)
DONNER
Watching The Colors Of The World
2pt cor CPP-BEL SV8426 $1.25 (D213)

DONNER LA LUMIERE see Correggia, Enrico

DON'T ASK ME see Berkowitz, Sol

DON'T BE WEARY, TRAVELER
(Seals, Karen) SATB,ob oct DEAN
HRD 133 $.85   (D214)

DON'T BLAME ME see Kunz

DON'T COUNT YOUR CHICKENS see Althouse

DON'T GET AROUND MUCH ANYMORE see
Ellington, Edward Kennedy (Duke)

DON'T PUT NO CHAINS ON ME see Johnson

DON'T SAY GOODBYE see McPheeters

DON'T YOU LET NOBODY TURN YOU 'ROUND
see McLin

DOO-WAH DAYS
(Scott) SATB CPP-BEL 5064DC1X $1.25,
accomp tape available   (D215)
(Scott) SSA CPP-BEL 5064DC2X $1.25,
accomp tape available   (D216)
(Scott) SAB CPP-BEL 5064DC3X $1.25,
accomp tape available   (D217)

DOOR DE BOSSEN, DOOR DE HEIDE (LENTE-
PARADE 3) see Beekum, Jan Van

DOORWAY, THE see Stine

D'ORLEANS, CH.
Ce Qui M'entre Par Une Oreille
(composed with Grimbert, Jacques)
wom cor/jr cor HEUGEL HE 31953
(D218)

En Yver Du Feu Du Feu (composed with
Grimbert, Jacques)
SSMezA HEUGEL HE 32546   (D219)

Plus Penser Que Dire (composed with
Grimbert, Jacques)
wom cor/jr cor HEUGEL HE 31953
(D220)

Quant N'ont Assez Fait Dodo (composed
with Grimbert, Jacques)
wom cor/jr cor HEUGEL HE 31953
(D221)

DORMENDO UN GIORNO A BAIA see Arcadelt,
Jacob

DORMEUR DU VAL, LE see Andriessen,
Hendrik

DORMIR see Daniel, Etienne

DORMOLEN, JAN WILLEM VAN (1956-   )
Sesimi Kaybeden Sehir
SATB,acap [8'30"] DONEMUS (D222)

DORS MON ENFANT SAGE see Barblan,
Emmanuel

DORT UNTEN AN DEM RHEINE see Miller,
Franz R., Ausserlich Und Innerlich

DOSSETT, TOM
Christmas Warmth
2pt cor JACKMAN JMC7047   (D223)

Cooperation
SAB,pno THOMAS C42-8706 $.75 (D224)

DOSTAL
Es Wird In Hundert Jahren Wieder So
Ein Fruhling Sein
(Grieshaber) mix cor,pno LEUCKART
LSB 516   (D225)

DOSTAL, NICO (1895-   )
Weihnacht, Weihnacht *Xmas
men cor,opt kbd LEUCKART NWL 103
f.s.   (D226)
mix cor,opt kbd LEUCKART NWL 503
f.s.   (D227)

DOTRENE see Sivertsen, Kenneth

DOTTY DITTIES see Kopelent, Marek

DOUBS, LE see Huguenin, Charles

DOUCETTE, SUCRINE see Grimbert, Jacques

DOULCE MEMOIRE see Klerk, Albert de

DOULCE MEMOIRE see Kox, Hans

DOULCE MEMOIRE see Sandrin, Pierre

DOUW, ANDRE (1951-   )
Erinnerung
TTB,A solo,ob/fl,English horn,clar,
bsn,horn,vln [20'] DONEMUS (D228)

DOUX CHAGRIN, LE see Fombonne, Jacques

DOUX CHAGRIN, LE see Vigneault, Gilles

DOUZE CANONS DU 16 SIECLE *CC12U
(Dottin, G.) 4pt mix cor HEUGEL 32221
(D229)

DOVE, THE see Holst, Gustav

DOWLAND
Come Again
see Gastoldi, Giovanni Giacomo,
Amor Vittorioso

Stay, Time, A While Thy Passing
SAB DEAN HRD 203   (D230)

DOWLAND, JOHN (1562-1626)
Away With These Self-Loving Lads
SATB,opt inst BROUDE BR. CR 41
(D231)

Eveille-Toi
SATB,acap HUGUENIN EB 11   (D232)

Fine Knacks For Ladies
(McCray) SATB,acap NEW MUSIC
NMA-158 $.55   (D233)

Flow Not So Fast, Ye Fountains
(Thoburn, Crawford R.) SSAB,acap
CPP-BEL OCT 02558 $1.10   (D234)

In Praise Of Cynthia *CCU
(Young, P.M.) [Eng/Ger] 4pt cor sc
BREITKOPF-L 7502   (D235)

Meidlein Tet Mir Klagen, Ein
mix cor BREITKOPF-L 7692 (D236)

DOWN BY DE RIVERSIDE
(Scherer) SSAA,pno,gtr MULLER 2753
see from Volkslieder Aus Aller Welt
(D237)

DOWN BY DE RIVERSIDE: LAY DOWN
(Scherer, E.) [Eng] SATB,pno,gtr
MULLER 2762   (D238)

DOWN BY THE RIVERSIDE (I'M GOIN' TO LAY
DOWN MY HEAVY LOAD) see Rutter,
John

DOWN THE RIVER *Greek
B&2camb CAMBIATA U485182 $.70 (D239)

DOWN THE RIVER see Van Iderstine,
Arthur Prentice

DOWNWARD ROAD IS CROWDED, THE see
Mcintyre

DRAAIERSJONGEN, EEN see Hol, Richard

DRAAIERSJONGEN, EEN see Holman, F.

DRAESEKE, FELIX (1835-1913)
Heinzelmannchen, Die *Op.41
SATB,acap KISTNER 7162 f.s. (D240)

DRAGONS see Crawley, Clifford

DRAGONS DE NOAILLES, LES
(Herr, F.) 2-3pt jr cor,Orff inst
HEUGEL HE 32399   (D241)

DRAPEAU, LE see Laur, F.

DRAUSS IST ALLES SO PRACHTIG see Reger,
Max, Mailied

DREAM, THE see Schumann, Robert
(Alexander)

DREAM A DREAM see Robertson, Ed

DREAM OF GERONTIUS, THE see Elgar,
[Sir] Edward (William)

DREAM OF THE CIRCLES see Tal, Joseph,
Halom Ha'igulim

DREAM SO FAIR, A
(Malewicki) SSA/SA KJOS C8621 $.70
(D242)
(Malewicki) SATB KJOS C8710 $.60
(D243)

DREAMCANON I see Crosse, Gordon

DREAMIN' see Montgomery, Lisa

DREI BECHER see Reinl, Franz

DREI BESINNLICHE GESANGE see Kutzer,
Ernst

DREI CHORE see Schumann, Clara (Wieck)

DREI CHORE, OP. 6 see Reger, Max

DREI CHORE, OP. 39 see Reger, Max

DREI GEDICHTE VON EMANUEL GEIBEL, OP.
29 see Schumann, Robert (Alexander)

DREI GELLERT-LIEDER see Beethoven,
Ludwig van

DREI GESANGE see Brahms, Johannes

DREI HOCHZEITSMADRIGALE NACH
MITTELALTERLICHEN MELODIEN see
Monter, Josef

DREI IRISCHE VOLKSLIEDER see Kelemen,
Milko

DREI JAGERLIEDER FUR MANNERCHOR see
Kelling, Hajo

DREI JUNGE LEUTE see Rubben,
Hermannjosef

DREI KLASSISCHE CHORE see Gluck,
Christoph Willibald, Ritter von

DREI KLASSISCHE CHORE see Gluck,
Christoph Willibald, Ritter von

DREI KLASSISCHE CHORE see Gluck,
Christoph Willibald, Ritter von

DREI LAUB AUF EINER LINDEN see Gebhard,
Hans

DREI LAUB AUF EINER LINDEN see
Hollfelder, Waldram

DREI LIEDER, OP. 114 see Schumann,
Robert (Alexander)

DREI LUSTIGE LIEDER see Beekum, Jan Van

DREI MANNERCHORE NACH VOLKSLIEDTEXTEN
see Dvorak, Antonin

DREI MINNELIEDER see Hollfelder,
Waldram

DREI PFALZISCHE VOLKSLIEDER see Klein,
Richard Rudolf

DREI QUARTETTE see Brahms, Johannes

DREI RUSSISCHE VOLKSLIEDER *see
Halmchen Kann Am Grossen Halme;
Kuckuck, Der; Schliesse, Schliesse
Dich, Zyklus   (D244)

DREI SCHONE DINGE FEIN see Friderici,
Daniel

DREI SCHWABISCHE LIEDER see Miller,
Franz R.

DREI SEEMANNSLIEDER see Deutschmann,
Gerhard

DREI SPIRITUALS
(Lampart, R.) mix cor,solo voice,pno,
opt inst BOHM   (D245)

DREI STERNE: SO VIEL STERNLEIN ALS DA
WALLEN see Weber, Carl Maria von

DREI TRAKL-GESANGE see Hellden, Daniel

DREI VOLKSLIEDER *see Bunt Sind Schon
Die Walder; Es Dunkelt Schon In Der
Heide; Sommers Abschied   (D246)

DREI WIEGENLIEDER see Rabe, Gerhard

DREI WIEGENLIEDER NACH ALTEN WEISEN see
Jochum, Otto

DREIFACH IST DER SCHRITT DER ZEIT see
Schubert, Franz (Peter)

DRENTSE METAMORFOSEN see Masseus, Jan

DRIE CANZONETTAS see Maessen, Antoon

DRIE NATIONALE LIEDEREN
(Penders, J.) SATB MOLENAAR 08177508
(D247)

DRIE OUDNEDERLANDSE LIEDEREN I see
Schrijvers, Jean

DRIE OUDNEDERLANDSE LIEDEREN II see
Schrijvers, Jean

DRIE OUDNEDERLANDSE LIEDEREN III see
Schrijvers, Jean

DRIED FLOWER see Sveinsson, Atli Heimir

DRILL, YE TARRIERS see Casey, Thomas

DRINK MIJ NIET TOE see Vermulst, Jan,
Drink To Me Only With Thine Eyes

DRINK TO ME ONLY see Willcocks, David
Valentine

DRINK TO ME ONLY WITH THINE EYES *folk
song,Eng
(Lawrence) BB&camb CAMBIATA U485181
$.75   (D248)

DRINK TO ME ONLY WITH THINE EYES see
Vermulst, Jan

DRINKHAIL see Liebergen, Patrick

DRINKING SONG see Deale, Edgar

DRINKING SONG see Yegorov

DRIVDALEN see Kvandal, Johan

DROM OM ELYSIUM see Ahlin, Sven

DROMMAR see Sandstrom, Sven-David

DRUMMER, THE
see Soldier, Soldier

DRUMS OF WAR, THE see Weigl, [Mrs.]
Vally

DRUON, M.
Galerien, Le (composed with Poll)
(Terral, F.) 3 eq voices HEUGEL
HE 32509   (D249)

DRY BONES see Gearhart

DRYVER, MICHAEL
Jericho
SATB LEONARD-US 08603345 $.95
(D250)

DU BIST AUF DIESER WELT NUR GAST see
Gebhard

DU BOYS, FRANCOISE
J'aime Bien Mon Ami
(Agnel, A.) 3 eq voices HEUGEL
HE 31989   (D251)

DU COEUR LE DON see Anonymous

DU, DU LIEGST MIR IM HERZEN
(Wind, Gerhard) TTBB MULLER 513
(D252)

DU FRAGSCH, WAS I MOCHT SINGE
(Willisegger, H.R.) 4pt men cor,acap
PELIKAN PE1199   (D253)
(Willisegger, H.R.) 4pt wom cor,acap
PELIKAN PE1200   (D254)
(Willisegger, H.R.) 3pt jr cor,acap
PELIKAN PE 1201   (D255)

DU FUGL SOM FLYVER
(Weaver, David) SATB MUSIKK MH 2469
(D256)

DU HAST DIAMANTEN UND PERLEN see
Andriessen, Jurriaan

DU HOGE FJELL see Knutsen, Torbjorn

DU MAINE, LA see Hemmerling, Carlos

DU MEIN EINZIG LICHT see Gebhard, Hans

DU SKA ITTE TRO I GRASET see Lyssand,
Henrik

DU SKA ITTE TRO I GRASET see Volle,
Bjarne

DU SKA ITTE TRO I GRASET see Volle,
Bjarne

DU SOM AR... see Andersson, Tommy B.

DU TOUT PLONGIET: FORS SEULEMENT see
Brumel, Antoine

DUBOIS, PIERRE-MAX (1930-   )
Pauvre Aveugle
4pt cor BILLAUDOT   (D257)

DUBOST
Delta
cor,acap HEUGEL HE 31995 (D258)

DUBRAVIN, Y.
Children's Choruses *CCU
[Russ] jr cor,acap/pno MEZ KNIGA
238   (D259)

Whence Comes Music? *CCU
[Russ] jr cor MEZ KNIGA 524 (D260)

DUCARROZ, M.
Ami, Un
SATB,acap HUGUENIN CH 2053 (D261)

Archer Du Roi, L'
SATB HUGUENIN CH 2061   (D262)

Au Grenier
SATB HUGUENIN CH 2062   (D263)

Fete, La
SATB,acap HUGUENIN CH 2052 (D264)

DUDELE, A
  [Yiddish/Eng] SATB,T solo SCHIRM.G
  455120 $.70   (D265)

DUETS see Laburda, Jiri

DUETTO BUFFO DI DUE GATTI see Rossini,
  Gioacchino

DUFAY, GUILLAUME (ca. 1400-1474)
  Ce Moys De May
    (Turellier, Jean) 3pt cor,opt 3rec
    HEUGEL HE 31934   (D266)

  Flos Florum
    (Turellier, Jean) SMezT,rec HEUGEL
    HE 32594   (D267)

  Je Ne Vis Oncques La Pareille,
    Rondeau
    (Turellier, Jean) AT,bsn,opt inst
    HEUGEL HE 32569   (D268)

DUFOURT, HUGUES
  Mort De Procris, La
    12pt mix cor [17'] SALABERT (D269)

DUKAS, PAUL (1865-1935)
  Bon Jour, Bon Mois
    (Turellier, Jean) 2pt cor,rec
    HEUGEL HE 32007 contains also:
    Langree, Alain, Or, Vous
    Tremoussez, Pasteurs   (D270)

DULCIS AMICA see Certon, Pierre

DUMONT, HENRI (1610-1684)
  Absent De Vous Je Languis De
    Tristesse
    (Turellier, J.) SAB,inst HEUGEL
    HE 32568   (D271)

  Je Ne Sais Que C'est D'un Fa Ni D'un
    Sol
    (Turellier, J.) SAB,inst HEUGEL
    HE 32567   (D272)

D'UN VANNEUR DE BLE
  (Grimbert, J.) 4pt mix cor HEUGEL
  HE 32463   (D273)

DUNAYEVSZKY, ISAAK O. (1900-1955)
  Isaak Dunayevsky And His Songs *CCU
    [Russ] jr cor,pno MEZ KNIGA 525
                                       (D274)

DUNBAR
  Once The Rain Has Fallen
    SATB SHAWNEE 1799 $.85   (D275)

DUNKELROTE ROSEN see Millocker

DUNQUE ROMPER LA FE DUNQUE DEGGIO IO
  see Marenzio, Luca

DUR ACIER ET DIAMONT see Janequin,
  Clement

DURCH DAS JAHR see Knorrn, Horst-Dieter

DURCH FELD AND BUCHENHALLEN see Mutter,
  Gerbert

DURSTIG JAHR, DAS see Biebl, Franz

DUSON, DEDE (1938-   )
  American Earth, The
    SATB,brass KJOS 8671 $.90, ipa
                                       (D276)
  Elusive Quest, The
    SATB KJOS 8687 $.80   (D277)

  Green
    2pt cor KJOS 6201 $.80   (D278)

  In Unison
    SSAA,clar,ob KJOS 6200 f.s.   (D279)

  River, The
    SATB KJOS 8688 $.95   (D280)

  Sense Of Kinship, A
    SATB KJOS 8653 $.70   (D281)

DUST OF SNOW see Kearns, Ann

DUTEIL, YVES
  Langue De Chez Nous, La
    (Ott, Norbert) 3 eq voices A COEUR
    JOIE 1032   (D282)

  Petit Pont De Bois, Le
    (Passaquet, R.) 3 eq voices HEUGEL
    HE 32576   (D283)

  Prendre Un Enfant
    (Passaquet, R.) 4pt mix cor HEUGEL
    HE 32577   (D284)

DVORAK, ANTONIN (1841-1904)
  Christmas Tree, The
    (Allen) 2pt cor GALLEON GCS 4006
    $.60   (D285)

  Come Let Us Sing
    mix cor CRANZ f.s. see from Songs
    Of Nature   (D286)

DVORAK, ANTONIN (cont'd.)
  Dawn In The Forest
    mix cor CRANZ f.s. see from Songs
    Of Nature   (D287)

  Drei Mannerchore Nach Volksliedtexten
    *Op.43
    [Czech] TTBB,2pno BAREN. AP 277
                                      (D288)
  Goin' Home
    SATB HARRIS HC-4010 $.75   (D289)

  Golden Cornfields
    mix cor CRANZ f.s. see from Songs
    Of Nature   (D290)

  On The Green Hillside
    mix cor CRANZ f.s. see from Songs
    Of Nature   (D291)

  Poursuite, La *Op.32,No.1
    2pt cor,pno HUGUENIN EB 464 (D292)

  Song To The Moon (from Rusalka)
    (Goldman) mix cor LAWSON LG 52087
    $.75   (D293)

  Songs Of Nature *see Come Let Us
    Sing; Dawn In The Forest; Golden
    Cornfields; On The Green
    Hillside; Why Do Sweet Songs
                                      (D294)
  Why Do Sweet Songs
    mix cor CRANZ f.s. see from Songs
    Of Nature   (D295)

DWAINE THE REINDEER see Lawrence,
  Stephen L.

DYING ROSES see Pieper, Rene

DYLAN, ROBERT (BOB) (1941-   )
  Jour Ou Le Bateau Viendra, Le *see
    Aufray, H.

DYLAN THOMAS SETTINGS see Gerber,
  Steven R.

DYRENE I STALLEN see Hovland, Egil

E

E-RI-E IS ARISIN', THE see Klouse,
  Andrea

E TEMPO DI PARTIRE, L'
  (Estermann, J.) mix cor,acap PELIKAN
  PE 1193   (E1)

EARCH MAGICIAN see Fritschel, James
  Erwin

EARLY ONE MORNING
  (Willisegger, H.R.) mix cor,acap
  PELIKAN PE1180   (E2)

EARLY ONE MORNING see Hopkins, Anthony

EARLY ONE MORNING see Willcocks, David
  Valentine

EARLY PART SONGS, THE see Elgar, [Sir]
  Edward (William)

EARTH see Shaw, Marshall L.

EAST, MICHAEL (ca. 1580-ca. 1648)
  Nous Sommes Les Bergers Au Coeur
    Joyeux
    TTBB HUGUENIN EB 48   (E3)
    men cor HUGUENIN EB 49   (E4)

  What Doth My Dainty Darling?
    SATB NATIONAL NMP-190 $.85   (E5)

EASTER SONGS THAT TICKLE YOUR FUNNY
  BONE! see Roberts, Ruth

EASY MIX 'N' MATCH: INSTANT PART
  SINGING see Jenkins, David

EBEN, PETR (1929-   )
  By The Pool
    SATB UNITED MUS see from Desire Of
    Ancient Things   (E6)

  Desire Of Ancient Things *see By The
    Pool; On An Air By Rameau; Tune,
    A   (E7)

  In Honorem Caroli *cant
    [Czech/Lat] men cor,0.6.3.0.
    0.3.3.0. timp,perc,strings
    [12'0"] SUPRAPHON H 6615   (E8)

  Music For Children's Choir *see
    Zelena Se Snitka

  On An Air By Rameau
    SATB UNITED MUS see from Desire Of
    Ancient Things   (E9)

  Tune, A
    SATB UNITED MUS see from Desire Of
    Ancient Things   (E10)

  Zehn Poetische Duette *CC10U
    [Czech/Ger] SA,pno BAREN. AP 3140
                                      (E11)
  Zelena Se Snitka
    "Music For Children's Choir" jr cor
    SUPRAPHON   (E12)

EBENEZER SCROOGE see Gould, Raymond

EBENHOH, HORST (1930-   )
  Schuster Franz, Der *Op.23,No.2
    SATB DOBLINGER 690   (E13)

ECCARD
  Winter Cantabile (composed with
    Snyder)
    SSATB,acap CPP-BEL SV8825 $1.10
                                      (E14)
ECCARD, JOHANNES (1553-1611)
  Heitere Weltliche Chorsatze *CC4U,
    madrigal
    (Bocker, Christine) 4pt cor BAREN.
    6934   (E15)

ECCE, TU PULCHRA ES see Des Prez,
  Josquin

ECCO L'AURORA see Perez, David

ECCO MORMORAR L'ONDE see Monteverdi,
  Claudio

ECHO see Hurnik, Ilja

ECHO, DAS
  (Hilfrich) SATB, solo voices MULLER
  882   (E16)

ECHO, THE see Seroussi, Ruben

ECHOES see Pfautsch, Lloyd Alvin

ECHOING GREEN, THE see Mathias, William

ECLATANTE TROMPETTE, PUBLIEZ LA
    VICTOIRE see Rameau, Jean-Philippe

ECLIPSE see Parmentier, F. Gordon

ECO see Lassus, Roland de (Orlandus)

ECOUTEZ LA CHANSON BIEN DOUCE see
    Mozart, Wolfgang Amadeus

EDDLEMAN, DAVID (1936-   )
    I Saw Old Autumn
        3pt treb cor,acap FISCHER,C CM8126
                                        (E17)

    Leprechaun, The
        2pt cor,kbd (easy) FISCHER,C CM8212
        $.85   (E18)

    Listen To The Music °Xmas
        2pt wom cor/mix cor&opt desc,pno,
        fl,bongos FISCHER,C CM8041   (E19)

    Music, When Soft Voices Die
        SSA KJOS GC134 $.70   (E20)

    Round And Round The Dreydl Spins
        2pt cor KJOS GC173 $.90   (E21)

    Sea Moods
        SSA KJOS GC137 $.70   (E22)

    There Is A Lady
        3pt mix cor,pno,bongos FISCHER,C
        CM7999   (E23)

    Time And Again
        4pt mix cor,kbd FISCHER,C SG120
                                        (E24)

    Winter Is Here
        2pt treb cor/2pt mix cor,pno,
        sleigh bells FISCHER,C CM7998
                                        (E25)

EDEN see Remsier

EDLER, ROBERT (1912-   )
    Amon
        SATB,2.2.2.2. 4.2.3.1. perc,harp,
        strings SEESAW   (E26)

EDUCATION SENTIMENTALE see Kernoa, J.P.

EDUCATION SENTIMENTALE see Le
    Forestier, Maxime

EDWARDS
    Invocation To Sleep
        SATB WILLIS 10953 $.75   (E27)

    Lullaby Of The Shepherds, The °Xmas
        SATB oct DEAN HRD 267 $.95   (E28)

    See You In September (composed with
        Wayne)
        (Strommen) SSA SHAWNEE 0525 $.90
                                        (E29)

    Sweet Suffolk Owl
        SATB WILLIS 10952 $.60   (E30)

EENZAME SCHAATSER, DE see Spierdijk, J.

EEUWIG DANKBAAR ZIJN see Wyrtzen, Don,
    Yesterday, Today And Tomorrow

EGNER, HERMANN
    Lieder Uber Die Grenzen °medley
        jr cor,pno/acord SCHULZ,FR 1037
                                        (E31)

EH AYE AYE AYE
    see Tour, Prends Garde, La

EHRE GOTTES AUS DER NATUR, DIE see
    Beethoven, Ludwig van

EHRLICH, ABEL (1915-   )
    As Fast As Thou Shalt Wane °see
        Sonnet 11 By Shakespeare

    Expense Of Spirit, The °see Sonnet
        129 By Shakespeare

    Like As The Waves °see Sonnet 60 By
        Shakespeare

    Sonnet 11 By Shakespeare
        "As Fast As Thou Shalt Wane" [Eng]
        cor,acap [2'] ISR.MUS.INST. 6239
                                        (E32)

    Sonnet 60 By Shakespeare
        "Like As The Waves" [Eng] cor,acap
        [4'] ISR.MUS.INST. 6240   (E33)

    Sonnet 129 By Shakespeare
        "Expense Of Spirit, The" [Eng] cor,
        acap [1'30"] ISR.MUS.INST. 6241
                                        (E34)

EI, WIE GEHT'S IM HIMMEL ZU °Op.38
    (Gebhard, L.) men cor BOHM see from
    Was Scheren Mich Sorgen: Drei
    Heitere Volkslieder   (E35)

EI, WIE SCHEINT DER MOND SO HELL see
    Weber, Carl Maria von

EIDOLA see Borishansky, Elliot

EIELSEN, STEINAR
    Mori Som Song
        SSA NORSK   (E36)

    Nar Strie Stormar Mot Deg Jagar
        men cor NORSK NMO 10077   (E37)
        mix cor NORSK NMO 9986   (E38)

    Nye Songen, Den
        TTBB NORSK   (E39)

    Setja Meg Pa Sullarkrakk: Folk Song
        From Bjerkrheim
        men cor NORSK NMO 10072   (E40)

EIFER see Naegeli, Hans Georg

EIGHT ORISONS see Friedell

EIGHT RIDDLES FROM SYMPHOSIUS AND A
    CODETTA see Bialosky, Marshall H.

EIGHT SONGS FROM THE PLAY "JON ARASON"
    see Sigurbjornsson, Thorkell

EIGHT SONGS TO THE WORDS BY MARIA
    KONOPNICKA see Ryling, Franciszek,
    Osiem Piesni Do Slow Marii
    Konopnickiej

EIGHTEEN-NINETY MUSIC HALL REVIEW, THE
    see Roberts, Ruth

EIGHTY ENGLISH FOLKSONGS °CCU,folk
    song
    (Sharp; Karpeles) cor FABER 10048 1
    f.s.   (E41)

EIGHTY'S GOLD: A MEDLEY
    (Brymer, Mark) SATB LEONARD-US
        08637551 $1.95   (E42)
    (Brymer, Mark) SAB LEONARD-US
        08637552 $1.95   (E43)
    (Brymer, Mark) 2pt cor LEONARD-US
        08637553 $1.95, ipa, accomp tape
        available   (E44)

EILEEN AROON
    see Two Irish Songs

EILERS, JOYCE ELAINE
    see BACAK, JOYCE EILERS

EINSAMKEIT, DU STUMMER BRONNEN:
    CHORFANTASIE see Lemacher, Heinrich

EINSAMKEIT (SOLITUDE) see Ligeti,
    Gyorgy, Magany

EIRIKSDOTTIR, KAROLINA (1951-   )
    Two Little Pieces For Choir °CC2U
        mix cor ICELAND 037-12   (E45)

EISLER, HANNS (1898-1962)
    Lob Der Dialektik
        mix cor,MezBar soli,fl,clar,horn,
        trp,perc,banjo,pno,db BREITKOPF-L
                                        (E46)

    Wie Die Krahe
        mix cor,Mez solo,fl,clar,horn,trp,
        perc,pno,banjo,db BREITKOPF-L
                                        (E47)

EKELUNDIANA XII see Blomberg, Erik

EKELUNDIANA XIV see Blomberg, Erik

ELDORADO see Hagemann, Philip

ELEGIE see Koester, Werner

ELEGY see Gallagher, Jack

ELEGY see Hansen, Theodore Carl

ELEGY see Wilson, R.

ELEMENTER see Kruse, Bjorn Howard

ELEMENTS, THE see Shaw, Marshall L.

ELEPHANTS see Crawley, Clifford

ELEPHANTS, CLOWNS AND CIRCUS SOUNDS see
    Roberts, Ruth

ELEVEN BALLATE see Perugia, Niccolo da

ELEVEN PART-SONGS AND SECULAR CHORUSES
    see Tchaikovsky, Piotr Ilyich

ELFENLIED see Bossler, Kurt

ELFENLIED see Wolf, Hugo

ELGAR, [SIR] EDWARD (WILLIAM)
    (1857-1934)
    As Torrents In Summer
        SSA NOVELLO f.s.   (E48)
        SS NOVELLO f.s.   (E49)
        SSA,pno CORONET 392-41569 $.90
                                        (E50)
    Dream Of Gerontius, The
        mix cor NOVELLO 07 0102   (E51)

ELGAR, [SIR] EDWARD (WILLIAM) (cont'd.)
    Early Part Songs, The °CCU
        SATB NOVELLO   (E52)

    Klange Der Freude
        (Trapp, Willy) mix cor,pno,org/orch
        BRAUN-PER 1073   (E53)
        (Trapp, Willy) men cor,pno,org/orch
        BRAUN-PER 1072   (E54)

    Snow, The
        SSA NATIONAL CMS-128 $.95   (E55)

    Three Unaccompanied Part-Songs
        SATB NOVELLO   (E56)

ELIASSON, ANDERS (1947-   )
    Breathing Room: July
        mix cor,acap REIMERS   (E57)

ELIJAH, ROCK! see Johnson, H.

ELIS see Delnooz, Henri

ELLE S'EN VA DE MOI LA MIEUX AIMEE see
    Castro, Jean de

ELLE S'EN VA DE MOI LA MIEUX AIMEE see
    Le Blanc, Didier

ELLE VOYANT APPROCHER SON DEPART see
    Gervaise, Claude

ELLINGTON, EDWARD KENNEDY (DUKE)
    (1899-1974)
    Don't Get Around Much Anymore
        (Behnke, Martin) SATB CPP-BEL
        5096DC1X $1.25, accomp tape
        available   (E58)

    It Don't Mean A Thing (If It Ain't
        Got That Swing)
        (Huff) SAB CPP-BEL 6684IC3X $1.25,
        accomp tape available   (E59)
        (Huff) SATB CPP-BEL 6684IC1X $1.25,
        accomp tape available   (E60)
        (Huff) SSA CPP-BEL 6684IC2X $1.25,
        accomp tape available   (E61)

    Portrait Of Duke Ellington
        (Cacavas) SATB,opt gtr,opt db,opt
        drums CPP-BEL 64393 $2.50   (E62)

    Satin Doll
        (Chinn, Teena) SATB CPP-BEL
        0199SC1X $1.25, accomp tape
        available   (E63)
        (Chinn, Teena) SAB CPP-BEL 0199SC3X
        $1.25, accomp tape available
                                        (E64)

ELUARD, P.
    A Peine Defiguree
        (Grimbert, J.) 5pt mix cor HEUGEL
        HE 32466   (E65)

ELUSIVE QUEST, THE see Duson, Dede

EMERSON MOTETS see Zallman, Arlene
    (Proctor)

EMIG, LOIS IRENE (MYERS) (1925-   )
    Violets Are For Picking
        2pt treb cor (med) GENTRY JG2085
        $.90   (E66)

EMILY see Kitzke, Jerome P.

EMMERIK, IVO VAN (1961-   )
    Lecture
        SATB,2clar,horn,2db [21'] DONEMUS
                                        (E67)

EMMERT, FRANTISEK (1940-   )
    Blazing Torches Of The Sun, The
        °CC3U
        men cor CESKY HUD.   (E68)

    Bread Will Grow In Those Fields
        °CC3U
        jr cor CESKY HUD.   (E69)

    Dawn
        mix cor,ABar soli,orch [18'] CESKY
        HUD.   (E70)

    Moment And Eternity °CC3U
        men cor CESKY HUD.   (E71)

    Mother's Eyes °CC3U
        wom cor CESKY HUD.   (E72)

    Singing Landscape
        mix cor,solo voice,string quar
        [10'] CESKY HUD.   (E73)

    Space Bells: Fifth Symphony
        men cor,S solo,electronic tape,orch
        [23'] CESKY HUD.   (E74)

    Sunny Land
        mix cor,narrator&S solo,orch [52']
        CESKY HUD.   (E75)

    White Roads °CC3U
        men cor,A solo,org CESKY HUD.   (E76)

EN ALLANT A LA FOIRE see Lauber, Emile

EN ALS DE BOER EEN PAAR BLOKSKENS HEEFT
see Anonymous

EN AVILA see Anonymous

EN BATEAU see Ronfort, Jean-Christophe

EN LA SAISON JOLIE see Weber, Gustav

EN REVENANT DE LA FOIRE see Cornaz,
Emmanuel

EN REVENANT DU BOIS see Richafort,
Joannes

EN ROUTE see Zollner, Karl Friedrich

EN VAIN LA SEVERE RAISON
(Will, M.) SATB,acap HUGUENIN CH 975
(E77)

EN YVER DU FEU DU FEU see D'Orleans,
Ch.

ENDYMION see Horowitz

ENFANT DE BOHEME, L' see Cornaz,
Emmanuel

ENFANTILLAGES see Jolas

ENFANTS QUI PLEURENT, LES see Marnay

ENFANTS TRISTES, LES see Vanderlove,
Anne

ENGEL, YEHUDA (1924-   )
Life In The Seasonal Orbit
jr cor ISRAELI IMP 1701   (E78)

ENGELMANN, HANS ULRICH (1921-   )
Stele Fur Buchner °Op.52
SATB,ABar soli,1.1+English
horn.1.1. 4.4.3.1. 2perc,harp,
strings [30'] BREITKOPF-W   (E79)

ENGLISH ANYONE? see Grob, Anita Jean

ENGLISH ROMANTIC PARTSONGS °CC30U
(Hillier, Paul) SATB OXFORD
19 3436507 contains works by
Stanford, Elgar, Sullivan and
others   (E80)

ENGLISH STREET CRY
(Kicklighte) SSB&camb CAMBIATA
U978110 $.75   (E81)

ENGLUND, EINAR (1916-   )
Aforismeja Sekakuorolle Ja
Orkesterille
mix cor,acap FAZER F 06989-8 (E82)

ENTFLIEH MIT MIR see Mendelssohn-
Bartholdy, Felix

ENTFUHRUNG, DIE see Brahms, Johannes

ENTOURAGE INTIMES, L' see Leroux,
Philippe

ENTSAGEN see Bruckner, Anton

ENVERS DE PARIS, L' see Havard de la
Montagne,Joachim

EPHROS, GERSHON (1890-1978)
New Birth Of Freedom
[Heb/Eng] SATB,kbd TRANSCON. 981016
$2.00   (E83)

EPIGRAMS TO THE TEXTS BY JAN
KOCHANOWSKI see Fotek, Jan, Fraszki
Do Tekstow Jana Kochanowskiego

EPISCOPIUS, L.
All Fancies From Your Mind Deporting
°see Laet Varen Alle Fantasie

Bier, Een Bier, Een Bierenbroyken,
Een
"More Ale" SATTB ZENGERINK 1431
(E84)

Joy And Virtue Fill My Heart °see
Vruecht En Duecht Myn Hert
Verhuecht

Laet Varen Alle Fantasie
(Lagas, R.) "All Fancies From Your
Mind Deporting" SATB,acap (diff)
ZENGERINK G 523   (E85)

More Ale °see Bier, Een Bier, Een
Bierenbroyken, Een

More Ale, More Ale And Cake
(Lagas, R.) SATTB (med diff)
ZENGERINK G 526   (E86)

Vruecht En Duecht Myn Hert Verhuecht
(Lagas, R.) "Joy And Virtue Fill My
Heart" SATB,acap (diff) ZENGERINK
G 533   (E87)

EPITHALAME see Jolivet, Andre

EPITHALAMION see Vaughan Williams,
Ralph

EQUALIS ETERNO see Willaert, Adrian

ER IST'S see Reger, Max

ER RUISCHT DOOR 'S HEMELS ZALEN see
Schaik, Johan Ant. Stephanus Van

ERDMANN, GUNTHER
Gepfefferte Spruche °song cycle
sc BREITKOPF-L 7693   (E88)

Heissa, Kathreinerle
mix cor,acap sc BREITKOPF-L 7701
(E89)

ERDMANN-ABELE, VEIT (1944-   )
Ich Weiss Ein Maidlein Hubsch Und
Fein
TTBB MULLER 554   (E90)

Mit Lust Tat Ich Ausreiten
SATB MULLER 555   (E91)

Rheinweinlied
men cor BOHM   (E92)

Wir Alle Leben In Gestundeter Zeit
(Miller, Franz R.) men cor,2trp,
2trom BOHM   (E93)

EREMENKO, SERHIJ (1912-   )
Conquerors Of The Prairies
[Ukranian] mix cor,Bar solo,pno
DUMA $10.00   (E94)

ERFULLTE ZEIT see Seeger, Peter

ERICKSON, FRANK WILLIAM (1923-   )
America Stands Free
SATB,opt band CPP-BEL OCT 02520
$1.10   (E95)
SA,opt band CPP-BEL OCT 02519
$1.10, ipa   (E96)

Americana °medley
mix cor CPP-BEL BD 00769 f.s. (E97)

ERIE CANAL, THE °folk song,US
(De Cormier, Robert) eq voices,pno,
perc LAWSON LG 52073 $.70   (E98)
(Halferty) KJOS C8610 $.70   (E99)
(Moore) SATB CPP-BEL SV8812 $1.10,
accomp tape available   (E100)
(Rifflinger, Donald H.) SATB UNIVERSE
392-00652   (E101)

ERIKSON, AKE (1937-   )
Skapelse Utelamnad; En Ekologisk
Betraktelse
mix cor&jr cor,Mez solo,orch STIM
(E102)

ERINDRINGER see Lunde, Ivar

ERINNERUNG see Douw, Andre

ERLAUBE MIR see Brahms, Johannes

ERMITE, L' see Apotheloz, Jean

ERNTELIED: ES STEHT EIN GOLDNES
GARBENFELD see Strauss-Konig,
Richard

ERNTELIED: FLUR IST GEMAHT see
Deutschmann, Gerhard

ERSTES LIEDERWERK WANDERSCHAFT see
Siegl, Otto

ES BLIES EIN JAGER IN SEIN HORN see
Kanetscheider, Artur

ES BLIES EIN JAGER WOHL IN SEIN HORN
see Clemens, Adolf

ES DUNKELT SCHON IN DER HEIDE
mix cor BRAUN-PER 1078 see from Drei
Volkslieder   (E103)

ES FIEL EIN REIF see Burthel, Jakob

ES FIEL EIN REIF see Scherber, M.

ES FLOG EIN KLEIN'S WALDVOGELEIN
(Schneider, Walther) SATB MULLER 664
f.s. see from Zwei Altdeutsche
Liebeslieder   (E104)

ES FLOG EIN KLEIN'S WALDVOGELEIN see
Bauer

ES GEHT EIN' DUNKLE WOLK' HIEREIN see
Poos, Heinrich

ES GEHT EIN WEHEN DURCH DEN WALD see
Brahms, Johannes

ES GING SICH UNSRE FRAUE see Brahms,
Johannes

ES IST DIE SCHONSTE FRUJAHRSZEIT
cor HIEBER MH 5025   (E105)

ES IST FUR UNS EINE ZEIT ANGEKOMMEN
(Willisegger, H.R.) mix cor,acap
PELIKAN PE1189   (E106)

ES KRIBBELT UND WIBBELT WEITER see
Poos, Heinrich

ES LEBE DIE LIEBE see Stolz, Robert

ES SASS EIN SCHNEEWEIS VOGELEIN see
Brahms, Johannes

ES STEHT EIN LIND see Gebhard, Hans

ES STUNDEN DREI ROSEN see Brahms,
Johannes

ES TONT EIN VOLLER HARFENKLANG see
Brahms, Johannes

ES WANDELS SICH DIE REICHE see Zipp,
Friedrich

ES WAR EINMAL EIN KLEINER MANN see
Backer, Hans

ES WAR EINMAL EIN ZIMMERGESELL see
Brahms, Johannes

ES WAR EINMAL EINE MAUS see Schwaen,
Kurt

ES WAREN ZWEI KONIGSKINDER see
Schroeder, Hermann

ES WIRD IN HUNDERT JAHREN WIEDER SO EIN
FRUHLING SEIN see Dostal

ES WOLLT' EIN JAGERLEIN JAGEN see
Jochum, Otto

ES WOLLT EIN JAGERLEIN JAGEN see
Kelling, Hajo

ES WOLLT EIN JAGERLEIN JAGEN see
Kracke, Hans

ESCENA see Pablo, Luis de

ESKELIN
Jim, Jam, Jump °see Carey

ESPERANCE see Bezencon, G.

ESPRESSIONI MUSICALI see Even-Or, Mary

ESQUISSE PATRIOTIQUE see Beauverd

ESSEY, G.
Madame Automne (composed with
Passaquet, Raphael)
3pt jr cor HEUGEL HE 32372   (E107)

ESTES
Sing, Sing! (composed with Holder)
SAB SHAWNEE 0407 $.95   (E108)

ET POURTANT C'EST VRAI see Bleuse, Marc

ET YOU, YOU, YOU see Apotheloz, Jean

ETERNAL FLAME, THE °CCU
(Yablonev, E.) [Russ] cor,acap MEZ
KNIGA 176   (E109)

ETERNITE see Ninnin, Francois

ETIENNE, L.
Porc, Le °see Queneau, R.

ETOILE QUI SOURIT, UNE see Defossez,
Rene

ETUDES see Goeb, Roger

ETYDE see Brevik, Tor

EURYDICE see Biscardi, Chester

EVAS ERSTGEBURT see Stockhausen,
Karlheinz

EVAS ZAUBER see Stockhausen, Karlheinz

EVAS ZWEITGEBURT see Stockhausen,
Karlheinz

EVEIL see Veysseyre, Henri

EVEILLE-TOI see Dowland, John

EVEILLE-TOI RENAUD see Daniel, Etienne

EVEN-OR, MARY
Espressioni Musicali
[It] cor,acap [3'30"] ISR.MUS.INST.
6376   (E110)

Holy Curtain
jr cor ISRAELI IMP 1703   (E111)

EVEN-OR, MARY (cont'd.)

Sheshet Ha-Yamim Veshivat Hashe'arim
"Six Days And The Seven Gates, The"
[Heb] jr cor [5'] ISR.MUS.INST.
6698   (E112)

Six Days And The Seven Gates, The
*see Sheshet Ha-Yamim Veshivat
Hashe'arim

EVENING WATCH, THE see Hamilton, Iain

EVENINGTIME MEDLEY
(Ashton) SS&camb,SA soli CAMBIATA
U483173 $.75   (E113)

EVENSEN, BERNT KASBERG (1944-   )
Slow Song
[Eng] mix cor,acap NORGE   (E114)

EVERTSE, J.
Avondlied
SSA MOLENAAR 15024303   (E115)

Voermanslied
SSA MOLENAAR 15023703   (E116)

Winter Is Verganghen, Die
SSA MOLENAAR 15023603   (E117)

EVERY HEART WAS MADE FOR SONG see
Ydstie

EVERY HOUR THAT THIS DAY GIVES ME see
Nystedt, Knut

EVERYBODY DANCE see Johnson, Jesse

EVERYBODY LOVES MY BABY
(Shaw, Kirby) SATB LEONARD-US
08657281 $.95   (E118)
(Shaw, Kirby) SAB LEONARD-US 08657282
$.95   (E119)
(Shaw, Kirby) SSA LEONARD-US 08657283
$.95, ipa, accomp tape available
                                       (E120)

EVERYBODY LOVES SATURDAY NIGHT
(Scott, Michael) SAB CPP-BEL SV8815
f.s.   (E121)

EVETT, ROBERT (1922-1975)
Monadnock
SATB,2(pic).2(English horn).2(bass
clar).2. 0.0.0.0. perc,strings
[5'] AM.COMP.AL.   (E122)

EVIGE BAND, DE see Fongaard, Bjorn

EVOLENE see Miche, Paul

EV'RYDAY THINGS see Crawley, Clifford

EWIG ZURNT DIE GOTTHEIT NICHT see
Gluck, Christoph Willibald, Ritter
von

EWIGES WANDERN see Weiss-Steinberg,
Hans

EXPENSE OF SPIRIT, THE see Ehrlich,
Abel, Sonnet 129 By Shakespeare

EXTASE see Piantoni, Louis

EXTASE see Simoncini, Ernest D.

EYE IN THE SKY
(Riley; Wilson) SATB CPP-BEL 9005EC1X
$1.25   (E123)

EZOP see Hurnik, Ilja

F

FABELEN NAAR EEUWENOUDE VERDICHTSELS IN
VOLKSTRANT: EERSTE REEKS see Vocht,
Lodewijk de

FABELEN NAAR EEUWENOUDE VERDICHTSELS IN
VOLKSTRANT: TWEEDE REEKS see Vocht,
Lodewijk de

FABELEN NAAR EEUWENOUDE VERDICHTSELS IN
VOLKSTRANT: DERDE REEKS see Vocht,
Lodewijk de

FABELN DES ASOP, DIE see Poser, Hans

FABLE see Ballou, Philip

FABREZ, E.
Bolleras Sevillanas
SATB CAILLARD PC 211   (F1)

FACTEUR, LE see Hadjidakis, Manos

FAIN
Love Is A Many- Splendored Thing
*see Webster

FAIN, SAMMY (1902-1990)
Let A Smile Be Your Umbrella (On A
Rainy Day)
(Madsen) SATB CPP-BEL 1622LC1X
$1.25, accomp tape available (F2)
(Madsen) 2pt cor CPP-BEL 1622LC5X
$1.25, accomp tape available (F3)

FAIR LISA see Hoddinott, Alun

FAIR PHYLLIS see Farmer, John

FAIR PHYLLIS I SAW see Farmer, John

FAIREST ROSE IN ALL THE GARDEN see
Deale, Edgar, O Du Schoner
Rosengarten

FAIRY-TALE ABOUT A SICK PUSSY-CAT, A
see Wallek-Walewski, Boleslaw,
Bajeczka O Chorym Kotku

FALCONS OF ARCOS DE LA FRONTERA, THE
see Nuernberger, L. Dean

FALIK, YURI (1936-   )
Autumn Storm (from Four Songs Of
Autumn: No. 3)
SATB SCHIRM.G 232660 $.75   (F4)

Cranberries (from Four Songs Of
Autumn)
SATB SCHIRM.G 232650 $.70   (F5)

FALK, KARL-AXEL
Se, Nu Stiger Solen Ur Havets Famn
[Swed] SATB NORGE   (F6)

FALL
Und Der Himmel Hangt Voller Geigen
(Grieshaber) mix cor,pno LEUCKART
LSB 527   (F7)

FALL see Mathias, William

FALL, THE see Williams, Julius A.

FALL ON ME LIKE A SILENT DEW see
Coleridge-Taylor, Samuel

FALSE SIR JOHN see Burton

FAMILY AT CHRISTMAS, THE see Bacon,
Boyd

FAMILY (SOAR WITH EAGLES)
(Baker, Jonathan) SATB,opt gtr/pno
CPP-BEL 0156FC1X $1.25, accomp tape
available   (F8)
(Baker, Jonathan) SSA,opt gtr/pno
CPP-BEL 0156TC2X $1.25, accomp tape
available   (F9)
(Baker, Jonathan) SAB,opt gtr/pno
CPP-BEL 0156FC3X $1.25, accomp tape
available   (F10)

FAMOUS NEGRO SPIRITUALS
cor CPP-BEL TMF0027 $4.95 contains
Deep River, Nobody Knows The
Trouble and others   (F11)

FAMOUS VOYAGE OF CHRISTOPHER COLUMBUS,
THE see Kay, Heather

FANCHETTE, LA
1-4pt cor HUGUENIN see from Chansons
Pour La Jeunesse, Sixieme Cahier
                                   (F12)

FANCHON see Boller, Carlo

FANFARE FOR PEACE see Thomson, Virgil
Garnett

FANFARNETO see Caillat, Stephane

FANSHAWE, DAVID
Ring Out The Bells
SATB,2trp,3-4perc,org,elec bass,
harp,kbd [5'] OXFORD rent   (F13)

FANTAISIE POUR CHOEUR A BOUCHE FERMEE
see Alain, Jehan

FANTASIE C-MOLL see Beethoven, Ludwig
van

FANTOCHES see Ronfort, Jean-Christophe

FARANDOLE see Kef, Kees

FARARSNID see Sigurbjornsson, Thorkell

FAREWELL, DEAR LOVE see Jones, Robert
[1]

FAREWELL GIFT, A see Takemitsu, Toru

FAREWELL MY SUMMER LOVE
(Strommen) TTB CPP-BEL 0108FC4X $1.25
                                   (F14)

FAREWELL TO THE FOREST see Mendelssohn-
Bartholdy, Felix

FARFALLA, LA see Campra, Andre

FARKAS, FERENC (1905-   )
Deutsche Lieder *CCU
mix cor sc BREITKOPF-L 7666   (F15)

FARMER, JOHN (fl. 1591-1601)
Fair Phyllis
SATB HARMONIA 3644   (F16)

Fair Phyllis I Saw
(Fellowes, Edmund) ATTB STAINER
3.3208 $.95   (F17)

FARMER IS THE MAN, THE *folk song,US
(De Cormier, Robert) mix cor LAWSON
LG 51918 $.70   (F18)

FARONIKA SYMPHONY see Bravnicar, Matija

FARROW, LARRY
Jamaican Market Place
SATB (med) GENTRY JG2092 $.95 (F19)

FAST
Music Sweet Music
SAB CPP-BEL SV8508 $.95   (F20)
2pt cor CPP-BEL SV8509 $.95   (F21)

FAT MAN'S COMING, THE see Feldstein,
Saul (Sandy)

FATA MORGANA see Hurum, Helge

FATHER, FATHER
see Songs Of Papua New Guinea

FATHER WILLIAM see Berkowitz, Sol

FAURE
Source, La *see Djian, H.

FAURE, GABRIEL-URBAIN (1845-1924)
Clair De Lune
(Noyon, Joseph) SSA,pno A COEUR
JOIE 9006   (F22)

FAUTE D'ARGENT, C'EST DOULEUR NON
PAREILLE see Anonymous

FAVEZ, DANIEL
Chasseral
SATB,acap HUGUENIN CH 1183   (F23)

FEAST OF LANTERNS see Jennings

FEAST OF LIGHTS see Sargon, Simon A.

FEEL THE POWER see Rothenberg, Irv

FEELS LIKE CHRISTMAS see Lightfoot,
Mary Lynn

FEESTCANTATE SINT-CECILIA see Bots, J.

FEESTZANG BIJ DE GEBOORTE VAN EEN
KONINGSKINDJE see Pelt, R.A. van

FEESTZANG: HIJ LEVE LANG see Algra,
Joh.

FEIN SEIN, BEINANDER BLEIBEN see
Strecke, Gerhard

FEINBERG, SAMMY
see FAIN, SAMMY

FELDSTEIN, SAUL (SANDY) (1940-   )
Fat Man's Coming, The
SATB ALFRED 7670 $.95, accomp tape
available   (F24)
1-2pt cor ALFRED 7672 $.95, accomp
tape available   (F25)
SAB ALFRED 7671 $.95, accomp tape
available   (F26)

FELDSTEIN, SAUL (SANDY) (cont'd.)

Festival Of Lights
cor ALFRED   (F27)

Music Fact Rap, The
ALFRED   (F28)

Sing A New Song
ALFRED   (F29)

We, The Children Of America
unis cor,opt band,opt strings oct
ALFRED 7434 $.95, pts ALFRED 3198
$40.00   (F30)

FELICE PASTORELLA see Jeffreys, G.

FELLER
Snow, Snow, Beautiful Snow (composed
with Sigman)
(Shaw) SATB SHAWNEE 1880 $1.25
(F31)
(Shaw) SSA SHAWNEE 0542 $1.25 (F32)
(Shaw) SAB SHAWNEE 0409 $1.25 (F33)

FENNELLY, BRIAN (1937-   )
Love's Philosophy
SATB [4'] AM.COMP.AL. $4.60   (F34)

Music, When Soft Voices Die
SATB [4'] (Shelley) AM.COMP.AL.
$4.60   (F35)

Winterkill...
SATB,pno [7'] AM.COMP.AL. $5.40
(F36)

FERRAT, JEAN
Heureux Celui Qui Meurt D'aimer
(Ott, Norbert) SATB A COEUR JOIE
044   (F37)

Hourrah
(Lavoisy-Drouot, Ch.) 4pt mix cor
HEUGEL HE 32195   (F38)

Montagne, La
(Lenoble, J.) 4pt mix cor HEUGEL
(F39)

Nous Dormirons Ensemble °see Aragon,
L.

Nuit Et Brouillard
(Grindel, J.) 4-7pt mix cor HEUGEL
HE 32254   (F40)

FERRE, LEO
Merde A Vauban
(Leleu, F.) 3-4pt mix cor HEUGEL
HE 32062   (F41)

FEST-CANTATE see Bruckner, Anton

FEST UND GEDENKSPRUCHE see Brahms,
Johannes

FESTA, COSTANZO (ca. 1480-1545)
Altro Non E'l Mio Amor
(Agnel, A.) 3pt mix cor HEUGEL
HE 32402   (F42)

Madonna, Io V'amo E Taccio °madrigal
3 eq voices HEUGEL HE 32597   (F43)

FESTAS DE FOLIADAS °CCU
4pt mix cor,tamb ALPUERTO 1610 (F44)

FESTAS DE MUINEIRAS °CCU
4pt mix cor,tamb ALPUERTO 1609 (F45)

FESTAS DE PANDEIRADAS °CCU
4pt mix cor,tamb ALPUERTO 1608 (F46)

FESTES VENITIENNES, LES see Campra,
Andre

FESTGANG AN DIE KUNSTLER see
Mendelssohn-Bartholdy, Felix

FESTGESANG (JODOK-KANTATE) see
Bruckner, Anton

FESTIN DU JEUDI GRAS see Banchieri,
Adriano

FESTIVAL LEOPOLD ROBERT see Pantillon,
G.L.

FESTIVAL OF LIGHTS see Feldstein, Saul
(Sandy)

FESTIVAL SANCTUS see Leavitt, John

FESTIVE MADRIGAL see Perry

FESTIVE SONGS see Chudova, T.

FETE, LA see Ducarroz, M.

FETE DES OURS, LA
see Banuwa

FETE DES OURS, LA see Sonthonay, F.

FETE DES TRAVAILLEURS, LA see Huguenin,
Charles

FETES GALANTES see Ronfort, Jean-
Christophe

FETLER
All Day I Hear
4pt mix cor LAWSON 682   (F47)

April
4pt mix cor LAWSON 779   (F48)

FEUERREITER, DER see Wolf, Hugo

FEUERSPRUCH UBER DIE TOTEN GENOSSEN see
Meyer, Ernst Hermann

FEVIN, ANTOINE DE (ca. 1474-1512)
Chanson Du Petit Chien
see Fevin, Antoine de, J'ai Vu La
Beaute M'amie

J'ai Vu La Beaute M'amie
(Dottin, G.) 3 eq voices HEUGEL
HE 31838 contains also: Chanson
Du Petit Chien   (F49)

On A Mal Dit De Mon Ami
(Agnel, A.) 3 eq voices HEUGEL
HE 32236   (F50)

FIALAIRA, LA see Blanchard

FIANCEE DU TIMBALIER, LA see Bigot, P.

FIBICH, ZDENEK (ZDENKO) (1850-1900)
Jarni Romance, Op. 23
mix cor, solo voices,2.2.2.2.
4.2.4.0. timp,perc,strings
[12'0"] SUPRAPHON H 2062   (F51)

FICOCELLI, MICHAEL V.
Showing Us The Way
SATB,pno SOMERSET SP-801 $.80 (F52)
2pt cor SOMERSET SP-802 $.80 (F53)

FIFTEEN RUSSIAN FOLK SONGS, OP. 19 see
Rimsky-Korsakov, Nikolai

FIFTEEN RUSSIAN FOLK SONGS, OP. 19 see
Rimsky-Korsakov, Nikolai

FIFTEEN SISTERS °CCU
[Russ] jr cor MEZ KNIGA 504   (F54)

FILAS, JURAJ (1955-   )
Canzone Dell'amore, La
mix cor,SBar soli,org,orch [22']
CESKY HUD. 8110 0535   (F55)

Lauretti: Altre Canzone Amorose
cor,2vln,vcl,pno [12'] CESKY HUD.
(F56)

Old Oak's Last Dream
jr cor,orch [12'] CESKY HUD.   (F57)

Spring Song
mix cor,pno [11'] CESKY HUD.   (F58)

FILHARMONICO see Meneely-Kyder, Sarah

FILLE DU VIGNERON, LA see Weckerlin,
Jean-Baptiste-Theodore

FILLE MORTE DANS SES AMOURS, LA see
Apotheloz, Jean

FILLED WINE CUP see O'Leary, Jane

FILLES DE LA ROCHELLE, LES see
Blanchard

FILLES DE LORIENT, LES
(Turellier, J.) 4pt mix cor HEUGEL
HE 32412   (F59)

FILLES DE LORIENT, LES see Turellier,
Jean

FILLES DE TOULON, LES see Caillat,
Stephane

FILLES DU HAMEAU
(Huguenin, Charles) 1-4pt cor
HUGUENIN see from Chansons Pour La
Jeunesse, Troisieme Cahier   (F60)

FILLETTE, UNE
(Koller, Martin) mix cor BREITKOPF-W
CHB 5181 see from Vier Franzosische
Liebeslieder   (F61)

FILLETTES DE CHAMPAGNE see Blanchard

FILS DU CAPITAINE ACHAB, LE see Yvart,
J.

FINAL CHORUS see Smith, Gregg

FINCKEL
Snowfall
SSA BOURNE B240226 $.65   (F62)

FIND A WAY see Lojeski

FIND THE MISSING CHILDREN see Harwood,
Chris

FINDIN' A WAY TO YOU see Madsen

FINDING MY WAY see Schwartz

FINE KNACKS FOR LADIES see Dowland,
John

FINGERS OF THE LIGHT, THE see Van Wijk,
Jan

FINI LE BIEN see Gardane, Antonio

FINK
Keepin' Good Company
(Duncan) 2pt cor SHAWNEE 0069 $.85
(F63)

FINKENLIED, DAS see Rosenstengel,
Albrecht

FINNEGAN'S FLORAS see Buller, John

FINNEGIN'S FUGUE see Silverberg,
Frederick Irwin

FINNISSY, MICHAEL (1946-   )
Australian Sea Shanties
SAB UNITED MUS   (F64)

Ngano
SATB,MezT soli,2perc UNITED MUS
(F65)

FINNS EN GLADJE, DET see Grandert,
Johnny

FIRE see Shaw, Marshall L.

FIRE SLATTER FOR KOR °see Brurelat Fra
Vaga; Mazurka Fra Lom; Springdans
Fra Bergen I; Springdans Fra Bergen
II   (F66)

FIRE UP see Pollack, Lisa Lauren

FIRENZE, GHIRARDELLO DA
Tosto Che L'alba
(Turellier, Jean) 2 eq voices,trom/
vcl HEUGEL HE 32356   (F67)

FIRST BOOK OF SONGS OF AIRS OF FOUR
PARTS: VOL. 1, NO 1-7 see
Pilkington, Francis

FIRST BOOK OF SONGS OF AIRS OF FOUR
PARTS: VOL. 2, NO 8-14 see
Pilkington, Francis

FIRST BOOKE OF CANZONETS TO TWO VOYCES
see Morley, Thomas

FIRST CHRISTMAS see Ray, Jerry

FIRST DAY OF CHOIR, THE see Quesnel,
Steven R.

FIRST ENCOUNTER see Johansson, Bengt

FIRST SPRING DAY, THE see Smith, Robert
Edward

FIRST THANKSGIVING, THE see Roberts,
Ruth

FISCHBACH, KLAUS (1935-   )
An Die Musik
SATB MULLER 574   (F68)

FISHER
It's Time To Ring Those Christmas
Bells! °see Price

Magic To Do °see Schwartz

When You're Smiling (composed with
Goodwin; Shay)
(Althouse) SAB SHAWNEE 0357 $1.00
(F69)
(Althouse) 2pt cor SHAWNEE 0078
$1.00   (F70)
(Althouse) SATB SHAWNEE 1809 $1.00
(F71)

FISHER, IRWIN
Statement: 1976
SATB,S solo,4horn,3trp,3trom,1tuba,
3timp,perc,strings [15']
AM.COMP.AL. $21.35   (F72)

FITCH
Trains
S&camb,SA soli CAMBIATA T 978117
$.65   (F73)

Words
SAB&camb CAMBIATA C17799 $.75 (F74)

FITZMARTIN
Ride The Wave
SSATB CPP-BEL SV8429 $2.25   (F75)

Take The Time
3pt cor CPP-BEL SV8627 $.95, accomp
tape available   (F76)

FIVE AMERICAN ECHOES see Wallach, Joelle

FIVE ANGLO-NORMAN MOTETS *CC5U,13th cent
(Everist, Mark) ANTICO AE24   (F77)

FIVE CANADIAN FOLK SONGS FOR YOUTH CHOIR see Han, Isaac

FIVE FOLK SONGS see Willcocks, David Valentine

FIVE LIMERICKS see Palsson, Pall P.

FIVE OFF THE WALL see Fritschel, James Erwin

FIVE SHAKESPEARE LYRICS see Lane, Philip

FIVE SHAKESPEARE SONGS FOR VOICES AND PERCUSSION see Gill, R.

FIVE SONGS IN 5 MINUTES see Warren, B.

FIVE SUMMER MADRIGALS see Walker, Robert

FIVE SYSTEMS see Meneely-Kyder, Sarah

FIVE WALTZES see Brahms, Johannes

FJELLTRALLEN OG TO ANDRE SANGER see Storbekken, Egil

FLAHERTY, THOMAS (1950-   )
Break, Break, Break
SSA,pno [4'] AM.COMP.AL. $6.90
(F78)

FLAMME VON MANSFELD, DIE see Geissler, Fritz

FLEA AND A FLY, A see Goemanne

FLECHA, MATEO (1530-1604)
Primo Libro De Madrigali, Il *CCU
ALPUERTO   (F79)

FLEDERMAUS-WALZER see Strauss, Johann, [Jr.]

FLEE, FLORET, FLORENS see Ceely, Robert Paige

FLEISCHER, TZIPPI
Clock Wants To Sleep, The
jr cor ISRAELI IMP 34-1   (F80)

Girl Dreamed, A *see Halma Na'ara

Halma Na'ara (from Girl, Butterfly, Girl)
"Girl Dreamed, A" [Heb/Eng] unis
cor [3'] ISR.MUS.INST. 6228M
(F81)

FLETCHER, PERCY EASTMAN (1879-1932)
Ring Out, Wild Bells
SSA,pno NOVELLO 29 0618   (F82)

FLEURS DE LA PIERRE see Grimbert, Jacques

FLIES, J. BERNHARD (1770- ?)
Wiegenlied
(Gotter, F.W.) SATB MOLENAAR
15010202   (F83)

FLIGHT see Liddell, Claire

FLOH, DER see Widmann, Erasmus

FLOHE WIMMELN MEINEM WEIBE
(Hollfelder, Waldram) men cor BOHM
see from Vier Heitere Europaische
Volkslieder   (F84)

FLOR DE CHANER *folk song
(Leleu, Francoise) 3 eq voices,gtr,
perc HEUGEL HE 32601   (F85)

FLOR DE LA MIEL, LA see Grau, Alberto

FLORA GAVE ME FAIREST FLOWERS see Wilbye, John

FLORILEGE TROIS VOIX MIXTES *CC70U
3pt mix cor A COEUR JOIE   (F86)

FLOS FLORUM see Dufay, Guillaume

FLOTHUIS, MARIUS (1914-   )
Laatste Brief, De
mix cor [3'] DONEMUS   (F87)

FLOW GENTLY SWEET AFTON
(Leavitt, John) SATB CPP-BEL SV8841
$1.10   (F88)

FLOW NOT SO FAST, YE FOUNTAINS see Dowland, John

FLOW, O MY TEARS see Latham, William Peters

FLOWER, A see Oliver, Harold

FLOWERS O' THE FOREST, THE see Roberton, Hugh Stevenson

FLUIST'REND VERLANGEN see Winner, Septimus ("Alice Hawthorne"), Whispering Hope

FLY OFF WITH ME see Mendelssohn-Bartholdy, Felix

FLYAWAY HILL see Gwynne, Una

FLYING DREAMS (FROM SECRET OF NIMH) see Goldsmith, Jerry

FODT PA NY - I "GREVENS TID" see Kvam, Oddvar S.

FOGERTY, J.C.
Proud Mary
(Billingsley, Alan) SATB CPP-BEL
5758PC1X $1.40, accomp tape
available   (F89)
(Billingsley, Alan) SSA CPP-BEL
5758PC2X $1.40   (F90)
(Billingsley, Alan) 3pt mix cor
CPP-BEL 5758PC3X $1.40   (F91)

FOLK BOUQUETS see Lidl, Vaclav

FOLK MUSIC OF THE WORLD *CCU
cor CAMBIATA $13.95   (F92)

FOLK SONG TRILOGY
(Ray) cor ALFRED   (F93)

FOLK SONGS ARRANGED BY ALEXANDER SVESHNIKOV *CCU
(Kalinin, S.) [Russ] cor,acap MEZ
KNIGA 178   (F94)

FOLK-SONGS FOR CHOIRS 1 *CC12L
(Rutter, John) mix cor,acap OXFORD
343718-X f.s. contains works by
Byrt, James, Rutter and others
(F95)

FOLK-SONGS FOR CHOIRS 2 *CC13L
(Rutter, John) mix cor,acap OXFORD
343719-8 f.s. contains works by
Willcocks, Grainger, Holst and
others   (F96)

FOLKEVISE see Soderlind, Ragnar

FOLKSONG TRANSFORMATIONS *CC39U
(Parker, Alice) unis cor GALAXY
1.3052 $4.50   (F97)

FOLKSONGS FROM MANY LANDS see Weigl, Karl

FOLKVISA: SA ODSLIGT MOLNEN PA FASTET GA see Lilja, Bernhard

FOLLOW see Wilson, Mark

FOLLOW THE CAT see Braun, Yeheskiel, Be'ikvot Hehatul

FOMBONNE, JACQUES
Doux Chagrin, Le
4pt mix cor,opt rec,opt gtr HEUGEL
HE 32154   (F98)

FOMENKO, MYKOLA (1895-1961)
Willow, The
[Ukranian] wom cor,S solo,pno DUMA
$3.50   (F99)

FOND AFFECTION see Crocker

FONGAARD, BJORN (1919-1981)
Aphorism 1: Concerning The
Interpretation Of Nature And The
Kingdom Of Man *Op.31,No.1
[Eng] men cor,acap [2'] NORGE
(F100)

Aphorism 23: Concerning The
Interpretation Of Nature And The
Kingdom Of Man *Op.31,No.4
[Eng] men cor,acap [2'] NORGE
(F101)

Evige Band, De
[Norw] men cor,acap NORGE   (F102)

Now And Here
[Eng] men cor,acap NORGE   (F103)

Sne
[Norw] men cor,acap NORGE   (F104)

FONTENAY AUX ROSES see Le Forestier, Maxime

FOOD see Crawley, Clifford

FOOTLOOSE
(Madsen) SATB CPP-BEL SV8459 $1.25
(F105)
(Madsen) SAB CPP-BEL SV8464 $1.25
(F106)

FOOTLOOSE (BEST OF) MEDLEY
(Strommen) SATB CPP-BEL C0092C1X
$2.25   (F107)

(Strommen) SSA CPP-BEL C0092C2X $2.25
(F108)
(Strommen) SAB CPP-BEL C0092C3X $2.25
(F109)

FOR A THOUSAND BLOSSOMS see Lidl, Vaclav

FOR JEFFERSON AND LIBERTY
(Goldman) mix cor LAWSON LG 51863
$.70   (F110)

FOR JUST A MOMENT (LOVE THEME FROM ST. ELMO'S FIRE)
(Chinn) SATB CPP-BEL 5231LC1X $1.25,
accomp tape available   (F111)
(Chinn) SAB CPP-BEL 5231LC3X $1.25,
accomp tape available   (F112)

FOR ME AND MY GAL (A MEDLEY OF HITS FROM THE TWENTIES)
(Madsen) SATB CPP-BEL C0105C1X $2.25,
accomp tape available   (F113)
(Madsen) SAB CPP-BEL C0105C3X $2.25,
accomp tape available   (F114)

FOR MORE THAN ONE see Rudi, Joran

FOR SPACIOUS SKIES see Zaninelli

FOR THE FREEDOM OF MAN see North

FOR WHOM SHALL I WEEP? see Stanley, John

FORBES, SEBASTIAN (1941-   )
Approaching Winter
SATB,acap STAINER W140 see from
Seasonal Roundelay   (F115)

Autumn
SATB,acap STAINER W140 see from
Seasonal Roundelay   (F116)

Seasonal Roundelay *see Approaching
Winter; Autumn; Summer Night;
Thaw; Time Of Roses, The   (F117)

Summer Night
SATB,acap STAINER W140 see from
Seasonal Roundelay   (F118)

Thaw
SATB,acap STAINER W140 see from
Seasonal Roundelay   (F119)

Time Of Roses, The
SATB,acap STAINER W140 see from
Seasonal Roundelay   (F120)

FORD, RONALD (1959-   )
Foy Porter (from Virelay Of Machaut)
cor,S solo [10'] DONEMUS   (F121)

FORELLE, DIE see Schubert, Franz (Peter)

FORESTERS, SOUND THE CHEERFUL HORN see Shearer, C.M.

FOREVER
(Huff) SATB CPP-BEL 4821FC1X $1.25
(F122)
(Huff) SSA CPP-BEL 4821FC2X $1.25
(F123)
(Huff) SAB CPP-BEL 4821FC3X $1.25
(F124)

FOREVER EVERLY
(Besig) SATB SHAWNEE 1783 $1.50
(F125)

FORGE, LA see Lachner, Franz

FORGERONS, LES see Aeschbacher, Walther

FORHANDLINGER I ET MAGERT LAND see Sonstevold, Gunnar

FORK, GUNTER (1930-   )
Weinschroterlied
mix cor,T solo MULLER 412   (F126)

FORMULA, THE see De Cormier, Robert

FORSELV, RANDI
Vinterland
2 eq voices MUSIKK MH 2504   (F127)

FORSTA MAJ see Bergman, Erik

FORSTE SNE, DEN see Aas, Esle Berntsen

FORSTER, PETER
Da Drunten In Jenem Tale
mix cor BOHM   (F128)

Kein Feuer, Keine Kohle
mix cor,acap BOHM   (F129)

FORTUNA see Termos, Paul

FORTUNE HELAS see Certon, Pierre

FORWARD, TOWARDS THE DAWN! *CCU
[Russ] jr cor,pno MEZ KNIGA 493
(F130)

FOSTER
  Foster Mania
    (Ashton) SSB&camb CAMBIATA U485184
    f.s.   (F131)

  Nelly Bly
    (Cooper) SSB&camb CAMBIATA U117571
    $.65   (F132)

FOSTER, STEPHEN COLLINS (1826-1864)
  Alter Joe
    (Cadow, P.) mix cor ZIMMER. 631
                                      (F133)

  Beautiful Dreamer
    (Harris, Ron) SSAATTBB,acap WOODL
    A050207 $.85   (F134)
    (Kubik) SATB SCHIRM.G 390160 $.70
                                      (F135)

  Camptown Races
    (Halloran, Jack) SSAATTBB (med
    diff) GENTRY JG2095 $.95   (F136)

  Camptown Races, The
    (Depue) TTBB CPP-BEL SV8518 $1.25
                                      (F137)

  Fosterama *Suite
    (De Cormier, Robert) SATB,acap
    (includes Ring The Banjo, Gentle
    Annie, Some Folks, Camptown
    Races) LAWSON 52442   (F138)

  Jeanie With The Light Brown Hair
    (Harris, Ron) SATB,acap WOODL
    A050208 $.85   (F139)
    (Mattson) SATB KJOS C8525 $.60
                                      (F140)

  Oh Susanna
    (Heywood) SATB CPP-BEL SV8537 $.95
                                      (F141)

  Some Folks
    (Krone) 1-2pt cor KJOS 6188 $.70
                                      (F142)

  Stephen Foster- Immortal Melodies
    *CCUL
    4pt cor CPP-BEL TPF0076   (F143)

  Swanee River
    (Cadow, P.) mix cor ZIMMER. 630
                                      (F144)

FOSTER MANIA see Foster

FOSTERAMA see Foster, Stephen Collins

FOT MOT JORD see Sipila, Eero

FOTEK, JAN (1928-   )
  Epigrams To The Texts By Jan
    Kochanowski *see Fraszki Do
    Tekstow Jana Kochanowskiego

  Fraszki Do Tekstow Jana
    Kochanowskiego
    "Epigrams To The Texts By Jan
    Kochanowski" [Polish] mix cor,
    acap POLSKIE   (F145)

FOUGSTEDT, NILS-ERIC (1910-1961)
  Tersen
    (Grasbeck, Gottfrid) wom cor&men
    cor&mix cor AKADEM   (F146)

FOUR AZTEC DANCES see Kelly, Robert T.

FOUR CHILDREN'S CHORUSES see Zamecnik,
  Evzen

FOUR CORONATION ANTHEMS (ZADOK THE
  PRIEST AND OTHERS) see Handel,
  George Frideric

FOUR ELIZABETHAN SONGS see Mollicone,
  Henry

FOUR FOLK SONGS FROM CHINA *CC4U
  (Roff, Joseph) 2pt cor,pno,fl,opt
  perc (med) THOMAS 1C107906 $.80
                                      (F147)
FOUR FOLKTUNES FROM SOUTHERN NORWAY see
  Slogedal, Bjarne

FOUR INDONESIAN FOLKSONGS *CCU
  (Nieland, H.) mix cor BROEKMANS
  BP 1088   (F148)

FOUR INNOCENT AIRS see Bacon, Ernst L.

FOUR LOVE SONGS see Austin, John

FOUR LULLABYES see Meneely-Kyder, Sarah

FOUR MADRIGALS (BLAKE) see Austin, John

FOUR ODES see Rinehart, John

FOUR PART SONGS see Holst, Gustav

FOUR PIECES see Schoenberg, Arnold

FOUR ROUNDS see Haufrecht, Herbert

FOUR SONGS see Pleskow, Raoul

FOUR SONGS see Stewart, Robert

FOUR SONGS FOR THREE VOICES see Brahms,
  Johannes

FOUR SONGS FROM EASTER ISLAND *CC4U
  (Roff, Joseph) 2pt cor,pno,opt fl,opt
  perc (med) THOMAS 1C108409 $1.20
                                      (F149)
FOUR SONGS FROM INDONESIA *CC4U
  (Roff, Joseph) 2pt cor,pno,opt fl,opt
  perc (med) THOMAS 1C108410 $.90
                                      (F150)
FOUR SONGS FROM TWELFTH NIGHT see
  Hagemann, Philip

FOUR SONGS TO VERSE BY VITEZSLAV NEZVAL
  see Kopelent, Marek

FOUR SONNETS OF FENG ZHI see MacBride,
  David Huston

FOUR SPIRITUALS see Wheeler, Janet

FOUR STATEMENTS see Ogdon, Wilbur L.

FOUR THREE-PART CHORUSES FOR MALE
  VOICES, OP. 23 see Rimsky-Korsakov,
  Nikolai

FOUR TRADITIONAL SONGS see Asgeirsson,
  Jon

FOUR VOCALISES OP. 100 see Bergman,
  Erik

FOUR WELSH SONGS see Hoddinott, Alun

FOURTEEN ICELANDIC FOLK SONGS *CC14U
  (Asgeirsson, Jon) mix cor ICELAND
  010-15   (F151)

FOY PORTER see Ford, Ronald

FRA NORSK LANDSKAP see Sommerfeldt,
  Oistein

FRADKIN, LESLIE MARTIN (1951-   )
  Neem Mijn Hand
    (Verheijen, J.) "Song Of A Thousand
    Voices" SATB MOLENAAR 13000803
                                      (F152)
  Song Of A Thousand Voices *see Neem
    Mijn Hand

FRAGA see Blomberg, Erik

FRAGMENT UIT HET LIED DER ACHTTIEN
  DODEN: EEN CEL IS MAAR TWEE METER
  LANG see Vranken, Joseph

FRAGMENTE see Rosell, Lars-Erik

FRAGMENTS OF A LOST SONG see Cowles,
  Darleen

FRANCAIX, JEAN (1912-   )
  Coq Et Le Renard, Le
    TTBB,pno TRANSAT. TR000893-1 (F153)

  Grenouille Qui Veut Se Faire Aussi
    Grosse Que Le Boeuf, La
    TTBB,pno TRANSAT. TR000892-1 (F154)

FRANCION VINT L'AUTRE JOUR see Bonnet,
  Pierre

FRANCIS, CLEVE
  Martin
    SATB CPP-BEL 0385MC1X $1.25, accomp
    tape available   (F155)
    SSA CPP-BEL 0385MC2X $1.25, accomp
    tape available   (F156)
    SAB CPP-BEL 0385MC3X $1.25, accomp
    tape available   (F157)

FRANCK
  Do Not Be Amazed
    (Frischman) SATB CPP-BEL 4951DC1X
    $.95   (F158)

FRANCK, CESAR (1822-1890)
  Premier Sourire De Mai
    3pt cor,pno HUGUENIN EB 298   (F159)

  Psyche
    [Fr] SAT,orch KALMUS K 06707 $3.50
                                      (F160)
FRANCO, CESARE
  see FRANCK, CESAR

FRANCO, JOHAN (1908-   )
  Autumn And The Raindrop's Adventure
    jr cor,pno [2'] AM.COMP.AL. $1.60
                                      (F161)
  Passacaglia
    SATB,electronic tape [5']
    AM.COMP.AL. $3.85   (F162)

  Stars Look Down, The
    SATBB,boy solo,2.2.2.2. 3.3.2.0.
    timp,harp,strings [60']
    AM.COMP.AL.   (F163)

  Water-Go-Round, The *round
    3pt cor,pno [2'] AM.COMP.AL. $.80
                                      (F164)

FRANK, MARCEL [GUSTAVE] (1909-   )
  As Soon As The Moon Lifts Out Of The
    Sea
    4pt men cor,pno BOSTON 14011 $.60
                                      (F165)
FRANKE-BLOM, LARS-AKE (1941-   )
  Sjung Frid
    men cor STIM   (F166)

FRANKEN, WIM (1922-   )
  Deluge, Le
    SATB,acap [10'] DONEMUS   (F167)

  In Weer En Wind
    jr cor,opt pno [7'30"] DONEMUS
                                      (F168)

  Vloed In Klank, De *ora
    8pt mix cor&4pt men cor,SATB&3
    speaking voices,6rec,2.2.2.2.
    4.3.3.0. perc,harp,3org,strings,
    electronic tape [150'] DONEMUS
                                      (F169)
FRANKIE AND JOHNNY
  (De Cormier, Robert) mix cor LAWSON
  LG 52040 $.85   (F170)

FRANKLIN
  I Knew You Were Waiting
    (Ray) cor ALFRED   (F171)

FRANKS WILLIAMS, JOAN (1930-   )
  Gulliver In Lilliput
    jr cor,acap ISR.MUS.INST. 6736
                                      (F172)
FRANSISKA
  (Asgeirsson, Jon) cor ICELAND 010-20
                                      (F173)
FRANSSENS, JOEP (1955-   )
  Phasing
    SATB,3.2.3.2. 2.2.2.1. strings
    [21'] DONEMUS   (F174)

FRASZKI DO TEKSTOW JANA KOCHANOWSKIEGO
  see Fotek, Jan

FRAUEN VON RAVENNA, DIE see Watkinson,
  Percy Gerd

FRAZEE, J.
  Baker's Dozen, A (composed with
    Steen)
    cor,rec,Orff inst CPP-BEL
    SCHBK 09058 $6.25   (F175)

  Singing In The Season *CC15U
    jr cor,Orff inst MMB SE-0882 $4.00
                                      (F176)

FREDENS LYS: ET JULESPILL see Brevik,
  Tor

FREDSKJEMPERENS DOD see Sonstevold,
  Gunnar

FREE, AND GLAD TO BE ME! see Price

FREE I AM ONCE AGAIN see Regnart

FREEDMAN, HARRY (1922-   )
  Keewaydin
    SATB ANERCA   (F177)

FREEDOM see Lojeski

FREEDOM FOR ALL see Tester, Wayne

FREEDOM! FREEDOM! see Burroughs

FREEDOM'S FLAME see Davidson, Charles
  Stuart

FRESH IS THE MAYTIME see Schein

FREUDE, HOLDE FREUDE see Distler, Hugo

FREUNDE DER BERGE see Herborg, Dieter

FREUNDE, VERNEHMET DIE GESCHICHTE see
  Trapp, Willy

FREUNDE, WASSER MACHET STUMM see Haydn,
  [Franz] Joseph

FREUT EUCH ALLE see Bach, Johann
  Sebastian

FREUT EUCH DES LEBENS see Trapp, Willy

FREY
  Bell Noel
    SATB CPP-BEL FEC 10123 $1.50 (F178)

FRICK
  Christmas Lullabye, A
    2pt cor CPP-BEL SV8437 $.95 (F179)

FRIDERICI, DANIEL (1584-1638)
  Drei Schone Dinge Fein
    SSA HARMONIA 3718   (F180)

FRIEDELL
  Eight Orisons
    SATB,acap CPP-BEL GCMR 02693 $.95
                                      (F181)
FRIEDEN, DER see Treibmann, Karl
  Ottomar

FRIEDEN - HALFTE DES LEBENS, DER see
    Domhardt, Gerd

FRIEMEL, G.
    Mein Schatzlein Kommt Von Ferne
        mix cor BOHM   (F182)

    Wenn Ich Ein Voglein War
        3 eq voices BOHM   (F183)

FRIEND LIKE YOU, A see Snyder, Audrey

FRIENDS FOREVER see McPheeters

FRIENDS THAT ARE FEATHERED, FURRY AND
    FINE see Roberts, Ruth

FRISCH AUF, IHR KLOSTERBRUDER MEIN see
    Schein, Johann Hermann

FRISCH AUF UND LASST UNS SINGEN see
    Peuerl

FRITSCHEL, JAMES ERWIN (1929-   )
    Earch Magician
        SSAATTBB,acap MUSIC SEV. M70-430
        $.85   (F184)

    Five Off The Wall
        2pt mix cor,pno MUSIC SEV. M70-527
        $.90   (F185)

FROCHAUX, JEAN-CHS.
    Marche Des Soldats De Turenne
        (Langree, Alain) TTBB HUGUENIN
        CH 2026   (F186)

FROG, THE see Shur, Yekutiel

FROGS AND THE BULL, THE see Smith,
    Gregg

FROHLICHE MUSICUS, DER see Bruch, Max

FROHLICHE WEIHNACHT UBERALL *Xmas,Eng/
    US
    (Deutschmann, Gerhard) eq voices BOHM
                                       (F187)

FROM MY WINDOW see Bacon, Boyd

FROM SATURDAY TO SATURDAY see Pauer,
    Jiri

FROM SCI-FI NOTES see Kvech, Otomar

FROM SEA TO SHINING SEA see Althouse,
    Jay

FROM THE DIARY OF A NORTHERN WINDOW see
    Parmentier, F. Gordon

FROM THE FAR CORNERS see Weigl, [Mrs.]
    Vally

FROM THE GAY TWENTIES see Mandelieu, M.
    De

FROM THE HEART: A MEDLEY OF LOVE SONGS
    *medley
    (Hanson, Mark) 3-4pt mix cor CPP-BEL
    C0142C1X $2.50, accomp tape
    available   (F188)

FROM THE MUSICIAN'S YEARBOOK see
    Brandon, Seymour (Sy)

FROM THE REPERTOIRE OF THE MEN'S CHORUS
    OF THE MOSCOW ENGINEERING AND
    PHYSICS INSTITUTE *CCU
    (Ryvkina, E.; Malyavina, N.) [Russ]
    men cor,acap/pno MEZ KNIGA 169
                                       (F189)

FROM THE REPERTOIRE OF THE USSR
    MINISTRY OF CULTURE CHAMBER CHORUS
    *CCU
    (Bogdanov, Y.) [Russ] cor,acap MEZ
    KNIGA 168   (F190)

FROZEN DECEMBER, THE see Miller

FRUHE see Schumann, Robert (Alexander)

FRUHLING see Weiss-Steinberg, Hans

FRUHLING IN WIEN see Grothe

FRUHLINGS-PARADE see Beekum, Jan Van,
    Lente-Parade

FRUHLINGSBLICK see Reger, Max

FRUHLINGSBOTSCHAFT: KUCKUCK RUFT AUS
    DEM WALD see Schumann, Robert
    (Alexander)

FRUHLINGSCHOR see Wolf, Hugo

FRUHLINGSGRUSS see Reinecke, Carl

FRUHLINGSLIED see Mendelssohn-
    Bartholdy, Felix

FRUHLINGSSINFONIE see Theodorakis,
    Mikis, Sinfonie Nr. 7

FRUHMORGENS, WENN DAS JAGDHORN SCHALLT
    see Deutschmann, Gerhard

FRUHZEITIGER FRUHLING see Hensel, Fanny
    Mendelssohn

FRUHZEITIGER FRUHLING see Mendelssohn-
    Bartholdy, Felix

FRUITCAKE see Hagemann, Philip

FRY
    Solid As A Rock
        SATB SHAWNEE 1672 $1.15   (F191)
        SAB SHAWNEE 0398 $1.15   (F192)

FUGA see Kyllonen, Timo-Juhani

FUGAIN, MICHEL
    Printemps, Le *see Vidalin, M.

FUGAL CAROL see Boodle

FUGUE see Jeanquartier, Marianne

FUGUE IN C MINOR see Bach, Johann
    Sebastian

FUGUE IN D MAJOR (FROM THE WELL
    TEMPERED CLAVIER) see Bach, Johann
    Sebastian

FUGUE SANDWICH see Manners, Richard

FUGUES ARE FUN see Keil, Kevin

FULL FATHOM FIVE see Lane, Philip

FULLER, JEANNE WEAVER (1917-   )
    Lake Isle Of Innisfree, The
        SATB,acap LAWSON 52365 $.90   (F193)

FUNCK-BRENTANO, FR.
    Victoire En Chantant, La *cant
        cor, solo voices&narrator,orch cor
        pts HUGUENIN CH 440, voc sc
        HUGUENIN CH 451   (F194)

FUNERAL SINFONIA AND CANTATA FOR GUSTAF
    III see Kraus, Joseph Martin

FUNF CHORE NACH GEDICHTEN VON THEODOR
    STORM see Walter, Fried

FUNF LANDER- FUNF LIEDER see Rubben,
    Hermannjosef

FUNF LIEDEREN see Bremer, Jetse

FUNF NEUE LIEDER see Habersack, Karl

FUNF VILLANELLEN see Watkinson, Percy
    Gerd

FUNNY THING HAPPENED ON THE WAY TO THE
    SEDER, A see Davidson, Charles
    Stuart

FUR MARIE see Schmidt, Helmut

FURCHTSAME JAGER, DER see Lamy, Rudolf

FUSEAU DE MA GRAND-MERE, LE see Bovet,
    Joseph

FUYONS TOUS D'AMOUR LE JEU see Lassus,
    Roland de (Orlandus)

FUYONS TOUS D'AMOUR LE JEU see Le
    Jeune, Claude

FYNSK FORAR see Nielsen, Carl

FYRA VISOR AV MATS PAULSON see Paulson

G

GAA see Wolters, Karl-Heinz

GAATHAUG, MORTEN (1955-   )
    Min Bregne
        [Norw] SSA NORGE   (G1)

    Nocturne
        jr cor,pno NORSK NMO 9767   (G2)
        [Norw] jr cor,pno NORGE   (G3)

    Potpourri Over Norske Barne- Og
        Folkeviser
        SSA NORSK NMO 9867   (G4)

    Potpurri Over Norske Barne- Og
        Folkeviser
        SSA NORSK   (G5)

    Siste Visa, Den
        [Norw] SSA NORGE   (G6)

    Stanzas For Lovers
        [Eng] mix cor,acap NORGE   (G7)

    Under Linden
        wom cor,pno NORSK 9791   (G8)

GAB, MARC
    Boites A Musique, Les *see Blanche

GABEL, GERALD L. (1950-   )
    Labyrinth
        SATB,2perc,string quar SEESAW (G9)

    Wicked Walk On Every Side
        SATB SEESAW   (G10)

GABRIELI, ANDREA (1510-1586)
    Battaglia
        (Grimbert, J.) dbl cor HEUGEL
        HE 32159   (G11)

GAELIC RHAPSODY
    (Lojeski, Ed) SATB LEONARD-US
        08403131 $.95   (G12)
    (Lojeski, Ed) SAB LEONARD-US 08403132
        $.95   (G13)
    (Lojeski, Ed) SSA LEONARD-US 08403133
        $.95   (G14)

GAGARIN see Schwaen, Kurt

GAGLIANO, MARCO DA (1582-1643)
    Trois Madrigaux
        (Grimbert, J.) 5pt mix cor HEUGEL
        HE 32157   (G15)

GAGNEBIN, HENRI (1886-1977)
    Dansez
        TTBB HUGUENIN CH 677 see from
        Jeunes Filles   (G16)

    Jeunes Filles *see Dansez; Prologue;
        Promeneur, Le   (G17)

    Prologue
        TTBB HUGUENIN CH 677 see from
        Jeunes Filles   (G18)

    Promeneur, Le
        TTBB HUGUENIN CH 677 see from
        Jeunes Filles   (G19)

GAI LABOUREUR, LE see Schumann, Robert
    (Alexander)

GAILLARD, PAUL-ANDRE
    C'etait Le Bon Temps
        SATB,acap HUGUENIN EB 445   (G20)
        mix cor,pno/orch HUGUENIN EB 444
                                       (G21)

    Joli Village, Le
        3pt cor HUGUENIN EB 481   (G22)

GAILLARDE: TANZEN UND SPRINGEN see
    Hassler

GAINSBOURG, S.
    Poinconneur Des Lilas, Le
        (Grindel, J.) 4pt mix cor HEUGEL
        HE 31924   (G23)

GAL, HANS (1890-1987)
    Motet *see Motette

    Motette (Motet) Op.19
        SSAATTBB SCHAUR EE 4006   (G24)
        8pt mix cor,acap LENGNICK 4715
                                       (G25)

GALAY, DANIEL (1945-   )
    Amanda *ballet
        cor,fl,perc,pno [15'] ISR.MUS.INST.
        6217R rent   (G26)

GALERE, LA (from Quatre Chansons)
    (Pagot, Jean) SATB A COEUR JOIE 046
                                       (G27)

GALERIEN, LE see Druon, M.

GALILEO GALILEI see Laderman, Ezra

GALLAGHER, JACK
  Elegy
    SATB,acap LAWSON 52364 $.80   (G28)

GALLINA
  Holiday Blessing
    2pt cor SHAWNEE 0081   (G29)

  It's A Great Big, Wonderful World
    SA SHAWNEE 0308 $.80   (G30)

  Just A Little Baby
    SAB SHAWNEE   (G31)

GALLINA, JILL C. (1946-   )
  Give Thanks, America (composed with
    Gallina, Michael)
    SA,pno WIDE WORLD $.75, accomp tape
      available   (G32)
    SAB,pno WIDE WORLD $.75, accomp
      tape available   (G33)

  Love Makes The World Go 'Round
    SA,pno WIDE WORLD $.75   (G34)

  My Ship And I
    see Three Robert Louis Stevenson
      Settings

  Night And Day
    see Three Robert Louis Stevenson
      Settings

  Swing, The
    see Three Robert Louis Stevenson
      Settings

  Three Robert Louis Stevenson Settings
    SA/SAB,pno WIDE WORLD $1.00
      contains: My Ship And I; Night
      And Day; Swing, The   (G35)

GALLINA, MICHAEL
  Give Thanks, America *see Gallina,
    Jill C.

GALLOPING GODIVA see Carter, Andrew

GAMES see Zamecnik, Evzen

GAMOT, PIERRE
  Chante, Antilles Chante
    2-3pt mix cor,4rec ZURFLUH AZ 1199
                                  (G36)

GAMSTORP, GORAN (1957-   )
  Jaguaren
    5pt men cor STIM   (G37)

  Morgonrodnad
    mix cor,Mez solo,harp,strings STIM
                                  (G38)

GANG SKALL JAG STILLA SOMNA, EN see
  Paulson

GANG ZUM LIEBCHEN, DER see Brahms,
  Johannes

GANG ZUR LIEBSTEN see Brahms, Johannes

GANGLAT see Sjoblom, Heimer

GANZE WELT IST HIMMELBLAU, DIE see
  Stolz, Robert

GARA MEMO AGNIATA see Kjellsby, Erling

GARCIN
  D'Autres Oiseaux
    jr cor [35'] SALABERT EAS18335X
                                  (G39)

GARDANE, ANTONIO (ca. 1500-1571)
  Fini Le Bien
    (Agnel, A.) 2pt mix cor HEUGEL
      HE 31888   (G40)

  M'amie Un Jour
    (Agnel, A.) 2-3 eq voices HEUGEL
      HE 32017   (G41)

  Quatre Duos A Voix Egles *CC4U
    (Agnel, A.) 2 eq voices HEUGEL
      HE 39404   (G42)

  Si J'ai Du Bien
    (Agnel, A.) 2 eq voices HEUGEL
      HE 32237   (G43)

  Six Duos A Voix Mixtes *CCU
    (Agnel, A.) mix cor HEUGEL HE 32405
                                  (G44)

GARGOUILLE, LA see Suc, P.

GARLAND
  In The Mood
    (Sterling) SAB SHAWNEE 0350 $1.00
                                  (G45)

GARLAND OF FLOWERS, A see Braun,
  Yeheskiel, Zer Prahim

GARNER, ERROLL (1923-1977)
  Misty
    (Snyder) SSATB CPP-BEL 2887MC1X
      $1.25   (G46)

GARTNER, DER see Brahms, Johannes

GARVIA, ISABEL
  Canco De La Tempestat
    4pt mix cor CLIVIS AC181   (G47)

GARVIN, JOYCE
  Once Upon A Christmas *see Yolleck,
    Mary

GASCONGNE, MATHIEU
  J'ai Dormi La Matinee
    (Agnel, A.) 3pt mix cor HEUGEL
      HE 32238   (G48)

GASTOLDI, GIOVANNI GIACOMO
  (ca. 1556-1622)
  Amor In Het Bootje *see Amor Nel
    Battello

  Amor Nel Battello
    (Elsenaar, E.) SSA MOLENAAR
      15024204   (G49)
    (Lemarc, A.) "Amor In Het Bootje"
      TTBB MOLENAAR 15011203   (G50)

  Amor Vittorioso
    SSATB CAILLARD PC 43 contains also:
      Dowland, Come Again; Hassler,
      Gaillarde: Tanzen Und Springen
                                  (G51)

  Balletti A Cinque Voci *CCU
    (Sanvoisin, Michel) 5pt cor HEUGEL
      HE 33352   (G52)

  Look Upon Me, My Beloved
    SSATB CPP-BEL SV8719 f.s.   (G53)

  Questa Dolce Sirena
    SATB CAILLARD PC 144   (G54)

GATES, CRAWFORD (1921-   )
  Oh My Luve's Like A Red, Red Rose
    SSAATTBB,acap (med diff) THOMAS
      1C137728 $.90   (G55)

  Ring O Bell Of Freedom
    SATB,pno/org (med diff) THOMAS
      1C138607 $.90   (G56)

GATHER LITTLE CHILDREN see Sangster, D.

GATHER ROUND THE CHRISTMAS TREE see
  Sangster, D.

GATHER YOUR ROSEBUDS see Shearer

GAUD, A.
  Chansons Populaires Pour Les Poilus
    Et Les Ecoles, 25 *CC25U
    cor HUGUENIN CH 449   (G57)

GAUDEAMUS: BRUDER, LASST UNS LUSTIG
  SEIN see Strauss-Konig, Richard

GAUDEAMUS CHORUS SINGS, THE *CCU
  [Russ] MEZ KNIGA 157   (G58)

GAUDEAMUS IGITUR
  see Three Arrangements

GAUFFRIAU, JEAN
  Arc En Ciel *CC11L
    eq voices A COEUR JOIE   (G59)

  Blues Du Mangeur De Citron, Le
    3pt mix cor A COEUR JOIE 1033 (G60)

  Dans Le Coeur De Chaque Homme
    SATB A COEUR JOIE CA 22   (G61)

  Lion Et L'escargot, Le
    4 eq voices,pno A COEUR JOIE MA 8
                                  (G62)
    4pt mix cor,pno A COEUR JOIE CA 16
                                  (G63)

  Sardana Dels Forasters, La
    SATB A COEUR JOIE 356   (G64)

GAUGLER, THEODOR (1840-1892)
  Depart De L'Emigrant, Le
    TTBB HUGUENIN EB 300   (G65)

GAWTHROP
  There Is Sweet Music
    SSAA CPP-BEL SCHCH 77111 $1.10
                                  (G66)

GAY 90'S FANTASY
  (Ehret) 2pt cor CPP-BEL PROCH 02108
    $.95   (G67)

GAYLE, CRYSTAL
  Nobody Wants To Be Alone
    (Althouse) SATB CPP-BEL 4867NC1X
      $1.25, accomp tape available
                                  (G68)
    (Althouse) SSA CPP-BEL 4867NC2X
      $1.25, accomp tape available
                                  (G69)
    (Althouse) SAB CPP-BEL 4867NC3X
      $1.25, accomp tape available

GAYLE, CRYSTAL (cont'd.)
                                  (G70)

GEARHART
  Dry Bones
    SATB SHAWNEE 0064 $1.30   (G71)
    SAB SHAWNEE 0048 $.85   (G72)
    TTBB SHAWNEE 0061 $1.35   (G73)

GEBHARD
  Du Bist Auf Dieser Welt Nur Gast
    *Op.8c
    3pt cor BOHM see from Vom Leben
                                  (G74)

  Ich Leb' Und Weiss Nicht, Wie Lang
    *Op.8c
    3pt cor BOHM see from Vom Leben
                                  (G75)

  Mensch Lebt So Hin, Der *Op.8c
    3pt cor BOHM see from Vom Leben
                                  (G76)

  Vom Leben *see Du Bist Auf Dieser
    Welt Nur Gast, Op.8c; Ich Leb'
    Und Weiss Nicht, Wie Lang, Op.8c;
    Mensch Lebt So Hin, Der, Op.8c
                                  (G77)

GEBHARD, HANS (1929-   )
  All Mein Gedanken
    men cor,opt inst BOHM see from
      Lieder Der Minne   (G78)

  Drei Laub Auf Einer Linden
    men cor,opt inst BOHM see from
      Lieder Der Minne   (G79)

  Du Mein Einzig Licht
    mix cor,acap BOHM   (G80)

  Es Steht Ein Lind
    men cor,opt inst BOHM see from
      Lieder Der Minne   (G81)

  Ich Fahr Dahin
    men cor,opt inst BOHM see from
      Lieder Der Minne   (G82)

  Lieder Der Minne *CC5U
    men cor,inst BOHM
    see also: All Mein Gedanken; Drei
      Laub Auf Einer Linden; Es Steht
      Ein Lind; Ich Fahr Dahin; Wach
      Auf, Wach Auf Mit Heller Stimm
                                  (G83)

  Schwabisches Bilderbuch *cant
    mix cor/men cor, solo voices,pno/
      strings/2clar&2trp BOHM   (G84)

  Wach Auf, Wach Auf Mit Heller Stimm
    men cor,opt inst BOHM see from
      Lieder Der Minne   (G85)

GEBURTSTAGSWUNSCH: EIN BISSCHEN MEHR
  FRIEDE see Brugk, Hans Melchior

GEE, IT'S A WONDERFUL DAY see Althouse

GEELEN, MATHIEU (1933-   )
  Berichten... Tot Ons Gekomen In De
    Eerste Helft Van De Maand Januari
    SATB,Bar solo,pno 4-hands [25']
      DONEMUS   (G86)

  In Illo Tempore
    4pt mix cor,AB soli,2.2.2.2.
      2.2.3.1. timp,2-3perc,strings
      [27'] DONEMUS   (G87)

GEESTELIJK EN EEN GEESTIG OUDNEDERLANDS
  LIED, EEN see Schrijvers, Jean

GEESTELIJK EN EEN GEESTIG OUDNEDERLANDS
  LIED, EEN, NR. 2 see Zeg Kwezelken,
  Wilde Gij Dansen

GEFUNDEN see Track, Gerhard

GEHT SCHLAFEN see Telemann, Georg
  Philipp

GEISSLER, FRITZ (1921-1984)
  Chorsinfonie *see Sinfonie Nr. 8

  Flamme Von Mansfeld, Die *ora
    cor,ABar soli,orch AUTOGR   (G88)

  Sinfonie Nr. 8
    "Chorsinfonie" mix cor,SATBar soli,
      3.3.3.3. 4.3.3.1. timp,perc,pno,
      harp,strings [40'] BREITKOPF-L
                                  (G89)

GEIST DER LIEBE see Schubert, Franz
  (Peter)

GEISTESGRUSS see Wolf, Hugo

GEITOSTEN see Albertsen, Per Hjort

GELBES MONDLICHT UND SCHALMEIEN *folk
  song,Isr
  (Scherer) SSAA MULLER 2405   (G90)

GELBRUN, ARTHUR (1913-1985)
  Ricercare
    [Ger] mix cor,acap ISR.MUS.INST.
      6648   (G91)

GELBRUN, ARTHUR (cont'd.)

Three Pieces °CC3U
[Ger] mix cor,acap ISR.MUS.INST.
6646 texts by Reiner Maria Rilke
(G92)

Two Pieces °CC2U
[Ger] mix cor,acap ISR.MUS.INST.
6647 texts by Reiner Maria Rilke
(G93)

GELEITE DURCH DIE WELLEN see
Brantschen, Gregor

GELUCKIG IS HET LAND see Anonymous

GEMS see White, Gary C.

GENEE, RICHARD (1823-1895)
Italian Salad
[It] SATB,Bar solo,acap [7']
ROBERTON 392-00507 $1.50   (G94)

GENESE see Metral, Pierre

GENOM VASENSDJUPET see Ahlin, Sven

GENTIL COQUELICOT
(Ponsot, O.) S,Orff inst HEUGEL
HE 31864 contains also: Bonjour
Mademoiselle   (G95)

GENTLE RAIN see Stroman, Scott

GENZMER, HARALD (1909-   )
Am Abend
[Ger] mix cor,acap SCHOTTS C 46570
see from Sieben Holderlin-Chore
(G96)

An Ihren Genius
[Ger] mix cor,acap SCHOTTS C 46571
see from Sieben Holderlin-Chore
(G97)

Halfte Des Lebens
[Ger] mix cor,acap SCHOTTS C 46567
see from Sieben Holderlin-Chore
(G98)

Hyperions Schicksalslied
[Ger] mix cor,acap SCHOTTS C 46569
see from Sieben Holderlin-Chore
(G99)

Lebenslauf: Gebet Fur Die
Unbelehrbaren
[Ger] mix cor,acap SCHOTTS C 46566
see from Sieben Holderlin-Chore
(G100)

Sieben Holderlin-Chore °see Am
Abend; An Ihren Genius; Halfte
Des Lebens; Hyperions
Schicksalslied; Lebenslauf: Gebet
Fur Die Unbelehrbaren;
Sonnenuntergang   (G101)

Sonnenuntergang
[Ger] mix cor,acap SCHOTTS C 46568
see from Sieben Holderlin-Chore
(G102)

GEOFFRAY, CESAR (1901-1972)
Merveilleuses Creatures, Les
3pt wom cor A COEUR JOIE 32 (G103)

GEORGE, AMANDA
Let's Give The World A Chance °see
Papoulis, Jim

GEORGE, EARL ROBERT (1924-   )
All In Green Went My Love Riding
TTBB,acap MUSIC SEV. M70-463 $.95
(G104)

GEORGIA ON MY MIND see Carmichael,
Hoagy

GEPFEFFERTE SPRUCHE see Erdmann,
Gunther

GERAEDTS, HENRI
'T Avondt: Tenden 'S Werelds Palen
SSAA ZENGERINK 61   (G105)

'T Is Stille Allengerhand
[Dutch] 3 eq voices,acap ZENGERINK
V 62   (G106)

Zacht Is Uw Hand, O Windeke
[Dutch] 3 eq voices,acap ZENGERINK
V 63   (G107)

GERAEDTS, JAAP (1924-   )
Aloeette, Voghel Clein
"Aloette, My Thrush, My Sweet" SSA/
TTB,acap (med diff) ZENGERINK
V 380   (G108)

Aloette, My Thrush, My Sweet °see
Aloeette, Voghel Clein

GERARD
C'est A L'aube
(Passaquet, R.) 3 eq voices HEUGEL
HE 31923   (G109)

GERBER, STEPHEN EDWARD (1948-   )
Saison En Enfer, Une
SATB,T solo,pno [16'] AM.COMP.AL.
$13.05   (G110)

GERBER, STEVEN R. (1948-   )
Ceremony After A Fire Raid
SATB [7'0"] APNM sc $4.75, cor pts
rent   (G111)

Dylan Thomas Settings
SATB [9'0"] APNM sc $4.75, cor pts
rent   (G112)

Illuminations
SATB [7'0"] APNM sc $4.00, cor pts
rent   (G113)

GERHARDT, EMIL
Lenz, Der
men cor BRAUN-PER 1063   (G114)

GERMAN ACTION SONGS °CCU
[Russ/Ger] jr cor MEZ KNIGA 520
(G115)

GERMAN FOLK SONGS °CC14U
(Brahms, Johannes) [Ger] SATB,acap
KALMUS K 06104 $3.50   (G116)

GERMAN FOLK SONGS see Brahms, Johannes

GERMANENZUG see Bruckner, Anton

GERMETEN, GUNNAR (1947-   )
Sans Og Samling
[Norw] mix cor,acap [15'] NORGE
(G117)

Siokate
2 children's choirs, 2perc, tape
NORGE   (G118)

GERO, IHAN (fl. ca. 1555)
Au Joli Son Du Sansonnet
(Agnel, A.) 2 eq voices HEUGEL
HE 32073 contains also:
Contentez-Vous   (G119)

Contentez-Vous
see Gero, Ihan, Au Joli Son Du
Sansonnet

Incessamment Mon Pauvre Coeur Lamente
(Agnel, A.) 2pt mix cor HEUGEL
HE 32306 see from Quatre Chansons
A 2 Voix Mixtes   (G120)

J'ai Mis Mon Coeur
(Agnel, A.) 2pt mix cor HEUGEL
HE 32048 contains also: Je
Recommence Mes Douleurs   (G121)

Je L'ai Aimee Bien Sept Ans Et Demi
(Agnel, A.) 2pt mix cor HEUGEL
HE 32306 see from Quatre Chansons
A 2 Voix Mixtes   (G122)

Je M'y Complains De Mon Ami
(Agnel, A.) 2pt mix cor HEUGEL
HE 31986 contains also: Tant Que
Vivray En Age Florissant (G123)

Je Recommence Mes Douleurs
see Gero, Ihan, J'ai Mis Mon Coeur

La, La, Maitre Pierre
(Agnel, A.) 2 eq voices HEUGEL
HE 31843   (G124)

Mort Et Fortune
(Agnel, A.) 2pt mix cor HEUGEL
HE 32457 contains also: Vrai Dieu
D'amour   (G125)

Ne Sais Pourquoi Votre Grace Ai Perdu
(Agnel, A.) 2 eq voices,opt 2rec
HEUGEL HE 32305   (G126)

Pauvre Coeur, Tant Il M'ennoie
(Agnel, A.) 2pt mix cor HEUGEL
HE 32306 see from Quatre Chansons
A 2 Voix Mixtes   (G127)

Quand Je Bois Du Vin Claret
(Agnel, A.) 2pt mix cor/2 eq voices
HEUGEL HE 32239   (G128)

Quand Je Vois Du Vin Claret
(Agnel, A.) 2 eq voices/2pt mix cor
HEUGEL HE 32239   (G129)

Quatre Chansons A 2 Voix Mixtes °see
Incessamment Mon Pauvre Coeur
Lamente; Je L'ai Aimee Bien Sept
Ans Et Demi; Pauvre Coeur, Tant
Il M'ennoie; Sur Tous Regrets
(G130)

Sur Tous Regrets
(Agnel, A.) 2pt mix cor HEUGEL
HE 32306 see from Quatre Chansons
A 2 Voix Mixtes   (G131)

Tant Que Vivray En Age Florissant
see Gero, Ihan, Je M'y Complains De
Mon Ami

Trist' Et Pensi
(Agnel, A.) ST HEUGEL HE 32554
(G132)

Vrai Dieu D'amour
see Gero, Ihan, Mort Et Fortune

GERSCHEFSKI, EDWIN (1909-   )
Dedication °Op.36,No.3a
SSA,pno [5'] AM.COMP.AL. $4.60
(G133)

Man Overboard! A Sea Tale
SATB,pno,perc [14'] AM.COMP.AL.
$10.70   (G134)

October
wom cor/jr cor,org [3'] AM.COMP.AL.
$3.10   (G135)

Six Songs °Op.39
jr cor/SSA/SATB,pno,opt perc [15']
AM.COMP.AL. $13.80   (G136)

GERSHWIN, GEORGE (1898-1937)
Sing Of Spring
(Smith, Gregg) SATB LAWSON LG 51964
f.s.   (G137)

GERVAISE, CLAUDE (fl. ca. 1550)
Elle Voyant Approcher Son Depart
(Agnel, A.) 3pt mix cor HEUGEL
HE 31987   (G138)

GESANG AUS FINGAL see Brahms, Johannes

GESANG DER GEISTER UBER DEN WASSERN,
"DES MENSCHEN SEELE" see Schubert,
Franz (Peter)

GESANG DER GEISTERN UBER DEN WASSERN
see Schubert, Franz (Peter)

GESANG DER PARZEN see Brahms, Johannes

GESANG VOM FRIEDEN see Seckinger,
Konrad

GESANGE AUS ALTER ZEIT °CC15L
cor HELBLING C4128 f.s.   (G139)

GESCHICHTE VON DEN ZWEI HASEN, DIE see
Heinrichs, Wilhelm

GESCHWINDE, IHR WIRBELNDEN WINDE see
Bach, Johann Sebastian

GESELLEN, STIMMET ALL MIT EIN see
Trapp, Willy, Gesellen-Trinklied

GESELLEN-TRINKLIED see Trapp, Willy

GESICHT JESAJAS, DAS see Burkhard,
Willy

GESSENEY, ANDRE
Monsieur Printemps
3pt cor HUGUENIN EB 466   (G140)

GESSENEY-RAPPO, DOMINIQUE
Bonsoir Princesse
TTBB,acap HUGUENIN CH 2081 (G141)

Couler Des Rois, La
4pt men cor HUGUENIN CH 2073 (G142)

Noel Aujourd'hui
4pt men cor HUGUENIN CH 2072 (G143)

GESTA MACHABAEORUM see Pinos, Alois

GESUALDO, [DON] CARLO (DA VENOSA)
(ca. 1560-1613)
Resta Didar Mi Noia
5pt mix cor HEUGEL HE 32373 (G144)

GET ON BOARD, LITTLE CHILDREN °spir
(Farrow, Larry) SATB (med diff)
GENTRY JG2091 $.75   (G145)

GET READY
(Huff) SATB CPP-BEL 1417GC1X $1.25,
accomp tape available   (G146)
(Huff) SAB CPP-BEL 1417GC3X $1.25,
accomp tape available   (G147)

GETTY, GORDON
All Along The Valley
see Six Choruses On Poems By
Tennyson And Housman

Along The Field As We Came By
see Six Choruses On Poems By
Tennyson And Housman

Annabel Lee
TB,pno [5'] PRESSER 392-00498 $1.95
(G148)

Blow, Bugle, Blow
see Six Choruses On Poems By
Tennyson And Housman

Loveliest Of Trees
see Six Choruses On Poems By
Tennyson And Housman

Rue My Heart Is Laden
see Six Choruses On Poems By
Tennyson And Housman

Six Choruses On Poems By Tennyson And
Housman
2pt cor,horn/pno PRESSER 492-00005
$4.00

GETTY, GORDON (cont'd.)

contains: All Along The Valley;
Along The Field As We Came By;
Blow, Bugle, Blow; Loveliest Of
Trees; Rue My Heart Is Laden;
Time Draws Near The Birth Of
Christ, The   (G149)

Time Draws Near The Birth Of Christ,
The
see Six Choruses On Poems By
Tennyson And Housman

GHIJ MEYSKENS DIE VAN DER COMENSCHAP
SIJT see Turnhout, Jan-Jacobvan

GHOST OF ABEL, THE see Willingham,
Lawrence

GHOSTBUSTERS see Snyder

GHOSTBUSTIN': A MEDLEY OF SUPERSTITION,
THRILLER AND GHOSTBUSTERS
(Chinn) SATB CPP-BEL CO115C1X $2.25,
accomp tape available   (G150)
(Chinn) SAB CPP-BEL CO115C3X $2.25,
accomp tape available   (G151)
(Chinn) 2pt cor CPP-BEL CO115C5X f.s.
(G152)

GHOSTS, FIRE, WATER see Mews, (Eric)
Douglas Kelson

GIA TORNA see Marenzio, Luca

GIASSON, PAUL EMILE (1921-   )
Sleighbells And Snow
SATB,pno GALLEON GCS-4007 $.80
(G153)

GIBBONS, ORLANDO (1583-1625)
Cygne D'Argent, Le
SATB,acap HUGUENIN CH 919   (G154)

Madrigals And Motets For Five Parts
°CCU
5pt cor PERF.ED. PF 50 $40.00 sold
in set of five part-books (G155)

Mon Amour, Pourquoi Partir?
SATB,acap HUGUENIN EB 57   (G156)

GIBBS, ALAN
Mountain, The
SATB,acap LAWSON 52367 $.90 (G157)

GIDEON, MIRIAM (1906-   )
Slow, Slow Fresh Fount
SATB [4'] AM.COMP.AL. $3.50 (G158)
TTBB [4'] AM.COMP.AL. $1.95 (G159)

Where Wild Carnations Blow
SATB,fl,ob,trp,timp,strings [12']
AM.COMP.AL. sc $16.75, pts
$17.95, pno red $10.30   (G160)

GIFT, THE see Wilson

GIFT OF LIFE, THE see McCray, James

GIFT OF LOVE WE BRING, A see Graham

GIFT OF SONG, THE see Ingalls

GIFT OF SPRING see Burgess

GIFT TO BE SIMPLE, THE
(Sateren, Leland) SATB AMSI 419 $.70
(G161)

GIFTS THAT ARE MINE TO GIVE see Allen,
David Len

GILBERT
We Will Walk With Mother And Morn
SATB oct DEAN HRD 250 $.95   (G162)

GILDEBROEDERS, MAAKT PLEZIEREN see
Anonymous

GILDEMARSCH-JAGERSKOOR see Potgieser,
P.

GILES
Poor Lonesome Cowboy
BB&2camb CAMBIATA U97446 $.75
(G163)

GILL, R.
Five Shakespeare Songs For Voices And
Percussion °CC5U
jr cor,perc MMB SE-0914 $8.50
(G164)

Nine New Canons °CC9U
jr cor MMB SE-0046 $4.00   (G165)

GILLESPIE
Santa Claus Is Comin' To Town
(composed with Coots)
SATB CPP-BEL SV8329 $.95   (G166)

Santa Claus Is Comin' To Town: A
Medley (composed with Coots)
°medley
(Scott, Michael) SATB CPP-BEL
CO125C1X $2.25, accomp tape
available   (G167)
(Scott, Michael) 2pt cor CPP-BEL
CO125C5X $2.25, accomp tape

GILLESPIE (cont'd.)

available   (G168)
(Scott, Michael) SAB CPP-BEL
CO125C3X $2.25, accomp tape
available   (G169)

GILPIN, GREG
Celebrate Tonight!
SATB CPP-BEL 1426CC1X $1.25, accomp
tape available   (G170)
2pt cor CPP-BEL 1426CC5X $1.25,
accomp tape available   (G171)
SAB CPP-BEL 1426CC3X $1.25, accomp
tape available   (G172)

I Dream Music
SATB CPP-BEL SV8561 $.95, accomp
tape available   (G173)

In The Night
SATB CPP-BEL 4808IC1X $1.25, accomp
tape available   (G174)

Love Can Never Say Goodbye
SATB CPP-BEL SV8746 $1.10, accomp
tape available   (G175)

Make Some Excitement
SATB CPP-BEL 0383MC1X $1.25, accomp
tape available   (G176)

(Movin' To The Beat) Everybody Dance!
SATB CPP-BEL 7139EC1X $1.25, accomp
tape available   (G177)

Sail Away
SA CPP-BEL SV8636 $.95, accomp tape
available   (G178)
TB CPP-BEL SV8637 $.95, accomp tape
available   (G179)

Secret Dream, A
SATB CPP-BEL SV8710 $.95, accomp
tape available   (G180)

Slave To The Music
SATB CPP-BEL 3760SC1X $1.25, accomp
tape available   (G181)

We Must Say Goodbye
SATB CPP-BEL SV8621 $1.10, accomp
tape available   (G182)

Winter Fantasy
SATB CPP-BEL 4835WC1X $1.40, accomp
tape available   (G183)

You Smile
3pt cor CPP-BEL SV8736 $1.10,
accomp tape available   (G184)

You're Dancing (In My Soul)
SATB,opt alto sax CPP-BEL 5236YC1X
$1.25, accomp tape available (G185)

GIORDANI, TOMMASO (1730-1806)
Caro Mio Ben, Credi Mi Almen
(Smeets, Leo) [It] 3 eq voices,acap
ZENGERINK V 227   (G186)

GIORDANO, UMBERTO (1867-1948)
Sweet Shepherdess, Addio (from Andrea
Chenier)
(Goldman) SSA LAWSON LG 51978 $.70
(G187)

GIPSIES see Schumann, Robert
(Alexander)

GIRAUDOUX, J.
Chanson De Tessa (composed with
Jaubert, Maurice)
(Ziberlin, F.) 4pt mix cor,rec,gtr
HEUGEL HE 32038   (G188)

Chansons De Tessa (composed with
Jaubert, Maurice)
(Ziberlin, F.) 3 eq voices/4pt mix
cor,rec,opt gtr HEUGEL HE 33592
(G189)

GIRL DREAMED, A see Fleischer, Tzippi,
Halma Na'ara

GIROD, VINCENT
Tout Au Long Du Doubs
SATB,acap HUGUENIN CH 2048   (G190)

Vie, La
mix cor HUGUENIN CH 2075   (G191)

GIUFFRE, GAETANO (1918-   )
Hiroshima-Poem
cor,B solo,2.2.2.2. 4.1.3.1. harp,
perc,strings SEESAW   (G192)

GIVE A LITTLE LOVE AWAY see Reese

GIVE ALL TO LOVE see Clarke, Henry
Leland

GIVE EAR UNTO MY WORDS see Bach, Johann
Sebastian

GIVE ME THE KEYS see Lewis, Huey

GIVE THANKS, AMERICA see Gallina, Jill
C.

GJENDINES BANLAT
(Eielsen, Steinar) SATB MUSIKK
MH 2488 see from To Folketoner
(G193)

GJEV MEG JORDA see Am, Magnar

GJEV MEG JORDA see Medaas, Ivar

GLADJEN see Blomberg, Erik

GLADJENS DANSANDE STRANG see Hallberg,
Bengt

GLADSOME MIND, A see Davidson

GLANZBERG, N.
Grands Boulevards
(Passaquet, R.) 5pt mix cor HEUGEL
HE 31852   (G194)

GLASER, WERNER WOLF (1910-   )
Cielo, El
"Sky, The" SA,SA soli,fl,clar,vla,
vcl,3perc STIM   (G195)

Hav Och Host °CC3U
men cor STIM   (G196)

Pastorale
3pt wom cor,instrumental ensemble
STIM   (G197)

Sky, The °see Cielo, El

GLAUBE, HOFFNUNG UND LIEBE see
Schubert, Franz (Peter)

GLIMMANDE NYMF see Sagvik, Stellan

GLINKA, MIKHAIL IVANOVICH (1804-1857)
Choral Works °CCU
[Russ] cor,pno MEZ KNIGA 162 (G198)

GLOBOKAR, VINKO (1934-   )
Concerto Grosso
cor,5 solo voices,chamber orch
AUTOGR   (G199)

GLOCKENTURMERS TOCHTERLEIN see
Schumann, Robert (Alexander)

GLOCKNER, GOTTFRIED
Storch Von Storkow, Der °CCU
jr cor,opt pno sc BREITKOPF-L 7947
(G200)

GLOIRE AU VIN see Moreillon, H.P.

GLORIA! see Althouse

GLORY OF LOVE
(Chinn) SATB CPP-BEL 3722GC1X $1.25,
accomp tape available   (G201)
(Chinn) SAB CPP-BEL 3722GC3X $1.25,
accomp tape available   (G202)
(Chinn) TTB CPP-BEL 3722GC4X $1.25,
accomp tape available   (G203)

GLORY TO UKRAINE see Hayvoronsky,
Mykhajlo

GLOVES see Beebe, Hank

GLUCK, CHRISTOPH WILLIBALD, RITTER VON
(1714-1787)
Amour Triomphe, L' (from Orphee)
SATB,acap HUGUENIN CH 611   (G204)
TTBB HUGUENIN CH   (G205)

C'est L'Amour (from Armide)
SATB,acap HUGUENIN EB 162   (G206)

Chor Der Selige Geister (from Orfeo)
(Stalmeier, P.) SATB MOLENAAR
08168107   (G207)

Choruses From Operas °CCU
[Russ/Fr] MEZ KNIGA 172 includes
choruses from Orpheus, Alkestis,
and Iphigenia In Taurus   (G208)

Drei Klassische Chore °CC3U
(Beekum, J.V.) SATB,band MOLENAAR
08 1707 08   (G209)

Drei Klassische Chore °see Zur Feier
(from Iphigenie In Aulis)   (G210)

Drei Klassische Chore °see Ewig
Zurnt Die Gottheit Nicht   (G211)

Ewig Zurnt Die Gottheit Nicht
(Beekum, J.V.) SATB,band MOLENAAR
08 1707 53 see from Drei
Klassische Chore   (G212)

Hymne A L'Amour
SATB,acap HUGUENIN CH 612   (G213)
TTBB HUGUENIN CH   (G214)

Zur Feier (from Iphigenie In Aulis)
(Beekum, J.V.) SATB,band MOLENAAR
08 1707 51 see from Drei
Klassische Chore   (G215)

GLUCK, FR.
Untreue
(Silcher, Friedrich) TTBB HARMONIA
3821   (G216)

GLUCK IST WIE EIN SONNENBLICK see
Schneider, W.

GLUCK ZUM NEUEN JAHR see Bauer

GLUCKLICHE STUNDE see Schneider, W.

GNAT, THE see Tate, Phyllis

GNUS AND GNATS see Belyea, H.

GO HOME see Morris, Stevland (Stevie
Wonder)

GO, LOVELY ROSE see Bainton, Edgar
Leslie

GO, LOVELY ROSE see Scott, K. Lee

GO NOW, MY LOVE see De Sermisy, Amours,
Partes

GO OUT AND FIND A FRIEND see McPheeters

GO 'WAY FROM MY WINDOW see Reese, Jan

GO WITH A SONG IN YOUR HEART see Price

GOD BLESS AMERICA see Berlin, Irving

GOD BLESS AMERICA (FESTIVAL EDITION)
see Berlin, Irving

GOD BLESS THE U.S.A. see Greenwood

GOD NATT see Tveitt, Geirr

GOD NATT ALLE BLOMAR see Lyssand,
Henrik

GOD SAVE THE QUEEN
(MacMillan, Ernest) SATB HARRIS
HC-W04008 $.50   (G217)

GOD SAVE THE QUEEN see Williamson,
Malcolm

GODE LANDET, DET see Tveit, Sigvald

GODOY, ROLF INGE (1952-   )
Sangen Om Vannhjulet
[Norw] SATB,clar,sax,trp,trom,perc,
pno [9'] NORGE   (G218)

GOD'S CHRISTMAS TREE see Lippman

GOD'S COUNTRY see Brymer, Mark

GOEB, ROGER (1914-   )
Etudes
SATB,brass [12'] AM.COMP.AL. sc
$11.45, pts $7.70   (G219)

Phrases From Blake I & II
SSATB [7'] AM.COMP.AL. $4.60 (G220)

GOEDEN NACHT EN WIEGENLIED see Brahms,
Johannes

GOEHR
Imitations Of Baudelaire
SATB SCHOTT ED 12282   (G221)

GOEMANNE
Flea And A Fly, A (from Jeu De Mots
(Play On Words))
see Two Tongue Twisters

Swim, Sam (from Jeu De Mots (Play On
Words))
see Two Tongue Twisters

Two Tongue Twisters (from Jeu De Mots
(Play On Words))
TTBB OXFORD 385756-1 $1.00
contains: Flea And A Fly, A;
Swim, Sam   (G222)

We, The Children (A Prayer For Peace)
1-2pt cor KJOS GC139 $.70   (G223)

GOETZE, M.
Sing We Noel *CC6U
2-3pt jr cor,Orff inst MMB SE-0892
$4.50   (G224)

GOIN' HOME see Dvorak, Antonin

GOLD
Thank You For Being A Friend
(Strommen) SATB SHAWNEE 1831 $.90
(G225)
(Strommen) SSA SHAWNEE 0531 $.90
(G226)
(Strommen) SAB SHAWNEE 0378 $.90
(G227)
(Strommen) 2pt cor SHAWNEE 0091
$.90   (G228)

GOLDEN CLOUDLET, THE see Tchaikovsky,
Piotr Ilyich

GOLDEN CORNFIELDS see Dvorak, Antonin

GOLDEN ORIOLE, THE see Handelsman,
Smadar, Zehavan

GOLDEN SEQUENCE, THE see McBride,
Robert Guyn

GOLDEN SLUMBERS
(Goldman) mix cor LAWSON LG 51884
$.70   (G229)
(Goldman; Erg) SSA,S solo LAWSON
LG 51876 $.70   (G230)

GOLDEN SLUMBERS see Dewhurst, Robin

GOLDEN SLUMBERS see Vermulst, Jan

GOLDEN VANITY, THE see Skolnik, Walter

GOLDENE BLUTENZEIT see Jochum, Otto

GOLDMAN
Beside The Golden Door
(Wagner, Roger) mix cor LAWSON
LG 52036 $.70   (G231)

Tchum Bi-Ri Tchum
LAWSON LG 51888 $.75   (G232)

GOLDMANN
Actualites *see Vidalie

GOLDSMITH, JERRY (1929-   )
Flying Dreams (From Secret Of Nimh)
(Snyder) 2pt cor CPP-BEL SV8603
$1.25, accomp tape available
(G233)
(Snyder) SSA CPP-BEL SV8604 $1.25,
accomp tape available   (G234)

GOLDSMITH, OWEN
Chiome D'oro *Renaissance
SA oct DEAN HRD 132 $.85   (G235)

GOLLE, JURGEN
Menagerie *song cycle
jr cor sc BREITKOPF-L 7667   (G236)

GOLLER, FRITZ (1914-   )
Ich Trag Ein Goldnes Ringelein
mix cor BOHM see from Von Gold Ein
Ringelein   (G237)

Ich Wollt, Wenn's Kohlen Schneit
mix cor BOHM see from Von Gold Ein
Ringelein   (G238)

Mein Schatzlein Hor Ich Singen
mix cor BOHM see from Von Gold Ein
Ringelein   (G239)

Von Gold Ein Ringelein *see Ich Trag
Ein Goldnes Ringelein; Ich Wollt,
Wenn's Kohlen Schneit; Mein
Schatzlein Hor Ich Singen   (G240)

GOLOWALJ MOJA
(Klos, Ton) "Mein Lieber Gatte"
[Russ/Ger] TTBB BANK 11.413.001 see
from Bojarenliederen 1   (G241)

GOLSON, BENNY
I Remember Clifford
mix cor CPP-BEL SVJ8501 $26.00
(G242)

GONDELFAHRRER, DER, "ES TANZEN MOND UND
STERN" see Schubert, Franz (Peter)

GONDELFAHRT see Mozart, Wolfgang
Amadeus

GONDOLIERI, I see Rossini, Gioacchino

GONNA SIT DOWN AND REST AWHILE see
Scott

GOOD ALE see Rutter, John

GOOD-BYE, OUR ABC! *CCU
[Russ] jr cor MEZ KNIGA 539   (G243)

GOOD FOR YOU AND ME see Jergenson

GOOD MORROW FAIR LADIES see Morley,
Thomas

GOOD MORROW TO YOU, SPRINGTIME see
Roberton, Hugh Stevenson

GOOD NEWS see Brown, Gary

GOOD NIGHT LADIES
(Perisson, Jean) SATB HEUGEL HE 32590
(G244)

GOOD NIGHT LADIES (THE OLD TIMERS
MEDLEY 4) see Beekum, Jan Van

GOOD TIMES see Ray, Jerry

GOODBYE OLD FRIEND (THE GRADUATION
SONG) see Scott, Michael

GOODMAN, BENNY (BENJAMIN DAVID)
(1909-1986)
Stompin' At The Savoy (composed with
Webb, Chick (William); Sampson,
Edgar M.)
(Chinn) SATB CPP-BEL T6790SC1X
$1.25, accomp tape available
(G245)
(Chinn) SSA CPP-BEL T6790SC2X
$1.25, accomp tape available
(G246)
(Chinn) SSAB CPP-BEL T6790SCWX
$1.25, accomp tape available
(G247)

GOODRICH, JEFF
I Heard Him Come
(Runyan, Michael) SATB JACKMAN
JMC7042   (G248)

GOODWILL TO ALL THIS YEAR see Terhune,
Charles

GOODWIN
When You're Smiling *see Fisher

GOORHUIS, ROB (1948-   )
Trovatore, Il
4pt mix cor,A/B solo [18'] DONEMUS
(G249)

GOOSSENS, FRANK
Kubla Khan
SATB [5'] (Coleridge) AM.COMP.AL.
$6.90   (G250)

GORDY, BERRY
Shop Around (composed with Robinson,
William (Smokey))
(Billingsley, Alan) SATB CPP-BEL
2452SC1X $1.40, accomp tape
available   (G251)
(Billingsley, Alan) SSA CPP-BEL
2452SC2X $1.40   (G252)
(Billingsley, Alan) SAB CPP-BEL
2452SC3X $1.40   (G253)

GORL, WILLIBALD
Lullaby, A *see Wiegenlied, Ein

Wiegenlied, Ein
"Lullaby, A" SATB PRO MUSICA INTL
146 $.60   (G254)

GOSPEL JUBILEE! see Musser

GOSSEC, FRANCOIS JOSEPH (1734-1829)
Hymne A La Nature
mix cor HUGUENIN CH 804   (G255)

Hymne A L'Etre Supreme
mix cor HUGUENIN CH   (G256)

Peuple, Eveille-Toi
SATB,acap HUGUENIN CH 937   (G257)
TTBB HUGUENIN CH 937   (G258)

GOTT BHUTE DICH see Lechner

GOTTIN DER FREUDE, DIE see Aeschbacher,
Walther

GOULD, MORTON (1913-   )
A Cappella For Double Chorus
dbl cor,acap [12'20"] SCHIRM.G
(G259)
Solfegging
dbl cor,acap LAWSON 52478 $2.95   (G260)
Tolling
dbl cor,acap (extended setting of
John Donne's "For Whom The Bell
Tolls") LAWSON 52477 $2.95 (G261)

GOULD, RAYMOND
Ebenezer Scrooge
2pt cor LESLIE 2055 f.s.   (G262)

GOUNOD, CHARLES FRANCOIS (1818-1893)
Chant De Louanges (from Judex)
TTBB HUGUENIN CH 983   (G263)

Choeur Des Magnanerelles (from
Mireille)
3pt cor,pno/orch HUGUENIN EB 319
(G264)
Choeur Des Soldats (from Faust)
TTBB HUGUENIN EB 397   (G265)

Hymne A La Paix
SATB,acap HUGUENIN CH 668B   (G266)
TTBB HUGUENIN CH 813   (G267)

Judex (Mors Et Vita)
(Leeuwen, A.C.) [Lat] SATB,band
MOLENAAR 08 0094 02   (G268)

Loup Et L'Agneau, Le
TTBB HUGUENIN EB 406   (G269)

Ouvrez Vos Portes Eternelles
TTBB HUGUENIN CH 675   (G270)

Soldatenkoor Uit Faust
(Diepenbeek, Fr.) [Fr/Dutch] TTBB
MOLENAAR 08047105   (G271)

GRAD AUS DEM WIRTSHAUS KOMM ICH HERAUS
see Mullich, Hermann,
Bedenklichkeiten

GRADUATION DAY see Sherman, Joe

GRAF WALDERSEE see Oertel, L.

GRAF WALDERSEE see Oertel, L., U Zij De
Glorie

GRAHAM
Gift Of Love We Bring, A
2pt cor CPP-BEL SV8504 $.95, accomp
tape available   (G272)

GRAINGER, PERCY ALDRIDGE (1882-1961)
Country Gardens
(Tall, David) SATB,acap ROBERTON
63179   (G273)

I'm Seventeen Come Sunday
cor,perc,4horn,3trp,3trom,tuba [3']
KALMUS sc $10.00, cor pts $2.00
(G274)
GRAND DESIR D'AIMER ME TIENT, LE see
Mouton, Jean

GRAND IS THE SEEN see Stearns, Peter
Pindar

GRANDE VALSE CHORALE; MARCHE see
Swider, Jozef, Wielki Walc
Choralny; Marsz

GRANDERT, JOHNNY (1939-   )
Finns En Gladje, Det
4pt wom cor [2'30"] STIM 8511-017
(G275)

Marionetterna
mix cor STIM   (G276)

GRANDES: SUITE DE 7 CHANTS DE LABOUR
(Filleul, Jacques) mix cor A COEUR
JOIE 286   (G277)

GRANDIS, RENATO DE
see DE GRANDIS, RENATO

GRANDMA GOT RUN OVER BY A REINDEER see
Brooks, Randy

GRANDS BOULEVARDS see Glanzberg, N.

GRASBECK, GOTTFRID (1927-   )
Kvallen
mix cor AKADEM   (G278)

Mellanbindaren
wom cor AKADEM   (G279)

GRASS IS ALWAYS GREENER see Crawley,
Clifford

GRASSHOPPER, THE see Thornton

GRASSI, A.
Complainte Du Corsaire, La °see
Contet, H.

GRAU, ALBERTO
Flor De La Miel, La
6 eq voices A COEUR JOIE 9007
(G280)
GRAVE PEN'IN AMOR see Rore, Cipriano de

GRAVI PENE IN AMOR see Arcadelt, Jacob

GRAY, CHAUNCEY
Bye Bye Blues °see Hamm, Fred

GREAN
Thing, The
(Althouse) SATB SHAWNEE $.90 (G281)

GREAT DAY
(Kirk, Theron) SSAB CPP-BEL
PROCH 03004 $1.10   (G282)

GREAT DAY see Youmans, Vincent Millie

GREAT GRANDAD °folk song,US
(De Cormier, Robert) jr cor,speaking
voice LAWSON LG 52074 $.70 (G283)

GREAT GRANDMA see Cable, Howard

GREAT GRANNY'S SEASIDE SONGS see
Vinson, Harvey

GREAT PRETENDER, THE see Ram, Samuel
(Buck)

GREAT SON OF THE GREAT LAND, THE °CCU
[Russ] jr cor,pno MEZ KNIGA 222
(G284)
GREATEST LOVE OF ALL, THE see Masser,
Michael

GREEN see Duson, Dede

GREEN GROW THE RUSHES, OH
(Suerte) SSB&camb CAMBIATA U 97206
$.80   (G285)

GREEN GROW'TH THE HOLLY see Smith,
Robert Edward

GREEN-STEMMED WORLD see Jennings, C.

GREENSLEEVES
(Holstein) CAILLARD PC 1080   (G286)
(Willisegger, H.R.) mix cor,acap
PELIKAN PE 1184   (G287)

GREENWICH FUNK TIME see Taylor, Lemoyne

GREENWOOD
God Bless The U.S.A. (composed with
Brymer, Mark)
SSA LEONARD-US 08637723 $.95, ipa,
accomp tape available   (G288)
SATB LEONARD-US 08637721 $.95
(G289)
SAB LEONARD-US 08637722 $.95 (G290)

GREETING CARD MADRIGALS see Brandon,
Seymour (Sy)

GREGOIRE OU SEBASTIEN see Sylvestre,
Anne

GREGOR, CESTMIR (1926-   )
Children Of The Sea, The
mix cor [10'] CESKY HUD. 8112 0133
(G291)
You And Me
men cor [3'] CESKY HUD.   (G292)

GREGSON, EDWARD
In The Beginning
SATB,pno NOVELLO 20 0195   (G293)

GREMLINS see Crawley, Clifford

GRENOUILLE QUI VEUT SE FAIRE AUSSI
GROSSE QUE LE BOEUF, LA see
Francaix, Jean

GRETRY, ANDRE ERNEST MODESTE
(1741-1813)
Nachtegaal, De °see Rossignol, Le

Rossignol, Le
(Evertse, J.) "Nachtegaal, De" SATB
MOLENAAR 15008702   (G294)

GRETSCH, PEGGY
Sing A Song Of Love
2pt cor,pno,fl/treb inst CPP-BEL
SV8805 $.95   (G295)

GRIEG, EDVARD HAGERUP (1843-1907)
Song For The Christmas Tree
(Grundahl) SATB KJOS C8920 $.90
(G296)
Vals °Op.12,No.2
(Lyssand, Henrik) mix cor MUSIKK
MH 2498   (G297)

Varen
(Lyssand, Henrik) SATB MUSIKK
MH 2448   (G298)

GRIFFIN, ELINOR REMICK WARREN
see WARREN, ELINOR REMICK

GRIGORIU, THEODOR
Canti Per Europa °ora
cor,orch [40'0"] sc TRANSAT.
TRP01544 f.s., perf mat rent
(G299)
GRIMBERT, JACQUES
Bouquet, Le °see Prevert, J.

Ce Qui M'entre Par Une Oreille °see
D'Orleans, Ch.

Cricket's World
cor,pno,gtr,db,perc HEUGEL HE 32063
(G300)
Doucette, Sucrine
(Grimbert, J.) SAT HEUGEL HE 31893
(G301)
En Yver Du Feu Du Feu °see
D'Orleans, Ch.

Fleurs De La Pierre (composed with
Seferis)
SMezATBarB HEUGEL HE 32566 (G302)

Plus Penser Que Dire °see D'Orleans,
Ch.

Quant N'ont Assez Fait Dodo °see
D'Orleans, Ch.

Qui Vient Ce Jour °see Tamaris

Slow Rock
3 eq voices,gtr,db,perc HEUGEL
HE 32064   (G303)

GRISELDA, THE REINDEER NOBODY KNOWS see
Joseph

GROB, ANITA JEAN (1927-   )
English Anyone?
2pt cor LEONARD-US 08565053 $.85
(G304)

GROB, ANITA JEAN (cont'd.)

Limerick Song, The
2pt cor LEONARD-US 08565713 $.85
(G305)
Long, Long Ago
2pt cor LEONARD-US 08565723 $.85
(G306)
Mr. Nobody
2pt cor LEONARD-US 08565733 $.85
(G307)
Mouse, The Frog And The Little Red
Hen, The
2pt cor LEONARD-US 08565739 $.85
(G308)
On The State Line
2pt cor LEONARD-US 08565751 $.85
(G309)
Santa Claus
2pt cor LEONARD-US 08565803 $.85
(G310)

GROBA, ROGELIO (1934-   )
Cancionero Gallego °CC11L
4pt mix cor ALPUERTO 1035   (G311)

GRONFUR, BJARNE
Kvifor Blinkar Stjernone?
(Solberg, Leif) SSA NORSK   (G312)

GROOTE HOND EN DE KLEINE KAT, DE see
Oberstadt, Carolus Detmar

GROS MOINE, LE see Blanchard

GROSSE LALULA, DAS see Hiller, Wilfried

GROSSFADER'S HISTORIKERVERSEN see
Pfautsch, Lloyd Alvin

GROTHE
An Der Donau, Wenn Der Wein Bluht
(composed with Melichar, Alois)
(Grieshaber) mix cor,opt pno
LEUCKART LSB 522   (G313)
(Grieshaber) men cor,opt pno
LEUCKART LSB 122 f.s.   (G314)

Fruhling In Wien
(Hess) men cor,opt pno LEUCKART
LSB 118 f.s.   (G315)
(Hess) mix cor,opt pno LEUCKART
LSB 518   (G316)

Mitternachtsblues
(Grieshaber) men cor,pno LEUCKART
LSB 121 f.s.   (G317)
(Grieshaber) mix cor,pno LEUCKART
LSB 521   (G318)

Postillion-Lied
(Hess) mix cor,opt pno LEUCKART
LSB 520   (G319)
(Hess) men cor,opt pno LEUCKART
LSB 120 f.s.   (G320)

So Schon Wie Heut', So Musst' Es
Bleiben
(Grieshaber) mix cor,pno LEUCKART
LSB 528   (G321)

Walzer Fur Dich Und Fur Mich, Einen
(Hess) mix cor,opt pno LEUCKART
LSB 519   (G322)
(Hess) men cor,opt pno LEUCKART
LSB 119 f.s.   (G323)

GROV, MAGNE (1938-   )
Tre Songar Til Dikt Av Ivar Orgland
°CC3U
[Norw] mix cor,acap NORGE   (G324)

GROVEN, EIVIND (1901-1977)
Mot Ballade (from Gjoa And The Giant)
mix cor cor pts LYCHE 914   (G325)

GRUNDAHL
'Tis Winter Now
SATB KJOS C8716 $.80   (G326)
'Twas The Night Before Christmas (The
Night Big Daddy Dropped In)
SATB KJOS C8628 f.s.   (G327)

GUANTANAMERA
(Grimbert, J.) 4pt mix cor,gtr,opt
perc HEUGEL HE 32165   (G328)

GUERRE DE 14-18, LA see Brassens,
Georges

GUGLER, LES see Vuataz, Roger

GUIDA
School Is Out °see Barge

GUIGNOLOT
(Grimbert
(Grimbert, J.) unis jr cor,gtr/pno
HEUGEL HE 32288   (G329)

GUILLAUME SE VA CHAUFER see Anonymous

GUILLO, PRENDS TON TAMBOURIN
jr cor,Orff inst HEUGEL HE 32078
(G330)

GULDNE ROSENKRANZ, DER
cor HIEBER MH 5041   (G331)

GULDNE SONNE, VOLL FREUD UND WONNE, DIE
°see Koch, Johannes H.E., Guldne
Sonne, Voll Freud Und Wonne, Die;
Koch, Johannes H.E., Im Fruhtau Zu
Berge; Watkinson, Percy Gerd, Ich
Bin Der Junge Hirtenknab   (G332)

GULDNE SONNE, VOLL FREUD UND WONNE, DIE
see Koch, Johannes H.E.

GULL AND I, THE see Barley

GULLIVER IN LILLIPUT see Franks
Williams, Joan

GUNSENHEIMER, GUSTAV (1934-   )
Alleweil Ein Wenig Lustig
mix cor,rec,opt gtr BOHM   (G333)

Ich Wollt, Dass Ich Ein Jager War
men cor BOHM   (G334)

Jagen Ist Die Schonste Lust
men cor BOHM   (G335)

Musikantengruss °see Singet Dem
Herrn Ein Neues Lied; Stimmt An
Den Lobgesang   (G336)

Singet Dem Herrn Ein Neues Lied
3-6pt mix cor,winds/strings BOHM
see from Musikantengruss   (G337)

Stimmt An Den Lobgesang
3-6pt mix cor,winds/strings BOHM
see from Musikantengruss   (G338)

GURSCHING, ALBRECHT (1934-   )
Poems De Gosses
SSAATTBB,acap PEER   (G339)

GUSS
Take Care
SSA LAWSON LG 52283 $.70   (G340)

GUT NACHT see Silcher, Friedrich

GUTE NACHT
(Kjelson) SA/TB CPP-BEL OCT 02092
$.95   (G341)

GUTE NACHT see Seckinger, Konrad

GUTEN ABEND, GUT NACHT
SATB MULLER 534   (G342)
(Wind) TTBB,T solo MULLER 623 (G343)

GUTEN ABEND, GUT' NACHT see Brahms,
Johannes

GUTHRIE
This Land Is Your Land- A Panorama
Americana
(Ringwald) SATB SHAWNEE   (G344)

GUY, NOA
Lemuel's Words
jr cor ISRAELI IMP 1707   (G345)

GUYOT
Trois Comptines Pour Anne (composed
with Bleuse, Marc)
2 eq voices,Orff inst HEUGEL
HE 32081   (G346)

GWINNER, VOLKER (1916-   )
Cantata (from Weihnachtspsalm)
mix cor,S solo,vln,org FAZER
W 12810-8   (G347)

GWYNNE, UNA
Flyaway Hill
unis cor&opt desc,opt pno [1'45"]
ROBERTON 75155   (G348)

GYPSIE LADDIE see Daniel, Etienne

GYPSY LOVE SONG see Herbert, Victor

H

HA-ZOHAR HA-RAKIA see Hamburg, Jeff

HAB MEIN' WAGE VOLL GELADE... see
Ketterer, Ernst

HABBESTAD, KJELL (1955-   )
Om De Sidste Ting, Og Om Laengselen
Efter Det Himmelske Faedreland
[Norw] SATB,trp,2sax,pno,db,perc
NORGE   (H1)

HABERSACK, KARL
Funf Neue Lieder (composed with Last,
Gert) °CC5U
mix cor&men cor WELT   (H2)

HABET ACHT! see Schumann, Robert
(Alexander)

HABITANT DE SAINT-BARBE, L' see Jones,
Robert Frederick

HADJIDAKIS, MANOS
Facteur, Le (composed with Moustaki,
Georges)
(Lavoisy-Drouot, Ch.) 4 eq voices,S
solo HEUGEL HE 32335   (H3)

HADNLIED, DAS
cor HIEBER MH 5026   (H4)

HAGEMANN, PHILIP
Come Away, Death
TTBB,pno OXFORD 19 385765 0 see
from Four Songs From Twelfth
Night   (H5)

Eldorado
SATB,pno OXFORD 19 3857669 (H6)

Four Songs From Twelfth Night °see
Come Away, Death; I Am Gone, Sir;
O Mistress Mine; Rain It Raineth,
The   (H7)

Fruitcake
5pt cor CPP-BEL PROCH 02276 $1.10
                            (H8)

SSATB CPP-BEL PROCH 02449 $1.25
                            (H9)

I Am Gone, Sir
TTBB,pno OXFORD 19 385765 0 see
from Four Songs From Twelfth
Night   (H10)

O Mistress Mine
TTBB,pno OXFORD 19 385765 0 see
from Four Songs From Twelfth
Night   (H11)

Rain It Raineth, The
TTBB,pno OXFORD 19 385765 0 see
from Four Songs From Twelfth
Night   (H12)

HAHOFESH HAGADOL see Braun, Yeheskiel

HAIKU'S & WAKA'S see Holtslag, Ron

HA'IR MESAHEKET MAHBOYIM see Avni, Tzvi

HAKAMAASSA see Madetoja, Leevi

HALFERTY
Arise And Sing
cor ALFRED   (H13)

Liberty
cor ALFRED   (H14)

Song For America
ALFRED   (H15)

HALFTE DES LEBENS see Genzmer, Harald

HALLBERG, BENGT (1932-   )
Dancing String Of Joy, The °see
Gladjens Dansande Strang

Gladjens Dansande Strang
"Dancing String Of Joy, The" men
cor,pno,orch STIM   (H16)

HALLELUJA see Handel, George Frideric

HALLELUJAH
(De Cormier, Robert) mix cor LAWSON
LG 51272 $.75   (H17)

HALLELUJAH CHRISTMAS PARTY see
Mitchell, Bob

HALLELUJAH, I'M A BUM see Cobb

HALLO, SCHOOL! see Partzkhaladze, M.

HALLOWEEN SONGS THAT TICKLE YOUR FUNNY
BONE! see Roberts, Ruth

HALMA NA'ARA see Fleischer, Tzippi

HALMCHEN KANN AM GROSSEN HALME
(Fleig, G.) wom cor ZIMMER. 607 see
from Drei Russische Volkslieder
                            (H18)

HALOM HA'IGULIM see Tal, Joseph

HALSOKALLAN see Lindgren, Olof

HAMBURG
Snow-Storm, The
SATB,trp KJOS C8810 $.90   (H19)

HAMBURG, JEFF (1956-   )
Ha-Zohar Ha-Rakia
SATB,4.4.4.4. 4.3.3.1. 4perc,harp,
2pno,strings [30'] DONEMUS (H20)

HAMBURGER ADMIRALITATSMUSIK 1723 see
Telemann, Georg Philipp

HAMEAU, LE see Berat, F.

HAMECHONIT see Weidberg, Ron

HAMEL, PETER MICHAEL (1947-   )
Klangvorstellung
mix cor,English horn,bass clar,bsn,
2pno,orch BAREN. 7128   (H21)

Stimmen Fur Den Frieden
SSAATTBB,vln,pno BAREN. BA 7135
                            (H22)

HAMILTON, IAIN (1922-   )
Careless Rambles
SATB,acap,opt winds PRESSER
312-41530 $.90 see from Summer
Fields, The   (H23)

Convergence Of The Twain, The
SATB,pno [4'30"] PRESSER 312-41483
$.90   (H24)

Evening Watch, The
mix cor,2ob,English horn,2bsn,2trp,
3trom KALMUS,A see from Morning
Watch, The   (H25)

Heat Of Noon, The
SATB,acap,opt winds PRESSER
312-41532 $.80 see from Summer
Fields, The   (H26)

Lamp, The
mix cor,2ob,English horn,2bsn,2trp,
3trom KALMUS,A see from Morning
Watch, The   (H27)

Midnight
mix cor,2ob,English horn,2bsn,2trp,
3trom KALMUS,A see from Morning
Watch, The   (H28)

Midsummer
SATB,acap,opt winds PRESSER
312-41529 $.85 see from Summer
Fields, The   (H29)

Morning Watch, The °see Evening
Watch, The; Lamp, The; Midnight;
Morning Watch, The   (H30)

Morning Watch, The
mix cor,2ob,English horn,2bsn,2trp,
3trom KALMUS,A see from Morning
Watch, The   (H31)

Nightingale, The
SATB,acap,opt winds PRESSER
312-41533 $.85 see from Summer
Fields, The   (H32)

Prometheus
SATB,SMezTBar soli,3.3.3.3.
4.3.3.1. timp,perc,harp,strings
voc sc KALMUS,A f.s.   (H33)

Summer Fields, The °see Careless
Rambles; Heat Of Noon, The;
Midsummer; Nightingale, The;
Summer Happiness; Twilight In
Summer   (H34)

Summer Fields, The
SATB,acap (may be performed with
the following inst:.0222 4230.)
KALMUS,A f.s.   (H35)

Summer Happiness
SATB,acap,opt winds PRESSER
312-41531 $.95 see from Summer
Fields, The   (H36)

Twilight In Summer
SATB,acap,opt winds PRESSER
312-41534 $.85 see from Summer
Fields, The   (H37)

HAMLISCH, MARVIN F. (1944-   )
Ice Castles: Theme (Through The Eyes
Of Love)
(Besig) SATB CPP-BEL SV8327 $1.25
                            (H38)

HAMM, FRED
Bye Bye Blues (composed with Bennett,
David; Lown, Bert; Gray,
Chauncey)
TTBB BOURNE B239954-355 f.s.   (H39)

HAMMERTH, JOHAN (1953-   )
Kronbruden
mix cor STIM   (H40)

HAN, ISAAC
Five Canadian Folk Songs For Youth
Choir
SATB HARRIS HC-6008 $1.50   (H41)

HAN DU SKAL TAKKA see Jordan, Sverre

HANBY
Up On The Housetop
(Althouse) 2pt cor SHAWNEE 0112
$.95   (H42)

HAND, COLIN (1929-   )
Moon Is Up, The
unis cor,pno STAINER 3.3261 $.95
(H43)

HAND IN HAND see Rogers

HAND 'N HAND see Ross

HANDEL, GEORGE FRIDERIC (1685-1759)
A La Musique (from La Fete
D'Alexandre)
3pt cor,pno/orch HUGUENIN EB 394
(H44)
Acis And Galatea
[Ger/Eng] SATTB,STTB soli,kbd min
sc KALMUS K 01296 $11.50   (H45)
[Eng/Fr] SATTB,STTB soli KALMUS
K 06208 $8.75   (H46)

Alceste: Incidental Music
[Ger/Eng] SATB,SSTB soli,kbd min sc
KALMUS K 01294 $6.00   (H47)

Alexander Balus
[Ger/Eng] SATB,SSATB soli,kbd min
sc KALMUS K 01306 $14.25   (H48)

Alexander's Feast
[Eng] SATB,SATB soli,orch KALMUS
K 06203 $5.75   (H49)
[Ger/Eng] SATB,SATB soli,kbd/orch
min sc KALMUS K 01297 $15.25,
ipa, ipr   (H50)

Allegro, Il Penseroso And Il
Moderato, L'
[Ger/Eng] SATB,SATB soli,kbd/orch
min sc KALMUS K 01298 $17.25,
ipa, ipr   (H51)

Allegro, Il Penseroso Ed Il Moderato,
L'
(James, S.; Martin, V.) cor,soli,
org/hpsd,timp,strings DEUTSCHER
3110   (H52)

Caecilien-Ode
(Siegmund-Schultze, W.) "Ode For
St. Cecilia's Day" [Eng/Ger]
SATB,ST soli,2trp,timp,fl,2ob,
bsn,2vln,vla,cont BREITKOPF-L
(H53)
Choeur Patriotique
SATB,acap HUGUENIN CH 654   (H54)

Choice Of Hercules, The
[Ger/Eng] SATB,SSAT soli min sc
KALMUS K 01299 $8.75   (H55)

Chor Der Jungfrauen: Seht, Er Kommt
Im Siegesglanz *see Chorus Of
Virgins: See The Godlike Youth
Advance

Chor Der Junglinge: Seht Den Sieger
Ruhmgekront *see Chorus Of
Youths: See, The Conqu'ring Hero
Comes

Chorus Of Virgins: See The Godlike
Youth Advance
(Zengerink, Herman) "Chor Der
Jungfrauen: Seht, Er Kommt Im
Siegesglanz" [Eng/Ger] SA/TB
ZENGERINK V 220   (H56)

Chorus Of Youths: See, The Conqu'ring
Hero Comes
(Zengerink, Herman) "Chor Der
Junglinge: Seht Den Sieger
Ruhmgekront" SSA/TTB ZENGERINK
220   (H57)

Four Coronation Anthems (Zadok The
Priest And Others) *CC4U
cor min sc LEA 165   (H58)

Halleluja
(Brissler, F.F.) SATB,pno [6'] voc
sc BREITKOPF-W EB2419   (H59)

Hercules
[Ger/Eng] SATB,SSATBB soli,kbd/orch
min sc KALMUS K 01301 $15.00,

HANDEL, GEORGE FRIDERIC (cont'd.)
ipa, ipr   (H60)

Ode For St. Cecilia's Day
[Ger/Eng] SATB,ST soli,orch/kbd min
sc KALMUS K 01303 $7.00, ipa, ipr
(H61)
Ode For St. Cecilia's Day *see
Caecilien-Ode

Ode For St. Cecilia's Day; Praise Of
Harmony
cor min sc LEA 164   (H62)

Ode For The Birthday Of Queen Anne
[Ger/Eng] 4-6pt cor,SATB soli min
sc KALMUS K 01302 $6.00   (H63)

Ode On St. Cecilia's Day
SATB, solo voices CPP-BEL GB 00476
$3.50   (H64)

Ode To St. Cecilia
[Eng] SATB,ST soli,orch KALMUS
K 06202 $5.75   (H65)

Seht, Der Morgen Mit Gekose (from
Alcina)
3pt wom cor,instrumental ensemble
BOHM   (H66)

Semele
SATB,SSAATTBBB soli,orch (abridged
concert version) KALMUS K 06876
$11.50   (H67)
[Ger/Eng] SSAAATTBB min sc KALMUS
K 01305 $17.25   (H68)

Silent Worship
(Somervell, Arthur) unis cor,pno
[2'] ROBERTON 75364   (H69)

Sing With Songs Of Joy
(Hopson) 2pt cor SHAWNEE 5070 $.80
(H70)
Sound An Alarm (from Judas
Maccabaeus)
(Noble) TTBB OXFORD 340886-4 $2.90
(H71)
Susanna *ora
[Eng/Ger] sc BAREN. BA 4013   (H72)

Zadok The Priest
SSAATBB CPP-BEL GCMR 02646 $1.25
(H73)

HANDELINGEN see Poort, Hans

HANDELSMAN, SMADAR (1954-   )
Golden Oriole, The *see Zehavan

Zehavan
"Golden Oriole, The" [Heb] jr cor
[11'] ISR.MUS.INST. 6735   (H74)

HANDMADE PROVERBS see Takemitsu, Toru

HANDS ACROSS AMERICA
(Chinn) SATB CPP-BEL 0217HC1X $1.25,
accomp tape available   (H75)

HANDSCHUH, DER see Schumann, Robert
(Alexander)

HANG IN THERE, BUT HANG LOOSE see
Collins

HANGET SOI see Sarmanto, Heikki

HANNISIAN
Carry On
SATB CPP-BEL SV8516 $.95   (H76)

Movin' On
SATB SHAWNEE 1150 $.85   (H77)
SSAA SHAWNEE 0336 $.85   (H78)
TTBB SHAWNEE 0225 $.85   (H79)
SAB SHAWNEE 0154 $.85   (H80)
2pt cor SHAWNEE 0114 $.85   (H81)

HANRYCKNING see Sundin, Nils Goran

HANSEN, GREG
Love Of Christmas, The
SAB JACKMAN JMC7045   (H82)

HANSEN, THEODORE CARL (1935-   )
Elegy
SATB,3trp,2trom,org SEESAW   (H83)

HANSON, HOWARD (1896-1981)
Lament For Beowulf *Op.25
mix cor,pno FISCHER,C 04879   (H84)

Sea Symphony, A
mix cor,pno,opt band FISCHER,C
05027 f.s., ipr   (H85)

HANUKAH, FESTIVAL OF LIGHTS see Blatt

HANUKKAH NIGUN see Davidson, Charles
Stuart

HANUKKAH'S CHILD see Swears

HAPPY BIRTHDAY TO OUR YOUNG PIONEER
GROUP *CCU
[Russ] jr cor MEZ KNIGA 508   (H86)

HAPPY BIRTHDAY, U.S.A. see Barlow,
Betty

HAPPY CHRISTMAS COMES ONCE MORE, THE
(Phelps) SATB KJOS C8917 $.90   (H87)

HAPPY IS see Parnes

HAPPY LOVE (GREAT LAKES SEA SONG)
(Langejans) MUSIC SEV. M70-456 $.90
(H88)
HAPPY MUSIC IN THE AIR see Artman

HAR AR STUNDEN, DET see Alldahl, Per-
Gunnar

HARBINGERS OF SPRING see Weigl, [Mrs.]
Vally

HARD TO SAY I'M SORRY
(Strommen) SSA CPP-BEL 0141HC2X $1.25
(H89)
HARDI LES GARS! see Blanchard

HARES AND THE FROGS, THE see Smith,
Gregg

HARK ALL YE LOVELY SAINTS see Weelkes,
Thomas

HARLAN
Be Joyful And Sing
SATB SHAWNEE 6449 $.95   (H90)

HARLAO, AHARON
Two Choral Settings *CC2U
jr cor ISRAELI IMP 1702   (H91)

HARLAP, AH'ARON (1941-   )
Still Remembering Names
treb cor,acap [4'] ISR.MUS.INST.
6734   (H92)

HARLEQUIN SALAD see Bucci

HARLEQUINADE see De Cormier, Robert

HARLIGA ROSTEN, DEN see Runnstrom,
William

HARLINE, LEIGH (1907-1969)
When You Wish Upon A Star (composed
with Washington, Ned)
(Porter) SATB BOURNE B240382 $.80
(H93)
HARNICK, SHELDON (1924-   )
Sunrise, Sunset *see Bock, Jerry

HARPER OF CHAO, THE see Heilner, Irwin

HARRIET TUBMAN see Robinson

HARRIS
Break Forth Into Singing
(Hayes) SHAWNEE 6412 $.85   (H94)

Keep The Dream Alive, America
2pt cor SHAWNEE 0100 $.95   (H95)
SATB SHAWNEE 1855 $.95   (H96)

Three Renaissance Pieces For Treble
Voices *CCU
SSA SHAWNEE 0407 $.95   (H97)

Three Renaissance Pieces For Treble
Voices, Vol. 2 *CCU
SSA SHAWNEE 0538 $1.25   (H98)

HARRIS, LOUIS
Christmas! Yes, It's Christmas
cor ALFRED   (H99)

Christmastime!
cor ALFRED   (H100)
SAB ALFRED 7447 f.s., accomp tape
available   (H101)
SATB ALFRED 7446 f.s., accomp tape
available   (H102)

Come, Sing A Carol
SATB ALFRED 7622 $.95   (H103)

Someone
ALFRED   (H104)

We're Number One!
SATB ALFRED 7594 $.95, accomp tape
available   (H105)

HARRIS, ROBERT A. (1938-   )
Oh, How Can I Keep From Singing?
SATB OXFORD 19 385793 6   (H106)

HARRIS, RONALD S. (1941-   )
Do Not Stand At My Grave And Weep
SATB,acap WOODL A050210 $.85 (H107)

HARRISON, LOU (1917-   )
Koro Sutro, La
SATB, 6 member gamelan PEER $30.00
(H108)

HARRISON, LOU (cont'd.)
    Three Songs
        TBarB,string orch,pno,org PEER
        $12.00   (H109)

HARRY, LYN
    Land Of Song (composed with Davies,
        David)
        SAA,pno WEINBERGER   (H110)

HARTE
    Who Needs Christmas?
        SATB CPP-BEL DMC 01121 $.95   (H111)
        SA/TB CPP-BEL DMC 08032 $.95   (H112)

HARTER
    Two Wings
        SATB oct DEAN HRD 167 $.95   (H113)

HARTMANN, CHRISTIAN (1910-   )
    Sommertrall
        SSA/TTBB NORSK   (H114)

    Sov, Du Vesle Guten Min
        3 eq voices,pno NORSK NMO 10071
                                        (H115)

HARVEST FEAST °CCU
    [Russ] jr cor,pno MEZ KNIGA 232
                                        (H116)

HARWOOD, CHRIS
    Find The Missing Children
        2pt cor GENTRY JG2096 $.90   (H117)

HASELBACH, B.
    Blessed Are Those Who Work For Peace
        °see Regner, Hermann

HASSLER
    Gaillarde: Tanzen Und Springen
        see Gastoldi, Giovanni Giacomo,
        Amor Vittorioso

HASSLER, HANS LEO (1564-1612)
    Dansen En Springen °see Tanzen Und
        Springen

    Herz Tut Mir Aufspringen, Das
        (Kaplan, Abraham) mix cor LAWSON
        LG 51851 $.70   (H118)

    Herzlieb, Zu Dir Allein
        see MADRIGALE FUR GEMISCHTEN CHOR A
        CAPPELLA: BLATT VI

    Komt Makkers Altezaam °see Nun
        Fanget An

    Nun Fanget An
        (Evertse, J.) "Komt Makkers
        Altezaam" TTBB MOLENAAR 15012503
                                        (H119)
    O Toi Dont La Beaute
        SATB,acap HUGUENIN EB 88   (H120)

    Tanzen Und Springen
        (Lemarc, A.) "Dansen En Springen"
        SATB MOLENAAR 15001802   (H121)
        (Trapp, Willy) men cor BOHM   (H122)

HATCH
    Christmas Bell Waltz
        SA KJOS C8705 $.80   (H123)

    Singin' A New Song
        3pt treb cor CPP-BEL SV7937 $.95
                                        (H124)

HATHOR-SUITE see Bergman, Erik

HAUFRECHT, HERBERT (1909-   )
    Four Rounds
        SATB,acap [3'] AM.COMP.AL. $1.60
                                        (H125)
    Little Hawk
        mix cor,woodwinds,trp,vln,vcl,perc
        [7'] AM.COMP.AL. $15.30   (H126)

    Magic Clock, The
        SATB,narrator,ob,bsn,2trp,perc [6']
        AM.COMP.AL. $7.70   (H127)

    Robin Hood
        TTBB,narrator,woodwinds,brass,perc,
        gtr,vln [12'] AM.COMP.AL. f.s.
                                        (H128)

    We've Come From The City °show
        cor, solo voices,1.1.2+3sax.1.
        0.0.0.0. timp,perc,strings [25']
        AM.COMP.AL. $22.90   (H129)
        cor,1.1.2+opt 3sax.1. 2.3.1.0.
        timp,perc,strings [25']
        AM.COMP.AL. $23.00   (H130)

HAUGLAND, GLENN ERIK (1961-   )
    Denne Vesle Jenta
        [Norw] SSAA manuscript NORGE (H131)

    Hulderkall
        SATB,SATB&narrator,electronic tape
        manuscript NORGE   (H132)

HAUPTMANN, MORITZ (1792-1868)
    An Der Kirche Wohnt Der Priester
        (Groth, Klaus) [Ger] mix cor,acap
        SCHOTTS C 46302 see from Sechs
        Chorlieder, Opus 47   (H133)

HAUPTMANN, MORITZ (cont'd.)
    Aus "Mirza Schaffy"
        (Groth, Klaus) [Ger] mix cor,acap
        SCHOTTS C 46307 see from Sechs
        Chorlieder, Opus 47   (H134)

    Coeurs Amoureux
        see Brahms, Johannes, Jour
        S'enfuit, Le

    Hell Ins Fenster Scheint
        (Groth, Klaus) [Ger] mix cor,acap
        SCHOTTS C 46303 see from Sechs
        Chorlieder, Opus 47   (H135)

    Im Holz
        (Groth, Klaus) [Ger] mix cor,acap
        SCHOTTS C 46306 see from Sechs
        Chorlieder, Opus 47   (H136)

    Lerchenbaum, Der
        (Groth, Klaus) [Ger] mix cor,acap
        SCHOTTS C 46304 see from Sechs
        Chorlieder, Opus 47   (H137)

    Sechs Chorlieder, Opus 47 °see An
        Der Kirche Wohnt Der Priester;
        Aus "Mirza Schaffy"; Hell Ins
        Fenster Scheint; Im Holz;
        Lerchenbaum, Der; Wenn Zweie Sich
        Gut Sind   (H138)

    Wenn Zweie Sich Gut Sind
        (Groth, Klaus) [Ger] mix cor,acap
        SCHOTTS C 46305 see from Sechs
        Chorlieder, Opus 47   (H139)

HAUS, K.
    Jager Lust Und Freud, Der
        "Wer Immer Annehmliche Freuden Will
        Haben" men cor BOHM   (H140)

    Kantate Zum Hausbau
        2-3pt jr cor,strings,pno,perc BOHM
                                        (H141)
    Wer Immer Annehmliche Freuden Will
        Haben °see Jager Lust Und Freud,
        Der

HAUS, KARL (1928-   )
    Komm, Stiller Abend, Nieder
        [Ger] mix cor,acap SCHOTTS CHBL 433
                                        (H142)
    Vier Ruckert-Lieder °CC4U
        mix cor BOHM   (H143)

HAUS STEHT JETZT VOLLENDET, DAS see
    Vigl, Karl H.

HAUSIERER, DER
    (Biebl) men cor ZIMMER. 605   (H144)

HAUSMANN
    Tanz Mir Nicht Mit
        see MADRIGALE FUR GEMISCHTEN CHOR A
        CAPPELLA: BLATT VII

HAV OCH HOST see Glaser, Werner Wolf

HAVARD DE LA MONTAGNE,JOACHIM
    Envers De Paris, L'
        SATB HUGUENIN CH 2063   (H145)

HAVE A GOOD TIME TONIGHT
    (Simms, Patsy Ford) 2pt cor (med
    easy) GENTRY JG2099 $1.00   (H146)

HAVE A JOLLY, JOLLY, JOLLY, JOLLY see
    Lawrence, Steve

HAVE A MERRY MERRY MERRY MERRY
    CHRISTMAS see Brymer, Mark

HAVE YOU SEEN MY MAN?
    (Kunz) SSA CPP-BEL SV8514 $.95 (H147)

HAVE YOURSELF A MERRY LITTLE CHRISTMAS
    see Hunsecker, Ralph Blane

HAVU MAYIM see Shapira, Sergiu

HAWTHORNE, ALICE
    see WINNER, SEPTIMUS

HAWTHORNE, GRACE (1939-   )
    Be Smart, Don't Start (composed with
        Wilson, John Floyd)
        jr cor HOPE pt $2.50, sc $9.95,
        accomp tape available   (H148)

HAXTON, KENNETH
    Autumn Tune
        SATB [3'] AM.COMP.AL. $4.25   (H149)

HAY, AY see Rutter, John

HAYDN, [FRANZ] JOSEPH (1732-1809)
    Aime! °canon
        3pt cor,pno HUGUENIN CH 805   (H150)

    An Den Vetter
        (Vancil) "To A Cousin" SSA SOUTHERN
        $.85   (H151)

HAYDN, [FRANZ] JOSEPH (cont'd.)
    An Die Frauen
        (Vancil) TTB SOUTHERN f.s.   (H152)

    Ceder? °canon
        3pt cor,pno HUGUENIN CH 806   (H153)

    Chagrin! °canon
        3pt cor,pno HUGUENIN CH 807   (H154)

    Chor Des Landvolks °see Komm, Holder
        Lenz!

    Consolation °canon
        3pt cor,pno HUGUENIN CH 808   (H155)

    Deutschlandlied
        (Seeger, Peter) SATB MULLER 2515
                                        (H156)

    Freunde, Wasser Machet Stumm
        SATB DOBLINGER NR 212   (H157)

    Homo Sum °canon
        4pt cor,pno HUGUENIN CH 809   (H158)

    Komm, Holder Lenz!
        "Chor Des Landvolks" SATB MOLENAAR
        15001304   (H159)

    Minor Masterpiece, A
        (Depue, Wallace) [Ger/Eng] 3-5pt
        mix cor,acap CPP-BEL SV8816 f.s.
                                        (H160)

    Moment Present, Le °canon
        5pt cor,pno HUGUENIN CH 810   (H161)

    O Wondrous Harmony
        (Goldman) LAWSON LG 52065 $.75
                                        (H162)

    Piercing Eyes
        (Hines) SA MUSIC SEV. M70-482 f.s.
                                        (H163)

    Recollection
        (Hines, Robert S.) SSA,pno LAWSON
        52402 $1.10   (H164)

    Sturm, Der
        "Tempesta, La" [Ger/Eng] SATB,kbd/
        orch KALMUS K 06938 $3.50, ipr,
        ipa   (H165)

    Tempesta, La °see Sturm, Der

    Tempete, La
        mix cor HUGUENIN EB 54   (H166)

    To A Cousin °see An Den Vetter

    Viens, Doux Printemps (from Les
        Saisons)
        3pt cor,pno/orch HUGUENIN EB 393
                                        (H167)

HAYES
    Christmas Joy!
        SATB SHAWNEE 1879   (H168)

    Deck The Hall
        SATB SHAWNEE 1878 $.85   (H169)

HAYOM TEAMTZENU see Lind

HAYS
    Two White Horses (composed with
        Krause)
        (De Cormier, Robert) SATB,Bar solo
        LAWSON LG 52327 $.85   (H170)

HAYVORONSKY, MYKHAJLO (1892-1949)
    Glory To Ukraine
        see Three Songs For Satb Chorus

    Three Songs For Satb Chorus
        [Ukranian] DUMA $2.50
        contains: Glory To Ukraine;
        Ukraine!; Yikhav Strilets
                                        (H171)
    Ukraine!
        see Three Songs For Satb Chorus

    Yikhav Strilets
        see Three Songs For Satb Chorus

HAZE see MacBride, David Huston

HAZEGRAUWT, HET: VROEG AVONDT HET see
    Zwager, Piet

HAZENBOSCH, ANTOON CORNELIUS
    Naar Het Bosch: Wij Trekken Vroolijk
        [Dutch] 3 eq voices,acap ZENGERINK
        V 110   (H172)

HAZZARD, PETER PEABODY (1949-   )
    Praise Book
        SATB,2trp,tuba,3perc SEESAW   (H173)

HE IS LOOKING FOR SOMETHING
    see Songs Of Papua New Guinea

HE SET MY LIFE TO MUSIC
    (Madsen) SATB CPP-BEL SV8450 $.95
                                        (H174)

HEADIN' WEST (THREE COWBOY SONGS) see
    Althouse

HEART IN THE JAR, THE see Bialosky,
Marshall H.

HEART IS NOT SO SMART, THE
(Hanson) SATB CPP-BEL 1714HC1X $1.25
(H175)
(Hanson) TTB CPP-BEL 1714HC4X $1.25
(H176)

HEART WE WILL FORGET HIM see
Mulholland, James

HEART'S CONTENT see Weigl, [Mrs.] Vally

HEAT OF NOON, THE see Hamilton, Iain

HEAVEN
(Chinn) SATB CPP-BEL 1647HC1X $1.25,
accomp tape available   (H177)
(Chinn) SAB CPP-BEL 1647HC3X $1.25,
accomp tape available   (H178)

HEAVEN-HAVEN see Paynter, John P.

HEAVEN IN YOUR EYES
(Buchholz) SATB CPP-BEL 1732HC1X
$1.25, accomp tape available (H179)
(Buchholz) SSA CPP-BEL 1732HC2X
$1.25, accomp tape available (H180)
(Buchholz) SAB CPP-BEL 1732HC3X
$1.25, accomp tape available (H181)

HEAVENLY AEROPLANE, THE see Rutter,
John

HEBAKES: FIVE SAPPHIC LYRICS see
Biscardi, Chester

HEBREW REQUIEM see Ma'ayani, Ami

HEGAR, FRIEDRICH (1841-1927)
Minuet, Op. 35, No. 1
TTBB HUGUENIN CH 8329   (H182)

HEGDAL, MAGNE (1944-   )
Ringer
[Norw] treb cor [18'] NORGE (H183)

HEI SUSU see Biebl, Franz

HEIDENROSLEIN
(Wind) TTBB MULLER 533   (H184)

HEIDENROSLEIN see Schumann, Robert
(Alexander)

HEIDENROSLEIN: SAH EIN KNAB EIN ROSLEIN
STEHN see Poos, Heinrich

HEIDER, WERNER (1930-   )
Sensemaya
3 eq voices/3pt mix cor,clar,bongos
BOSSE 105 sc f.s., cor pts f.s.(H185)

HEILBUT, P.
Kanons, Seventy (composed with Ruhl,
Herbert) °CC70U
cor HUG GH 11333   (H186)

HEILMANN, HARALD (1924-   )
Liebe Ist Das Hochste, Die
SATTB MULLER 2151   (H187)

Schneeblume, Die: Inmitten Weissen
Schnees
SSA MULLER 2046   (H188)

HEILNER, IRWIN (1908-   )
Black Is °round
3pt cor [1'] (Turner Brown, Jr.)
AM.COMP.AL. $.30   (H189)

Harper Of Chao, The
SSAATBB [3'] AM.COMP.AL. $5.40
(H190)

Hey There °round
3pt cor [3'] AM.COMP.AL. $.80 (H191)

Ivory Tower Trilogy °round
SSAATB [3'] AM.COMP.AL. $4.10
(H192)

HEIMAN, N.
Vagues De La Mer, Les °see Lama, S.

HEIMAT, LAND DER LIEDER see Kollo

HEIMLICHE LIEBE see Brahms, Johannes

HEIMLICHE LIEBE see Lang, H.

HEIN, H.
Kein Schoner Land
men cor BOHM   (H193)

Wenn Alle Brunnlein Fliessen
men cor BOHM   (H194)

HEINE-SZENEN see Kratzschmar, Wilfried

HEINRICHS, WILHELM (1914-   )
Geschichte Von Den Zwei Hasen, Die
men cor BRAUN-PER 1054   (H195)

Heut Soll Das Grosse Flachsernten
Sein
wom cor/jr cor BRAUN-PER 1099 (H196)

HEINRICHS, WILHELM (cont'd.)

Ich Denke Dein
men cor BRAUN-PER 1075   (H197)

In Mutters Stubele
wom cor/jr cor BRAUN-PER 1070
(H198)

Marjatta
men cor BRAUN-PER 1010   (H199)

Musica Zu Ehren
men cor BRAUN-PER 1079   (H200)
mix cor BRAUN-PER 1080   (H201)
wom cor BRAUN-PER 1081   (H202)

Schneeballschlacht
wom cor/jr cor BRAUN-PER 1008
(H203)

Tanz, Ma Mila
men cor BRAUN-PER 1048   (H204)

Weihnachtsuhr, Die °see Lang, Hans

HEINZELMANNCHEN, DIE see Beckerath,
Alfred von

HEINZELMANNCHEN, DIE see Draeseke,
Felix

HEISSA, KATHREINERLE see Erdmann,
Gunther

HEITERE WELTLICHE CHORSATZE see Eccard,
Johannes

HELAN
(Grasbeck, Gottfrid) wom cor&mix cor
AKADEM   (H205)

HELAS, MADAME, FAITES-LUI QUELQUE BIEN
see Hesdin, Nicolle Des Celliers D'

HELDMAN, KEITH
One And Twenty
SATB oct DEAN HRD 171 $.95 (H206)

HELGOLAND see Bruckner, Anton

HELL INS FENSTER SCHEINT see Hauptmann,
Moritz

HELLAN, ARNE (1953-   )
Isa
mix cor,acap NORGE   (H207)

HELLDEN, DANIEL (1917-   )
Drei Trakl-Gesange °CCU
men cor,acap STIM   (H208)

Kordans
cor MUSIKK   (H209)

Ro Fjorden
SSA/eq voices MUSIKK   (H210)

HELLE WEISE see Beguelin

HELLINCK, LUPUS (ca. 1496-1541)
Janne Moye, Al Claer
(Lagas, R.) "Tom The Tiddler, All
Clear" SATB,acap (diff) ZENGERINK
G 521   (H211)

Tom The Tiddler, All Clear °see
Janne Moye, Al Claer

HELLO, GIRLS °folk song,US
(Pfautsch, Lloyd) SSA,pno LAWSON
52453 $1.10   (H212)

HELLO, MY BROTHER see Sprunger, David

HELLO, SUNSHINE see McPheeters

HELMSCHROTT, ROBERT M. (1938-   )
Hesse-Lieder °see Manchmal; Morgen;
Nachtgefuhl; Schones Heute (H213)

Manchmal
[Ger] mix cor,acap SCHOTTS C 46425
see from Hesse-Lieder   (H214)

Morgen
[Ger] mix cor,acap SCHOTTS C 46426
see from Hesse-Lieder   (H215)

Nachtgefuhl
[Ger] mix cor,acap SCHOTTS C 46428
see from Hesse-Lieder   (H216)

Schones Heute
[Ger] mix cor,acap SCHOTTS C 46427
see from Hesse-Lieder   (H217)

HELOE! KOMM DU AUF UNSRE HEIDE see
Schumann, Robert (Alexander)

HELP, HELP VATELOT see Landowski, M.

HELVEZ, E.
Alchimiste, L' °see Morin, M.

HEMBERG, ESKIL (1938-   )
Manadsjournal I Mitten Av Attiotalet,
En °Op.71
mix cor STIM   (H218)

HEMMERLING, CARLOS
Du Maine, La
SATB,acap HUGUENIN EB 425   (H219)

Hymne A La Terre
TTBB HUGUENIN EB 485   (H220)

J'ai Demande Z'a La Vieille
SATB,acap HUGUENIN EB 424   (H221)

Jardin D'Amour, Le
SATB,acap HUGUENIN EB 437   (H222)

Je Vis...
TTBB HUGUENIN H2   (H223)

Jeunes Filles De La Rochelle, Les
TTBB HUGUENIN EB 172   (H224)

Lai Pour Bercer
SATB,acap HUGUENIN EB 275   (H225)

O Petit Pays
TTBB HUGUENIN EB 30   (H226)

Prieres Du Vigneron, Les
TTBB HUGUENIN EB 244   (H227)

HEMPEL, ROLF
Jahreskreis
TTBB,2trp,trom MULLER 2355 (H228)

Wenn Wir Unterm Fiedelbogen
SATB HEIDELBERGER 121   (H229)

HENCHOZ, EMILE
Pays En Marche, Un
TTBB HUGUENIN CH 2045   (H230)

HENRIKSEN, JOSEF
Jack Be Nimble °CCU,round
ST.GREG.   (H231)

HENRY VIII, KING OF ENGLAND (1491-1547)
O My Heart
(Owens) SAB,acap CPP-BEL SV8567
$1.25   (H232)

HENSEL, FANNY MENDELSSOHN (1805-1847)
Fruhzeitiger Fruhling
mix cor BREITKOPF-W CHB 5235 (H233)

Unter Des Laubdachs Hut
mix cor BREITKOPF-W CHB 5234 (H234)

HENSEL, WALTHER (1887-1956)
Jungbrunnlein, Das °see Kein Schoner
Land In Dieser Zeit; Und In Dem
Schneegebirge   (H235)

Kein Schoner Land In Dieser Zeit
3-4 eq voices BAREN. 95 see from
Jungbrunnlein, Das   (H236)

Und In Dem Schneegebirge
3-4 eq voices BAREN. 95 see from
Jungbrunnlein, Das   (H237)

HERBERT
I Got Me Flowers (composed with
Burton)
SATB CPP-BEL SV8486 $.95   (H238)

I Want What I Want
TTBB LAWSON LG 52320 $.85   (H239)

HERBERT, VICTOR (1859-1924)
Gypsy Love Song
SATB LAWSON LG 52319 $.85   (H240)

Italian Street Song
SATB LAWSON LG 52318 $.95   (H241)

Kiss In The Dark
SATB LAWSON LG 52317 $1.00 (H242)

HERBORG, DIETER
Freunde Der Berge (composed with
Buttner, Rudi)
1-2pt cor SCHULZ,FR 988   (H243)

HERBST see Mendelssohn, Arnold

HERBST see Monter, Josef, Bunt Sind
Schon Die Walder

HERBST, DER see Bose, Hans-Jurgen Von

HERBST: BUNT SIND SCHON DIE WALDER see
Miller, Franz R.

HERBST IM SEETAL
(Jenny, Albert) mix cor,acap PELIKAN
PE 1205   (H244)

HERBSTESZEIT, REICHE ZEIT see Ziegler,
Josef W.

HERCULES see Handel, George Frideric

HERE I AM see Strommen, Carl

HERE WE COME A-CAROLING
(North) SATB CPP-BEL OCT 02507 $1.10
(H245)
(Tishman) KJOS C8615 $.70   (H246)

HERE WE COME A-WASSAILING see Rutter,
John

HERE WITHIN MY HEART see McPheeters

HERMAN
Building A Pyramid Of Musicianship
KJOS C8829 $25.00   (H247)

HERNANDO'S HIDEAWAY see Adler, Richard

HEROLD ENGEL, WEIHNACHTSLIED see
Mendelssohn-Bartholdy, Felix

HERR, FRANCOISE
Mon Bateau
unis jr cor,Orff inst HEUGEL
HE 32573   (H248)

Solferino, Sol, Fa, Re, Ut
2pt jr cor,perc HEUGEL HE 32544
(H249)

HERR, SCHICKE WAS DU WILLT see
Micheelsen, Hans Friedrich

HERRMANN, PETER (1941-   )
Sinfonie Der Kinder
jr cor,2.2.2.2. 4.3.3.1. gtr,harp,
timp,perc,strings [30']
BREITKOPF-L   (H250)

HERVIG, RICHARD B. (1917-   )
Woman With A Torch
SATB,kbd SCHIRM.G 50541070 $.95
(H251)

HERZ TUT MIR AUFSPRINGEN, DAS see
Hassler, Hans Leo

HERZLIEB, ZU DIR ALLEIN see Hassler,
Hans Leo

HE'S GONE AWAY
(Lojeski, Ed) SATB LEONARD-US
08401871 $.85   (H252)
(Lojeski, Ed) SSA LEONARD-US 08401873
$.85   (H253)

HE'S THE MAN FOR ME
(De Cormier, Robert) SAB,opt Bar
solo,vln LAWSON LG 51974 $.70
(H254)

HESDIN, NICOLLE DES CELLIERS D'
(?   -1538)
Helas, Madame, Faites-Lui Quelque
Bien
(Agnel, A.) 3pt mix cor HEUGEL
HE 32240   (H255)

Mon Pere M'a Tant Battu
(Agnel, A.) 3 eq voices HEUGEL
HE 32241   (H256)

HESDIN, PIERRE
see HESDIN, NICOLLE DES CELLIERS D'

HESELTINE, PHILIP ("PETER WARLOCK")
(1894-1930)
Birds, The
(Ferguson, Barry) SATB,org STAINER
W134   (H257)

HESS, KARLHEINZ
Kolumbus *cant
men cor/jr cor/wom cor BOHM (H258)

HESSE-LIEDER see Helmschrott, Robert M.

HESSENBERG
Mein Schonste Zier
mix cor,acap SCHOTT C 46424 (H259)

Mond Ist Aufgegangen, Der
(Claudius) mix cor,acap SCHOTT
C 46423   (H260)

HEUREUX CELUI QUI MEURT D'AIMER see
Ferrat, Jean

HEUT SOLL DAS GROSSE FLACHSERNTEN SEIN
see Heinrichs, Wilhelm

HEUTE SING ICH EUCH EIN LIEDCHEN *folk
song/song cycle,Span
(Backer, H.) men cor BOHM   (H261)

HEWITT-JONES, TONY (1926-   )
Busy Ben By The Sea *see Vinson,
Harvey

Great Granny's Seaside Songs *see
Vinson, Harvey

Paddling *see Vinson, Harvey

Sandcastle Cake *see Vinson, Harvey

Sea Shell Song *see Vinson, Harvey

HEY ANNA MAE
(Roff, Joseph) 2pt cor,pno (med)
THOMAS 1C107715 $.35   (H262)

HEY! BABY!
(Althouse, Jay) SAB CPP-BEL 1767HC3X
$1.25, accomp tape available (H263)
(Althouse, Jay) TBB CPP-BEL 1767HC4X
$1.25, accomp tape available (H264)

HEY, GOOD LOOKIN' see Williams, Hank

HEY! LOOK ME OVER: A MEDLEY OF CY
COLEMAN HITS see Coleman, Cy

HEY THERE see Heilner, Irwin

HEYMANN
Das Gibt's Nur Einmal
(Hess) men cor,opt pno LEUCKART
LSB 123 f.s.   (H265)
(Hess) mix cor,opt pno LEUCKART
LSB 523   (H266)

Das Muss Ein Stuck Vom Himmel Sein
(Grieshaber) mix cor,pno LEUCKART
LSB 529   (H267)

HI HO, IT'S CHRISTMAS see Besig, Don

HI HO, JERUM
(Yannerella, Charles) 2pt cor,pno
SOMERSET SP-795 $.90   (H268)

HI-NEY MA TOV
(Goldman) "How Good It Is" SSA LAWSON
LG 51959 $.70   (H269)

HIC HOMO SUM see Lidl, Vaclav

HICKEN, KEN L.
Three Spoofs In Classical Style
*CC3U
SATB,pno (med) THOMAS 1C017605
$2.25
see also: Thy Body; Weed, The
(H270)
Thy Body
SATB,pno (med) THOMAS 1C017605A
$.90 see also Three Spoofs In
Classical Style   (H271)

Weed, The
SATB,pno (med) THOMAS 1C017605C
$.90 see also Three Spoofs In
Classical Style   (H272)

HIER AU SOIR J'AI TANT DANSE
(Burdet, Jacques) SATB,acap HUGUENIN
EB 327   (H273)

HIER BUITEN IN HET GROENE BOS see
Purcell, Henry

HIER MOCHT ICH STUNDEN VERTREIBEN see
Watkinson, Percy Gerd

HIGH FLIGHT see Adler, Samuel Hans

HIGH ROAD HOME see Strommen, Carl

HILDEN, SAKARI
Viihdesovituksia Mieskuorolle
men cor FAZER F.M. 07763-6   (H274)

HILL, J.
Calm Is The Morn
SATB SCHIRM.G 501560 $.95   (H275)

HILL, THE see Ireland, John

HILLER
Hush My Dear
SATB STAINER 3.3166   (H276)

HILLER, WILFRIED (1941-   )
Grosse Lalula, Das
[Ger] wom cor,acap SCHOTTS C 46435
(H277)

HILLIARD
Bouquet Of Roses *see Nelson

I'm In Favor Of Friendship (composed
with Mann; Swietlicki)
2pt cor BOURNE B240770 $1.15 (H278)

HIMMEL RUHMEN DES EWIGEN EHRE, DIE see
Beethoven, Ludwig van, Ehre Gottes
Aus Der Natur, Die

HIROSHIMA-POEM see Giuffre, Gaetano

HIRTEN-BOARISCHER see Langer, J.

HIRTENCHOR NO. 7, "HIER AUF DEN FLUREN"
see Schubert, Franz (Peter)

HISTOIRE see Massis

HISTORIC MARCH
see Chernyhivs'ki Sichovyky And Other
Songs

HISTORY OF OUR LIVES, THE *CCU
[Russ] jr cor MEZ KNIGA 522 (H279)

HIT ME WITH A HOT NOTE AND WATCH ME
BOUNCE!
(Shaw, Kirby) SATB CPP-BEL 2794HC1X
$1.25, accomp tape available (H280)
(Shaw, Kirby) SSA CPP-BEL 2794HC2X
$1.25, accomp tape available (H281)
(Shaw, Kirby) SAB CPP-BEL 2794HC3X
$1.25, accomp tape available (H282)
(Shaw, Kirby) 2pt cor CPP-BEL
2794HC5X $1.25, accomp tape
available   (H283)

HIVER SERA, ET L'ETE, VARIABLE, L' see
Villiers, Pierre de

HJARTSTILLA see Andersson, Tommy B.

HO, FIREFLY see Hotaru Koi

HOAGY CARMICHAEL CHORAL FESTIVAL, A see
Carmichael, Hoagy

HOAMGEHN ZU DIR see Muthspiel, K.

HOBBIT SUITE see King, Patricia W.

HOBBS, JAMES
Annabel Lee
SATB A COEUR JOIE CA 23   (H284)

HOCH AUF DEM GELBEN WAGEN see Neelen,
J.

HOCHZEIT WAR BEIM MUCKELEIN see
Hollfelder, Waldram, Muckenhochzeit

HOCHZYTER, DER *Swiss
(Barblan, Emmanuel) TTBB HUGUENIN
EB 67   (H285)

HODDINOTT, ALUN (1929-   )
Fair Lisa (from Four Welsh Songs)
see Four Welsh Songs
TTBB,pno OXFORD 385716-2 $.50
(H286)

Four Welsh Songs
TTBB,pno/orch OXFORD 343653-1 $5.25
contains: Fair Lisa; Lazy Wife;
Poet's Dream; Yellow Sheepskin
(H287)
Lazy Wife
see Four Welsh Songs

Poet's Dream
see Four Welsh Songs

Silver Swimmer, The
SATB,2pno OXFORD 336840-4 $6.20
(H288)
Voyagers
TTBB,Bar solo,orch OXFORD rent
(H289)
Yellow Sheepskin
see Four Welsh Songs

HODGETTS, COLIN
Moon's Alight, The
SATB,opt org STAINER 3.3199 (H290)

HODKINSON, SYDNEY P. (1934-   )
Alte Liebeslieder, Book 1 *CCU
SATB,clar,horn,vcl,perc AM.COMP.AL.
$41.15   (H291)

Alte Liebeslieder, Book 2 *CCU
SATB AM.COMP.AL. $24.40   (H292)

Alte Liebeslieder, Book 3 *CC4U,
madrigal
SATB,pno AM.COMP.AL. f.s.   (H293)

HOE SCHITTERDE IN 'T VERLEDEN see
Schaik, Johan Ant. Stephanus Van

HOEZEE *folk song/medley,Dutch
(Penders, J.) TTBB MOLENAAR 08177608
(H294)

HOHE LIED-MOTETTEN see Schroeder,
Hermann

HOKEY POKEY MEDLEY, THE
(Ray, Jerry) SATB ALFRED 7690 $1.25,
accomp tape available   (H295)
(Ray, Jerry) SAB ALFRED 7691 $1.25,
accomp tape available   (H296)
(Ray, Jerry) 1-2pt cor ALFRED 7692
$1.25, accomp tape available (H297)

HOL, RICHARD (1825-1904)
Avondlied: O Plechtig Uur, Gij Doet
Ons Zielrust Smaken
mix cor ZENGERINK 23   (H298)

Draaiersjongen, Een
(Hoogerwerf, N.) TTBB MOLENAAR
15022103   (H299)

HOLA MON COEUR see Weber, Gustav

HOLD IT FAST see Beebe, Hank

HOLD ME (IN YOUR ARMS)
(Strommen) SATB CPP-BEL 4955HC1X
$1.25   (H300)
(Strommen) SSA CPP-BEL 4955HC2X $1.25
(H301)

(Strommen) TTB CPP-BEL 4955HC4X $1.25
(H302)
HOLD ON
(Roberts, Howard) SATB,opt perc
LAWSON LG 51666 $.70   (H303)

HOLD ON see Marsh, Mary Val

HOLD ON TO A STAR see Jensen

HOLD ON TO THE NIGHTS see Marx, Richard

HOLD ON TO YOUR DREAM see Althouse, Jay

HOLD YOUR HEAD UP HIGH see Snyder

HOLDER
Sing, Sing! *see Estes

HOLDSTOCK, JAN
Dick Whittington *show
jr cor UNIVER. UE 17698 $3.95
(H304)

Teddy's Christmas
jr cor UNIVER. UE 17697 $2.95
(H305)

HOLE TOWARD SPACE, A see Plompen, Peter

HOLIDAY BLESSING see Gallina

HOLIDAYLAND see Roberts, Ruth

HOLLA, GUT GESELL see Schein, Johann
Hermann

HOLLA, MEIN BRUDERLEIN: GUTEN TAG!
*folk song
(Schmid, Reinhold) SATB,SS soli
DOBLINGER 761   (H306)

HOLLAND see Laetantius, Br.

HOLLAND: GRAUW IS UW HEMEL EN STORMIG
UW STRAND see Schmitz, J.

HOLLAND IS EEN HEERLIJK LAND see
Anonymous

HOLLANDS LIED, EEN see Tetterode, L.
Adr. von

HOLLANDS LIEDJE
(Abramsz, S.; Lemarc, A.) SATB
MOLENAAR 15021702   (H307)

HOLLANDS VLAG see Wierts, J.P.J.

HOLLFELDER, WALDRAM (1924-   )
Abendmusik
men cor,2trp,2trom BOHM   (H308)

Ach Elslein, Liebes Elselein
mix cor BOHM see from Drei
Minnelieder   (H309)

Drei Laub Auf Einer Linden
mix cor BOHM see from Drei
Minnelieder   (H310)

Drei Minnelieder *see Ach Elslein,
Liebes Elselein; Drei Laub Auf
Einer Linden; Ich Weiss Ein
Maidlein   (H311)

Hochzeit War Beim Muckelein *see
Muckenhochzeit

Ich Weiss Ein Maidlein
mix cor BOHM see from Drei
Minnelieder   (H312)

Lobpreis Der Musik
6pt mix cor/3pt men cor/3pt wom
cor,brass/pno BOHM   (H313)

Muckenhochzeit
(Miller, Franz R.) "Hochzeit War
Beim Muckelein" mix cor,clar,db
BOHM   (H314)

Musikanten, Warum Schweigt Ihr *see
Musikantenstandchen

Musikantenstandchen
(Miller, Franz R.) "Musikanten,
Warum Schweigt Ihr" men cor,acord
BOHM   (H315)

Sonntag Ist Heute
mix cor,tamb BOHM   (H316)

Von Schelmen Und Spitzbuben *CC4U
wom cor/jr cor,pno,perc BOHM (H317)

Wanderkantate
wom cor,strings/pno SCHOTT ED 7623
(H318)
HOLMAN, F.
Draaiersjongen, Een
SATB MOLENAAR 15021102   (H319)

Liedje Van De Koppelstok, Een
SATB MOLENAAR 15020903   (H320)

HOLMAN, F. (cont'd.)

Mijn Nederland
SATB MOLENAAR 15021202   (H321)

Zilvervloot, De
SATB MOLENAAR 15021003   (H322)

HOLMES
All-American (Choral Review) *see
Brymer

HOLST, GUSTAV (1874-1934)
Dove, The
SATB SCHIRM.G 316340 $.80   (H323)

Four Part Songs *CC4U
mix cor NOVELLO   (H324)

HOLST, IMOGEN (1907-1984)
Nineteen Songs *CC19U
unis cor NOVELLO 0743 $3.50 (H325)

HOLSTEIN, JEAN-PAUL (1939-   )
Aussi Bien Que De Pluie
2pt cor,opt pno CAILLARD PC 166
(H326)

Dis-Moi, Bon Charbonnier
see Bleuse, Marc, Derriere La
Montagne

N'etait Peut-Etre Par Venue
2pt cor,opt pno CAILLARD PC 165
(H327)

Pas Par Le Plafond
2pt cor,opt pno CAILLARD PC 167
(H328)

HOLTSLAG, RON
Haiku's & Waka's *CC4U
[Jap] SATB BANK DVE 001 text is
transliterated   (H329)

HOLY CURTAIN see Even-Or, Mary

HOLY LOVE see Sviridov, Georgy

HOLY MICHAEL see Parker, Alice

HOLY NATION see Davis

HOLY WAS THE NIGHT see Kocher, Konrad

HOME FOR THE HOLIDAYS see Allen

HOMEWARD BOUND see Olson, Lynn Freeman

HOMO SUM see Haydn, [Franz] Joseph

HONESTY
(Chinn, Teena) SATB CPP-BEL 5025HC1X
$1.40   (H330)
(Chinn, Teena) SSA CPP-BEL 5025HC2X
$1.40   (H331)
(Chinn, Teena) 2pt cor CPP-BEL
5025HC5X $1.40   (H332)
(Chinn, Teena) 3pt mix cor CPP-BEL
5025HC3X $1.40   (H333)

HONGISTO, MAURI
Koyhista Vanhemmista
mix cor,acap FAZER F 07831-1 (H334)

HONIGMAN, SAUL
Apples
SATB,acap LAWSON 52307 $1.00 (H335)

HONVED BANDA see Abraham

HOOG OP DE GELE WAGEN (LENTE-PARADE 1)
see Beekum, Jan Van

HOOP OP VREDE see Naberman, J.

HOOR, DE MUZIKANTEN..SPELEN IN DE
STRAAT see Stenz, Herman

HOOR TROMPETGESCHAL see Purcell, Henry,
Trumpet Voluntary

HOPE FOR AMERICA, THE see Pollack, Lisa
Lauren

HOPE IS A THING WITH FEATHERS see
Rasley

HOPE IS FOREVER see Leisy, James
Franklin

HOPE OF THE WORLD, THE see Clarke,
Henry Leland

HOPE SPRINGS ETERNAL see Powell

HOPKINS
Christmas Comes Again
(Krumnach) SA KJOS C8927 $.80
(H336)
HOPKINS, ANTHONY (1921-   )
Early One Morning *cant
wom cor,opt orch WEINBERGER (H337)

School (from Early One Morning)
SSAA,pno WEINBERGER   (H338)

HOPSON
Christmas Canon
3pt cor SHAWNEE   (H339)

HORA ALI see Cossetto, Emil

HORA JERUSALEM *folk song,Isr
(Scherer) [Ger/Heb] SATB,opt pno/gtr
MULLER 2639   (H340)

HORCH, DER WIND KLAGT see Brahms,
Johannes

HORNPIPE see Wolff, H. de, Doedelzak

HORNSBY, G.F.
Way It Is, The
(Ray) ALFRED   (H341)

HOROWITZ
Endymion
SSAATTBB NOVELLO 0720 $5.25 (H342)

HORSE WITH VIOLIN IN MOUTH, THE see
Yavelow, Christopher Johnson

HORSES see Crawley, Clifford

HOSPODINE see Janacek, Leos

"HOT DOG" FUGUE, THE see Olson, Lynn
Freeman

HOTARU KOI
(Ogura) "Ho, Firefly" [Eng/Jap] SSA,
acap [1'15"] PRESSER 312-41520 f.s.
(H343)

HOURRAH see Ferrat, Jean

HOURS see Podesva, Jaromir

HOUSE AND HOME see Tate, Phyllis

HOUSE WAS QUIET AND WORLD WAS CALM see
Borishansky, Elliot

HOUSTON, JARI
Do You Believe In Miracles? *see
Lawrence, Stephen L.

HOVI, SEPPO
Ikava Sun Olla On Yksinas
cor FAZER F 06984-9   (H344)

HOVLAND, EGIL (1924-   )
Dyrene I Stallen *Op.106
[Norw/Swed] SSAA,2clar,2vcl,db,
2harp,cel [19'] NORGE   (H345)

Se, Dagen Kommer
[Norw] jr cor NORGE   (H346)

Vi Vil Ga Ut
cor,instrumental ensemble NORSK
(H347)
HOW A SONG WAS BORN see Sviridov,
Georgy

HOW GOOD IT IS see Hi-Ney Ma Tov

HOW GREAT DELIGHT see Tomkins

HOW HAPPY THE LOVER see Purcell, Henry

HOW LIKE A WINTER see Beale, James

HOW LONG WILL HOVER THE HAWK OF WOE see
Shaporin, Yuri Alexandrovich

HOW LOVELY IS THE ROSE
(Crocker) SAB&camb CAMBIATA U485189
$.90   (H348)

HOW MANY SEASONS? see McPheeters

HOW NICE TO MARCH SINGING *CCU
[Russ] jr cor,pno/acord MEZ KNIGA 535
(H349)

HOW SMALL A BABE see Nygard

HOW WE ARE TO BEHAVE see Zamecnik,
Evzen

HOW WILL I KNOW see Roscoe

HOWARD
Medley Christmas
ALFRED   (H350)

HOWELLS, HERBERT NORMAN (1892-1983)
In Youth Is Pleasure
SSATB NOVELLO 0714 $1.55   (H351)

HOYR KOR KYRKJEKLOKKA LOKKAR see Baden,
Conrad

HUBER, F.
Soir En Montagne
TTBB HUGUENIN EB 193   (H352)

HUBERS, ANDRIES (1933-   )
Nog Is Er Een Tijd..
mix cor,SMezB soli,orch,opt pno
[35'] DONEMUS   (H353)

HUCKLEBERRY FINN see Collins

HUCKLEBERRY FINN ALBUM see Collins

HUDSON, WILL (1908-)
Moonglow (composed with DeLange,
Edgar (Eddie); Mills, Irving;
Cassey)
(Chinn, Teena) SATB CPP-BEL SVJ8601
$1.25, accomp tape available
(H354)
(Chinn, Teena) SAB CPP-BEL SVJ8602
$1.25, accomp tape available
(H355)

HUFF, MAC
Disney Spectacular (composed with
Jacobson, John)
SAB LEONARD-US 08426512 $2.95
(H356)
SATB LEONARD-US 08426511 $2.95
(H357)
1-2pt cor LEONARD-US 08426513
$2.95, ipa, accomp tape available
(H358)
Start A New Life
SATB LEONARD-US 08603702 $.95, ipa
(H359)

HUGHES
Reach Out (composed with Thygerson)
SATB CPP-BEL SCHCH 01215 $.95
(H360)

HUGHES-JONES, LLIFON (1918-)
Can Y Melinydd
"Miller's Song, The" SATB,pno [2']
ROBERTON 63157
(H361)
Migildi Magildi
SSAA,acap [2'] ROBERTON 75303
(H362)
Miller's Song, The *see Can Y
Melinydd

HUGUENIN, CHARLES (1870-1939)
A L'heure Solennelle
see Huguenin, Charles, Tour De
Constance, Le
Alleluia
see Huguenin, Charles, Tour De
Constance, Le
Au Large
TTBB HUGUENIN CH
(H363)
Aveugle
SATB,acap HUGUENIN C 2088 H
contains also: Laisse Tes Cheveux
(H364)
Chanson A La Mariee
SATB,acap HUGUENIN CH 601
(H365)
Chansons Jeunes *CC24U
eq voices,pno cor pts HUGUENIN
CH 827, sc HUGUENIN CH 825 (H366)
Chansons Populaires Poitevines, 23
*CC23U
eq voices,pno cor pts HUGUENIN
CH 449
(H367)
Chants D'alsace *CCU
eq voices,pno cor pts HUGUENIN
CH 426, sc HUGUENIN 425
(H368)
Desir Du Printemps, Le
3pt cor HUGUENIN CH 858
(H369)
Doubs, Le
SATB,acap HUGUENIN CH 600
(H370)
Fete Des Travailleurs, La
TTBB HUGUENIN CH
(H371)
Laisse Tes Cheveux
see Huguenin, Charles, Aveugle
Laissez Venir A Moi Les Petits
Enfants
1-4pt cor HUGUENIN see from
CHANSONS POUR LA JEUNESSE,
SEPTIEME CAHIER
(H372)
Monsieur D'Charette A Dit
SATB,acap HUGUENIN CH 289
(H373)
Nuages, Les
men cor HUGUENIN C 2087
(H374)
Printemps, Le
unis cor,pno HUGUENIN CH 220 (H375)
Provence, La
SATB,acap HUGUENIN CH 299
(H376)
TTBB HUGUENIN CH462
(H377)
Renouveau, Le
3pt cor HUGUENIN CH 825
(H378)
Ronde Des Saisons, La *CCU
eq voices,pno cor pts HUGUENIN
CH 949, sc HUGUENIN CH 950 (H379)
Sur Le Calvaire
see Huguenin, Charles, Tour De
Constance, Le

HUGUENIN, CHARLES (cont'd.)
Tour De Constance, La
men cor/mix cor HUGUENIN CH 613
(H380)
Tour De Constance, Le
TTBB HUGUENIN CH 447 contains also:
Sur Le Calvaire; Alleluia; A
L'heure Solennelle
(H381)

HULDEGEDICHT AAN SINGER see Toebosch,
Louis

HULDERKALL see Haugland, Glenn Erik

HULTBERG, SVEN (1912-)
Sjunga Ar Silver, Dirigera Ar Guld
men cor, solo voices STIM
(H382)

HULTQVIST, ANDERS (1955-)
Winter Afternoons
12pt cor STIM
(H383)

HUMORESKE see Trapp, Willy

HUMORESQUE see Asgeirsson, Jon

HUMPTY DUMPTY see Collins, David

HUNDSNES, SVEIN (1951-)
Lyrisk Suite
[Norw] SA,solo voice,ob,vcl,pno
NORGE
(H384)

HUNFELD, XANDER (1949-)
Magnificat
mix cor [4'45"] DONEMUS
(H385)

HUNSECKER, RALPH BLANE (1914-)
Have Yourself A Merry Little
Christmas
(Huff) SATB,pno CPP-BEL T1723HC1
$1.25, accomp tape available
(H386)
(Huff) 2pt cor CPP-BEL T1723HC5
$1.25, accomp tape available
(H387)
(Huff) SAB CPP-BEL T1723HC3 $1.25,
accomp tape available
(H388)

HUOKAUS see Palmgren, Selim

HURD, MICHAEL (1928-)
Captain Coram's Kids
mix cor NOVELLO
(H389)
Looking Glass, The
2pt cor,pno,rec,perc NOVELLO rent
(H390)
Once In A Dream
SA,pno NOVELLO 16 0199
(H391)
Parley Of Owls, A
mix cor NOVELLO
(H392)

HURNIK, ILJA (1922-)
Carp, The Flea And So On, The *CCU
jr cor,pno PANTON
(H393)
Children's Terzettos
3pt jr cor,fl,harp,db [12']
SUPRAPHON
(H394)
Choral Music For Children *see
Detske Sbory
Conversations Between Mother And
Child
jr cor [12'] CESKY HUD.
(H395)
Detske Sbory
"Choral Music For Children" jr cor
SUPRAPHON
(H396)
Echo
girl cor, solo voices,chamber orch,
string orch,ob,pno [15'] CESKY
HUD.
(H397)
Ezop *cant
mix cor,S solo,2.2.2.2. 4.2.3.0.
timp,perc,pno,strings [18'0"]
SUPRAPHON H 4357
(H398)
Pastorella
jr cor,chamber orch [15'] BAREN.
(H399)
Scenes For Children's Chorus
jr cor [15'] CESKY HUD.
(H400)
Seasonal Madrigals
mix cor,instrumental ensemble [14']
CESKY HUD.
(H401)
Sun-Warmed Balk
girl cor,pno PANTON
(H402)
Water, Little Water
jr cor [8'] CESKY HUD.
(H403)

HURRY, HURRY NOW TO BETHLEHEM see
Kauffman

HURUM, HELGE (1936-)
Fata Morgana
[Eng] SSAATTBB,fl,ob,alto sax,tenor
sax,trp,gtr,db,drums,pno NORGE
(H404)

HUSH, MISSUS TEENAGE MARY see Medema

HUSH MY DEAR see Hiller

HUSH! SOMEBODY'S CALLIN' MY NAME see
Dennard

HUSH SWEET LUTE see Stanford, Charles
Villiers

HUSH TO PEACE see Arne, Thomas
Augustine

HUSTAVLE, EN see Lyssand, Henrik

HUT DU DICH see Strauss, Richard

HUTCHINSON, J.E.
Uncle Sam's Farm
(De Cormier, Robert) jr cor,vln,pno
LAWSON LG 52144 $.85
(H405)

HUWELIJKSLIED: OP HET HOOGFEEST VAN UW
LEVEN see Stenz, Herman

HUWILER, PIERRE
C'est Toi, Neuchatel
SATB,acap HUGUENIN CH 2036
(H406)
Conquerants, Les
men cor HUGUENIN
(H407)
TTBB,acap HUGUENIN CH 2082
(H408)
Printemps, Le
mix cor HUGUENIN CH 2068
(H409)

HVOR LENGE? see Slogedal, Bjarne

HVOSLEF, KETIL (1939)
Balladen Om Narkis Och Eko
[Swed] mix cor,acap [16'] NORGE
(H410)
Concerto For Choir And Chamber
Orchestra
cor,orch NORSK NMO 9314B
(H411)
Nattlig Madonna
men cor NORSK NMO 9984
(H412)
Spillemaend
[Norw] SATB,org,vln NORGE
(H413)

HYMN TO FREEDOM see Peterson, Oscar

HYMNE A LA JOIE see Beethoven, Ludwig
van

HYMNE A LA NATURE see Gossec, Francois
Joseph

HYMNE A LA PAIX see Gounod, Charles
Francois

HYMNE A LA PATRIE see Lauber, Emile

HYMNE A LA TERRE see Hemmerling, Carlos

HYMNE A LA TERRE NATALE see Pantillon,
G.L.

HYMNE A L'AMOUR see Gluck, Christoph
Willibald, Ritter von

HYMNE A L'ETRE SUPREME see Gossec,
Francois Joseph

HYMNE A PESTALOZZI see Lauber, Emile

HYMNE AN DIE NACHT see Beethoven,
Ludwig van

HYMNE AU SOLEIL see Rameau, Jean-
Philippe

HYMNE AU VULLY see Pantillon, G.L.

HYMNE DE FRATERNITE see Lancen, Serge

HYMNE DU 10 AOUT (CHUTE DE LA ROYAUTE)
see Catel, Charles Simon

HYMNS AND DANCES see Slothouwer, Jochem

HYMNS FOR THE AMUSEMENT OF CHILDREN see
Oldham, Arthur

HYPERIONS SCHICKSALSLIED see Genzmer,
Harald

HYRDER STIRRER I NATTEN UT, DE see
Karlsen, Kjell Mork

I

I AM A ROCK see Strommen, Carl

I AM DRAWING THE ELEPHANT *CCU
[Russ] MEZ KNIGA 188 (I1)

I AM GONE, SIR see Hagemann, Philip

I AM HE THAT ACHES WITH AMOROUS LOVE
see Brooks, Richard James

I AM NO LONGER WHO I WAS see Berger

I AM NOBODY see Welin, Karl-Erik

I AM ONLY ONE see Clarke, Henry Leland

I BATEN see Killengreen, Christian

I BEEN IN THE STORM SO LONG
(De Cormier, Robert) mix cor LAWSON
LG 51282 $.70 (I2)

I BELIEVE IN YOU AND ME see Riley

I BELIEVE (QUODLIBET WITH BACH-GOUNOD
AVE MARIA) see Beard

I BUTIKKENS SKOGER see Mostad, Jon

I CAN'T GIVE YOU ANYTHING BUT LOVE see
McHugh

I DON'T WANT TO BE A NUMBER see Blake,
Howard

I DREAM MUSIC see Gilpin, Greg

I DREAMED OF A CITY INVINCIBLE see
Dello Joio, Norman

I FEEL A SONG COMIN' ON
(Speta) SATB CPP-BEL T11201C8 $1.25
(I3)

I FELT A CLEAVAGE IN MY MIND see
Kitzke, Jerome P.

I GAMLE DAGE see Ohrn, Konrad M.

I GET ALONG WITHOUT YOU VERY WELL see
Snyder

I GO TO RIO
(Huff) SATB CPP-BEL 2021IC1X $1.25,
accomp tape available (I4)
(Huff) SAB CPP-BEL 2021IC3X $1.25,
accomp tape available (I5)

I GOE BEFORE MY DARLING see Morley,
Thomas

I GOT ME FLOWERS see Herbert

I HAD A LITTLE PUP see Berkowitz, Sol

I HAVE A DREAM see Donnelly, Mary

I HAVE A SONG TO SING see Wyatt

I HAVE A WISH, DEAR MOTHER see Brahms,
Johannes

I HAVE NOT SEEN MY LOVE OF LATE see
Wolff

I HEAR A SIGHING IN THE TREES see
Brahms, Johannes, Es Geht Ein Wehen
Durch Den Wald

I HEAR A SKY-BORN MUSIC see Land

I HEAR MUSIC see Loesser

I HEAR THE MINSTRELS IN OUR STREET see
Waxman, J'entends Par Notre Rue

I HEARD EIGHT REINDEER HOOFING see Kern

I HEARD HIM COME see Goodrich, Jeff

I HEARD IT THROUGH THE GRAPEVINE
(Chinn) SATB CPP-BEL 2410IC1X $1.25,
accomp tape available (I6)
(Chinn) SAB CPP-BEL 2410IC3X $1.25,
accomp tape available (I7)

I JUST CALLED TO SAY I LOVE YOU
(Althouse) SATB CPP-BEL 3025IC1X
$1.25 (I8)
(Althouse) SSA CPP-BEL 3025IC2X $1.25
(I9)
(Althouse) SAB CPP-BEL 3025IC3X $1.25
(I10)

I JUST CAN'T SAY GOODBYE TO YOU see
Althouse

I KNEW YOU WERE WAITING see Franklin

I KNEW YOU WERE WAITING (FOR ME)
(Chinn) SATB CPP-BEL 3419IC1X $1.25,
accomp tape available (I11)
(Chinn) SAB CPP-BEL 3419IC3X $1.25,
accomp tape available (I12)

I KNOW WHERE I'M GOING
(Fraser, Shena) SATB,acap [2']
ROBERTON 63171 (I13)

I LAID ME DOWN TO REST *folk song,Norw
(Haugland, Oscar) SATB HOA $.75 (I14)

I LIKE CAMP FIRES *CCU
[Russ] cor MEZ KNIGA 177 (I15)

I LIKE DOGS see Ohlin, Camille

I LIKE MUSIC see Butler, Eugene Sanders

I LIVE FOR YOUR LOVE
(Snyder, Audrey) SAB CPP-BEL 3869IC3X
$1.25, accomp tape available (I16)
(Snyder, Audrey) SATB CPP-BEL
3869IC1X $1.25, accomp tape
available (I17)
(Snyder, Audrey) SSA CPP-BEL 3869IC2X
$1.25, accomp tape available (I18)

I LOVE A BROADWAY SHOW see Leavitt,
John

I LOVE, ALAS, I LOVE THEE see Morley,
Thomas

I LOVE CHRISTMAS see Bacak, Joyce
Eilers

I LOVE THEE see Beethoven, Ludwig van,
Ich Liebe Dich

I NEVER SAW A MOOR see Constantinides,
Dinos Demetrios

I NEVER SAW ANOTHER BUTTERFLY see
Davidson, Charles Stuart

I REMEMBER CHRISTMAS see Jensen

I REMEMBER CLIFFORD see Golson, Benny

I SAW OLD AUTUMN see Eddleman, David

I SING FOR YOU see Cooper

I STILL BELIEVE see Armato

I STUMBLE see Kopelent, Marek, Vacillat
Pes Meus

I THINK CONTINUALLY OF THOSE see Adler,
Samuel Hans

I THINK I NEED A FRIEND see Besig, Don

I THINK I UNDERSTAND WHAT LOVE IS see
Lord, Suzanne

I WAKE AND FEEL THE FELL OF DARK see
Bialosky, Marshall H.

I WALK THE UNFREQUENTED ROAD
(Kjelson) SA/TB,pno/org CPP-BEL
OCT 02207 $.95 (I19)

I WANNA DANCE WITH SOMEBODY (WHO LOVES
ME)
(Billingsley, Alan) SATB CPP-BEL
7542IC1X $1.25, accomp tape
available (I20)
(Billingsley, Alan) SSA CPP-BEL
7542IC2X $1.25, accomp tape
available (I21)
(Billingsley, Alan) SAB CPP-BEL
7542IC3X $1.25, accomp tape
available (I22)

I WANT JESUS TO WALK WITH ME
(Roberts, Howard) SATB LAWSON
LG 51572 $.70 (I23)

I WANT TO BE FREE see Snyder

I WANT TO BE READY *spir
(Scherer) SSAA,S solo MULLER 2751 see
from Volkslieder Aus Aller Welt
(I24)
(Scherer, E.) [Eng] SATB MULLER 2765
(I25)

I WANT TO BE READY see Bolt

I WANT TO SEE THE WORLD see Melrose,
Ronald

I WANT TO SING see Robb

I WANT WHAT I WANT see Herbert

I WENT TO THE MARKET see Anonymous

I WILL BE WITH YOU EVERY CHRISTMAS see
Scott

I WILL FOREVER SING see Marcello

I WILL GIVE MY LOVE AN APPLE see
Williams

I WILL SING OF MERCY AND JUDGMENT see
Diemer, Emma Lou

I WISH YOU WERE HERE WITH ME see
McPheeters

I WOULD BE TRUE see Siltman, Bobby L.

IBARRONDO, FELIX (1943-)
Canto
mix cor,SAT soli,instrumental
ensemble [20'] JOBERT (I26)

ICARUS see Silsbee, Ann

ICE CASTLES: THEME (THROUGH THE EYES OF
LOVE) see Hamlisch, Marvin F.

ICH BIN DAS GANZE JAHR VERGNUGT see
Seckinger, Konrad

ICH BIN DER JUNGE HIRTENKNAB see
Watkinson, Percy Gerd

ICH BIN IN MIR VERGNUGT see Bach,
Johann Sebastian

ICH BRECH DREI DURRE REISELEIN see
Distler, Hugo

ICH DENKE DEIN see Heinrichs, Wilhelm

ICH FAHR DAHIN see Biebl, Franz

ICH FAHR DAHIN see Brahms, Johannes

ICH FAHR DAHIN see Gebhard, Hans

ICH GEFALL MIR see Bernstein, Leonard

ICH GING AN EINEM FRUHMORGEN see Zoll,
Paul

ICH HAB' MEIN HERZ IN HEIDELBERG
VERLOREN see Raymond

ICH KENN' EINE QUELLE see Pappert,
Robert

ICH LEB OHNE RUH IM HERZEN see Bose,
Hans-Jurgen Von

ICH LEB' UND WEISS NICHT, WIE LANG see
Gebhard

ICH LIEBE DICH see Beethoven, Ludwig
van

ICH SCHELL MEIN HORN see Brahms,
Johannes

ICH SING' MEIN LIED HEUT' NUR FUR DICH!
see Stolz, Robert

ICH SPRING IN DIESEM RINGE
(Schneider, Walther) SATB MULLER 665
f.s. see from Zwei Altdeutsche
Liebeslieder (I27)

ICH STUND AN EINEM MORGEN see Senfl,
Ludwig

ICH TANZE MIT DIR IN DEN HIMMEL HINEIN
see Schroder

ICH TRAG EIN GOLDNES RINGELEIN see
Goller, Fritz

ICH WEISS EIN MAIDLEIN see Hollfelder,
Waldram

ICH WEISS EIN MAIDLEIN HUBSCH UND FEIN
see Erdmann-Abele, Veit

ICH WILL DEN NAGENDEN BESCHWERDEN see
Bose, Hans-Jurgen Von

ICH WOLLT, DASS ICH EIN JAGER WAR see
Gunsenheimer, Gustav

ICH WOLLT, ICH LAG UND SCHLIEF see
Reger, Max, Liebeslied

ICH WOLLT' MEINE LIEB' see Mendelssohn-
Bartholdy, Felix

ICH WOLLT, WENN'S KOHLEN SCHNEIT see
Goller, Fritz

ICICLES see Rutter, John

I'D LIKE TO TEACH THE WORLD TO SING see
Bacharach, Burt F.

I'D PAINT YOU A PICTURE see McPheeters

IDAR, INGEGERD
Korsang Fra Bladet- Til Norsk Ved
Oystein Arva
cor MUSIKK (I28)

IDEGEN FOLDON see Ligeti, Gyorgy

IERSE SELECTIE (VAN BEKENDE IERSE
   LIEDJES) see Wolff, H. de

IF EVER YOU'RE IN MY ARMS AGAIN
   (Strommen) SSA CPP-BEL 1861IC2X $1.25
                                        (I29)
   (Strommen) SATB CPP-BEL 1861IC1X
   $1.25   (I30)

IF I HAD-A MY WAY see Morris

IF I WERE SANTA CLAUS see Cacavas

IF IT WEREN'T FOR YOU see Lubetkin

IF YOU HAD A THOUGHT IN YOUR HEAD see
   Anderson, Beth

IF YOU RING ONE BELL see McLaughlin

IF YOU SAY MY EYES ARE BEAUTIFUL
   (Chinn) SATB CPP-BEL 1887IC1X $1.25,
      accomp tape available   (I31)
   (Chinn) SSA CPP-BEL 1887IC2X $1.25,
      accomp tape available   (I32)
   (Chinn) SAB CPP-BEL 1887IC3X $1.25,
      accomp tape available   (I33)

IF YOU SHOULD MEET A CROCODILE see
   Telfer, Nancy

IF YOU TRY see Besig

IF YOU WERE COMING IN THE FALL see
   Silverberg, Frederick Irwin

IF YOUR HEART ISN'T IN IT
   (Smith) SATB CPP-BEL 1877IC1X $1.25,
      accomp tape available   (I34)
   (Smith) SSA CPP-BEL 1877IC2X $1.25,
      accomp tape available   (I35)
   (Smith) SAB CPP-BEL 1877IC3X $1.25,
      accomp tape available   (I36)

IHR BERGE LEBT WOHL see Baumann, Ludwig

IHR BRUDER, LIEBEN BRUDER MEIN see
   Schein, Johann Hermann

IHR BURSCHEN UND IHR FRAUEN see
   Watkinson, Percy Gerd

IK ZAG CECILIA KOMEN see Vermulst, Jan

IK ZEG ADIEU, WIJ MOETEN SCHEIDEN see
   Anonymous

IK ZEG ADIEU, WIJ TWEE WIJ MOETEN
   SCHEIDEN see Anonymous

IKAVA SUN OLLA ON YKSINAS see Hovi,
   Seppo

IL EST BEL ET BON see Passereau

IL EST EN VOUS see Richafort, Joannes

IL EST TROP TARD see Moustaki, Georges

IL ETAIT UNE FILLE, UNE FILLE D'HONNEUR
   (Mermoud, Robert) 3pt cor HUGUENIN
   EB 337 see from Trois Chansons
   Populaires   (I37)

IL ETAIT UNE FILLETTE see Janequin,
   Clement

IL FAUT VOULOIR see Weber, Gustav

IL N'EST PLAISIR see Janequin, Clement

IL S'APPELAIT RICHARD see Sylvestre,
   Anne

IL SE FAIT TARD, IL PLEUT, IL VENTE see
   Janequin, Clement

IL Y AVAIT UN JARDIN see Moustaki,
   Georges

I'LL BE HOME FOR CHRISTMAS
   (Strommen) SATB CPP-BEL SV8414 $1.25
                                        (I38)
   (Strommen) SSA CPP-BEL SV8415 $1.25
                                        (I39)
   (Strommen) SAB CPP-BEL SV8416 $1.25
                                        (I40)
I'LL GIVE MY LOVE AN APPLE
   (Han, Isaac) SATB,acap HARRIS HC-5032
   $.95   (I41)

(I'LL NEVER FIND) A BETTER FRIEND see
   Roscoe

I'LL REMEMBER YOU see McPheeters

I'LL REMEMBER YOU see Nygard, Carl J.

ILLUMINATIONS see Gerber, Steven R.

ILS ETAIENT TROIS PETITS ENFANTS see
   Merlet, Michel

ILS S'AIMENT see Lavoie, Daniel

ILS S'EN VONT, CES ROYS DE MA VIE see
   Piantoni, Louis

ILTALAULU; JAG SJUNGER ENSAM HAR MIN
   SANG see Palmgren, Selim

IM ANFANG WAR DER RHYTHMUS see Roeder,
   Toni

I'M BOUND AWAY
   (Owen) TTBB EARTHSNG EM-7 $.50 (I42)

I'M CONFESSIN
   (Minihane) SSAA (women's barbershop)
   BOURNE B239129 $.50   (I43)

IM FRUHTAU ZU BERGE see Koch, Johannes
   H.E.

I'M GOIN' TO SING!
   (Kjelson, Lee) SATB,acap CPP-BEL
   OCT 02061 $.95   (I44)
   (Kjelson, Lee) SA/TB CPP-BEL
   OCT 02229 $.95   (I45)

I'M GONNA SING see Nygard

IM HERBST see Brahms, Johannes

IM HOLZ see Hauptmann, Moritz

I'M IN FAVOR OF FRIENDSHIP see Hilliard

I'M IN THE MOOD FOR LOVE see McHugh,
   Jimmy

IM KRUG ZUM GRUNEN KRANZE see
   Deutschmann, Gerhard

IM MAI see Kubizek, Augustin

I'M MAKIN' MY MOVE! see Beebe

IM PRATER BLUH'N WIEDER DIE BAUME see
   Stolz, Robert

I'M PROUD TO CALL AMERICA MY HOME see
   Donnelly

I'M SEVENTEEN COME SUNDAY see Grainger,
   Percy Aldridge

IM SOMMER see Wolf, Hugo

IM VOLKSTON see Zoll, Paul

IM WALD, IM HELLEN SONNENSCHEIN see
   Biebl, Franz

IM WALDE see Mendelssohn-Bartholdy,
   Felix

IM "WEISSEN ROSSL" AM WOLFGANGSEE see
   Benatzky

IMAGO see Campana, Jose Luis

IMI MENAGENET VALZ see Weisenberg,
   Menachem

IMITATIONE DEL VENETIANO see Vecchi

IMITATIONS OF BAUDELAIRE see Goehr

IMPORTANT, C'EST LA ROSE, L' see
   Becaud, Gilbert

IMPRESSIONS OF THE HOLLOW MEN see
   Larsson, Martin

IMPROMPTU see Lilja, Bernhard

IMPROMPTU, "DER DU DIE STERNE LEITEST"
   see Sibelius, Jean

IMPROMTUS I see Zamecnik, Evzen

IMPROMTUS II see Zamecnik, Evzen

IMPROVISATION see McBride, Robert Guyn

IN A LITTLE RED SCHOOLHOUSE see
   Roberts, Ruth

IN CELEBRATION see Rudd-Moore, Dorothy

IN DE MAAND VAN MEI see Zwager, Piet

IN DEFENCE OF THE NATIVE LAND °CCU
   [Russ] jr cor MEZ KNIGA 522   (I46)

IN DEN HEMEL IS EENEN DANS see
   Schrijvers, Jean

IN DER FREMDE (FAR FROM HOME) see
   Ligeti, Gyorgy, Idegen Foldon

IN DER HEIMAT IST'S SO SCHON see Biebl,
   Franz

IN DER TAVERNE see Rosenstengel,
   Albrecht

IN EINEM ALTEN GARTEN see Watkinson,
   Percy Gerd

IN EXTREMIS: TRIPTYCH see Pinos, Alois

IN FLANDERS FIELD see Moses, Leonard

IN FLANDERS FIELDS see Tilley,
   Alexander

IN HONOREM CAROLI see Eben, Petr

IN IHM SEI'S BEGONNEN see Micheelsen,
   Hans Friedrich

IN ILLO TEMPORE see Geelen, Mathieu

IN IOWA see MacBride, David Huston

IN KOMMER FAR see Anonymous

IN MEMORIAM see Lauber, Emile

IN MUTTERS STUBELE see Heinrichs,
   Wilhelm

IN NACHT UND DUNKEL see Thoma, A.

IN PRAISE OF CYNTHIA see Dowland, John

IN PRAISE OF PEACE see Clarke, Henry
   Leland

IN PRIDE OF MAY see Weelkes, Thomas

IN SPRINGTIME see Stensaas, Janet

IN STILLER NACHT see Brahms, Johannes

IN STILLER NACHT see Schroeder, Hermann

IN 'T VOORJAAR see Altink, H.

IN 'T VOORJAAR: BLIJDE DALEN
   ZONNESTRALEN see Zwager, Piet

IN THE ATTIC see Mitchell

IN THE BEGINNING see Gregson, Edward

IN THE MERRY MONTH OF MAY see Youll

IN THE MOOD see Garland

IN THE MYSTIC LAND OF EGYPT see
   Ketelbey, Albert William

IN THE NIGHT see Gilpin, Greg

IN THESE DELIGHTFUL PLEASANT GROVES see
   Purcell, Henry

IN THESE TIMES... see Asgeirsson, Jon

IN UNISON see Duson, Dede

IN WEER EN WIND see Franken, Wim

IN WINTER'S COLD EMBRACES DYE see
   Steptoe, Roger

IN YOUTH IS PLEASURE see Howells,
   Herbert Norman

IN ZONEN see Karkoschka, Erhard

INCANTATIONS see Milhaud, Darius

INCESSAMMENT, JE M'Y TOURMENTE see
   Anonymous

INCESSAMMENT MON PAUVRE COEUR LAMENTE
   see Gero, Ihan

INDEROYA see Kvandal, Johan

INDES GALANTES, LES see Rameau, Jean-
   Philippe, Hymne Au Soleil

INDIAN SUMMER see Zamecnik, Evzen

INDIFFERENCE see Wyton

INDOLENTS, LES see Ronfort, Jean-
   Christophe

INDOVINELLO see Biscardi, Chester

INFERNO see Larsson, Martin

INFINITE SHINING HEAVENS, THE see
   Vaughan Williams, Ralph

INFINITO, L' see Mellnas, Arne

INGA LITIMOR
   (Eielsen, Steinar) SATB MUSIKK
   MH 2488 see from To Folketoner
                                        (I47)
INGALLS
   Gift Of Song, The
   (Ades) SATB SHAWNEE 1218 $.85 (I48)
   (Ades) TTBB SHAWNEE 0233 $.85 (I49)
   (Ades) 2pt cor SHAWNEE 0136 $.85
                                        (I50)
   (Ades) SAB SHAWNEE 0175 $.85   (I51)

INGEN ER SA TRYGG I FARE see Tveit, Sigvald

INNO DELLE NAZIONI see Verdi, Giuseppe

INT GROENE MET U ALDERLIEFSTE see Belle, J.

INTERROTE SPERAZANE see Monteverdi, Claudio

INTO THE GREENWOOD I GO, WITH MY DEAR BELOVED see Belle, J., Int Groene Met U Alderliefste

INTRADA FOR VOICES see Weinhorst, Richard

INTRODUCTION see Smith, Gregg

INVIOLATA see Dijker, Mathieu

INVIOLATA II see Dijker, Mathieu

INVITATION TO MADRIGALS, BOOK 3A
 °CC23U,madrigal
 TTB GALAXY 1.5256 f.s. includes works by Byrd, Morley, and others   (I52)

INVITATION TO THE PARTSONG 4: GLEES & MADRIGALS °CCU
 (Bush, Geoffrey; Hurd, Michael) SATB STAINER 3.3264 $7.95 contains works by Horsley, Mornington, Sir Arthur Sullivan and others   (I53)

INVOCATION see Pinos, Alois

INVOCATION TO SLEEP see Edwards

IO PIANGO see Lauridsen, Morten Johannes

IRELAND, JOHN (1879-1962)
 Hill, The
  SATB,acap STAINER W159   (I54)

 Sea Fever
  (Thomas, Mansel) TBarB,Bar solo,pno STAINER W 179   (I55)

IRIS see Kreiger, Arthur V.

IRISCHE LIEBESGESCHICHTEN see Schallehn, Hilger

IRISH HEIR, AN see Kreutz

IRISH SLUMBER SONG
 (Vantine, Bruce) SATB,acap PRESSER 312-41453 $.65   (I56)

IRON AGE, THE see Sallinen, Aulis

IRREVERIES FROM SAPPHO see Vercoe, Elizabeth

IRRGANG, HORST (1929-   )
 Schneemann Ladislaus °song cycle
  jr cor,child solo,perc,pno sc BREITKOPF-L 7942   (I57)

 Von Reh Und Fuchs °song cycle
  jr cor sc BREITKOPF-L 7661   (I58)

IRVING BERLIN- A CHORAL PORTRAIT see Berlin, Irving

IS see Slettholm, Yngve

ISA see Hellan, Arne

ISAACSON, MICHAEL NEIL (1946-   )
 Cradle Of Fire: Five Settings Of Holocaust Songs °CC5U
  treb cor,orch/pno TRANSCON. 991276 $8.00   (I59)

ISAAK DUNAYEVSKY AND HIS SONGS see Dunayevszky, Isaak O.

ISABEAU S'Y PROMENE
 (Grimbert, J.) 7pt mix cor HEUGEL HE 32264   (I60)

I'SE THE B'Y °folk song
 (De Cormier, Robert) mix cor LAWSON LG 52051 $.75   (I61)
 (Swift) SATB CPP-BEL DMC 08194 $1.10   (I62)

I'SE THE B'Y, BONAVIST' HARBOUR see Cable, Howard

ISN'T IT STRANGE? see Artman

ISOGLOSS see Torstensson, Klas

IST ETWAS SO MACHTIG see Seckinger, Konrad

IT ALL BEGINS WITH ME see Althouse

IT DON'T MEAN A THING (IF IT AIN'T GOT THAT SWING) see Ellington, Edward Kennedy (Duke)

IT EVEN SOUNDS LIKE CHRISTMAS see Murray

IT HAPPENED IN HELM see Davidson, Charles Stuart

IT MAY NOT ALWAYS BE SO see Rabe, Folke

IT MUST BE SPRING see North, Jack King

IT WAS A LOVER AND HIS LASS see Lane, Philip

ITALIAN SALAD see Genee, Richard

ITALIAN STREET SONG see Herbert, Victor

ITE see Consoli, Marc-Antonio

IT'S A GREAT BIG, WONDERFUL WORLD see Gallina

IT'S A HAPPY DAY see Avalos

IT'S A LONG WAY TO TIPPERARY (THE OLD TIMERS MEDLEY 3) see Beekum, Jan Van

IT'S A WONDERFUL, WONDERFUL FEELING see Besig

IT'S ALMOST TIME FOR CHRISTMAS see Besig

IT'S CHRISTMAS TIME see McCamley, Ursulene

IT'S DECEMBER ONCE AGAIN see Ydstie

IT'S FINE TO BE A YOUNG PIONEER see Peskov, N.

IT'S HARD TO SAY GOODBYE see Besig, Don

IT'S LOVE THAT MAKES THE WORLD GO 'ROUND see Lewis, A.

IT'S MY MUSIC see Ray, Jerry

IT'S NOT EASY see Crawley, Clifford

IT'S SO EASY see Bach

IT'S THE HOLIDAY TIME OF YEAR! see Snyder

IT'S THE TIME OF YEAR see Bellson, Louie

IT'S TIME FOR MOVIN' ON see Besig

IT'S TIME TO GO see Althouse

IT'S TIME TO RING THOSE CHRISTMAS BELLS! see Price

IT'S WITH YOU ALL THE TIME see Blevins, Patsy Ford

I'VE BEEN REACHIN' HIGHER see Klouse

I'VE BEEN TO HARLEM see Anonymous

I'VE BEEN WORKING ON THE RAILROAD
 °folk song,US
 (De Cormier, Robert) mix cor LAWSON LG 52386 $.85   (I63)

I'VE GOT MUSIC IN MY SOUL see Donnelly

I'VE GOT THE WORLD ON A STRING
 (Behnke) SATB CPP-BEL $1.25, accomp tape available   (I64)

(I'VE HAD) THE TIME OF MY LIFE
 (Chinn, Teena) 2pt mix cor CPP-BEL 2874TC5X $1.25, accomp tape available   (I65)
 (Chinn, Teena) SATB CPP-BEL 2874TC1X $1.25, accomp tape available (I66)
 (Chinn, Teena) SAB CPP-BEL 2874TC3X $1.25, accomp tape available   (I67)

I'VE TOLD EVERY LITTLE STAR see Kern

IVENS, J.
 Kwam, Een °see Meisje Dat Van Schevingen

 Meisje Dat Van Schevingen
  "Kwam, Een" SATB MOLENAAR 15006702   (I68)

IVORY TOWER TRILOGY see Heilner, Irwin

J

JACK BE NIMBLE see Henriksen, Josef

JACOBS
 This Is My Country
  (Bergman) SSA SHAWNEE 0298 $.60   (J1)
  (Raye) TTBB SHAWNEE 0192 $.85   (J2)
  (Scott) TTBB SHAWNEE 0013 $.85   (J3)
  (Scott) SATB SHAWNEE A0001 f.s.   (J4)
  (Scott) SSA SHAWNEE B0001 $.85   (J5)

JACOBSON
 All-American (Choral Review) °see Brymer

JACOBSON, JOHN
 Disney Spectacular °see Huff, Mac

JACOT, PIERRE
 Chanson De Route
  TTBB HUGUENIN CH 1091   (J6)

JACOTIN, JACQUES (? -1529)
 Amour De Moi, L'
  see Jacotin, Jacques, Dame D'honneur

 Amour Me Point
  (Agnel, A.) 3pt mix cor HEUGEL HE 31889   (J7)

 Dame D'honneur
  (Agnel, A.) 3pt mix cor HEUGEL HE 32130 contains also: Amour De Moi, L'   (J8)

 Je Suis Desheritee
  (Agnel, A.) 2-3 eq voices HEUGEL HE 31890   (J9)

 Mon Triste Coeur
  SATB,acap HUGUENIN EB 100   (J10)

 Qui Veut Aimer
  (Agnel, A.) 3pt mix cor HEUGEL HE 32131   (J11)

JACQUEMIN, C.
 Choral De Printemps
  3pt cor HUGUENIN CH 1083   (J12)

 Choral D'hiver
  3pt cor HUGUENIN CH 1059   (J13)

JACQUES DE COURTION
 (Mermoud, Robert) 3pt cor HUGUENIN EB 336   (J14)

JAGDLIEDER see Schumann, Robert (Alexander)

JAGDLIEDER, OP. 137 see Schumann, Robert (Alexander)

JAGDMORGEN see Schumann, Robert (Alexander)

JAGEN IST DIE SCHONSTE LUST see Gunsenheimer, Gustav

JAGER AUS KURPFALZ, DER see Kelling, Hajo

JAGER AUS KURPFALZ, EIN see Kanetscheider, Artur

JAGER LANGS DEM WEIHER GING, EIN see Lamy, Rudolf, Furchtsame Jager, Der

JAGER LUST UND FREUD, DER see Haus, K.

JAGUAREN see Gamstorp, Goran

JAHN, THOMAS (1940-   )
 'Tis A Pity She's A Whore: Ballet
  SSATB,band PEER   (J15)

JAHR UND TAG see Maierhofer, L.

JAHRESKREIS see Hempel, Rolf

J'AI CUEILLI LA BELLE ROSE
 (Pantillon, Georges-Louis) SATB,acap HUGUENIN CH 1116   (J16)

J'AI DANS LE COEUR UN GRAND AMOUR see Touati, Raymond

J'AI DE TOI UNE IMAGE see Waeber, Michel

J'AI DEMANDE Z'A LA VIEILLE
 (Hemmerling, Carlo) SATB,acap HUGUENIN   (J17)

J'AI DEMANDE Z'A LA VIEILLE see Hemmerling, Carlos

J'AI DORMI LA MATINEE see Gascongne, Mathieu

J'AI DU BON TABAC °folk song,Fr (Scherer, E.) SATB,kbd/acord,opt gtr MULLER 2747   (J18)

J'AI DU CHAGRIN (Grimbert, J.) 4pt mix cor HEUGEL HE 31904   (J19)

J'AI MIS MON COEUR see Anonymous

J'AI MIS MON COEUR see Gero, Ihan

J'AI PAR TROP LONGUEMENT AIME see Moulu, Pierre

J'AI PLANTE UNE ARBALETE see Barblan, Emmanuel

J'AI PRIS LA CLEF DE MON JARDIN see Blanchard

J'AI TANT DANSE see Caillard, Philippe

J'AI VU LA BEAUTE M'AMIE see Fevin, Antoine de

J'AI VU LE LOUP see Blanchard

J'AI VU LE LOUP, LE R'NARD, LE LIEVRE (Lallement, B.) SSA/SAB,opt fl HEUGEL HE 31861 contains also: A La Volette   (J20)

JAILHOUSE ROCK (Shaw, Kirby) SATB LEONARD-US 08657893 $.95   (J21) (Shaw, Kirby) SAB LEONARD-US 08657894 $.95   (J22) (Shaw, Kirby) SSA LEONARD-US 08657895 $.95   (J23) (Shaw, Kirby) TBB LEONARD-US 08657896 $.95, ipa, accomp tape available   (J24)

J'AIME BIEN MIEUX SOUFFRIR LA MORT see Costeley, Guillaume

J'AIME BIEN MON AMI see Du Boys, Francoise

J'AIME LE COEUR DE M'AMIE see Sermisy, Claude de (Claudin)

J'AIME PAR AMOUR see Willaert, Adrian

JALKANEN, PEKKA Piika Pikkarainen cor FAZER F 06972-4   (J25)

Vagehens Otetut Neidizet cor FAZER F 06950-0   (J26)

JAM RARA MICANT SIDERA see Brotons I Soler, Salvador

JAMAICA FAREWELL see Turellier, Jean

JAMAICAN MARKET PLACE see Farrow, Larry

JAMAICAN NOEL see Shaw, Kirby

JAMAICAN SPRING see Thliveris, Elizabeth Hope (Beth)

JAMES Roberta Lee (Whalum, Wendall) TTBB,T solo LAWSON LG 51866 $.85   (J27)

JAMFORELSE, EN see Blomberg, Erik

JANACEK, LEOS (1854-1928) Hospodine dbl cor,SATB soli,0.0.0.0. 0.3.3.1. harp,org SUPRAPHON H 4700   (J28)

Mannerchore, Band 1 °CCU [Czech/Ger/Eng] BAREN. AP 3005   (J29)

Na Solani Cartak "Schenke In Den Bergen" sc SUPRAPHON   (J30)

Schenke In Den Bergen °see Na Solani Cartak

JANEQUIN, CLEMENT (ca. 1485-ca. 1560) Au Joli Jeu Du Pousse Avant CAILLARD PC 219   (J31)

Au Joly Jeu SATB A COEUR JOIE 671   (J32)

Ce Mois De Mai SATB,acap HUGUENIN EB 479   (J33) (Thijsse, W.H.) TTBB MOLENAAR 15012603   (J34)

Ce Moys De Mai (Huguenin, C) TTBB HUGUENIN CH 633   (J35)

C'est Mon Ami (Agnel, A.) 3pt mix cor HEUGEL HE 32242   (J36)

JANEQUIN, CLEMENT (cont'd.)

Dur Acier Et Diamont (Guentner) SATB BOURNE B240507 $.65   (J37)

Il Etait Une Fillette CAILLARD R 30   (J38) (Guentner, Francis J.) cor BOURNE B239327-357 $.70   (J39)

Il N'est Plaisir (Guentner, Francis J.) cor BOURNE B239319-357 $.65   (J40)

Il Se Fait Tard, Il Pleut, Il Vente SATB,acap HUGUENIN EB 415   (J41)

Je Ne Connais Femme see Bonnet, Pierre, Francion Vint L'autre Jour

Nature Ornant La Dame (from Polyphonia) (Ouvrard, J.P.) SATB HEUGEL 509   (J42)

Or Sus, Or Sus, L'alouette A 3 (Agnel, A.) SAT HEUGEL HE 32564   (J43)

Ouvrez-Moi L'huis SATB CAILLARD PC 140   (J44)

Plus Belle De La Ville, La SSATB CAILLARD PC 100 contains also: Tu As Tout Seul   (J45)

Rossignol, Le: En Coutant (Guentner) SATB BOURNE B240515 $.95   (J46)

Si Le Coucou En Ce Mois (Guentner) SATB BOURNE B240499 $.70   (J47)

Toutes Les Nuits SATB A COEUR JOIE 670   (J48)

Tu As Tout Seul see Janequin, Clement, Plus Belle De La Ville, La

JANNE MOYE, AL CLAER see Hellinck, Lupus

JANSON, ALFRED (1937-   ) Ky Og Vakre Madame Ky [Norw] SATB,B solo,pno,db,2perc,sax NORGE   (J49)

Tre Dikt Av Ebba Lindquist °CC3U [Swed] mix cor,acap NORGE   (J50)

Vinger SATB,fl/sax,trp,trom,kbd,elec gtr, vcl,db,2perc [13'] NORGE   (J51)

JANSSEN, GUUS (1951-   ) Zonder chamber choir [9'] DONEMUS   (J52)

JAPANESE POEMS see Sveinsson, Atli Heimir

JAPANISCHE JAHRENZEITEN see De Grandis, Renato

JARDIN D'AMOUR, LE see Hemmerling, Carlos

JARDIN DES PLANTES, LE see Bonneau, Paul

JARDIN EXTRAORDINAIRE, LE see Trenet, Charles

JARNI ROMANCE, OP. 23 see Fibich, Zdenek (Zdenko)

JASON AND THE ARGONAUTS see Bailey

JASON AND THE GOLDEN FLEECE see Benton

JASTRZEBSKA, ANNA (1950-   ) Sma Eventyr [Norw] jr cor,Orff inst [10'] NORGE   (J53)

JAUBERT, MAURICE (1900-1940) Ballade Sur La Paix (from Polyphonia) SATB HEUGEL 507   (J54)

Chanson De Tessa °see Giraudoux, J.

Chansons De Tessa °see Giraudoux, J.

Complainte De France (from Polyphonia) SATB HEUGEL 506   (J55)

JAUCHZE, JUBILIER UND SINGE see Telemann, Georg Philipp

J'AURAIS GRAND TORT see Anonymous

JAVA DES HOMMES GRENOUILLES, LA (Grindel, J.) 4pt mix cor HEUGEL HE 31851   (J56)

JAZZ, BLUES, SWING, BOP see Salerno, Chris Paquin

JE CHANTE POUR VOUS see Beaucarne, Julos

JE DEMEURE SEULE EGAREE see Anonymous

JE L'AI AIMEE BIEN SEPT ANS ET DEMI see Gero, Ihan

JE L'AIME BIEN see Castro, Jean de

JE L'AIME BIEN see Verdonk, Jan

JE ME COMPLAINS see Des Prez, Josquin

JE M'Y COMPLAINS DE MON AMI see Gero, Ihan

JE NE CONNAIS FEMME see Janequin, Clement

JE NE FUS JAMAIS SI AISE see Certon, Pierre

JE NE L'OSE DIRE see Certon, Pierre

JE NE ME CONFESSERAI POINT see Arcadelt, Jacob

JE NE PUIS TENIR D'AIMER see Temps Qui Court, Le

JE NE SAIS PAS COMMENT see Anonymous

JE NE SAIS QUE C'EST D'UN FA NI D'UN SOL see Dumont, Henri

JE NE VEUX PLUS A MON MAL CONSENTIR (Agnel, A.) 3pt mix cor HEUGEL HE 32043 contains also: Pastorella, La   (J57)

JE NE VIS ONCQUES LA PAREILLE, RONDEAU see Dufay, Guillaume

JE PENSE A NOEL see Sylvestre, Anne

JE POSSEDE UN REDUIT OBSCUR (Barblan, Emmanuel) SATB,acap HUGUENIN EB 93 see from Trois Chansons D'autrefois   (J58) (Lauber, Emile) TTBB HUGUENIN SP 7   (J59) (Lauber, Emile) TTBB HUGUENIN SP 114   (J60)

JE RECOMMENCE MES DOULEURS see Gero, Ihan

JE SOUFFRE UN SI CRUEL MARTYRE see Bonnet, Pierre

JE SUIS (Frochot, J.) SATB HEUGEL HE 32549   (J61)

JE SUIS DESHERITEE see Jacotin, Jacques

JE SUIS TROP JEUNETTE (Koller, Martin) mix cor BREITKOPF-W CHB 5181 see from Vier Franzosische Liebeslieder   (J62)

JE VEUX A BOIRE see Schumann, Robert (Alexander)

JE VIS... see Hemmerling, Carlos

JE VOIS NEUCHATEL see Volery, Francis

JE VOY DES GLISSANTES EAUX see Costeley, Guillaume

JEAN DA LA "BOILLETTA" see Bovet, Joseph

JEAN P'TIT JEAN (Opienski, Henryk) "Au Flanc Du Coteau" SATB,acap HUGUENIN EB 69   (J63)

JEAN P'TIT JEAN see Barblan, Emmanuel

JEANIE WITH THE LIGHT BROWN HAIR see Foster, Stephen Collins

JEANNE see Brassens, Georges

JEANQUARTIER, MARIANNE Chanson "Lied" SATB,acap HUGUENIN 2084 H   (J64)

Fugue SATB,acap HUGUENIN   (J65)

Lied °see Chanson

JECHALI BOJARE (Klos, Ton) "Aus Nowgorod Zogen Bojaren" [Russ/Ger] TTBB BANK 11.413.001 see from Bojarenliederen 1   (J66)

JEEP, JOHANN (1581-1644)
Musica, Die Ganz Lieblich Kunst
4pt mix cor BAREN. 136   (J67)

O Music, Thou Most Lovely Art
(Harris, Jerry W.) [Eng/Ger] SSAA,
acap CPP-BEL OCT 02503 f.s. (J68)

JEFFERS
Anyone Lived In A Pretty How Town
unis cor EARTHSNG EW-3 $.50   (J69)

Roethke Songs: The Sloth And The
Serpent
SATB EARTHSNG ES-5 $.75   (J70)

This We Know
[Eng/Ger/Fr/Span] SATB/TTBB (also
available in fin, gael, heb, hun,
jap, kor, pol, rus, swe, wol for
25 cents each) EARTHSNG ES-2 $.50
(J71)
SSA EARTHSNG $.60   (J72)
TTBB EARTHSNG ES-2 $.50   (J73)

Whitman Credo
SATB,pno EARTHSNG ES-3 $1.00   (J74)

JEFFERSON
Christmas Day
SSA CPP-BEL SV8305 $.95   (J75)

JEFFREYS, G.
Felice Pastorella
(Aston, Peter) SSATB,STB soli,
strings,cont NOVELLO   (J76)

JEG LAGDE MEG SA SILDIG: FOLK TUNE FROM
VAGA see Nystedt, Knut

JEG MINNES see Kjeldaas, Arnljot

JENIN L'AVENU see Turellier, Jean

JENKINS, DAVID
Easy Mix 'N' Match: Instant Part
Singing (composed with Visocchi,
Mark) *CCU
UNIVER. UE 17953 $9.95   (J77)

JENNEFELT, THOMAS (1954-   )
Tre Etyder Tillagnada Det Patafysiska
Kollegiet *CC3U
mix cor,acap STIM 8511-062   (J78)

JENNER, GUSTAV (1865-1920)
Meeresleuchten
[Ger] wom cor,harp [3'] sc SCHOTTS
C 45916, cor pts SCHOTTS C 45917,
pt SCHOTTS C 45918   (J79)

Wohl Dem Menschen, Der Weisheit
Findet
SSAATTBB SCHOTT SKR 19001   (J80)

JENNINGS
Feast Of Lanterns
SATB LAWSON LG 52343 $.90   (J81)

JENNINGS, C.
Green-Stemmed World
unis cor,kbd KJOS C8813 f.s.   (J82)

JENNY JENKINS *folk song,US
(De Cormier, Robert) mix cor LAWSON
LG 51612 $.85   (J83)

JENSEN
Hold On To A Star
cor ALFRED   (J84)

I Remember Christmas
cor ALFRED   (J85)

J'ENTENDS PAR NOTRE RUE see Waxman

JERAKINA
(Becker, G.) men cor,acap ZIMMER. 562
(J86)

JERGENSON
Good For You And Me
SA LAWSON LG 52333 $.85   (J87)

JERICHO see Dryver, Michael

J'ESPERE ET CRAINS see Certon, Pierre

JESSLER, FRITZ
Sangerprolog: Gegrusset Alle, Die Das
Schone Lieben
men cor/mix cor BOHM   (J88)

Spatabends: Busch Und Falter Schlafen
mix cor BOHM   (J89)

JESUS' BLOEMHOF see Schrijvers, Jean

JESUS IS NU EEN KINDEKIJN CLEIN see
Schrijvers, Jean

JETZT FANGT DAS SCHONE FRUHJAHR AN
(Haus, Karl) SATB MULLER 522 f.s. see
from Volksliedsatze   (J90)

JETZT GANG I ANS BRUNNELE see
Deutschmann, Gerhard

JETZT KOMMT DIE FROHLICHE SOMMERZEIT
see Kracke, Hans

JETZT KOMMT DIE ZEIT see Lampart,
Reinhold

JEU, LE RIS, LE PASSETEMPS, LE see
Costeley, Guillaume

JEUNE AURORE, LA see Perez, David, Ecco
L'aurora

JEUNE DAME S'EN VA AU MOULIN, LA see
Willaert, Adrian

JEUNE MOINE, UN see Lassus, Roland de
(Orlandus)

JEUNES FILLES see Gagnebin, Henri

JEUNES FILLES DE LA ROCHELLE, LES
(Rochat, Jean) SATB,acap HUGUENIN
CH 2044   (J91)

JEUNES FILLES DE LA ROCHELLE, LES see
Hemmerling, Carlos

JEUNESSE see Pantillon, G.L.

JEUX see Massis

JEUX ET CHANSONS see Dere, Jean

JEVERUD, JOHAN (1962-   )
Att Bli Gammal Under Diskussion
mix cor,winds,elec bass,opt combo
STIM   (J92)

JIM, JAM, JUMP see Carey

JINGLE BELLS (THE OLD TIMERS MEDLEY 2)
see Beekum, Jan Van

JOCHUM, OTTO (1898-1969)
Aus Unserem Singschulgarten, Heft 1:
Im Reigen Des Jahres *CCU
2-3pt jr cor BOHM   (J93)

Aus Unserem Singschulgarten, Heft 2:
Heitere Muse *CCU
1-3pt jr cor BOHM   (J94)

Aus Unserem Singschulgarten, Heft 3:
Um Liebe Und Wiege *CCU
1-4pt jr cor BOHM   (J95)

Aus Unserem Singschulgarten, Heft 4:
Standelieder *CCU
1-3pt jr cor BOHM   (J96)

Drei Wiegenlieder Nach Alten Weisen
*Op.183
3pt wom cor,inst BOHM   (J97)

Es Wollt' Ein Jagerlein Jagen
*Op.44,No.1
men cor BOHM   (J98)

Goldene Blutenzeit *Op.117, cant
wom cor/jr cor,fl,clar,horn,opt pno
BOHM   (J99)

O Musika! Dir Wird Gross Lob Gegeben
*Op.148, Suite
jr cor,chamber orch/pno BOHM (J100)

Viva La Musica
4-8pt cor BOHM   (J101)

Waldkantate *Op.124, cant
mix cor,2fl,2horn,opt strings,opt
pno BOHM   (J102)

JODEL, SING
cor HIEBER MH 5029   (J103)

JOGO (AFRO-BRAZILIAN RITUAL) see Nobre,
Marlos

JOHANNA SEBUS see Zelter, Carl
Friedrich

JOHANSEN, BERTIL PALMAR (1954-   )
Mot En Ny Verden
[Norw] SATB,bass clar,string quar,
perc,trp NORGE   (J104)

JOHANSEN, KAI LENNART
Play Together 1
cor,rec,gtr,Orff inst NORSK
NMO 9329   (J105)

JOHANSSON, BENGT (1914-   )
First Encounter
mix cor FAZER (CH 32) F 05297-7
(J106)

Second Encounter
mix cor FAZER (CH 39) F 05445-2
(J107)

JOHN ANDERSON see Schumann, Robert
(Alexander)

JOHN HARDY see Bacon, Ernst L.

JOHN HENRY *folk song,US
(De Cormier, Robert) mix cor,SBar
soli LAWSON LG 52310 $1.25   (J108)

JOHNER, HANS-RUDOLF
Nachtmusikanten: Hier Sind Wir Arme
Narren
SATB HEIDELBERGER 120   (J109)

JOHNNY HAS GONE FOR A SOLDIER
(Hall) SSAA,fl,harp/pno CPP-BEL
FEC 09344 $.95   (J110)
(Jeffers) SSA EARTHSNG EW-2 $.50
(J111)
(Williams, Wendy) SATB NEW MUSIC
NMA-201 $.70   (J112)

JOHNNY ONE NOTE
(Puerling, Gene) SATB LEONARD-US
08624171 $1.25, ipa, accomp tape
available   (J113)

JOHN'S GONE TO HILO
(Mason, Roger) men cor HEUGEL
HE 32011 contains also: When Jesus
Wept   (J114)

JOHN'S LULLABY see Bruynel, Ton

JOHNSEN, HALLVARD (1916-   )
August *Op.84
[Norw] men cor,acap NORGE   (J115)

Juninatt *Op.100b
[Norw] men cor,acap NORGE   (J116)

JOHNSON
Don't Put No Chains On Me
cor ALFRED   (J117)

No Time Like The Present
ALFRED   (J118)

One Step At A Time
ALFRED   (J119)

Road Less Traveled, The
ALFRED   (J120)

JOHNSON, ALBERT R.
Advice From "Poor Richard": Courtship
And Marriage
SATB KJOS C8613 $1.00   (J121)

JOHNSON, H.
Elijah, Rock!
8pt cor SCHIRM.G 305960 $.80 (J122)

JOHNSON, JESSE
Everybody Dance
SATB CPP-BEL 7131EC1X $.95, accomp
tape available   (J123)
SAB CPP-BEL 7131EC3X $.95, accomp
tape available   (J124)
SSA CPP-BEL 7131EC2X $.95, accomp
tape available   (J125)

JOHNSON, ROBERT SHERLAW (1932-   )
Anglorum Feriae
SATB,ST soli,2ob,2trp,timp,strings
OXFORD 337170-7 $15.00   (J126)

JOHNSON, VERONICA
Christmas Tree, The *see Coslett,
Martin

JOIE see Veysseyre, Henri

JOIE, LA see Aeschbacher, Walther,
Gottin Der Freude, Die

JOIE PRINTANNIERE see Vocht, Lodewijk
de, Lentevreugd

JOIN THE WORLD see Brunet

JOLAS
Enfantillages
SSA,acap LEDUC AL 227226   (J127)

JOLEKVELD see Brevik, Tor

JOLI VILLAGE, LE see Gaillard, Paul-
Andre

JOLIVET, ANDRE (1905-1974)
Coeur De La Matiere, Le *cant
cor, solo voices,orch [30'0"]
BILLAUDOT   (J128)

Epithalame
12pt mix cor BILLAUDOT   (J129)

JONES, LLIFON HUGHES
see HUGHES-JONES, LLIFON

JONES, ROBERT [1]
Farewell, Dear Love
SATB NATIONAL NMP-195 $.85   (J130)

JONES, ROBERT FREDERICK
Habitant De Saint-Barbe, L'
SATB HARRIS HC-5029 $1.25   (J131)

JONES, STEPHEN
Mother's Eyes, A
SATB JACKMAN JMC7052   (J132)

JONES, TREVOR (1899-   )
Come Awa' Dear Old Granny
SATB HARRIS HCWO-4002 $.75   (J133)

JONG, F. DE
Spotlied
SATB MOLENAAR 15009103   (J134)

JONGE JAAR, HET see Vocht, Lodewijk de

JONQUILLES see Bovet, Joseph

JOPLIN, SCOTT (1868-1917)
Ragtime Fantasy (from Mapleleaf Rag)
(Adler, James) SATB,pno MUSIC SEV.
M70-591 $.90   (J135)

JORDAN
America The Beautiful
SSAATTBB oct DEAN HRD 152 $.95
                             (J136)

JORDAN, SVERRE (1889-1972)
Han Du Skal Takka
[Norw] 3pt mix cor,acap NORGE
                             (J137)

Pa Solsida
[Norw] mix cor,Bar solo NORGE
                             (J138)

JORGENSEN, BRENT
When I Think Of Christmas
SATB UNIVERSE 392-00647   (J139)

JOSEPH
Griselda, The Reindeer Nobody Knows
(Siegel) 2pt cor CPP-BEL DMC 08047
$.95   (J140)

JOSEPH OF ARIMATHEA see Bush, Geoffrey

JOSEPHS, WILFRED (1927-   )
Lilliputian Boating Song, The (from
The Return Of The Antelope)
unis cor,pno NOVELLO 12 0645 f.s.
                             (J141)

Rebecca
mix cor NOVELLO   (J142)

JOSHUA FIT DE BATTLE OB JERICHO
(Howorth, Wayne) SA/TB CPP-BEL
OCT 00934 $.95   (J143)

JOSQUIN
see DES PREZ, JOSQUIN

JOTHEN, MICHAEL JON (1944-   )
Over The Sea To Skye
2pt mix cor BECKEN 116   (J144)

JOUBERT, JOHN (1927-   )
Autumn Rain *Op.105
SSAA,pno NOVELLO rent   (J145)

Music For A Pied-Piper
6pt men cor,7inst NOVELLO   (J146)

South Of The Line *Op.109
mix cor,SBar soli,2pno,timp,perc
NOVELLO   (J147)

JOUR DE JOIE *CC10U
2-3pt mix cor ZURFLUH AZ 1103 (J148)

JOUR JE M'EN ALLAI, UN see Wert,
Giaches de (Jakob van)

JOUR OU LE BATEAU VIENDRA, LE see
Aufray, H.

JOUR S'ENFUIT, LE see Brahms, Johannes

JOURNEY THROUGH THE NIGHT see Matys,
Jiri

JOY AND PEACE see Schnabel, Artur

JOY AND VIRTUE FILL MY HEART see
Episcopius, L., Vruecht En Duecht
Myn Hert Verhuecht

JOYEUSE ET EDIFIANTE HISTOIRE DU GALANT
VENDU AUX ENCHERES see Bron,
Patrick

JUBILATE DEO! see Praetorius, Michael

JUDEX (MORS ET VITA) see Gounod,
Charles Francois

JUDY'S TURN TO CRY see Lewis

JUGABA LA NINA AQUELLA see Balzonelli,
Alberto

JUKE-BOX SATURDAY NIGHT see Perry

JULNATT see Sjoblom, Heimer

JUNG, HELGE (1943-   )
Tibulli Elegia Pacis *Op.42
12pt cor,speaking voice sc
BREITKOPF-L 7698   (J149)

JUNG BIN ICH *Op.38
(Gebhard, L.) men cor BOHM see from
Was Scheren Mich Sorgen: Drei
Heitere Volkslieder   (J150)

JUNG SAN MA! FESCH SAN MA! see Stolz,
Robert

JUNG SEIN UND LACHEN see Rosenstengel,
Albrecht

JUNGBRUNNLEIN, DAS see Hensel, Walther

JUNGGESELLE, DER
(Hollfelder, Waldram) men cor BOHM
see from Vier Heitere Europaische
Volkslieder   (J151)

JUNGLING LIEBT EIN MADCHEN, EIN see
Andriessen, Jurriaan

JUNINATT see Johnsen, Hallvard

JUST A LITTLE BABY see Gallina

JUST A LITTLE BIT see Kinsale

JUST BEYOND THE RAINBOW'S END see
Snyder

JUST FOR TODAY see Strommen, Carl

JUST GOTTA TRY see Derwingson, Richard

JUST MAKE MUSIC! see Stephens, Michele

JUST ONE PERSON
(Brymer, Mark) SATB LEONARD-US
08638181 $.85   (J152)
(Brymer, Mark) 3pt mix cor LEONARD-US
08638182 $.85   (J153)
(Brymer, Mark) 2pt cor LEONARD-US
08638183 $.85, accomp tape
available   (J154)

JUST YOU WAIT!, VOL. 5 *CCUL
[Russ] jr cor,pno MEZ KNIGA 499
                             (J155)

JUST YOU WAIT!, VOL. 6 *CCU
[Russ] jr cor,pno MEZ KNIGA 529
                             (J156)

JUST YOU WAIT! VOL. 7 *CCU
[Russ] jr cor,pno MEZ KNIGA 226
                             (J157)

K

'K HEB MIJN WAGEN VOLGELADEN see
Anonymous

KAAIJ, WILLEM HENDRIK V. D.
Als Ge In Blijdschap *see Ode Aan De
Muziek

Ode Aan De Muziek
"Als Ge In Blijdschap" [Dutch] 2 eq
voices,acap ZENGERINK V 337 (K1)

KABELAC, MILOSLAV (1908-1977)
Neustupujte *Op.7
men cor,0.0.0.2. 4.3.3.1. timp,perc
[9'0"] SUPRAPHON H 4611   (K2)

KAGEL, MAURICIO (1931-   )
Rrrrrr...; Sieben Chorstucke *CC7U
mix cor,opt pno PETERS 8530 (K3)

KAISER-WALZER see Strauss, Johann,
[Jr.]

KALABIS, VIKTOR (1923-   )
Autum *Op.60
mix cor [3'] CESKY HUD.   (K4)

KALINKA
(Asgeirsson, Jon) cor,solo voice
ICELAND 010-19   (K5)
(Grimbert, J.) 4 eq voices HEUGEL
HE 32345   (K6)
(Ham, J.) TTBB,band MOLENAAR 08181704
                             (K7)

KALINKA see Pitfield

KALLAN see Lilja, Bernhard

KANDER, JOHN
New York, New York: Theme
(Kern, Philip) SATB CPP-BEL
T0450TC1 $1.25, accomp tape
available   (K8)
(Kern, Philip) SSA CPP-BEL T0450TC2
$1.25, accomp tape available (K9)
(Kern, Philip) SAB CPP-BEL T0450TC3
$1.25, accomp tape available (K10)

KANETSCHEIDER, ARTUR
Als Wir Jungst In Regensburg Waren
*Op.138
men cor BOHM see from Zu Regensburg
                             (K11)

Es Blies Ein Jager In Sein Horn
*Op.148
men cor BOHM see from Zwei
Jagerlieder   (K12)

Jager Aus Kurpfalz, Ein *Op.148
men cor BOHM see from Zwei
Jagerlieder   (K13)

Schneider Jahrtag, Der: Zu Regensburg
Auf Der Kirchturmspitz *Op.138
men cor BOHM see from Zu Regensburg
                             (K14)

Zu Regensburg *see Als Wir Jungst In
Regensburg Waren, Op.138;
Schneider Jahrtag, Der: Zu
Regensburg Auf Der
Kirchturmspitz, Op.138   (K15)

Zwei Jagerlieder *see Es Blies Ein
Jager In Sein Horn, Op.148; Jager
Aus Kurpfalz, Ein, Op.148   (K16)

KANKAINEN, JUKKA
Koulukuoro 6 *see Sillanpaa, Anna-
Maija

Koulukuoro 8-Kun Pimenevat Illat...
SSA FAZER F 07814-7   (K17)

Lapsi
SSAA FAZER F.M. 07864- 2R   (K18)

KANKAINEN, TAUNO
Koulukuoro 6 *see Sillanpaa, Anna-
Maija

KANN MAN NOCH SINGEN IN DIESER WELT?
see Seckinger, Konrad

KANNO, YOSHIHIRO (1953-   )
Mythe D'hiver 2
cor,SMezT soli,perc [21'9"] JAPAN
7903   (K19)

KANONS, 187 *CCU
(Jung) PETERS 9435   (K20)

KANONS, SEVENTY see Heilbut, P.

KANTATA NA TEXT FRANZE KAFKY see
Vostrak, Zbynek

KANTATE ZUM HAUSBAU see Haus, K.

KANTATEN UND CHORWERKE I see Bruckner,
Anton

KANTATEN UND CHORWERKE II see Bruckner,
Anton

KAPER, BRONISLAW (1902-1983)
On Green Dolphin Street
(Behnke, Martin) SATB CPP-BEL
T52850C1 $1.25   (K21)

KARACHEVSKY
Agada
(Coopersmith) "Legend, A" [Heb/Eng]
TRANSCON. 990743 f.s.   (K22)

Legend, A °see Agada

KARKOSCHKA, ERHARD (1923-   )
In Zonen
SATB,2fl,clar,vcl,perc,pno SEESAW
(K23)

KARLEKEN TILL LIVET see Totari, Georg

KARLINS, M. WILLIAM (1932-   )
Concert Music No. 2
SATB,2.2.2.2. 4.2.3.1. timp,harp,
strings [14'] AM.COMP.AL. $22.90
(K24)

KARLSEN, KJELL MORK (1947-   )
Hyrder Stirrer I Natten Ut, De
SATB NORSK NMO 9951   (K25)

Kvitsunn   °Op.72
[Norw] SATB,S solo,rec,vln,hpsd
[17'] NORGE   (K26)

Three Songs For Mixed Choir
mix cor NORSK   (K27)

Tirukkural-Suite   °Op.67
[Swed] mix cor,pno [11'] NORGE
(K28)

To Folketonebearbeidelser   °Op.9,
No.9-10, CC2U
[Norw] mix cor,acap NORGE   (K29)

Tri Gjeterviser Fra Gudbrandsdalen
jr cor,fl,pno NORSK   (K30)

KARLSEN, ROLF (1911-1982)
Raven Og Lambet
mix cor,T solo NORSK   (K31)

KARMA CHAMELEON see Madsen

KARPATS'KI SICHOVYKY
see Chernyhivs'ki Sichovyky And Other
Songs

KASPERSMA, G.
Auld Lang Syne
TTBB MOLENAAR 13017103   (K32)

KATER SCHNURRIBUM see Kleine-
Mollenbick, Heinz

KATTENE see Brevik, Tor

KATTNIGG, RUDOLF (1895-1955)
Leise Erklingen Glocken Vom Campanile
(Grieshaber) mix cor,pno LEUCKART
LSB 533   (K33)
(Grieshaber) men cor,pno LEUCKART
LSB 129 f.s.   (K34)

KAUFFMAN
Hurry, Hurry Now To Bethlehem
SATB SHAWNEE 6064 $.70   (K35)

KAUFMAN
Poetry In Motion   °see Anthony

KAUFMANN, DIETER (1941-   )
Quodlibet
[Ger] mix cor,acap REIMERS   (K36)

Try
mix cor,electronic tape REIMERS
AVANTI ER 9   (K37)

Wanderlied Der Zeit
[Ger] mix cor,acap REIMERS   (K38)

KAY, HEATHER
Famous Voyage Of Christopher
Columbus, The (composed with Kay,
Peter)   °cant
cor,pno,gtr,perc voc sc UNIVER.
UE 17641 $14.95   (K39)

KAY, PETER
Famous Voyage Of Christopher
Columbus, The   °see Kay, Heather

KEARNS, ANN (1939-   )
Change Of Mood, A: Two Frost Poems
SATB BROUDE BR. f.s.
contains: Dust Of Snow; My
November Guest   (K40)

Conversation Hearts
see Three For The Children

KEARNS, ANN (cont'd.)

Dust Of Snow
see Change Of Mood, A: Two Frost
Poems

Laria Rhyme
see Three For The Children

My November Guest
see Change Of Mood, A: Two Frost
Poems

Naomi's Song
see Three For The Children

Three For The Children
SATB BROUDE BR. f.s.
contains: Conversation Hearts;
Laria Rhyme; Naomi's Song (K41)

KEEP CHRISTMAS AROUND see Thliveris,
Elizabeth Hope (Beth)

KEEP IN THE MIDDLE OF THE ROAD
(Hansen) SA KJOS C8925 $.80 (K42)

KEEP ON BELIEVING see Snyder

KEEP THE DREAM ALIVE, AMERICA see
Harris

KEEPER OF THE EDDYSTONE LIGHT, THE
(Churchill, Stuart) SAB/3pt boy cor
CPP-BEL OCT 01894 $.95   (K43)

KEEPIN' GOOD COMPANY see Fink

KEEWAYDIN see Freedman, Harry

KEF, KEES (1894-1961)
Farandole
SSA MOLENAAR 15014804   (K44)

KEIL, KEVIN
Fugues Are Fun
SAB (med) THOMAS 1C598901 $.85
(K45)

KEIN FEUER, KEINE KOHLE see
Deutschmann, Gerhard

KEIN FEUER, KEINE KOHLE see Forster,
Peter

KEIN HALMLEIN WACHST AUF ERDEN see
Bach, Wilhelm Friedemann

KEIN SCHONER LAND see Burkhart, F.

KEIN SCHONER LAND see Hein, H.

KEIN SCHONER LAND IN DIESER ZEIT see
Hensel, Walther

KEIN SCHONERES LEBEN see Biebl, Franz,
Schaferlied

KEINEN TROPFEN IM BECHER MEHR see Abt,
Franz

KELEMEN, MILKO (1924-   )
Drei Irische Volkslieder   °CC3U
mix cor,acap PETERS 8467   (K46)

KELLING, HAJO (1907-1982)
Auf, Auf Zum Frohlichen Jagen
men cor BOHM see from
Jagerlieder Fur Mannerchor   (K47)

Drei Jagerlieder Fur Mannerchor   °see
Auf, Auf Zum Frohlichen Jagen; Es
Wollt Ein Jagerlein Jagen; Jager
Aus Kurpfalz, Der   (K48)

Es Wollt Ein Jagerlein Jagen
men cor BOHM see from Drei
Jagerlieder Fur Mannerchor   (K49)

Jager Aus Kurpfalz, Der
men cor BOHM see from Drei
Jagerlieder Fur Mannerchor (K50)

KELLY, ROBERT T. (1916-   )
Four Aztec Dances (from The White
Gods)
SATB [27'] AM.COMP.AL.   (K51)

Walden Pond
cor,S&narrator,fl,pic,pno,cel,perc
[33'] AM.COMP.AL. sc $6.90, pts
$54.10   (K52)

KELTERBORN, LOUIS
A La Suisse
TTBB HUGUENIN CH 1164   (K53)

KENDALL
Over The Rainbow
SATB CPP-BEL T87850C1 $1.25 (K54)
2pt cor CPP-BEL T87850C5 $1.25
(K55)

KENINS, TALIVALDIS (1919-   )
Bon Homme!
SATB HARRIS HC-W04007 $.60   (K56)

KENNEDY, JAMES I.
Let There Be Peace
SATB,pno WEINBERGER   (K57)
SA,pno WEINBERGER   (K58)

KERN
Christmas Comes Anew!
SAB SHAWNEE 0362 $.95   (K59)

I Heard Eight Reindeer Hoofing
2pt cor CPP-BEL DMC 08198 $.95
(K60)

I've Told Every Little Star
(Ringwald) SATB SHAWNEE 1588 $.60
(K61)

KERNOA, J.P.
Education Sentimentale (composed with
Le Forestier, Maxime)
(Fourcaud, G.) 4pt mix cor HEUGEL
HE 32513   (K62)

KERR, ANITA
see GROB, ANITA JEAN

KERSTENS, HUUB (1947-   )
Crudele Acerba
SMezATB [4'] DONEMUS   (K63)

Monde Du Sommeil
cor,inst [18'] DONEMUS   (K64)

Mort, La   °Op.20
5pt mix cor,2.2.2.2. 2.2.1.0.
3perc,harp,pno,strings [14']
DONEMUS   (K65)

Mortels, Les
5-6pt mix cor [5'] (five-pt is Op.
29b; six-pt is Op. 29a) DONEMUS
(K66)

Schlaf Und Tod   °Op.22
8pt mix cor [13'20"] DONEMUS (K67)

Temps Perdu, Le   °Op.21
5pt mix cor,3.3.3.4. 4.4.4.1. timp,
3-4perc,strings [20'30"] DONEMUS
(K68)

KERSTERS, WILLEM (1929-   )
Zonnelied, Het   °Op.81
mix cor,trp,2pno,timp [10'] CBDM
f.s.   (K69)

KETELBEY, ALBERT WILLIAM (1875-1959)
In The Mystic Land Of Egypt
(Meij, J. De) MOLENAAR 08168908
(K70)

KETTERER, ERNST (1898-   )
Hab Mein' Wage Voll Gelade...
men cor BOHM   (K71)

KEYS
Mother Of Mine, I Still Have You
(composed with Szabo)
TTBB (barbershop) BOURNE B238931
$.50   (K72)

KIDS ARE SPECIAL see Bray, Jo Marie

KIEV AND OTHER SONGS see Borodievych,
Roman

KIJK NAAR DE HEMEL see Whittaker,
Roger, Show Me Your Mountain

KILLENGREEN, CHRISTIAN (1954-   )
Aftenvind
[Norw] SSSSAAAA,pno,perc manuscript
NORGE   (K73)

I Baten
[Norw] SATB NORGE   (K74)

Tidleg Varsong
[Norw] SSA NORGE   (K75)

Vingeslag
unis cor NORSK NMO 9649   (K76)

Voggevise
[Norw] men cor,acap NORGE   (K77)

KILLMAYER, WILHELM (1927-   )
Sonntagsausflug
[Ger] mix cor,acap SCHOTTS
SKR 20013 see from
Sonntagsgeschichten   (K78)

Sonntagsgedanken
[Ger] mix cor,acap SCHOTTS
SKR 20014 see from
Sonntagsgeschichten   (K79)

Sonntagsgeschichten   °see
Sonntagsausflug;
Sonntagsgedanken;
Sonntagsnachmittagskaffee   (K80)

Sonntagsnachmittagskaffee
[Ger] mix cor,acap SCHOTTS
SKR 20004 see from
Sonntagsgeschichten   (K81)

KIND BEETLE, A
[Russ] jr cor MEZ KNIGA 501 see from
Picture Songs, Vol. 5   (K82)

KINDER, HEUT' IST WOCHENMARKT see
Coenen, Hans

KINDERFANGER, DER see Stockhausen,
Karlheinz

KINDJE: OP DE PEUL MIJNS HERTEN RUST UW
HOOFDEKE see Zaagmans, Jan

KING, PATRICIA W.
Hobbit Suite
SATB,pno [5'30"] PRESSER 312-41463
$1.95   (K83)

KING AND I, THE: A MEDLEY see Rodgers,
Richard

KING GOES FORTH TO FRANCE, THE see
Sallinen, Aulis

KING HAL see Langford, Gordon

KINGFISHER, THE see Liddell, Claire

KINGMA, PIET (1926-   )
Rilke Lieder
SATB,3.3.2.2. 2.2.2.0. timp,2-
3perc,strings [18'] DONEMUS (K84)

KINSALE
Just A Little Bit
2pt cor CPP-BEL SV8633 $.95, accomp
tape available   (K85)

KIRBY
What Do All Of These Things
SAB&camb, solo voices CAMBIATA
L117208 f.s.   (K86)
BB&2camb CAMBIATA L97443 f.s. (K87)

KIRBYE, GEORGE
See What A Maze Of Error
SSATB NATIONAL CMS-127 $.85   (K88)

KIRK
Christmas Is A Time For Joy
S&camb CAMBIATA T979129 $.75 (K89)

Laughing Song
SSA SOUTHERN $1.00   (K90)

Stars Are With The Voyager, The
SATB SOUTHERN f.s.   (K91)

When It's Love
SAB&camb CAMBIATA A981159 $.75
                               (K92)

KIRK, THERON WILFORD (1919-   )
Bring A Little Joy
SS&camb,SA soli CAMBIATA A979128
$.70   (K93)

Sound The Trumpet
mix cor,opt tamb,opt bells,opt pno
FISCHER,C CM8196   (K94)

Travelin'
4pt mix cor,solo voice,acap
FISCHER,C CM8052   (K95)

KISS IN THE DARK see Herbert, Victor

KISTLER
Song Of Myself
SA CPP-BEL SV8607 $1.10   (K96)

KITES ARE FUN see Dedrick

KITSCHPOSTILLE, DIE see Kunad, Rainer

KITTELSEN, GUTTORM (1951-   )
Pa Trinn
[Norw] men cor,solo voice,fl,pno,
perc,timp NORGE   (K97)

KITZKE, JEROME P.
And Miles To Go Before I Sleep
SSAA,S solo,2+pic.0.2.0. 1.0+
baritone horn.0.0. 2perc,
handbells,pno,harp,strings [13']
AM.COMP.AL. $31.20   (K98)

Emily
SATB [6'] (Dickinson) AM.COMP.AL.
$5.00   (K99)

I Felt A Cleavage In My Mind
SATB [2'] (Dickinson) AM.COMP.AL.
$3.50   (K100)

KJAERLIGHETENS VEI see Sonstevold, Maj

KJELDAAS, ARNLJOT (1916-   )
Bonn
[Norw] SATB,acap [2'0"] NORGE
                            (K101)
Jeg Minnes
SATB [2'0"] NORGE   (K102)

Kyrkjeklokkun I Dal Kyrkje °Op.36
[Norw] men cor,TBar soli,pno NORGE
                            (K103)
Rjomegrauten
"Sagn Um "Maristigen" Fra
Tinnstoga" [Norw] TTBB [2'] NORGE
                            (K104)

KJELDAAS, ARNLJOT (cont'd.)

Sagn Um "Maristigen" Fra Tinnstoga
°see Rjomegrauten

Solsong Fra Tinn
[Norw] SATB [3'] NORGE   (K105)

Staren
[Norw] SATB,acap [3'] NORGE (K106)

Sverre-Luren
[Norw] SATB [3'] NORGE   (K107)

Three Hovden-Songs °CC3U
[Norw] mix cor NORGE   (K108)

Ved En Milepel
[Norw] SATB,acap [2'] NORGE (K109)

KJELLSBY, ERLING (1901-1976)
Gara Memo Agniata
mix cor,acap [2'] NORGE   (K110)

KJERRINGVISE MOT VINTER'N see Bergh,
Sverre

KJERULF, HALFDAN (1815-1868)
Cortege Nuptial Norvegien
SATB,acap HUGUENIN CH 661   (K111)
TTBB HUGUENIN   (K112)

Serenade
TTBB,Bar solo HUGUENIN EB 235
                            (K113)

KLANG UM KLANG see Poos, Heinrich

KLANGE DER FREUDE see Elgar, [Sir]
Edward (William)

KLANGVORSTELLUNG see Hamel, Peter
Michael

KLEIBERG, STALE (1958-   )
All-Tid
[Norw] SSAA NORGE   (K114)

Alt I Universet
[Norw] SATB manuscript NORGE (K115)

Sonetto Di Tasso
[It] SATB,org NORGE   (K116)

Tonen
[Norw] SATB,2vln,vla,vcl manuscript
NORGE   (K117)

Vaer Hilset
[Norw] SATB,2vln,vla,vcl manuscript
NORGE   (K118)

KLEIN, LEONARD
Reflections On The Days Of Christmas
mix cor,cel,harp [10'0"] (may also
be performed with 2pno or 2vibr +
harp) sc APNM $13.75, perf mat
rent   (K119)

KLEIN, RICHARD RUDOLF (1921-   )
Drei Pfalzische Volkslieder °CCU
[Ger] mix cor,pno cor pts SCHOTTS
C 46002 f.s., ipa   (K120)

KLEINE LACHMUSIK, EINE see Trapp, Willy

KLEINE-MOLLENBICK, HEINZ
Kater Schnurribum
wom cor/jr cor BRAUN-PER 1041
                            (K121)

KLEINE WEISSE MOWE see Schultze,
Norbert

KLEINE ZOO, DER see Micheelsen, Hans
Friedrich

KLEINERTZ, HANNS (1905-   )
Sing Dein Lied: In Die Dunkle Schale
Der Nacht
mix cor BOHM   (K122)

KLEINES LIED, EIN see Schallehn, Hilger

KLEINES LIED FUR DICH, EIN: DU BIST DAS
LIEBSTE MEIN see Seckinger, Konrad

KLERK, ALBERT DE (1917-   )
Doulce Memoire
SATB,acap HARMONIA HU 3811 (K123)

KLERKX, WIM (1956-   )
Variety Of Curses And A Blessing, A
mix cor [12'] DONEMUS   (K124)

KLING AUF, MEIN LIED UND SINGE °CCU
(Mahling, Christoph- Hellmuth) mix
cor BAREN. 6379   (K125)

KLINGE LIEBLICH UND SACHT see Biebl,
Franz

KLINGE LIEBLICH UND SACHT see Kuntz, M.

KLOEK, D.
Raak Mij Niet Kwijt
(Hoogeveen,G.H.) SATB MOLENAAR
13035903   (K126)

KLOKGEBED, HET: HOE HELDER KLINKT DE
KLOKKENTAAL see Maassen, Johannes
Ant.

KLOKKENVREUGD see Moerenhout, J.

KLOUSE
I've Been Reachin' Higher
SATB CPP-BEL SV8729 $1.10, accomp
tape available   (K127)

KLOUSE, ANDREA
E-Ri-E Is Arisin', The
2pt cor LEONARD-US 08598490 $.85
                            (K128)

Let Us Sing!
SATB CPP-BEL SV8707 $.95, accomp
tape available   (K129)

Never Will I Rove
2pt cor LEONARD-US 08599451 $.85
                            (K130)

KLUSMEIER, R.T.A.
Man Is Not Alone
unis cor HARRIS HC-4064 $.50 (K131)

KNOCK, KNOCK see Lewis, A.

KNORRN, HORST-DIETER
Durch Das Jahr °song cycle
4pt jr cor sc BREITKOPF-L 7691
                            (K132)

KNOW WHO YOU ARE see Ward, Norman

KNOWN ONLY TO GOD see Siltman, Bobby L.

KNOX
Follow °see Wilson, Mark

Gift, The °see Wilson

Spanish Carol, A
(Wilson) 2pt cor SHAWNEE 0323 $.95
                            (K133)

KNOX-OM-PAX see Scelsi, Giacinto

KNUMANN, JO
Trav'ler °see Wilson, Mark

KNUTSEN, TORBJORN (1904-   )
Du Hoge Fjell
[Norw] men cor,acap NORGE   (K134)

KOCH, ERLAND VON (1910-   )
Cantilena
3pt wom cor [2'30"] STIM 8511-033
                            (K135)

KOCH, JOHANNES H.E. (1918-   )
Guldne Sonne, Voll Freud Und Wonne,
Die
3-4pt mix cor BAREN. 174 see from
GULDNE SONNE, VOLL FREUD UND
WONNE, DIE   (K136)

Im Fruhtau Zu Berge
3-4pt mix cor BAREN. 174 see from
GULDNE SONNE, VOLL FREUD UND
WONNE, DIE   (K137)

Lustig, Ihr Bruder
5pt mix cor BAREN. 142   (K138)

Tanz, Madchen, Tanz...Und Andere
Chorlieder °CCU
3-6pt mix cor BAREN. 6371   (K139)

KOCHER, KONRAD
Holy Was The Night
(North, Jack) SSA ALFRED 7631 $.95
                            (K140)

KOCHER-KLEIN, HILDA (1894-1975)
Altdeutsche Liebeslieder °Op.59
3pt wom cor BOHM   (K141)

KOEPKE, ALLEN
Lord, I Wanna Climb, But I Keep
Slippin' Away
SATB CPP-BEL OCT 02505 $1.10 (K142)

Sea Is Now Calling, The
1-4pt men cor,fl,rec,pno CPP-BEL
SV8846 f.s.   (K143)

KOESTER, WERNER
Elegie
wom cor/jr cor BRAUN-PER 1027
                            (K144)

Wie Schon Ist Doch Die Weite Welt
wom cor/jr cor BRAUN-PER 997 (K145)

KOHELETH see Nuernberger, L. Dean

KOHLER, SIEGFRIED (1927-   )
Unser Das Land Und Die Zeit °Op.52,
song cycle
mix cor sc BREITKOPF-L 7670 (K146)

Von Baumen, Knospen Und Nachtigallen
°Op.51, song cycle
jr cor/wom cor sc BREITKOPF-L 7662
                            (K147)

KOHLER, SIEGFRIED (cont'd.)

Vor Dem Gewitter
mix cor sc BREITKOPF-L 7665 (K148)

KOHS, ELLIS BONOFF (1916-   )
Two Medieval Latin Songs
TTBB [8'] AM.COMP.AL. $4.60 (K149)

KOLBERG, KARE (1936-   )
Se Solens Skjonne Lys Og Prakt
[Norw] mix cor,acap [5'] NORGE
(K150)

KOLEDZIOLKI BESKIDZKIE (CHRISTMAS
CAROLS FROM THE BESKID MOUNTAINS)
see Wiechowicz, Stanislaw

KOLENDEN: SECHZEHN POLNISCHE
WEIHNACHTSLIEDER *CC16U
(Moller; Zoller) mix cor,pno/org
PETERS S 2400 (K151)

KOLLO
Heimat, Land Der Lieder
(Stegen) men cor,opt pno LEUCKART
LSB 125 f.s. (K152)
(Stegen) mix cor,opt pno LEUCKART
LSB 526 (K153)

KOLLO, RENE
Weihnachtsfriede *Xmas
men cor,opt kbd LEUCKART NWL 104
f.s. (K154)
mix cor,opt kbd LEUCKART NWL 504
f.s. (K155)

KOLME VENALAISTA KANSANLAULUA see
Mirola, Pekka

KOLNEDER, WALTER
Singen Nach Noten: Ein Lehrwerk Fur
Chorsanger (composed with
Schmitt, Karl Heinz)
[Ger] SCHOTTS ED 7396 (K156)

KOLUMBUS see Hess, Karlheinz

KOM TILL MIG see Rosenbluth, Leo

KOMM, HOLDER LENZ! see Haydn, [Franz]
Joseph

KOMM, STILLER ABEND, NIEDER see Haus,
Karl

KOMM, TANZ MIT MIR see Reinl, Franz

KOMM ZU KOLO see Biebl, Franz

KOMM ZUM TANZ see Bader, K.

KOMM ZUM TANZ see Kubizek, Augustin

KOMMT DIR MANCHMAL see Brahms, Johannes

KOMMT MIT, WOHIN DIE FREUDE ZIEHT! see
Backer, Hans

KOMT MAKKERS ALTEZAAM see Hassler, Hans
Leo, Nun Fanget An

KOMT TROMPETTEN see Purcell, Henry,
Sound The Trumpet

KOMT VRIENDEN IN HET RONDE see
Anonymous

KON-TAKTE (JAZZ CANTATA) see Puetz,
Eduard

KONIG DAGOBERT, DER
(Hollfelder, Waldram) men cor BOHM
see from Vier Heitere Europaische
Volkslieder (K157)

KONIG VON THULE, DER see Schumann,
Robert (Alexander)

KONIGE, DIE see Cornelius, Peter

KONING MIDAS KRIJGT EZELSOREN see
Burgers, Simon

KOOIJ, DANIEL
Liedjes Van En Voor Soldaten, 27
*CC27U
unis cor,gtr ZENGERINK Z 606 (K158)

KOORFANTASIE see Strating, S.

KOOTEN, GERARD VAN
Broeders Willen Wij Worden
see Kooten, Gerard Van, Onder Den
Helm

Onder Den Helm
unis cor,pno ZENGERINK Z 602
contains also: Broeders Willen
Wij Worden (K159)

KOP OP: 'T LEVEN IS NIET ALTIJD LICHT
see Stenz, Herman

KOPELENT, MAREK (1932-   )
Amusing Song
mix cor [4'] CESKY HUD. (K160)

Daybreak
jr cor [7'] CESKY HUD. (K161)

Dotty Ditties
jr cor [5'] CESKY HUD. (K162)

Four Songs To Verse By Vitezslav
Nezval
jr cor,pno [7'] CESKY HUD. (K163)

I Stumble *see Vacillat Pes Meus

Laudatio Pacis
cor,SMezTB&narrator,orch [40']
CESKY HUD. (K164)

Matka
"Mother" mix cor,fl [11'] CESKY
HUD. (K165)

Messaggio Della Bonta
cor,soli,orch BREITKOPF-W f.s., ipr
(K166)

Mother *see Matka

Ona Skutecne Jest
"She Really Exist" mix cor&jr cor,
TB&narrator,orch [45'] CESKY HUD.
(K167)

Plants
mix cor,trp,opt timp [14'] CESKY
HUD. (K168)

She Really Exist *see Ona Skutecne
Jest

Stone Prayer
dbl cor,narrator,3tom-tom [4']
CESKY HUD. (K169)

Syllabes Mouvementees
"Syllables On The Move" 12pt cor
[9'] CESKY HUD. (K170)

Syllables On The Move *see Syllabes
Mouvementees

Vacillat Pes Meus
"I Stumble" mix cor [11'] CESKY
HUD. (K171)

Woman's Lament, A
14pt wom cor&jr cor,7brass, actress
[15'] CESKY HUD. (K172)

KOR UTEN ORD see Asheim, Nils Henrik

KORDANS see Hellden, Daniel

KORINGER, FRANZ (1921-   )
Sieben Neue Madrigale *CC7U
SATB DOBLINGER 44 742 (K173)

Steirische Mundartlieder Zur Mess
*CCU
mix cor DOBLINGER 07 581 (K174)

KORN, SEBASTIAN
Massstabe: Miss Nicht Dein Leben
mix cor BOHM (K175)

KORO SUTRO, LA see Harrison, Lou

KORSANG FRA BLADET- TIL NORSK VED
OYSTEIN ARVA see Idar, Ingegerd

KORTEKANGAS, OLLI (1955-   )
Metamatiikkaa
SA,opt inst FAZER F 06935-1 (K176)

Tuutulaulu
SA FAZER F 06782- 7 (K177)

KOSAKEN- REITERMARSCH
(Karpowitsch) men cor,Bar solo
ZIMMER. 604 (K178)

KOSCHAT
Schneewalzer
(Hunger) men cor,opt pno LEUCKART
LSB 101 f.s. (K179)
(Hunger) mix cor,opt pno LEUCKART
LSB 501 (K180)

KOULUKUORO 3, KUUSI LAULUA
NUORISOKUOROLLE see Tormala, Jouko

KOULUKUORO 4, VIIHDESOVITUKSIA
KOULUKUOROLLE see Sipila, Erkki

KOULUKUORO 5, KANSANLAULUJA KAUKOMAILTA
see Papp, Akos G.

KOULUKUORO 6 see Sillanpaa, Anna-Maija

KOULUKUORO 7, SEITSEMAN JOULULAULUA see
Sillanpaa, Anna-Maija

KOULUKUORO 8-KUN PIMENEVAT ILLAT... see
Kankainen, Jukka

KOULUKUORO 9 see Arvola, Tapani

KOX, HANS (1930-   )
Doulce Memoire
4pt mix cor [6'] (text: 16th cent)
DONEMUS (K181)

Schalmei, De
4pt mix cor [6'] DONEMUS (K182)

KOYHISTA VANHEMMISTA see Hongisto,
Mauri

KRACKE, HANS (1910-   )
Ach Blumlein Blau Verdorre Nicht
3pt wom cor BOHM (K183)

Es Wollt Ein Jagerlein Jagen
men cor BOHM (K184)

Jetzt Kommt Die Frohliche Sommerzeit
men cor BOHM (K185)

Morgen Will Mein Schatz Verreisen
men cor BOHM (K186)

Schon Ist Die Welt
men cor BOHM (K187)

Weiss Mir Ein Blumlein Blaue
men cor BOHM (K188)

Wohlauf In Gottes Schone Welt
men cor BOHM (K189)

KRAKEVISE
(Eielsen, Steinar) SATB MUSIKK
MH 2466 see from Tre Folkeviser Fra
Rogaland (K190)

KRANZELKRAUT: SECHS VOLKSLIEDER VON DER
LIEBE see Kuppelmayer, Alfred

KRAPF, GERHARD (1924-   )
Bit Of Advice, A (from Three Bits)
SATB,acap LAWSON 52433 $.90 (K191)

Bit Of Bliss, A (from Three Bits)
SATB,acap LAWSON 52434 $.90 (K192)

Bit Of Wisdom, A (from Three Bits)
SATB,acap LAWSON 52435 $.90 (K193)

Wit And Wisdom
(Whalum, Wendall) TTBB LAWSON
LG 52289 $.95 (K194)

KRATOCHWIL, HEINZ (1932-   )
Abschiedslied
SATB DOBLINGER G 787 (K195)

Spiegelbild, Das *Op.156a
(Kuprian, H.) SATB DOBLINGER G 788
(K196)

KRATZSCHMAR, WILFRIED (1944-   )
Heine-Szenen *CCU
mix cor,Bar solo,string quar,harp,
prepared pno,perc,org,4.0.4.2.
4.0.0.2. strings sc BREITKOPF-L
1136 (K197)

KRAUS, JOSEPH MARTIN (1756-1792)
Funeral Sinfonia And Cantata For
Gustaf III
mix cor,orch REIMERS
MONUMENTA MUSICAE SUECICAE (K198)

KRAUSE
Two White Horses *see Hays

KREIGER, ARTHUR V. (1945-   )
Complaint
SATB,electronic tape [6'0"] APNM sc
$5.00, accomp tape available, cor
pts rent (K199)

Iris
SATB,electronic tape [5'0"] APNM sc
$5.00, cor pts rent (K200)

Passacaglia On Spring And All
SATB,electronic tape [5'0"] APNM sc
$4.75, cor pts rent (K201)

KREJCI, ISA (1904-1968)
Zpev Zastupu
[Czech] mix cor,3.2.2.2. 4.3.3.1.
timp,perc,strings SUPRAPHON
H 5714 (K202)

KREMER, CLEMENS (1930-   )
A Midi: En Souvenir D'aix
SATB,acap A COEUR JOIE 172 (K203)

KREUTZ
Irish Heir, An
SA KJOS 6186 $.80 (K204)

Who Has Seen The Wind?
SA KJOS 6187 $.70 (K205)

KREUTZER, KONRADIN (1780-1849)
Schafers Sonntagslied: Das Ist Der
Tag Des Herrn
mix cor BOHM (K206)

KROKODILROMANZE: ICH BIN EIN ARMES
    KROKODIL see Mutter, Gerbert

KROME
    Zu Rudesheim In Der Drosselgass
        (Grieshaber) men cor,opt pno
        LEUCKART LSB 126 f.s.   (K207)

KRONBRUDEN see Hammerth, Johan

KRUSE, BJORN HOWARD (1946-   )
    Elementer
        [Norw] 3 eq voices NORGE   (K208)

    Luft, Die
        [Ger] mix cor,acap NORGE   (K209)

    Orde Fer Vidare Enn Mannen
        [Norw] SATB,sax,3elec gtr,pno,elec
        bass,perc NORGE   (K210)

    Vaer Utalmodig Menneske
        [Norw] mix cor,acap NORGE   (K211)

KUBIK
    Monotony Song
        TTBB LAWSON LG 52153 $.85   (K212)

    When I Was But A Maiden
        SATB LAWSON LG 52152 $1.25   (K213)

KUBIZEK, AUGUSTIN (1918-   )
    Im Mai
        SATB DOBLINGER 44 761   (K214)

    Komm Zum Tanz
        SATB DOBLINGER 44 759   (K215)

    Liebessehnsucht
        SATB DOBLINGER 44 760   (K216)

    Nec Morti Esse Locum °Op.46
        mix cor,orch,opt org [6'] DOBLINGER
        46 058   (K217)

    Wach Auf, Mein Hort
        SATB DOBLINGER 44 758   (K218)

KUBLA KHAN see Goossens, Frank

KUCKUCK, DER
    (Fleig, G.) wom cor ZIMMER. 607 see
        from Drei Russische Volkslieder
                                      (K219)

KUHNAU, JOHANN (1660-1722)
    Tristis Est Anima Mea
        SSATB CAILLARD PC 57   (K220)

KULVERS, J.
    Te Kieldrecht
        TTBB MOLENAAR 15014303   (K221)

KUM BAH YA
    (Koepke, Allen) SATB CPP-BEL
        OCT 02524 $1.20   (K222)

KUNAD, RAINER (1936-   )
    Kitschpostille, Die °ora
        (Hubner, W.) mix cor,ST soli,
        0.0.1.0. 4.4.4.1. timp,perc,harp,
        6vcl [14'] voc sc BREITKOPF-L
        6116   (K223)

    Stimmen Der Volker °ora
        (Hubner, W.) SATB,2.2.2.2. 3.3.3.1.
        harp,pno,org,perc,strings [70']
        voc sc BREITKOPF-L   (K224)

KUNAK
    (Karpowitsch) men cor,T solo ZIMMER.
        612   (K225)

KUNST DES KUSSENS: NIRGENDS HIN ALS AUF
    DEN MUND see Burkhart, F.

KUNTZ, M.
    Klinge Lieblich Und Sacht
        mix cor BOHM see from Zwei
        Abendlieder   (K226)

    Mond Ist Aufgegangen, Der
        mix cor BOHM see from Zwei
        Abendlieder   (K227)

    Zwei Abendlieder °see Klinge
        Lieblich Und Sacht; Mond Ist
        Aufgegangen, Der   (K228)

KUNZ
    Alleluia
        SATB CPP-BEL SV8527 $1.10   (K229)

    Come On! °see Caletti

    Cross-Bearing Child, The
        SATB SCHIRM.G 320670 $.70   (K230)

    Daydreamin' Me °see Caletti

    Don't Blame Me
        SATB CPP-BEL SV8511 $.95   (K231)

    Look Around
        SATB CPP-BEL SV8501 $.95   (K232)
        SSAA CPP-BEL SV8502 $.95   (K233)

KUNZ (cont'd.)

    There's Nothin' Like Summer
        TTB CPP-BEL SV8421 $.95   (K234)

KUNZ, JACK
    Simplest Of Gifts
        SATB,pno CPP-BEL SV8732 $.95,
        accomp tape available   (K235)

KUPFERSCHMID, STEVEN
    Christmas On The Isthmus Of Panama
        (Althouse) 2pt cor SHAWNEE 0075
        $.85   (K236)

    Come Follow Me
        SATB SHAWNEE 6441 $.95   (K237)

    Santa Claus, Santa Claus (You Are
        Much Too Fat)
        SAB SHAWNEE 0355 $.90   (K238)

    Twinkle, Twinkle, Christmas Star
        2pt cor SHAWNEE 0309 $.85   (K239)

    Wake Up, It's Springtime (composed
        with Althouse, Jay)
        2pt cor CPP-BEL SV8552 $.95, accomp
        tape available   (K240)

KUPPELMAYER, ALFRED (1918-1978)
    Kranzelkraut: Sechs Volkslieder Von
        Der Liebe °Op.16, CC6U
        wom cor/jr cor,fl,ob,horn,opt bsn
        BOHM   (K241)

    Ruhloses Jahr: Vier Herbstgesange
        °Op.9, CC4U
        men cor BOHM   (K242)

KURZ, IVAN
    Blue Sky Is Lovely, The °CC5U
        unis jr cor CESKY HUD.   (K243)

    Moravian Contemplations °CC4U
        mix cor,2vln,vcl,bongos,triangle
        CESKY HUD.   (K244)

KURZE FRUHLING, DER see Mendelssohn,
    Arnold

KUTZER, ERNST (1918-   )
    Bauernwerk °Op.21, CC3U
        mix cor,4winds/pno BOHM   (K245)

    Drei Besinnliche Gesange °CC3U
        mix cor BOHM   (K246)

    Landlicher Tag °Op.95
        wom cor/jr cor,S/T solo,pno/
        instrumental ensemble BOHM   (K247)

    Lieben Bringt Gross' Freud, Das
        °Op.37, cant
        mix cor,solo voice,rec,Orff inst
        BOHM   (K248)

    Tageskreis, Der °Op.53
        mix cor BOHM   (K249)

    Und Als Die Schneider Jahrstag Hatt'n
        "Zu Regensburg Auf Der
        Kirchturmspitz" men cor BOHM
                                      (K250)
    Zu Regensburg Auf Der Kirchturmspitz
        °see Und Als Die Schneider
        Jahrstag Hatt'n

KVALLEN see Grasbeck, Gottfrid

KVAM, ODDVAR S. (1927-   )
    Atlantis °Op.18,No.4
        [Norw] men cor,acap NORGE   (K251)

    Fodt Pa Ny - I "Grevens Tid" °Op.80,
        No.1
        [Norw] SATB manuscript NORGE (K252)

    Landskapets Forvandling °Op.61
        [Swed] mix cor,acap NORGE   (K253)

    Min Onkel Hadde En Bondegard °see
        Old McDonald Had A Farm

    Morgenen °Op.49,No.2
        [Norw] men cor,acap [7'] NORGE
                                      (K254)
    Old McDonald Had A Farm
        "Min Onkel Hadde En Bondegard"
        [Norw] men cor,acap NORGE (K255)

KVANDAL, JOHAN (1919-   )
    Ballade Om Freden °Op.72
        [Fr/Norw] SATB,acap manuscript
        NORGE   (K256)

    Drivdalen
        [Norw] mix cor,acap NORGE   (K257)

    Inderoya
        [Norw] mix cor,acap NORGE   (K258)

    Ormen Lange: Faeroyisk Sogekvad
        [Norw] men cor,acap NORGE   (K259)

KVAR SKAL EG VEL AV?: VARIATIONS ON A
    NORWEGIAN FOLK TUNE see Waring, Rob

KVECH, OTOMAR (1950-   )
    From Sci-Fi Notes
        wom cor [4'] CESKY HUD.   (K260)

    Spring Motifs °CCU
        mix cor CESKY HUD.   (K261)

KVERNDOKK, GISLE
    Og Englehaerar Styrde Ut
        [Norw] SATB,pno NORGE   (K262)

KVIFOR BLINKAR STJERNONE? see Gronfur,
    Bjarne

KVITSUNN see Karlsen, Kjell Mork

KWAM, EEN see Ivens, J., Meisje Dat Van
    Schevingen

KWELLER, LEE
    Ain't Too Tired To Dance
        (Strommen, Carl) SATB ALFRED 7657
        $.95, accomp tape available
                                      (K263)
        (Strommen, Carl) 1-2pt cor ALFRED
        7659 $.95, accomp tape available
                                      (K264)
        (Strommen, Carl) SAB ALFRED 7658
        $.95, accomp tape available
                                      (K265)
    Crystal Voice
        (Strommen) SSA ALFRED 7603 $.95,
        accomp tape available   (K266)
        (Strommen) SATB ALFRED 7602 $.95,
        accomp tape available   (K267)

KWEZELKEN, HET see Lemarc, A.

KY OG VAKRE MADAME KY see Janson,
    Alfred

KYLLONEN, TIMO-JUHANI
    Alfarero °Op.5
        mix cor FAZER (CH 83) F 07759-4 see
        from Ciclo   (K268)

    Cancion Del Retorno °Op.5
        mix cor FAZER (CH 83) F 07759-4 see
        from Ciclo   (K269)

    Ciclo °see Alfarero, Op.5; Cancion
        Del Retorno, Op.5; Fuga, Op.5
                                      (K270)
    Fuga °Op.5
        mix cor FAZER (CH 83) F 07759-4 see
        from Ciclo   (K271)

KYRIE see Leavitt, John

KYRKJEKLOKKUN I DAL KYRKJE see
    Kjeldaas, Arnljot

L

LA-HAUT SUR LA MONTAGNE
(Mayor, Charles) 3pt cor HUGUENIN
EB 411 (L1)

LA, LA, MAITRE PIERRE see Gero, Ihan

LAAT ONS SAMEN NU GAAN ZINGEN see
Stenz, Herman

LAATSTE BRIEF, DE see Flothuis, Marius

LABORAVI see Rameau, Jean-Philippe

LABOUR, LE see Lauber, Emile

LABOURS, LES see Piantoni, Louis

LABURDA, JIRI (1931-   )
Brigands' Songs *see Rebellenlieder

Carmina
[Lat] wom cor [16'30"] CESKY HUD.
(L2)

Duets
wom cor,pno [13'] CESKY HUD. (L3)

Lime-Tree Has Blossomed, The
wom cor [6'] CESKY HUD. (L4)

Memento
men cor,pno [4'] CESKY HUD. (L5)

Rebellenlieder
"Brigands' Songs" mix cor [10']
CESKY HUD. (L6)

Ut Omnes Homines Virant Humaniter
mix cor [6'] CESKY HUD. (L7)

Wedding
3pt wom cor,soli,pno [35'] CESKY
HUD. (L8)

LABYRINTH see Gabel, Gerald L.

LAC LOMOND, LE
(Geoffray, Cesar) TTBB A COEUR JOIE
357 (L9)

LACHNER, FRANZ (1803-1890)
Forge, La
TTBB HUGUENIN EB 277 (L10)

LACHSIAN SONGS see Macha, Otmar, Lasske
Halekacky

LACRIMOSA SON IO see Schubert, Franz
(Peter)

LAD UP THE HILL, THE *folk song,Norw
(Haugland, Oscar) SATB HOA $.75 (L11)

LADERMAN, EZRA (1924-   )
Galileo Galilei (composed with
Darion, Joseph)
SATB,7 solo voices,2.2.2.2.
2.2.1.1. timp,perc,harp,org,
strings voc sc OXFORD 385224-1
$85.00 (L12)

LADY AND THE SWINE, THE (NURSERY
RHYMES, NO.3) see Walters, Edmund

LADY IN NEW YORK HARBOR see Wurtzel

LADY OF THE HARBOR see Bacak, Joyce
Eilers

LADY STANDS FOR LIBERTY, THE see
Robinson, Russ

LADY WITH SORE EYES, THE see Smith,
Gregg

LADY, YOUR WORDS DO SPITE ME see
Wilbye, John

LAET ONS NU AL VERBLIJDEN see Belle, J.

LAET VAREN ALLE FANTASIE see
Episcopius, L.

LAETANTIUS, BR.
Als In Ons Hart
(Biersma, P.) "Lied Weerklinkt,
Een" SATB MOLENAAR 15000402 (L13)

Holland
(Schreuder) SATB MOLENAAR 15004103
(L14)
Lied Weerklinkt, Een *see Als In Ons
Hart

Nachtegaal, De
(Biersma, P.) SATB MOLENAAR
15006902 (L15)

LAETANTIUS, BR. (cont'd.)
Orgellied, Het
(Hildebrand) SATB MOLENAAR 15007704
(L16)

LAFARGE, GUY
Boites A Musique, Les *see Blanche

LAGA'AT MAKOM see Tal, Joseph

LAGGER, OSCAR
Danse Macabre
SATB,acap HUGUENIN CH 2000 (L17)
TTBB HUGUENIN CH 2025 (L18)

Villanelle
SATB,acap HUGUENIN CH 1199 (L19)

LAI POUR BERCER see Hemmerling, Carlos

LAINE, LA
(Grimbert, J.) 4 eq voices HEUGEL
HE 31895 (L20)

LAINE DES MOUTONS, LA
(Perret, Francis) SATB,acap HUGUENIN
CH 2030 (L21)

LAISSE TES CHEVEUX see Huguenin,
Charles

LAISSEZ LA MORT ME PRENDRE see
Monteverdi, Claudio, Lasciate Mi
Morire

LAISSEZ VENIR A MOI LES PETITS ENFANTS
see Huguenin, Charles

LAKE ISLE OF INNISFREE, THE see Fuller,
Jeanne Weaver

LAMA, S.
Vagues De La Mer, Les (composed with
Heiman, N.)
(Passaquet, R.) 4pt mix cor HEUGEL
HE 32604 (L22)

LAMBERT
When Johny Comes Marching Home
SSA,pno FISCHER,C CM5322 (L23)

LAMBERT, MICHEL
Pour Estre Ayme
(Sanvoisin, M.) 3pt cor,2treb inst,
cont HEUGEL HE 31937 (L24)

LAMENT FOR BEOWULF see Hanson, Howard

LAMENTATION see Cossetto, Emil

LAMENTATIONS FOR JULIET see Plunkett,
Elizabeth Kuhn

LAMENTO see Welin, Karl-Erik

LAMENTO-BURLETTA see Bergman, Erik

LAMENTO DI ARIANA ABBANDONATA see
Neumann, Veroslav, Narek Opustene
Ariadny

LAMENTO DI ORLANDO see Bialas, Gunter

LAMP, THE see Hamilton, Iain

LAMPART, KARL (1900-1974)
Aus Dem Jahreslauf *Op.128, CC6U
unis jr cor,pno/strings,fl,horn,opt
perc BOHM (L25)

Mai Ist Da!, Der *Op.88, CC5U
jr cor,pno/3inst BOHM (L26)

Seltsame Geschichten *Op.90
unis jr cor,2vln,vcl,pno BOHM (L27)

LAMPART, REINHOLD
Jetzt Kommt Die Zeit
mix cor,pno&combo/strings BOHM
(L28)

Lob Des Sommers
1-3pt jr cor/wom cor,pno BOHM (L29)

LAMY, RUDOLF (1905-1962)
Furchtsame Jager, Der *Op.2
"Jager Langs Dem Weiher Ging, Ein"
mix cor BOHM (L30)

Jager Langs Dem Weiher Ging, Ein
*see Furchtsame Jager, Der

LANAUVE, G. DE
Chant Du Grillon (composed with
Passaquet, Raphael)
see Delarue-Mardrus, Lucie, Automne

LANCE
Night Carol *Xmas
SATB oct DEAN HRD 260 $1.10 (L31)

LANCEN, SERGE (1922-   )
Hymne De Fraternite (from Poeme
Oecumenique)
(Thirault, R.) SATB MOLENAAR
13022404 (L32)

LANCHA NUEVA ESPARTA, LA
(Fourcaud, G.) mix cor HEUGEL
HE 32518 (L33)

LAND
I Hear A Sky-Born Music
SATB SOUTHERN $.55 (L34)

Let Me Go
SATB SOUTHERN $.55 (L35)

LAND OF CHILDREN, THE *CCU
[Russ] jr cor,pno MEZ KNIGA 494 (L36)

LAND OF SONG see Harry, Lyn

LAND OF THE OCTOBER REVOLUTION, THE
*CCU
[Russ] MEZ KNIGA 156 (L37)

LAND OF THE SILVER BIRCH
(Han, Isaac) SATB HARRIS HC-5034
$1.25 (L38)

LANDLICHE KONZERTPROBE, DIE see Suppe,
Franz von

LANDLICHER TAG see Kutzer, Ernst

LANDLORD, FILL THE FLOWING BOWL
(Jeffers) TTBB EARTHSNG EM-5 $.50
(L39)

LANDOWSKI, M.
Help, Help Vatelot
mix cor,inst [5'] SALABERT
EAS18338P (L40)

LANDRY, FREDY
Au Pays
SATB,acap HUGUENIN CH 1033 (L41)
TTBB HUGUENIN CH 1032 (L42)

Cabane, La
"Wildhorn" TTBB HUGUENIN CH 912
(L43)

Ce Petit Village
1-2pt cor,pno,fl HUGUENIN CH 1063
(L44)

Chanson Du Vigneron, La
SATB,acap HUGUENIN CH 1051 (L45)

Chante! Mon Village...
TTBB HUGUENIN CH 1128 (L46)
SATB,acap HUGUENIN CH 1129 (L47)

Salut! Terre Des Monts!
SATB,acap HUGUENIN CH 877 (L48)

Terre Promise
SATB,acap HUGUENIN CH 1127 (L49)

Wildhorn *see Cabane, La

LANDSCAPES see Paynter, John P.

LANDSKAP MED SNE see Soderlind, Ragnar

LANDSKAPETS FORVANDLING see Kvam,
Oddvar S.

LANE
I Hear Music *see Loesser

LANE, PHILIP (1950-   )
Blow, Blow, Thou Winter Wind
SSA,pno ROBERTON 3073 see from Five
Shakespeare Lyrics (L50)

Five Shakespeare Lyrics *see Blow,
Blow, Thou Winter Wind; Full
Fathom Five; It Was A Lover And
His Lass; Tell Me Where Is Fancy
Bred; Where The Bee Sucks (L51)

Full Fathom Five
SSA,pno ROBERTON 3073 see from Five
Shakespeare Lyrics (L52)

It Was A Lover And His Lass (from
Five Shakespeare Lyrics)
SSA,pno ROBERTON 3073 see from Five
Shakespeare Lyrics (L53)
SSA,pno [1'30"] ROBERTON 75348
(L54)

Tell Me Where Is Fancy Bred
SSA,pno ROBERTON 3073 see from Five
Shakespeare Lyrics (L55)

Where The Bee Sucks
SSA,pno ROBERTON 3073 see from Five
Shakespeare Lyrics (L56)

LANG, H.
Aus Grauer Stadte Mauern
men cor BOHM (L57)

Heimliche Liebe
men cor BOHM (L58)

LANG, HANS
Weihnachtsuhr, Die (composed with
Heinrichs, Wilhelm)
wom cor/jr cor BRAUN-PER 1017 (L59)

LANG, HERMANN
  Chanson Tendre (from Ruy Blas)
    TTBB HUGUENIN EB 259   (L60)
    3pt cor HUGUENIN EB 260   (L61)

LANGER, J.
  Hirten-Boarischer
    cor HIEBER MH 5031   (L62)

LANGFORD, GORDON
  King Hal
    TTBB,pno ROBERTON 53138   (L63)

LANGREE, ALAIN
  Bourree Auvergnate
    (Turellier, Jean) SAB,3inst HEUGEL
    HE 31915   (L64)

  Or, Vous Tremoussez, Pasteurs
    see Dukas, Paul, Bon Jour, Bon Mois

LANGUE DE CHEZ NOUS, LA see Duteil,
  Yves

LANNER, JOSEF (1801-1843)
  Schonbrunner, Die
    (Scholtys, H.) cor,pno cor pts,voc
    sc DOBLINGER 46 827   (L65)

LAPINHAS-CHRISTMAS SONGS see Prado,
  Jose-Antonio (Almeida)

LAPLANTE, PIERRE
  Three Dishes And Six Questions
    SATB BOURNE B238709 $1.10   (L66)

LAPRUS, LUCJAN
  Do Matki: Kolysanka Polska, U Moji
    Matusi
    "To Mother: Polish Cradle-Song, At
    My Mother's Home" [Polish]
    POLSKIE PLCH 303   (L67)

  To Mother: Polish Cradle-Song, At My
    Mother's Home *see Do Matki:
    Kolysanka Polska, U Moji Matusi

LAPSI see Kankainen, Jukka

LARIA RHYME see Kearns, Ann

LARK IN A NET, THE see Smith, Gregg

LARK IN THE CLEAR AIR, THE see Deale,
  Edgar

LARSEN, PAT
  White Star A Bright Star
    2pt cor JACKMAN JMC7090   (L68)

LARSON
  Crescent Moon Now Floating
    SATB LAWSON LG 52357 $.85   (L69)

LARSSON, BJORN (1958-   )
  Bortbytingarna
    cor, solo voices,orch SUECIA (L70)

LARSSON, LARS-ERIK (1908-1986)
  Norge I Rodt, Hvitt Og Blatt
    mix cor,opt kbd MUSIKK MH 2436
                                  (L71)
    3-4pt jr cor MUSIKK MH 2435   (L72)

LARSSON, MARTIN (1967-   )
  Impressions Of The Hollow Men
    mix cor STIM   (L73)

  Inferno
    8pt mix cor STIM   (L74)

LAS, JE N'IRAI PLUS, JE N'IRAI PAS see
  Costeley, Guillaume

LAS! VOULEZ-VOUS QU'UNE PERSONNE
  CHANTE? see Lassus, Roland de
  (Orlandus)

LASCIATE MI MORIRE see Monteverdi,
  Claudio

LASCIATEMI MORIRE see Monteverdi,
  Claudio

LASCIATI I MONTI see Monteverdi,
  Claudio

LASS FROM THE LOW COUNTRY, THE
  (LaMance) SSA,horn LAWSON LG 52187
  $.85   (L75)

LASS, O LASS see Distler, Hugo

LASS OF RICHMOND HILL see Willcocks,
  David Valentine

LASSKE HALEKACKY see Macha, Otmar

LASSO, ORLANDO DI
  see LASSUS, ROLAND DE

LASST UNS WANDERN see Pappert, Robert

LASSUS, ROLAND DE (ORLANDUS)
  (1532-1594)
  Bauer Von Eselskirchen, Der
    (Mayer, H.) SATB MOLENAAR 15000803
                                  (L76)
  Bonjour Mon Coeur
    SATB CAILLARD PC 194   (L77)

  Ce Beau Printemps
    SATB,acap HUGUENIN EB 95   (L78)
    TTBB HUGUENIN EB 94   (L79)

  Day After Day They All Say "Sing"
    *see Tutto Lo Di Mi Dici

  Deus Qui Bonum Vinum Creasti (from
    Polyphonia)
    (Ouvrard, J.P.) SATB HEUGEL 510
                                  (L80)
  Eco
    CAILLARD PC 220   (L81)

  Fuyons Tous D'amour Le Jeu
    SATB,acap HUGUENIN EB 152   (L82)

  Jeune Moine, Un
    SATB CAILLARD PC 195   (L83)

  Las! Voulez-Vous Qu'une Personne
    Chante?
    see Brahms, Johannes, Jour
    S'enfuit, Le

  Lucescit; Nunc Bibamus (from
    Polyphonia)
    (Ouvrard, J.P.) SATB HEUGEL 511
                                  (L84)
  Madrigal
    10pt mix cor HEUGEL HE 32269 (L85)
    SATB,acap HUGUENIN EB 31B   (L86)
    (Perret, F.) TTBB HUGUENIN EB 487
                                  (L87)
  Mailied
    TTBB HUGUENIN EB 24   (L88)

  Mon Coeur Se Recommande A Vous
    SATB HARMONIA 3658   (L89)

  Ne T'y Fie Pas
    SATB,acap HUGUENIN EB 99   (L90)

  Nuit Froide Et Sombre, La
    SATB CAILLARD PC 216   (L91)

  O Doux Parlez
    (Grimbert, J.) dbl cor HEUGEL
    HE 32158   (L92)

  Pronuba Juno (from Polyphonia)
    (Ouvrard, J.P.) 4pt mix cor HEUGEL
    512   (L93)

  Quand Mon Mari Vient De Dehors
    see Brahms, Johannes, Jour
    S'enfuit, Le
    SATB,acap HUGUENIN EB 168F   (L94)

  Quel Rossignuol
    (Stevens) SSATB,acap OXFORD
    19 385723 5   (L95)

  Soyons Joyeux Sur La Plaisant Verdure
    SATB CAILLARD PC 148   (L96)

  Toi Qui M'es Chere
    SATB,acap HUGUENIN EB 14   (L97)

  Tutto Lo Di Mi Dici
    "Day After Day They All Say "Sing""
    [Eng/Lat] 8pt cor SCHIRM.G 320870
                                  (L98)
LAST, GERT
  Funf Neue Lieder *see Habersack,
    Karl

LAST FAREWELL, THE see Whittaker, Roger

LAST FLEETING CLOUD OF THE STORM see
  Rimsky-Korsakov, Nikolai

LAST INVOCATION, THE see Danner

LAST OF THE LITTERBUGS, THE see
  Roberts, Ruth

LAST ROSE OF SUMMER, THE *folk song,Ir
  (Ierswoud, Frederik Van) SATB,S solo
    HARMONIA 3672   (L99)
  (Thijsse, Wim Herman) "Letzte Rose"
    SSA,acap (med diff) ZENGERINK V 448
                                  (L100)
  (Wielakker, Gerhard) TTBB,T solo
    HARMONIA 3775   (L101)

LAST ROSE OF SUMMER, THE see Lightfoot,
  Mary Lynn

LAST SHOPPING DAY UNTIL CHRISTMAS, THE
  see Albrecht

LATHAM, WILLIAM PETERS (1917-   )
  Flow, O My Tears
    SATB,acap PRESSER 352-00173 $.85
                                  (L102)

LAUBER, EMILE
  Agneau Blanc, L'
    TTBB HUGUENIN SP 108   (L103)

  Au Bord D'une Tombe
    TTBB HUGUENIN SP 113   (L104)

  Au Pressoir (from La Fete De La
    Vigne)
    TTBB HUGUENIN SP 14   (L105)

  Aube, L'
    TTBB HUGUENIN SP   (L106)

  Chansons Tirees De "La Gloire Qui
    Chante" *CC30L
    HUGUENIN   (L107)

  Chant De Printemps
    TTBB HUGUENIN SP 9   (L108)

  Chant Des Moissonneurs
    TTBB HUGUENIN SP 103   (L109)

  Chant Des Paysans (from Pestalozzi)
    TTBB HUGUENIN SP 105   (L110)

  Chant Du Berger
    TTBB HUGUENIN SP see from Quatuors
    Pour Voix D'hommes: C.1   (L111)

  Chant Du Bucheron
    TTBB HUGUENIN SP 102   (L112)

  Chant Du Premier Aout 1914
    TTBB HUGUENIN SP 1   (L113)

  Chant Du Printemps
    TTBB HUGUENIN SP 106   (L114)

  Chasse Au Cerf
    TTBB HUGUENIN SP see from Quatuors
    Pour Voix D'hommes: C.4   (L115)

  Chasseur, Le
    TTBB HUGUENIN SP see from Quatuors
    Pour Voix D'hommes: C.2   (L116)

  Cher Pays
    TTBB HUGUENIN SP 10   (L117)
    TTBB HUGUENIN SP 111   (L118)

  Cloche Du Soir
    TTBB HUGUENIN SP see from Quatuors
    Pour Voix D'hommes: C.2   (L119)

  Croix En Valais, Une
    TTBB HUGUENIN SP see from Quatuors
    Pour Voix D'hommes: C.1   (L120)

  Dans La Foret
    TTBB HUGUENIN SP see from Quatuors
    Pour Voix D'hommes: C.4   (L121)

  Depart Des Hirondelles
    TTBB HUGUENIN SP see from Quatuors
    Pour Voix D'hommes: C.2   (L122)

  En Allant A La Foire
    TTBB HUGUENIN SP see from Quatuors
    Pour Voix D'hommes: C.1   (L123)

  Hymne A La Patrie
    TTBB HUGUENIN SP 12   (L124)

  Hymne A Pestalozzi
    TTBB HUGUENIN SP 16B   (L125)
    men cor HUGUENIN SP   (L126)

  In Memoriam
    TTBB HUGUENIN SP 8   (L127)

  Labour, Le
    TTBB,T solo HUGUENIN SP 101   (L128)

  Mare Aux Elfes, La
    TTBB HUGUENIN SP see from Quatuors
    Pour Voix D'hommes: C.4   (L129)

  Notre Terre
    TTBB HUGUENIN SP 110   (L130)

  Nous Chanterons, Nature
    TTBB HUGUENIN CH 992   (L131)

  O Divin Soleil (Chanson De Labour)
    TTBB HUGUENIN SP 5   (L132)

  Octobre
    TTBB HUGUENIN SP 11   (L133)

  Pays, Le
    TTBB HUGUENIN SP 109   (L134)

  Quand Je Vais Au Bois
    SATB,acap HUGUENIN EB 89   (L135)

  Quand On Y Pense
    TTBB HUGUENIN SP see from Quatuors
    Pour Voix D'hommes: C.3   (L136)

  Quatuors Pour Voix D'hommes: C.1
    *see Chant Du Berger; Croix En
    Valais, Une; En Allant A La Foire
                                  (L137)

LAUBER, EMILE (cont'd.)

Quatuors Pour Voix D'hommes: C.2
*see Chasseur, Le; Cloche Du
Soir; Depart Des Hirondelles
(L138)

Quatuors Pour Voix D'hommes: C.3
*see Quand On Y Pense; Sur
L'alpe; Tilleul, Le (L139)

Quatuors Pour Voix D'hommes: C.4
*see Chasse Au Cerf; Dans La
Foret; Mare Aux Elfes, La (L140)

Ronde Des Vendanges
SATB,acap HUGUENIN SP (L141)

Sempach
TTBB,Bar solo HUGUENIN SP 3 (L142)

Serenade
TTBB HUGUENIN SP (L143)

Soir D'ete (from Pestalozzi)
TTBB HUGUENIN CH 2020 (L144)
TTBB HUGUENIN SP 15 (L145)

Soleil De Juin
TTBB HUGUENIN SP 11 (L146)
TTBB HUGUENIN CH 2021 (L147)

Sur L'alpe
TTBB HUGUENIN SP see from Quatuors
Pour Voix D'hommes: C.3 (L148)

Terre Haute (from La Gloire Qui
Chante)
TTBB HUGUENIN SP (L149)

Tilleul, Le
TTBB HUGUENIN SP see from Quatuors
Pour Voix D'hommes: C.3 (L150)

Tout A L'entour De Nos Remparts
TTBB HUGUENIN SP (L151)

Vieille Maison Vol. 1, La *CC12L
eq voices,pno HUGUENIN SP (L152)

Vieille Maison Vol. 2, La *CC12L
eq voices,pno HUGUENIN SP (L153)

Vins Du Pays Romand, Les (from La
Fete De La Vigne)
TTBB HUGUENIN SP 13 (L154)

Voila L'beau Temps
TTBB HUGUENIN SP 117 (L155)

LAUBER, JOSEPH (1864-1952)
Chanson De Printemps
TTBB HUGUENIN EB 213 (L156)

Sur L'alpe
TTBB HUGUENIN CH 993 (L157)

Travaillons
TTBB HUGUENIN CH 994 (L158)

LAUD AL PUR E MEISTER GRISCHUN see
Aeschbacher, Walther

LAUDATE PACEM see Matthus, Siegfried

LAUDATIO PACIS see Kopelent, Marek

LAUFET ALL, IHR KINDER *Xmas,Span
(Deutschmann, Gerhard) mix cor BOHM
(L159)

LAUGHING MATTER, A see Chinn, Teena

LAUGHING SONG see Kirk

LAUGHING SONG see Pfautsch, Lloyd Alvin

LAUGHING SONG see Wetzler

LAULU LEMMINKAISELLE see Sibelius, Jean

LAULUJA SEKAKOORILLE see Sibelius, Jean

LAUR, F.
Drapeau, Le
1-4pt cor HUGUENIN see from
CHANSONS POUR LA JEUNESSE,
TROISIEME CAHIER (L160)

LAURA
(Buchholz) SATB CPP-BEL TO945LC1
$1.25, accomp tape available (L161)
(Buchholz) SSA CPP-BEL TO945LC2
$1.25, accomp tape available (L162)
(Buchholz) SAB CPP-BEL TO945LC3
$1.25, accomp tape available (L163)

LAURETTI: ALTRE CANZONE AMOROSE see
Filas, Juraj

LAURIDSEN, MORTEN JOHANNES (1943-   )
Amor, Io Sento L'alma (from
Madrigali: Six Fire-Songs On
Italian Renaissance Poems)
SATB oct PEER 61651-121 $.85 (L164)

LAURIDSEN, MORTEN JOHANNES (cont'd.)

Io Piango (from Madrigali: Six Fire-
Songs On Italian Renaissance
Poems)
SATB oct PEER 61646-121 $.85 (L165)

Luci Serene E Chiare (from Madrigali:
Six Fire-Songs On Italian
Renaissance Poems)
SATB oct PEER 61652-121 $.85 (L166)

Ov'e, Lass', Il Bel Viso? (from
Madrigali: Six Fire-Songs On
Italian Renaissance Poems)
SATB oct PEER 61649-121 $.95 (L167)

Quando Son Piu Lonton (from
Madrigali: Six Fire-Songs On
Italian Renaissance Poems)
SATB oct PEER 61650-121 $.95 (L168)

Se Per Havervi, Oime (from Madrigali:
Six Fire-Songs On Italian
Renaissance Poems)
SATB oct PEER 61653-121 $.95 (L169)

LAVOIE, DANIEL
Ils S'aiment
(Ott, Norbert) SAB,acap A COEUR
JOIE 050 (L170)

LAWRENCE
With A Ring And A Jingle And A Pop
SATB CPP-BEL SV8714 $1.10, accomp
tape available (L171)

LAWRENCE, STEPHEN L.
Concerto For Singing Chickens And
Piano
2-4pt mix cor CPP-BEL SV8837 $.95
(L172)
Do You Believe In Miracles? (composed
with Houston, Jari)
SATB ALFRED 7585 (L173)

Dwaine The Reindeer
1-2pt cor CPP-BEL SV8809 $.95,
accomp tape available (L174)
3pt mix cor CPP-BEL SV8808 $.95,
accomp tape available (L175)

Sing A Little Song
2-3pt treb cor CPP-BEL SV8828 $1.10
(L176)
Valentine Song, The
SATB CPP-BEL SV8734 $1.25, accomp
tape available (L177)

LAWRENCE, STEVE
Have A Jolly, Jolly, Jolly, Jolly
cor ALFRED (L178)

LAWSON, PETER (1951-   )
Supertoad *educ/show
jr cor voc sc UNIVER. UE 17640
$9.95 (L179)

LAY OF THE BELL, THE see Bruch, Max,
Lied Von Der Glocke, Das

LAYOLLE, FRANCESCO (fl. 1530-1540)
Bourguignons, Les
(Agnel, A.) 2 eq voices HEUGEL
HE 32596 (L180)

LAZY KINDA BLUES see Moore, Donald

LAZY RIVER see Carmichael, Hoagy

LAZY WIFE see Hoddinott, Alun

LE BARON, ANNE
Concerto For Active Frogs
4-8pt mix cor,inst,perc,electronic
tape [10'] AM.COMP.AL. $5.40
(L181)

LE BLANC, DIDIER (fl. ca. 1580)
Avecques Vous Mon Amour Finira
see Le Blanc, Didier, Mon Coeur Se
Recommande A Vous

Elle S'en Va De Moi La Mieux Aimee
(Agnel, A.) 2-3pt mix cor HEUGEL
HE 32144 (L182)

Mignonnette
(Grimbert, J.) 4pt mix cor HEUGEL
HE 32411 (L183)

Mon Coeur Se Recommande A Vous
(Agnel, A.) 2 eq voices HEUGEL
HE 32142 contains also: Avecques
Vous Mon Amour Finira (L184)

LE CANNU, G.
Rat, Le
(Tritsch, J.) 4 eq voices HEUGEL
HE 32253 (L185)

LE FANU, NICOLA
see LEFANU, NICOLA

LE FEBVRE, JACQUES
Aime-Moi, Bergere
(Gounod, Charles) CAILLARD PC 127
(L186)

LE FORESTIER, MAXIME
Dialogue
(Holstein, Jean-Paul) SAB,opt pno
CAILLARD PC 174 (L187)

Education Sentimentale
(Holstein, Jean-Paul) SAB,opt pno
CAILLARD PC 173 (L188)

Education Sentimentale *see Kernoa,
J.P.

Fontenay Aux Roses
(Holstein, Jean-Paul) SAB,opt pno
CAILLARD PC 175 (L189)

LE JEUNE, CLAUDE (1528-1600)
Amour, Quand Fus-Tu Ne?
(Grimbert, J.) 7pt mix cor HEUGEL
HE 32196 (L190)

Fuyons Tous D'amour Le Jeu
SATB,acap HUGUENIN EB 360 (L191)

O Occhi Mansa Mia-Toi Seule En Qui
J'espere
SATB,acap HUGUENIN EB 372 (L192)

O Vilanella-Gente Pastourelle
SATB,acap HUGUENIN EB 62 (L193)

Puce, La
SATB,acap HUGUENIN EB 448 (L194)

LE LACHEUR, REX
Seagulls
SATB HARRIS HC-6005 $.95 (L195)

LEADEN ECHO AND THE GOLDEN ECHO, THE
see Milner, Anthony

LEADEN SKY see Permont, Haim, Shmei
Oferet

LEAF
Beware The Wind Of Spring
SATB KJOS 8680 $.80 (L196)

LEARSONGS see Mathias, William

LEAVING MOTHER RUSSIAN see Solomon,
Robert

LEAVITT, JOHN
Christmas Pickle Rhapsody, A: Jolly
Old Saint Pickle-Less
3pt mix cor,pno CPP-BEL SV8910
$1.10 (L197)

Country Corn
SATB CPP-BEL SV8919 $1.10, accomp
tape available (L198)

Festival Sanctus
SATB CPP-BEL SV8821 $.95 (L199)

I Love A Broadway Show
SATB CPP-BEL SV8806 $.95, accomp
tape available (L200)

Kyrie
SATB CPP-BEL SV8904 $1.10 (L201)
SSA CPP-BEL SV8906 $1.10 (L202)
SAB CPP-BEL SV8905 $1.10 (L203)

Singin' You A Song
SATB CPP-BEL SV8932 $1.10, accomp
tape available (L204)
SAB CPP-BEL SV8933 $1.10, accomp
tape available (L205)

You're Looking Good, America
3pt mix cor CPP-BEL SV8922 $1.10,
accomp tape available (L206)
2pt cor CPP-BEL SV8923 $1.10,
accomp tape available (L207)
SATB CPP-BEL SV8920 $1.10, accomp
tape available (L208)
TTB CPP-BEL SV8921 $1.10, accomp
tape available (L209)

LEB WOHL, MEIN TABOR
(Karpowitsch) men cor ZIMMER. 611
(L210)

LEBENSLAUF: GEBET FUR DIE UNBELEHRBAREN
see Genzmer, Harald

LEBENSREGELN see Biebl, Franz

LECHNER
Gott Bhute Dich
see MADRIGALE FUR GEMISCHTEN CHOR A
CAPPELLA: BLATT VII

LECTURE see Emmerik, Ivo Van

LEE
Advent Legend, An (composed with
Wagner)
SAB SHAWNEE 5390 $.95 (L211)

LEE (cont'd.)

Pretty Little Angel Eyes °see Boyce

LEECH, BRYAN JEFFERY (1931-   )
To The Hills
(Gay, Ruth Morris) SATB BOCK BG2057
$.85   (L212)

LEEF VANDAAG see Wyrtzen, Don, Love Is
Now

LEEUW, TON DE (1926-   )
Transparence
18pt cor,3trp,3trom [15'] DONEMUS
(L213)

LEEUWERIK, DE: DE SNEEUWKLOK BLOEIT see
Zwager, Piet

LEFANU, NICOLA (1947-   )
Story Of Mary O'neill, The
17pt cor NOVELLO rent   (L214)

LEFARGE, G.
Seine, La
(Ziberlin, F.) 4pt mix cor HEUGEL
HE 31885   (L215)

LEFEBVRE
Chute, La
mix cor,B solo,pno,electronic tape
[40'] SALABERT   (L216)

LEGACY see De Cormier, Robert

LEGEND, A see Karachevsky, Agada

LEGEND FOR SPRING see Starr, [Paul]
Douglas

LEGEND OF THE TWELVE MOONS, THE see
Roberts, Ruth

LEGENDE DE SAINT-NICOLAS, LE
(Frochaux, Jean-Bernard) SATB,acap
HUGUENIN CH 2041   (L217)

LEGENDEN OM KRISTI see Lindgren, Olof

LEGRAND, MICHEL (1932-   )
Enfants Qui Pleurent, Les °see
Marnay

Little Boy Lost (Pieces Of Dreams)
(Chinn, Teena) SATB CPP-BEL
T3452LC1 $1.40, accomp tape
available   (L218)
(Chinn, Teena) SSA CPP-BEL T3452LC2
$1.40   (L219)
(Chinn, Teena) SAB CPP-BEL T3452LC3
$1.40   (L220)

LEHRNDORFER, F.
Wenn Ich Ein Voglein War
mix cor BOHM   (L221)

LEIGHTON, KENNETH (1929-1988)
Six Elizabethan Lyrics
SSAA,acap NOVELLO   (L222)

LEISE ERKLINGEN GLOCKEN VOM CAMPANILE
see Kattnigg, Rudolf

LEISY, JAMES FRANKLIN (1927-   )
Hope Is Forever (from Pandora)
SA/SAB/SATB,pno,opt fl WIDE WORLD
$.80   (L223)

Me And You
(Besig) 2pt cor SHAWNEE 0102 $.95
(L224)
Miracles Still Happen At Christmas
(Lambert) SAB SHAWNEE 0358 $.85
(L225)
Talkin' 'Bout America
2 speaking cor WIDE WORLD $.85
(L226)
2 speaking cor,pno,pic,drums WIDE
WORLD $2.25   (L227)

LELEU, FRANCOISE
Six Chansons A Repondre Et A Sonner
Du Pays Guerandais
4pt mix cor,opt inst HEUGEL
HE 32468   (L228)

LEMACHER, HEINRICH (1891-1966)
Auf, Du Junger Wandersmann °Op.123,
No.1
men cor BOHM   (L229)

Einsamkeit, Du Stummer Bronnen:
Chorfantasie °Op.182
men cor,pno,strings BOHM   (L230)

LEMARC, A.
Kwezelken, Het
SSA MOLENAAR 15024703   (L231)

LEMARQUE, F.
Marjolaine (composed with Revil,
Rudi)
(Frochot, J.) SATB HEUGEL HE 32548
(L232)

LEMARQUE, F. (cont'd.)

Quand Un Soldat
(Tritsch, J.) 4pt mix cor HEUGEL
HE 32187   (L233)

Temps Du Muguet, Le (composed with
Sodoi; Matoussouski)
(Gaudin, J.Y.) 4pt mix cor HEUGEL
HE32479   (L234)

LEMUEL'S WORDS see Guy, Noa

LENELI DU SIMMELIBERG see Bovet, Joseph

LENNON, JOHN (1940-1980)
All You Need Is Love (composed with
McCartney, [John] Paul)
(Averre, Dick) SATB,pno,opt combo
PRESSER 312-41473 f.s.   (L235)

Blackbird (composed with McCartney,
[John] Paul)
(Averre, Dick) SATB,pno,opt combo
PRESSER 312-41474 f.s.   (L236)

Norwegian Wood (composed with
McCartney, [John] Paul)
(Averre, Dick) SATB,pno,opt combo
PRESSER 312-41475 $.75   (L237)

LENNON, JOHN ANTHONY (1950-   )
Passage To Thereafter
[Lat] SA,3.3.3.3. 4.3.3.2. 3perc,
cel,2harp,strings [20']
AM.COMP.AL. $46.50   (L238)

LENOIR, JEAN
Parlez-Moi D'amour
(Ott, Norbert) SAB A COEUR JOIE
1027   (L239)

LENSELINK, HAROLD
Love's Day
SSAATTBB,opt pno HARMONIA 3736
(L240)

LENTE-MARS see Vaal, O. de

LENTE-PARADE see Beekum, Jan Van

LENTE-WALS VOOR LILITH see Beurden,
Bernard van

LENTELIEDJE see Stenz, Herman

LENTELIEDJE: WELKOM, LIEVE LENTEBODEN
see Bogert, Hans Van Den

LENTEMARS see Vaal, O. de

LENTEMORGEN: O, HOE HEERLIJK IS 'T NU
BUITEN see Brune, Joseph Frederik

LENTEVREUGD see Vocht, Lodewijk de

LENTEZANG: STIL, IN WAZIG NEVELGRAUWEN
see Zwager, Piet

LENTZ
Come Along!
2pt cor CPP-BEL SV8528 $.95, accomp
tape available   (L241)

Ted E. Bear And Me (composed with
Truesdale)
2pt cor CPP-BEL SV8505 $.95 (L242)

LENTZ, ROGER G.
Like A Shining Light
SATB,pno SOMERSET SP-798 $.90
(L243)
Maybe We Can
3pt mix cor CPP-BEL SV8632 $1.25,
accomp tape available   (L244)

LENZ, DER see Gerhardt, Emil

LEONTOVICH, MYKOLA (1877-1921)
Carol Of The Bells
TTBB,acap FISCHER,C CM2270   (L245)
SSA,acap FISCHER,C CM5276   (L246)
jr cor,acap FISCHER,C CM7989 (L247)
SATB,acap FISCHER,C CM4604   (L248)
SAB,acap FISCHER,C CM4747   (L249)

LEPRECHAUN, THE see Eddleman, David

LERCHENBAUM, DER see Hauptmann, Moritz

LERCHESGESANG see Mendelssohn-
Bartholdy, Felix

LEROUX, PHILIPPE (1959-   )
Entourage Intimes, L'
12pt mix cor BILLAUDOT   (L250)

LERSTAD, TERJE B. (1955-   )
Confiture De Genevriers °Op.175
[Norw] mix cor,fl,clar,pno [8']
NORGE   (L251)

Ti Arstider, De °Op.106
[Norw] mix cor,acap [5'] NORGE
(L252)

LESSARD, JOHN AYRES (1920-   )
Pastimes And An Alleluia
unis men cor,2.1.1.1. 2.2.2.0.
harp,pno/cel,2perc,strings [15']
AM.COMP.AL. $24.45   (L253)

LET A SMILE BE YOUR UMBRELLA (ON A
RAINY DAY) see Fain, Sammy

LET IT FLY AWAY see Miller, Dave

LET IT SNOW! LET IT SNOW! LET IT SNOW!
see Cahn, Sammy

LET ME DANCE FOR YOU
(Shaw, Kirby) SSA LEONARD-US 08657963
$.95, ipa, accomp tape available
(L254)
(Shaw, Kirby) SATB LEONARD-US
08657961 $.95   (L255)
(Shaw, Kirby) SAB LEONARD-US 08657962
$.95   (L256)

LET ME GO see Land

LET MY COUNTRY AWAKE see Weigl, [Mrs.]
Vally

LET PEACE ENCIRCLE ALL THE WORLD see
Clarke, Henry Leland

LET SOUNDS OF JOY BE HEARD see
Pfautsch, Lloyd Alvin

LET THE RIVER RUN (NEW JERUSALEM) see
Simon, Carly

LET THE TINY BABY COME IN see Price

LET THERE ALWAYS BE SUNSHINE! see
Ostrovski, A.

LET THERE BE MUSIC see Young

LET THERE BE PEACE see Kennedy, James
I.

LET THOSE MERRY BELLS RING! see Swears

LET US REMEMBER see Crawley, Clifford

LET US SING! see Klouse, Andrea

LET US SING see Perry, Dave

LET'S CREATE A LAND OF SONG see
Zamecnik, Evzen

LET'S GIVE THE WORLD A CHANCE see
Papoulis, Jim

LET'S GO! MOVIE CLASSICS ON THE MOVE
(Chinn, Teena) SATB (contains On The
Atcheson, Topeka And The Santa Fe;
The Trolley Song; Chattanooga Choo
Choo) CPP-BEL C0148C1X $2.50,
accomp tape available   (L257)
(Chinn, Teena) SAB (contains On The
Atcheson, Topeka And The Santa Fe;
The Trolley Song; Chattanooga Choo
Choo) CPP-BEL C0148C3X $2.50 (L258)
(Chinn, Teena) 2pt mix cor (contains
On The Atcheson, Topeka And The
Santa Fe; The Trolley Song;
Chattanooga Choo Choo) CPP-BEL
C0148C5X $2.50   (L259)

LET'S HEAR IT FOR AMERICA! see Artman,
Ruth Eleanor

LET'S SING, FRIENDS! VOL. 8 °CCU
[Russ] cor,pno/acord/gtr MEZ KNIGA
178   (L260)

LET'S SING, FRIENDS! VOL. 9 °CCU
[Russ] cor,pno/acord/gtr MEZ KNIGA
177   (L261)

LET'S SING, FRIENDS! VOL. 10 °CCU
[Russ] cor,acap/pno/acord/gtr MEZ
KNIGA 175   (L262)

LET'S SING, FRIENDS! VOL. 11 °CCU
(Fyodorov, V.) [Russ] cor,pno/acord/
gtr MEZ KNIGA 186   (L263)

LET'S TAKE A CHRISTMAS TRIP see Chiara,
Jo

LET'S TELL THE WORLD ABOUT CHRISTMAS
see North, Jack King

LETTER FROM PATMOS see Prado, Jose-
Antonio (Almeida)

LETTERS TO LINDBERGH see Bennett

LETZTE LEI, DIE see Biebl, Franz

LETZTE ROSE see Last Rose Of Summer,
The

LEUTNANT WARST DU EINST BEI DEN HUSAREN
see Stolz, Robert

LEVEL, PIERRE YVES
A.E.I.O.U.
3 eq voices,opt 3rec,opt tamb
HEUGEL HE 31981 contains also:
Level, Pierre Yves, Am, Stram,
Gram (2-4 eq voices,2rec) (L264)

Am, Stram, Gram
see Level, Pierre Yves, A.E.I.O.U.

Ce Que J'aime
see Level, Pierre Yves, Quatrain

Chaton Et La Souris, Le °see
Massepin, A.

Quatrain
4pt cor,2rec,xylo,opt tamb HEUGEL
HE 32024 contains also: Ce Que
J'aime (L265)

LEVENE
It's Time To Ring Those Christmas
Bells! °see Price

LEVENSWONDER see Naberman, Mar

LEVI
Mark Twain - Awful German Language
°CCU
SATB LAWSON LG 52350 $2.50 (L266)

Mark Twain - Golden Arm °CCU
SATB LAWSON LG 52351 $2.50 (L267)

Mark Twain - Great Joust °CCU
SATB LAWSON LG 52349 $2.95 (L268)

Mark Twain - Sunrise On Miss °CCU
SATB LAWSON LG 52348 $1.95 (L269)

LEVI, PAUL ALAN (1941-   )
Natural History Of The Water Closet,
The
SATB,1.0.1.1. 1.1.1.0. harp,timp,
perc,strings [25'] AM.COMP.AL.
$46.35 (L270)

LEVINAS, M.
Barberine
mix cor,orch [5'] SALABERT
EAS18167P (L271)

LEWIN, FRANK (1925-   )
Music For The White House
STB/SATB,woodwinds,brass,timp,perc,
gtr,vln solo [28'] AM.COMP.AL.
(L272)

Seasons
unis girl cor,Bar solo,3.1.0.0.
1.1.0.0. pno,perc,2vln,2vcl [20']
AM.COMP.AL. (L273)

LEWIS
Judy's Turn To Cry (composed with
Ross)
(Nowak) SSA SHAWNEE 0536 $1.00
(L274)
Rock-A-Bye Your Baby With A Dixie
Melody (composed with Young;
Schwartz)
SATB CPP-BEL 64419 $.95 (L275)
TTBB CPP-BEL 60760 $.95 (L276)

LEWIS, A.
It's Love That Makes The World Go
'Round
2pt cor,pno (med easy) THOMAS
1C258516 $.75 (L277)

Knock, Knock
2pt cor,pno,opt wood blocks THOMAS
1C258422 $.80 (L278)

Pic-Co-Lo-Min-I
2pt cor,pno (med) THOMAS 1C258411
$.85 (L279)

LEWIS, ADEN G. (1924-   )
No One In The House
2pt cor/mix cor, solo voices,kbd
CORONET 392-41390 $.90 (L280)

LEWIS, HUEY
Give Me The Keys
(Strommen, Carl) SATB ALFRED 7627
$1.25 (L281)
(Strommen, Carl) 1-2pt cor ALFRED
7629 $1.25 (L282)
(Strommen, Carl) SAB ALFRED 7628
$1.25 (L283)

Naturally
(Strommen) ALFRED (L284)

Perfect World
(Strommen) 1-2pt cor ALFRED 7606
$1.25, accomp tape available
(L285)
(Strommen) SATB ALFRED 7604 $1.25,
accomp tape available (L286)
(Strommen) SAB ALFRED 7605 $1.25,
accomp tape available (L287)

LEWIS, W. REES
Boot, Saddle To Horse
TTBB,pno [2'30"] ROBERTON 53077
(L288)

LIADOV, ANATOL KONSTANTINOVICH
(1855-1914)
Children's Songs °CCU
[Russ] jr cor,pno MEZ KNIGA 527
(L289)

LIBELLULES, LES see Pierne

LIBERTY see Halferty

LICHT, MYRTHA B.
Spring Leads Death To Life
SATB/SAB/jr cor FISCHER,C CM7196
$.70 (L290)

LICHTMATROOS VAN LIMMEN see Mever, P.
Van

LICHTSCHOPFER, DER see Naegeli, Hans
Georg

LICORNE, LA °Ir
(Burnand, Alain) SATB,acap HUGUENIN
CH 2005 (L291)

LIDDELL, CLAIRE
Blackbird
SSA,pno ROBERTON 75304 see from
Flight (L292)

Butterfly
SSA,pno ROBERTON 75304 see from
Flight (L293)

Cuckoo
SSA,pno ROBERTON 75304 see from
Flight (L294)

Flight °see Blackbird; Butterfly;
Cuckoo; Kingfisher, The; To A
Skylark; Visit From The Sea, A
(L295)
Kingfisher, The
SSA,pno ROBERTON 75304 see from
Flight (L296)

To A Skylark
SSA,pno ROBERTON 75304 see from
Flight (L297)

Visit From The Sea, A
SSA,pno ROBERTON 75304 see from
Flight (L298)

LIDICE see Bachorek, Milan

LIDL, VACLAV (1922-   )
Bridge
mix cor,acap CESKY HUD. (L299)

Folk Bouquets
mix cor CESKY HUD. (L300)

For A Thousand Blossoms °CCU
jr cor,instrumental ensemble CESKY
HUD. (L301)

Hic Homo Sum
[Lat] mix cor,T solo,pno,perc
SUPRAPHON (L302)

Song From War
men cor CESKY HUD. (L303)

LIEB, J.G.
Salut! Glaciers Sublimes
1-4pt cor HUGUENIN see from
CHANSONS POUR LA JEUNESSE,
TROISIEME CAHIER (L304)

LIEBE see Strauss, Richard

LIEBE IST DAS HOCHSTE, DIE see
Heilmann, Harald

LIEBE UND WEIN see Mendelssohn-
Bartholdy, Felix

LIEBEN BRINGT GROSS' FREUD, DAS see
Kutzer, Ernst

LIEBERGEN
As The Leaves Fall
SATB CPP-BEL SCHCH 77106 $1.10
(L305)
What Shall We Sing?
SATB SHAWNEE 6482 $1.25 (L306)

LIEBERGEN, PATRICK
Drinkhail
SATB,acap (med) THOMAS 1C308509
$.75 (L307)

'Tis The Season To Be Jolly °Xmas
SAB,pno (med) THOMAS 1C308816 $.90
(L308)

LIEBESERFAHRUNG see Schallehn, Hilger

LIEBESGLUCK see Schallehn, Hilger

LIEBESLIED see Schallehn, Hilger

LIEBESLIED see Reger, Max

LIEBESLIEDER WALZER SUITE see Brahms,
Johannes

LIEBESQUAL see Reger, Max

LIEBESQUALEN DES CATULL, DIE see
Matthus, Siegfried

LIEBESSEHNSUCHT
(Opienski, Henryk) TTBB HUGUENIN
EB 23 (L309)

LIEBESSEHNSUCHT see Kubizek, Augustin

LIEBESWERBUNG see Schallehn, Hilger

LIEBLICH HAT SICH GESELLET see
Anonymous

LIEBLINGSPLATZCHEN see Mendelssohn-
Bartholdy, Felix

LIED see Jeanquartier, Marianne,
Chanson

LIED see Schumann, Robert (Alexander)

LIED IST UBER DEM WORT see Zipp,
Friedrich

LIED VAN DE DORSCHERS, DE see
Bastiannse, F.

LIED VAN DE DROGE HARING see Vermulst,
Jan

LIED VAN ZUID-HOLLAND, HET see Lukkien,
Hendrik Gerard

LIED VON DER GLOCKE, DAS see Bruch, Max

LIED VON SHAKESPEARE see Brahms,
Johannes

LIED WEERKLINKT, EEN see Laetantius,
Br., Als In Ons Hart

LIEDER DER MINNE see Gebhard, Hans

LIEDER FUR FRAUENCHOR NACH GEDICHTEN
VON EDUARD MORIKE see Micheelsen,
Hans Friedrich

LIEDER FUR MANNERCHOR A CAPPELLA see
Wolf, Hugo

LIEDER UBER DIE GRENZEN see Egner,
Hermann

LIEDER VON NORBERT WALLNER, HEFT 1
°CC10L
cor HELBLING C4185 f.s. (L310)

LIEDER VON NORBERT WALLNER, HEFT 2
°CC9L
cor HELBLING C4188 f.s. (L311)

LIEDJE see Boedijn, Gerard H.

LIEDJE VAN DE KOPPELSTOK, EEN see
Holman, F.

LIEDJES VAN EN VOOR SOLDATEN, 27 see
Kooij, Daniel

LIEPIN, A.
Our Cherished Dreams °CCU
[Russ] jr cor,pno MEZ KNIGA 526
(L312)

LIFE see Clarke, Henry Leland

LIFE HAS LOVELINESS TO SELL see Clarke,
Henry Leland

LIFE IN THE SEASONAL ORBIT see Engel,
Yehuda

LIFE IS A SONG see Norton

LIFERMAN, G.
Lune Est Morte, La °see Mareuil, J.

LIFT UP THINE EYES ROUND ABOUT AND SEE
see Shur, Yekutiel

LIGETI, GYORGY (1923-   )
Einsamkeit (Solitude) °see Magany

Idegen Foldon
"In Der Fremde (Far From Home)"
[Hung/Eng/Ger] wom cor,acap
[3'20"] SCHOTTS C 46165 (L313)

In Der Fremde (Far From Home) °see
Idegen Foldon

Magany
"Einsamkeit (Solitude)" [Hung/Ger/
Eng] mix cor,acap [3'] SCHOTTS
SKR 20019 (L314)

Out In The Woods
see Songs From Matraszentimre

LIGETI, GYORGY (cont'd.)
  Papaine
    "Witwe Papai (Widow Papai)" [Hung/
    Ger/Eng] mix cor,acap [3']
    SCHOTTS SKR 20018   (L315)

  Pom-Pom
    see Songs From Matraszentimre

  Songs From Matraszentimre °folk
    song,Hung
    2-3pt treb cor SCHOTTS CO 45593
    f.s.
    contains: Out In The Woods; Pom-
    Pom; Three Barrels; True Love
                                 (L316)
  Three Barrels
    see Songs From Matraszentimre

  True Love
    see Songs From Matraszentimre

  Witwe Papai (Widow Papai) °see
    Papaine

LIGHT, THE see White, Gary C.

LIGHT A CANDLE see Strommen, Carl

LIGHT INVISIBLE, THE see Wills, Arthur

LIGHT OF MORNING see Cooper, Steve

LIGHT ONE CANDLE see Yarrow, Peter

LIGHTFOOT, MARY LYNN
  Feels Like Christmas
    2pt cor LEONARD-US 08598570 $.85
                                 (L317)
  Last Rose Of Summer, The
    SSA HOFFMAN,R H2044 $.95   (L318)

LIGHTS! see Albrecht

LIGHTS see Crawley, Clifford

LIGHTS AND HARMONIES see
  Sigurbjornsson, Thorkell

LIJNSCHOOTEN, H.V.
  Acht Klankstudies °CC8U
    SATB MOLENAAR 03120707   (L319)

  Choral Figure
    (Zwart, W.) SATB MOLENAAR 13033403
                                 (L320)
LIKE A SHINING LIGHT see Lentz, Roger
  G.

LIKE AN AUTUMN SKY see Wright, Maurice

LIKE AS THE WAVES see Ehrlich, Abel,
  Sonnet 60 By Shakespeare

LIKE THE FLIGHT OF AN EAGLE see Bacon,
  Boyd

LIKE VENUS FAIR, BEYOND COMPARE see
  Clemens, Jacobus (Clemens non
  Papa), Venus Schoon, Een

LI'L LIZA JANE °folk song
  (Shaw, Robert; Hunter, Ralph) TTBB,T
  solo LAWSON LG 535 $.85   (L321)
  (Swenson) B&2camb CAMBIATA U979134
  f.s.   (L322)

LILITH DIE IS LIEF see Beurden, Bernard
  van

LILJA, BERNHARD (1895-   )
  Dofta, Dofta Vit Syren
    men cor STIM   (L323)

  Folkvisa: Sa Odsligt Molnen Pa Fastet
    Ga
    mix cor STIM   (L324)

  Impromptu
    men cor STIM   (L325)

  Kallan
    mix cor STIM   (L326)

LILLIPUTIAN BOATING SONG, THE see
  Josephs, Wilfred

LIME-TREE HAS BLOSSOMED, THE see
  Laburda, Jiri

LIMERICK SONG, THE see Grob, Anita Jean

LIMERICKS (TONGUE TWISTERS A LA
  TARANTELLA) see McAfee, D.

LIND
  Hayom Teamtzenu
    (Kaplan, Abraham) mix cor LAWSON
    LG 51553 $.70   (L327)

LINDEN TREE, THE see Schubert, Franz
  (Peter)

LINDENFELD, HARRIS NELSON (1945-   )
  And The Eagles
    SATB,3.3.3.4. 4.3.4.0. timp,perc,
    strings [13'] AM.COMP.AL. $28.95
                                 (L328)
LINDGREN, OLOF (1934-   )
  Att Likna Dig
    mix cor [2'] STIM 8511-053 (L329)

  Bada Regnen, De
    wom cor STIM 8511-054 see from
    Trohjartat   (L330)

  Dag Ska Jag, En
    3pt cor [2'] STIM 8511-052 (L331)

  Halsokallan
    wom cor STIM 8511-054 see from
    Trohjartat   (L332)

  Legenden Om Kristi
    wom cor STIM 8511-054 see from
    Trohjartat   (L333)

  Navervisor
    men cor,TBar soli,winds,string orch
    SUECIA   (L334)

  Trohjartat °see Bada Regnen, De;
    Halsokallan; Legenden Om Kristi
                                 (L335)
LINDSAY FOLK BOOK °CC1OL
  (Coombes, Douglas) 2pt cor,gtr
  LINDSAY folksongs from around the
  world   (L336)

LINIEN DES LEBENS, DIE see Poos,
  Heinrich

LION ET L'ESCARGOT, LE see Gauffriau,
  Jean

LIONS see Belyea, H.

LIONS, see Crawley, Clifford

LIPPMAN
  God's Christmas Tree
    (Dahle) SATB KJOS C8922 $.90 (L337)

LISSMANN, KURT (1902-1983)
  Aus Der Traube In Die Tonne
    (Davies, Bryan) "Tribute To Mr.
    Curwen, A" TTBB,pno [1'55"]
    ROBERTON 53085   (L338)

  Tribute To Mr. Curwen, A °see Aus
    Der Traube In Die Tonne

LISTEN see Crawley, Clifford

LISTEN TO ME see Clarke, Henry Leland

LISTEN TO THE MUSIC see Eddleman, David

LISTEN TO THE WIND A-BLOWIN' see
  Matheny, Gary

LISZT, FRANZ (1811-1886)
  O Lieb So Lang Du Lieben Kannst:
    Nocturne
    men cor,solo voice,pno BOHM (L339)

LITANEI see Schubert, Franz (Peter)

LITANY FOR AMERICA, A see Pfautsch,
  Lloyd Alvin

LITEN NORSK KORRAPSODI
  (Ugland, Johan Varen) SATB MUSIKK
  MH 2477   (L340)

LITEN VISE, EN see Volle, Bjarne

LITTLE BABE, DO YOU KNOW? see Peninger

LITTLE BLACK BOY, THE see Crawford,
  John Charlton

LITTLE BOY BLUE see Thliveris,
  Elizabeth Hope (Beth)

LITTLE BOY LOST (PIECES OF DREAMS) see
  Legrand, Michel

LITTLE DAVID
  (Daniel, Etienne) SATB CAILLARD
  PC 130 see from Deux Negro
  Spirituals   (L341)
  (Wilkinson, Scott) SATB,acap CPP-BEL
  OCT 02348 $1.10   (L342)

LITTLE DRUMMER BOY see Davis

LITTLE EVENING MUSIC see Bachorek,
  Milan

LITTLE HAWK see Haufrecht, Herbert

LITTLE KINDNESS, A see Snyder

LITTLE LAMB see Allen, David Len

LITTLE LEPRECHAUN see Crawley, Clifford

LITTLE LOST CHRISTMAS HARMONY see
  Roberts, Ruth

LITTLE LOVE GOES A LONG WAY, A see
  Balkin, Alfred

LITTLE ONE, TINY ONE see Price

LITTLE RED RIDING HOOD see Boshkoff,
  Ruth

LITTLE SAINT NICK see Wilson, Brian

LITTLE SONGS FOR BIG CHILDREN see Bar-
  Am, Benjamin

LITTLE WHEEL A-TURNIN'
  (Kirk, Theron) SATB,acap CPP-BEL
  PROCH 01574 $1.10   (L343)
  (Kirk, Theron) SA/TB CPP-BEL
  PROCH 01775 $.95   (L344)

LITTLE WHEEL A-TURNIN' see Pfautsch,
  Lloyd Alvin

LITTLE WHEEL A-TURNING °spir
  (McNeil, Albert) SATB (med) GENTRY
  JG2027 $.65   (L345)

LITTLE WOODLARK, THE see Wienhorst,
  Richard

LITTLEST CHRISTMAS TREE see Pickell

LIVE FOR THE MOMENT see Porterfield,
  Sherrie

LIVING IN AMERICA
  (Chinn) SATB CPP-BEL T4280LC1 $1.25,
  accomp tape available   (L346)

LIVINGSTON
  Sing, Alleluia!
    SATB oct DEAN HRD 162 $.75 (L347)

LIVINGSTON, JAY HAROLD (1915-   )
  Silver Bells
    (Snyder) 3pt mix cor,pno CPP-BEL
    SV8720 $1.25, accomp tape
    available   (L348)

LIVRE D'HEURES see Canat De Chizy,
  Edith

'LIZA JANE see Althouse, Jay

LLANTO POR IGNACIO SANCHEZ MEIJAS see
  Ohana, Maurice

LLOYD, GEORGE
  Pervigilium Veneris °see Vigil Of
    Venus, The

  Vigil Of Venus, The
    "Pervigilium Veneris" cor,ST soli,
    orch voc sc UNITED MUS $15.50
                                 (L349)
LOB AUF DIE MUSIK see Distler, Hugo

LOB DER DIALEKTIK see Eisler, Hanns

LOB DER MEISTER: FROHLICHE
  HANDWERKSKANTATE see Backer, Hans

LOB DES LIEDES see Zipp, Friedrich

LOB DES SOMMERS see Lampart, Reinhold

LOBPREIS DER MUSIK see Hollfelder,
  Waldram

LOCKLAIR, DAN STEVEN (1949-   )
  Tapestries
    SATB,handbells MUSIC SEV. M70-493
    $.90   (L350)

LOCKWOOD, NORMAND (1906-   )
  Shine, Perishing Republic
    SATB,org,3trp,trom,2vla,timp,2perc
    [11'] AM.COMP.AL. $24.45   (L351)

LOESSER
  I Hear Music (composed with Lane)
    (Kerr) SSA CPP-BEL 2440IC2X $1.25,
    accomp tape available   (L352)
    (Kerr) SATB CPP-BEL 2440IC1X $1.25,
    accomp tape available   (L353)
    (Kerr) SAB CPP-BEL 2440IC3X $1.25,
    accomp tape available   (L354)

LOGGINS, KENNY
  Nobody Loves Me Like You Do °see
    Murray

LOITSUJA see Bergman, Erik

LOJESKI
  Find A Way
    SATB LEONARD-US 08215796 $.85
                                 (L355)
    SAB LEONARD-US 08215797 $.85 (L356)

  Freedom
    SAB LEONARD-US 08217202 $.95 (L357)
    SATB LEONARD-US 08217201 $.95
                                 (L358)

LOJESKI (cont'd.)

    2pt cor LEONARD-US 08217204 $.95,
    ipa, accomp tape available (L359)

LOKEN
    Pass It Along
    SAB KJOS C8821 $.80   (L360)

LOMBARDO, ROBERT M. (1932-)
    Rosalia *madrigal
    24pt cor [6'] AM.COMP.AL. f.s.
    (L361)

LONDON, EDWIN (1929-)
    Christmas Music By Bjorne Enstabile
    mix cor,T solo,bells,org [13'0"]
    GUNMAR GM 08 $1.50   (L362)

LONDONDERRY AIR
    (Mattson) SATB KJOS C8923 $.80 (L363)
    (Penders, J.) SATB MOLENAAR 13034004
    (L364)

LONELINESS see Wright, Maurice

LONELY STEPPE, THE see Davies, Bryan

LONESOME COWBOY: GOODBYE OLD PAINT see
    Blair, Dean

LONESOME SAIL, THE *CCU
    [Russ] jr cor MEZ KNIGA 509   (L365)

LONG DAY CLOSES, THE see Sullivan,
    [Sir] Arthur Seymour

LONG, LONG AGO see Grob, Anita Jean

LONG TIME AGO see Neaum, Michael

LONG TIME AGO IN BETHLEHEM see Moore,
    Donald

LOOK AROUND see Kunz

LOOK BEYOND TOMORROW see Wiser

LOOK DOWN FAIR MOON see Wallach, Joelle

LOOK TO THE WIND see Page

LOOK TO THIS DAY see Sateren, Leland
    Bernhard

LOOK UP see Clarke, Henry Leland

LOOK UPON ME, MY BELOVED see Gastoldi,
    Giovanni Giacomo

LOOKING GLASS, THE see Hurd, Michael

LOOKING UP see McPheeters

LOOS, ARMIN (1904-1971)
    Elegy
    (Schubert, Peter) SSATB APNM sc
    $3.50, cor pts rent   (L366)

LOPER
    Take In The Sunshine
    SS&camb,SA soli CAMBIATA A982167
    $.65   (L367)

LORD, SUZANNE
    I Think I Understand What Love Is
    1-2pt cor LEONARD-US 08599230 $.85
    (L368)
    Morning Star
    2pt cor LEONARD-US 08599444 $.85
    (L369)

LORD, I WANNA CLIMB, BUT I KEEP
    SLIPPIN' AWAY see Koepke, Allen

LORD LOVELACE see Richards, Goff

LORELEI, DIE see Silcher, Friedrich

LORELEY, DIE see Silcher, Friedrich

LOST DOUBLE BASS, THE see Pauer, Jiri

LOST IN LOVE see Robb

LOST SWEETHEART AND SWEET JACK see
    Bachorek, Milan

LOTOSBLUME, DIE see Schumann, Robert
    (Alexander)

LOTUS FLOWER, THE see Schumann, Robert
    (Alexander)

LOUGHTON, LYNNETTE
    Sing Praises To The King
    SATB ALFRED 7421 $.95   (L370)

LOUIS ARMSTRONG STORY, THE see Roberts,
    Ruth

LOUP ET L'AGNEAU, LE see Gounod,
    Charles Francois

LOUPIAS, H.P.
    A Paris
    2S,2fl HEUGEL HE 31863 contains
    also: Balalin   (L371)

LOUPIAS, H.P. (cont'd.)

    Balalin
    see Loupias, H.P., A Paris

LOVE ALWAYS
    (Roscoe) SATB CPP-BEL 5262LC1X $1.25,
    accomp tape available   (L372)
    (Roscoe) SSA CPP-BEL 5262LC2X $1.25,
    accomp tape available   (L373)
    (Roscoe) SAB CPP-BEL 5262LC3X $1.25,
    accomp tape available   (L374)

LOVE CAME TO US see Rinehart, John

LOVE CAN NEVER SAY GOODBYE see Gilpin,
    Greg

LOVE IS see McCray, James

LOVE IS A MANY- SPLENDORED THING see
    Webster

LOVE IS COLDER THAN DEATH see Violette,
    Andrew

LOVE IS NOW see Wyrtzen, Don

LOVE IS THE KEY see Stephens, Michele

LOVE IS THE MEANING OF CHRISTMAS see
    Besig

LOVE IS THE WAY see Olson, Lynn Freeman

LOVE LEARNS BY LAUGHING see Morley

LOVE MAKES THE WORLD GO 'ROUND see
    Gallina, Jill C.

LOVE OF CHRISTMAS, THE see Hansen, Greg

LOVE SONG see Vidar, Jorunn

LOVE SONG, A see Telfer, Nancy

LOVE-SONG WALTZES, OP. 52 see Brahms,
    Johannes

LOVE UKRAINE see Sonevytsky, Ihor

LOVE WILL SAVE THE DAY
    (Hanson, Mark) SAB CPP-BEL 5304LC3X
    $1.40   (L375)

LOVE WILL TURN YOU AROUND see Madsen

LOVELIEST OF TREES see Getty, Gordon

LOVERS LOVE THE SPRING see Dickau

LOVE'S DAY see Lenselink, Harold

LOVE'S LESSON see Nowak, Lionel

LOVE'S MUSIC see McRae, Shirley W.

LOVE'S PHILOSOPHY see Fennelly, Brian

LOVE'S PLEA, A see Albert, Prince
    Consort of Queen Victoria

LOVE'S THE REASON WHY see Nelson

LOWN, BERT (1903-1962)
    Bye Bye Blues *see Hamm, Fred

LUBETKIN
    If It Weren't For You (composed with
    Oliver)
    SATB CPP-BEL SV8214 $.95   (L376)

    Tale Of Millington River, The
    SATB NEW MUSIC NMA-213 $.85   (L377)

LUCESCIT; NUNC BIBAMUS see Lassus,
    Roland de (Orlandus)

LUCI SERENE E CHIARE see Lauridsen,
    Morten Johannes

LUCI SERENE E CHIARE see Monteverdi,
    Claudio

LUCILLE-ANNE; JEFF see Adler, Samuel
    Hans

LUDUS FLORALIS see Pinos, Alois

LUEDEKE, RAYMOND (1944-)
    Of Him I Love...And A Noiseless
    Patient...
    SATB,4sax,db,2perc [10']
    AM.COMP.AL. sc $15.30, pts $19.10
    (L378)

LUENING, OTTO (1900-)
    When In The Languor Of Evening
    SATB,S solo,pno,4inst [8']
    AM.COMP.AL. $4.60   (L379)

LUFT, DIE see Kruse, Bjorn Howard

LUKKIEN, HENDRIK GERARD
    Lied Van Zuid-Holland, Het
    unis cor,pno ZENGERINK Z 620 (L380)
    4 eq voices,acap ZENGERINK 345
    (L381)

LUKOWSKY, ROLF (1926-)
    Sine Musica Nulla Vita
    4pt treb cor/4-8pt mix cor sc
    BREITKOPF-L 7689   (L382)

LULLABY see Bergstrome, Flora

LULLABY see Dollarhide, Theodore

LULLABY see Telfer, Nancy

LULLABY, A see Gorl, Willibald,
    Wiegenlied, Ein

LULLABY, GENTLE BREEZE see Butler

LULLABY-LOO see Crawley, Clifford

LULLABY OF THE LEAVES
    (Anderson) SSAA (women's barbershop)
    BOURNE B238725 $.50   (L383)

LULLABY OF THE SHEPHERDS, THE see
    Edwards

LULLY, JEAN-BAPTISTE (LULLI)
    (1632-1687)
    Bourgeois Gentilhomme, Le
    4pt mix cor,string orch HEUGEL
    HE 32359   (L384)

    Cadmus Et Hermione
    (Rollin, J.) 2-4pt cor HEUGEL
    HE 32349   (L385)

    Monsieur De Pourceaugnac
    4pt mix cor,string quar,cont HEUGEL
    HE 32251   (L386)

    Tanz-Chor
    SATB MOLENAAR 15020703   (L387)

LUND, EDDIE
    Tahiti Nui
    (Ott, Norbert) SATB,acap A COEUR
    JOIE 355   (L388)

LUND, LYNN S.
    She Is The Mother
    SATB JACKMAN JMC7155   (L389)

LUNDE, IVAR (1944-)
    Erindringer *Op.68
    [Norw] mix cor,acap NORGE   (L390)

    Nocturne *Op.46
    [Eng] SATB,narrator,ob,clar,2perc,
    2electronic tape [12'] NORGE
    (L391)

    Tonen - The Song *Op.6
    [Norw/Eng] 3pt wom cor NORGE   (L392)

    Two The Same *Op.81
    [Eng] SSA/SSSSAA [6'] NORGE   (L393)

LUNE BLANCHE, LA see Aeschbacher,
    Walther

LUNE EST MORTE, LA see Mareuil, J.

LUSTELIJCKE MEY, DE see Clemens,
    Jacobus (Clemens non Papa)

LUSTIG, IHR BRUDER see Koch, Johannes
    H.E.

LUSTIG IHR BRUDER see Schlerf, L.

LUSTIG, LUSTIG, IHR LIEBEN BRUDER:
    SIEBEN FRANKISCHE VOLKSLIEDER
    *CC7L
    (Haus, K.) eq voices/mix cor,opt
    instrumental ensemble BOHM   (L394)

LUSTIGE GESCHICHTE see Trapp, Willy

LUTZ, LAWRENCE
    Math Test Boogie, The
    SAB DVM 2188-2 f.s., accomp tape
    available   (L395)
    SSA DVM 2188-3 f.s., accomp tape
    available   (L396)

    Rhythm's Everywhere, The
    SAB DVM 2088-2 f.s., accomp tape
    available   (L397)
    SSA DVM 2088-3 f.s., accomp tape
    available   (L398)
    SATB DVM 2088-1 f.s., accomp tape
    available   (L399)

    That Old Hat And Cane
    SSA DVM 1988-3 f.s., accomp tape
    available   (L400)
    SAB DVM 1988-2 f.s., accomp tape
    available   (L401)

LUX NOCTIS see Ohana, Maurice

LUYSTERBURG, THEO
  Overal Feestgeschal
    mix cor ZENGERINK 73   (L402)

LYDIA'S CAROL see Beaudrot

LYRISK SUITE see Hundsnes, Svein

LYSER EN STJARNA, DET see Paulson

LYSSAND, HENRIK
  Du Ska Itte Tro I Graset
    mix cor MUSIKK MH 2439   (L403)
    men cor MUSIKK MH 2443   (L404)

  God Natt Alle Blomar
    mix cor MUSIKK MH 2452   (L405)

  Hustavle, En
    men cor MUSIKK MH 2442   (L406)

  Rodstrupe
    2pt jr cor MUSIKK MH 2501 see from
    Tre Barnesanger Av Inger Hagerup
                                 (L407)

  Sangen Om Fuglene
    2pt jr cor MUSIKK MH 2501 see from
    Tre Barnesanger Av Inger Hagerup
                                 (L408)

  Seks Inger Hagerup Sanger
    eq voices MUSIKK   (L409)

  Stille
    5pt men cor MUSIKK MH 2441   (L410)
    mix cor MUSIKK MH 2440   (L411)

  Tre Barnesanger Av Inger Hagerup
    °see Rodstrupe; Sangen Om
    Fuglene; Vi Troster   (L412)

  Vi Troster
    2pt jr cor MUSIKK MH 2501 see from
    Tre Barnesanger Av Inger Hagerup
                                 (L413)

LYSTRUP, GEIRR
  Diger Dag
    (Amundsen, Lars) mix cor MUSIKK
    MH 2497 see from To Viser   (L414)

  Songen Om Kjaerligheta
    (Amundsen, Lars) mix cor MUSIKK
    MH 2497 see from To Viser   (L415)

  To Viser °see Diger Dag; Songen Om
    Kjaerligheta   (L416)

M

MA LIBERTE see Moustaki, Georges

MA MIE see Monteverdi, Claudio, Cor
  Mio! Mentre Vi Miro

MA MIE see Weber, Gustav

MA NORMANDIE see Berat, F.

MAASSEN, JOHANNES ANT.
  Als De Ziele Luistert
    [Dutch] 3 eq voices,acap ZENGERINK
    V 358   (M1)

  Klokgebed, Het: Hoe Helder Klinkt De
    Klokkentaal
    mix cor ZENGERINK 357   (M2)

  Vleug'len: Een Lied, Een Lied, Uw
    Leven Lang
    mix cor ZENGERINK 358   (M3)

MA'AYANI, AMI (1936-   )
  Hebrew Requiem (Symphony No. 3)
    cor,Mez solo,orch [40'] voc sc
    ISR.MUS.INST. 6255B   (M4)

  Symphony No. 3 °see Hebrew Requiem

MABRY, JOHN (1926-   )
  Camptown Races
    SATB BECKEN 115   (M5)

MCAFEE
  Poor Richard's Almanack
    SA/TB CPP-BEL DMC 08040 $1.10 (M6)

MCAFEE, D.
  Limericks (Tongue Twisters A La
    Tarantella)
    SATB CPP-BEL DMC 08130 $1.10   (M7)

MACBRIDE, DAVID HUSTON (1951-   )
  Four Sonnets Of Feng Zhi
    SATB,ST soli,3.3.3.3. 4.3.3.1.
    timp,3perc,pno/cel,harp,strings
    [18'] AM.COMP.AL. $33.50   (M8)

  Haze
    SATB [5'] (Thoreau) AM.COMP.AL.
    $4.60   (M9)

  In Iowa
    SSAATTBB,2pno [8'] AM.COMP.AL.
    $16.85   (M10)

MCBRIDE, ROBERT GUYN (1911-   )
  Golden Sequence, The
    SATB,org [2'] AM.COMP.AL. $3.85
                                 (M11)
  Improvisation
    boy cor/SSA,pno [3'] AM.COMP.AL.
    $1.60   (M12)

MCCABE
  Siberia
    SATB,acap NOVELLO 0806-30 $2.45
                                 (M13)

MCCAMLEY, URSULENE
  It's Christmas Time
    2pt cor LEONARD-US 08599285 $.85
                                 (M14)

MCCARTHY
  You Made Me Love You °see Monaco

MCCARTNEY, [JOHN] PAUL (1942-   )
  All You Need Is Love °see Lennon,
    John

  Blackbird °see Lennon, John

  Norwegian Wood °see Lennon, John

MCCRAY
  New Day
    SAB&camb CAMBIATA A979130 $.75
                                 (M15)

MCCRAY, JAMES
  Child Said, A
    SATB NATIONAL NMP-151 $.90   (M16)
    SSA NATIONAL NMP-130 $.90   (M17)

  Gift Of Life, The
    SATB,chimes,timp NEW MUSIC NMA-148
    $.80   (M18)

  Love Is
    SATB NEW MUSIC NMA-189 $.80 (M19)

  Never Doubt My Love
    SATB NATIONAL NMP-181 $.80   (M20)

  Passages
    SATB NATIONAL NMP-177 $.95   (M21)

MACFARREN
  You Stole My Love
    (Harris) SSA BOURNE B239061 $.70
                                 (M22)

MACHA, OTMAR (1922-   )
  Lachsian Songs °see Lasske Halekacky

  Lasske Halekacky
    "Lachsian Songs" SUPRAPHON   (M23)

MACHAUT, GUILLAUME DE (ca. 1300-1377)
  De Tout Suis Si Confortee
    (Turellier, Jean) ST,rec,opt vcl
    HEUGEL HE 31911 contains also:
    Brouillards De Noel, Les   (M24)

  Qui Es Promesse °mot
    (Turellier, Jean) SA,rec/strings
    HEUGEL HE 32250   (M25)

  Se Je Souspire
    (Turellier, Jean) S/T,rec/strings
    HEUGEL HE 32249   (M26)

MACHT DER MUSIK, DIE see Mutter,
  Gerbert

MCHUGH
  I Can't Give You Anything But Love
    (composed with Rutherford,
    Edward)
    SATB CPP-BEL 64400 $.95   (M27)

MCHUGH, JIMMY (1894-1969)
  I'm In The Mood For Love
    (Behnke, Martin) SATB,combo CPP-BEL
    SVC8701 f.s., accomp tape
    available   (M28)

MCINTYRE
  Downward Road Is Crowded, The
    SATB SHAWNEE 1853 $1.25   (M29)

MCKAY
  Come, Dance And Sing
    SATB SCHIRM.G 315470 $.70   (M30)

MCLAUGHLIN
  If You Ring One Bell
    SSA CPP-BEL SV8566 $1.10, accomp
    tape available   (M31)

MACLEOD
  Dance And Sing!
    2pt cor CPP-BEL SV8210 $.95 (M32)

MCLIN
  Don't You Let Nobody Turn You 'Round
    SATB KJOS GC166 $.90   (M33)

  Reach Up!
    SATB KJOS GC157 $.90   (M34)

MCPHEETERS
  Born With The Beat To Dance On The
    Street
    SATB CPP-BEL 4838BC1X $1.25, accomp
    tape available   (M35)

  Don't Say Goodbye
    SATB CPP-BEL SV8649 $1.40, accomp
    tape available   (M36)
    3pt mix cor CPP-BEL SV8648 $1.40
                                 (M37)

  Friends Forever
    SAB CPP-BEL SV8432 $1.25   (M38)

  Go Out And Find A Friend
    2pt cor CPP-BEL SV8565 $.95, accomp
    tape available   (M39)

  Hello, Sunshine
    SAB CPP-BEL SV8534 $.95   (M40)

  Here Within My Heart
    SSA CPP-BEL SV8724 $1.10, accomp
    tape available   (M41)

  How Many Seasons?
    SATB CPP-BEL SV8515 $.95   (M42)

  I Wish You Were Here With Me
    SSA CPP-BEL SV8602 $.95   (M43)

  I'd Paint You A Picture
    SAB CPP-BEL SV8411 $.95   (M44)

  I'll Remember You
    SAB CPP-BEL SV8404 $1.25   (M45)

  Looking Up
    3pt cor CPP-BEL SV8725 $.95, accomp
    tape available   (M46)

  More Than A Friend
    3pt cor,pno CPP-BEL SV8743 $.95,
    accomp tape available   (M47)

  My Special Friend
    SAB CPP-BEL SV8206 $.95   (M48)

  River Runnin' Free
    SAB CPP-BEL SV8618 $.95, accomp
    tape available   (M49)
    SSA CPP-BEL SV8617 $.95, accomp
    tape available   (M50)

MCPHEETERS (cont'd.)

Sing Me A Song About Christmas
SA CPP-BEL SV8315 $.95 (M51)

Sunny Day
SAB CPP-BEL SV8316 $1.10 (M52)

(Tell Me) When Will I See You Again
"When Will I See You Again" SAB
CPP-BEL SV8555 $1.20, accomp tape
available (M53)

Very Golden Season, A
SATB CPP-BEL SV8536 $.95 (M54)

When Will I See You Again °see (Tell
Me) When Will I See You Again

MCRAE, SHIRLEY W. (1933-   )
Love's Music
SSAA,pno/harp [2'] BROUDE BR. $.95
(M55)

MADAME AUTOMNE see Essey, G.

MADCHEN MIT DEN BLAUEN AUGEN see
Ophoven, Hermann

MADCHEN VOM LANDE, DAS see Biebl, Franz

MADCHEN VON MISOX, DAS see Ammann,
Benno

MADCHENLIED see Zoll, Paul

MADCHENPROZESSION see Stockhausen,
Karlheinz

MADEL HABT KEINE ANGST see Nje
Boitjessia Djewizy

MADETOJA, LEEVI (1887-1947)
Hakamaassa
wom cor,acap FAZER FO7805-5 (M56)

MADONNA (GEBET DER FISCHER) see
Watkinson, Percy Gerd

MADONNA, IO V'AMO E TACCIO see Festa,
Costanzo

MADRIGAL see Adams, Leslie

MADRIGAL see Lassus, Roland de
(Orlandus)

MADRIGAL see Weigl, [Mrs.] Vally

MADRIGALE FUR GEMISCHTEN CHOR A
CAPPELLA: BLATT V see Schein,
Johann Hermann

MADRIGALE FUR GEMISCHTEN CHOR A
CAPPELLA: BLATT VI °madrigal
mix cor,acap HANSSLER 40.404-60 f.s.
contains: Hassler, Hans Leo,
Herzlieb, Zu Dir Allein; Senfl,
Ludwig, Ach, Elslein, Liebes
Elselein; Senfl, Ludwig, Mag Ich,
Herzlieb, Erwerben Dich;
Steuerlein, Johann, Mit Lieb Bin
Ich Umfangen (M57)

MADRIGALE FUR GEMISCHTEN CHOR A
CAPPELLA: BLATT VII °madrigal
mix cor,acap HANSSLER 40.404-70 f.s.
contains: Anonymous, Lieblich Hat
Sich Gesellet; Arbeau, Thoinot
(Jehan Tabourot), Pavane: "Bella,
Qui Tiens Ma Vie"; Hausmann, Tanz
Mir Nicht Mit; Lechner, Gott
Bhute Dich (M58)

MADRIGALI E CANZONETTE: LIBRO 9 see
Monteverdi, Claudio

MADRIGALI GUERRIERI ET AMOROSI: ALTRI
CANTI D'AMOR see Monteverdi,
Claudio

MADRIGALI GUERRIERI ET AMOROSI: ALTRI
CANTI DI MARTE see Monteverdi,
Claudio

MADRIGALI: LIBRO 3 see Monteverdi,
Claudio

MADRIGALI: LIBRO 5 see Monteverdi,
Claudio

MADRIGALI: LIBRO 6 see Monteverdi,
Claudio

MADRIGALS see Wright, Maurice

MADRIGALS AND MOTETS FOR FIVE PARTS see
Gibbons, Orlando

MADSEN
Christmas Feast
SATB CPP-BEL SV8302 $.95 (M59)

Findin' A Way To You
SSA CPP-BEL SV8563 $.95, accomp
tape available (M60)

MADSEN (cont'd.)

Karma Chameleon
SAB CPP-BEL SV8461 $.95 (M61)

Love Will Turn You Around
SAB CPP-BEL SV8349 $.95 (M62)

Song Of Noel, A
SATB CPP-BEL SV8535 $.95 (M63)

Time Will Reveal
SATB CPP-BEL SV8462 $.95 (M64)

Waitin' For The Robert E. Lee
SATB CPP-BEL SV8345 $1.25, accomp
tape available (M65)

What's Forever For
SATB CPP-BEL SV8354 $.95 (M66)

You Touched My Life
SATB CPP-BEL SV8435 $.95 (M67)

MAES, JEF (1905-   )
Zomer
mix cor,acap [3'] CBDM f.s. (M68)

MAESSEN, ANTOON (1919-   )
Drie Canzonettas
4pt mix cor,fl,ob,clar,bsn [6']
DONEMUS (M69)

MAG ICH, HERZLIEB, ERWERBEN DICH see
Senfl, Ludwig

MAGANY see Ligeti, Gyorgy

MAGIC CARPET see Crawley, Clifford

MAGIC CLOCK, THE see Haufrecht, Herbert

MAGIC DREAM SONG see Poorman, Sonja

MAGIC HOUR, THE see Read, Gardner

MAGIC IN THE AIR see Crawley, Clifford

MAGIC OF BELIEVING, THE see Monath,
Norman

MAGIC STORE see Tilley, Alexander

MAGIC TO DO see Schwartz

MAHEL, JEAN
Campeur Chante, Le
2-4pt mix cor,acap ZURFLUH AZ 1104
(M70)

MAI IST DA!, DER see Lampart, Karl

MAI TRITT EIN MIT FREUDEN, DER
(Haus, Karl) SATB MULLER 521 f.s. see
from Volksliedsatze (M71)

MAIERHOFER, L.
Jahr Und Tag °CCU
mix cor/3 eq voices DOBLINGER
07 582 (M72)

MAIGLOCKEN UND DIE BLUMELEIN see
Mendelssohn-Bartholdy, Felix

MAILIED see Lassus, Roland de
(Orlandus)

MAILIED see Reger, Max

MAILIED see Wolf, Hugo

MAKE A JOYFUL NOISE see Walter

MAKE BELIEVE see Otey

MAKE SOME EXCITEMENT see Gilpin, Greg

MAKE YOUR DREAMS COME TRUE see Snyder

MAKING FRIENDS WITH SONGS, VOL. 6 °CCU
[Russ] jr cor,pno MEZ KNIGA 490 (M73)

MAKING FRIENDS WITH SONGS, VOL. 7 °CCU
[Russ] jr cor,pno MEZ KNIGA 519 (M74)

MAKING FRIENDS WITH SONGS, VOL. 8 °CCU
[Russ] jr cor,pno MEZ KNIGA 221 (M75)

MAKING LOVE see Nadelson, Andrew

MAL SO, MAL SO see Bibus, Ludwig

MALCANTONESINA see Castelnuovo, V.

MALDOROR-REQUIEM see Wittinger, Robert

MALIN see Nilsson, Torsten

MALLOW, MONTI
Reach Out °see Steffy, Thurlow

You Can Be (composed with Steffy,
Thurlow)
SAB CPP-BEL SV8312 $.95 (M76)

MALMLOF-FORSSLING, CARIN (1916-   )
Ars Longa Vita Brevis
mix cor STIM see from Tre Bevingade
Ord (M77)

Tre Bevingade Ord °see Ars Longa
Vita Brevis; Vita Sine Proposito
Vaga Est; Vivas Crescas, Floreas
(M78)

Vita Sine Proposito Vaga Est
mix cor STIM see from Tre Bevingade
Ord (M79)

Vivas Crescas, Floreas
mix cor STIM see from Tre Bevingade
Ord (M80)

MAMAN see Romieux, Charles

MAMAN NE VEUT PAS QUE J'AILLE AU BOIS
(Pantillon, Georges-Louis) SATB,acap
HUGUENIN CH 1123 (M81)

MAMIE ET MOY see Regnard, Francois

M'AMIE UN JOUR see Anonymous

M'AMIE UN JOUR see Gardane, Antonio

MAN IN MOTION (from St. Elmo's Fire)
SAB CPP-BEL 6686SC3X $1.25, accomp
tape available (M82)
SATB CPP-BEL 6686SC1X $1.25, accomp
tape available (M83)
SSA CPP-BEL 6686SC2X $1.25, accomp
tape available (M84)

MAN IS NOT ALONE see Klusmeier, R.T.A.

MAN OVERBOARD! A SEA TALE see
Gerschefski, Edwin

MANADSJOURNAL I MITTEN AV ATTIOTALET,
EN see Hemberg, Eskil

MANCHMAL see Helmschrott, Robert M.

MANCINI
Thank You, Santa
(Lojeski) 2pt cor LEONARD-US
08266753 $.95 (M85)
(Lojeski) 3pt mix cor LEONARD-US
08266754 $.95 (M86)

MANCINI, HENRY (1924-   )
Moon River
(Chinn) SATB CPP-BEL SV8471 $1.25
(M87)

MANDEL, JOHNNY ALFRED (1925-   )
Shadow Of Your Smile, The
mix cor CPP-BEL SVGP501 $1.25 (M88)

MANDELIEU, M. DE
From The Gay Twenties
SATB MOLENAAR 08185206 (M89)

MANN
I'm In Favor Of Friendship °see
Hilliard

Our Lady Of Liberty
SATB,opt narrator CPP-BEL OCT 02511
$1.10 (M90)
TTBB,opt narrator CPP-BEL OCT 02512
$1.10 (M91)

MANNERCHOR DE STEFFISBOURG, LE see
Villard, Jean (Gilles)

MANNERCHORE, BAND 1 see Janacek, Leos

MANNERS
Stopping By Woods
SATB CPP-BEL OCT 02529 $1.20 (M92)

MANNERS, RICHARD
Fugue Sandwich
SATB CPP-BEL SVC8601 f.s., accomp
tape available (M93)

MAN'S FANCY see Smith, Robert Edward

MANUSCRIT ITALIEN DE FROTTOLE (1502)
°sac/sec,CC114U
[It] 2-4pt cor fac ed MINKOFF
ISBN 2-8266-0665-4 contains works
by Cara, Tromboncino, Isaac and
Fogliano (M94)

MANZANO ALONSO, MIGUEL
Canciones Zamoranas, 24 °CCU
4-5pt mix cor ALPUERTO 1619 (M95)

MAR-CHAIM, JOSEPH (1940-   )
Bird Dances
jr cor ISRAELI IMP 1709 (M96)

Declaration Of Independence °ora
[Heb] mix cor&jr cor,Bar solo,
brass,orch,electronic tape [23']
ISR.MUS.INST. 6756R rent (M97)

MARATHON see Muller-Weinberg, Achim

MARCELLO
  I Will Forever Sing
    SAB oct DEAN HRD 164 $.95   (M98)

MARCHE
    cor HIEBER MH 5032   (M99)

MARCHE DES SOLDATS DE TURENNE
    see Chanson Du Couturier

MARCHE DES SOLDATS DE TURENNE see
    Frochaux, Jean-Chs.

MARCY, ROBERT
  Queue Du Chat, La
    (Grindel, J.) 4pt mix cor HEUGEL
    HE 32575   (M100)

MARE AUX ELFES, LA see Lauber, Emile

MARE DE DEU, LA
    (Agnel, A.) jr cor HEUGEL 32504
    contains also: Voila Le Printemps
                                   (M101)

MARENZIO, LUCA (1553-1599)
  Care Lagrime Mie
    SATTB BROUDE BR. CD 16 $.95   (M102)

  Dunque Romper La Fe Dunque Deggio Io
    [It] SATTB BROUDE BR. CD 15 $.75
                                   (M103)

  Gia Torna *madrigal
    SSATB CAILLARD R 71   (M104)

  Occhi Dolci E Soavi
    3pt mix cor HEUGEL HE 32600   (M105)
    3 eq voices HARMONIA 3643   (M106)

MAREUIL, J.
  Lune Est Morte, La (composed with
    Liferman, G.)
    (Lenoble, J.) 3 eq voices/4pt mix
    cor HEUGEL HE 32427   (M107)

MAREZ OYENS, TERA DE (1932-   )
  Sinfonia Testimonial
    4pt mix cor,3.3.3.3. 4.3.3.1. timp,
    3-4perc,harp,pno,strings,
    electronic tape [40'] DONEMUS
                                   (M108)

MARGIT HJUKSE
    (Weaver, David) SATB MUSIKK MH 2470
                                   (M109)

MARGOLIS, JEROME N.
  Christmas Song
    unis cor MOD ART MA-001 $.50   (M110)

MARGOT see Arcadelt, Jacob

MARIEN-LEGENDE see Schmidt-Duisburg, M.

MARIETTE see Barblan, Emmanuel

MARIN ET LA ROSE, LE see Pingault, Cl.

MARINS DES ETOILES see Volery, Francis

MARIONETTERNA see Grandert, Johnny

MARI'S KULOKK OG BRUREMARSJ see
    Sommerfeldt, Oistein

MARJATTA see Heinrichs, Wilhelm

MARJATTA MATALA NEITI see Rautavaara,
    Einojuhani

MARJOLAINE see Lemarque, F.

MARK TWAIN - AWFUL GERMAN LANGUAGE see
    Levi

MARK TWAIN - GOLDEN ARM see Levi

MARK TWAIN - GREAT JOUST see Levi

MARK TWAIN - SUNRISE ON MISS see Levi

MARK WELL, MY HEART see Vick

MARKET STREET, THE see Rasiuk, Moshe,
    Rehov Hashuk

MARNAY
  Cent Mille Chansons
    (Magne; Hille) "Nieuwe Dag, De"
    SATB MOLENAAR 13039704   (M111)

  Enfants Qui Pleurent, Les (composed
    with Legrand, Michel)
    (Gaudin, J.Y.) 4-7pt mix cor HEUGEL
    HE 32478   (M112)

  Nieuwe Dag, De *see Cent Mille
    Chansons

MAROS, RUDOLF (1917-   )
  Tiny Cantata, A
    [Ger/Eng] 3pt mix cor,pno,string
    orch [7'] PEER 61459-116 f.s.,
    ipr   (M113)

MARSEILLAISE, LA: CHANT DU DEPART
    (Chailley, Jacques) SATB,pno A COEUR
    JOIE CA 20   (M114)

MARSH, MARY VAL
  Hold On
    SAB ALFRED 7586 $.95, accomp tape
    available   (M115)
    unis cor/2pt cor ALFRED 7587 $.95,
    accomp tape available   (M116)

  Yellow Sun, The
    ALFRED   (M117)

MARSHALL, IAN
  Multi-Mix Music *CCU
    UNIVER. UE 17630 $7.95 teacher's
    ed., includes record   (M118)

MARTIAL-EPIGRAMME see Wolschina,
    Reinhard

MARTIN
  Warmland
    SATB KJOS 8655 $.70   (M119)

MARTIN see Francis, Cleve

MARTIN, GILBERT M. (1941-   )
  Ring Christmas Bells! *Xmas
    SSAATTBB oct DEAN HRD 263 $.95
                                   (M120)

MARTIN, JAMES
  Our School Chorus Song
    2pt jr cor LUDWIG L-1225 $.85
                                   (M121)
    3pt jr cor LUDWIG L-1226 $.85
                                   (M122)

MARTINO, DONALD JAMES (1931-   )
  White Island, The
    mix cor,1.1.2.1. 1.1.2.0. 2perc,
    pno,cel,string quin (5 pious
    texts by Robert Herrick) sc
    DANTALIAN DSE303 f.s., study sc
    DANTALIAN DSE303A f.s., voc sc
    DANTALIAN DSE303B f.s., perf mat
    rent   (M123)

MARX, RICHARD
  Hold On To The Nights
    (Ray) SATB ALFRED 7610 $1.25,
    accomp tape available   (M124)
    (Ray) SSA ALFRED 7613 $1.25, accomp
    tape available   (M125)
    (Ray) SAB ALFRED 7611 $1.25, accomp
    tape available   (M126)
    (Ray) 1-2pt cor ALFRED 7613 $1.25,
    accomp tape available   (M127)

MARY HAD A LITTLE CAT
    (Jackman, Jerry) 2pt cor BUGZY
    BGZ-1015   (M128)

MASCHA
    (Karpowitsch; Ignatieff) men cor
    ZIMMER. 622   (M129)

MASKERDANS see Neve, F.D.

MASLANKA, DAVID HENRY (1943-   )
  April Is In My Mistress' Face (from
    Spring Rain)
    SATB KJOS GC143 $.80   (M130)

  Rain, Rain (from Spring Rain)
    SATB KJOS GC142 $.70   (M131)

MASON
  Fete Des Ours, La *see Sonthonay, F.

  O Music (composed with Wyatt)
    3pt cor,pno CPP-BEL PROCH 03016
    $.95   (M132)

MASQUERADE see Taylor, Clifford Oliver

MASS OF THE SEA see Patterson, Paul

MASSAZANG, EN see Beekum, Jan Van, Old
    Timers Medley, The

MASSEPIN, A.
  Chaton Et La Souris, Le (composed
    with Level, Pierre Yves)
    4pt cor,2rec,xylo,opt tamb HEUGEL
    HE 32076   (M133)

MASSER, MICHAEL (1941-   )
  Greatest Love Of All, The (composed
    with Creed, Linda)
    (Chinn, Teena) SAB CPP-BEL 5724GC3X
    $1.40   (M134)
    (Chinn, Teena) SATB CPP-BEL
    5724GC1X $1.40, accomp tape
    available   (M135)
    (Chinn, Teena) SSA CPP-BEL 5724GC2X
    $1.40   (M136)

MASSEUS, JAN (1913-   )
  Drentse Metamorfosen
    SATB,0.0.0.0. 4.3.3.3. 4sax,4bugle,
    timp,2perc [15'] DONEMUS   (M137)

MASSIS
  Ballade
    2pt cor,pno JOBERT see from Six
    Enfantines   (M138)

MASSIS (cont'd.)

  Dispute
    2pt cor,pno JOBERT see from Six
    Enfantines   (M139)

  Histoire
    2pt cor,pno JOBERT see from Six
    Enfantines   (M140)

  Jeux
    2pt cor,pno JOBERT see from Six
    Enfantines   (M141)

  Promenades En Foret
    2pt cor,pno JOBERT see from Six
    Enfantines   (M142)

  Ronde
    2pt cor,pno JOBERT see from Six
    Enfantines   (M143)

  Six Enfantines *see Ballade;
    Dispute; Histoire; Jeux;
    Promenades En Foret; Ronde   (M144)

MASSON, ASKELL (1953-   )
  Visions
    wom cor,perc [8'40"] ICELAND 003-3
                                   (M145)

MASSSTABE: MISS NICHT DEIN LEBEN see
    Korn, Sebastian

MASTERS, DAVID
    see BURGER, DAVID MARK

MATEJ, JOZKA (JOSEF) (1922-   )
  Creators
    cor, solo voices,orch [14'] CESKY
    HUD.   (M146)

MATH TEST BOOGIE, THE see Lutz,
    Lawrence

MATHENY, GARY
  Listen To The Wind A-Blowin'
    SAB/3pt men cor,acap SOMERSET
    SP-794 $.60   (M147)

MATHEWS, PETER
  Birds Of Paradise
    SA,pno LAWSON 52326 $.90   (M148)

MATHEY, PAUL
  C'est Par Vous
    TTBB HUGUENIN EB 164   (M149)

  Soleil Miraculeux- Sonnenkraft
    TTBB HUGUENIN CH 1097   (M150)

MATHIAS, WILLIAM (1934-   )
  Ceremony After A Fire Raid
    SATBB,solo voice,pno,perc OXFORD
    337434-X $8.75   (M151)

  Echoing Green, The
    SSAA,pno OXFORD W103 19342603 X
                                   (M152)

  Fall
    see This Worlde's Joie

  Learsongs *CC5U
    SA,2pno OXFORD rent   (M153)

  May Magnificat, A
    dbl cor,opt chimes OXFORD 337442-0
    $12.00   (M154)

  O Aula Nobilis
    SA,3trp,timp,3perc,pno 4-hands
    OXFORD 19 3374412   (M155)

  Spring
    see This Worlde's Joie

  Summer
    see This Worlde's Joie

  This Worlde's Joie
    SATB&jr cor,STBar soli,3.2.2.3.
    4.3.3.1. timp,4perc,pno,cel,harp,
    org,strings OXFORD 337437-4
    $20.00
    contains: Fall; Spring; Summer;
    Winter   (M156)

  Three Medieval Lyrics *CC3U
    SATB,2trp,perc,org OXFORD   (M157)

  Winter
    see This Worlde's Joie

MATIN, LE see Miche, Paul

MATKA see Kopelent, Marek

MATOUSSOUSKI
  Temps Du Muguet, Le *see Lemarque,
    F.

MATTHEWS, MICHAEL
  Song Of Cornwall
    TTBarB,acap STAINER W101   (M158)

MATTHUS, SIEGFRIED (1934-   )
  Laudate Pacem
    dbl cor&jr cor,3.3.3.3. 4.6.4.1.
    pno,org,timp,perc,strings [75']
    BREITKOPF-L   (M159)

  Liebesqualen Des Catull, Die
    mix cor,SBar soli,2fl,2clar,2harp,
    2pno,2perc,2elec gtr,4vcl,elec
    bass [38'] BREITKOPF-L   (M160)

  Musica Et Vinum °Variations
    mix cor sc BREITKOPF-L 7665   (M161)

  Wir Zwei
    12pt mix cor sc BREITKOPF-L 7668
                                  (M162)
MATTSON
  Sebastopol Carol
    SATB CPP-BEL SV8224 $.95   (M163)

  Simple Gifts
    SATB CPP-BEL SV8220 $.95   (M164)

MATYS, JIRI (1927-   )
  Journey Through The Night °CC3U
    wom cor/girl cor,acap CESKY HUD.
    8112 0190   (M165)

  Red Toadstool, The
    jr cor,solo voice,pno,fl [6'] CESKY
    HUD. 1 39 9807   (M166)

MAUDUIT, JACQUES (1557-1627)
  Voici Le Vert Et Beau Mai
    SATB,acap HUGUENIN EB 287   (M167)

  Vous Me Tuez Si Doucement
    see Costeley, Guillaume, Puisque Ce
    Beau Mois
    SATB,acap HUGUENIN EB 87   (M168)

MAUSCHEN MIT DEM ABGEBISSENEN
  SCHWANZCHEN, DAS see Schwaen, Kurt

MAUSFALLEN- SPRUCHLEIN see Scherber, M.

MAUVAISE REPUTATION, LA see Brassens,
  Georges

MAXI-MIN see Welin, Karl-Erik

MAY, KARL
  Vergiss Mich Nicht!
    [Ger] mix cor,acap [4'] SCHOTTS
    CHBL 436   (M169)

MAY DAY CAROL
  (Taylor, Deems) SATB,pno CPP-BEL
    FEC 04838 $1.20   (M170)

MAY MAGNIFICAT see Paynter, John P.

MAY MAGNIFICAT, A see Mathias, William

MAY MORNING see Smith, Robert Edward

MAY SONG, A see Crosse, Gordon

MAY THE ROAD RISE UP TO MEET YOU see
  Burton

MAYA PROPHECY, A see Mindel, Meir,
  Nevu'at Maya

MAYBE WE CAN see Lentz, Roger G.

MAYR-KANTATE see Bruckner, Anton

MAZURKA FRA LOM
  (Rormark, Joar) mix cor MUSIKK
    MH 2434 see from Fire Slatter For
    Kor   (M171)

MAZURKA SOUTO LI PINS, LA
  (Langree, A.) SAB A COEUR JOIE 1022
                                  (M172)
ME AND MY BEST FRIEND see Rench

ME AND MY SHADOW
  (Driscoll) TTBB (barbershop) BOURNE
    B238949 $.50   (M173)

ME AND YOU see Leisy, James Franklin

MECHEM, KIRKE LEWIS (1925-   )
  Choral Tribute, A °Op.49
    SATB,opt pno SCHIRM.G 502140 $2.25
                                  (M174)
  Christmas Past And Christmas Present
    2pt treb cor,pno SCHIRM.G 50488838
    $.95   (M175)
    SATB,pno SCHIRM.G 50488839 $.95
                                  (M176)
  Professor Nontroppo's Music
    Dictionary
    SATB,opt pno kbd pt PRESSER
    312-41012A $5.00   (M177)

MEDAAS, IVAR
  Gjev Meg Jorda
    TTBB/SATB NORSK   (M178)

MEDEK, TILO (1940-   )
  An Den Aether
    3pt cor [15'] MOECK 5301   (M179)

  Bitte Am Morgen
    4pt cor [3'] MOECK 5282   (M180)

MEDEMA
  Hush, Missus Teenage Mary
    SATB SHAWNEE   (M181)

MEDLEY CHRISTMAS see Howard

MEERESLEUCHTEN see Jenner, Gustav

MEERESSTILLE UND GLUCKLICHE FAHRT see
  Beethoven, Ludwig van

MEET MY FOLKS! (8 PORTRAITS) see
  Crosse, Gordon

MEHUL
  Chant Du Depart
    (Langree, Alain) SATB A COEUR JOIE
    283   (M182)

MEHUL, ETIENNE-NICOLAS (1763-1817)
  Aux Accents De Notre Harmonie (from
    Joseph)
    SATB,acap HUGUENIN CH 623   (M183)
    TTBB HUGUENIN CH 662   (M184)

  Dieu D'Israel (from Joseph)
    SATB,acap HUGUENIN CH 419   (M185)

MEIDLEIN TET MIR KLAGEN, EIN see
  Dowland, John

MEIJERING, CHIEL (1954-   )
  Ahnung Des Endes
    4pt mix cor,3.3.3.3. 8.4.3.1.
    4perc,pno/cel,2harp,strings,vla
    solo [60'] DONEMUS   (M186)

MEIMA, HERMAN (1905-   )
  Tien Kinderliedjes °CC10L
    unis jr cor,pno ZENGERINK Z 605
                                  (M187)
MEIN HERZ, ICH WILL DICH FRAGEN see
  Zoll, Paul

MEIN HERZ RUFT IMMER NUR NACH DIR, O
  MARITA! see Stolz, Robert

MEIN LIEBER GATTE see Golowalj Moja

MEIN LIEBESLIED MUSS EIN WALZER SEIN
  see Stolz, Robert

MEIN SCHATZLEIN HOR ICH SINGEN see
  Goller, Fritz

MEIN SCHATZLEIN KOMMT VON FERNE see
  Friemel, G.

MEIN SCHONES HOLLAND see Stolz, Robert,
  Mijn Dierbaar Holland

MEIN SCHONSTE ZIER see Hessenberg

MEINE FREUNDIN IST SCHON see Bach,
  Johann Christoph

MEISJE DAT VAN SCHEVINGEN see Ivens, J.

MEISKEN JONG, MIJN MAEGDEKEN TEER see
  Schrijvers, Jean

MEIZANG: 'T IS LENTE, 'T IS LENTE see
  Zwaan, J.

MELANCOLIE see Perrinjaquet, G.

MELCHERS, WALTER
  Standchen
    mix cor BRAUN-PER 1021   (M188)

MELCHIOR ET BALTHAZAR
  see Dis-Moi, Jeannette
    (Brasseur, M.A.; Teniere, C.) unis jr
    cor,Orff inst HEUGEL HE 32374
    contains also: Dis-Moi Jeannette
                                  (M189)
MELICHAR, ALOIS (1896-1976)
  An Der Donau, Wenn Der Wein Bluht
    °see Grothe

MELIN, STEN (1957-   )
  Vivisektion
    8pt mix cor [10'] STIM 8511-064
                                  (M190)
MELLANBINDAREN see Grasbeck, Gottfrid

MELLNAS, ARNE (1933-   )
  Infinito, L'
    mix cor,acap [8'] REIMERS
    AVANTI ER 93   (M191)

  Wind Has Blown, A
    mix cor,acap [4'] REIMERS
    AVANTI ER 62   (M192)

MELODY MAKER see Ross, Brad

MELROSE, RONALD
  I Want To See The World
    SATB,kbd,opt band FISCHER,C CM8211
    $.95   (M193)
MELTON, WILLIAM E.
  Autumn Song, An
    SATB oct DEAN HRD 136 $.75   (M194)

MEMENTO see Laburda, Jiri

MEMORIES OF CHRISTMAS see Reese

MEMORY see Bezanson, Philip

MEN OF IWO JIMA see Siltman, Bobby L.

MEN ROEPT VAN GROENLANDS BERGEN see
  Anonymous

MENAGE DE LA SAINTE FAMILLE, LE see
  Blanchard

MENAGERIE see Golle, Jurgen

MENDELSSOHN, ARNOLD (1855-1933)
  Herbst
    see Mendelssohn, Arnold, Kurze
    Fruhling, Der

  Kurze Fruhling, Der
    SSAA,acap HARMONIA 3695 contains
    also: Herbst   (M195)

MENDELSSOHN, FANNY
  see HENSEL, FANNY MENDELSSOHN

MENDELSSOHN-BARTHOLDY, FELIX
  (1809-1847)
  Abendlied
    SA/TB NATIONAL NMP-144 $.80   (M196)

  Abschied Vom Walde
    SATB CAILLARD PC 170   (M197)

  Andenken
    SATB LAWSON LG 52322 $.85   (M198)

  Antigone °Op.55
    (Draheim, J.) TTTTBBBB,soli&
    narrator,pno [60'] voc sc
    BREITKOPF-W EB 135   (M199)

  Auf Dem See °Op.14,No.6
    SATB NATIONAL NMP- 184 $.95   (M200)
    (Walker) "On The Sea" [Ger/Eng] 4pt
    mix cor LAWSON 52181   (M201)

  Autumn Song
    (Holcombe) SA&opt TB MUSICIANS PUB
    ES-101 $.85   (M202)

  Entflieh Mit Mir
    SATB CAILLARD PC 169   (M203)

  Farewell To The Forest
    (Reed, Everett) cor ASPEN 3002 $.75
                                  (M204)
  Festgang An Die Kunstler °Op.68
    men cor,soli,brass BREITKOPF-W
    CHB 3423   (M205)

  Fly Off With Me
    SATB LAWSON LG 52362 $.70   (M206)

  Fruhlingslied
    SATB CAILLARD PC 171   (M207)

  Fruhzeitiger Fruhling
    SATB NATIONAL NMP-167 $.90   (M208)

  Herold Engel, Weihnachtslied
    mix cor,acap CRON   (M209)

  Ich Wollt' Meine Lieb'
    SA/TB NATIONAL NMP-146 $.80   (M210)

  Im Walde
    SATB CAILLARD PC 168   (M211)

  Lerchesgesang
    SATB NATIONAL NMP-168 $.85   (M212)

  Liebe Und Wein °Op.50,No.5
    men cor PETERS 8534   (M213)

  Lieblingsplatzchen
    (Altink) TTBB MOLENAAR 15012702
                                  (M214)
  Maiglocken Und Die Blumelein
    SA NATIONAL NMP-193 $.85   (M215)

  Morgengebed
    (Evertse) SSA MOLENAAR 15023003
                                  (M216)
  Musik Zu Antigone Von Sophokles
    °Op.55
    men cor,orch/pno voc sc AUTOGR
                                  (M217)
  Neujahrslied
    SATB NATIONAL NMP-182 $.85   (M218)

  On The Sea °see Auf Dem See

MENDELSSOHN-BARTHOLDY, FELIX (cont'd.)

Turkisches Schenkenlied °Op.50,No.1
TTBB HARMONIA 3808   (M219)

Upon Her Grave
SATB LAWSON LG 52368 $.85   (M220)

MENEELY-KYDER, SARAH
Filharmonico
SSAATTBB,pno,vibra,gamelan [10']
AM.COMP.AL. $13.80   (M221)

Five Systems
SSA,3perc [5'] AM.COMP.AL. $2.70
(M222)

Four Lullabyes
SA,pno, tubular chimes [12']
AM.COMP.AL. $10.70   (M223)

MENGELBERG, KAREL (1902-1984)
'T Was Niets Dan Zonnig Ritme °see
Valse De La Poupee

Valse De La Poupee
"'T Was Niets Dan Zonnig Ritme"
unis cor,pno ZENGERINK Z 613
(M224)

MENNIN, PETER (MENNINI) (1923-1983)
Reflections Of Emily °song cycle
3pt treb cor,harp,pno,perc (texts
by Emily Dickinson) FISCHER,C
05173 f.s.   (M225)

MEN'S CHORUS OF THE MOSCOW ENGINEERING
AND PHYSICS INSTITUTE SINGS, THE
°CCU
[Russ] TTBB,pno MEZ KNIGA 161 (M226)

MENSCH BEI WEIBERN NICHTS ERREICHT, EIN
see Scheck, Helmut, Variationen

MENSCH LEBT SO HIN, DER see Gebhard

MENUET POUR LA JOCONDE see Brafford, P.

MERDE A VAUBAN see Ferre, Leo

MERE GODICHON, LA see Vuataz, Roger

MERE NOEL see Perret, P.

MEREL IN DE MORGEN: IK SLIEP IN
FRISSCHEN DRUIVELAAR see Vocht,
Lodewijk de

MERIKESS MYKONOS see Sagvik, Stellan

MERK TOCH HOE STERK
(Thijsse, Wim Herman) [Dutch] 3 eq
voices,acap ZENGERINK V 146 (M227)

MERK TOCH HOE STERK see Anonymous

MERK TOCH HOE STERK see Thijsse, Wim

MERLET, MICHEL (1939-   )
Ils Étaient Trois Petits Enfants
SATB,fl,2clar,bsn,cont HEUGEL
HE 32098   (M228)

MERMAN, JOYCE
Happy Birthday, U.S.A. °see Barlow,
Betty

MERRY CHRISTMAS, DARLING see Carpenter,
Richard Lynn

MERRY CHRISTMAS, ONCE AGAIN see
Strommen, Carl

MERRY CHRISTMAS WALTZ see Walter

MERRY-GO-ROUND, A: VOL. 4 °CCUL
[Russ] jr cor,pno MEZ KNIGA 491
(M229)

MERRY-GO-ROUND, A: VOL. 6 °CCU
[Russ] jr cor,pno MEZ KNIGA 520
(M230)

MERRY-GO-ROUND, A: VOL. 7 °CCU
[Russ] cor,pno MEZ KNIGA 223 (M231)

MERRY LESSONS FROM THE "RADIO NANNY"
PROGRAMME °CCU
[Russ] jr cor MEZ KNIGA 492 (M232)

MERRY LESSONS FROM THE "RADIO NANNYA"
PROGRAMME, VOL. 2 °CCU
[Russ] jr cor,pno MEZ KNIGA 521
(M233)

MERRY MONTH OF MAY, THE see Clemens,
Jacobus (Clemens non Papa),
Lustelijcke Mey, De

MERRY MOUNTAIN RAINDROPS see Ahrold,
Frank A.

MERRY WAS THE MUSIC see North

MERRY WIND
[Russ] jr cor MEZ KNIGA 501 see from
Picture Songs, Vol. 5   (M234)

MERVEILLEUSES CREATURES, LES see
Geoffray, Cesar

MES VERTS PATURAGES see Cossetto, Emil

MESKILL
What! No Women? (composed with Ness;
Bloom; Strum)
TTBB (barbershop) BOURNE B240788
$.50   (M235)

MESSAGE, LE see Prevert, J.

MESSAGE D'AMOUR
(Vuataz, Roger) SATB,acap HUGUENIN
CH 778   (M236)

MESSAGGIO DELLA BONTA see Kopelent,
Marek

MET HUN POOTEN IN DE VAART see
Schellevis, Antoon

MET JE HANDEN see Warnaar, D.J.

METAMATIIKKAA see Kortekangas, Olli

METAMORPHOSEN see Delft, Marc van

METAMORPHOSIS see Rypdal, Terje

METRAL, PIERRE (1936-   )
Genese
SATB,solo,4trom,4perc SEESAW (M237)

Noche Serena
SATB,B solo,harp,trp,2trom,4perc
SEESAW   (M238)

MEVER, P. VAN
Lichtmatroos Van Limmen
TTBB MOLENAAR 15027204   (M239)

MEWS, (ERIC) DOUGLAS KELSON (1918-   )
Ghosts, Fire, Water
SATB,A solo,acap OXFORD   (M240)

MEYER, ERNST HERMANN (1905-   )
Feuerspruch Uber Die Toten Genossen
mix cor sc BREITKOPF-L 7665   (M241)

MEYERS, RANDALL
Prayer Offering For Large Choir
cor,acap NORGE   (M242)

MI Y'MALEIL see Barnett, Steve

MI ZEH HIDLIK see Barnett, Steve

MICH ZIEHT ES see Schumann, Robert
(Alexander)

MICHAEL °spir
(Grimbert, J.) 4-6pt mix cor HEUGEL
HE 32462   (M243)

MICHAEL, EDWARD (1921-   )
Petite Suite
wom cor TRANSAT. TR000779   (M244)

MICHAEL, ROW THE BOAT ASHORE
(Chinn, Teena) SATB CPP-BEL
SV8928 F 110 $1.10, accomp tape
available   (M245)
(Chinn, Teena) SAB CPP-BEL SV8929
$1.10, accomp tape available (M246)

MICHAELS, DAVID JULIAN
Children Of The World
SAB (med) GENTRY JG2103 $.95,
accomp tape available   (M247)

Move To The Music
2pt cor (med easy) GENTRY JG2082
$.95, accomp tape available
(M248)
Shout!
SATB (med) GENTRY JG2108 $1.15,
accomp tape available   (M249)

Sing Out
SAB GENTRY JG2081 $.85, accomp tape
available   (M250)
2pt cor GENTRY JG2055 $.75, accomp
tape available   (M251)

MICHANS, CARLOS (1950-   )
Zes Gelderse Gedichten
mix cor [16'] DONEMUS   (M252)

MICHE, PAUL
Evolene
TTBB HUGUENIN CH 1092   (M253)

Matin, Le
TTBB HUGUENIN CH 996   (M254)

Trois Roses, Les
SATB,acap HUGUENIN CH 1154   (M255)
TTBB HUGUENIN CH 995   (M256)

MICHEELSEN, HANS FRIEDRICH (1902-1973)
Herr, Schicke Was Du Willt
SSA MULLER SM 2133 see from Lieder
Fur Frauenchor Nach Gedichten Von
Eduard Morike   (M257)

MICHEELSEN, HANS FRIEDRICH (cont'd.)

In Ihm Sei's Begonnen
SSA MULLER SM 2134 see from Lieder
Fur Frauenchor Nach Gedichten Von
Eduard Morike   (M258)

Kleine Zoo, Der °cant
mix cor,instrumental ensemble
SIKORSKI 406 f.s.   (M259)

Lieder Fur Frauenchor Nach Gedichten
Von Eduard Morike °see Herr,
Schicke Was Du Willt; In Ihm
Sei's Begonnen   (M260)

MICHEL ET CHRISTINE
(Lauber, Emile) TTBB HUGUENIN SP 6
(M261)
MIDDLEMAS
Passing By
SA&camb CAMBIATA A180142 $.75
(M262)

MIDNIGHT see Hamilton, Iain

MIDSUMMER see Hamilton, Iain

MIDSUMMER SPELL see Roberton, Hugh
Stevenson

MIGILDI MAGILDI see Hughes-Jones,
Llifon

MIGNONNE see Curti, F.

MIGNONNE, ALLONS VOIR SI LA ROSE see
Costeley, Guillaume

MIGNONNETTE see Le Blanc, Didier

MIJN BOERENLAND see Bos-Maurer, A. Van
De

MIJN DIERBAAR HOLLAND see Stolz, Robert

MIJN NEDERLAND see Holman, F.

MILHAUD, DARIUS (1892-1974)
Incantations °Op.201
(Carpentier) men cor SCHOTT ME 8066
(M263)

MILLER
Cat Came Back, The
(Sumner) SAB,kbd [2'45"] CORONET
392-41407 $.95   (M264)

Frozen December, The
SATB,acap NEW MUSIC $.60   (M265)

Stanzas For Music
TBB SOUTHERN $1.00   (M266)

MILLER, DAVE
Let It Fly Away
2pt cor,pno CPP-BEL SV8731 $.95,
accomp tape available   (M267)

MILLER, FRANZ R.
Ausserlich Und Innerlich
(Miller, Franz R.) "Dort Unten An
Dem Rheine" men cor,4winds BOHM
(M268)
Boarischer Bauer
men cor BOHM   (M269)

Dort Unten An Dem Rheine °see
Ausserlich Und Innerlich

Drei Schwabische Lieder
3pt wom cor BOHM   (M270)

Herbst: Bunt Sind Schon Die Walder
2pt wom cor,inst BOHM   (M271)

Musikanten Wollen Wandern
men cor BOHM   (M272)

Muss I Denn Zum Stadtele 'Naus
mix cor BOHM   (M273)

Narren, Scherz, Und Liebe °cant
men cor&wom cor&mix cor,Bar solo,
orch BOHM   (M274)

Schwabische Liebeslieder
2pt mix cor,6winds,perc,opt pno
BOHM   (M275)

Sprich, O Herz
4-5pt men cor BOHM   (M276)

Von Den Sieben Schwaben: Horet Die
Geschichte °cant
mix cor/men cor,pno BOHM   (M277)

Zeit Und Ewigkeit °cant
4-8pt mix cor,pno/orch BOHM   (M278)

MILLER, HAROLD
Trelawny
TTBB,acap STAINER W100   (M279)

MILLER'S SONG, THE see Hughes-Jones,
Llifon, Can Y Melinydd

MILLER'S TEARS, THE
(Goldman) SATB,Bar solo LAWSON
LG 52329 $.70   (M280)

MILLOCKER
Dunkelrote Rosen
(Hess) mix cor,opt pno LEUCKART
LSB 517   (M281)
(Hess) men cor,pno LEUCKART LSB 117
f.s.   (M282)

MILLS, IRVING (1894-   )
Moonglow *see Hudson, Will

MILNER, ANTHONY (1925-   )
Leaden Echo And The Golden Echo, The
*Op.30
cor,acap [10'] NOVELLO   (M283)

Motet For Peace *Op.29
TTBB,2trp,2horn,3trom,euphonium,
tuba [10'] NOVELLO   (M284)

Out Of Your Sleep Arise And Wake
2pt jr cor,pno NOVELLO   (M285)

MIN BREGNE see Gaathaug, Morten

MIN ONKEL HADDE EN BONDEGARD see Kvam,
Oddvar S., Old McDonald Had A Farm

MINCED TURKEY see Bucci

MINDEL, MEIR (1946-   )
Maya Prophecy, A *see Nevu'at Maya

Nevu'at Maya
"Maya Prophecy, A" [Heb] mix cor,
acap [11'] ISR.MUS.INST. 6565
(M286)

MINER'S LAMENT
(De Cormier, Robert) mix cor LAWSON
LG 51975 $.70   (M287)

MINKOV, M.
Perpetuum Mobile *CCU
[Russ] jr cor,pno MEZ KNIGA 496
(M288)

MINNELIED see Brahms, Johannes

MINNESANG see Nunes, Emmanuel

MINNESINGERS, THE see Schumann, Robert
(Alexander)

MINNESPIEL see Schumann, Robert
(Alexander)

MINOR BIRD, A see Abraham, Diana

MINOR MASTERPIECE, A see Haydn, [Franz]
Joseph

MINSTREL BOY, THE
(Jeffers) TTBB EARTHSNG EM-4 $.25
(M289)

MINUIT SONNE
see Daniel, Etienne, Chanson A Virer

MINUIT SONNE see Daniel

MIRACLE AND A TEAR, A see Am, Magnar

MIRACLES STILL HAPPEN AT CHRISTMAS see
Leisy, James Franklin

MIRANTE, T.
Night Is Darkening Round Me
SATB,acap MUSIC SEV. M70-476 $.85
(M290)

MIRAVAL, RAYMOND DE
Sehl Que No Vol
(Turellier, J.) men cor,inst HEUGEL
HE 32150   (M291)

MIRJAMS SIEGESGESANG, "RUHRT DIE
CYMBEL" see Schubert, Franz (Peter)

MIROLA, PEKKA
Kolme Venalaista Kansanlaulua
men cor,acap FAZER F 06988-0 (M292)

MIS SCHATZELI, MIS HAARZELI
(Willisegger, H.R.) mix cor,opt inst
PELIKAN PE 1204   (M293)

MISCH-MASCH see Bovet, J.

MISSA
Allons Dans Les Grands Bois: Feuilles
D'automne
2pt cor,pno JOBERT   (M294)

MISSA ANTIPHONICA see Badings, Henk

MISTER MUSIC MAN see Asplund, David

MR. NOBODY see Grob, Anita Jean

MISTY see Garner, Erroll

MISTY ISLE, THE see Roberton, Hugh
Stevenson

MISTY TAKES ME WALKING see Ohlin,
Camille

MIT GESANG UND RHYTHMUS see Roeder,
Toni

MIT GEWITTER UND STURM see Wagner,
Richard

MIT LIEB BIN ICH UMFANGEN see
Steuerlein, Johann

MIT LUST TAT ICH AUSREITEN see Erdmann-
Abele, Veit

MIT MUSIK GEHT ALLES BESSER see
Bochmann

MIT UNS SPRINGT, TANZT UND SINGT see
Seckinger, Konrad

MITCHELL
In The Attic
SA CPP-BEL SV8313 $.95   (M295)

Santa's A Cool Guy
SA SHAWNEE 0310 $.85   (M296)

MITCHELL, BOB
"Ayes" Have It, The (composed with
Mitchell, Mary)
SAB ALFRED 7435 f.s., accomp tape
available   (M297)

Best Friends
SA,pno WIDE WORLD $.80   (M298)

Cold Feet
cor ALFRED   (M299)

Hallelujah Christmas Party
1-2pt cor ALFRED 7630 $.95, accomp
tape available   (M300)

Spring Fever
1-2pt treb cor,pno WIDE WORLD $.80
(M301)
World Sings Christmas, The (composed
with Mitchell, Mary) *Xmas
1-2pt cor ALFRED 7436   (M302)

MITCHELL, MARY
"Ayes" Have It, The *see Mitchell,
Bob

World Sings Christmas, The *see
Mitchell, Bob

MITTAG: AM WALDESSAUME see Pappert,
Robert

MITTANTIER
Tel En Medit
(Agnel, A.) ST HEUGEL HE 32552
contains also: Vous Perdez Temps
(M303)
Vous Perdez Temps
see Mittantier, Tel En Medit

MITTELBACH, OTTO
Weiss Mir Ein Schones Roselein
mix cor BOHM   (M304)

MITTERNACHTSBLUES see Grothe

MIZMORIM UFIZMONOT (VOL. 1) see Braun,
Yeheskiel

MIZMORIM UFIZMONOT (VOL. 2) see Braun,
Yeheskiel

MIZMORIM UFIZMONOT (VOL. 3) see Braun,
Yeheskiel

MMM, WINTER (THE COCOON) see Berger,
Jean

MOBY DICK see Procter, Leland

MODUS VIVENDI see Schoonenbeek, Kees

MOEDERLIEDJE see Stenz, Herman

MOERENHOUT, J. (1909-1985)
Klokkenvreugd *Suite
SATB MOLENAAR 08053306   (M305)

MOET JE VAREN: DAAR GING ER EEN MEISJE
see Verhulst, Johannes

MOI, GARDAIS LES CHEVRES
(Brasseur, M.A.; Teniere, C.) 2 eq
voices,Orff inst HEUGEL HE 32367
contains also: Autre Jour J'etais
En Route, L'   (M306)

MOI JE GARDAIS LES CHEVRES
see Autre Jour, J'etais En Route, L'

MOJA DIRIDIKA see Cossetto, Emil

MOLEN, DE: ZIE DEN MOLEN DRAAIEN see
Appeldoorn, Dina

MOLENAARS DOCHTERKEN.. KLIMT OP DEN HIL
see Smeets, Leo

MOLENTJE; HEI MOLENTJE, HOOG IN DE WIND
see Coljee, Jan

MOLLICONE, HENRY (1946-   )
Four Elizabethan Songs
SATB,S solo,2vln,vla,opt perc [10']
AM.COMP.AL. $10.70   (M307)

MOLLY MALONE see Crouch

MOMENT AND ETERNITY see Emmert,
Frantisek

MOMENT FOR MORRICONE see Morricone,
Ennio

MOMENT PRESENT, LE see Haydn, [Franz]
Joseph

MOMENTS TO REMEMBER
(Ray, Jerry) SATB ALFRED 7673 $.95
(M308)
(Ray, Jerry) SAB ALFRED 7674 $.95
(M309)
(Ray, Jerry) 1-2pt cor ALFRED 7675
$.95   (M310)

MON AMOUR, POURQUOI PARTIR? see
Gibbons, Orlando

MON BATEAU see Herr, Francoise

MON BEAU SAPINE see O Tannenbaum

MON CHER TROUPEAU see Anonymous

MON COEUR EST DANS LA PEINE
(Kremser, Edouard) TTBB HUGUENIN
EB 413   (M311)

MON COEUR EST LAS see Schubert, Franz
(Peter), Sehnsucht

MON COEUR SE RECOMMANDE A VOUS see
Castro, Jean de

MON COEUR SE RECOMMANDE A VOUS see
Lassus, Roland de (Orlandus)

MON COEUR SE RECOMMANDE A VOUS see Le
Blanc, Didier

MON DIEU, MON DIEU, QUE MA MAISTRESSE
EST BELLE see Bertrand, Antoine de

MON MARI EST PARTI see Sylvestre, Anne

MON MARI VA A LA TAVERNE see Daniel,
Etienne

MON PAYS see Simoncini, Ernest D.

MON PAYS see Vigneault, Gilles

MON PER' M'A ENVOYEE AU BOIS
(Mimet, A.M.) 3 eq voices HEUGEL
HE 31898   (M312)

MON PERE A FAIT BATIR MAISON
3pt mix cor HEUGEL HE 31950 contains
also: Quand Ti-Jean Revient Des
Bois   (M313)

MON PERE M'A TANT BATTU see Hesdin,
Nicolle Des Celliers D'

MON PERE N'AVAIT FILLE QUE MOI
see C'est Dans Le Mois De Mai

MON PERE TOT M'A MARIEE
(Lallement, B.) S,fl HEUGEL HE 31940
contains also: Chanson De Quete De
Champagne   (M314)

MON TRISTE COEUR see Jacotin, Jacques

MONACO
You Made Me Love You (composed with
McCarthy)
(Strommen) SAB SHAWNEE 0404 $.95
(M315)
(Strommen) SSA SHAWNEE 0540 $.95
(M316)
(Strommen) SATB SHAWNEE 1874 $.95
(M317)

MONADNOCK see Evett, Robert

MONATH, NORMAN (1920-   )
Magic Of Believing, The
(Britt) SATB BOURNE B239178 $.65
(M318)

MOND, DER see Naegeli, Hans Georg

MOND IM WASSER, DER see Bossler, Kurt

MOND IST AUFGEGANGEN, DER see
Hessenberg

MOND IST AUFGEGANGEN, DER see Kuntz, M.

MOND IST AUFGEGANGEN, DER see Mutter,
Gerbert

MOND IST AUFGEGANGEN, DER see
  Rothschuh, F.

MONDAY'S CHILD see Rutter, John

MONDE DU SOMMEIL see Kerstens, Huub

MONIN, CLAUDE
  Belles Fleurs, Les
    SATB,rec,S rec HEUGEL HE 31909
                                      (M319)

MONKEYS AND DUCKS see Belyea, H.

MONNIKENKOOR see Verdi, Giuseppe

MONOTONY SONG see Kubik

MONROE
  What Is Your Choice
    SATB,acap (med) THOMAS 1C318525
    $.65   (M320)

MONSIEUR D'CHARETTE A DIT
  1-4pt cor HUGUENIN see from Chansons
    Pour La Jeunesse, Sixieme Cahier
                                      (M321)

MONSIEUR D'CHARETTE A DIT see Huguenin,
  Charles

MONSIEUR DE POURCEAUGNAC see Lully,
  Jean-Baptiste (Lulli)

MONSIEUR PRINTEMPS see Gesseney, Andre

MONTAGNE, LA see Ferrat, Jean

MONTAGS-ABSCHIED (EVA-ABSCHIED) see
  Stockhausen, Karlheinz

MONTE, PHILIPPE DE (1521-1603)
  Comme La Tourterelle
    (Grimbert, J.) 5pt mix cor HEUGEL
    HE 32340   (M322)

MONTER, JOSEF (1931-)
  Bunt Sind Schon Die Walder
    "Herbst" mix cor BOHM   (M323)

  Drei Hochzeitsmadrigale Nach
    Mittelalterlichen Melodien
    2-3pt wom cor, solo voices,org/pno,
    2vln,2vcl BOHM   (M324)

  Herbst *see Bunt Sind Schon Die
    Walder

  Sascha, Hor Die Balalaika
    mix cor,opt combo BOHM   (M325)

MONTEVERDI, CLAUDIO (ca. 1567-1643)
  A Che Tormi Il Ben Mio
    (Vree) "Pain, Thou Causeth,
    Beloved" 5pt mix cor LAWSON 51153
                                      (M326)

  Ah, Dolente Partita
    "Ah, In Sadness I Now Leave" SSATB
    SCHIRM.G 320950 $1.20   (M327)

  Ah, In Sadness I Now Leave *see Ah,
    Dolente Partita

  Amor Che Deggio Far
    SATB,2treb inst,cont HEUGEL
    HE 32096   (M328)

  Amor-Lamento Della Ninfa
    STTB,cont HEUGEL HE 32360   (M329)

  Cor Mio! Mentre Vi Miro
    "Ma Mie" SSATB HUGUENIN EB 377
                                      (M330)
  Ecco Mormorar L'onde *madrigal
    SSATB CAILLARD R 62   (M331)

  Interrote Sperazane
    2 eq voices oct DEAN HRD 163 $.85
                                      (M332)
  Laissez La Mort Me Prendre *see
    Lasciate Mi Morire

  Lasciate Mi Morire
    "Laissez La Mort Me Prendre" SSATB
    HUGUENIN EB 386   (M333)

  Lasciatemi Morire
    (Goldman) mix cor LAWSON LG 51805
    $.70   (M334)

  Lasciati I Monti (from Orfeo)
    see Monteverdi, Claudio, Vieni
    Imenco

  Luci Serene E Chiare
    SATBB HARMONIA 3732   (M335)

  Ma Mie *see Cor Mio! Mentre Vi Miro

  Madrigali E Canzonette: Libro 9 *CCU
    (Vacchelli, Anna Maria Monterosso)
    MONTEVERDI   (M336)

  Madrigali Guerrieri Et Amorosi: Altri
    Canti D'amor *CCU
    (Grimbert, J.) mix cor HEUGEL
    HE 32294   (M337)

MONTEVERDI, CLAUDIO (cont'd.)

  Madrigali Guerrieri Et Amorosi: Altri
    Canti Di Marte *CCU
    (Grimbert, J.) mix cor HEUGEL
    HE 32295   (M338)

  Madrigali: Libro 3 *CCU
    (Barezzani, Maria Teresa Rosa) mix
    cor MONTEVERDI   (M339)

  Madrigali: Libro 5 *CCU
    (Caraci, Maria) mix cor MONTEVERDI
                                      (M340)
  Madrigali: Libro 6 *CCU
    mix cor MONTEVERDI   (M341)

  Pain, Thou Causeth, Beloved *see A
    Che Tormi Il Ben Mio

  Scherzi Musicali
    (Turellier, J.) 3pt cor,2treb inst,
    cont HEUGEL HE 32514   (M342)

  Se Nel Partir Da Voi
    "Si Loin De Vous Je Pars" SATB,acap
    HUGUENIN EB 385   (M343)

  Sfogava Con Le Stelle
    SSATB,acap OXFORD 19 385724 3
                                      (M344)
  Si Loin De Vous Je Pars *see Se Nel
    Partir Da Voi

  Su, Su, Su, Pastorelli Vezzosi
    (Turellier, Jean) 3pt cor,cont
    HEUGEL HE 32146   (M345)

  Svogava Con Le Stelle
    SATB NATIONAL RCS-103 $.90   (M346)

  Vieni Imenco (from Orfeo)
    (Sanvoisin, M.) SSTTB,opt 5inst,
    gtr,cont HEUGEL HE 32056 contains
    also: Lasciati I Monti   (M347)

MONTGOMERY, LISA
  Dreamin' (composed with Paschal,
    Geneva)
    (Chinn, Teena) SATB CPP-BEL
    5796DC1X $1.40, accomp tape
    available   (M348)
    (Chinn, Teena) SSA CPP-BEL 5796DC2X
    $1.40, accomp tape available
                                      (M349)
    (Chinn, Teena) SAB CPP-BEL 5796DC3X
    $1.40, accomp tape available
                                      (M350)

MOON FLOATS see Rimsky-Korsakov,
  Nikolai

MOON IS UP, THE see Hand, Colin

MOON RIVER see Mancini, Henry

MOONGLOW see Hudson, Will

MOON'S ALIGHT, THE see Hodgetts, Colin

MOORE
  American Creed, The
    2pt cor CPP-BEL SV8844 $1.10,
    accomp tape available   (M351)
    SAB CPP-BEL SV8843 $1.10, accomp
    tape available   (M352)
    SATB CPP-BEL SV8842 $1.10, accomp
    tape available   (M353)

MOORE, CARMAN (1936-   )
  American Nebula, The
    SATB,orch [35'] PEER   (M354)

MOORE, DONALD
  Bye, Bye, Sleep Little One
    SATB CPP-BEL SV8914 $1.10   (M355)
    2pt cor CPP-BEL SV8915 $1.10   (M356)

  Dancin' At The Rock
    SATB CPP-BEL SV8829 $1.10   (M357)
    3pt mix cor CPP-BEL SV8831 $1.10
                                      (M358)
    SSA CPP-BEL SV8830 $1.10   (M359)

  Lazy Kinda Blues
    3pt mix cor CPP-BEL SV8811 $.95,
    accomp tape available   (M360)

  Long Time Ago In Bethlehem
    SATB,pno CPP-BEL SV8901 $1.10
                                      (M361)
    SA,pno CPP-BEL SV8903 $1.10   (M362)
    SAB,pno CPP-BEL SV8902 $1.10   (M363)

MOORE, DONALD P.
  Rockin' The Glory
    ALFRED   (M364)

MOORE, DOROTHY RUDD
  see RUDD-MOORE, DOROTHY

MORAVIAN CONTEMPLATIONS see Kurz, Ivan

MORBIHAN see Daniel, Etienne

MORE ALE see Episcopius, L., Bier, Een
  Bier, Een Bierenbroyken, Een

MORE ALE, MORE ALE AND CAKE see
  Episcopius, L.

MORE INDISPENSABLE INCIDENTALS see
  Whitworth

MORE THAN A FRIEND see McPheeters

MORE THAN YOU KNOW
  (Huff, Mac) SATB CPP-BEL T5385MC1
    f.s., accomp tape available   (M365)

MOREILLON, H.P.
  Chasseur, Le
    SATB,acap HUGUENIN EB 435   (M366)

  Gloire Au Vin
    TTBB HUGUENIN EB 430   (M367)

  Rideau De Ma Voisine, Le
    SATB,acap HUGUENIN EB 216   (M368)
    4pt mix cor HUGUENIN EB 409   (M369)

MORGAN, DENNIS
  With Just One Look In Your Eyes *see
    Davis, Stephen

MORGAN, HILDA
  Snowdrop And Lamb
    unis cor,pno ROBERTON 75343   (M370)

MORGEN see Helmschrott, Robert M.

MORGEN MUSS ICH FORT VON HIER see
  Brahms, Johannes

MORGEN WILL MEIN SCHATZ VERREISEN see
  Kracke, Hans

MORGENEN see Kvam, Oddvar S.

MORGENGEBED see Mendelssohn-Bartholdy,
  Felix

MORGENGROET: WAT FLUITEN DAAR BUITEN
  see Smeets, Leo

MORGENHYMNUS see Wolf, Hugo

MORGONRODNAD see Gamstorp, Goran

MORGONSTUND see Vea, Ketil

MORI SOM SONG see Eielsen, Steinar

MORIKE-TRIVIUM see Schroeder, Hermann

MORIN, JEAN BAPTISTE (1677-1745)
  Belle Corinne
    (Turellier, Jean) SATB,2vln,cont
    HEUGEL HE 32057   (M371)

  Charmant Amour
    (Turellier, Jean) 3pt cor,cont
    HEUGEL HE 32151   (M372)

MORIN, M.
  Alchimiste, L' (composed with Helvez,
    E.)
    (Passaquet, R.) 3 eq voices HEUGEL
    HE 32337   (M373)

MORLEY
  Love Learns By Laughing
    ATB STAINER 3.3193   (M374)

MORLEY, THOMAS (1557-1602)
  Allons Danser Aussi
    SATB,acap HUGUENIN EB 60   (M375)

  Allons Danser Aussi (Chant De Mai)
    TTBB HUGUENIN EB 192   (M376)

  April Is In My Mistress' Face
    SATB,acap HARMONIA 3671   (M377)

  Au Bois Qui Chante
    2pt cor HUGUENIN EB 45   (M378)

  Come Lovers Follow Me
    SSAT STAINER 3.3191   (M379)

  First Booke Of Canzonets To Two
    Voyces *CCU
    2pt cor PERF.ED. PF 39 $20.00 sold
    in set of two part-books   (M380)

  Good Morrow Fair Ladies
    ATB STAINER 3.3209 $.95   (M381)

  I Goe Before My Darling
    SA EARTHSNG EW-1 $.50   (M382)

  I Love, Alas, I Love Thee
    ATTBB STAINER 3.3211 $.95   (M383)

  My Bonny Lass She Smileth
    (Dorff) SSATB,acap [1'30"] PRESSER
    312-41492 $.85   (M384)

  Now Is The Month
    see Bennet, John, Weep, O Mine Eyes

MORLEY, THOMAS (cont'd.)

Now Is The Month Of Maying
SATB HARRIS HC-5013 $.50   (M385)
(Kingsbury) SAB,acap PRESSER
312-41541 see from TWO MADRIGALS
(M386)

Rossignol Chante, Le
men cor HUGUENIN EB 218A   (M387)

Round Around About A Wood
ATTB STAINER $.95   (M388)

MORNING DEW
(Han, Isaac) SATB HARRIS HC-5033 $.95
(M389)

MORNING SERENADE see Butler

MORNING STAR see Lord, Suzanne

MORNING WATCH, THE see Hamilton, Iain

MORNING WATCH, THE see Hamilton, Iain

MORRICONE, ENNIO (1928-   )
Moment For Morricone
(Mey, J. De) SATB MOLENAAR 08162808
(M390)

MORRIS
If I Had-A My Way
(De Cormier, Robert) mix cor LAWSON
OC 51530 $.70   (M391)

MORRIS, STEVLAND (STEVIE WONDER)
(1950-   )
Go Home
(Chinn, Teena) SAB CPP-BEL 4976GC3X
$.95, accomp tape available
(M392)
(Chinn, Teena) SSA CPP-BEL 4976GC2X
$.95, accomp tape available
(M393)
(Chinn, Teena) SATB CPP-BEL
4976GC1X $.95, accomp tape
available   (M394)

MORT, LA see Kerstens, Huub

MORT DE BALE, LA
(Barblan, Emmanuel) TTBB HUGUENIN
EB 160   (M395)

MORT DE PROCRIS, LA see Dufourt, Hugues

MORT DES PAUVRES, LA see Soderlind,
Ragnar

MORT ET FORTUNE see Gero, Ihan

MORTELS, LES see Kerstens, Huub

MORTENSEN, FINN (1922-   )
Tre Ved Stranden °Op.20
[Norw] SA [4'] NORGE   (M396)

MORTENSEN, OTTO (1907-   )
Sence You Went Away
"Since You Went Away" SATB A COEUR
JOIE 353   (M397)

Since You Went Away °see Sence You
Went Away

MOSCOW see Tchaikovsky, Piotr Ilyich

MOSES, LEONARD
In Flanders Field
SATB,acap MUSIC SEV. M70-561 $.85
(M398)

MOST SPECIAL TIME OF THE YEAR, THE see
Snyder

MOST WNDERFUL TIME OF THE YEAR, THE see
Brymer, Mark

MOSTAD, JON (1942-   )
Canon
SSAATB [5'] NORGE   (M399)

I Butikkens Skoger
[Norw] men cor,acap [2'] NORGE
(M400)

MOT BALLADE see Groven, Eivind

MOT EN NY VERDEN see Johansen, Bertil
Palmar

MOT LJUSET see Runnstrom, William

MOTET see Pimmer, Hans

MOTET FOR PEACE see Milner, Anthony

MOTETTE see Gal, Hans

MOTETTI NOVI E CHANZONI FRANCIOSE A
QUATRO SOPRA DOI °CCU
(Antico, Andrea) MINKOFF
ISBN 2-8266-0814-2 contains canonic
chansons & motets by Willaert,
Mouton, Prioris, Divitis, Vassoris,
P. de La Rue, and others   (M401)

MOTETUS see Straesser, Joep

MOTHER see Kopelent, Marek, Matka

MOTHER GOOSE see Collins, David

MOTHER OF MINE, I STILL HAVE YOU see
Keys

MOTHER'S EYES see Emmert, Frantisek

MOTHER'S EYES, A see Jones, Stephen

MOTS DE LA MER see Daniel, Etienne

MOTTO - SOMMER OG REGN see Arnestad,
Finn

MOULTON, JEAN
see MOUTON, JEAN

MOULU, PIERRE
J'ai Par Trop Longuement Aime
(Agnel, A.) 3pt mix cor HEUGEL
HE 32243   (M402)

MOUNTAIN, THE see Gibbs, Alan

MOUNTAIN AND THE SQUIRREL, THE see
Clarke, Henry Leland

MOUNTAIN SONG see Nygard, Carl J.

MOUSE, THE FROG AND THE LITTLE RED HEN,
THE see Grob, Anita Jean

MOUSSORGSKY, MODEST PETROVITCH
see MUSSORGSKY, MODEST PETROVICH

MOUSTAKI, GEORGES
Danse
(Passaquet, R.) 3pt mix cor HEUGEL
HE 32338   (M403)

Facteur, Le °see Hadjidakis, Manos

Il Est Trop Tard
(Turellier, J.) 2-3pt mix cor,fl,
gtr HEUGEL HE 32426   (M404)

Il Y Avait Un Jardin
(Passaquet, R.) 4pt mix cor HEUGEL
HE 32199   (M405)

Ma Liberte
(Turellier, J) 2-3pt mix cor,gtr
HEUGEL HE 32258   (M406)

Requiem Pour N'importe Qui
(Passaquet, R.) 3 eq voices HEUGEL
HE 32200   (M407)

MOUTON, JEAN (ca. 1470-1522)
Grand Desir D'aimer Me Tient, Le
(Agnel, A.) 3 eq voices HEUGEL
HE 32075   (M408)

MOVE TO THE MUSIC see Michaels, David
Julian

MOVIE CLASSICS: THE BEST OF THE 80'S
°medley
(Chinn) SATB CPP-BEL C0126C1X $2.25,
accomp tape available   (M409)
(Chinn) SAB CPP-BEL C0126C3X $2.25,
accomp tape available   (M410)
(Chinn) 2pt cor CPP-BEL C0126C5X
$2.25, accomp tape available (M411)

MOVIE CLASSICS: THROUGH THE EYES OF
LOVE °medley
(Chinn) SATB CPP-BEL C0112C1X $2.25,
accomp tape available   (M412)
(Chinn) SSA CPP-BEL C0112C2X $2.25,
accomp tape available   (M413)
(Chinn) SAB CPP-BEL C0112C3X $2.25,
accomp tape available   (M414)

MOVIN' ON see Hannisian

(MOVIN' TO THE BEAT) EVERYBODY DANCE!
see Gilpin, Greg

MOWING THE BARLEY
(Williamson, Malcolm) SATB,2.2.2.2.
2.2.0.0. harp,strings [3']
WEINBERGER   (M415)

MOZART, WOLFGANG AMADEUS (1756-1791)
Ecoutez La Chanson Bien Douce
2pt cor,pno/strings HEUGEL HE 32534
(M416)
(Turellier, Jean) 2pt cor,pno
HEUGEL HE 32512   (M417)

Gondelfahrt
(Rollin, J.) 3-4pt cor HEUGEL
HE 32350   (M418)

Minuet (from Eine Kleine Nachtmusik)
(Hugo, John W.) SATB,opt kbd THOMAS
C41-38620 $.75   (M419)

Notturno °K.346
SAB,3strings/3winds HEUGEL HE 32595
(M420)

MOZART, WOLFGANG AMADEUS (cont'd.)

O Isis Und Osiris (from Die
Zauberfloete)
[Ger/It/Dutch] 3 eq voices
ZENGERINK M 2   (M421)

Overture From "Die Zauberflote"
(Jurgens, Jurgen) [Ger] men cor,
acap [8'] SCHOTTS C 46077 (M422)
(Jurgens, Jurgen) [Ger] mix cor,
acap [8'] SCHOTTS C 46078 (M423)

Songs And Choruses °CCU
[Russ] jr cor MEZ KNIGA 542 (M424)

Warnung: Manner Suchen Stets Zu
Naschen °K.433
mix cor BOHM   (M425)

Wiegenlied
SATB MOLENAAR 15020404   (M426)

MRS. SANTA CLAUS see Dellasandro, G.

MUCKENHOCHZEIT see Hollfelder, Waldram

MUGE
(Larson, David) [Chin/Eng] SATB,acap
LAWSON 52315 $.90   (M427)

MULHOLLAND, JAMES
Bredon Hill
SATB NATIONAL NMP-174 $.90   (M428)

Heart We Will Forget Him
SSA NATIONAL WHC-153 $.80   (M429)

Nobody Knows This Little Rose
SSA NATIONAL WHC-151 $.80   (M430)

Oh See How Thick The Goldcup Flowers
SATB NATIONAL NMP-172 $.85   (M431)

So I Let Him Lead Me Home
SSA NATIONAL WHC-152 $.80   (M432)

White In The Moon
SATB NATIONAL NMP-171 $.80   (M433)

With Rue My Heart Is Laden
SATB NATIONAL NMP-157 $.80   (M434)

MULLER-MEDEK, TILO
see MEDEK, TILO

MULLER-WEINBERG, ACHIM
Marathon
mix cor,1.1.1.1. 2.2.1.0. 2vln,vla,
vcl,db,7perc,pno,elec gtr [12']
BREITKOPF-L   (M435)

MULLICH, HERMANN (1943-   )
Bedenklichkeiten
"Grad Aus Dem Wirtshaus Komm Ich
Heraus" men cor,brass BOHM (M436)

Grad Aus Dem Wirtshaus Komm Ich
Heraus °see Bedenklichkeiten

Schulersongs
1-2pt jr cor,pno/Orff inst BOHM
(M437)

MULTI-MIX MUSIC see Marshall, Ian

MUNDY, JOHN (? -1630)
Of All The Birds That I Have Heard
°madrigal
(Rumery, L.) SAB,acap (med) THOMAS
1C288511 $.80   (M438)

MURRAY
Christmas, A Wonderful Time Of The
Year
SA,fl KJOS C8724 $.80   (M439)

It Even Sounds Like Christmas
SATB KJOS C8617 $.70   (M440)

Nobody Loves Me Like You Do (composed
with Loggins, Kenny)
(Althouse) 2pt cor CPP-BEL 4861NC5X
$1.25   (M441)
(Althouse) SAB CPP-BEL 4861NC3X
$1.25   (M442)
(Althouse) SATB CPP-BEL 4861NC1X
$1.25   (M443)

MUSIC ALONE SHALL LIVE see Rodby,
Walter

MUSIC AT THE KINDERGARTEN °CCU
[Russ] jr cor MEZ KNIGA 484   (M444)

MUSIC BOX CAROL, A see Besig

MUSIC FACT RAP, THE see Feldstein, Saul
(Sandy)

MUSIC FOR A PIED-PIPER see Joubert,
John

MUSIC FOR CHILDREN'S CHOIR see Eben,
Petr, Zelena Se Snitka

MUSIC FOR CONCERT CHOIR AND CARILLON
see Udow, Michael William

MUSIC FOR SOPRANO & CHOIR see Bialosky,
Marshall H.

MUSIC FOR THE WHITE HOUSE see Lewin,
Frank

MUSIC IS FULL OF DREAMS see Walter,
Lana

MUSIC IS MY LIFE see Butler, Eugene
Sanders

MUSIC IS OUR HERITAGE see Bialomizy,
Stan

MUSIC MAKES THE WORLD GO 'ROUND see
Butler, Eugene Sanders

MUSIC! MUSIC! MUSIC! see Weiss

MUSIC OF GOODBYE, THE
(Lojeski) SATB LEONARD-US 08243861
$.95   (M445)
(Lojeski) SAB LEONARD-US 08243862
$.95, ipa   (M446)

MUSIC RESOUNDS see Calvisius, Seth(us),
Musiken Klang

MUSIC SWEET MUSIC see Fast

MUSIC, SWEET MUSIC see Ray, Jerry

MUSIC TO GOETHE'S "EGMONT" see
Beethoven, Ludwig van

MUSIC TO MOVE see Delft, Marc van

MUSIC TO TWO FRAGMENTS TO MUSIC BY
SHELLEY see Nordheim, Arne

MUSIC, WHEN SOFT VOICES DIE see
Eddleman, David

MUSIC, WHEN SOFT VOICES DIE see
Fennelly, Brian

MUSIC, YOU GAVE ME MUSIC see Bacon,
Boyd

MUSICA, DIE GANZ LIEBLICH KUNST see
Jeep, Johann

MUSICA ET VINUM see Matthus, Siegfried

MUSICA POPULAR DE ZAMORA *CCU
ALPUERTO   (M447)

MUSICA ZU EHREN see Heinrichs, Wilhelm

MUSICAL HOUR, THE: VOL. 2 *CCUL
[Russ] jr cor,pno 4-hands MEZ KNIGA
497   (M448)

MUSICAL THEATRE, THE: VOL. 2 *CCU
[Russ] jr cor MEZ KNIGA 518 theatre
shows with music by Abramov,
Popatenko, Lebedev and others
                                  (M449)

MUSICIANS OF BREMEN, THE see
Williamson, Malcolm

MUSICIENS QUI CHANTEZ see Waelrant,
Hubert

MUSIK ZU ANTIGONE VON SOPHOKLES see
Mendelssohn-Bartholdy, Felix

MUSIKALISCHE FAMILIE, DIE
(Scheidegger, J.) unis jr cor,opt
inst PELIKAN PE 1207   (M450)

MUSIKANTEN, WARUM SCHWEIGT IHR see
Hollfelder, Waldram,
Musikantenstandchen

MUSIKANTEN WOLLEN WANDERN see Miller,
Franz R.

MUSIKANTENGRUSS see Gunsenheimer,
Gustav

MUSIKANTENSTANDCHEN see Hollfelder,
Waldram

MUSIKEN KLANG see Calvisius, Seth(us)

MUSIQUE POUR NICOLAS FLAMEL see
Challulau, Patrice

MUSS I DENN ZUM STADTELE 'NAUS see
Miller, Franz R.

MUSSER
Gospel Jubilee!
SAB SHAWNEE 0396 $.95   (M451)

R-A-G-T-I-M-E!
3pt cor SHAWNEE 0333 $.80   (M452)

MUSSORGSKY, MODEST PETROVICH
(1839-1881)
Children's Songs And Choruses *CCU
[Russ] jr cor,pno MEZ KNIGA 240
                                  (M453)
Coronation Scene (from Boris Godunov)
SSAATTBB,TBar soli voc sc KALMUS
K 06354 $3.50   (M454)

Selected Choruses *CCU
(Ptitsa, K.) [Russ] cor MEZ KNIGA
161   (M455)

Sonnen-Hymne
TTBB MOLENAAR 15022204   (M456)

MUTHSPIEL, K.
Hoamgehn Zu Dir *CCU
mix cor/eq voices DOBLINGER 42 861
                                  (M457)
Stellt's Enk Z'samm Und Hiaz Sing Ma
Oans *CCU
mix cor/eq voices DOBLINGER 07 585
                                  (M458)

MUTTER, GERBERT (1923-   )
Durch Feld And Buchenhallen *song
cycle
mix cor BOHM   (M459)

Krokodilromanze: Ich Bin Ein Armes
Krokodil
3pt wom cor BOHM   (M460)

Macht Der Musik, Die (from Augsburger
Tafelkonfekt)
men cor,winds/pno BOHM   (M461)

Mond Ist Aufgegangen, Der
mix cor BOHM   (M462)

Viva La Musica: Musica, Du Schone
Zier
men cor BOHM   (M463)

Wenn Alle Brunnlein Fliessen
mix cor BOHM   (M464)

MUUTAMAT KEVAAN PAIVAT see Bashmakov,
Leonid

MY BONNIE IS OVER THE OCEAN (BONNIE'S
MEDLEY 1) see Beekum, Jan Van

MY BONNIE LASS SHE SMELLETH see
Schickele, Peter

MY BONNY LASS SHE SMILETH see Morley,
Thomas

MY CHRISTMAS WISH see Allen, David Len

MY DEAREST LOVE see Sermisy, Claude de
(Claudin)

MY DOOR IS ALWAYS OPEN see Williams

MY GOD, WHAT IS A HEART? see Weigl,
[Mrs.] Vally

MY HEART CAN'T TELL YOU NO
(Keveren, Phillip) SATB ALFRED 7665
$1.25   (M465)
(Keveren, Phillip) SAB ALFRED 7666
$1.25   (M466)

MY HOME TOWN see Althouse, Jay

MY LORD, WHAT A MORNIN' *spir
(Scherer) SSAA MULLER 2752 see from
Volkslieder Aus Aller Welt   (M467)
(Scherer, E.) SATB,pno,opt gtr MULLER
2766   (M468)

MY LOVE ASLEEP see Shearer, C.M.

MY LOVE FOR YOU see Beethoven, Ludwig
van, Ich Liebe Dich

MY LOVE HAS SOFT SKIN see Wolff

MY LOVE IS LIKE A RED, RED ROSE see
Cutter, Bill

MY LOVELY CELIA see Deale, Edgar

MY MOTHER PLAYS A WALTZ see Weisenberg,
Menachem, Imi Menagenet Valz

MY MOTHERLAND'S VOICE *CCU
[Russ] jr cor MEZ KNIGA 511   (M469)

MY NOVEMBER GUEST see Kearns, Ann

MY OLD KENTUCKY HOME
(Turellier, J.) 4pt mix cor,opt gtr
HEUGEL HE 32247   (M470)

MY ONLY LOVE
see Songs Of Papua New Guinea

MY PIGEON HOUSE
(Plank) SATB KJOS C8914 $.90   (M471)

MY ROOSTER
see Songs Of Papua New Guinea

MY SECRET LOVE see Vogel, Roger Craig

MY SHINING HOUR see Strommen, Carl

MY SHIP AND I see Gallina, Jill C.

MY SOUL, THERE IS A COUNTRY see
Nystedt, Knut

MY SPECIAL FRIEND see McPheeters

MY VISTULA RIVER, A LITTLE QUAIL FLEW
AWAY see Sulej, Michal, Wislo Moja,
Uciekla Mi Przepioreczka

MY WISH FOR YOU see Carter, John

MYSTERY
(Zegree, Steve) SATB LEONARD-US
07357770 $.95   (M472)
(Zegree, Steve) SAB LEONARD-US
07357771 $.95, ipa, accomp tape
available   (M473)

MYTHE D'HIVER 2 see Kanno, Yoshihiro

N

NA SOLANI CARTAK see Janacek, Leos

NAAR HET BOSCH: WIJ TREKKEN VROOLIJK
see Hazenbosch, Antoon Cornelius

NAAR OOSTLAND WILLEN WIJ RIJDEN see
Anonymous

NABERMAN, J.
Hoop Op Vrede
SATB MOLENAAR 13021004 (N1)

NABERMAN, MAR
Levenswonder
SATB MOLENAAR 15006402 (N2)

Trouw (Oud Ballade)
SATB MOLENAAR 15009403 (N3)

Zacht Zingt De Zee
SATB MOLENAAR 15010402 (N4)

Zwaluwen, De
SATB MOLENAAR 15010502 (N5)

NACHKLANGE see Poos, Heinrich

NACHT, DE: DOOR HEEL DE OMTREK MELDEN
see Abt, Franz

NACHT, DE: HOE WONDERGOED see Schubert,
Franz (Peter), Nacht, Die: Wie
Schon Bist Du

NACHT, DIE see Schubert, Franz (Peter)

NACHT, DIE: WIE SCHON BIST DU see
Schubert, Franz (Peter)

NACHTEGAAL, DE see Gretry, Andre Ernest
Modeste, Rossignol, Le

NACHTEGAAL, DE see Laetantius, Br.

NACHTEGAAL IN ECHTERNACH, EEN see
Strategier, Herman

NACHTGEFUHL see Helmschrott, Robert M.

NACHTGESANG see Badings, Henk

NACHTGESANG see Cacioppo, Curt

NACHTGESANG IM WALDE, "SEI UNS STETS
GEGRUSST" see Schubert, Franz
(Peter)

NACHTGRUSS see Poos, Heinrich

NACHTHELLE, "DIE NACHT IST HEITER" see
Schubert, Franz (Peter)

NACHTIGALL, DIE see Alabieff, A.

NACHTIGALL, SAG see Brahms, Johannes

NACHTLICHTER SIND WIR ALLZUMAL see
Deutschmann, Gerhard, Chor Der
Nachtlichter

NACHTLIED see Schumann, Robert
(Alexander)

NACHTMUSIKANTEN: HIER SIND WIR ARME
NARREN see Johner, Hans-Rudolf

NADAL TINDAIRE
(Herr, F.) 4pt mix cor HEUGEL
HE 32412 (N6)

NADELSON, ANDREW
Making Love
SSSMezAAATTTTTBBB [10'0"] APNM sc
$5.00, cor pts rent (N7)

NAEGELI, HANS GEORG (1773-1836)
Am Herbstabend
men cor HUGUENIN EB 222 see from
Perlen Der Mannerchor-Literatur
(N8)

Auf Dem See
men cor HUGUENIN EB 222 see from
Perlen Der Mannerchor-Literatur
(N9)

Chant De La Foret, Le
TTBB HUGUENIN EB 267 (N10)

Eifer
men cor HUGUENIN EB 222 see from
Perlen Der Mannerchor-Literatur
(N11)

Lichtschopfer, Der
TTBB HUGUENIN EB 353 (N12)

Mond, Der
men cor HUGUENIN EB 222 see from
Perlen Der Mannerchor-Literatur
(N13)

NAEGELI, HANS GEORG (cont'd.)

Perlen Der Mannerchor-Literatur °see
Am Herbstabend; Auf Dem See;
Eifer; Mond, Der; Waldesklang;
Zur Wasserfahrt (N14)

Waldesklang
men cor HUGUENIN EB 222 see from
Perlen Der Mannerchor-Literatur
(N15)

Zur Wasserfahrt
men cor HUGUENIN EB 222 see from
Perlen Der Mannerchor-Literatur
(N16)

NAKI GREIN, EI see Solberg, Leif

NAMNSDAGSVISA
see Sol Och Mane

NANIE see Schumann, Robert (Alexander)

NAOMI'S SONG see Kearns, Ann

NAPRAVNIK, EDUARD (1839-1916)
Selected Choruses °CCU
[Russ] cor MEZ KNIGA 162 (N17)

NAR STRIE STORMAR MOT DEG JAGAR see
Eielsen, Steinar

NAREK OPUSTENE ARIADNY see Neumann,
Veroslav

NARREN, SCHERZ, UND LIEBE see Miller,
Franz R.

NATHALIE see Becaud, Gilbert

NATIONAL ANTHEM, THE
(Popplewell, R) SATB,winds,brass,
perc,harp,org NOVELLO (N18)

NATTLIG MADONNA see Hvoslef, Ketil

NATURAL HISTORY OF THE WATER CLOSET,
THE see Levi, Paul Alan

NATURALLY see Lewis, Huey

NATURE see Weigl, Karl

NATURE OF THE CAT, THE see Vogel, Roger
Craig

NATURE ORNANT LA DAME see Janequin,
Clement

NATY, JEAN
Au Chateau
(Fombonne, J.) 4pt mix cor,A rec,
pno/gtr HEUGEL HE32410 (N19)

NATY-BOYER, JEAN
Chemin De La Plage, Le
(Daniel, Etienne) 2 eq voices,fl,
pno A COEUR JOIE CA 7 (N20)

NAVERVISOR see Lindgren, Olof

NE ME QUITTE PAS see Brel, Jacques

NE SAIS POURQUOI VOTRE GRACE AI PERDU
see Gero, Ihan

NE T'Y FIE PAS see Lassus, Roland de
(Orlandus)

NEAR THE TINY HEARTH
(Goldman) SATB,MezBar soli LAWSON
LG 52328 $.85 (N21)

NEARNESS OF YOU, THE see Carmichael,
Hoagy

NEAUM, MICHAEL (1939-)
A La Rurru Nino
SSA cor ROBERTON 75327 see from Two
Spanish Traditional Songs (N22)

Boleras Sevillanas
SSA cor ROBERTON 75327 see from Two
Spanish Traditional Songs (N23)

Didn't It Rain
SSA,pno [2'] ROBERTON 75328 (N24)

Long Time Ago
SSA,pno [2'45"] ROBERTON 75329
(N25)
Two Spanish Traditional Songs °see A
La Rurru Nino; Boleras Sevillanas
(N26)

NEC MORTI ESSE LOCUM see Kubizek,
Augustin

NEDERLAND LET OP UW SAECK, O see
Smeets, Leo

NEDERLANDSE MADRIGALEN see Padbrue,
Cornelis Thymans

NEDILSKYJ, IVAN (1895-1970)
Selected Works For Chorus A Cappella
°CC7L
[Ukranian] cor DUMA $12.00 (N27)

NEEDLESS NEEDLES see Rausch, Carlos

NEELEN, J.
Hoch Auf Dem Gelben Wagen
SATB MOLENAAR 15021402 (N28)

NEEM MIJN HAND see Fradkin, Leslie
Martin

NELLY BLY see Foster

NELSON
Bouquet Of Roses (composed with
Hilliard; Cassey)
SAB BOURNE B239343 $1.10 (N29)

Love's The Reason Why
SAB&camb CAMBIATA L117448 $.80
(N30)

NELSON, HAVELOCK (1917-)
Shivery Sarah
unis cor,pno [1'20"] ROBERTON 75321
(N31)

NESS
What! No Women? °see Meskill

N'ESSE PAS UN GRANT DESPLAISIR see Des
Prez, Josquin

NEST EGGS see Williams-Wimberly, Lou

N'ETAIT PEUT-ETRE PAR VENUE see
Holstein, Jean-Paul

NEUCHATEL see Torche, Ch.

NEUE LIEBESLIEDER, OP. 65 see Brahms,
Johannes

NEUEN CHORLIEDERBUCH see Distler, Hugo

NEUES KLEID ZUR LUST UND FREUD, EIN see
Backer, Hans

NEUF CHANSONS SUR DES POEMES
CONTEMPORAINS see Daniel, Etienne

NEUJAHRSLIED see Mendelssohn-Bartholdy,
Felix

NEUMANN, VEROSLAV (1931-)
Lamento Di Ariana Abbandonata °see
Narek Opustene Ariadny

Narek Opustene Ariadny
"Lamento Di Ariana Abbandonata" wom
cor SUPRAPHON (N32)

Soleils Couchants
mix cor A COEUR JOIE MA 5 (N33)

NEUN ALPENLANDISCHE WEIHNACHTSLIEDER
°CC9L
cor HELBLING C4017 f.s. (N34)

NEUN HIRTENLIEDER °CC9L
cor HELBLING C4016 f.s. (N35)

NEUSTUPUJTE see Kabelac, Miloslav

NEUWEINLIED: DAS HAT GOTT VATER GUT
GEMACHT see Pappert, Robert

NEVE, F.D.
Maskerdans
SSA MOLENAAR 15015104 (N36)

NEVER DOUBT MY LOVE see McCray, James

NEVER GONNA GIVE YOU UP
(Hanson, Mark) SATB CPP-BEL 1533NC1X
$1.25, accomp tape available (N37)
(Hanson, Mark) SAB CPP-BEL 1533NC3X
$1.25, accomp tape available (N38)

NEVER SURRENDER
(Althouse) SATB CPP-BEL 1504NC1X
$1.25, accomp tape available (N39)
(Althouse) SSA CPP-BEL 1504NC2X
$1.25, accomp tape available (N40)
(Althouse) SAB CPP-BEL 1504NC3X
$1.25, accomp tape available (N41)

NEVER WEATHER-BEATEN SAIL see Campian,
Thomas (Campion)

NEVER WILL I ROVE see Klouse, Andrea

NEVEUX DE JEAN BART, LES see Blanchard

NEVU'AT MAYA see Mindel, Meir

NEW AGE DAWNING see Strommen, Carl

NEW BIRTH OF FREEDOM see Ephros,
Gershon

NEW DAY see McCray

NEW HAMPSHIRE see Paynter, John P.

NEW RIVER TRAIN   *folk song,US
  (Vance, Margaret) SATB,pno LAWSON
  52465 $1.10   (N42)

NEW SHOES see Woodward, Ralph, Jr.

NEW YORK, NEW YORK: THEME see Kander,
  John

NEWBURY, KENT ALAN (1925-   )
  Travelin' Man
    SATB,pno,opt strings,brass,fl NEW
    MUSIC NMA-123 $.70   (N43)

NEZ DE MARTIN, LE
  (Holstein, J.P.) 2-4pt jr cor HEUGEL
  HE 32080   (N44)

NGANO see Finnissy, Michael

NICOLETTE see Ravel, Maurice

NIELSEN, CARL (1865-1931)
  Fynsk Forar *Op.42
    "Springtime In Funen" SATB,SATB
    soli,2.2.2.2. 4.2.0.0. strings,
    timp [19'] sc KALMUS $20.00 (N45)

  Springtime In Funen *see Fynsk Forar

NIEUWE DAG, DE see Marnay, Cent Mille
  Chansons

NIGGLI, FRIEDRICH
  Que Veut Un Suisse Au Coeur Hardi?
    SATB,acap HUGUENIN EB 179   (N46)

NIGHT see Reed, Everett

NIGHT AND DAY see Gallina, Jill C.

NIGHT CAROL see Lance

NIGHT IMAGES see White, Gary C.

NIGHT IS DARKENING ROUND ME see
  Mirante, T.

NIGHT SONG FOR THE MOUNTAINS
  (Gates, C.) SA,pno/org (med) THOMAS
  1C137729 $.70   (N47)

NIGHT VOYAGES see Aird, Donald

NIGHT WATCH IN THE CITY OF BOSTON see
  Warren, B.

NIGHT WILL NEVER STAY, THE see Weigl,
  [Mrs.] Vally

NIGHTINGALE, THE see Hamilton, Iain

NIGHTINGALE SO PLEASANT, THE see Byrd,
  William

NIGHTINGALES *CCU
  [Russ] jr cor MEZ KNIGA 546   (N48)

NIGHTSHIFT (COMMODORES)
  (Chinn) SATB CPP-BEL 2776NC1X $1.25,
    accomp tape available   (N49)
  (Chinn) SSA CPP-BEL 2776NC2X $1.25,
    accomp tape available   (N50)
  (Chinn) SAB CPP-BEL 2776NC3X $1.25,
    accomp tape available   (N51)

NIIN KUIN PITSIA VALOA VASTEN... see
  Bruk, Fridrich

NIJMEGEN, NIJMEGEN see Dijk, Jan van

NILL
  Live For The Moment *see
    Porterfield, Sherrie

NILSSON, TORSTEN (1920-   )
  Corda Natus Ex Parentis (Evigt Fodd
    Ur Faderns Hjarta)
    wom cor,S solo,org STIM   (N52)

  Malin
    mix cor,orch SUECIA   (N53)

NINE MEN SLEPT IN A BOARDINGHOUSE BED
  (Roff, Joseph) 2pt cor,pno (med easy)
  THOMAS 1C107806 $.80   (N54)

NINE NEW CANONS see Gill, R.

NINETEEN SONGS see Holst, Imogen

NINNIN, FRANCOIS
  Bonheur, Le
    SATB A COEUR JOIE 167   (N55)

  Eternite
    SATB A COEUR JOIE 168   (N56)

NINTH SYMPHONY: CHORAL SECTION see
  Beethoven, Ludwig van

NIRVANA DHARMA see Rautavaara,
  Einojuhani

NJE BOITJESSIA DJEWIZY
  (Klos, Ton) "Madel Habt Keine Angst"
  [Russ/Ger] TTBB BANK 11.413.001 see
  from Bojarenliederen 1   (N57)

NO GREAT, NO SMALL see Clarke, Henry
  Leland

NO ONE IN THE HOUSE see Lewis, Aden G.

NO TIME LIKE THE PRESENT see Johnson

NO WANT SHALL I KNOW see Peterson

NO WORST, THERE IS NONE see Bialosky,
  Marshall H.

NOBODY KNOWS see Owen, John Warren

NOBODY KNOWS THIS LITTLE ROSE see
  Mulholland, James

NOBODY LOVES ME LIKE YOU DO see Murray

NOBODY WANTS TO BE ALONE see Gayle,
  Crystal

NOBRE, MARLOS (1939-   )
  Ago Lona (Afro-Brazilian)
    SATB SEESAW   (N58)

  Canceiro De Lampiao
    SATB SEESAW   (N59)

  Jogo (Afro-Brazilian Ritual)
    TB SEESAW   (N60)

  Yanomani
    SATB,T solo,gtr SEESAW   (N61)

NOCES, LES see Stravinsky, Igor

NOCHE SERENA see Metral, Pierre

NOCTURNE see Gaathaug, Morten

NOCTURNE see Richli, E.

NOCTURNE FOR FOUR VOICES see Tate,
  Phyllis

NOEL! see Telfer, Nancy

NOEL AUJOURD'HUI see Gesseney-Rappo,
  Dominique

NOEL, NOEL EST VENU see Alin, Pierre

NOEL NOUVEAU
  see Quand La Mer Rouge

NOG IS ER EEN TIJD.. see Hubers,
  Andries

NOISE see Telfer, Nancy

NOISELESS PATIENT SPIDER, A see
  Warfield, Gerald Alexander

NOISETTES, LES see Renard, Georges

NOLA, G. DOMENICO DA
  Tre Ciechi Siamo
    3 eq voices HEUGEL HE 32599 (N62)

NON PAPA, JACOBUS CLEMENS
  see CLEMENS, JACOBUS

NONNETTE, LA
  (Lauber, Emile) TTBB HUGUENIN SP 116
                                  (N63)

NONSENSE see Bennett, Richard Rodney

NORDENSTEN, FRANK TVEOR (1955-   )
  Pieces For Evidence *Op.33
    [Eng] SATB,elec pno [25'] NORGE
                                  (N64)
  Seven Or Eight Yeasty Cadenzas For
    Multivoice Choir *Op.14b
    [Eng] [16'] NORGE   (N65)

NORDHEIM, ARNE (1931-   )
  Music To Two Fragments To Music By
    Shelley
    SSAA HANSEN-DEN WH 29889   (N66)

NOREGS VAKT see Beck, Thomas Ludvigsen

NORGE I RODT, HVITT OG BLATT see
  Larsson, Lars-Erik

NORSKE DANSEVISER *CC9L
  (Rormark, Joar) jr cor,pno MUSIKK
  MH 2437   (N67)

NORTH
  For The Freedom Of Man
    SSB/camb,S solo CAMBIATA P978111
    f.s.   (N68)

  Merry Was The Music
    2pt cor SHAWNEE 0077 $.90   (N69)

NORTH, JACK KING (1908-   )
  Bonita Pinata
    cor ALFRED   (N70)

  Bye, Bye Lully Lullay
    cor ALFRED   (N71)

  It Must Be Spring
    SSA,pno,opt cym (med) THOMAS
    1C177905 $.80   (N72)

  Let's Tell The World About Christmas
    cor ALFRED   (N73)

NORTH COUNTRY SONGS *CC4U
  (Williamson, Malcolm) SATB WEINBERGER
                                  (N74)

NORTHWARD see Crawley, Clifford

NORTON
  Life Is A Song
    SAB CPP-BEL SV8430 $.95   (N75)

  You're My Friend
    SA CPP-BEL SV8318 $.95   (N76)

NORTON, OMAR C.
  Place I Call My Home, A
    TTBB NEW MUSIC NMC-3003 $.60 (N77)

NORWEGIAN WOOD see Lennon, John

NOTAIRE DE CORTAILLOD, LE see Bron,
  Patrick

NOTHIN' SWEETER see Taylor, Lemoyne

NOTRE TERRE see Lauber, Emile

NOTRE VIE EST UN PASSAGE see
  Aeschbacher, Walther

NOUS CHANTERONS, NATURE see Lauber,
  Emile

NOUS DORMIRONS ENSEMBLE see Aragon, L.

NOUS ETIONS DIX DEDANS UN PRE see
  Blanchard

NOUS SOMMES LES BERGERS AU COEUR JOYEUX
  see East, Michael

NOW AND FOREVER (YOU AND ME)
  (Chinn) SSA CPP-BEL 4877NC2X $1.25,
    accomp tape available   (N78)
  (Chinn) SAB CPP-BEL 4877NC3X $1.25,
    accomp tape available   (N79)

NOW AND HERE see Fongaard, Bjorn

NOW I AM HAPPY *folk song
  (Kristinsson, Sigursveinn D.) men cor
  ICELAND 021-8   (N80)

NOW IS THE MONTH see Morley, Thomas

NOW IS THE MONTH OF MAYING see Morley,
  Thomas

NOW LET THERE BE REJOICING THIS MERRY
  TIME OF MAY see Belle, J., Laet Ons
  Nu Al Verblijden

NOW MAKE WE MERTHE, BOOK 1: 12-14TH
  CENT. LATIN *CCU
  (Harrison, Frank L.) men cor OXFORD
  353192-5 f.s.   (N81)

NOW MAKE WE MERTHE, BOOK 2: 14-15TH
  CENT. ENGLISH *CCU
  (Harrison, Frank L.) men cor OXFORD
  353193-3 f.s.   (N82)

NOW MAKE WE MERTHE, BOOK 3: 15-16TH
  CENT. CONTINENTAL *CCU
  (Harrison, Frank L.) men cor OXFORD
  353194-1 f.s.   (N83)

NOW, O NOW I NEEDS MUST PART see
  Crocker, Emily

NOW SING WE ALL NOEL see Young, G.

NOW SPRING IN ALL HER GLORY see
  Arcadelt, Jacob

NOWAK, LIONEL (1911-   )
  Love's Lesson
    [Greek/Eng] SSSSAA [5'] AM.COMP.AL.
    $5.40   (N84)

NU BREEKT UIT ALLE TWIJGEN (LENTE-
  PARADE 2) see Beekum, Jan Van

NU DAAGT HET IN HET OOSTEN see Boekel,
  M.

NU VOOR 'T OOG VAN GOD EN DE ENGLEN see
  Schaik, Johan Ant. Stephanus Van

NUAGES, LES see Huguenin, Charles

NUERNBERGER, L. DEAN
Falcons Of Arcos De La Frontera, The
SSATBB,SSS soli [5'0"] APNM sc
$4.00, cor pts rent   (N85)

Koheleth
dbl cor,SSATB&narrator [10'0"] APNM
sc $10.00, cor pts rent   (N86)

Slouthe: A Portraite
SSATTB [5'0"] APNM sc $3.25, cor
pts rent   (N87)

NUIT D'ETOILES see Debussy, Claude

NUIT ET BROUILLARD see Ferrat, Jean

NUIT FROIDE ET SOMBRE, LA see Lassus,
Roland de (Orlandus)

NUKU, NUKU NURMEN ALLA; SLUMRA UNDER
BLOMSTERKULLEN see Palmgren, Selim

NUN FANGET AN see Hassler, Hans Leo

NUN IST APRIL UND FREUDENZEIT
(Becker, G.) men cor,T solo,acap
ZIMMER. 564   (N88)

NUNES, EMMANUEL (1941-   )
Minnesang
12pt mix cor [30'] JOBERT   (N89)

NUR DIESE EINE SCHWALBE see
Theodorakis, Mikis

NUR EIN WENIG GEDULD see Backer, Hans

NURSE'S SONG see Reed, Everett

NUTCRACKER (YOUTH MUSICAL) see Artman

NYE SONGEN, DEN see Eielsen, Steinar

NYGARD
How Small A Babe
SSA SHAWNEE 0523 $.85   (N90)

I'm Gonna Sing
SAB SHAWNEE 0352 $.85   (N91)

Shepherds On A Hill
SATB SHAWNEE 1803 $.85   (N92)

NYGARD, CARL J.
I'll Remember You
SATB ALFRED 7520 $.95   (N93)

Mountain Song
2pt cor LEONARD-US 08599447 $.85
                             (N94)

One More Road
SAB,pno ALFRED 7521 $.95   (N95)

NYSTEDT, KNUT (1915-   )
Brenn Sol
3 eq voices LYCHE 943   (N96)

Brumbaskon I Bumba: Folk Tune From
Valdres
2 eq voices,pno NORSK NMO 10039
                             (N97)
Every Hour That This Day Gives Me
[Eng] SATB manuscript NORGE (N98)

Jeg Lagde Meg Sa Sildig: Folk Tune
From Vaga
SSA NORSK   (N99)

My Soul, There Is A Country *Op.112
[Eng] SATB [7'] NORGE   (N100)

Rideregle
[Norw] jr cor NORGE   (N101)

Toro Liti: Folk Tune From Valdres
SSA NORSK NMO 10038   (N102)

Tretten Troll- Trillinger
SSA LYCHE   (N103)
[Norw] jr cor NORGE   (N104)

Var Je Og Det Var Du, Det: Folk Tune
From Elverum
SA,pno NORSK   (N105)

Wall Is Down, The *Op.104
SATB ROBERTON   (N106)
[Eng] [9'] NORGE   (N107)

O

O AMOUREUSICH MONDEKEN ROOT see Belle,
J.

O ARRANMORE see Daniel, Etienne

O AULA NOBILIS see Mathias, William

O CAILLE, PAUVRE CAILLE
(Brasseur, M.A.; Teniere, C.) unis
cor,perc HEUGEL HE 32365 contains
also: Belle Marion   (O1)

O CANADA
(Cooper, Gwyneth) SSB&camb HARRIS
HCWO-4003 $.50   (O2)
(Le Lacheur, Rex) SATB HARRIS HC-4080
$.50   (O3)

O CHE SPLENDOR see Palestrina, Giovanni
Pierluigi da

O COME, MODERN MAN see Burroughs

O DEAR, WHAT CAN THE MATTER BE?
(Artman) SSA KJOS C8625 $.70 (O4)

O DIVIN SOLEIL (CHANSON DE LABOUR) see
Lauber, Emile

O DOUX PARLEZ see Lassus, Roland de
(Orlandus)

O DU GNADENREICHE ZEIT see Ophoven,
Hermann

O DU SCHONER ROSENGARTEN see Deale,
Edgar

O GUTER VINZENZ
cor HIEBER MH 5035   (O5)

O HEER DIE DAER DES HEMELS TENTE
SPREIJT see Schrijvers, Jean

O ISIS UND OSIRIS see Mozart, Wolfgang
Amadeus

O IT'S GOODBYE LIZA JANE
(Ehret) SAB&camb,S solo CAMBIATA
U97231 $.75   (O6)
(Ehret) S&camb,SA soli CAMBIATA
T981160 $.75   (O7)

O LET US SING, I PRAY YOU see Waxman,
Chantons, Je Vous Prie

O LIEB SO LANG DU LIEBEN KANNST:
NOCTURNE see Liszt, Franz

O LIED see Strategier, Herman

O MA BELLE AURORE
(Perret, Francis) SATB,acap HUGUENIN
CH 2029   (O8)

O MISTRESS MINE see Criswell

O MISTRESS MINE see Dickau

O MISTRESS MINE see Hagemann, Philip

O MUSIC see Mason

O MUSIC, THOU MOST LOVELY ART see Jeep,
Johann

O MUSIKA! DIR WIRD GROSS LOB GEGEBEN
see Jochum, Otto

O MY HEART see Henry VIII, King of
England

O NEDERLAND! LET OP U SAECK see
Anonymous

O NO JOHN *folk song
(Gates, C.) SATB,pno (med) THOMAS
1C137722 $.80   (O9)

O NUIT PLUS BELLE QUE LE JOUR see
Bousset, de

O OCCHI MANSA MIA-TOI SEULE EN QUI
J'ESPERE see Le Jeune, Claude

O PETIT PAYS see Hemmerling, Carlos

O SHENANDOAH see Diemer, Emma Lou

O, SHENANDOAH see Parker, Alice

O SOJEK KORALOWYCH OCZACH see
Wiechowicz, Stanislaw

O SOV'REIGN OF MY DAYS see Rimsky-
Korsakov, Nikolai

O SUISSE, O MA PATRIE see Cornaz,
Emmanuel

O SWEETEST NIGHTTIME see Verdelot,
Phillippe

O SWIFTLY GLIDES THE BONNY BOAT see
Beethoven, Ludwig van

O TANNENBAUM *Xmas
(Brubaker) SATB,kbd,opt band CPP-BEL
OCT 02557 $1.10, ipa   (O10)
(Brubaker) SATB,opt band CPP-BEL
OCTO2557 $1.10, ipa   (O11)
(Rehak, Jeno) "Mon Beau Sapine" SATB
A COEUR JOIE 468   (O12)

O TO MAKE THE MOST JUBILANT SONG see
Diemer, Emma Lou

O TOI DONT LA BEAUTE see Hassler, Hans
Leo

O TRUBE DIESE TAGE NICHT see Pappert,
Robert

O VILANELLA-GENTE PASTOURELLE see Le
Jeune, Claude

O VOUX, BEAUX YEUX see Regnard,
Francois

O VRIJHEID: HET VOLK VAN NEERLAND & O
NEDERLAND see Smit, Theo

O WALY, WALY see Rutter, John

O WALY, WALY see Tilley, Alexander

O WONDROUS HARMONY see Haydn, [Franz]
Joseph

O ZALOTACH OCZAROWANYCH see Wiechowicz,
Stanislaw

OATAS EIMI see Skouen, Synne

OB BLOND, OB BRAUN, ICH LIEBE ALLE
FRAU'N see Stolz, Robert

OBBIRGER-LIED
(Leuthold, H.J.) mix cor,acap CRON
                             (O13)

OBENDRAUF, DER see Strecke, Gerhard

OBERSTADT, CAROLUS DETMAR
Groote Hond En De Kleine Kat, De
SATB,S solo ZENGERINK 50   (O14)

OCCHI DOLCI E SOAVI see Marenzio, Luca

OCEAN ZERO-ZERO see Bleuse, Marc

OCH DET VART MORGON see Alldahl, Per-
Gunnar

OCTOBER see Cox

OCTOBER see Gerschefski, Edwin

OCTOBRE see Lauber, Emile

ODE see Sigurbjornsson, Thorkell

ODE A VILLON see Reibel, Guy

ODE AAN DE MUZIEK see Kaaij, Willem
Hendrik V. D.

ODE AN DAS LEBEN see Zimmermann, Udo

ODE AUPRES DE ROSEAUX see Sutermeister,
Heinrich

ODE DE RONSARD see Balmer, Luc

ODE FOR ST. CECILIA'S DAY see Handel,
George Frideric

ODE FOR ST. CECILIA'S DAY see Handel,
George Frideric, Caecilien-Ode

ODE FOR ST. CECILIA'S DAY; PRAISE OF
HARMONY see Handel, George Frideric

ODE FOR THE BIRTHDAY OF QUEEN ANNE see
Handel, George Frideric

ODE: LA TERRE DE JAVA see Badings, Henk

ODE ON ST. CECILIA'S DAY see Handel,
George Frideric

ODE ON ST. CECILIA'S DAY 1692 see
Purcell, Henry

ODE TO FREEDOM see Washburn, Robert
Brooks

ODE TO JOY see Beethoven, Ludwig van

ODE TO JOY see Tchaikovsky, Piotr
Ilyich

ODE TO POSTUMUS see Sir, N.

ODE TO ST. CECILIA see Handel, George Frideric

ODE TO ST. CECILIA'S DAY see Purcell, Henry

ODE TO THE WESTWIND see Weigl, [Mrs.] Vally

ODE TO YOUTH see Track, Gerhard

ODE: WE ARE THE MUSIC MAKERS see Weigl, [Mrs.] Vally

ODEGAARD, HENRIK
Play Your Joy
jr cor,instrumental ensemble NORSK NMO 9582   (015)

Three Poems By Jan Erik Vold
mix cor NORSK NMO 9550   (016)

Velsigna Band Som Bind
[Norw] jr cor&cong,fl,vcl,hpsd NORGE   (017)

OEDIPUS TEX see Schickele, Peter

OERTEL, L.
Graf Waldersee
(Rijken, J.) "U Zij De Glorie" SATB,band MOLENAAR 05 0436 02
(018)

Graf Waldersee *see U Zij De Glorie

U Zij De Glorie
(Rijken, J.) "Graf Waldersee" SATB, band MOLENAAR 05 0436 50   (019)

U Zij De Glorie *see Graf Waldersee

OF ALL THE BIRDS THAT I HAVE HEARD see Mundy, John

OF ENCHANTED COURTSHIP see Wiechowicz, Stanislaw, O Zalotach Oczarowanych

OF HIM I LOVE...AND A NOISELESS PATIENT... see Luedeke, Raymond

OF MY LOST CHILDHOOD see Sviridov, Georgy

OF THE JAY'S CORAL-RED EYES see Wiechowicz, Stanislaw, O Sojek Koralowych Oczach

OF THE PEOPLE see Brandon, Seymour (Sy)

OFFRANDE see Beethoven, Ludwig van

OFFRANDE LYRIQUE see Vaillant, Raymond

OG ENGLEHAERAR STYRDE UT see Kverndokk, Gisle

OGDON, WILBUR L. (1921-   )
Four Statements
SATB [5'0"] APNM sc $4.75, cor pts rent   (020)

Three Sea Choruses
SATB [10'0"] APNM sc $3.25, cor pts rent   (021)

Three Statements
SATB [4'0"] APNM sc $3.50, cor pts rent   (022)

OH FARE YOU WELL, MY OWN TRUE LOVE
*folk song,US
(Ehret, Walter) SATB,pno LAWSON 52284 $.80   (023)

OH HAPPY DAY
(Shaw) SATB,opt synthesizer CPP-BEL T07630C1 $1.25, accomp tape available   (024)
(Shaw) SAB,opt synthesizer CPP-BEL T07630C3 $1.25, accomp tape available   (025)

OH, HOW CAN I KEEP FROM SINGING? see Harris, Robert A.

OH! I WANT TO GO
(Daniel, Etienne) SATB CAILLARD PC 130 see from Deux Negro Spirituals   (026)

OH, LOVE OF MINE *madrigal,15th cent
(Rice, Martin) SATB,acap (med diff) FISCHER,C CM8309 $.95   (027)

OH MY LUVE'S LIKE A RED, RED ROSE see Gates, Crawford

OH, OH, FALL (THE CRICKET) see Berger, Jean

OH SEE HOW THICK THE GOLDCUP FLOWERS see Mulholland, James

OH SHENANDOAH
(Stocker, D.) SATB,pno,opt 2fl (med) THOMAS 1C368615 $.85   (028)

OH, SPRING! (THE CATERPILLAR) see Berger, Jean

OH STAR see Stainbrook

OH SUSANNA see Foster, Stephen Collins

OH, SUSANNA! OH ELIZA! see Strid

OH, THE SUMMER see Coleridge-Taylor, Samuel

OH! WHAT A BEAUTIFUL CITY
(Anders) SSA,acap CPP-BEL SV8619 $.95   (029)

OH! YOU BEAUTIFUL DOLL see Brown

OHANA, MAURICE (1914-   )
Llanto Por Ignacio Sanchez Meijas
8-12pt wom cor,Bar&speaking voice, 1.1.2.1. 2.1.0.0. timp,perc [39'0"] voc sc BILLAUDOT   (030)

Lux Noctis
SATB&SATB&SATB&SATB,org [12'] JOBERT   (031)

OHE, MEUNIER
(Langree, Alain) 2-3 eq voices A COEUR JOIE 9 016 see from Quartre Chansons Populaires Hongroises
(032)

OHLIN, CAMILLE
I Like Dogs
unis cor LESLIE 1138 f.s.   (033)

Misty Takes Me Walking
unis cor LESLIE 1139 f.s.   (034)

OHRN, KONRAD M.
I Gamle Dage
SSA MUSIKK MH 2401   (035)

Pa Byens Runde Torg
SSA MUSIKK MH 2402   (036)

OISEAU, L' see Beausonge, Lucid

OISEAU BLEU, L' see Aeschbacher, Walther

OITO CANTIGAS
4pt mix cor ALPUERTO 1611   (037)

OKTOBERLIED: DER NEBEL STEIGT see Pappert, Robert

OL' DAN TUCKER *folk song,US
(De Cormier, Robert) jr cor LAWSON LG 52075 $.85   (038)

OLD FAMILIAR FACES
(Franceschi) SSAA (easy, women's barbershop) BOURNE B239111 $.50
(039)

OLD FASHIONED CHRISTMAS see Strommen, Carl

OLD IRONSIDES see Bacon, Boyd

OLD KING COLE see Collins, David

OLD MCDONALD HAD A FARM see Kvam, Oddvar S.

OLD MUSIC FOR QUIET HEARTS see Bender

OLD OAK'S LAST DREAM see Filas, Juraj

OLD, OLD MAN, AN
(Thliveris, B.) SATB,pno (med easy) THOMAS 1C128205 $.80   (040)

OLD ORDER CHANGETH, THE see Shephard, Richard

OLD SONG, AN see Rimsky-Korsakov, Nikolai

OLD SUE'S PANDA see Carter, John

OLD-TIME WALTZES *CCU
[Russ] cor MEZ KNIGA 163   (041)

OLD TIMERS MEDLEY, THE see Beekum, Jan Van

OLD WOMAN see Collins, David

OLDHAM, ARTHUR (1926-   )
Hymns For The Amusement Of Children
SATB,S solo,org/orch OXFORD   (042)

O'LEARY, JANE (1946-   )
Begin
SATB,fl [5'0"] APNM sc $4.75, cor pts rent   (043)

Filled Wine Cup
cor [9'0"] APNM sc $4.75, cor pts rent   (044)

OLIPHANT
All Ye Who Music Love (composed with Donato)
SATB,acap CPP-BEL 60650 $.95   (045)

OLIVE TREES STAND see Atsey Zeytim Omdin

OLIVER
If It Weren't For You *see Lubetkin

OLIVER, HAROLD (1942-   )
Flower, A
SATB [2'0"] sc APNM $2.50   (046)

Walden - 1974
wom cor&speaking cor,pno,perc [15'0"] APNM sc $9.00, cor pts rent   (047)

OLIVER, STEPHEN (1950-   )
Beauty And The Beast
mix cor NOVELLO   (048)

Ricercare No. 4
TTBar,countertenor NOVELLO   (049)

OLIVER CROMWELL
(Locke) SATB,acap WOODL A050208 $.95   (050)

OLIVEROS, PAULINE (1932-   )
Sound Patterns
SATB SEESAW   (051)

OLLANTA, LA *folk song
(Leleu, Francoise) 3 eq voices,4rec, gtr,perc,opt vcl HEUGEL HE 32602
(052)

OLLIVIER, J.
Chanson Du Printemps Retourne *see Ronsard

OLSON, LYNN FREEMAN (1938-1987)
Discover Joy!
3pt cor,pno FISCHER,C CM8027   (053)

Homeward Bound
SAB,pno FISCHER,C CM8143   (054)

"Hot Dog" Fugue, The
2pt cor,pno FISCHER,C CM8061   (055)

Love Is The Way
SAB,pno FISCHER,C CM8060   (056)

OM DE SIDSTE TING, OG OM LAENGSELEN EFTER DET HIMMELSKE FAEDRELAND see Habbestad, Kjell

OMENS OF SPRING see Anderson, William H.

OMENS OF SPRING see Anderson, William H.

ON A MAL DIT DE MON AMI see Fevin, Antoine de

ON AN AIR BY RAMEAU see Eben, Petr

ON AN OLD DREAM'S HEATHER-SLOPE see Ragnarsson, Hjalmar H.

ON COMING SLEEP see Tchaikovsky, Piotr Ilyich

ON EN DIRA CE QU'ON VOUDRA see Sermisy, Claude de (Claudin)

ON GREEN DOLPHIN STREET see Kaper, Bronislaw

ON THE ATCHESON, TOPEKA AND THE SANTA FE see Warren, Harry

ON THE ECHOING GREEN see Warren, Elinor Remick

ON THE GREEN HILLSIDE see Dvorak, Antonin

ON THE SEA see Mendelssohn-Bartholdy, Felix, Auf Dem See

ON THE SHORE OF BODENSEE see Schumann, Robert (Alexander)

ON THE STATE LINE see Grob, Anita Jean

ON THE SUNLIT GLADE *CCU
[Russ] jr cor,pno/acord MEZ KNIGA 487   (057)

ON THE WINGS OF LOVE
(Althouse) SATB CPP-BEL 45800C1X $1.25   (058)
(Althouse) SSA CPP-BEL 45800C2X $1.25   (059)
(Althouse) SAB CPP-BEL 45800C3X $1.25   (060)

ON TOP OF THE WORLD see Snyder

ONA SKUTECNE JEST see Kopelent, Marek

ONBEDUIDENDE POLKA EN TWEE WIEGELIEDJES see Dijk, Jan van

ONCE CANCIONES POPULARES ESPANOLAS see Angulo, Manuel

ONCE IN A DREAM see Hurd, Michael

ONCE MORE THE FLOWERS BLOOM see Schein

ONCE THE RAIN HAS FALLEN see Dunbar

ONCE UPON A CHRISTMAS see Yolleck, Mary

ONCE UPON A CHRISTMAS TIME see Crawley, Clifford

ONCE UPON A CHRISTMAS TIME see Crawley, Clifford

ONCE UPON A TIME (from All American) (Chinn, Teena) SATB,acap CPP-BEL T54600C1 $1.25 (061)

ONCQUES AMOUR see Crecquillon, Thomas

ONDER DEN HELM see Kooten, Gerard Van

ONE AND TWENTY see Heldman, Keith

ONE AND TWENTY PENNIES see De Cormier, Robert

ONE DAY AT A TIME SAB CPP-BEL 45330C3X $1.25 (062)

ONE HUNDRED SONGS OF THE PEOPLES OF THE USSR *CCU [Russ] jr cor MEZ KNIGA 483 (063)

ONE LITTLE CANDLE see Snyder

ONE LITTLE STAR see Sobaje, Martha

ONE MORE ROAD see Nygard, Carl J.

ONE MORE SONG see Strommen, Carl

ONE OF A KIND see Ross, Brad

ONE SMILING SUMMER MORNING see Verdelot, Phillippe, Vostr' Acuti Dardi, Il

ONE STEP see Perry

ONE STEP AT A TIME see Johnson

ONE THAT YOU LOVE, THE (Nowak) SATB CPP-BEL 45600C1X $1.25 (064)
(Nowak) SSA CPP-BEL 45600C2X $1.25 (065)
(Nowak) SAB CPP-BEL 45600C3X $1.25 (066)

ONE TO ONE SSA CPP-BEL SV8352 $.95 (067)

1-2-3 (Billingsley, Alan) SATB CPP-BEL 47200C1X $1.25 (068)
(Billingsley, Alan) SSA CPP-BEL 47200C2X $1.25 (069)

ONE VERSE AT A TIME see Tuttle, Billie G.

ONORATI Little Drummer Boy *see Davis

ONS LIED VAN NOORD-HOLLAND see Boedijn, Gerard H.

OOSTEN, ROEL VAN (1958-) Trois Chansons Parisiennes mix cor [11'] DONEMUS (070)

OP DE TOP VAN EEN WOLK see Carpenter, Richard Lynn, Top Of The World

OP EEN KAT see Strategier, Herman

OP EEN ZANGKRAAI see Strategier, Herman

OPEN THE DOOR see Ross

OPFERLIED see Beethoven, Ludwig van

OPHELIA'S SONG see Schultz, Donna Gartman

OPHOVEN, HERMANN (1914-) Madchen Mit Den Blauen Augen men cor BRAUN-PER 1015 (071)
mix cor BRAUN-PER 1016 (072)

O Du Gnadenreiche Zeit mix cor BRAUN-PER 1057 (073)
wom cor/jr cor BRAUN-PER 1058 (074)

Zieh, Schimmel, Zieh men cor BRAUN-PER 1045 (075)
mix cor BRAUN-PER 1046 (076)
wom cor/jr cor BRAUN-PER 1047 (077)

OPIENSKI, HENRYK (1870-1942) Vrai Dieu D'amour 4pt cor HUGUENIN EB 26 (078)

OPPERSTE HERDER, DE see Boekel, M.

OR SHALL WE DIE? see Berkeley, Michael

OR SUIS-JE BIEN AU PIRE see Willaert, Adrian

OR SUS, OR SUS, L'ALOUETTE A 3 see Janequin, Clement

OR, VOUS TREMOUSSEZ, PASTEURS see Langree, Alain

ORANGE, L' see Becaud, Gilbert

ORB, THE see White, Gary C.

ORDE FER VIDARE ENN MANNEN see Kruse, Bjorn Howard

ORGAD, BEN-ZION (1926-) Sha'ar Larashut cor,acap ISR.MUS.INST. 6712 (079)

Shirim Me'emek Hoshen *song cycle "Songs Out Of Hoshen Valley" [Heb] mix cor,acap [50'] ISR.MUS.INST. 6326 (080)

Songs Out Of Hoshen Valley *see Shirim Me'emek Hoshen

ORGELLIED, HET see Laetantius, Br.

ORLAND, HENRY (1918-) Christmas Candlelight SATB,2.2.2.2. 2.2.2.1. 2perc, strings SEESAW (081)

Christmas Legend SATB,2.2.2.2. 2.2.3.0. perc,strings SEESAW (082)

ORLOV At The Spinning Wheel SATB SCHIRM.G 232540 $.70 (083)

ORMEN LANGE: FAEROYISK SOGEKVAD see Kvandal, Johan

OSIEM PIESNI DO SLOW MARII KONOPNICKIEJ see Ryling, Franciszek

OSSEWAARDE, JACK HERMAN (1918-) Sing We Merrily SATB,org CPP-BEL GCMR 03074 $1.40 (084)

OSTERN, PER HROAR A Hvor Salig mix cor MUSIKK (085)

Returning (Canon Senza Parole) TTBB,pno NORSK (086)

Singing Is So Good A Thing TTBB MUSIKK MH 2438 (087)

Vaggsong mix cor NORSK (088)

OSTROVSKI, A. Let There Always Be Sunshine! *CCU [Russ] jr cor,pno MEZ KNIGA 531 (089)

OTEY Make Believe (Nygard) cor ALFRED (090)

OU VA L'EAU QUI S'EN VA? see Touati, Raymond

OU VAS-TU? see Daniel, Etienne

OUDE EN NIEUWE BEKENDEN *CC8L unis cor,pno ZENGERINK Z 615 (091)

OUR CHERISHED DREAMS see Liepin, A.

OUR CHRISTMAS DREAM see Stephens, Michele

OUR COUNTRY 'TIS OF THEE see Roberts, Ruth

OUR DAY WILL COME (Chinn) SATB CPP-BEL SV8623 $.95 (092)

OUR FEARFUL TRIP see Siltman, Bobby L.

OUR HOMESTEAD'S ON THE FLATLANDS see Crawley, Clifford

OUR LADY OF LIBERTY see Mann

OUR OWN SOVIET ARMY *CCU [Russ] MEZ KNIGA 536 (093)

OUR SCHOOL CHORUS SONG see Martin, James

OUR SONGS, 1989 *CCU [Russ] MEZ KNIGA 178 (094)

OUT IN THE WOODS see Ligeti, Gyorgy

OUT OF THE STARS see Clarke, Henry Leland

OUT OF YOUR SLEEP ARISE AND WAKE see Milner, Anthony

OUTLAW'S POEM see Thorarinsson, Leifur

OUTRAGEOUS, THAT SHORTNIN' BREAD see Taylor, Lemoyne

OUVREZ-MOI L'HUIS see Janequin, Clement

OUVREZ VOS PORTES ETERNELLES see Gounod, Charles Francois

OVADIA, TUVIA Speak Out Your Words, O Lonely One jr cor ISRAELI IMP 1713 (095)

OV'E, LASS', IL BEL VISO? see Lauridsen, Morten Johannes

OVER THE RAINBOW see Kendall

OVER THE RIVER AND THROUGH THE WOOD (Williams, Wendy) SATB,acap LAWSON 52288 $.80 (096)

OVER THE SEA TO SKYE see Jothen, Michael Jon

OVER THE SEA TO SKYE see Wagner

OVER THERE see Ray, Jerry

OVER YONDER (Christiansen, P.) SATB KJOS 8682 $.80 (097)

OVERAL FEESTGESCHAL see Luysterburg, Theo

OVERJOYED (Scott) SAB CPP-BEL 70250C3X $1.25, accomp tape available (098)
(Scott) SATB CPP-BEL 70250C1X $1.25, accomp tape available (099)
(Scott) SSA CPP-BEL 70250C2X $1.25, accomp tape available (0100)

OVERTURE FROM "DIE ZAUBERFLOTE" see Mozart, Wolfgang Amadeus

OWEN, JOHN WARREN Choice, A (from Hamlet) SATB EARTHSNG ES-10 $.60 (0101)

Nobody Knows SATB EARTHSNG ES-8 $.50 (0102)

Touch Them Softly SATB EARTHSNG ES-7 $.50 (0103)

Where, O Where Are The Hebrew Children? SATB EARTHSNG ES-9 $.50 (0104)

OXFORD BOOK OF FRENCH CHANSONS, THE *CC84U (Dobbins, Frank) 2-7pt cor OXFORD 19 343539 (0105)

OYENS, TERA DE MARZ see MAREZ OYENS, TERA DE

OZ-WIZ MEDLEY see Shaw

P

PA BYENS RUNDE TORG see Ohrn, Konrad M.

PA SOLSIDA see Jordan, Sverre

PA TRINN see Kittelsen, Guttorm

PABLO, LUIS DE (1930-   )
    Escena
        SATB,3perc,strings SEESAW   (P1)

PAC-MAN FEVER
    (Riley; Wilson) 2pt treb cor CPP-BEL
    0080PC5X $1.25   (P2)

PACHELBEL, JOHANN (1653-1706)
    Canon In D
        (Goemanne) SAB SHAWNEE 5316 $.95
                                         (P3)

    Canon On Alleluia
        (Hayes; Gooch) 3pt cor,treb inst,
        bass inst KJOS J5 $.80   (P4)

PACKER, RANDALL
    Bateau Ivre, Le
        SATB,2.1.2.0. 0.0.0.0. 2perc,harp,
        pno,strings [17'] AM.COMP.AL.
        $19.85   (P5)

PADBRUE, CORNELIS THYMANS (1592-1670)
    Nederlandse Madrigalen *CCU
        (Noske, Frits) 3-5pt cor
        VER.NED.MUS. MMN 5   (P6)

PADDLING see Vinson, Harvey

PAGE
    Look To The Wind
        SATB KJOS C8827 $.80   (P7)

    When Moments Were Gold
        SATB KJOS C8913 $.90   (P8)

PAGEANT see Ball, M.

PAIN OF LOVE, THE see Regnart

PAIN, THOU CAUSETH, BELOVED see
    Monteverdi, Claudio, A Che Tormi Il
    Ben Mio

PALESTRINA, GIOVANNI PIERLUIGI DA
    (1525-1594)
    Complete Works, Vol. 5: Madrigals For
        4 And 5 Voices *CCU
        [It] 4-5pt cor,acap KALMUS K 08004
        $5.75   (P9)

    Complete Works, Vol. 24: Madrigals
        For 5 Voices *sac/sec,CC26U
        [It] 4-5pt cor,acap KALMUS K 08023
        $5.75   (P10)

    Complete Works, Vol. 74: Madrigals
        For 4 Voices *CCU
        [It] 4pt cor,acap KALMUS K 08073
        $5.75   (P11)

    O Che Splendor
        mix cor ZENGERINK 240   (P12)

PALMER, HAP
    Carol Of The Shepherd Boy
        cor ALFRED   (P13)

    Chiapanecas (Mexican Hand- Clapping)
        cor ALFRED   (P14)

    Songs To Enhance Movement Vocabulary
        Of Young Children *CCU
        ALFRED 2072 $16.95   (P15)

    Turn On The Music *CC11U
        jr cor,pno,opt gtr ALFRED 3550
        $24.95   (P16)

PALMGREN, SELIM (1878-1951)
    Huokaus
        mix cor,acap FAZER F 06966-6   (P17)

    Iltalaulu; Jag Sjunger Ensam Har Min
        Sang
        mix cor,acap FAZER W 11243-3   (P18)

    Nuku, Nuku Nurmen Alla; Slumra Under
        Blomsterkullen
        mix cor,acap FAZER W 11244-1   (P19)

    Polku
        FAZER F 06967-4   (P20)

    Surren Laulelen
        mix cor,acap FAZER F 06965-8   (P21)

PALSSON, PALL P. (1928-   )
    Bridal Gown, The
        men cor ICELAND 020-14   (P22)

PALSSON, PALL P. (cont'd.)
    Five Limericks *CC5U
        men cor,pno ICELAND 020-13   (P23)

    Poet, The
        men cor ICELAND 020-15   (P24)

    Three Welsh Songs *CC3U
        men cor,harp ICELAND 020-20   (P25)

    To Reykjavik
        men cor ICELAND 020-12   (P26)

PANKIEWICZ, EUGENIUSZ (1857-1898)
    Six Polish Wedding Folk Songs In A
        Suite Form *see Szesc Piesni
        Weselnych Ludowych Polskich W
        Formie Suity

    Szesc Piesni Weselnych Ludowych
        Polskich W Formie Suity
        "Six Polish Wedding Folk Songs In A
        Suite Form" [Polish] wom cor,pno
        4-hands POLSKIE   (P27)

PANTILLON, G.L.
    Allons Danser Ma Belle
        SATB,acap HUGUENIN CH 1197   (P28)

    Bles Murs, Les
        SATB,acap HUGUENIN CH 1135   (P29)

    Chalets, Les
        SATB,acap HUGUENIN CH 1115   (P30)

    Chanson Des Tourbiers (from Festival
        Leopold Robert)
        TTBB HUGUENIN CH 986   (P31)

    Chanson Des Vieux-Pres, La
        SATB,acap HUGUENIN CH 1119   (P32)

    Chant Des Sonneurs, Le
        SATB,acap HUGUENIN CH 1120   (P33)

    Chaux De Fonds, La
        see Pantillon, G.L., Depuis La
        Citadelle Jusqu'a

    Creux-Du-Van, Le
        SATB,acap HUGUENIN CH 1121   (P34)

    Dammerung
        TTBB HUGUENIN CH 1090   (P35)

    Depuis La Citadelle Jusqu'a
        SATB,acap HUGUENIN CH 1122 contains
        also: Chaux De Fonds, La   (P36)

    Festival Leopold Robert *Suite
        mix cor&wom cor&jr cor&men cor,orch
        cor pts HUGUENIN CH 985   (P37)

    Hymne A La Terre Natale
        SATB,acap HUGUENIN CH 1124   (P38)

    Hymne Au Vully
        SATB,acap HUGUENIN CH 1125   (P39)

    Jeunesse
        TTBB HUGUENIN CH 1083   (P40)

PAPAINE see Ligeti, Gyorgy

PAPILLON, LE see Campra, Andre,
    Farfalla, La

PAPOULIS, JIM
    Let's Give The World A Chance
        (composed with George, Amanda)
        SA (easy) HHP   (P41)

PAPP, AKOS G.
    Koulukuoro 5, Kansanlauluja
        Kaukomailta
        SA FAZER F 07717-2   (P42)

PAPPERT, ROBERT (1930-   )
    Auf Die Pferde, Kosaken
        men cor BRAUN-PER 1059   (P43)

    Auf Wiedersehen
        SATB MULLER 874   (P44)
        TTBB MULLER 873   (P45)
        SAA MULLER 875   (P46)

    Berge Der Heimat
        men cor,TB soli BRAUN-PER 1083
                                         (P47)

    Des Herrgotts Weinkeller
        SATB MULLER 681   (P48)
        SSA MULLER 682   (P49)

    Ich Kenn' Eine Quelle
        4pt men cor MULLER SM 624   (P50)

    Lasst Uns Wandern
        wom cor/jr cor BRAUN-PER 1082   (P51)
        men cor BRAUN-PER 1024   (P52)

    Mittag: Am Waldessaume
        TTBB MULLER 712   (P53)

PAPPERT, ROBERT (cont'd.)
    Neuweinlied: Das Hat Gott Vater Gut
        Gemacht
        SATB MULLER 709   (P54)

    O Trube Diese Tage Nicht
        wom cor/jr cor BRAUN-PER 1060 (P55)

    Oktoberlied: Der Nebel Steigt
        TTBB MULLER 715   (P56)

    Weinlied
        mix cor BRAUN-PER 1064   (P57)

    Wie Leuchtet Es Uber Dem Walde
        SAA MULLER 821   (P58)
        TTBB MULLER 819   (P59)
        SATB MULLER 820   (P60)

PARADISE AND THE PERI see Schumann,
    Robert (Alexander)

PARADISE AND THE PERI: CHORUSES see
    Schumann, Robert (Alexander)

PARC MONCEAU, LE see Bonneau, Paul

PARCHET, A.
    Chanson Du Rouet
        see Brahms, Johannes, Jour
        S'enfuit, Le

PARIS... see Bigot, P.

PARKER, ALICE (1925-   )
    Holy Michael
        2pt cor,gtr,harp,kbd GALAXY 1.3105
        $.75   (P61)

    O, Shenandoah
        SATBB,opt ob,opt harp,opt strings
        GALAXY 1.3101   (P62)

    Songstream
        SATB,pno/pno 4-hands GALAXY 1.3051
        $3.95   (P63)

PARKINSON, REBECCA
    All That I Love Is Home
        SATB JACKMAN JMC7087   (P64)

PARLEY OF OWLS, A see Hurd, Michael

PARLEZ-MOI D'AMOUR see Lenoir, Jean

PARMENTIER, F. GORDON
    Eclipse
        SATB,BB soli,2.2+English horn.3.3.
        4.3.3.0. perc,strings,opt org
        [12'] AM.COMP.AL.   (P65)

    From The Diary Of A Northern Window
        SATB,2.2.2.2. 4.2.3.0. timp,perc,
        harp/pno,strings [18']
        AM.COMP.AL.   (P66)

PARNES
    Happy Is
        (Ray) cor ALFRED   (P67)

PAROLES QUE TU M'AS DITES, LES see
    Apotheloz, Jean

PARTIR AU BOUT DU MONDE see Rochat,
    Jean

PARTOS, ODON (1907-1977)
    Cantata
        [Heb/Eng] cor,S/T solo,orch [10']
        voc sc ISR.MUS.INST. 105B   (P68)

PARTY ALL THE TIME
    (Roscoe, Jeffrey) SATB CPP-BEL
    0113PC1X $1.25, accomp tape
    available   (P69)
    (Roscoe, Jeffrey) SAB CPP-BEL
    0113PC3X $1.25, accomp tape
    available   (P70)
    (Roscoe, Jeffrey) TTB CPP-BEL
    0113PC4X $1.25, accomp tape
    available   (P71)

PARTZKHALADZE, M. (1897-   )
    Choruses *CCU
        [Russ] wom cor,acap MEZ KNIGA 167
                                         (P72)

    Hallo, School! *CCU
        [Russ] jr cor,pno MEZ KNIGA 227
                                         (P73)

PARYS, GEORGES VAN
    see VAN PARYS, GEORGES

PAS PAR LE PLAFOND see Holstein, Jean-
    Paul

PASCAL, ANDRE
    Qu'il Est Beau Mon Pays
        wom cor/men cor TRANSAT. TR001192
                                         (P74)

PASCHAL, GENEVA
    Dreamin' *see Montgomery, Lisa

PASS IT ALONG see Loken

PASSACAGLIA IN BLUE see Berkowitz, Sol

PASSACAGLIA ON SPRING AND ALL see Kreiger, Arthur V.

PASSAGE TO THEREAFTER see Lennon, John Anthony

PASSAGES see McCray, James

PASSANT PAR PARIS
(Huguenin, Charles-Andre) TTBB,acap HUGUENIN C 2089A H   (P75)

PASSAQUAY, F.
Fils Du Capitaine Achab, Le *see Yvart, J.

PASSAQUET, RAPHAEL
Automne *see Delarue-Mardrus, Lucie

Chant Du Grillon *see Lanauve, G. De

Madame Automne *see Essey, G.

PASSEREAU
Il Est Bel Et Bon
SATB,acap HUGUENIN EB 15   (P76)

PASSING BY see Middlemas

PASTIMES AND AN ALLELUIA see Lessard, John Ayres

PASTORAL CAROL, A see Boodle

PASTORALE see Glaser, Werner Wolf

PASTORELA see Pinos, Alois

PASTORELLA see Hurnik, Ilja

PASTORELLA, LA
see Je Ne Veux Plus A Mon Mal Consentir

PASTURE, THE see Wagner, Douglas Edward

PATRE DES MONTAGNES
(Langree, Alain) 2-3 eq voices A COEUR JOIE 9 016 see from Quartre Chansons Populaires Hongroises
(P77)

PATRIE see Barblan, Emmanuel

PATRIOT PRIMER see Clarke, Henry Leland

PATRIOTIC MEDLEY
(Mann, Johnny) SATB CPP-BEL T1800PC $.95   (P78)

PATRIOTJES, DE: WAT ZULLEN ONS PATRIOTJES ETEN see Anonymous

PATRY, ANDRE J.
Amie, Ne Vous Soit Etrange
SAT HUGUENIN CH 932   (P79)

Ballade Des Trois Compagnons
TTBB HUGUENIN CH   (P80)

D'Amour Le Beau Visage
SAT HUGUENIN CH 931   (P81)

Quand Elle Est La, La Belle Dame
SAT HUGUENIN CH 933   (P82)

PATTERSON, PAUL (1947-   )
Mass Of The Sea *Op.47
cor,SB soli,2.2.2.2. 4.3.3.1. 2perc,timp,strings [43'0"]
UNIVER. UE 17644   (P83)

Te Deum *sac/sec
cor WEINBERGER   (P84)

Time-Piece, Op. 16
AATBarBarB,acap WEINBERGER (P85)

Voices Of Sleep *Op.40
SATB,S solo,1.1.1.1. 1.2.1.1. 4perc,timp,strings [45'0"]
UNIVER. UE 16252   (P86)

PAUER, JIRI (1919-   )
From Saturday To Saturday *CCU
jr cor CESKY HUD.   (P87)

Lost Double Bass, The
jr cor [8'] CESKY HUD.   (P88)

PAULL
Autumn (from The Seasons)
SATB KJOS GC146 $.90   (P89)

So Long Through The Night (from Through The Night)
(Maslanka) KJOS GC162 $.80 (P90)

Springtime (from The Seasons)
(Maslanka) SATB KJOS GC144 f.s.
(P91)

Summer (from The Seasons)
(Maslanka) SATB KJOS GC145 f.s.
(P92)

PAULL (cont'd.)
Whisper Song, The (from Through The Night)
(Maslanka) SA KJOS GC161 $.80 (P93)

Winter (from The Seasons)
(Maslanka) SATB KJOS GC147 $.90
(P94)

Your Lullaby (from Through The Night)
(Maslanka) KJOS GC160 $.80   (P95)

PAULSON
Fyra Visor Av Mats Paulson *see Gang Skall Jag Stilla Somna, En; Lyser En Stjarna, Det; Visa Om Rimfrost Och Vinterstra; Visa Vid Vindens Angar   (P96)

Gang Skall Jag Stilla Somna, En
(Lonna, Kjell) SATB PROPRIUS 7970 see from Fyra Visor Av Mats Paulson   (P97)

Lyser En Stjarna, Det
(Lonna, Kjell) SATB PROPRIUS 7970 see from Fyra Visor Av Mats Paulson   (P98)

Visa Om Rimfrost Och Vinterstra
(Lonna, Kjell) SATB PROPRIUS 7970 see from Fyra Visor Av Mats Paulson   (P99)

Visa Vid Vindens Angar
(Lonna, Kjell) SATB PROPRIUS 7970 see from Fyra Visor Av Mats Paulson   (P100)

PAULUS, STEPHEN HARRISON (1949-   )
Silver The River
2pt treb cor,pno/harp EUR.AM.MUS. EA00525 $.60   (P101)

PAUMANOK: A LONG ISLAND CANTATA see Pleskow, Raoul

PAUVRE AVEUGLE see DuBois, Pierre-Max

PAUVRE COEUR, TANT IL M'ENNOIE see Gero, Ihan

PAUVRE LABOUREUR, LE
(Vuataz, Roger) SATB,acap HUGUENIN CH 983   (P102)

PAUVRE LABOUREUR, LE see Vuataz, Roger

PAUVRE MARTIN see Brassens, Georges

PAUVRE SOLDAT
(Brasseur, M.A.; Teniere, C.) unis jr cor,Orff inst HEUGEL HE 32375
(P103)

PAVANE
(Grimbert, J.) 3 eq voices,opt cont HEUGEL HE 32164   (P104)

PAVANE: "BELLA, QUI TIENS MA VIE" see Arbeau, Thoinot (Jehan Tabourot)

PAVANE - BELLE QUI TIENS MA VIE see Arbeau, Thoinot (Jehan Tabourot)

PAYNTER, JOHN P.
Cape Ann
SATB,opt ob OXFORD see from Landscapes   (P105)

Heaven-Haven
see May Magnificat

Landscapes *see Cape Ann; New Hampshire; Usk; Virginia   (P106)

May Magnificat
SATB,acap OXFORD 343692-2 $2.90 contains: Heaven-Haven; Pied Beauty; Starlight Night (P107)

New Hampshire
SATB,opt ob OXFORD see from Landscapes   (P108)

Pied Beauty
see May Magnificat

Starlight Night
see May Magnificat

Usk
SATB,opt ob OXFORD see from Landscapes   (P109)

Virginia
SATB,opt ob OXFORD see from Landscapes   (P110)

PAYS, LE see Lauber, Emile

PAYS EN MARCHE, UN see Henchoz, Emile

PAYS, GARDE TES FILS! see Wuilleumier, Henri

PAYSANS, LES see Aeschbacher, Walther

PEACE BE MULTIPLIED see Ultan, Lloyd

PEACE BE TO THIS HOUSE see Strommen, Carl

PEACE MEANS see Clarke, Henry Leland

PEASANT'S PRAYER see Zamecnik, Evzen

PEASLEE, RICHARD (1930-   )
Reveille (from Seven Housman Songs)
SATB STAINER 7.0327 $.95   (P111)

PECHEUR, LE *Flemish
(Barblan, Emmanuel) SATB,acap HUGUENIN EB 446   (P112)
(Barblan, Emmanuel) TTBB HUGUENIN EB 475   (P113)

PELICANS see Crawley, Clifford

PELLETIER, R. OCTAVE
Si Mon Malheur M'y Continue
(Agnel, A.) 2 eq voices HEUGEL HE 32245 contains also: Souvent Amour   (P114)

Souvent Amour
see Pelletier, R. Octave, Si Mon Malheur M'y Continue

PELT, R.A. VAN
Blijde Mare, Een
SSA/TTB ZENGERINK 356 contains also: Feestzang Bij De Geboorte Van Een Koningskindje; Blijde Mare Klonk Door 'T Land, Een
(P115)

Blijde Mare Klonk Door 'T Land, Een
see Pelt, R.A. van, Blijde Mare, Een

Feestzang Bij De Geboorte Van Een Koningskindje
see Pelt, R.A. van, Blijde Mare, Een

PENDERECKI, KRZYSZTOF (1933-   )
Song Of Cherubum
SSAATTBB,acap SCHOTT SKR 20020 $4.95   (P116)

PENDERS, J.
Cantilenas Profanas
SATB MOLENAAR 08187007   (P117)

PENDUBIDU
(Grimbert, J.) 3 eq voices HEUGEL HE 31894   (P118)

PENDULUM OF TIME, THE see Slavicky, Milan

PENET, HILAIRE
Au Joly Bois
(Agnel, A.) MezMezT HEUGEL HE 32556
(P119)

PENINGER
Little Babe, Do You Know?
SATB SHAWNEE 1807 $.80   (P120)

Pirate Don Durk Of Dowdee
SAB&camb CAMBIATA C17674 $.80
(P121)

PENNY FIDDLE, THE see Yager, R. Stewart

PENSEZ DE FAIRE GARNISON see Anonymous

PEOPLE
(Puerling, Gene) SATB LEONARD-US 07359307 $.95   (P122)

PEOPLE IS A POLYCHROME, THE see Weigl, [Mrs.] Vally

PER FARE L'AMORE
(Ganter, C.) mix cor,acap PELIKAN PE 1186   (P123)

PERDER, KJELL (1954-   )
Aphorism
dbl cor,SBar soli STIM   (P124)

PEREZ, DAVID (1711-1778)
Ecco L'aurora
"Jeune Aurore, La" 2pt cor,pno/ strings HUGUENIN EB 279 (P125)

Jeune Aurore, La *see Ecco L'aurora

PERFECT WORLD see Lewis, Huey

PERGOLESI, GIOVANNI BATTISTA (1710-1736)
Canon
4pt mix cor,2gtr HEUGEL HE 32516
(P126)

PERHAPS LOVE see Deutschendorf, Henry John (John Denver)

PERKINS, FRANK
  Stars Fell On Alabama
    (Behnke, Martin) SATB CPP-BEL
    6424SC1X $1.40, accomp tape
    available   (P127)
    (Behnke, Martin) SSA CPP-BEL
    6424SC2X $1.40   (P128)
    (Behnke, Martin) SAB CPP-BEL
    6424SC3X $1.40   (P129)

PERLEN DER MANNERCHOR-LITERATUR see
  Naegeli, Hans Georg

PERMONT, HAIM (1950-   )
  Leaden Sky *see Shmei Oferet

  Shmei Oferet
    "Leaden Sky" [Heb] cor, solo
    voices,orch sc ISR.MUS.INST.
    6634, study sc ISR.MUS.INST.
    6634, voc sc ISR.MUS.INST. 6634B,
    set ISR.MUS.INST. 6634R   (P130)

PERPETUUM MOBILE see Minkov, M.

PERRET, P.
  Mere Noel
    (Passaquet, R.) 4pt mix cor HEUGEL
    HE 32339   (P131)

PERRINE ETAIT SERVANTE
  (Robert, F.) 6pt mix cor HEUGEL
  HE 32268   (P132)

PERRINJAQUET, G.
  Deux Choeurs A 4 Voix D'hommes *see
    Melancolie; Yeux, Les   (P133)

  Melancolie
    TTBB HUGUENIN EB 200 see from Deux
    Choeurs A 4 Voix D'hommes (P134)

  Yeux, Les
    TTBB HUGUENIN EB 200 see from Deux
    Choeurs A 4 Voix D'hommes (P135)

PERRUQUIERS see Bleuse, Marc

PERRY
  Alleluia! Sing With Joy
    2pt cor SHAWNEE 71 $.85   (P136)

  And I Came Alive
    SAB SHAWNEE 0354 $.90   (P137)

  Festive Madrigal
    2pt cor SHAWNEE 0113 $.95   (P138)

  Juke-Box Saturday Night
    cor ALFRED   (P139)

  One Step
    ALFRED   (P140)

  Star Shone Down, A
    2pt cor SHAWNEE 5071 $.90   (P141)

  Time To Be Goin'
    ALFRED   (P142)

PERRY, DAVE
  Let Us Sing (composed with Perry,
    Jean)
    SATB ALFRED 7588 $.95   (P143)

PERRY, JANICE KAPP
  What Is The Constitution
    SATB JACKMAN JMC7134   (P144)

PERRY, JEAN
  Let Us Sing *see Perry, Dave

PERSEN, JOHN (1941-   )
  Samesiidat Osv
    TTTBBB/SMezATBarB NORGE NC 3921
                                      (P145)

PERT, MORRIS
  Two Medieval Latin Lyrics, Op.1
    *CC2U
    SATB,acap WEINBERGER   (P146)

PERUGIA, NICCOLO DA
  Eleven Ballate *CC11U,14th cent
    (Kelly, Stephen) 2pt cor ANTICO
    AE26   (P147)

PERVIGILIUM VENERIS see Lloyd, George,
  Vigil Of Venus, The

PESKOV, N.
  It's Fine To Be A Young Pioneer
    *song cycle
    [Russ] jr cor,pno MEZ KNIGA 543
                                      (P148)

PETER GO RING DEM BELLS *spir
  (Scherer) SSAA,pno MULLER 2755 see
    from Volkslieder Aus Aller Welt
                                      (P149)
  (Scherer, E.) [Eng] SATB,pno,gtr
    MULLER 2763   (P150)

PETER PIPER see Rausch, Carlos

PETERSON
  No Want Shall I Know
    SAB SHAWNEE 5373 $.80   (P151)

PETERSON, OSCAR
  Hymn To Freedom
    cor,pno FAZER F 07752-9   (P152)

PETIT ATOME, LE see Brafford, P.

PETIT BOIS DE SAINT-AMAND, LE see
  Barbara

PETIT BONHOMME, LE see Vigneault,
  Gilles

PETIT JOUEUR DE FLUTEAU, LE see
  Brassens, Georges

PETIT MOUSSE, LE
  (Bleuse, M.) 2pt jr cor,2rec,perc
    HEUGEL HE 31982   (P153)

PETIT PONT DE BOIS, LE see Duteil, Yves

PETITE CAMUSETTE see Des Prez, Josquin

PETITE JEANNETON, LA
  (Mermoud, Robert) 3pt cor HUGUENIN
    EB 337 see from Trois Chansons
    Populaires   (P154)

PETITE LECON, UNE see Berkowitz, Sol,
  To Have And To Be

PETITE NYMPHE FOLATRE see Utendal,
  Alexander

PETITE SUITE see Michael, Edward

PETITE SUITE ROMANDE
  (Falquet, Rene) SATB,pno/orch HUG
    FF 8820   (P155)

PETITES D'ECHICHENS, LES see Reymond,
  Herny

PETKER, ALLAN R.
  Rejoice And Sing Noel! *medley
    SAB,pno,opt handbells oct BOCK
    BG2075 $.95, pts BOCK BG0831
    $1.50   (P156)
    SATB (med) BOCK BG2075 $.90   (P157)

  Sing Noel
    SSAA (med) BOCK BG2145 $1.15   (P158)

PETRON, DANIEL
  Discover
    SAB CPP-BEL SV8424 $1.25   (P159)

PETROUCHKA
  (Rochat, Jean) SATB,acap HUGUENIN
    CH 2043   (P160)
  (Rochat, Jean) TTBB HUGUENIN CH 2042
                                      (P161)

PETRUSCHKA
  (Hollfelder, Waldram) men cor BOHM
    see from Vier Heitere Europaische
    Volkslieder   (P162)

PEUERL
  Frisch Auf Und Lasst Uns Singen
    (Malin) SSATB,acap CPP-BEL
    OCT 02492 $1.10   (P163)

PEUPLE, EVEILLE-TOI see Gossec,
  Francois Joseph

PFAUTSCH, LLOYD ALVIN (1921-   )
  Be Careful What You Say (from Songs
    Of Experience)
    SATB LAWSON LG 52049 $.70   (P164)

  Beautiful But Truthful
    (Goldman) SSA LAWSON LG 549 $.85
                                      (P165)

  Echoes (from Three Songs Of Nature)
    SATB LAWSON LG 52372 $.70   (P166)

  Grossfader's Historikerversen
    SATB LAWSON LG 51208 $.75   (P167)

  Laughing Song
    SSAA,fl LAWSON LG 51949 $.70   (P168)

  Let Sounds Of Joy Be Heard
    TTBB LAWSON LG 52090 $.75 contains
    also: Schumann, Robert
    (Alexander), Lotus Flower, The   (P169)

  Litany For America, A (from Songs Of
    Experience)
    SATB LAWSON LG 52050 $.70   (P170)

  Little Wheel A-Turnin'
    SATB LAWSON LG 547 $.70   (P171)

  Salute To Heritage, A
    SATB LAWSON LG 52384 $.85   (P172)

  Seasonal Songs
    SATB LAWSON LG 52240 $1.40   (P173)

PFAUTSCH, LLOYD ALVIN (cont'd.)

  Set Me As A Seal
    SATB LAWSON LG 52029 $.70   (P174)

  Stars (from Three Songs Of Nature)
    SATB LAWSON LG 52374 $.85   (P175)

  Winds (from Three Songs Of Nature)
    SATB LAWSON LG 52373 $.70   (P176)

PFEIL, HEINRICH
  Calm Is The Sea
    (Williams) TTBB [2'] ROBERTON $.75
                                      (P177)

PHASING see Franssens, Joep

PHILADELPHIA-MARSCH see Weiss-
  Steinberg, Hans

PHILIPP, FRANZ (1890-1972)
  All Mein Gedanken
    men cor BOHM   (P178)

PHILOSOPHER, THE (PHILOSOPHICAL
  ANECDOTES) see Sowash

PHOEBUS UND PAN see Bach, Johann
  Sebastian

PHRASES see Vries, Klaas de

PHRASES FROM BLAKE I & II see Goeb,
  Roger

PIANO STUDENT, THE see Blair, Dean

PIANTO (LAMENT) see Roxburgh, Edwin

PIANTONI, LOUIS
  Extase
    SATB,acap HUGUENIN CH 751   (P179)

  Ils S'en Vont, Ces Roys De Ma Vie
    SATB,acap HUGUENIN CH 752   (P180)

  Labours, Les
    TTBB HUGUENIN CH 754   (P181)

  Voeu
    SATB,acap HUGUENIN CH 753   (P182)

PIC-CO-LO-MIN-I see Lewis, A.

PICK A BALE O' COTTON
  (Terhune, Charles) 2-3pt cor CPP-BEL
    SV8730 $1.20, accomp tape available
                                      (P183)

PICK THE CHERRIES RIPE
  (Goldman) SATB,Mez solo LAWSON
    LG 52331 $.85   (P184)

PICKELL
  Littlest Christmas Tree
    1-2pt cor CPP-BEL PROCH 02868 $.95
                                      (P185)

PICTURE SONGS, VOL. 5 *see Kind
  Beetle, A; Merry Wind; Setting Up
  Exercises; Song Of Gena, The
  Crocodile   (P186)

PICTURE SONGS, VOL. 6 *CCU
  [Russ] jr cor MEZ KNIGA 532   (P187)

PICTURE SONGS, VOL. 7 *CCU
  [Russ] jr cor MEZ KNIGA 229   (P188)

PIECES FOR EVIDENCE see Nordensten,
  Frank Tveor

PIED BEAUTY see Paynter, John P.

PIED PIPER, THE see Warnock, Colin

PIEPER, RENE (1955-   )
  Achterbergliederen
    4pt mix cor,fl,ob,clar,bsn,horn
    [17'30"] DONEMUS   (P189)

  Dying Roses
    mix cor,ob,2trp,org,perc [11'30"]
    DONEMUS   (P190)

PIERCING EYES see Haydn, [Franz] Joseph

PIERNE
  Libellules, Les
    2pt cor,pno JOBERT   (P191)

PIERPONT, J.
  Sounds Of Christmas, The
    (Chinn) 2-4pt mix cor CPP-BEL
    SV8907 $1.10   (P192)

PIERRE, TENEZ-MOI PRES DE VOUS see
  Vaccaro, Jean-Michel

PIGUET, R.
  A Un Aubespin
    TTBB HUGUENIN EB 80   (P193)

PIIKA PIKKARAINEN see Jalkanen, Pekka

PILEUR, G.
Compagnon, Le
TTBB HUGUENIN CH (P194)

Vin Vaudois, Le
TTBB HUGUENIN CH (P195)

PILGRIM'S CHORUS see Wagner, Richard

PILKINGTON, FRANCIS (ca. 1562-1638)
Amyntas With His Phyllis Fair
SATB STAINER 3.3190 (P196)

First Book Of Songs Of Airs Of Four
Parts: Vol. 1, No 1-7 °CCU
SATB,acap KALMUS K 06848 $3.50 (P197)

First Book Of Songs Of Airs Of Four
Parts: Vol. 2, No 8-14 °CCU
SATB,acap KALMUS K 06849 $3.50 (P198)

PIMMER, HANS (1931-)
Motet
mix cor ZIMMER. 563 (P199)

PINGAULT, CL.
Marin Et La Rose, Le
(Ziberlin, F.) 4pt mix cor HEUGEL
HE 31849 (P200)

PINOCCHIO, DON'T SMOKE THAT CIGARETTE!
see Roberts, Ruth

PINOS, ALOIS (1925-)
Apage, Satanas!
mix cor CESKY HUD. see from In
Extremis: Triptych (P201)

Criers
mix cor, solo voices,chamber orch,
actors [20'] CESKY HUD. (P202)

Gesta Machabaeorum
mix cor,opt inst [17'] CESKY HUD. (P203)

In Extremis: Triptych °see Apage,
Satanas!; Invocation; Sursum
Corda (P204)

Invocation
mix cor CESKY HUD. see from In
Extremis: Triptych (P205)

Ludus Floralis °CC5U
wom cor,B solo,perc,electronic tape
CESKY HUD. (P206)

Pastorela
mix cor,opt brass,opt perc [12']
CESKY HUD. (P207)

Sursum Corda
mix cor CESKY HUD. see from In
Extremis: Triptych (P208)

"PIONERIA" CHORUS SINGS, THE °CCU
(Struve, G.) [Russ] jr cor MEZ KNIGA
241 (P209)

PIPEAU, LE see Aufray, H.

PIPER, THE see Reed, Everett

PIQUE LA BALEINE see Blanchard

PIRATE DON DURK OF DOWDEE see Peninger

PISK, PAUL AMADEUS (1893-)
Two Sonnets
SATB,pno [4'] AM.COMP.AL. $4.10 (P210)

PITCHFORD, DEAN
After All (composed with Snow, Tom)
(Buchholz, Buck) 2pt mix cor CPP-
BEL 1738AC5X $1.40, accomp tape
available (P211)
(Buchholz, Buck) SATB CPP-BEL
1738AC1X $1.40, accomp tape
available (P212)
(Buchholz, Buck) SAB CPP-BEL
1738AC3X $1.40, accomp tape
available (P213)

PITFIELD
Kalinka
TTBB,pno OXFORD 341016-8 $.45 (P214)

PLACE DE LA CONCORDE see Thiriet,
Maurice

PLACE I CALL MY HOME, A see Norton,
Omar C.

PLAINT FOR A PRINCE AND KING see
Wallach, Joelle

PLAISIRS SONT DOUX, LES
(Corneloup, Marcel) SATB A COEUR JOIE
280 (P215)

PLANTONS LA VIGNE see Barblan, Emmanuel

PLANTS see Kopelent, Marek

PLAY TOGETHER 1 see Johansen, Kai
Lennart

PLAY TOGETHER 2 see Somdalen, Bjorn

PLAY YOUR JOY see Odegaard, Henrik

PLEASE DO NOT GO MY LOVE
(Bacon, Boyd) SATB NEW MUSIC NMA-181
$.75 (P216)

PLESKOW, RAOUL (1931-)
Cantata
SATB, ST soli,woodwinds,2pno,perc,
vla,vcl,db [12'] AM.COMP.AL. f.s. (P217)
Four Songs
S/SATB [12'] AM.COMP.AL. $10.70 (P218)
Paumanok: A Long Island Cantata
SATB,S solo,fl,clar,pno,timp,
strings [12'] AM.COMP.AL. $27.95 (P219)
Second Cantata
SATB,MezT soli,fl,2clar,vln,vla,
vcl,pno [11'] AM.COMP.AL. $16.75 (P220)

PLEUREZ YEUX NOIRS see Cossetto, Emil

PLOMPEN, PETER (1944-)
Hole Toward Space, A
SATB [4'] DONEMUS (P221)

PLORAR see Reyes, Fernando

PLOWSHARES see Clarke, Henry Leland

PLUISTER, SIMON (1913-)
Aan Silvestre Revueltas, Van Mexico,
Bij Zijn Dood
4-6pt mix cor,1.2.0.0.alto sax.
1.3.4.0. pno,strings [8'20"]
DONEMUS (P222)

Dagen Na Kruisiging, De (from Bar
Abbas)
3pt wom cor,3 soli,2.1.2.1.alto
sax. 1.2.2.1. harp,pno/cel,2perc,
strings [22'50"] DONEMUS (P223)

PLUNKETT, ELIZABETH KUHN
Lamentations For Juliet
SSA oct DEAN HRD 134 $.75 (P224)

PLUS BELLE DE LA VILLE, LA see
Janequin, Clement

PLUS PENSER QUE DIRE see D'Orleans, Ch.

POCKETFUL OF RHYMES, A see Price, Beryl

POD OKAPEM SNIEGU see Wiechowicz,
Stanislaw

PODESVA, JAROMIR (1927-)
Hours °CC5U
mix cor CESKY HUD. (P225)

Sinfonietta Of Nature
mix cor [10'] CESKY HUD. 8283 (P226)

Unseen, Unheard °CC4U
jr cor CESKY HUD. (P227)

POEM see Bordewijk-Roepman, Johanna

POEM IN MEMORY OF SERGEI YESENIN see
Sviridov, Georgy

POEM OF HUKVALDY, THE see Bachorek,
Milan

POEM OF OLEG THE WISE see Rimsky-
Korsakov, Nikolai

POEMS DE GOSSES see Gursching, Albrecht

POET, THE see Palsson, Pall P.

POETE, LE see Berat, F.

POETRY IN MOTION see Anthony

POET'S DREAM see Hoddinott, Alun

POET'S SOLILOQUY, THE
(Goldman) mix cor LAWSON LG 52230
$.70 (P228)

POINCONNEUR DES LILAS, LE see
Gainsbourg, S.

POLDERSTAD see Scheepmaker, N.

POLICE LOG OF THE IPSWICH CHRONICLE see
Wigglesworth, Frank

POLISH LULLABY
(Grundahl) SATB,fl KJOS C8803 $.80 (P229)

POLKA DES DIMANCHES, LA see Urfer,
Albert

POLKA DES TORTUES, LA see Brafford, P.

POLKU see Palmgren, Selim

POLL
Galerien, Le °see Druon, M.

POLLACK
We're So Cool!
SATB SHAWNEE 1856 $1.15 (P230)

POLLACK, BILL
Dance, Dance, Dance (composed with
Pollack, Lisa Lauren)
SATB CPP-BEL 0179DC1X $1.25, accomp
tape available (P231)

Fire Up °see Pollack, Lisa Lauren

Hope For America, The °see Pollack,
Lisa Lauren

POLLACK, LISA LAUREN
Christmastime Is Here
SATB CPP-BEL 2654CC1X $1.25, accomp
tape available (P232)

Dance, Dance, Dance °see Pollack,
Bill

Fire Up (composed with Pollack, Bill)
SATB CPP-BEL 2809FC1X $1.25, accomp
tape available (P233)

Hope For America, The (composed with
Pollack, Bill)
SSA CPP-BEL 5018HC7X $1.25, accomp
tape available (P234)
SATB CPP-BEL 5018HC6X $1.25, accomp
tape available (P235)
SAB CPP-BEL 5018HC8X $1.25, accomp
tape available (P236)

We've Got A Show For You
SATB LEONARD-US 08603821 $.95 (P237)
SSA LEONARD-US 08603823 $.95, ipa,
accomp tape available (P238)

POLLOCK, ROBERT EMIL (1946-)
Sketches: By The Sea
SATB [5'0"] sc APNM $5.75, perf mat
rent (P239)

POLNAREFF, M.
Qui A Tue Grand' Maman?
(Frochot, J.) 4pt mix cor HEUGEL
HE 32330 (P240)

POLTER TE CRESO see Carlsen, Philip

POM-POM see Ligeti, Gyorgy

POND, THE see Van de Vate, Nancy Hayes

POOR LONESOME COWBOY see Giles

POOR MARINERS see Shearer

POOR PAPA see Woods, Harry MacGregor

POOR RICHARD'S ALMANACK see McAfee

POORMAN, SONJA
Magic Dream Song
1-2pt cor,pno CPP-BEL SCHCH 77113
$.95 (P241)

Sing Noel!
SATB LEONARD-US 08603693 $.85 (P242)

Somebody Special
1-2pt cor CPP-BEL SV8601 f.s. (P243)

You And I
3pt mix cor LEONARD-US 08604001
$.85 (P244)

POORT, HANS (1954-)
Handelingen
mix cor,electronic tape [21']
DONEMUS (P245)

POOS, HEINRICH (1928-)
Abt, Der Reit, Der
mix cor,acap [3'] SCHOTTS C 46446 (P246)

Alter, Das
[Ger] mix cor,acap SCHOTTS C 46449
see from Nachklange (P247)

Es Geht Ein' Dunkle Wolk' Hierein
TTBB MULLER 1725 (P248)

Es Kribbelt Und Wibbelt Weiter
[Ger] men cor,acap [2'] SCHOTTS
C 46355 (P249)

Heidenroslein: Sah Ein Knab Ein
Roslein Stehn
SSA MULLER 1722 (P250)

Klang Um Klang
[Ger] mix cor,acap SCHOTTS C 45500
see from Nachklange (P251)

POOS, HEINRICH (cont'd.)

Linien Des Lebens, Die
[Ger] men cor [4'] SCHOTTS C 45833
(P252)

Nachklange *see Alter, Das; Klang Um
Klang; Nachtgruss; Traurige
Jager, Der; Weltlauf (P253)

Nachtgruss
[Ger] mix cor,acap SCHOTTS C 45501
see from Nachklange (P254)

Sonn' Ist Untergangen, Die
[Ger] men cor,acap SCHOTTS
C 46011 (P255)

Tochter Der Heide, Die
[Ger] wom cor,acap [3'] SCHOTTS
CHBL 621 (P256)

Traurige Jager, Der
[Ger] mix cor,acap SCHOTTS C 46447
see from Nachklange (P257)

...Und Des Friedens Kein Ende
SSA&SATB&TTBB,orch MULLER 2785
(P258)

Weltlauf
[Ger] mix cor,acap SCHOTTS C 46448
see from Nachklange (P259)

POPOV, V.
School Of Choral Singing, A: Vol. 2
*see Sokolov, Nikolai
Alexandrovich

POPP, ANDRE
Abecedaire *see Dimey, B.

POPULIER, DE: DAAR STAAT HIJ, 'T EDEL
HOOFD OMHOOG see Zwager, Piet

PORC, LE see Queneau, R.

PORTER
Christmas Story, The
cor ALFRED (P260)

PORTERFIELD, SHERRIE
Live For The Moment (composed with
Nill)
2pt cor CPP-BEL SV8744 $.95, accomp
tape available (P261)

We Are The Music Makers
SATB CPP-BEL 1598WC1X $1.40, accomp
tape available (P262)
SAB CPP-BEL 1598WC3X $1.40, accomp
tape available (P263)
SSA CPP-BEL 1598WC5X $1.40, accomp
tape available (P264)

PORTRAIT NO. 1 see Cohen, Edward

PORTRAIT OF DUKE ELLINGTON see
Ellington, Edward Kennedy (Duke)

POSCHIAVINA see Castelnuovo, V.

POSER, HANS (1917-1970)
Fabeln Des Asop, Die
TTBB,pno,perc SIKORSKI (P265)

POSTILLION-LIED see Grothe

POSTKOETS, DE see Cleber, Joseph

POTATO- VEGETABLE CHOWDER see Bucci

POTGIESER, P.
Gildemarsch-Jagerskoor
TTBB MOLENAAR 13006103 (P266)

POTPOURRI OVER NORSKE BARNE- OG
FOLKEVISER see Gaathaug, Morten

POTPURRI OVER NORSKE BARNE- OG
FOLKEVISER see Gaathaug, Morten

POTTAR, O.
Sirene Et Scaphandrier (composed with
Brafford, P.)
(Tritsch, J.) 4pt mix cor HEUGEL
HE 32429 (P267)

POUR ESTRE AYME see Lambert, Michel

POURSUITE, LA see Dvorak, Antonin

POWELL
Hope Springs Eternal
SAB CPP-BEL SV8212 $.95 (P268)

Send Some Music
SAB CPP-BEL SV8301 $.95 (P269)

You Need A Friend
SATB CPP-BEL SV8215 $.95 (P270)

PRADO, JOSE-ANTONIO (ALMEIDA)
(1943-)
Alegoria Buffa
SATB SEESAW (P271)

PRADO, JOSE-ANTONIO (ALMEIDA) (cont'd.)

Canticos De Amor
SATB SEESAW (P272)

Celebratio Americae
SATB SEESAW (P273)

Celebratio Amoris
SATB,gtr SEESAW (P274)

Ciranda
SA SEESAW (P275)

Lapinhas-Christmas Songs
SATB SEESAW (P276)

Letter From Patmos
SATB,S solo,org,3trp,2horn,2trom,
perc SEESAW (P277)

Villegagnon
SATB,SBar&narrator,2.2.2.2.
3.4.3.0. strings SEESAW (P278)

PRAETORIUS, MICHAEL (1571-1621)
Canon
(Owen, Harold) SATB CPP-BEL 64336
$1.25 (P279)
(Owen, Harold) SAB,acap CPP-BEL
SV8568 $.95 (P280)

Jubilate Deo!
(Wagner, Douglas E.) 2pt cor,kbd
CPP-BEL OCT 02543 $.95 (P281)

PRAIRIE WOMAN SINGS, A see Butler,
Eugene Sanders

PRAISE BOOK see Hazzard, Peter Peabody

PRAISES OF THE DAY see Avni, Tzvi

PRAISES OF THE NIGHT [1] see Avni, Tzvi

PRAISES OF THE NIGHT [2] see Avni, Tzvi

PRAY FOR PEACE see Clarke, Henry Leland

PRAY TELL ME, OH, PLEASE *Mex
(Collins) S&camb,SA soli CAMBIATA
U117696 $.70 (P282)

PRAYER FULL see Sviridov, Georgy

PRAYER OFFERING FOR LARGE CHOIR see
Meyers, Randall

PREISE DEIN GLUCKE, GESEGNETES SACHSEN
see Bach, Johann Sebastian

PREMIER LIVRE DES CHANSONS, LE: VOL.1
see Susato, Tielman

PREMIER LIVRE DES CHANSONS, LE: VOL.2
see Susato, Tielman

PREMIER SOURIRE DE MAI see Franck,
Cesar

PRENDRE UN ENFANT see Duteil, Yves

PRETTY LITTLE ANGEL EYES see Boyce

PRETTY SARO see Clausen

PREVERT, J.
Bouquet, Le (composed with Grimbert,
Jacques)
5pt mix cor HEUGEL HE 32010 (P283)

Message, Le
(Grimbert, J.) 6pt mix cor HEUGEL
HE 32465 (P284)

Tendre Et Dangereux Visage De
L'amour, Le (composed with
Thiriet, Maurice)
(Ziberlin, F.) 4 eq voices HEUGEL
HE 32035 (P285)

PRICE
All My Tomorrows *see Besig

As Long As I Have Music (composed
with Besig)
SATB SHAWNEE 1800 $.85 (P286)

Awake! Arise! Go Forth (composed with
Besig)
SATB SHAWNEE 6470 $.95 (P287)

Best Is Yet To Come, The (composed
with Besig)
SATB SHAWNEE 1805 $.95 (P288)

Free, And Glad To Be Me! (composed
with Besig)
SATB SHAWNEE 0384 $.90 (P289)

Go With A Song In Your Heart
(composed with Besig)
SAB SHAWNEE 0360 $.90 (P290)

PRICE (cont'd.)

If You Try *see Besig

It's Almost Time For Christmas *see
Besig

It's Time To Ring Those Christmas
Bells! (composed with Besig;
Fisher; Levene)
(Besig) SATB SHAWNEE 1882 (P291)

Let The Tiny Baby Come In (composed
with Besig)
SATB SHAWNEE 1814 $.95 (P292)

Little One, Tiny One (composed with
Besig)
SATB SHAWNEE 6407 $.85 (P293)

Music Box Carol, A *see Besig

Walk A Little Slower, My Friend
(composed with Besig)
2pt cor SHAWNEE 0105 $.95 (P294)

PRICE, BERYL (1912-)
Pocketful Of Rhymes, A
SATB,pno OXFORD 343097 $2.25 (P295)

Victoria Station
unis cor,pno [2'] ROBERTON 75228
(P296)

PRICE, NANCY
It's Hard To Say Goodbye *see Besig,
Don

PRIERE, LA see Brassens, Georges

PRIERE D'UN ENFANT DE CHOEUR MOURANT,
LA see Clemens, Henri

PRIERES DU VIGNERON, LES see
Hemmerling, Carlos

PRIMO LIBRO DE MADRIGALI, IL see
Flecha, Mateo

PRIMO LIBRO DELLE CANZONETTE A TRE
VOCI, IL see Rossi, Salomone

PRINS, J.
Bruid, De
(Potgieser, P.) TTBB MOLENAAR
13005803 (P297)

PRINTEMPS see Schubert, Franz (Peter)

PRINTEMPS see Vocht, Lodewijk de, Jonge
Jaar, Het

PRINTEMPS, LE see Huguenin, Charles

PRINTEMPS, LE see Huwiler, Pierre

PRINTEMPS, LE see Vidalin, M.

PRINTEMPS CAMPAGNARD see Chatton,
Pierre

PRISE DU HAVRE, LA see Costeley,
Guillaume

PRIZE WE SOUGHT, THE see Siltman, Bobby
L.

PROCTER, LELAND (1914-)
Moby Dick
SATB,3.3.3.3. 4.2.3.1. harp,timp,
perc,strings [60'] AM.COMP.AL.
(P298)
Three Songs Of Service *CCU
SATB AM.COMP.AL. $4.10 (P299)

PROESTANTS FUGITIFS see Assalinde

PROFESSOR NONTROPPO'S MUSIC DICTIONARY
see Mechem, Kirke Lewis

PROLOGUE see Gagnebin, Henri

PROLOGUE AND THE END OF THE WORLD see
Bell, Larry

PROLOOG EN TUSSENSTUK 1 see Bank,
Jacques

PROMENADES EN FORET see Massis

PROMENEUR, LE see Gagnebin, Henri

PROMETHEUS see Hamilton, Iain

PRONUBA JUNO see Lassus, Roland de
(Orlandus)

PROST! SCHENK EIN DEN KUHLEN WEIN see
Seckinger, Konrad

PROUD MARY see Fogerty, J.C.

PROVENCE, LA see Huguenin, Charles

PROVINS, J.
    Amour En Dix-Neuf Ponts
        (Passaquet, R.) 4pt mix cor HEUGEL
        HE 31846   (P300)

PSALMI see Slavicky, Klement

PSALMS OF ASCENT see Alwes, Chester

PSYCHE see Franck, Cesar

P'TIT BONNET CARRE see Ah! Si J'avais
    Un Sou

P'TIT QUINQUIN, LE
    (Holstein, J.P.) 3 eq voices HEUGEL
        HE 32033   (P301)

P'TIT VIN D'LAVAUX, LE see Bovet,
    Joseph

PUCE, LA see Le Jeune, Claude

PUCHNER, JOHANN
    see BUCHNER, JOHANN

PUEBLO BONITO see Balazs, Frederic

PUERLING, GENE
    Button Up Your Overcoat
        SATB CPP-BEL SVGP005 $1.25   (P302)

PUETZ, EDUARD
    Kon-Takte (Jazz Cantata)
        SATB,fl,sax,vibra,gtr,pno,db,perc
        SEESAW   (P303)

PUGET
    Retour Des Hirondelles, Le
        2pt cor,pno JOBERT   (P304)

PUISQUE CE BEAU MOIS see Costeley,
    Guillaume

PURCELL, HENRY (1658 or 59-1695)
    Hier Buiten In Het Groene Bos
        mix cor ZENGERINK 136   (P305)

    Hoor Trompetgeschal °see Trumpet
        Voluntary

    How Happy The Lover
        (McCray) SA&B NEW MUSIC NMA-196
        $.90   (P306)

    In These Delightful Pleasant Groves
        (Kingsbury) SAB,acap PRESSER
        312-41541 see from TWO MADRIGALS
                                         (P307)

    Komt Trompetten °see Sound The
        Trumpet

    Ode On St. Cecilia's Day 1692 (from
        The New Purcell Society Edition:
        Vol: 8)
        mix cor NOVELLO f.s.   (P308)

    Ode To St. Cecilia's Day
        4-6pt cor,SAATBB soli KALMUS
        K 06381 $7.00   (P309)

    Sound The Trumpet
        2pt mix cor,kbd FISCHER,C CM 8056
                                         (P310)
        (Zengerink, Herman) "Komt
        Trompetten" 2 eq voices,pno
        (diff) ZENGERINK V 136   (P311)

    Trumpet Voluntary
        (Kaspersma) "Hoor Trompetgeschal"
        TTBB MOLENAAR 13036506   (P312)
        (Lucas, C.) "Hoor Trompetgeschal"
        SATB MOLENAAR 13026906   (P313)

    Ye Tuneful Muses
        SATB,ATB soli KALMUS K 06383 $2.00
                                         (P314)

PUSSY CAT DUETS see Warren, B.

PUT A LITTLE LOVE IN YOUR HEART
    (Snyder) SATB CPP-BEL T8842PC1 $1.25,
        accomp tape available   (P315)
    (Snyder) SAB CPP-BEL T8842PC3 $1.25,
        accomp tape available   (P316)
    (Snyder) 2pt cor CPP-BEL T8842PC5
        $1.25, accomp tape available   (P317)

PUT YOUR DREAMS ON A BUTTERFLY see
    Clapp

PUTSCHE, THOMAS (1929-   )
    Cat And The Moon
        jr cor SEESAW   (P318)

PYRAMIDEN see Sommerfeldt, Oistein

Q

QUAND CE BEAU PRINTEMPS JE VOY see
    Turellier, Jean

QUAND ELLE EST LA, LA BELLE DAME see
    Patry, Andre J.

QUAND IL NEIGE see Chailley, Jacques

QUAND JE BOIS DU VIN CLARET see
    Anonymous

QUAND JE BOIS DU VIN CLARET see Gero,
    Ihan

QUAND JE MENAIS MES CHEVAUX BOIRE see
    Turellier, Jean

QUAND JE VAIS AU BOIS see Lauber, Emile

QUAND JE VAIS AU JARDIN D'AMOUR
    (Will, M.) SATB,acap HUGUENIN CH 974
                                         (Q1)

QUAND JE VOIS DU VIN CLARET see Gero,
    Ihan

QUAND J'ETAIS JEUNE see Blanchard

QUAND LA MARIE
    (Nahoum, J.) 4 eq voices HEUGEL
    HE 32418 contains also: Sommeil
                                         (Q2)

QUAND LA MER ROUGE
    (Nahoum, J.) 2 eq voices HEUGEL
    HE 32416 contains also: Noel
    Nouveau   (Q3)

QUAND LE GUERRIER see Couste, Francis

QUAND LE ROSSIGNOL CHANTE
    (Grimbert, J.) 3pt jr cor,opt inst
    HEUGEL HE 32287   (Q4)

QUAND MON MARI VIENT DE DEHORS see
    Castro, Jean de

QUAND MON MARI VIENT DE DEHORS see
    Lassus, Roland de (Orlandus)

QUAND ON Y PENSE see Lauber, Emile

QUAND TI-JEAN REVIENT DES BOIS
    see Mon Pere A Fait Batir Maison

QUAND TU SAURAS see Richli, E.

QUAND UN SOLDAT see Lemarque, F.

QUANDO SON PIU LONTON see Lauridsen,
    Morten Johannes

QUANT N'ONT ASSEZ FAIT DODO see
    D'Orleans, Ch.

QUARTRE CHANSONS POPULAIRES HONGROISES
    °see Au Marche De Yanochida; Ohe,
    Meunier; Patre Des Montagnes; Voici
    Le Gai Printemps   (Q5)

QUATRAIN see Level, Pierre Yves

QUATRE BALLADES FRANCAISES see
    Apotheloz, Jean

QUATRE CHANSONS A 2 VOIX MIXTES see
    Gero, Ihan

QUATRE CHANSONS POPULAIRES
    (Feuillie, J.) 2pt jr cor HEUGEL
    HE 32181   (Q6)

QUATRE CHANTS YOUGOSLAVES see Cossetto,
    Emil

QUATRE DUOS A VOIX EGLES see Gardane,
    Antonio

QUATRE-VINGTS CHASSEURS, LES
    (Lattion, Guy) SATB,acap HUGUENIN
    CH 1196   (Q7)
    (Lattion, Guy) TTBB HUGUENIN CH 1193
                                         (Q8)

QUATTRO PEZZI see Swider, Jozef

QUATUORS POUR VOIX D'HOMMES: C.1 see
    Lauber, Emile

QUATUORS POUR VOIX D'HOMMES: C.2 see
    Lauber, Emile

QUATUORS POUR VOIX D'HOMMES: C.3 see
    Lauber, Emile

QUATUORS POUR VOIX D'HOMMES: C.4 see
    Lauber, Emile

QU'AVONS-NOUS FAIT? see Brel, Jacques

QUE DE MARTYRE ET DE DOULEURS see
    Costeley, Guillaume

QUE DE PASSIONS ET DOULEURS see
    Costeley, Guillaume

QUE FAIS-TU LA, BEL OISEAU?
    (Barblan, Emmanuel) SATB,acap
    HUGUENIN EB 297 contains also: Che
    Fasch Qua Tu Bel Utschlin?   (Q9)

QUE L'ECHO REPONDE A NOS TRANSPORTS see
    Rameau, Jean-Philippe

QUE VEUT UN SUISSE AU COEUR HARDI? see
    Niggli, Friedrich

QUEL MAZZOLIN DI FIORI
    (Frochaux, Jean-Bernard) SATB,acap
    HUGUENIN CH 2028   (Q10)

QUEL ROSSIGNUOL see Lassus, Roland de
    (Orlandus)

QUENEAU, R.
    Porc, Le (composed with Etienne, L.)
    (Lenoble, J.) 3 eq voices/4pt mix
    cor,pno,db HEUGEL HE 32483   (Q11)

QUESNEL, STEVEN R. (1950-   )
    First Day Of Choir, The
        SATB (med) GENTRY JG2078 $.90,
        accomp tape available   (Q12)
        2pt cor (med) GENTRY JG0448 f.s.
                                         (Q13)

QUESTA DOLCE SIRENA see Gastoldi,
    Giovanni Giacomo

QUESTIONS see Distler, Hugo

QUEUE DU CHAT, LA see Marcy, Robert

QUI A TUE GRAND' MAMAN? see Polnareff,
    M.

QUI ES PROMESSE see Machaut, Guillaume
    de

QUI PEUT-ETRE
    (Lenoble, J.) 3pt mix cor HEUGEL
    HE 32161   (Q14)

QUI VEUT AIMER see Jacotin, Jacques

QUI VIENT CE JOUR see Tamaris

QUICK! WE HAVE BUT A SECOND see
    Stanford, Charles Villiers

QUIETT
    White Wings
        SAB CPP-BEL SV8113 $1.10   (Q15)

QU'IL EST BEAU MON PAYS see Pascal,
    Andre

QUIMEY, NEUQUEN see Berbel, Marcelo

QUISNAM CRASSUS EST see Riedstra, Tom

QUODLIBET see Kaufmann, Dieter

R

R-A-G-T-I-M-E! see Musser

RAAK MIJ NIET KWIJT see Kloek, D.

RABBITS see Belyea, H.

RABE, FOLKE (1935-   )
   It May Not Always Be So
      men cor,acap REIMERS   (R1)

   Sju Dikter *CC7U
      [Swed] mix cor,acap REIMERS   (R2)

   To Love
      [Eng] mix cor,acap REIMERS   (R3)

RABE, GERHARD
   Drei Wiegenlieder *CC3U
      wom cor/jr cor BRAUN-PER 1022 (R4)

RACHMANINOFF, SERGEY VASSILIEVICH
   (1873-1943)
   Bells, The *Op.35
      [Russ/Ger/Eng] SATB,solo,orch
      KALMUS K 09721 $8.75   (R5)

   Trois Chansons Russes *CC3U
      [Russ/Eng/Ger/Fr] 2pt mix cor BUDDE
      901   (R6)

RADETZKY-MARSCH see Strauss, Johann,
   [Sr.]

RADSTAKE, L.J.
   Ruhe Zum Herzen
      (Steen, J.) TTBB MOLENAAR 15014102
                                    (R7)

RAGNARSSON, HJALMAR H. (1952-   )
   On An Old Dream's Heather-Slope
      mix cor,acap ICELAND 030-10 see
      from Two Songs Of Love   (R8)

   Stone, The
      mix cor,acap ICELAND 030-10 see
      from Two Songs Of Love   (R9)

   Two Songs Of Love *see On An Old
      Dream's Heather-Slope; Stone, The
                                    (R10)

RAGTIME FANTASY see Joplin, Scott

RAICHL, MIROSLAV (1930-   )
   Children's Choir *see Detske Sbory

   Detske Sbory
      "Children's Choir" jr cor SUPRAPHON
                                    (R11)

RAIN IT RAINETH, THE see Hagemann,
   Philip

RAIN, RAIN see Maslanka, David Henry

RAINBOW-89 *CCU
   [Russ] MEZ KNIGA 186   (R12)

RAISE THE SONG see Shur, Yekutiel

RAISE THE SONG see Shur, Yekutiel

RAM, SAMUEL (BUCK) (1907-1991)
   Great Pretender, The
      (Shaw, Kirby) SAB CPP-BEL 5745GC3X
      $1.25, accomp tape available
                                    (R13)
      (Shaw, Kirby) SATB CPP-BEL 5745GC1X
      $1.25, accomp tape available
                                    (R14)
      (Shaw, Kirby) TTB CPP-BEL 5745GC4X
      $1.25, accomp tape available
                                    (R15)

RAMEAU, JEAN-PHILIPPE (1683-1764)
   A L'Amour Rendons Les Armes (from
      Hippolyte)
      SATB,acap HUGUENIN EB 401   (R16)

   Chantons Sur La Musette (from
      Hippolyte)
      SATB,acap HUGUENIN EB 296   (R17)

   Choeur Des Spartiates Et Menuet
      Chante (from Castor Et Pollux)
      SATB,acap HUGUENIN EB 161   (R18)

   Eclatante Trompette, Publiez La
      Victoire
      mix cor,solo voice HUGUENIN CH 453
                                    (R19)

   Hymne Au Soleil
      "Indes Galantes, Les" SATB,acap
      HUGUENIN EB 395   (R20)

   Indes Galantes, Les *see Hymne Au
      Soleil

   Laboravi
      SSATB,cont CAILLARD PC 133   (R21)

RAMEAU, JEAN-PHILIPPE (cont'd.)

   Que L'echo Reponde A Nos Transports
      SATB,acap HUGUENIN CH 620   (R22)

   Volez, Zephirs! Volez!
      mix cor HUGUENIN CH 623   (R23)

RAMMO, PEETER
   Spruche Des Konfuzius *Op.6
      [Ger] dbl cor NORGE   (R24)

RAMONEUR, LE
   (Passaquay, F.) 2pt jr cor HEUGEL
      HE 32371   (R25)

RANDALL, BRUCE
   see RODBY, WALTER

RAPOSO, JOSEPH G. (1937-1989)
   America Is (Official Statue Of
      Liberty Song)
      (Chinn) SA CPP-BEL 4063AC5X $1.25)
                                    (R26)
      (Chinn) SATB CPP-BEL 4063AC1X $1.25)
                                    (R27)
      (Chinn) SAB CPP-BEL 4063AC3X $1.25)
                                    (R28)
      (Chinn) SSA CPP-BEL 4063AC2X $1.25)
                                    (R29)

RAPTURES see Avshalomov, Jacob

RASIUK, MOSHE (1954-   )
   Market Street, The *see Rehov Hashuk

   Rehov Hashuk
      "Market Street, The" [Heb/Eng] mix
      cor,acap [7'] ISR.MUS.INST. 6344
                                    (R30)

RASLEY
   Hope Is A Thing With Feathers
      SATB,acap MUSIC SEV. M70-454 $.85
                                    (R31)

RAT, LE see Le Cannu, G.

RAUSCH, CARLOS
   Chitterabob
      SATB sc APNM $4.50 see from Rounds
                                    (R32)
   Needless Needles
      SATB sc APNM $3.00 see from Rounds
                                    (R33)
   Peter Piper
      SATB sc APNM $3.00 see from Rounds
                                    (R34)
   Rounds *see Chitterabob; Needless
      Needles; Peter Piper; Whistle
      Whistle   (R35)

   Whistle Whistle
      SATB sc APNM $3.00 see from Rounds
                                    (R36)

RAUTAVAARA, EINOJUHANI (1928-   )
   Marjatta Matala Neiti
      SA FAZER F 06994-8   (R37)

   Nirvana Dharma
      mix cor,S solo,fl FAZER
      (CH 81) F 06976-5   (R38)

   Suite De Lorca *Op.72
      jr cor FAZER F 06946-8   (R39)

   Viatonten Valssi
      "Waltz Of The Innocents" cor,S solo
      FAZER F 06974-0   (R40)

   Waltz Of The Innocents
      SA,vln FAZER F 06974-0   (R41)

   Waltz Of The Innocents *see
      Viatonten Valssi

RAVEL, MAURICE (1875-1937)
   Nicolette
      SATB,acap HARMONIA HU 3790 see from
      Trois Chansons   (R42)

   Ronde
      SATB,acap HARMONIA HU 3792 see from
      Trois Chansons   (R43)

   Trois Beaux Oiseaux Du Paradis
      SATB,SAB soli,acap HARMONIA HU 3791
      see from Trois Chansons   (R44)

   Trois Chansons *see Nicolette (R45)

   Trois Chansons *see Trois Beaux
      Oiseaux Du Paradis   (R46)

   Trois Chansons *see Ronde   (R47)

RAVEN AND THE FOX, THE see Smith, Gregg

RAVEN OG LAMBET see Karlsen, Rolf

RAVENSCROFT, THOMAS (1593-1635)
   We Be Three Poor Mariners
      (Owens) SAB,acap CPP-BEL
      SV8569 F 110 $1.20   (R48)
      (Owens) TTB,acap CPP-BEL SV8570
      $1.20   (R49)

RAWSTHORNE, ALAN (1905-1971)
   Canticle Of Man, A
      SATB,Bar solo,fl,strings OXFORD
                                    (R50)
   Carmen Vitale
      [Lat/Eng] SATB,S solo,3.2.2.2.
      4.3.3.1. timp,perc,harp,strings
      OXFORD   (R51)

RAY, JERRY
   Catch The Spirit
      cor ALFRED   (R52)

   Christmas Noel
      cor ALFRED   (R53)

   Common Ground
      SAB ALFRED 7680 $.95, accomp tape
      available   (R54)

   First Christmas
      cor ALFRED   (R55)

   Good Times
      cor ALFRED   (R56)

   It's My Music
      cor ALFRED   (R57)

   Music, Sweet Music
      ALFRED   (R58)

   Over There
      SAB ALFRED 7515 $.95   (R59)

   Sing Out With Joy
      SATB ALFRED 7607 $.95   (R60)

   We Hold The Future
      SATB ALFRED 7516 $.95, accomp tape
      available   (R61)
      SAB ALFRED 7517 $.95, accomp tape
      available   (R62)
      SSA ALFRED 7518 $.95, accomp tape
      available   (R63)
      1-2pt cor ALFRED 7519 $.95, accomp
      tape available   (R64)

RAYMOND
   Ich Hab' Mein Herz In Heidelberg
      Verloren
      (Grieshaber) men cor,pno,opt acord
      LEUCKART LSB 116 f.s.   (R65)

RAY'S ROCKHOUSE
   (Zegree, Steve) SATB LEONARD-US
      07357821 $.95   (R66)
   (Zegree, Steve) SAB LEONARD-US
      07357822 $.95, ipa, accomp tape
      available   (R67)

RAZZAMATAZZ
   (Buchholz) SATB CPP-BEL 0050RC1X
      $1.25, accomp tape available (R68)

REACH FOR A STAR see Ross, Brad

REACH OUT see Hughes

REACH OUT see Steffy, Thurlow

REACH OUT AND TOUCH (SOMEBODY'S HAND)
   see Ashford, Nickolas

REACH TO THE STARS see Terhune, Charles

REACH UP! see McLin

READ, GARDNER (1913-   )
   Magic Hour, The
      SSA,pno LAWSON 52295   (R69)

   When Moonlight Falls
      (Read, Vail) SSA,pno LAWSON 52436
      $.90   (R70)

REBECCA see Josephs, Wilfred

REBELLENLIEDER see Laburda, Jiri

REBSCHER, HELMUT (1928-   )
   Zum Meer "In Der Kleinen Stadt Am
      Hafen"
      SSA MULLER 407   (R71)

RECITATIVES AND CHORUS FROM AUBER'S "LE
   DOMINO NOIR"
   see Three Arrangements

RECITATIVES FROM "LE NOZZE DI FIGARO"
   see Three Arrangements

RECOLLECTION see Haydn, [Franz] Joseph

RED IRON ORE (MICHIGAN SEA SONG)
   (Langejans) TTBB,acap MUSIC SEV.
      M70-457 $.90   (R72)

RED-LETTER DAYS *CCU
   [Russ] jr cor,pno MEZ KNIGA 486 (R73)

RED RIVER VALLEY
   (Daniel, Etienne) 3-4pt mix cor
      CAILLARD PC 141 contains also: We
      Shall Overcome   (R74)

RED RIVER VALLEY see Cable, Howard

RED RIVER VALLEY; TRAIL TO MEXICO
(Blair, D.) SATB,pno (med) THOMAS
1C038418 $.90 (R75)

RED TOADSTOOL, THE see Matys, Jiri

REDEDICATION see Adler, Samuel Hans

REED
Your Imagination *see Donnelly

REED, EVERETT
Chimney Sweeper, The
cor ASPEN 2003 $.85 (R76)

Night
cor ASPEN 2005 $.65 (R77)

Nurse's Song
cor ASPEN 2004 $.75 (R78)

Piper, The
cor ASPEN 2001 $.75 (R79)

Shepherd, The
cor ASPEN 2002 $.75 (R80)

REESE
Anything You Want To Be
2pt cor CPP-BEL SV8422 $.95 (R81)

Give A Little Love Away
2pt cor SHAWNEE 0313 $.95 (R82)

Memories Of Christmas
SAB CPP-BEL SV8409 $.95 (R83)

REESE, JAN
Go 'Way From My Window
3pt cor LEONARD-US 08602918 $.85
(R84)

Texas
2pt cor LEONARD-US 08599508 $.85
(R85)
3pt mix cor LEONARD-US 08599509
$.85 (R86)

REFLECTIONS OF CANADA, VOL. 1: PINE
TREE GENTLY SIGH *CCU
2pt cor HARRIS HC-7013 $12.95 (R87)

REFLECTIONS OF CANADA, VOL. 2: THE
RAFTSMEN *CCU
3pt cor HARRIS HC-7014 $12.95 (R88)

REFLECTIONS OF CANADA, VOL. 3: IN THE
MOON OF WINTERTIME *CCU
SATB HARRIS HC-7015 $12.95 (R89)

REFLECTIONS OF EMILY see Mennin, Peter
(Mennini)

REFLECTIONS ON THE DAYS OF CHRISTMAS
see Klein, Leonard

REFLETS D'ENFANCE see Defossez, Rene

REFUGES see Berthomier, Michel

REGER, MAX (1873-1916)
Abendlied
mix cor,pno BREITKOPF-W CHB 5195
see from Drei Chore, Op. 6 (R90)
mix cor BREITKOPF-W CHB 5196 see
from Drei Chore, Op. 39 (R91)

Ach Baumchen, Du Stehst Grune
SATB,acap HANSSLER 40.299-20 f.s.
(R92)

Denk Ich Allweil *see Vergebens

Drauss Ist Alles So Prachtig *see
Mailied

Drei Chore, Op. 6 *see Abendlied;
Trost; Zur Nacht (R93)

Drei Chore, Op. 39 *see Abendlied;
Fruhlingsblick; Schweigen (R94)

Er Ist's
SSAA HARMONIA 3654 (R95)

Fruhlingsblick
mix cor BREITKOPF-W CHB 5196 see
from Drei Chore, Op. 39 (R96)

Ich Wollt, Ich Lag Und Schlief *see
Liebeslied

Liebeslied
"Ich Wollt, Ich Lag Und Schlief"
SATB,acap HANSSLER 40.299-30 f.s.
(R97)

Liebesqual
"Und Schau Ich Hin, So Schaust Du
Her" SATB,acap HANSSLER 40.298-30
f.s. (R98)

Mailied
"Drauss Ist Alles So Prachtig"
SATB,acap HANSSLER 40.299-10 f.s.
(R99)

REGER, MAX (cont'd.)
Schweigen
mix cor BREITKOPF-W CHB 5196 see
from Drei Chore, Op. 39 (R100)

Sternlein, Das
SATB,acap HANSSLER 40.298-20 f.s.
(R101)

Trost
mix cor,pno BREITKOPF-W CHB 5195
see from Drei Chore, Op. 6 (R102)

Und Schau Ich Hin, So Schaust Du Her
*see Liebesqual

Vergebens
"Denk Ich Allweil" SATB,acap
HANSSLER 40.298-40 f.s. (R103)

Volkslieder *CCU
(Pommer) mix cor PETERS 9449 (R104)

Zur Nacht
mix cor,pno BREITKOPF-W CHB 5195
see from Drei Chore, Op. 6 (R105)

REGN see Bergman, Erik

REGNARD, FRANCOIS (1540-1599)
Mamie Et Moy
(Grimbert, J.) 4pt mix cor HEUGEL
HE 32414 (R106)

O Voux, Beaux Yeux
(Grimbert, J.) 4pt mix cor HEUGEL
HE 32415 (R107)

REGNART
Free I Am Once Again
(Snyder) SAB CPP-BEL SV8615 $1.10
(R108)

Pain Of Love, The
TBB CPP-BEL SV8631 $1.10 (R109)
3pt mix cor CPP-BEL SV8630 $1.10
(R110)
SSA CPP-BEL SV8629 $1.10 (R111)

REGNART, JACOB (ca. 1540-1599)
Wenn Ich Gedenk Der Stund
SSA HARMONIA 3768 (R112)

REGNER, HERMANN (1928-)
Blessed Are Those Who Work For Peace
(composed with Haselbach, B.)
SATB (orff-schulwerk) MMB SE-0893
$2.00 (R113)

REGNEY, NOEL
Do You Hear What I Hear? (composed
with Shayne)
(Simeone) SATB SHAWNEE 0708 $.85
(R114)

REHNQVIST, KARIN (1957-)
Davids Nimm
treb cor,3 female soli SUECIA
SUE 351 (R115)

Sang Ur Sagan Om Fatumeh
12pt men cor STIM (R116)

Tilt. Drama
4pt mix cor,acap [8'-9'] STIM
8511-057 (R117)

REHOV HASHUK see Rasiuk, Moshe

REIBEL, GUY (1936-)
Balancements
mix cor,acap HEUGEL HE 31945 (R118)

Chambres De Cristal, Les
mix cor,inst,electronic tape [90']
SALABERT EAS18314P (R119)

Ode A Villon
mix cor,electronic tape [20']
SALABERT EAS18374P (R120)

REICH' MIR ZUM ABSCHIED NOCH EINMAL DIE
HANDE see Abraham

REICH UND ARM
(Estermann, J.) mix cor,acap PELIKAN
PE1191 (R121)

REILLY
Two By Two
2-3pt cor,fl KJOS C8802 $.80 (R122)

REINECKE, CARL (1824-1910)
Fruhlingsgruss *Op.14,No.2
SATB HARMONIA 3773 (R123)

REINL, FRANZ (1903-)
Drei Becher
men cor,acap ZIMMER. 613 (R124)

Komm, Tanz Mit Mir
mix cor ZIMMER. 624 (R125)
men cor,acap ZIMMER. 623 (R126)

Sanger Und Ein Gitarrist, Ein
men cor,gtr ZIMMER. 618 (R127)

REITER UND DER BODENSEE, DER see
Schroeder, Hermann

REJOICE AND BE MERRY see Ryden

REJOICE AND SING NOEL! see Petker,
Allan R.

RELUCTANT DRAGON, THE see Rutter, John

REMEMBER THIS ONE see Scott

REMEMBRANCE see Agay, Denes

REMINDER see De Cormier, Robert

REMSIER
Eden
SATB SCHIRM.G 316020 $.70 (R128)

RENARD see Stravinsky, Igor

RENARD, GEORGES
Coin Bleu, Le
TTBB HUGUENIN PG 4136 (R129)

Noisettes, Les
SATB,acap HUGUENIN PG 4455 (R130)

RENCH
Me And My Best Friend
cor ALFRED (R131)

RENOUVEAU see Apotheloz, Jean

RENOUVEAU, LE see Huguenin, Charles

REPENTANCE see Sviridov, Georgy

REPERTOIRE OF AMATEUR CHORUSES, VOL. 10
*CCU
(Selivanov, B.) [Russ] cor,acap/pno
MEZ KNIGA 185 (R132)

REPERTOIRE OF RUSSIAN FOLK CHORUSES,
VOL. 10 *CCU
(Shirokov, A.) [Russ] cor,acap/pno/
acord MEZ KNIGA 184 (R133)

REQUIEM see Shearer, C.M.

REQUIEM FOR MIGNON see Schumann, Robert
(Alexander)

REQUIEM POUR N'IMPORTE QUI see
Moustaki, Georges

REQUIEM VOOR EEN LEVENDE see Bank,
Jacques

RESPECT YOURSELF
(Buchholz) SATB CPP-BEL 1550RC1X
$1.25, accomp tape available (R134)
(Buchholz) SAB CPP-BEL 1550RC3X
$1.25, accomp tape available (R135)

REST FOR ALL ETERNITY see Cooper, Steve

RESTA DIDAR MI NOIA see Gesualdo, [Don]
Carlo (da Venosa)

RETOUR DES HIRONDELLES, LE see Puget

RETURN OF SPRING see Bacon, Ernst L.

RETURNING (CANON SENZA PAROLE) see
Ostern, Per Hroar

RETZEL, FRANK (1948-)
Break Forth
SATB,T solo,org [6'0"] sc APNM
$4.50, perf mat rent (R136)

REUZEGOM see Vermulst, Jan

REUZEGOM (OUD VLAAMS VOLKSLIED) see
Vermulst, Jan

REVEILLE see Peaslee, Richard

REVEILLEZ-VOUS PICARDS
(Herr, Francoise) 2pt jr cor,Orff
inst HEUGEL HE 32543 (R137)

REVEILLEZ-VOUS PICARDS ET BOURGUIGNONS
(Holstein, J.P.) 4pt mix cor HEUGEL
HE 32034 (R138)

REVELATION IS NOT SEALED see Clarke,
Henry Leland

REVER see Bovet, Joseph

REVIL, RUDI
A La Saint-Medard
(Bereau, J.S.) 3pt mix cor HEUGEL
HE 31921 (R139)

Marjolaine *see Lemarque, F.

REY, L.
Dans La Marine Suisse (composed with
Clausier, R.)
(Tritsch, J.) 4 eq voices HEUGEL
HE 32332 (R140)

REYES, FERNANDO
  Plorar
    4pt cor CLIVIS AC231   (R141)

REYMOND, HERNY
  Avril
    SATB,acap HUGUENIN EB 211   (R142)

  Petites D'Echichens, Les
    SATB,acap HUGUENIN EB 210   (R143)

  Rose Rosette
    SATB,acap HUGUENIN EB 212   (R144)

RHEINWEIN MUSS ES SEIN see Cadow, Paul

RHEINWEINLIED see Erdmann-Abele, Veit

RHODES, PHILLIP (1940-   )
  Wind Songs
    unis jr cor,Orff inst UNIVER.
      STAP 197 $4.95   (R145)

RHYMES see Swider, Jozef, Rymowanki

RHYTHM IN MY SOUL see Simms

RHYTHM IS GONNA GET YOU
  (Hanson, Mark) SATB,opt db,gtr,drums
    CPP-BEL 2412RC1X $1.25, accomp tape
    available   (R146)
  (Hanson, Mark) SAB,opt db,gtr,drums
    CPP-BEL 2412RC3X $1.25, accomp tape
    available   (R147)

RHYTHM OF LIFE, THE see Coleman, Cy

RHYTHM OF THE NIGHT
  (Chinn) SATB CPP-BEL 2408RC1X $1.25,
    accomp tape available   (R148)
  (Chinn) SSA CPP-BEL 2408RC2X $1.25,
    accomp tape available   (R149)
  (Chinn) SAB CPP-BEL 2408RC3X $1.25,
    accomp tape available   (R150)

RHYTHM'S EVERYWHERE, THE see Lutz,
  Lawrence

RIBBON IN THE SKY
  (Levine) SATB CPP-BEL 2756RC1X $1.25
                                 (R151)

RIBON, RIBONBAINE
  (Grombert, J.) 4pt mix cor HEUGEL
    HE 31903   (R152)

RICHAFORT, JOANNES (1490-1548)
  En Revenant Du Bois
    (Agnel, A.) 3 eq voices HEUGEL
      HE 32128   (R153)

  Il Est En Vous
    (Agnel, A.) 3 eq voices HEUGEL
      HE 32045   (R154)

  Trut Avant, Il Faut Boire
    (Dottin, G.) 3 eq voices HEUGEL
      HE 31840 contains also:
      Anonymous, Faute D'argent, C'est
      Douleur Non Pareille   (R155)

RICHARDS, GOFF
  Lord Lovelace
    TTBB,pno ROBERTON 53131   (R156)

RICHIE, LIONEL
  Ballerina Girl
    (Strommen, Carl) cor ALFRED (R157)

  Deep River Woman
    (Ray) cor ALFRED   (R158)

RICHLI, E.
  Nocturne
    TTBB HUGUENIN CH 823   (R159)

  Quand Tu Sauras
    SATB,acap HUGUENIN CH 824   (R160)

RIDDLE OF THE WORLD, THE see Willcocks,
  Jonathan

RIDDLE SONG, THE *folk song,US
  (Dusing, David) SA,kbd (easy) LAWSON
    52379 $1.25   (R161)

RIDE THE WAVE see Fitzmartin

RIDE THE WIND see Strommen, Carl

RIDEAU DE MA VOISINE, LE see Moreillon,
  H.P.

RIDEREGLE see Nystedt, Knut

RIDIAMO CANTIAMO see Rossini,
  Gioacchino

RIEDSTRA, TOM (1957-   )
  Quisnam Crassus Est
    mix cor, toy piano [4'] DONEMUS
                                 (R162)

RIETZ, JULIUS (1812-1877)
  Au Mois De Mai
    TTBB HUGUENIN EB 40   (R163)

RIETZ, R.
  Bonheur Craintif
    1-4pt cor HUGUENIN see from
    CHANSONS POUR LA JEUNESSE,
    TROISIEME CAHIER   (R164)

RILEY
  I Believe In You And Me (composed
    with Wilson)
    SATB CPP-BEL SV8348 $.95   (R165)

RILEY, DENNIS (1943-   )
  Three Little Commentaries
    SAB,string orch [5'] AM.COMP.AL.
                                 (R166)

RILKE LIEDER see Kingma, Piet

RIMSKY-KORSAKOV, NIKOLAI (1844-1908)
  Alone In The North
    see Six A Cappella Choruses, Op. 16

  Bacchanalian Song
    see Six A Cappella Choruses, Op. 16

  Boyarina Vera Sheloga *Op.54
    [Russ] cor KALMUS K 05259 $11.50
                                 (R167)

  Choruses From Operas, Vol. 2 *CCU
    [Russ] cor,pno MEZ KNIGA 162
      includes choruses from The Snow
      Maiden and Mlada   (R168)

  Choruses From Operas, Vol. 3 *CCU
    [Russ] cor,pno MEZ KNIGA 164 (R169)

  Choruses From Operas, Vol. 4 *CCU
    (Kopylova, V.) [Russ] cor,pno MEZ
      KNIGA 173   (R170)

  Fifteen Russian Folk Songs, Op. 19
    *CC15U
    [Russ] cor,acap MEZ KNIGA 163
                                 (R171)
  Fifteen Russian Folk Songs, Op. 19
    see Two Choral Works

  Four Three-Part Choruses For Male
    Voices, Op. 23
    see Three Choral Works

  Last Fleeting Cloud Of The Storm
    see Six A Cappella Choruses, Op. 16

  Moon Floats
    see Six A Cappella Choruses, Op. 16

  O Sov'reign Of My Days
    see Six A Cappella Choruses, Op. 16

  Old Song, An
    see Six A Cappella Choruses, Op. 16

  Poem Of Oleg The Wise *Op.58
    [Russ] men cor,TB soli,orch voc sc
      MEZ KNIGA 473   (R172)

  Six A Cappella Choruses, Op. 16
    [Eng/Russ] KALMUS K 05281 $8.75
      contains: Alone In The North
      (SATB); Bacchanalian Song
      (TTBB); Last Fleeting Cloud Of
      The Storm (SSAA); Moon Floats
      (SATB); O Sov'reign Of My Days
      (SSAATTBB); Old Song, An
      (SSAATTBB)   (R173)

  Song Of The Highwaymen
    see Three Choral Works

  Switezianka *Op.44
    [Russ] cor KALMUS K 05267 $28.75
                                 (R174)

  Three Choral Works
    [Russ/Eng] KALMUS K 05283 $8.75
      contains: Four Three-Part
      Choruses For Male Voices, Op.
      23 (3pt men cor,acap); Song Of
      The Highwaymen (TTB,acap); Two
      Choruses For Children's Voices
      (SSA,acap)   (R175)

  Two Choral Works
    [Russ/Eng] mix cor,acap KALMUS
      K 05282 $11.50
      contains: Fifteen Russian Folk
      Songs, Op. 19; Two Choruses For
      Mixed Voices, Op. 18   (R176)

  Two Choruses For Children's Voices
    see Three Choral Works

  Two Choruses For Mixed Voices, Op. 18
    see Two Choral Works

RINEHART, JOHN (1937-   )
  Four Odes
    SATB [9'] AM.COMP.AL. $9.15 (R177)

  Love Came To Us
    SATB [2'] AM.COMP.AL. $1.95 (R178)

  Vivas!
    SATB,brass [7'] AM.COMP.AL. $11.45
                                 (R179)

RINEHART, JOHN (cont'd.)

  With Music Strong
    SATB,brass,opt timp [10']
      AM.COMP.AL. $7.70   (R180)

RING CHRISTMAS BELLS! see Martin,
  Gilbert M.

RING O BELL OF FREEDOM see Gates,
  Crawford

RING OUT THE BELLS see Fanshawe, David

RING OUT THE OLD, RING IN THE NEW see
  Strommen, Carl

RING OUT, WILD BELLS see Fletcher,
  Percy Eastman

RINGER see Hegdal, Magne

RINGIN' IN CHRISTMAS COUNTRY STYLE see
  Buck

RIP VAN WINKLE see Bryan, John

RIPPEN, PIET
  Zommer
    SATB MOLENAAR 13054904   (R181)

RISE UP see Siltman, Bobby L.

RITCHIE, JEAN (1922-   )
  Courtin' Song, The
    (Dusing, David) SATB,acap LAWSON
      52323 $1.25   (R182)

RIVAT
  Vent Et La Jeunesse, Le
    (Thomas; Chevallier) SATB MOLENAAR
      13039905   (R183)

RIVER, THE see Duson, Dede

RIVER RUNNIN' FREE see McPheeters

RIVERS see Zamecnik, Evzen

RIVIER, JEAN (1896-   )
  Dolor
    mix cor,orch [20'0"] TRANSAT.
      TR001316 f.s., perf mat rent (R184)

RJOMEGRAUTEN see Kjeldaas, Arnljot

RO FJORDEN see Hellden, Daniel

ROAD LESS TRAVELED, THE see Johnson

ROAD OF MASTERS, THE *CCU
  [Russ] jr cor,pno/acord MEZ KNIGA 523
                                 (R185)
ROAD OF THE OCTOBER REVOLUTION, THE
  *show
  [Russ] cor,soli,pno/org,trp,
    concertina, perc ens MEZ KNIGA 472
                                 (R186)
ROBB
  I Want To Sing
    SATB CPP-BEL SV8467 $.95   (R187)
    SSA CPP-BEL SV8441 $.95   (R188)

  Lost In Love
    SSA CPP-BEL SV8356 $.95   (R189)

  You Can't Run From Love
    SAB CPP-BEL SV8335 $.95   (R190)

ROBERTA LEE see James

ROBERTON, HUGH STEVENSON (1874-1952)
  Barque Of Clanronald, The
    TTBB,acap ROBERTON 50783   (R191)

  Flowers O' The Forest, The
    SSA,acap [3'] ROBERTON 75359 (R192)

  Good Morrow To You, Springtime
    unis cor,pno [1'] ROBERTON 75019
                                 (R193)

  Midsummer Spell
    SATB,acap [1'15"] ROBERTON 61330
                                 (R194)

  Misty Isle, The
    SATB,acap [5'] ROBERTON 63026
                                 (R195)

  Softly Fall The Shades Of Evening
    unis cor,pno [1'] ROBERTON 75019
                                 (R196)

ROBERTS, JASON
  see BOCK, FRED

ROBERTS, RUTH (1930-   )
  Alexander Graham Bell, Teacher Of The
    Deaf *CCU
    cor sc BRENT 210601 $9.95, student
      bk BRENT 210602 $2.50   (R197)

  Animal Songs That Tickle Your Funny
    Bone! *CCU
    cor BRENT 290401 f.s.   (R198)

  Benny Bunny's Band
    jr cor [30'] student bk BRENT
      250101 $4.00   (R199)

ROBERTS, RUTH (cont'd.)

Brave And The Bold, The °CCU
cor sc BRENT 210401 $9.95, student
bk BRENT 210402 $2.50   (R200)

Cactus Christmas Tree, The °CCU
cor student bk BRENT 292001 $1.00
(R201)

Christmas Cookies And Holiday Hearts
°CCU
jr cor pt BRENT 230101 $4.00 (R202)

Christmas Songs That Tickle Your
Funny Bone! °CCU
cor BRENT 290101 $4.95   (R203)

Columbus Day Songs That Tickle Your
Funny Bone! °CCU
cor BRENT 290901 $4.95   (R204)

Easter Songs That Tickle Your Funny
Bone! °CCU
cor BRENT 290701 $4.95   (R205)

Eighteen-Ninety Music Hall Review,
The °CCU
cor sc BRENT 210501 $9.95, student
bk BRENT 210502 $2.50   (R206)

Elephants, Clowns And Circus Sounds
°CCU
cor student bk BRENT 270101 $2.50
(R207)

First Thanksgiving, The °CCU
cor sc BRENT 211201 f.s., student
bk BRENT 211202 f.s.   (R208)

Friends That Are Feathered, Furry And
Fine °CCU
jr cor pt BRENT 250301 $4.00 (R209)

Halloween Songs That Tickle Your
Funny Bone! °CCU
cor BRENT 290201 $4.95   (R210)

Holidayland °CCU
cor BRENT 230201 $4.00   (R211)

In A Little Red Schoolhouse
jr cor [30'] student bk BRENT
251001 $4.00   (R212)

Last Of The Litterbugs, The °CCU
cor sc BRENT 211301 $9.95, student
bk BRENT 211302 $1.95   (R213)

Legend Of The Twelve Moons, The °CCU
cor sc BRENT 210201 $9.95, student
bk BRENT 210202 $2.50   (R214)

Little Lost Christmas Harmony °CCU
cor student bk BRENT 230801 $1.00
(R215)

Louis Armstrong Story, The °CCU
cor student bk BRENT 210702 $1.00
(R216)

Our Country 'Tis Of Thee °CCU
cor sc BRENT 210101 $9.95, student
bk BRENT 210102 $2.50   (R217)

Pinocchio, Don't Smoke That
Cigarette! °CCU
cor sc BRENT 210903 $9.95, student
bk BRENT 210904 $2.50   (R218)

Saint Patrick's Day Songs That Tickle
Your Funny Bone! °CCU
cor BRENT 290601 $4.95   (R219)

Santa And The Three Scrooges
jr cor [30'] sc BRENT 211001 $9.95,
student bk BRENT 211002 $2.50
(R220)

Sis! Boom! Bah! °CCU
cor sc BRENT 210801 $9.95, student
bk BRENT 210802 $2.50   (R221)

Spring Songs That Tickle Your Funny
Bone! °CCU
cor BRENT 290501 $4.95   (R222)

Tall Tom Jefferson °CCU
cor sc BRENT 210301 $9.95, pt BRENT
210302 $2.50   (R223)

Thanksgiving Songs That Tickle Your
Funny Bone! °CCU
cor BRENT 290301 $4.95   (R224)

Three O'clock Rehearsal °CCU
jr cor pt BRENT 230701 $4.00 (R225)

Valentine Songs That Tickle Your
Funny Bone! °CCU
cor BRENT 290801 $4.95   (R226)

What Shall We Do For A Christmas
Play?
jr cor [25'] student bk BRENT
230301 f.s.   (R227)

Winter Holiday
jr cor [25'] sc BRENT 212001 $9.95,
pt BRENT 212002 $2.50   (R228)

ROBERTSON
Sing Noel!
SSAB CPP-BEL SV8406 $.95   (R229)

Together
2pt cor CPP-BEL SV8742 $.95, accomp
tape available   (R230)

ROBERTSON, ED
Dream A Dream
SA CPP-BEL SV7716 $.95   (R231)
SATB CPP-BEL SV7701 $.95   (R232)

ROBIN, MARIE-THERESE
Vague Emporte Au Loin, La
(Daniel, Etienne) 3 eq voices A
COEUR JOIE 9012   (R233)

ROBIN HOOD see Haufrecht, Herbert

ROBINSON
Harriet Tubman
(Coates) SATB SHAWNEE 1621 $.85
(R234)
(Coates) SSA SHAWNEE 0469 $.65
(R235)

ROBINSON, RUSS
Lady Stands For Liberty, The
SATB,narrator,brass,perc CPP-BEL
OCT 02525 $1.20, ipa   (R236)

ROBINSON, WILLIAM (SMOKEY) (1940-   )
Shop Around °see Gordy, Berry

When Smokey Sings: A Tribute To
Smokey Robinson
(Chinn, Teena) SAB CPP-BEL C0134C3X
$1.95, accomp tape available
(R237)
(Chinn, Teena) SATB CPP-BEL
C0134C1X $1.95, accomp tape
available   (R238)

ROBYN, GENTIL ROBYN, A
TBB EARTHSNG EM-6 $.25   (R239)

ROCHAT, JEAN
Chanson De L'amoureux
TTBB HUGUENIN CH 2001   (R240)

Partir Au Bout Du Monde
TTBB HUGUENIN CH 2001   (R241)

Vieilles Maisons, Les
TTBB HUGUENIN CH 2002   (R242)

ROCHON, G.
Beau Voyageur °see Vigneault, Gilles

ROCK, THE see Roxburgh, Edwin

ROCK-A-BYE YOUR BABY WITH A DIXIE
MELODY see Lewis

ROCK AND ROLL DRUMMER see Bacon, Boyd

ROCK AND ROLL GIRLS
(Althouse) SAB CPP-BEL 4888RC3X
$1.25, accomp tape available (R243)
(Althouse) 2pt cor CPP-BEL 4888RC5X
f.s., accomp tape available (R244)
(Althouse) SATB CPP-BEL 4888RC1X
$1.25, accomp tape available (R245)

ROCKIN' THE GLORY see Moore, Donald P.

ROCKIN' THE PARADISE see Brymer, Mark

ROCKMAKER, JODY
Wild Swans At Coole, The
SATB,fl,horn,vcl,harp [15'0"] APNM
sc $7.25, cor pts rent   (R246)

RODBY, WALTER (1917-   )
Music Alone Shall Live °round
(Roff, Joseph) SAB,pno (med) THOMAS
1C108215 $.80   (R247)

RODE SARAFAAN, DE see Wolff, H. de

RODGERS, RICHARD (1902-1979)
King And I, The: A Medley
(Kerr, Anita) SATB LEONARD-US
08565671 $1.75   (R248)
(Kerr, Anita) SSA LEONARD-US
08565673 $1.75, ipa, accomp tape
available   (R249)
(Kerr, Anita) SAB LEONARD-US
08565672 $1.75   (R250)

Some Enchanted Evening (from South
Pacific)
(Mey) TTBB MOLENAAR 08170507 (R251)

This Nearly Was Mine (from South
Pacific)
(Mey) [Eng] TB MOLENAAR 08170607
(R252)

RODSTRUPE see Lyssand, Henrik

ROED, IVAR A.
Bonnen
SATB/TTBB NORSK   (R253)

ROEDER, TONI
Im Anfang War Der Rhythmus °CCU
mix cor,perc ZIMMER. 2146   (R254)

Mit Gesang Und Rhythmus °CCU
mix cor,pno,gtr,db,drums ZIMMER.
2147   (R255)

ROEPT DE PLICHT (LENTE-PARADE 4) see
Beekum, Jan Van

ROETHKE SONGS: THE SLOTH AND THE
SERPENT see Jeffers

ROFF
Sail On O Ship Of State
SAB&camb CAMBIATA P978112 $.75
(R256)

ROFF, JOSEPH (1910-   )
Song Of The Azores
SAB,pno (med) THOMAS 1C108007 $.90
(R257)

ROGER, DENISE
Chanson De La Plus Haute Tour
mix cor [3'15"] A COEUR JOIE 175
(R258)

ROGERS
Hand In Hand (composed with Walker)
(Shaw) SAB SHAWNEE 0376 $.95 (R259)
(Shaw) SATB SHAWNEE 1828 $.95
(R260)

ROI DES ETOILES, LE see Stravinsky,
Igor

ROI D'YVETOT, LE see Cornaz, Emmanuel

ROI RENAUD, LE
(Grizey, G.) 3pt cor HEUGEL HE 31951
(R261)

ROLLIN
David Of The White Rock
TTBB BOURNE B239202 $.70   (R262)

Springtime Is Returning
TTBB BOURNE B239210 $.80   (R263)

ROMAN WAR SONG, A see Wagner, Richard

ROMANCES see Schumann, Robert
(Alexander)

ROMANCES, OP. 69 see Schumann, Robert
(Alexander)

ROMANZEN FUR FRAUENSTIMMEN, OP. 69 see
Schumann, Robert (Alexander)

ROMANZEN UND BALLADEN see Schumann,
Robert (Alexander)

ROMEO AND JULIET see Berlioz, Hector
(Louis)

ROMIEUX, CHARLES
Maman
2-3 eq voices,pno HUGUENIN CH 927
(R264)
unis cor,pno HUGUENIN CH 925 (R265)
TTBB HUGUENIN CH 936   (R266)
SATB,acap HUGUENIN CH 926   (R267)

RONDE see Cornaz, Emmanuel

RONDE see Massis

RONDE see Ravel, Maurice

RONDE, LA see Schubert, Franz (Peter)

RONDE DES SAISONS, LA see Huguenin,
Charles

RONDE DES VENDANGES see Lauber, Emile

RONDEAU OF LIFE, A see Williams-
Wimberly, Lou

RONFORT, JEAN-CHRISTOPHE
En Bateau
mix cor A COEUR JOIE MA 6 see from
Fetes Galantes   (R268)

Fantoches
mix cor A COEUR JOIE MA 6 see from
Fetes Galantes   (R269)

Fetes Galantes °see En Bateau;
Fantoches; Indolents, Les; Sur
L'herbe   (R270)

Indolents, Les
mix cor A COEUR JOIE MA 6 see from
Fetes Galantes   (R271)

Sur L'herbe
mix cor A COEUR JOIE MA 6 see from
Fetes Galantes   (R272)

RONNES, ROBERT (1959-   )
Three Self-Portraits Of Odd Nerdrum
°see Trois Images

Trois Images
"Three Self-Portraits Of Odd
Nerdrum" wom cor NORGE   (R273)

RONSARD
　Chanson Du Printemps Retourne
　　(composed with Breton, G.;
　　Ollivier, J.)
　　(Lavoisy-Drouot) 4 eq voices, solo
　　voices HEUGEL HE 32188　　(R274)

RORE, CIPRIANO DE (1516-1565)
　Although When I Depart
　　(Handrickson) SATB BOURNE B240523
　　$.70　　(R275)

　Datemi Pace
　　[It/Eng] SATB BROUDE BR. CR 39
　　$1.10　　(R276)

　Grave Pen'in Amor
　　(Agnel, A.) 3pt mix cor HEUGEL
　　HE 32461　　(R277)

ROS OCH TYSTNAD DOFTAR JORDEN see
　Blomberg, Erik

ROSA see Blanchard

ROSA OF SHARON see Billings, William

ROSALIA see Lombardo, Robert M.

ROSCOE
　Beat Goes On, The
　　SATB CPP-BEL 1609BC1X $1.25, accomp
　　tape available　　(R278)

　Breakway
　　SATB CPP-BEL 5858BC1X $1.25, accomp
　　tape available　　(R279)

　How Will I Know
　　SATB CPP-BEL 4983HC1X $1.25, accomp
　　tape available　　(R280)
　　SAB CPP-BEL 4983HC3X $1.25, accomp
　　tape available　　(R281)
　　SSA CPP-BEL 4983HC2X $1.25, accomp
　　tape available　　(R282)

　(I'll Never Find) A Better Friend
　　SATB CPP-BEL 0421AC1X $1.25, accomp
　　tape available　　(R283)
　　SATB CPP-BEL 0421AC1X $1.25　　(R284)

ROSE, PETER
　African Jigsaw (composed with Conlon,
　　Anne)
　　cor/camb WEINBERGER　　(R285)

　Yanomamo (composed with Conlon, Anne)
　　cor/jr cor WEINBERGER　　(R286)

ROSE AU BOUE, LA see Blanchard

ROSE DE DECEMBRE, LA see Sylvestre,
　Anne

ROSE PILGERFAHRT, DER see Schumann,
　Robert (Alexander)

ROSE ROSETTE see Reymond, Herny

ROSE SAUVAGE see Denereaz, Alexandre

ROSEBUD IN JUNE　*Renaissance
　(Davis, Craig) 3pt mix cor,acap,opt
　rec,opt drums (easy) CPP-BEL SV8925
　$1.10　　(R287)

ROSELL, LARS-ERIK (1944-　)
　Fragmente
　　mix cor STIM　　(R288)

ROSENBLUTH, LEO (1904-　)
　Kom Till Mig
　　mix cor,org STIM　　(R289)

ROSENGLAUBE see Weber, Gustav

ROSENKRANZKONIGIN see Brantschen,
　Gregor

ROSENSTENGEL, ALBRECHT (1912-　)
　Finkenlied, Das
　　wom cor,gtr ZIMMER. 627　　(R290)

　In Der Taverne
　　mix cor,pno,perc ZIMMER. 1931
　　　　(R291)

　Jung Sein Und Lachen
　　3pt jr cor,gtr,tamb BOHM　　(R292)

　Willst Du Mit Mir Singen
　　mix cor,opt gtr BOHM　　(R293)

ROSES DE SAADI, LES see Barblan-
　Opienska, Lydia

ROSEWALL, RICHARD B.
　Spring! Come, Spring, Again!
　　SSATTB,pno LAWSON 52369 $.90 (R294)

ROSLAGEN: KANTAT see Sjoblom, Heimer

ROSS
　Hand 'N Hand (composed with Averre)
　　SAB CPP-BEL DMC 08199 $1.10 (R295)

ROSS (cont'd.)
　Judy's Turn To Cry　*see Lewis

　Open The Door (composed with Tisch)
　　(Shaw) SATB SHAWNEE 1859 $.95
　　　　(R296)
　　(Shaw) SAB SHAWNEE 0399 $.95 (R297)
　　(Shaw) SSA SHAWNEE 0537 $.95 (R298)

ROSS, BRAD
　Bright New Day, A
　　(Strommen) 2pt cor,kbd [2'] CORONET
　　392-41430 $.85　　(R299)

　Christmas Is Comin' Along
　　(Thygerson) 2pt cor,kbd [2']
　　CORONET 392-41440 $.90　　(R300)

　Melody Maker
　　(Kern, Philip) SA,pno CPP-BEL
　　DMC 08197 $.85　　(R301)

　One Of A Kind
　　(Snyder) 2pt cor,pno CPP-BEL SV8717
　　$.95, accomp tape available
　　　　(R302)

　Reach For A Star
　　(Snyder, Audrey) 3pt mix cor CPP-
　　BEL SV8807 $.95, accomp tape
　　available　　(R303)

　Stepping Out Together
　　(Thygerson) 2pt cor,kbd CORONET
　　392-41549 $.90　　(R304)

ROSSEM, ANDRIES VAN (1957-　)
　Canto
　　SATB,2.2.2.2. 2.1.1.0. perc,pno,
　　strings [13'30"] DONEMUS　　(R305)

ROSSI, LUIGI (1597-1653)
　Berceuse (from Orfeo)
　　(Turellier, Jean) 3pt cor,cont
　　HEUGEL HE 33248　　(R306)

ROSSI, SALOMONE (ca. 1570-ca. 1630)
　Primo Libro Delle Canzonette A Tre
　　Voci, Il　*CC19U
　　[It/Heb] 3pt cor,opt winds
　　ISR.MUS.INST. 1013　　(R307)

　Secondo Libro De Madrigali A Cinque
　　Voci, Il　*CC20U
　　[It] 5pt mix cor,opt cont
　　ISR.MUS.INST. 1016　　(R308)

ROSSIGNOL, LE see Gretry, Andre Ernest
　Modeste

ROSSIGNOL, LE see Schubert, Franz
　(Peter)

ROSSIGNOL, LE: EN COUTANT see Janequin,
　Clement

ROSSIGNOL CHANTE, LE see Morley, Thomas

ROSSIGNOL, MON MIGNON see Chailley,
　Jacques

ROSSIGNOLET GENTIL
　(Haug, Hans) SATB,acap HUGUENIN
　　EB 226　　(R309)

ROSSINI, GIOACCHINO (1792-1868)
　Carnivale Di Venezia, Il
　　SSTB,pno HANSSLER 40.281-40 f.s.
　　　　(R310)
　Comic Duet For Two Cats　*see Duetto
　　Buffo Di Due Gatti

　Dall'oriente L'astro Del Giorno
　　STTB,pno HANSSLER 40.281-50 f.s.
　　　　(R311)
　Duetto Buffo Di Due Gatti
　　(Coombes, Douglas) "Comic Duet For
　　Two Cats" 2pt treb cor,pno
　　LINDSAY　　(R312)

　Gondolieri, I
　　SATB,pno HANSSLER 40.281-10 f.s.
　　　　(R313)
　Ridiamo Cantiamo
　　STTB,pno HANSSLER 40.281-60 f.s.
　　　　(R314)
　Tyrolienne (from Guillaume Tell)
　　(Evertse, J.) SA MOLENAAR 15009503
　　　　(R315)

ROTAS, NIKIFOROS
　Sonnengesang
　　SSAATTBB,winds,brass SEESAW (R316)

ROTE SARAFAN, DER see Cadow, Paul

ROTHENBERG, IRV
　Feel The Power
　　(Althouse, Jay) 1-2pt cor (opt horn
　　or accomp. tape) ALFRED 7626
　　$.95, accomp tape available
　　　　(R317)
　　(Althouse, Jay) SSA (opt horn or
　　accomp. tape) ALFRED 7625 $.95,
　　accomp tape available　　(R318)
　　(Althouse, Jay) SAB (opt horn or
　　accomp. tape) ALFRED 7624 $.95,

ROTHENBERG, IRV (cont'd.)
　　accomp tape available　　(R319)
　　(Althouse, Jay) SATB (opt horn or
　　accomp. tape) ALFRED 7623 $.95,
　　accomp tape available　　(R320)

ROTHSCHUH, F.
　Mond Ist Aufgegangen, Der
　　mix cor BOHM　　(R321)

　Und In Dem Schneegebirge
　　mix cor BOHM　　(R322)

ROUND AND ROUND THE DREYDL SPINS see
　Eddleman, David

ROUND AROUND ABOUT A WOOD see Morley,
　Thomas

ROUND ROBIN see Barnes

ROUNDS see Rausch, Carlos

ROUSEE DU MOIS DE MAI, LA see Willaert,
　Adrian

ROUSSAKIS, NICOLAS (1943-　)
　Voyage
　　8pt cor [18'] AM.COMP.AL. $19.85
　　　　(R323)

ROVING GAMBLER, THE see Bialosky,
　Marshall H.

ROXBURGH, EDWIN
　Pianto (Lament)
　　SATB UNITED MUS　　(R324)

　Rock, The
　　cor, solo voices,orch voc sc UNITED
　　MUS　　(R325)

ROY A FAIT BATTRE TAMBOUR, LE see
　Blanchard

ROY S'EN VA-T-EN CHASSE, LE see
　Turellier, Jean

ROY'S WIFE OF ALDIVALLOCH
　(Willisegger, H.R.) mix cor,acap
　　PELIKAN PE 1183　　(R326)

RRRRRR...; SIEBEN CHORSTUCKE see Kagel,
　Mauricio

RUBBEN, HERMANNJOSEF (1928-　)
　Drei Junge Leute
　　TTBB MULLER 1040　　(R327)

　Funf Lander- Funf Lieder　*CCU
　　wom cor/jr cor BRAUN-PER 1090
　　　　(R328)

RUDD-MOORE, DOROTHY (1940-　)
　In Celebration
　　SB/SATB,pno [7'] AM.COMP.AL. $6.90
　　　　(R329)

RUDI, JORAN (1954-　)
　For More Than One
　　SSAATTBB,electronic tape manuscript
　　NORGE　　(R330)

RUDINGER, GOTTFRIED (1886-1946)
　Waldkantate　*Op.84
　　3pt wom cor,inst BOHM　　(R331)

RUE MY HEART IS LADEN see Getty, Gordon

RUHE ZUM HERZEN see Radstake, L.J.

RUHL, HERBERT
　Kanons, Seventy　*see Heilbut, P.

RUHLOSES JAHR: VIER HERBSTGESANGE see
　Kuppelmayer, Alfred

RULE BRITANNIA see Arne, Thomas
　Augustine

RULE BRITTANNIA
　TTBB MOLENAAR 13029404　　(R332)

RUN, RABBIT, RUN
　(Lewis, A.) 2pt cor,pno (med easy)
　　THOMAS 1C258421 $.80　　(R333)

RUNDGANGEN: KATRIN- EN PLOMMONVALS see
　Sjoblom, Heimer

RUNNSTROM, WILLIAM (1951-　)
　Harliga Rosten, Den
　　men cor STIM　　(R334)

　Mot Ljuset　*Op.25
　　mix cor,3 soli,org,pno, film STIM
　　　　(R335)

　Tre Stycken, Op. 19　*CC3U
　　mix cor STIM　　(R336)

RUSE PETIT JEAN, LE see Weber

RUSSAVAGE, KATHY
　Social Commentary
　　SATB,acap BRAVE NM 08-R1 $.80
　　　　(R337)

RUSSIAN CANDLE CAROL
(Grundahl) SATB KJOS C8807 $.80
                                    (R338)
RUSSIAN FOLK CHORUS SINGS, A: VOL. 8
  °CCU
  [Russ] cor,opt acord MEZ KNIGA 176
                                    (R339)
RUSSIAN FOLK CHORUS SINGS, A: VOL. 9
  °CCU
  [Russ] cor,acap/acord/pno MEZ KNIGA
  173   (R340)
RUSSIAN FOLK SONGS °CCU
  [Russ] MEZ KNIGA 187   (R341)
RUSSIAN FOLK SONGS NOTED DOWN BY
  MITROFAN PYATNITSKY °CCU
  [Russ] cor,acap/acord MEZ KNIGA 174
                                    (R342)
RUSSIAN PEACE SONGS
  (Grundahl) SATB KJOS C8921 $.90
                                    (R343)
RUTHERFORD, EDWARD
  I Can't Give You Anything But Love
     °see McHugh

RUTTER, JOHN
  Blow, Blow, Thou Winter Wind
    see When Icicles Hang

  British Grenadiers, The
    SATBarB,acap OXFORD 385759-6 $1.00
                                    (R344)
  Dashing Away With The Smoothing Iron
    SATBarB,acap OXFORD   (R345)
  Down By The Riverside (I'm Goin' To
    Lay Down My Heavy Load) (from
    Three American Folk-Songs)
    SATB,pno/orch OXFORD 343049-5 $1.50
                                    (R346)
  Good Ale (from When Icicles Hang)
    see When Icicles Hang
    SATB,pno/orch OXFORD 19 385634 4
                                    (R347)
  Hay, Ay
    see When Icicles Hang

  Heavenly Aeroplane, The
    2pt cor,pno,opt drums,db/bass gtr
      OXFORD 341514-3 $1.00, ipa (R348)

  Here We Come A-Wassailing
    SATB,acap OXFORD 343119-X   (R349)

  Icicles
    see When Icicles Hang

  Monday's Child
    SATB,acap OXFORD 19 385694 8 see
    from Two Songs From "Five
    Childhood Lyrics"   (R350)

  O Waly, Waly (from Five Traditional
    Songs)
    SATBarB,acap OXFORD 19 385651 4
                                    (R351)
  Reluctant Dragon, The
    mix cor,soli&narrator,instrumental
    ensemble/pno [23'] OXFORD
    19 338056 0 f.s., ipr   (R352)

  Sing A Song Of Sixpence
    SATB,acap OXFORD 19 385694 8 see
    from Two Songs From "Five
    Childhood Lyrics"   (R353)

  Two Songs From "Five Childhood
    Lyrics" °see Monday's Child;
    Sing A Song Of Sixpence   (R354)

  When Icicles Hang
    SATB,T solo,chamber orch voc sc
    OXFORD 338073-0 f.s.
      contains: Blow, Blow, Thou Winter
      Wind; Good Ale; Hay, Ay;
      Icicles; Winter Nights; Winter
      Wakeneth All My Care   (R355)

  Wind In The Willows, The
    mix cor,5 soli&narrator [32']
    OXFORD 19 338058 7 rent   (R356)

  Winter Nights
    see When Icicles Hang

  Winter Wakeneth All My Care
    see When Icicles Hang

RUYSSEN
  Berceuse Savoyarde
    see Caillard, Philippe, Vla L'bon
    Vent

RYDEN
  Rejoice And Be Merry °Xmas
    SATB BOURNE B238782 $.80   (R357)

RYLING, FRANCISZEK (1902-   )
  Eight Songs To The Words By Maria
    Konopnicka °see Osiem Piesni Do
    Slow Marii Konopnickiej

  Osiem Piesni Do Slow Marii
    Konopnickiej
    "Eight Songs To The Words By Maria

RYLING, FRANCISZEK (cont'd.)

    Konopnicka" [Polish] mix cor
    POLSKIE PLCH 304   (R358)

RYMOWANKI see Swider, Jozef

RYPDAL, TERJE (1947-   )
  Metamorphosis
    [Eng] wom cor [6'] NORGE   (R359)

  Vardoger
    [Norw] men cor,trp,synthesizer,perc
    [21'] NORGE   (R360)

S

'S BUSSIN see Deutschmann, Gerhard

'S IST ALLES DUNKEL see Deutschmann,
  Gerhard

S' LUZARNERBIET
  (Zihlmann, H.) jr cor,clar,acord/gtr
    PELIKAN PE 1206   (S1)

SABOTS D'HELENE, LES see Brassens,
  Georges

SAD SONG OF THE SEA
  (Brandon, G.) SSA,acap (med) THOMAS
    1C117802 $.60   (S2)

SAENU see Davidson, Charles Stuart

SAFE AND WARM see Anderson, Gaylene

SAGN UM "MARISTIGEN" FRA TINNSTOGA see
  Kjeldaas, Arnljot, Rjomegrauten

SAGVIK, STELLAN (1952-   )
  April °Op.146
    mix cor STIM   (S3)

  Glimmande Nymf °Op.84b
    mix cor STIM   (S4)

  Merikess Mykonos °Op.148
    mix cor STIM   (S5)

SAIL AWAY see Gilpin, Greg

SAIL ON O SHIP OF STATE see Roff

SAILOR'S CHORUS see Wagner, Richard,
  Mit Gewitter Und Sturm

SAILOR'S SWEETHEART, THE see Telfer,
  Nancy

SAINT-GILLES see Blanchard

SAINT JACQUES see Curti, F.

SAINT MARTHA AND THE DRAGON see Tate,
  Phyllis

SAINT PATRICK'S DAY SONGS THAT TICKLE
  YOUR FUNNY BONE! see Roberts, Ruth

SAISON EN ENFER, UNE see Gerber,
  Stephen Edward

SAISONS A LA SAGNE, LES
  (Landry, Fredy) unis cor,pno HUGUENIN
    CH 1054   (S6)

SAISONS PARISIENNES see Serrand-
  Gribenski, Isabelle

SALADINO, DAVID
  Three Oriental Pieces
    SATB,acap FISCHER,C CM8311 $.85
                                  (S7)
SALERNO, CHRIS PAQUIN
  Jazz, Blues, Swing, Bop
    SAB BUGZY BGZ-1009   (S8)

  Twinkle, Twinkle Little Star
    SATB BUGZY BGZ-1016   (S9)

SALLINEN, AULIS (1935-   )
  Beaufort Scale, The
    SATB,acap NOVELLO   (S10)

  Iron Age, The °Op.55
    mix cor&jr cor,S solo,orch NOVELLO
                                  (S11)
  King Goes Forth To France, The
    mix cor NOVELLO   (S12)

  Songs From The Sea
    SSAA,acap NOVELLO 07 0463 06 (S13)

SALMODIA FINALE see Boito, Arrigo

SALOME see Stolz, Robert

SALTIMBANQUES see Baeriswyl, Henri

SALUT! GLACIERS SUBLIMES see Lieb, J.G.

SALUT! TERRE DES MONTS! see Landry,
  Fredy

SALUT VIGNERON
  (Huguenin, Charles-Andre) TTBB,acap
    HUGUENIN C 2089B H   (S14)

SALUTE TO HERITAGE, A see Pfautsch,
  Lloyd Alvin

SALVA, TADEAS (1937-   )
  Symfonia Pastoralis In E
    cor,trp,timp,org,string orch [35']
    SLOV.HUD.FOND P-135, 0-620 (S15)

SALVADOR, HENRI
  Chagrin D'amour, Un °see Teze, M.

SALVADOR, MATILDE
  Deixeu La Terra
    4pt mix cor PILES 424   (S16)

SALZ-BALLADE, DIE see Vermulst, Jan,
  Ballade Van Het Zout, De

SAMESIIDAT OSV see Persen, John

SAMOGLOSKI see Swider, Jozef

SAMPSON, EDGAR M. (1907-1973)
  Stompin' At The Savoy °see Goodman,
    Benny (Benjamin David)

SAMUIL MARSHAK AND CHILDREN'S MUSIC
  °CCU
    [Russ] jr cor,pno MEZ KNIGA 517 (S17)

SANCTA LUCIA see Cottrau, Teodoro

SAND, CARY J.
  Uncle Dean
    (Sand, Edward J.) 1-2pt cor CPP-BEL
    SV8836 $.95, accomp tape
    available   (S18)

SANDBRINK, AB (1953-   )
  Shadowvoices
    5pt mix cor,2clar,bass clar,3trom,
    2perc,pno [25'] DONEMUS   (S19)

SANDCASTLE CAKE see Vinson, Harvey

SANDCASTLES see Bock, Fred

SANDLER, F.
  Spring And Fall
    SATB,pno THOMAS 1C408619 $.95 (S20)

SANDRIN, PIERRE (ca. 1490-ca. 1561)
  Doulce Memoire
    [Fr/Eng] SATB BROUDE BR. CR 35 $.85
                                 (S21)

SANDSTROM, JAN (1954-   )
  Skuggsjon
    cor,winds,pno,opt electronic tape
    STIM   (S22)

  Tva Korpoem
    mix cor,acap REIMERS   (S23)

SANDSTROM, SVEN-DAVID (1942-   )
  Drommar
    mix cor,MezT soli,orch STIM (S24)

SANG TIL DEG, EN
  see Auld Lang Syne

SANG UR SAGAN OM FATUMEH see Rehnqvist,
  Karin

SANGEN OM FUGLENE see Lyssand, Henrik

SANGEN OM VANNHJULET see Godoy, Rolf
  Inge

SANGER TIL DIKT AV JOHAN FALKBERGET see
  Tveitt, Geirr

SANGER UND EIN GITARRIST, EIN see
  Reinl, Franz

SANGERLUST-POLKA see Strauss, Johann,
  [Jr.]

SANGERPROLOG: GEGRUSSET ALLE, DIE DAS
  SCHONE LIEBEN see Jessler, Fritz

SANGLARD, ABNER
  Chant De La Bergere
    SATB,S solo HUGUENIN C 2086 H (S25)

SANGSTER, D.
  Christmas Tree, The
    see Gather Round The Christmas Tree

  Gather Little Children
    see Gather Round The Christmas Tree

  Gather Round The Christmas Tree
    unis jr cor LESLIE 1150 f.s.
    contains: Christmas Tree, The;
      Gather Little Children; Santa
      Comes Tonight   (S26)

  Santa Comes Tonight
    see Gather Round The Christmas Tree

ST.-ANNA-LIED
  cor HIEBER MH 5036   (S27)

SANS OG SAMLING see Germeten, Gunnar

SANSLOSE, DEN see Ahlin, Sven

SANTA AND THE THREE SCROOGES see
  Roberts, Ruth

SANTA CLAUS see Grob, Anita Jean

SANTA CLAUS IS COMIN' TO TOWN see
  Gillespie

SANTA CLAUS IS COMIN' TO TOWN: A MEDLEY
  see Gillespie

SANTA CLAUS IS COMING TO TOWN
  (Shaw, Kirby) SAB,opt trp CPP-BEL
    T0510SC3 $1.25, accomp tape
    available   (S28)
  (Shaw, Kirby) SATB,opt trp CPP-BEL
    T0510SC1 $1.25, accomp tape
    available   (S29)
  (Shaw, Kirby) SSA,opt trp CPP-BEL
    T0510SC2 $1.25, accomp tape
    available   (S30)

SANTA CLAUS, SANTA CLAUS (YOU ARE MUCH
  TOO FAT) see Kupferschmid, Steven

SANTA COMES TONIGHT see Sangster, D.

SANTA, DON'T FORGET MY NAME! see Simms

SANTA LUCIA
  (Poos, Heinrich) men cor BRAUN-PER
    1052   (S31)

SANTA'S A COOL GUY see Mitchell

SANTA'S COMING see Bennett

SANTA'S PETS see Crawley, Clifford

SANTIAGO, RODRIGO DE
  Siete Cantos Corales Vascos °CC7L
    mix cor ALPUERTO 1374   (S32)

SARA
  (Lojeski) SATB LEONARD-US 08255901
    $.95   (S33)
  (Lojeski) SAB LEONARD-US 08255902
    $.95   (S34)
  (Lojeski) SSA LEONARD-US 08255903
    $.95, ipa, accomp tape available
                                 (S35)

SARDANA DELS FORASTERS, LA see
  Gauffriau, Jean

SARGON, SIMON A. (1938-   )
  Feast Of Lights
    2pt cor,kbd TRANSCON. 991254 $.85
                                 (S36)

SARMANTO, HEIKKI
  Hanget Soi
    "Singing Snow" cor FAZER F 07737-0
                                 (S37)

  Singing Snow °see Hanget Soi

SASCHA
  (Biebl) men cor ZIMMER. 599   (S38)

SASCHA, HOR DIE BALALAIKA see Monter,
  Josef

SATEREN, LELAND BERNHARD (1913-   )
  Look To This Day
    SATB,opt band KJOS C8928 $.90, ipa
                                 (S39)

SATIN DOLL see Ellington, Edward
  Kennedy (Duke)

SATYR ONCE, A see Ward, John

SAUFERBALLADE see Trapp, Willy

SAUH 3-4 see Scelsi, Giacinto

SAVETIER ET LE FINANCIER, LE see
  Chenaux, B.

SAY "NO" TO DRUGS see Atkinson

SCANDELLO, ANTONIO (SCANDELLUS,
  SCANDELLI) (1517-1580)
  Bonzorno, Madonna Benvegnua
    mix cor ZENGERINK 14   (S40)

SCARBOROUGH FAIR
  (Swenson) B&2camb CAMBIATA U97691
    $.70   (S41)

SCARBOROUGH FAIR see Cooper

SCARLET RIBBONS see Danzig, Evelyn

SCAT BOURREE see Bach, Johann Sebastian

SCAT SONG, THE see Taylor, Lemoyne

SCELSI, GIACINTO (1905-1988)
  Knox-Om-Pax
    mix cor, solo voices,orch [17']
    SALABERT EAS18441P   (S42)

  Sauh 3-4
    wom cor SALABERT EAS18435   (S43)

  Uaxuctum
    mix cor,orch SALABERT EAS18436P
                                 (S44)

SCENES FOR CHILDREN'S CHORUS see
  Hurnik, Ilja

SCHAATHUN, ASBJORN
  Virkeliggjorelse
    [Norw] SATB,fl,perc NORGE   (S45)

SCHAFERLIED see Biebl, Franz

SCHAFERS SONNTAGSLIED: DAS IST DER TAG
  DES HERRN see Kreutzer, Konradin

SCHAIK, JOHAN ANT. STEPHANUS VAN
  Bruiloftzangen I °see Er Ruischt
    Door 'S Hemels Zalen; Zoo Pas Had
    God Uw Ja Geschreven   (S46)

  Bruiloftszangen I: O Levensbron Der
    Liefde
    STB ZENGERINK 129   (S47)

  Er Ruischt Door 'S Hemels Zalen
    mix cor ZENGERINK 129 see from
    Bruiloftszangen I   (S48)

  Hoe Schitterde In 'T Verleden
    [Dutch] 2-3pt cor ZENGERINK R 130
    see from Zes Bruiloftszangen II
                                 (S49)

  Nu Voor 'T Oog Van God En De Englen
    SSA/TTB ZENGERINK 130 see from Zes
    Bruiloftzangen II   (S50)

  Zes Bruiloftzangen II °see Hoe
    Schitterde In 'T Verleden   (S51)

  Zes Bruiloftzangen II °see Nu Voor
    'T Oog Van God En De Englen (S52)

  Zoo Pas Had God Uw Ja Geschreven
    mix cor ZENGERINK 129 see from
    Bruiloftszangen I   (S53)

SCHALLEHN, HILGER (1936-   )
  Irische Liebesgeschichten °see
    Liebeserfahrung; Liebesgluck;
    Liebeslied; Liebeswerbung   (S54)

  Kleines Lied, Ein
    [Ger] mix cor,acap SCHOTTS CHBL 434
                                 (S55)

  Liebeserfahrung
    [Ger] men cor SCHOTTS ED 7517 see
    from Irische Liebesgeschichten
                                 (S56)

  Liebesgluck
    [Ger] men cor SCHOTTS ED 7517 see
    from Irische Liebesgeschichten
                                 (S57)

  Liebeslied
    [Ger] men cor SCHOTTS ED 7517 see
    from Irische Liebesgeschichten
                                 (S58)

  Liebeswerbung
    [Ger] men cor SCHOTTS ED 7517 see
    from Irische Liebesgeschichten
                                 (S59)

  Sommermorgenlied
    [Ger] mix cor,acap SCHOTTS C 45968
                                 (S60)

SCHALMEI, DE see Kox, Hans

SCHAPORIN, JURIJ
  see SHAPORIN, YURI ALEXANDROVICH

SCHATZ-WALZER see Strauss, Johann,
  [Jr.]

SCHECK, HELMUT (1938-   )
  Mensch Bei Weibern Nichts Erreicht,
    Ein °see Variationen

  Seht Doch, Wie Der Rheinwein Tanzt
    (Miller, Franz R.) men cor,6winds
    BOHM see from Zwei Lieder Vom
    Wein Auf Barocke Weisen   (S61)

  Variationen
    (Miller, Franz R.) "Mensch Bei
    Weibern Nichts Erreicht, Ein" men
    cor,acord BOHM   (S62)

  Wer Sich Vertreiben Will Schlechte
    Laune
    (Miller, Franz R.) men cor,6winds
    BOHM see from Zwei Lieder Vom
    Wein Auf Barocke Weisen   (S63)

  Zwei Lieder Vom Wein Auf Barocke
    Weisen °see Seht Doch, Wie Der
    Rheinwein Tanzt; Wer Sich
    Vertreiben Will Schlechte Laune
                                 (S64)

SCHEDL, GERHARD (1957-   )
  Bose Spruche °CCU
    mix cor,3winds DOBLINGER 46 077
                                 (S65)

SCHEEPMAKER, N.
  Polderstad
    (Vlak, K.) SATB MOLENAAR 08178405
                                 (S66)

SCHEIN
  Dame Nightingale
    (Malin) SSA,acap CPP-BEL OCT 02461
    $1.10   (S67)

SCHEIN (cont'd.)

Fresh Is The Maytime
(Malin) SSA,acap CPP-BEL OCT 02463
$1.10   (S68)

Once More The Flowers Bloom
(Malin) SSA,acap CPP-BEL OCT 02464
$.95   (S69)

SCHEIN, JOHANN HERMANN (1586-1630)
Die Mit Tranen Saen
(Porter) SATB SCHIRM.G 233740 $.80
                               (S70)

Frisch Auf, Ihr Klosterbruder Mein
see Madrigale Fur Gemischten Chor A
Cappella: Blatt V

Holla, Gut Gesell
see Madrigale Fur Gemischten Chor A
Cappella: Blatt V

Ihr Bruder, Lieben Bruder Mein
see Madrigale Fur Gemischten Chor A
Cappella: Blatt V

Madrigale Fur Gemischten Chor A
Cappella: Blatt V °madrigal,17th
cent
SSATB HANSSLER 40.404-50 f.s.
contains: Frisch Auf, Ihr
Klosterbruder Mein; Holla, Gut
Gesell; Ihr Bruder, Lieben
Bruder Mein; Sieh Da, Ihr
Lieben Herren; So Da, Mein
Liebes Bruderlein   (S71)

Sieh Da, Ihr Lieben Herren
see Madrigale Fur Gemischten Chor A
Cappella: Blatt V

So Da, Mein Liebes Bruderlein
see Madrigale Fur Gemischten Chor A
Cappella: Blatt V

SCHELLEVIS, ANTOON
Met Hun Pooten In De Vaart
mix cor ZENGERINK 249   (S72)

SCHENKE IN DEN BERGEN see Janacek,
Leos, Na Solani Cartak

SCHENKT EIN DEN KUHLEN WEIN see
Seckinger, Konrad

SCHERBER, M.
Es Fiel Ein Reif
mix cor ZIMMER. SK 3952   (S73)

Mausfallen- Spruchlein
SSATB ZIMMER. SK 3953   (S74)

Weihnacht
SSAT ZIMMER. SK 3954   (S75)

SCHERZI MUSICALI see Monteverdi,
Claudio

SCHICKELE, PETER (1935-   )
Birthday Ode To "Big Daddy" Bach
SATB,SATBar soli,chamber orch [8']
PRESSER 412-41067 $3.50, ipr
                               (S76)

My Bonnie Lass She Smelleth
SSATB,acap PRESSER 312-40795 $.95
                               (S77)

Oedipus Tex
SATB,solo voice,orch/pno PRESSER
412-41072 $9.95   (S78)

SCHICKSALSLIED see Brahms, Johannes

SCHIFFLEIN, DAS see Schumann, Robert
(Alexander)

SCHIMMERLING, H.A.
Beyond The Village
SATB SCHIRM.G 229300 $.70   (S79)

SCHLAF UND TOD see Kerstens, Huub

SCHLEIERMACHER, STEFFEN
Vier Chore °CC4U
mix cor, solo voices,acap sc
BREITKOPF-L 7696   (S80)

SCHLERF, L.
Bergwanderung °cant
wom cor/jr cor,narrator,strings,
winds,pno BOHM   (S81)

Lustig Ihr Bruder
mix cor BOHM   (S82)

Wohlauf, Die Luft Geht Frisch Und
Rein
men cor BOHM   (S83)

SCHLIESSE, SCHLIESSE DICH, ZYKLUS
(Fleig, G.) wom cor ZIMMER. 607 see
from Drei Russische Volkslieder
                               (S84)

SCHLUNZ, ANNETTE
Uber Die Hugel Wuchert Der Ginster
mix cor,Bar solo,2.2.0.0. 1.2.2.1.
perc,strings [12'] BREITKOPF-L
                               (S85)

SCHMID, A.
Wer Seine Heimat Liebt °cant
cor,pno ZIMMER. 582   (S86)

SCHMIDT, HELMUT
Fur Marie
mix cor sc BREITKOPF-L 7685   (S87)

SCHMIDT-DUISBURG, M.
Marien-Legende
wom cor/boy cor,S solo ZIMMER. 560
                               (S88)

SCHMIDT-WUNSTORF, RUDOLF (1916-   )
Au Chant Du Merle
mix cor,acap A COEUR JOIE MA 7 see
from Aubades   (S89)

Aubades °see Au Chant Du Merle;
Chanson De La Marjolaine; Chanson
De L'Amoureuse; Dactylos
Parisiennes, Les   (S90)

Chanson De La Marjolaine
mix cor,acap A COEUR JOIE MA 7 see
from Aubades   (S91)

Chanson De L'Amoureuse
mix cor,acap A COEUR JOIE MA 7 see
from Aubades   (S92)

Dactylos Parisiennes, Les
mix cor,acap A COEUR JOIE MA 7 see
from Aubades   (S93)

SCHMIED, DER see Brahms, Johannes

SCHMIEDE, DIE see Aeschbacher, Walther,
Forgerons, Les

SCHMITT, KARL HEINZ
Singen Nach Noten: Ein Lehrwerk Fur
Chorsanger °see Kolneder, Walter

SCHMITZ, J.
Daar Was Een Wuf Die Spon
SSA MOLENAAR 15023503   (S94)

Holland: Grauw Is Uw Hemel En Stormig
Uw Strand
4 eq voices,acap ZENGERINK 373
                               (S95)

SCHNABEL, ARTUR (1882-1951)
Dance And Secret
see Two Movements For Chorus With
Orchestra
see Two Movements For Chorus With
Orchestra

Joy And Peace
see Two Movements For Chorus With
Orchestra
see Two Movements For Chorus With
Orchestra

Two Movements For Chorus With
Orchestra
SATB,2+pic.2+English horn.2.2.
4.3.2.0. perc,pno,strings sc APNM
$24.00, ipr
contains: Dance And Secret; Joy
And Peace   (S96)

Two Movements For Chorus With
Orchestra
(Weber, Ben) SATB,pno 4-hands sc
APNM $12.75, perf mat rent
contains: Dance And Secret; Joy
And Peace   (S97)

SCHNEBEL, DIETER (1930-   )
Contrapunctus VI (from Kunst Der
Fuge)
SSSSSAAAAATTTTTBBBBB SCHOTT ED 6680
                               (S98)

SCHNEEBALLSCHLACHT see Heinrichs,
Wilhelm

SCHNEEBLUME, DIE: INMITTEN WEISSEN
SCHNEES see Heilmann, Harald

SCHNEEMANN LADISLAUS see Irrgang, Horst

SCHNEESTURM, DER see Buran

SCHNEEWALZER see Koschat

SCHNEIDER, W.
Gluck Ist Wie Ein Sonnenblick
(Miller, Franz R.) men cor,opt clar
BOHM see from Zwei Lieder Des
Glucks   (S99)

Gluckliche Stunde
(Miller, Franz R.) men cor,opt clar
BOHM see from Zwei Lieder Des
Glucks   (S100)

Zwei Lieder Des Glucks °see Gluck
Ist Wie Ein Sonnenblick;
Gluckliche Stunde   (S101)

SCHNEIDER JAHRTAG, DER: ZU REGENSBURG
AUF DER KIRCHTURMSPITZ see
Kanetscheider, Artur

SCHOEGGL, F.
Trout As You Like It
[Eng] mix cor (variations on
Schubert song) DOBLINGER 44 763
                               (S102)

SCHOEN, VICTOR R.
Chiu Yen
"Wine Feast" [Chin/Eng] TB oct DEAN
HRD 176 $.95   (S103)

Wine Feast °see Chiu Yen

SCHOENBERG, ARNOLD (1874-1951)
Four Pieces °Op.27, CCU
cor sc BELMONT UE-8549 $21.00, cor
pts BELMONT UE-8549A $5.50, ipr
                               (S104)

Three Satires °Op.28, CCU
cor BELMONT UE-8586 $16.00, ipr
                               (S105)

SCHOLA CANTORUM ALBUM, VOL. 1
mix cor BROEKMANS BP 1195   (S106)

SCHOLA CANTORUM ALBUM, VOL. 2
mix cor BROEKMANS BP 1196   (S107)

SCHOLA CANTORUM ALBUM, VOL. 3
mix cor BROEKMANS BP 1197   (S108)

SCHOLA CANTORUM ALBUM, VOL. 4
mix cor BROEKMANS BP 1198   (S109)

SCHOLARS' BOOK OF GLEES, THE °CC8U
(Johnson, David) mix cor,acap OXFORD
19 343659 0 contains works by
Beale, Callcott, Cooke and others
                               (S110)

SCHON IST DAS FEST DES LENZES see
Schumann, Robert (Alexander)

SCHON IST DIE WELT see Kracke, Hans

SCHON ROHTRAUT see Schumann, Robert
(Alexander)

SCHONBRUNNER, DIE see Lanner, Josef

SCHONE AUS DEM MAGGIA-TAL, DIE see
Ammann, Benno

SCHONE VON ONSERNONE, DIE see Ammann,
Benno

SCHONES HAMBURG see Beil, P.

SCHONES HEUTE see Helmschrott, Robert
M.

SCHOOL see Hopkins, Anthony

SCHOOL see Swietlicki

SCHOOL IS OUT see Barge

SCHOOL OF CHORAL SINGING, A: VOL. 2 see
Sokolov, Nikolai Alexandrovich

SCHOOL PARTY, A: VOL. 3 °CCU
[Russ] jr cor,pno/gtr MEZ KNIGA 506
                               (S111)

SCHOOL PARTY, A: VOL. 4 °CCU
[Russ] jr cor,pno/gtr MEZ KNIGA 538
                               (S112)

SCHOOLBOY, THE see Bacon, Ernst L.

SCHOON LIEVEKEN, WAER WAARDE GIJ see
Schrijvers, Jean

SCHOONENBEEK, KEES (1947-   )
Modus Vivendi
4pt mix cor,1.0.1.1. 0.0.0.0. pno,
perc,strings [15'] DONEMUS (S113)

SCHRAM
Come To Us, Little King
2pt cor SHAWNEE 5087 $.95   (S114)

SCHREBER PREVIEW see Tarenskeen,
Boudewijn

SCHRIJVERS, JEAN
Daar Was A Wuf Die Spon
[Dutch] 3 eq voices,acap ZENGERINK
R 632 see from Drie
Oudnederlandse Liederen II (S115)

Daer Was Een Kwezeltje
[Dutch] 3 eq voices,acap ZENGERINK
R 632 see from Drie
Oudnederlandse Liederen II (S116)

Daer Was Een Sneeuwwit Vogheltje
[Dutch] 3 eq voices,acap ZENGERINK
R 631 see from Drie
Oudnederlandse Liederen I (S117)

Den Soeten Tijdt
3 eq voices,acap ZENGERINK R 636
see from Twee Amoureuze En Een
Lustigh Liedeken   (S118)

SCHRIJVERS, JEAN (cont'd.)

Den Uyl Die Op Den Peerboom Zat
  [Dutch] 3 eq voices,acap ZENGERINK
  R 631 see from Drie
  Oudnederlandse Liederen I (S119)

Des Winters Als Het Regent
  [Dutch] 3 eq voices,acap ZENGERINK
  R 634 see from Twee
  Oudnederlandse Liederen (S120)

Drie Oudnederlandse Liederen I °see
  Daer Was Een Sneeuwwit Vogheltje;
  Den Uyl Die Op Den Peerboom Zat;
  Jesus Is Nu Een Kindekijn Clein (S121)

Drie Oudnederlandse Liederen II °see
  Daer Was A Wuf Die Spon; Daer Was
  Een Kwezeltje; In Den Hemel Is
  Eenen Dans (S122)

Drie Oudnederlandse Liederen III
  °see O Heer Die Daer Des Hemels
  Tente Spreijt; Schoon Lieveken,
  Waer Waarde Gij; Wilt Heden Nu
  Treden (S123)

Geestelijk En Een Geestig
  Oudnederlands Lied, Een °see
  Jesus' Bloemhof; Zeg Kwezelken,
  Wilde Gij Dansen (S124)

In Den Hemel Is Eenen Dans
  [Dutch] 3 eq voices,acap ZENGERINK
  R 632 see from Drie
  Oudnederlandse Liederen II (S125)

Jesus' Bloemhof
  [Dutch] 3 eq voices,acap ZENGERINK
  R 635 see from Geestelijk En Een
  Geestig Oudnederlands Lied, Een (S126)

Jesus Is Nu Een Kindekijn Clein
  [Dutch] 3 eq voices,acap ZENGERINK
  R 631 see from Drie
  Oudnederlandse Liederen I (S127)

Meisken Jong, Mijn Maegdeken Teer
  [Dutch] 3 eq voices,acap ZENGERINK
  R 634 see from Twee
  Oudnederlandse Liederen (S128)

O Heer Die Daer Des Hemels Tente
  Spreijt
  [Dutch] 3 eq voices,acap ZENGERINK
  R 633 see from Drie
  Oudnederlandse Liederen III (S129)

Schoon Lieveken, Waer Waarde Gij
  [Dutch] 3 eq voices,acap ZENGERINK
  R 633 see from Drie
  Oudnederlandse Liederen III (S130)

'T Haesken
  "Willen Wij 'T Haesken Jagen Door
  De Hei" [Dutch] 3 eq voices,acap
  ZENGERINK R 637 (S131)

Twee Amoureuze En Een Lustig
  Liedeken °see Den Soeten Tijdt;
  Waren Twee Coninckskinderen, Het;
  Winter Is Verganghen, Die (S132)

Twee Oudnederlandse Liederen °see
  Des Winters Als Het Regent;
  Meisken Jong, Mijn Maegdeken Teer (S133)

Waren Twee Coninckskinderen, Het
  3 eq voices,acap ZENGERINK R 636
  see from Twee Amoureuze En Een
  Lustigh Liedeken (S134)

Willen Wij 'T Haesken Jagen Door De
  Hei °see 'T Haesken

Wilt Heden Nu Treden
  [Dutch] 3 eq voices,acap ZENGERINK
  R 633 see from Drie
  Oudnederlandse Liederen III (S135)

Winter Is Verganghen, Die
  3 eq voices,acap ZENGERINK R 636
  see from Twee Amoureuze En Een
  Lustigh Liedeken (S136)

Zeg Kwezelken, Wilde Gij Dansen
  [Dutch] 3 eq voices,acap ZENGERINK
  R 635 see from Geestelijk En Een
  Geestig Oudnederlands Lied, Een (S137)

SCHRODER
Ich Tanze Mit Dir In Den Himmel
  Hinein
  (Hess) mix cor,opt pno LEUCKART
  LSB 525 (S138)

SCHROEDER, HERMANN (1904-1984)
Balladen °see Es Waren Zwei
  Konigskinder; Reiter Und Der
  Bodensee, Der (S139)

Es Waren Zwei Konigskinder
  TTBB MULLER 2743 see from Balladen (S140)

SCHROEDER, HERMANN (cont'd.)

Hohe Lied-Motetten °see Steig, O
  Steig Herab; Wie Schon Bist Du (S141)

In Stiller Nacht
  TTBB MULLER 667 (S142)

Morike-Trivium
  SMezA MULLER 2311 (S143)

Reiter Und Der Bodensee, Der
  TTBB MULLER 2742 see from Balladen (S144)

Steig, O Steig Herab
  TTBB HEIDELBERGER 116 see from Hohe
  Lied-Motetten (S145)

Vier Fruhlingslieder °CCU
  3pt jr cor,opt treb inst MULLER 646 (S146)

Vier Minnelieder °CCU
  3pt jr cor,opt treb inst MULLER 647 (S147)

Von Der Liebe Und Dem Suff
  TTBB MULLER 1887 (S148)

Wie Schon Bist Du
  TTBB HEIDELBERGER 117 see from Hohe
  Lied-Motetten (S149)

SCHTO MNJE SHIT'
  (Klos, Ton) "Wie Soll Ich Traurig
  Leben" [Russ/Ger] TTBB BANK
  11.413.001 see from Bojarenliederen
  1 (S150)

SCHUBERT, FRANZ (PETER) (1797-1828)
Aan De Kunst: O Heil'ge Kunst
  mix cor ZENGERINK 263 (S151)

Al Par Del Rustelletto (from Cantata
  D.936)
  (Bullock) "As A Brooklet" 6pt mix
  cor,pno LAWSON 52271 (S152)

Allons Vivre A La Campagne °Op.64,
  No.3
  TTBB HUGUENIN CH 947 (S153)

Am Brunnen Vor Dem Tore
  (Heilmann, Harald) SATB MULLER 687 (S154)

An Die Musik: Du Holde Kunst
  (Biebl, F.) mix cor BOHM (S155)

An Die Sonne
  SATB,pno CAILLARD PC 207 (S156)

As A Brooklet °see Al Par Del
  Rustelletto

Au Village °Op.11,No.1
  TTBB HUGUENIN CH 303 (S157)

Aubade °Op.135
  TTBB,A solo HUGUENIN CH 650 (S158)

Aubade °see Standchen

Begrabnislied
  SATB,pno CAILLARD PC 193 (S159)

C'est L'amour
  TTBB HUGUENIN CH 903 (S160)

Chanson Joyeuse
  TTBB HUGUENIN EB 451 (S161)

Chant Des Bardes
  TTBB HUGUENIN EB 239 (S162)

Chant Des Espirits Audessus Des Eaux
  °see Gesang Der Geistern Uber Den
  Wassern

Ciel Est Pur, Le
  TTBB HUGUENIN EB 240 see from Deux
  Chants De Mai (S163)
  eq voices HUGUENIN EB 266 see from
  Deux Chants De Mai (S164)

Coeur Joyeux
  TTBB HUGUENIN EB 175 see from Deux
  Choeurs (S165)

Debout, Folle Troupe
  TTBB HUGUENIN EB 175 see from Deux
  Choeurs (S166)

Des Fleurs En Couronne
  TTBB HUGUENIN EB 240 see from Deux
  Chants De Mai (S167)

Des Fleurs En Couronnes
  eq voices HUGUENIN EB 266 see from
  Deux Chants De Mai (S168)

Deux Chants De Mai °see Ciel Est
  Pur, Le; Des Fleurs En Couronne;
  Des Fleurs En Couronnes (S169)

Deux Choeurs °see Coeur Joyeux;
  Debout, Folle Troupe (S170)

SCHUBERT, FRANZ (PETER) (cont'd.)

Dreifach Ist Der Schritt Der Zeit
  3 eq voices,acap ZENGERINK V 263
  see from Vier Canons (S171)

Forelle, Die
  (Schreuder, G.) SATB MOLENAAR
  15002903 (S172)

Geist Der Liebe °D.447
  TTBB MULLER 1716 (S173)

Gesang Der Geister Uber Den Wassern,
  "Des Menschen Seele" °D.714,
  Op.Posth.167
  men cor,strings BREITKOPF-W
  CHB 5202 (S174)

Gesang Der Geistern Uber Den Wassern
  "Chant Des Espirits Audessus Des
  Eaux" TTBB HUGUENIN CH 1165 (S175)

Glaube, Hoffnung Und Liebe
  SATB,instrumental ensemble NATIONAL
  NMP-185 $.85, ipa (S176)

Gondelfahrer, Der, "Es Tanzen Mond
  Und Stern" °Op.28,D.809 (from
  Schubert- Chore)
  (Zender, Hans) TTBB,4perc,harp,
  strings BREITKOPF-W CHB 5130 (S177)

Hirtenchor No. 7, "Hier Auf Den
  Fluren"
  mix cor,orch BREITKOPF-W CHB 3577 (S178)

Lacrimosa Son Io
  3 eq voices,acap ZENGERINK V 263
  see from Vier Canons (S179)

Linden Tree, The
  (Averre) SATB BOURNE B239087 $.80 (S180)

Litanei
  (Linden, N.V.D.) TTBB MOLENAAR
  15012802 (S181)

Mirjams Siegesgesang, "Ruhrt Die
  Cymbel" °Op.Posth.136
  mix cor,S solo,pno BREITKOPF-W
  CHB 5144 (S182)

Mon Coeur Est Las °see Sehnsucht

Nacht, De: Hoe Wondergoed °see
  Nacht, Die: Wie Schon Bist Du

Nacht, Die
  TTBB oct DEAN HRD 179 $.75 (S183)

Nacht, Die: Wie Schon Bist Du
  "Nacht, De: Hoe Wondergoed" mix cor
  ZENGERINK 260 (S184)
  "Voorjaarsnacht: Gij Zijt Mijn
  Lust" 4 eq voices,acap ZENGERINK
  179 (S185)

Nachtgesang Im Walde, "Sei Uns Stets
  Gegrusst" °D.913,Op.Posth.139
  men cor,4horn BREITKOPF-W CHB 3520 (S186)

Nachthelle, "Die Nacht Ist Heiter"
  °D.892 (from Schubert- Chore)
  (Zender, Hans) TTBB,T solo,3.2.2.2.
  2.2.0.0. 2perc,harp,cel/
  harmonium,strings BREITKOPF-W
  CHB 5131 (S187)

Printemps
  SATB,acap HUGUENIN EB 462 (S188)

Ronde, La
  TTBB HUGUENIN CH 904 (S189)

Rossignol, Le °Op.11,No.2
  TTBB HUGUENIN CH 902 (S190)

Sehnsucht
  "Mon Coeur Est Las" TTBB HUGUENIN
  CH 1166 (S191)

Serenade
  SATB,opt pno CAILLARD PC 208 (S192)
  SATB,acap HUGUENIN EB 450 (S193)

Standchen
  "Aubade" men cor,A solo,pno
  HUGUENIN CH 1195 (S194)

Standchen: Selig Durch Die Liebe
  men cor DOBLINGER 54 020 (S195)

Streamlet, The °see Wohin?

Tout Est Joie
  SATB,acap HUGUENIN EB 449 (S196)
  TTBB HUGUENIN EB 174 (S197)

Tristesse
  TTBB HUGUENIN EB 178 (S198)

Two Paths Of Virtue
  (McCray) TBB,opt acap NEW MUSIC
  NMC- 3005 $.55 (S199)

SCHUBERT, FRANZ (PETER) (cont'd.)

Valse
SATB,acap HUGUENIN EB 454   (S200)

Viens, Printemps
TTBB HUGUENIN EB 238   (S201)

Vier Canons *see Dreifach Ist Der
Schritt Der Zeit; Lacrimosa Son
Io; Vreugde; Zonsondergang   (S202)

Voorjaarsnacht: Gij Zijt Mijn Lust
*see Nacht, Die: Wie Schon Bist
Du

Vreugde
3 eq voices,acap ZENGERINK V 263
see from Vier Canons   (S203)

Wohin?
(Reed, Everett) "Streamlet, The"
cor ASPEN 3001 $1.00   (S204)

Zonsondergang
3 eq voices,acap ZENGERINK V 263
see from Vier Canons   (S205)

SCHUBERT, MANFRED (1937-   )
Verwundbar Sind Wir, Aber Nicht
Besiegbar
mix cor,SBar soli,3.2.3.2. 4.2.3.0.
timp,perc,harp,strings BREITKOPF-
L   (S206)

SCHULERSONGS see Mullich, Hermann

SCHULMEISTER, DER see Telemann, Georg
Philipp

SCHULTZ, DONNA GARTMAN
Ophelia's Song
see Schultz, Donna Gartman, Under
The Greenwood Tree

Under The Greenwood Tree
SSA,pno LAWSON 52382 contains also:
Ophelia's Song   (S207)

SCHULTZE, NORBERT (1911-   )
Kleine Weisse Mowe
TTBB,pno SIKORSKI   (S208)

SCHUMAN, WILLIAM HOWARD (1910-   )
Singaling (from Esses)
SATB,acap PRESSER 342-40155 $.85
                             (S209)

SCHUMANN, CLARA (WIECK) (1819-1896)
Drei Chore
4pt cor BREITKOPF-W PB 3521 f.s.
                             (S210)

SCHUMANN, ROBERT (ALEXANDER)
(1810-1856)
A La Montagne
SATB,acap HUGUENIN CH 621   (S211)

An Die Sterne *Op.141
dbl cor HANSSLER 40.278-50 f.s.
                             (S212)

dbl cor BREITKOPF-W CHB 5122 see
from Vier Doppelchorige Gesange,
Op. 141   (S213)
(Jennings) "To The Stars" SATB
SCHIRM.G 322430 $1.40   (S214)

Au Bruit Des Brocs
TTBB HUGUENIN EB 176 see from Deux
Canons   (S215)

Bei Der Flasche *Op.137
men cor,4horn BREITKOPF-W CHB 5189
see from Jagdlieder   (S216)

Beim Abschied Zu Singen *Op.84
SATB,pno HANSSLER 40.280-60 f.s.
                             (S217)

Capelle, Die
SSAA,opt pno CAILLARD PC 163 see
from Romanzen Fur Frauenstimmen,
Op. 69   (S218)

Choruses *see Dream, The; Gipsies;
On The Shore Of Bodensee;
Paradise And The Peri: Choruses
                             (S219)

Des Sangers Fluch, Op. 139
see Schumann, Robert (Alexander),
Jagdlieder, Op. 137

Deux Canons *see Au Bruit Des Brocs;
Je Veux A Boire   (S220)

Dream, The
[Ger/Russ] cor MEZ KNIGA 174 see
from Choruses   (S221)

Drei Gedichte Von Emanuel Geibel, Op.
29 *see Lied   (S222)

Drei Lieder, Op. 114 *see Nanie;
Spuch; Triolett   (S223)

Fruhe *Op.137
men cor,4horn BREITKOPF-W CHB 5189
see from Jagdlieder   (S224)

SCHUMANN, ROBERT (ALEXANDER) (cont'd.)

Fruhlingsbotschaft: Kuckuck Ruft Aus
Dem Wald
[Ger] 3 eq voices,acap ZENGERINK
V 44   (S225)

Gai Laboureur, Le
(Ott, Norbert) 3pt mix cor A COEUR
JOIE 1034   (S226)

Gipsies
[Ger/Russ] cor MEZ KNIGA 174 see
from Choruses   (S227)

Glockenturmers Tochterlein
(Appel, Bernhard) [Ger] mix cor,
acap [2'] SCHOTTS C 46488   (S228)

Habet Acht! *Op.137
men cor,4horn BREITKOPF-W CHB 5189
see from Jagdlieder   (S229)

Handschuh, Der
(Appel, Bernhard) [Ger] mix cor,
acap [5'] SCHOTTS C 46487   (S230)

Heidenroslein *Op.67
mix cor BREITKOPF-W CHB 5208 see
from Romanzen Und Balladen   (S231)

Heloe! Komm Du Auf Unsre Heide
*Op.59,No.5
SSTT BREITKOPF-W CHB 5228 f.s.
                             (S232)

Jagdlieder *see Bei Der Flasche,
Op.137; Fruhe, Op.137; Habet
Acht!, Op.137; Jagdmorgen,
Op.137; Zur Hohen Jagd, Op.137
                             (S233)

Jagdlieder, Op. 137
[Ger] TTBB KALMUS K 06783 $3.00
contains also: Des Sangers Fluch,
Op. 139 (SATB,ATBarB soli)   (S234)

Jagdmorgen *Op.137
men cor,4horn BREITKOPF-W CHB 5189
see from Jagdlieder   (S235)

Je Veux A Boire
TTBB HUGUENIN EB 176 see from Deux
Canons   (S236)

John Anderson *Op.67
mix cor BREITKOPF-W CHB 5208 see
from Romanzen Und Balladen   (S237)

Konig Von Thule, Der *Op.67
mix cor BREITKOPF-W CHB 5208 see
from Romanzen Und Balladen   (S238)

Lied
SSA,pno CAILLARD PC 164 see from
Drei Gedichte Von Emanuel Geibel,
Op. 29   (S239)

Lotosblume, Die
TTBB HUGUENIN EB 351   (S240)

Lotus Flower, The
see Pfautsch, Lloyd Alvin, Let
Sounds Of Joy Be Heard

Mich Zieht Es (from Funf Lieder Von
Robert Burns, Op. 55)
3pt mix cor CAILLARD PC 189   (S241)

Minnesingers, The (from Three Songs
For Male Chorus)
(Pfautsch, Lloyd) LAWSON LG 52091
$.70   (S242)

Minnespiel *Op.101
see Schumann, Robert (Alexander),
Romances

Nachtlied *Op.108
see Schumann, Robert (Alexander),
Requiem For Mignon

Nanie
SSA,pno CAILLARD PC 182 f.s. see
from Drei Lieder, Op. 114   (S243)

On The Shore Of Bodensee
[Ger/Russ] cor MEZ KNIGA 174 see
from Choruses   (S244)

Paradise And The Peri *ora
[Russ] cor,soli,orch voc sc MEZ
KNIGA 476   (S245)

Paradise And The Peri: Choruses
[Ger/Russ] cor MEZ KNIGA 174 see
from Choruses   (S246)

Requiem For Mignon *Op.98b
[Ger] SSAATTBB KALMUS K 06782 $5.75
contains also: Nachtlied, Op.108;
Rose Pilgerfahrt, Der, Op.112 (S247)

Romances *Op.91
[Ger] 1-4pt cor KALMUS K 06788
$4.75 contains also: Spanish
Songs, Op.74; Minnespiel, Op.101
                             (S248)

SCHUMANN, ROBERT (ALEXANDER) (cont'd.)

Romances, Op. 69
see Schumann, Robert (Alexander),
Various Choral Works For Treble
Voices

Romanzen Fur Frauenstimmen, Op. 69
*see Capelle, Die   (S249)

Romanzen Und Balladen *see
Heidenroslein, Op.67; John
Anderson, Op.67; Konig Von Thule,
Der, Op.67; Schon Rohtraut,
Op.67; Ungewitter, Op.67   (S250)

Rose Pilgerfahrt, Der *Op.112
see Schumann, Robert (Alexander),
Requiem For Mignon

Schifflein, Das
SATB NATIONAL CMS-130 $.90   (S251)

Schon Ist Das Fest Des Lenzes
*Op.101
SATB,pno HANSSLER 40.280-40 see
from Zwei Quartette Aus Dem
Minnespiel   (S252)

Schon Rohtraut *Op.67
mix cor BREITKOPF-W CHB 5208 see
from Romanzen Und Balladen   (S253)

Singer
SATB LAWSON LG 52363 $.70   (S254)

So Wahr Die Sonne Scheinet *Op.101
SATB,pno HANSSLER 40.280-50 see
from Zwei Quartette Aus Dem
Minnespiel   (S255)

Spanish Songs *Op.74
see Schumann, Robert (Alexander),
Romances

Spuch
SSA,pno CAILLARD PC 184 f.s. see
from Drei Lieder, Op. 114   (S256)

Szenen Aus Goethes "Faust"
(Bargiel, Woldemar) cor, solo
voices,orch/pno voc sc AUTOGR
                             (S257)

Talismane *Op.141
dbl cor HANSSLER 40.278-80 f.s.
                             (S258)

dbl cor BREITKOPF-W CHB 5123 see
from Vier Doppelchorige Gesange,
Op. 141   (S259)

To The Stars *see An Die Sterne

Traume, Der
SATB LAWSON LG 52321 $.70   (S260)

Traumerei
(Dupuis, Alb.) TTBB MOLENAAR
13014303   (S261)

Triolett
SSA,pno CAILLARD PC 183 f.s. see
from Drei Lieder, Op. 114   (S262)

Ungewisses Licht *Op.141
dbl cor HANSSLER 40.278-60 f.s.
                             (S263)

dbl cor BREITKOPF-W CHB 5122 see
from Vier Doppelchorige Gesange,
Op. 141   (S264)

Ungewitter *Op.67
mix cor BREITKOPF-W CHB 5208 see
from Romanzen Und Balladen   (S265)

Various Choral Works For Treble
Voices
[Ger] 2-4pt treb cor KALMUS K 06787
$4.75 contains also: Romances,
Op. 69   (S266)

Veillee Des Confederes, La *Op.62,
No.1
TTBB HUGUENIN EB 98   (S267)

Vent D'orage, Le
(Weber, G.) TTBB HUGUENIN EB 237
                             (S268)

Vier Doppelchorige Gesange, Op. 141
*see An Die Sterne; Talismane;
Ungewisses Licht; Zuversicht (S269)

Vier Gesange *Op.59
4pt mix cor,acap BREITKOPF-W
CHB 5207 f.s.   (S270)

Volksliedchen
(Ierswoud, Frederik Van) "Wenn Ich
Fruh In Den Garten Geh'" SSA
HARMONIA 3817   (S271)

Wassermann, Der
wom cor,pno PETERS 8542   (S272)

Wenn Ich Fruh In Den Garten Geh'
*see Volksliedchen

SCHUMANN, ROBERT (ALEXANDER) (cont'd.)

Wiegenlied
SATB,opt pno CAILLARD PC 206 (S273)

Zur Hohen Jagd *Op.137
men cor,4horn BREITKOPF-W CHB 5189
see from Jagdlieder (S274)

Zuversicht *Op.141
dbl cor HANSSLER 40.278-70 f.s.
(S275)
dbl cor BREITKOPF-W CHB 5123 see
from Vier Doppelchorige Gesange,
Op. 141 (S276)

Zwei Quartette Aus Dem Minnespiel
*see Schon Ist Das Fest Des
Lenzes, Op.101; So Wahr Die Sonne
Scheinet, Op.101 (S277)

SCHUSTER FRANZ, DER see Ebenhoh, Horst

SCHWABISCHE ERBSCHAFT see Strauss,
Richard

SCHWABISCHE LIEBESLIEDER see Miller,
Franz R.

SCHWABISCHES BILDERBUCH see Gebhard,
Hans

SCHWAEN, KURT (1909-   )
Es War Einmal Eine Maus
1-4pt jr cor,pno sc BREITKOPF-L
7941 (S278)

Gagarin
mix cor sc BREITKOPF-L 7665 (S279)

Mauschen Mit Dem Abgebissenen
Schwanzchen, Das
jr cor,child solo,pno sc BREITKOPF-
L 7948 (S280)

Weltreise Im Zimmer, Die *cant
jr cor,child solo,acord,bsn,string
quar sc BREITKOPF-L 1092, pts
BREITKOPF-L 2092, cor pts
BREITKOPF-L 7092 (S281)

SCHWARTZ
Chanson De Grand-Pere
1-4pt cor HUGUENIN see from
CHANSONS POUR LA JEUNESSE,
SIXIEME CAHIER (S282)

Finding My Way (composed with Chiara,
Jo)
SATB CPP-BEL SV8557 $.95 (S283)

Let's Take A Christmas Trip *see
Chiara, Jo

Magic To Do (from Pippin) (composed
with Fisher)
SATB,pno,opt perc CPP-BEL OCT 02302
$1.25 (S284)

Rock-A-Bye Your Baby With A Dixie
Melody *see Lewis

Skyride
2pt cor CPP-BEL DMC 08155 $.95
(S285)

SCHWARZE HUSAREN
(Karpowitsch; Ignatieff) men cor
ZIMMER. 621 (S286)

SCHWEIGEN see Reger, Max

SCHWEINSBERG, FRANZ JOSEPH
Van Buiten Ijs, Van Binnen Gloed
4 eq voices,acap ZENGERINK 96
(S287)

SCOTT
Gonna Sit Down And Rest Awhile
SATB CPP-BEL SV8608 $1.10 (S288)

I Will Be With You Every Christmas
SATB,acap CPP-BEL SV8620 $.95
(S289)

Remember This One
SATB CPP-BEL 1531RC1X $1.25 (S290)

SCOTT, K. LEE
Go, Lovely Rose
SATB,acap GALAXY 1.3028 $.85 (S291)

SCOTT, MICHAEL
Goodbye Old Friend (The Graduation
Song)
SATB CPP-BEL 4990GC1X $1.40, accomp
tape available (S292)

SCULTHORPE, PETER [JOSHUA] (1929-   )
Autumn Song
SATBB SCHIRM.G 318470 $.70 (S293)

SE, DAGEN BRYTER FREM MED MAGT see
Soderlind, Ragnar

SE, DAGEN KOMMER see Hovland, Egil

SE JE SOUSPIRE see Machaut, Guillaume
de

SE! KROUTHEN see Alinder, Hakan

SE NEL PARTIR DA VOI see Monteverdi,
Claudio

SE, NU STIGER SOLEN UR HAVETS FAMN see
Falk, Karl-Axel

SE PER HAVERVI, OIME see Lauridsen,
Morten Johannes

SE SOLENS SKJONNE LYS OG PRAKT see
Kolberg, Kare

SEA DRIFT see Delius, Frederick

SEA FEVER see Ireland, John

SEA IS NOW CALLING, THE see Koepke,
Allen

SEA MOODS see Eddleman, David

SEA SHELL SONG see Vinson, Harvey

SEA SLEEPS, THE see Snetkov, B.

SEA SONG, A see Cunningham

SEA SUNSETS see Weigl, [Mrs.] Vally

SEA SYMPHONY, A see Hanson, Howard

SEAGULLS see Le Lacheur, Rex

SEARCH, THE (PHILOSOPHICAL ANECDOTES)
see Sowash

SEARCHING FOR A GIFT see Telfer, Nancy

SEASONAL CAROLS OLD & NEW VOLS. 1-3 see
Wilson, Alan

SEASONAL CAROLS VOL. 4 see Wilson, Alan

SEASONAL MADRIGALS see Hurnik, Ilja

SEASONAL ROUNDELAY see Forbes,
Sebastian

SEASONAL SONGS see Pfautsch, Lloyd
Alvin

SEASONS see Lewin, Frank

SEBASTOPOL CAROL see Mattson

SECHS CHORLIEDER, OPUS 47 see
Hauptmann, Moritz

SECKINGER, KONRAD (1935-   )
An Die Musikanten
4pt mix cor MULLER SM 1824 see from
Zwei Gesellige Lieder Nach
Barocken Weisen (S294)

Gesang Vom Frieden
SATB MULLER 1790 (S295)

Gute Nacht
SATB,fl,strings MULLER 2125 (S296)

Ich Bin Das Ganze Jahr Vergnugt
*cant
cor,string quar,2trp,2trom,opt pno
BOHM (S297)

Ist Etwas So Machtig
mix cor,winds/string quar BOHM
(S298)

Kann Man Noch Singen In Dieser Welt?
mix cor,2trp,2trom,opt pno BOHM
(S299)

Kleines Lied Fur Dich, Ein: Du Bist
Das Liebste Mein
TTBB MULLER 817 (S300)
SATB MULLER 818 (S301)

Mit Uns Springt, Tanzt Und Singt
4pt mix cor MULLER SM 1823 see from
Zwei Gesellige Lieder Nach
Barocken Weisen (S302)

Prost! Schenk Ein Den Kuhlen Wein
mix cor/men cor BOHM (S303)

Schenkt Ein Den Kuhlen Wein
SATB,Bar solo,brass,pno MULLER 2307
(S304)

Singet Leise: Kleine Abendmusik
SATB MULLER 736 (S305)

Zwei Gesellige Lieder Nach Barocken
Weisen *see An Die Musikanten;
Mit Uns Springt, Tanzt Und Singt
(S306)

SECOND CANTATA see Pleskow, Raoul

SECOND ENCOUNTER see Johansson, Bengt

SECONDO LIBRO DE MADRIGALI A CINQUE
VOCI, IL see Rossi, Salomone

SECRET DREAM, A see Gilpin, Greg

SECULAR WORKS FOR THREE VOICES see Des
Prez, Josquin

SEE THE CHERRY BLOSSOMS SWING see
Anderson, William H.

SEE WHAT A MAZE OF ERROR see Kirbye,
George

SEE YOU IN SEPTEMBER see Edwards

SEEGER, PETER (1919-   )
Dies Haus Ist Mein
2-4pt men cor MULLER SM 649 (S307)

Erfullte Zeit *cant
wom cor/jr cor,pno BOHM (S308)

Springtime: Madrigalvariationen
[Eng/Ger] SATB,SATB soli,db,perc
MULLER 2561 (S309)

Von Herz Und Schmerz
SSATBB,pno, opt plucked orch MULLER
2684 (S310)

SEFERIS
Fleurs De La Pierre *see Grimbert,
Jacques

SEGER, BOB
Shakedown
(Chinn, Teena) SATB,opt horn CPP-
BEL 2679SC1X $1.25, accomp tape
available (S311)
(Chinn, Teena) SAB CPP-BEL 2679SC3X
$1.25, accomp tape available
(S312)

SEHL QUE NO VOL see Miraval, Raymond De

SEHNSUCHT see Brahms, Johannes

SEHNSUCHT see Schubert, Franz (Peter)

SEHNSUCHT NACH DEN BERGEN see Biebl,
Franz

SEHT, DER MORGEN MIT GEKOSE see Handel,
George Frideric

SEHT DOCH, WIE DER RHEINWEIN TANZT see
Scheck, Helmut

SEIBER, MATYAS GYORGY (1905-1960)
Alle Leut' Sind Ausgegangen
[Ger] men cor [2'] SCHOTTS C 46029
(S313)
[Ger] wom cor [2'] SCHOTTS C 46028
(S314)

SEINE, LA see Lefarge, G.

SEIS CANTOS DE ARRIERO *CC6U
4pt mix cor ALPUERTO 1612 (S315)

SEKS INGER HAGERUP SANGER see Lyssand,
Henrik

SELECTED CHORALES, VOL. 2 see Bach,
Johann Sebastian

SELECTED CHORUSES see Borodin,
Alexander Porfirievich

SELECTED CHORUSES see Napravnik, Eduard

SELECTED CHORUSES see Mussorgsky,
Modest Petrovich

SELECTED CHORUSES see Antsev, M.

SELECTED CHORUSES see Alexandrov, A.

SELECTED WORKS FOR CHORUS A CAPPELLA
see Nedilskyj, Ivan

SELF CONTROL
(Strommen) TTB CPP-BEL 1523SC4X $1.25
(S316)

SELFISH GIANT, THE see Bryan, John

SELTSAME GESCHICHTEN see Lampart, Karl

SEMELE see Handel, George Frideric

SEMPACH see Lauber, Emile

SENCE YOU WENT AWAY see Mortensen, Otto

SEND SOME MUSIC see Powell

SENFL, LUDWIG (ca. 1490-1543)
Ach, Elslein, Liebes Elselein
see MADRIGALE FUR GEMISCHTEN CHOR A
CAPPELLA: BLATT VI

Bells At Speyer, The
(Glarum) 6pt cor SCHIRM.G 312990
$.80 (S317)

Ich Stund An Einem Morgen
[Ger/Eng] SATTB [2'] BROUDE BR.
CR 36 $.95 (S318)

SENFL, LUDWIG (cont'd.)

Mag Ich, Herzlieb, Erwerben Dich
see MADRIGALE FÜR GEMISCHTEN CHOR A
CAPPELLA: BLATT VI

SENSATION see Andriessen, Hendrik

SENSE OF KINSHIP, A see Duson, Dede

SENSEMAYA see Heider, Werner

SEPARATE LIVES
SATB CPP-BEL 1544SC1X $1.25, accomp
tape available   (S319)
SAB CPP-BEL 1544SC3X $1.25, accomp
tape available   (S320)
2pt cor CPP-BEL 1544SC5X $1.25,
accomp tape available   (S321)

SERENADE see Kjerulf, Halfdan

SERENADE see Lauber, Emile

SERENADE see Schubert, Franz (Peter)

SERENADE FOR A SUMMER EVENING see
Cohen, Edward

SERENATA EROICA see Telemann, Georg
Philipp

SERMISY, CLAUDE DE (CLAUDIN)
(ca. 1490-1562)
Ayez Pitie Du Grand Mal Que J'endure
(Agnel, A.) 2pt mix cor HEUGEL
HE 31887   (S322)

Changeons Propos
(Agnel, A.) 3pt mix cor HEUGEL
HE 32069   (S323)

Coeur De Vous, Le
(Agnel, A.) 2-3pt mix cor HEUGEL
HE 31884   (S324)

D'amour Je Suis Desheritee
(Agnel, A.) 2-3pt mix cor HEUGEL
HE 31988   (S325)

J'aime Le Coeur De M'amie
(Agnel, A.) 3pt mix cor HEUGEL
HE 32068   (S326)

My Dearest Love
(Campbell, Robert) SATB,acap
FISCHER,C CM8279 f.s.   (S327)

On En Dira Ce Qu'on Voudra
(Agnel, A.) 3pt mix cor HEUGEL
HE 31882   (S328)

Si Vous M'aimez
SATB A COEUR JOIE 678   (S329)

Tant Que Vivray
SATB NATIONAL NMP-192 $.90   (S330)

SEROUSSI, RUBEN (1959-   )
Echo, The
[Heb] jr cor,acap [5']
ISR.MUS.INST. 6739   (S331)

SERRAND-GRIBENSKI, ISABELLE
Saisons Parisiennes
2 eq voices A COEUR JOIE 9015
                                       (S332)

SERRURIERS see Bleuse, Marc

SERTORIUS
Aufbruch Aus Dem Wirtshause
mix cor HEUGEL HE 32467   (S333)

SERVER, JUAN PONS
Belen Tocan A Fuego, En
4pt mix cor PILES 421   (S334)

SESAME STREET
SATB CPP-BEL SVJ8305 $26.00   (S335)

SESIMI KAYBEDEN SEHIR see Dormolen, Jan
Willem van

SET ME AS A SEAL see Pfautsch, Lloyd
Alvin

SET MY SOUL FREE see Cutter, Bill

SETJA MEG PA SULLARKRAKK: FOLK SONG
FROM BJERKRHEIM see Eielsen,
Steinar

SETTING UP EXERCISES
[Russ] jr cor MEZ KNIGA 501 see from
Picture Songs, Vol. 5   (S336)

SEUFZER LIEF SCHLITTSCHUH, EIN see
Spranger, Jorg

SEVEN FAT FISHERMEN see Telfer, Nancy

SEVEN OR EIGHT YEASTY CADENZAS FOR
MULTIVOICE CHOIR see Nordensten,
Frank Tveor

SEVEN SEA SHANTIES °CCU
2pt men cor,pno OXFORD 380063-2 $2.00
                                       (S337)
SEVEN SPACE SONGS see Coombes, Douglas

SFOGAVA CON LE STELLE see Monteverdi,
Claudio

SHA'AR LARASHUT see Orgad, Ben-Zion

SHADOW OF YOUR SMILE, THE see Mandel,
Johnny Alfred

SHADOWS see Crawley, Clifford

SHADOWVOICES see Sandbrink, Ab

SHADY GROVE °folk song
(Nichol) SS&camb,S solo CAMBIATA
C981157 $.65   (S338)

SHAKEDOWN see Seger, Bob

SHAKESPEARIAN SONNET °mot
16pt cor,opt timp [8'] ZERBONI 9570
                                       (S339)
SHAME
(Roscoe) mix cor CPP-BEL 2646SRHX
$1.25, accomp tape available   (S340)

SHAPIRA, SERGIU (1931-   )
Havu Mayim °CC6U
2-3pt cor,acap ISR.MUS.INST. 6299
                                       (S341)

SHAPORIN, YURI ALEXANDROVICH
(1887-1966)
How Long Will Hover The Hawk Of Woe
°ora
[Russ] cor,soli,orch voc sc MEZ
KNIGA 475   (S342)

SHAW
Oz-Wiz Medley °medley
"Wiz-Oz Medley" SAB CPP-BEL SV8359
$2.25, accomp tape available
                                       (S343)
"Wiz-Oz Medley" SSA CPP-BEL SV8358
f.s., accomp tape available
                                       (S344)
"Wiz-Oz Medley" SATB CPP-BEL SV8357
$2.25, accomp tape available
                                       (S345)
Wiz-Oz Medley °see Oz-Wiz Medley

SHAW, KIRBY
Jamaican Noel
SATB LEONARD-US 08657902 $.85
                                       (S346)
3pt cor LEONARD-US 08657903 $.85
                                       (S347)
Tear Them Down
SATB LEONARD-US 08664421 $.95
                                       (S348)
SAB LEONARD-US 08664422 $.95   (S349)
SSA LEONARD-US 08664423 $.95, ipa,
accomp tape available   (S350)

SHAW, MARSHALL L.
Earth
see Elements, The

Elements, The
unis cor LESLIE 1155 f.s.
contains: Earth; Fire; Water;
Wind   (S351)

Fire
see Elements, The

Water
see Elements, The

Wind
see Elements, The

SHAY
When You're Smiling °see Fisher

SHAYNE
Do You Hear What I Hear? °see
Regney, Noel

SHE DWELT AMONG THE UNTRODDEN WAYS see
Boyd, Robert A.

SHE IS THE MOTHER see Lund, Lynn S.

SHE REALLY EXIST see Kopelent, Marek,
Ona Skutecne Jest

SHE STILL CARRIES THE TORCH see Wilbur,
Sandy

SHE WALKS IN BEAUTY see Brahms,
Johannes

SHE WANTS TO DANCE WITH ME see Astley,
Rick

SHEARER
Gather Your Rosebuds
3-4pt mix cor SOUTHERN $.50   (S352)

Poor Mariners
SATB/SAB SOUTHERN $.50   (S353)

SHEARER, C.M.
Foresters, Sound The Cheerful Horn
TTBB,acap SOUTHERN SC- 237 $.65
                                       (S354)
My Love Asleep
SAB SOUTHERN f.s.   (S355)

Requiem
SATB,acap SOUTHERN SC 192 $1.00
                                       (S356)
Tho' I Am Young
SATB,acap SOUTHERN SC-224 $.65
                                       (S357)

SHE'LL BE COMIN' 'ROUND THE MOUNTAIN
°folk song,US
(De Cormier, Robert) mix cor LAWSON
LG 51919 $.95   (S358)

SHE'LL BE COMIN' (THE OLD TIMERS MEDLEY
1) see Beekum, Jan Van

SHELTER FROM THE RAIN
(Mcpheeters) mix cor CPP-BEL SV8554
$.95   (S359)

SHENANDOAH
(Stone) SA/TB,pno CPP-BEL OCT 02141
$1.10   (S360)

SHEPHARD, RICHARD
Old Order Changeth, The
SATB oct DEAN HRD 168 $.95   (S361)

SHEPHERD, THE see Reed, Everett

SHEPHERDESS MOON see Weigl, [Mrs.]
Vally

SHEPHERD'S CAROL, A see Speight, John
A.

SHEPHERDS ON A HILL see Nygard

SHERIFF, NOAM (1935-   )
Shir Hama'alot
"Song Of Degrees" [Heb] boy cor,
acap [6'] ISR.MUS.INST. 6605
                                       (S362)
Song Of Degrees °see Shir Hama'alot

SHERLAW-JOHNSON, ROBERT
see JOHNSON, ROBERT SHERLAW

SHERMAN, JOE
Graduation Day
(Leavitt, John) SATB CPP-BEL
T7060GC1 $1.40, accomp tape
available   (S363)
(Leavitt, John) SSA CPP-BEL
T7060GC2 $1.40   (S364)
(Leavitt, John) SAB CPP-BEL
T7060GC3 $1.40   (S365)

SHE'S LIKE THE SWALLOW see Bray,
Kenneth I.

SHE'S LIKE THE SWALLOW see Cassils,
Craig

SHESHET HA-YAMIM VESHIVAT HASHE'ARIM
see Even-Or, Mary

SHINE FOR ME AGAIN see Carter, Dan

SHINE ON AMERICA see Strommen, Carl

SHINE, PERISHING REPUBLIC see Lockwood,
Normand

SHIP THAT NEVER RETURNED, THE see
Coombes, Douglas

SHIR HAMA'ALOT see Sheriff, Noam

SHIR KATALANI ATIK (OLD CATALAN SONG)
see Bertini, Gary

SHIRIM ME'EMEK HOSHEN see Orgad, Ben-
Zion

SHIVERY SARAH see Nelson, Havelock

SHMEI OFERET see Permont, Haim

SHOP AROUND see Gordy, Berry

SHORT SONGS FOR TINY TOTS °CCU
[Russ] jr cor,pno MEZ KNIGA 528
                                       (S366)

SHOUT! see Michaels, David Julian

SHOUT AMEN! see Althouse

SHOUTING PILGRIM see Bacon, Ernst L.

SHOW ME YOUR MOUNTAIN see Whittaker,
Roger

SHOWING US THE WAY see Ficocelli,
Michael V.

SHUR, YEKUTIEL
Bee, The
[Eng] wom cor/jr cor ISRAELI
IMP 802 see from Raise The Song
                                       (S367)

SHUR, YEKUTIEL (cont'd.)
Choir Of Cats, A
[Eng] wom cor/jr cor ISRAELI
IMP 802 see from Raise The Song
(S368)

Frog, The
[Eng] wom cor/jr cor ISRAELI
IMP 802 see from Raise The Song
(S369)

Lift Up Thine Eyes Round About And
See
[Eng] wom cor/jr cor ISRAELI
IMP 802 see from Raise The Song
(S370)

Raise The Song *CC20U
[Heb] wom cor/jr cor ISRAELI
IMP 802   (S371)

Raise The Song *see Bee, The; Choir
Of Cats, A; Frog, The; Lift Up
Thine Eyes Round About And See
(S372)

SI see Berthomier, Michel

SI J'AI DU BIEN see Gardane, Antonio

SI J'AI EU DU MAL OU DU BIEN see
Anonymous

SI J'AI EU DU MAL OU DU BIEN see Ysore,
Guillaume

SI J'ETAIS see Couste, Francis

SI LA FACE EST PALE, LA CAUSE EST AIMER
see Thijsse, Wim

SI LE COUCOU EN CE MOIS see Janequin,
Clement

SI LOIN DE VOUS JE PARS see Monteverdi,
Claudio, Se Nel Partir Da Voi

SI MES YEUX, SI MES MAINS see Daniel,
Etienne

SI MON MALHEUR M'Y CONTINUE see
Pelletier, R. Octave

SI SEULEMENT see Cornaz, Emmanuel

SI VOUS M'AIMEZ see Sermisy, Claude de
(Claudin)

SIBELIUS, JEAN (1865-1957)
Be Still, My Soul *Op.26 (from
Finlandia)
men cor,pno BREITKOPF-W CHB 5182
(S373)

Impromptu, "Der Du Die Sterne
Leitest" *Op.19
wom cor,orch BREITKOPF-W EB 8302
(S374)

Laulu Lemminkaiselle *Op.31,No.1
cor FAZER F 07749-5   (S375)

Lauluja Sekakoorille *Op.23
mix cor,acap FAZER F 00025-7 (S376)

SIBERIA see McCabe

SICK ROSE, THE see Sveinsson, Atli
Heimir

SIDEWALKS OF NEW YORK see Taylor,
Lemoyne

SIE HABEN MICH GEQUALET see Andriessen,
Jurriaan

SIEBEN HOLDERLIN-CHORE see Genzmer,
Harald

SIEBEN LIEDER FUR GEMISCHTEN CHOR see
Weber, Carl Maria von

SIEBEN NEUE MADRIGALE see Koringer,
Franz

SIEBEN STRASSEN WILL ICH GEHEN, SIEBEN
TAGE LANG *CC7U
mix cor,acap sc BREITKOPF-L 7699
(S377)

SIEBEN UND DREISSIG CHOR- ETUDEN see
Dessau, Paul

SIEG VON GUERNICA, DER see Zechlin,
Ruth

SIEGL, OTTO (1896-1978)
Erstes Liederwerk Wanderschaft
*Op.87
men cor,Bar solo,pno BOHM   (S378)

SIEGLER, WINFRIED
Bruder, Lasst Uns Lustig Sein
TTBB MULLER 931   (S379)

Steige Zu Mir In Den Nachen
TTBB MULLER 929   (S380)
SATB MULLER 930   (S381)

SIEH DA, IHR LIEBEN HERREN see Schein,
Johann Hermann

SIETE CANTOS CORALES VASCOS see
Santiago, Rodrigo de

SIGH NO MORE LADIES see Boyd, Robert A.

SIGHT IN CAMP IN THE DAYBREAK GRAY AND
DIM, A see Bialosky, Marshall H.

SIGMAN
Snow, Snow, Beautiful Snow *see
Feller

SIGNORE DELLE CIME see De Marzi, G.

SIGRID SLOKJEDALEN see Solberg, Leif

SIGURBJORNSSON, THORKELL (1938-   )
Beginning
mix cor ICELAND 022-49   (S382)

Eight Songs From The Play "Jon
Arason" *CC8U
mix cor,pno ICELAND 022-63 (S383)

Fararsnid
mix cor ICELAND 022-76   (S384)

Lights And Harmonies
mix cor ICELAND 022-61   (S385)

Ode
men cor,pno [23'35"] ICELAND 022-23
(S386)

SIJT NU VERBLIJT see Yperen, R. van

SILCHER, FRIEDRICH (1789-1860)
Gut Nacht
TTBB MOLENAAR 15022303   (S387)

Lorelei, Die
SSATB KJOS C8722 $.80   (S388)

Loreley, Die
(Evertse, J.) SSA MOLENAAR 15024002
(S389)

Waldhoorn, De
SATB MOLENAAR 15021302   (S390)
(Kooij, E.J.) SATB MOLENAAR
15009903   (S391)
(Kooij, E.J.) SSA MOLENAAR 15024904
(S392)

SILENCE OF THE NIGHT, THE see Butler,
Eugene Sanders

SILENT WORSHIP see Handel, George
Frideric

SILLANPAA, ANNA-MAIJA
Koulukuoro 6 (composed with
Kankainen, Tauno; Kankainen,
Jukka)
SSA FAZER F 07721-4   (S393)

Koulukuoro 7, Seitseman Joululaulua
SSA FAZER F 07748-7   (S394)

SILSBEE, ANN (1930-   )
Acre For A Bird, An
SSAATTBB [5'] (Dickinson)
AM.COMP.AL. $4.10   (S395)

Diffraction
SATB,S solo,fl,2perc,pno [16']
AM.COMP.AL. $11.45   (S396)

Icarus
SSAATTBB,3rec,bongos [7']
AM.COMP.AL. $7.70   (S397)

SILTMAN, BOBBY L.
Beacon, A Door, A
TTB SOUTHERN f.s.   (S398)

I Would Be True
TTB,acap SOUTHERN SC-239 $.65
(S399)

Known Only To God
TTB,acap SOUTHERN SC-240 $.65
(S400)

Men Of Iwo Jima
TB,acap SOUTHERN SC-241 $.45 (S401)

Our Fearful Trip
TB SOUTHERN f.s.   (S402)

Prize We Sought, The
TTB SOUTHERN f.s.   (S403)

Rise Up
TTB SOUTHERN f.s.   (S404)

SILVER, FREDERICK
see SILVERBERG, FREDERICK IRWIN

SILVER, S.
Cherry-Ripe (from Two Songs On
Elizabethan Poems)
SATB SCHIRM.G 233940 $.80   (S405)

SILVER BELLS see Livingston, Jay Harold

SILVER BELLS see Smith

SILVER SWIMMER, THE see Hoddinott, Alun

SILVER THE RIVER see Paulus, Stephen
Harrison

SILVER THREADS see Danks, Hart Pease

SILVERBERG, FREDERICK IRWIN (1936-   )
Finnegin's Fugue
SAB CPP-BEL DMC 07027 $1.20 (S406)

If You Were Coming In The Fall
SATB CPP-BEL DMC 01004 $1.10 (S407)

Twelve Days After Christmas
SATB CPP-BEL DMC 00138 $1.10 (S408)
SSA CPP-BEL DMC 00137 $1.10   (S409)
unis cor CPP-BEL DMC 00110 $1.10
(S410)
SAB CPP-BEL DMC 07008 $1.10   (S411)

Twelve Days Before Christmas
SATB CPP-BEL DMC 01008 $1.10 (S412)
1-2pt cor CPP-BEL DMC 08004 $1.10
(S413)

SILVIA see Dickau

SIMEONE
Little Drummer Boy *see Davis

SIMMS
Rhythm In My Soul
SAB SHAWNEE 0361 $.85   (S414)

Santa, Don't Forget My Name!
2pt cor SHAWNEE 0324 $.95   (S415)

Until We Meet Somewhere Again
SAB SHAWNEE 0392 $.85   (S416)

SIMMS, PATSY
see BLEVINS, PATSY FORD

SIMON, CARLY
Let The River Run (New Jerusalem)
(Althouse, Jay) SATB CPP-BEL
1649LC1X $1.40, accomp tape
available   (S417)
(Althouse, Jay) SSA CPP-BEL
1649LC2X $1.40, accomp tape
available   (S418)
(Althouse, Jay) SAB CPP-BEL
1649LC3X $1.40, accomp tape
available   (S419)

SIMON, RICHARD
Thin Snow, The
SATB,acap BOURNE B239293-357 $.80
(S420)

SIMONCINI, ERNEST D.
Cloches
SATB,acap HUGUENIN EB 420   (S421)

Extase
SATB,acap HUGUENIN EB 43   (S422)

Mon Pays
SATB,acap HUGUENIN EB 368   (S423)

SIMONSEN, MELVIN
Dikteren Og Fluen
[Norw] men cor,acap NORGE   (S424)

SIMPLE GIFTS
(Cooper) S&camb,SA soli (shaker)
CAMBIATA T978116 $.65   (S425)
(Monroe, A.) TTBB,Bar solo,acap (med)
THOMAS 1C318512 $.70   (S426)
(Terri, Salli) SSSAATTBB (triple
choir) LAWSON LG 51906 $.70 (S427)

SIMPLE GIFTS see Mattson

SIMPLE GIFTS see Strommen, Carl

SIMPLEST OF GIFTS see Kunz, Jack

SIMPLY MEANT TO BE
(Chinn) SAB CPP-BEL 2857SC3X $1.25,
accomp tape available   (S428)
(Chinn) SATB CPP-BEL 2857SC1X $1.25,
accomp tape available   (S429)

SIMPLY SUNG
(Goetze, Mary) 3pt jr cor SCHOTTS
ST 12242 $4.75   (S430)

SIMPSON, ROBERT
Tempi
SATB,acap [15'] ROBERTON 3078
(S431)

SIMPSON, VALERIE R. (1946-   )
Reach Out And Touch (Somebody's Hand)
*see Ashford, Nickolas

SIMS, EZRA (1928-   )
Bewties Of The Flute-Ball, The
5pt jr cor,rec,pno, idiophones [2']
AM.COMP.AL. sc $10.70, pts $3.10
(S432)

SSATB,opt fl,ob,horn,trom,2pno [2']
AM.COMP.AL. sc $11.45, pts $7.70
(S433)

SINCE ROBIN HOOD see Weelkes, Thomas

SINCE YOU WENT AWAY see Mortensen,
Otto, Sence You Went Away

SINE AMORE NIHIL see Zamecnik, Evzen

SINE MUSICA NULLA VITA see Lukowsky, Rolf

SINFONIA TESTIMONIAL see Marez Oyens, Tera de

SINFONIE DER KINDER see Herrmann, Peter

SINFONIE NR. 8 see Geissler, Fritz

SINFONIE NR. 3 see Theodorakis, Mikis

SINFONIE NR. 7 see Theodorakis, Mikis

SINFONIETTA OF NATURE see Podesva, Jaromir

SING A CHRISTMAS SONG see Thygerson

SING A LITTLE SONG see Lawrence, Stephen L.

SING A NEW SONG see Feldstein, Saul (Sandy)

SING A SONG OF LOVE see Gretsch, Peggy

SING A SONG OF SIXPENCE see Rutter, John

SING A SONG UNIVERSAL see Dello Joio, Norman

SING, ALLELUIA! see Livingston

SING DEIN LIED: IN DIE DUNKLE SCHALE DER NACHT see Kleinertz, Hanns

SING DEM HERRN
(Depue) 2-5pt cor CPP-BEL SV8640
$1.10 (S434)

SING JOYFULLY see Smith

SING, JUST SING
(Lojeski) SATB LEONARD-US 08258736
$.95 (S435)
(Lojeski) SAB LEONARD-US 08258737
$.95 (S436)

SING ME A SONG see Telfer, Nancy

SING ME A SONG ABOUT CHRISTMAS see McPheeters

SING N' DO SONGS, VOL II °CCU $12.95
(Albrecht) cor SHAWNEE 0096 $12.95
(S437)

SING NOEL see Petker, Allan R.

SING NOEL! see Poorman, Sonja

SING NOEL! see Robertson

SING OF SPRING see Gershwin, George

SING OUT see Michaels, David Julian

SING OUT FOR FREEDOM see Snyder, Michael

SING OUT THE NEWS! see Besig

SING OUT WITH JOY see Ray, Jerry

SING PRAISES TO THE KING see Loughton, Lynnette

SING, REJOICE, YE RIGHTEOUS see Viadana, Lodovico Grossi da

SING- SEA TO SEA see Cable, Howard

SING, SING! see Estes

SING, SING OF CHRISTMAS see Althouse, Jay

SING WE AT PLEASURE see Weelkes, Thomas

SING WE MERRILY see Ossewaarde, Jack Herman

SING WE NOEL see Goetze, M.

SING WITH SONGS OF JOY see Handel, George Frideric

SING YE MUSES see Blow, John

SINGALING see Schuman, William Howard

SINGEN NACH NOTEN: EIN LEHRWERK FUR CHORSANGER see Kolneder, Walter

SINGEND, KLINGEND RUFT DICH DAS GLUCK see Stolz, Robert

SINGER see Schumann, Robert (Alexander)

SINGET DEM HERRN EIN NEUES LIED see Gunsenheimer, Gustav

SINGET LEISE: KLEINE ABENDMUSIK see Seckinger, Konrad

SINGIN' A NEW SONG see Hatch

SINGIN' IN THE RAIN
(Simon) 2pt cor CPP-BEL SV8336 $1.25
(S438)

SINGIN' THAT SIMPLE MELODY
(Sand, Edward J.) 2pt cor,opt gtr
CPP-BEL SV8819 $1.10 (S439)

SINGIN' YOU A SONG see Leavitt, John

SINGING IN THE SEASON see Frazee, J.

SINGING IS SO GOOD A THING see Ostern, Per Hroar

SINGING LANDSCAPE see Emmert, Frantisek

SINGING OF ANGELS, A see Davidson, Charles Stuart

SINGING SNOW see Sarmanto, Heikki, Hanget Soi

SINGT IM CHOR °CC3OU
(Zimmer, Ulrich) SATB,acap BAREN.
6355 (S440)

SINTE CAECILIA see Strategier, Herman

SIOKATE see Germeten, Gunnar

SIPILA, EERO (1918-1972)
Fot Mot Jord
mix cor FAZER (CH 71) F 06753-8
(S441)

SIPILA, ERKKI
Koulukuoro 4, Viihdesovituksia Koulukuorolle
SAB FAZER F 06951-8 (S442)

SIPPING CIDER THROUGH A STRAW
(Roff, Joseph) 2pt cor,pno (easy)
THOMAS 1C107803 $.40 (S443)

SIR, N.
Ode To Postumus
SATB,2.2.4.2. 4.2.2.1. cel,harp, timp,xylo,vibra,strings [18'0"]
APNM sc $15.00, perf mat rent,
voc sc $9.50 (S444)

Upper Meadows °song cycle
SSAATTBB [18'0"] sc APNM $11.00,
perf mat rent (S445)

SIRENE ET SCAPHANDRIER see Pottar, O.

SIRENES see Debussy, Claude

SIRENS' SONG, THE see Butler, Martin

SIROTKIN, Y.
Songs °CCU
[Russ] jr cor,pno MEZ KNIGA 505
(S446)

SIS! BOOM! BAH! see Roberts, Ruth

SISTE VISA, DEN see Gaathaug, Morten

SIT EIN LITEN EINSAM FUGL, DET see Am, Magnar

(SITTIN' ON) THE DOCK OF THE BAY
(Strommen) SSA CPP-BEL 4751DC2X $1.25
(S447)
(Strommen) SAB CPP-BEL 4751DC3X $1.25
(S448)

SIVERTSEN, KENNETH (1961-)
Dotrene
[Norw] SATB,vln,gtr NORGE (S449)

SIX A CAPPELLA CHORUSES, OP. 16 see Rimsky-Korsakov, Nikolai

SIX CHANSONS A REPONDRE ET A SONNER DU PAYS GUERANDAIS see Leleu, Francoise

SIX CHILDREN'S SONGS see Weigl, Karl

SIX CHORUSES ON POEMS BY TENNYSON AND HOUSMAN see Getty, Gordon

SIX DAYS AND THE SEVEN GATES, THE see Even-Or, Mary, Sheshet Ha-Yamim Veshivat Hashe'arim

SIX DUOS A VOIX MIXTES see Gardane, Antonio

SIX ELIZABETHAN LYRICS see Leighton, Kenneth

SIX ENFANTINES see Massis

SIX ENGLISH LYRICS see Williamson, Malcolm

SIX POEMS OF EMILY DICKINSON see Warren, B.

SIX POEMS OF ROLLAND PIERRE see Belaubre, Louis-Noel

SIX POLISH WEDDING FOLK SONGS IN A SUITE FORM see Pankiewicz, Eugeniusz, Szesc Piesni Weselnych Ludowych Polskich W Formie Suity

SIX SONGS see Gerschefski, Edwin

SIX SONGS FROM THE YORK MYSTERY PLAY "THE ASSUMPTION OF THE VIRGIN"
°CC6U
(Rastall, Richard) 2 eq voices ANTICO
AE21 (S450)

SJOBLOM, HEIMER (1910-)
Ganglat
men cor STIM (S451)

Julnatt
mix cor,opt fl,opt org/pno STIM
(S452)

Roslagen: Kantat °Op.20
mix cor,orch SUECIA (S453)

Rundgangen: Katrin- En Plommonvals
cor STIM (S454)

Tre Glada Visor For Manskor °CC3U
men cor STIM (S455)

Vagorna
men cor STIM (S456)

SJU DIKTER see Rabe, Folke

SJUNG FRID see Franke-Blom, Lars-Ake

SJUNGA AR SILVER, DIRIGERA AR GULD see Hultberg, Sven

SKALASANGEN see Brevik, Tor

SKAPELSE UTELAMNAD; EN EKOLOGISK BETRAKTELSE see Erikson, Ake

SKETCHES: BY THE SEA see Pollock, Robert Emil

SKIP TO MY LOU
(Christiansen) SATB,opt pno CPP-BEL
SCHCH 07617 $1.10 (S457)

SKOLNIK, WALTER (1934-)
Blow The Man Down
see Three Songs Of The Sea

Blow Ye Winds
see Three Songs Of The Sea

Golden Vanity, The
see Three Songs Of The Sea

Three Songs Of The Sea
SATB MUSICUS f.s.
contains: Blow The Man Down; Blow
Ye Winds; Golden Vanity, The
(S458)

SKOUEN, SYNNE (1950-)
Bombardement: Et Dikt Av Pablo Neruda
[Norw] SATB,narrator,inst NORGE
(S459)

Oatas Eimi
wom cor NORSK NMO 10125 (S460)

SKUGGSJON see Sandstrom, Jan

SKY, THE see Glaser, Werner Wolf, Cielo, El

SKYRIDE see Schwartz

SLAAP KINDEKE, SLAAP see Vocht, Lodewijk de, Wiegezang

SLAVE TO THE MUSIC see Gilpin, Greg

SLAVENKOOR see Verdi, Giuseppe

SLAVICKY, KLEMENT (1910-)
Bird Year °CCU
jr cor,pno CESKY HUD. (S461)

Psalmi °CCU
cor, solo voices,org SUPRAPHON
(S462)

Summer Day °CCU
jr cor,pno CESKY HUD. (S463)

SLAVICKY, MILAN
Pendulum Of Time, The
6pt mix cor,instrumental ensemble,
electronic tape [8'] CESKY HUD.
(S464)

Spring Necklace
jr cor,gtr [4'] CESKY HUD. (S465)

SLEEP LITTLE BABY, SLEEP see Besig

SLEEP NOW, MY BABY see Cancion de Cuna

SLEEP ON, MY FRIEND see Clarke, Henry Leland

SLEEPERS WAKE: CHORALE-PRELUDE see
Bach, Johann Sebastian

SLEETH, NATALIE WAKELEY (1930-   )
This Land Of Ours
2-4pt cor,pno,2trp,snare drum
FISCHER,C CM7901   (S466)

What Would We Do Without Music?
mix cor,pno FISCHER,C CM7876 f.s.
(S467)
2pt cor,pno FISCHER,C CM7877 f.s.
(S468)

SLEIGH RIDE see Anderson, Leroy

SLEIGHBELLS AND SNOW see Giasson, Paul
Emile

SLETTHOLM, YNGVE (1955-   )
Is
[Norw] jr cor NORGE   (S469)

SLOGEDAL, BJARNE (1927-   )
Four Folktunes From Southern Norway
mix cor NORSK NMO 9479   (S470)

Hvor Lenge?
SSA NORSK   (S471)

SLOTHOUWER, JOCHEM (1938-   )
Hymns And Dances
mix cor,perc,pno [18'] DONEMUS
(S472)

SLOUTHE: A PORTRAITE see Nuernberger,
L. Dean

SLOW ROCK see Grimbert, Jacques

SLOW, SLOW FRESH FOUNT see Gideon,
Miriam

SLOW SONG see Evensen, Bernt Kasberg

SLUIMER ZACHT see Vermulst, Jan, Golden
Slumbers

SLUMBER SONG see Belyea, W.H.

SMA EVENTYR see Jastrzebska, Anna

SMEETS, LEO
Avondgebet: De Nacht, De Moeder Van
De Rust
SSAA,acap ZENGERINK 348   (S473)

Molenaars Dochterken.. Klimt Op Den
Hil
4 eq voices,acap ZENGERINK 346
(S474)
Morgengroet: Wat Fluiten Daar Buiten
[Dutch] 3 eq voices,acap ZENGERINK
V 347   (S475)

Nederland Let Op Uw Saeck, O
SSA MOLENAAR 15026403   (S476)

Sonnet: O Engel Die Met Schoonheid
Overtogen
mix cor ZENGERINK 337   (S477)

Voorjaar: De Winter Is Geweken
[Dutch] 3 eq voices,acap ZENGERINK
V 346   (S478)

SMETANA, BEDRICH (1824-1884)
Ceska Pisen
"Czech Song" pno red SUPRAPHON
(S479)
Czech Song °see Ceska Pisen

SMILE
(Calvin, Dot) SSAA (women's
barbershop) BOURNE B238758 $.50
(S480)
(Zegree, Steve) SATB LEONARD-US
08603699 $.85   (S481)

SMILE see Chaplin

SMIT, THEO
O Vrijheid: Het Volk Van Neerland & O
Nederland
2pt cor,pno ZENGERINK R 262 (S482)

SMITH
Silver Bells
SATB CPP-BEL SV8442 $1.25   (S483)

Sing Joyfully
(Lantz) SATB SHAWNEE 6435 $.95
(S484)
Star Spangled Banner, The
(Collins) SSB&camb CAMBIATA D978123
$.65   (S485)

SMITH, GREGG (1931-   )
Aesop's Fables °see Ass, Lion And
Cock, The; Boy And His False
Alarms, The; Death And The Old
Man; Final Chorus; Frogs And The
Bull, The; Hares And The Frogs,
The; Introduction; Lady With Sore
Eyes, The; Lark In A Net, The;
Raven And The Fox, The   (S486)

SMITH, GREGG (cont'd.)
Ass, Lion And Cock, The
SATB SCHIRM.G 319830 $.75 see from
Aesop's Fables   (S487)

Boy And His False Alarms, The
SATB SCHIRM.G 319880 $1.25 see from
Aesop's Fables   (S488)

Death And The Old Man
SATB SCHIRM.G 319840 $.70 see from
Aesop's Fables   (S489)

Final Chorus
SATB SCHIRM.G 319890 $.75 see from
Aesop's Fables   (S490)

Frogs And The Bull, The
SATB SCHIRM.G 319860 $1.25 see from
Aesop's Fables   (S491)

Hares And The Frogs, The
SATB SCHIRM.G 319820 $1.25 see from
Aesop's Fables   (S492)

Introduction
SATB SCHIRM.G 319800 $.75 see from
Aesop's Fables   (S493)

Lady With Sore Eyes, The
SATB SCHIRM.G 319850 $.75 see from
Aesop's Fables   (S494)

Lark In A Net, The
SATB SCHIRM.G 319870 $.75 see from
Aesop's Fables   (S495)

Raven And The Fox, The
SATB SCHIRM.G 319810 $.75 see from
Aesop's Fables   (S496)

SMITH, JOHN STAFFORD (1750-1836)
Star Spangled Banner
(Kral, Joseph) SATB,acap CPP-BEL
SV8641 $1.10   (S497)

SMITH, JULIA FRANCES (1911-1989)
Song For Texas, A
SATB,pno,opt band PRESSER 392-00441
$.65, ipr   (S498)

SMITH, ROBERT EDWARD (1946-   )
First Spring Day, The
SATB (med) THOMAS 1C328839A $.85
(S499)
Green Grow'th The Holly
SSA (med) THOMAS 1C328921 $.85
(S500)
Man's Fancy
SATB (med) THOMAS 1C328839B $.85
(S501)
May Morning
SATB,pno (med) THOMAS 1C328839C
$.85   (S502)

SNE see Fongaard, Bjorn

SNETKOV, B.
Sea Sleeps, The °CCU
[Russ] cor MEZ KNIGA 168   (S503)

SNOW, THE see Elgar, [Sir] Edward
(William)

SNOW, TOM
After All °see Pitchford, Dean

SNOW DISAPPEARED, THE °folk song
(Kristinsson, Sigursveinn D.) mix cor
ICELAND 021-3   (S504)

SNOW, SNOW, BEAUTIFUL SNOW see Feller

SNOW-STORM, THE see Hamburg

SNOWDROP AND LAMB see Morgan, Hilda

SNOWFALL see Finckel

SNOWY CLOUDS ON A SUMMER DAY see Artman

SNOWY FEATHERS see Chinn, Teena

SNYDER
Celebrate!
SSAB CPP-BEL SV8622 $.95, accomp
tape available   (S505)

Christmas Alleluia, A
2pt cor CPP-BEL SV8524 $.95 (S506)
SAB CPP-BEL SV8523 $.95   (S507)

Ghostbusters
2pt cor CPP-BEL SV8483 $1.25 (S508)

Hold Your Head Up High
2pt cor CPP-BEL SV8530 $.95 (S509)
SAB CPP-BEL SV8529 $.95   (S510)

I Get Along Without You Very Well
SSATB CPP-BEL SV8447 $1.25   (S511)

I Want To Be Free
2pt treb cor CPP-BEL SV7906 $.95
(S512)

SNYDER (cont'd.)
It's The Holiday Time Of Year!
2pt cor CPP-BEL SV8718 $1.10,
accomp tape available   (S513)
3pt cor CPP-BEL SV8711 $1.10,
accomp tape available   (S514)

Just Beyond The Rainbow's End
2pt cor CPP-BEL SV8407 $.95 (S515)

Keep On Believing
SA CPP-BEL SV8326 $1.10   (S516)

Little Kindness, A
2pt cor,opt gtr CPP-BEL SV8551
$.95, accomp tape available
(S517)
Make Your Dreams Come True
2pt treb cor CPP-BEL SV8203 $.95
(S518)
Most Special Time Of The Year, The
2pt cor CPP-BEL SV8408 $.95 (S519)

On Top Of The World
2pt cor CPP-BEL SV8564 $.95, accomp
tape available   (S520)

One Little Candle
2pt cor CPP-BEL SV8748 $1.10,
accomp tape available   (S521)
Warmth And Light
2pt treb cor CPP-BEL SV8101 $.95
(S522)
What Can I Do
SATB CPP-BEL SV8522 $.95   (S523)

When We Sing Together
SATB CPP-BEL SV8519 $.95   (S524)

Wind, The °see Stevenson

Winds Of Change
SATB CPP-BEL SV8560 $.95, accomp
tape available   (S525)

Winter Cantabile °see Eccard

Winter Celebration
2pt cor CPP-BEL SV8609 $.95, accomp
tape available   (S526)
SSA CPP-BEL SV8610 $.95, accomp
tape available   (S527)

Winter Snowflakes
SA CPP-BEL SV8204 $.95   (S528)

Wintertime Aglow
SATB CPP-BEL SV7917 $.95   (S529)
SA CPP-BEL SV7905 $.95   (S530)

SNYDER, AUDREY
America, My Home °see Brown, Raymond

Audrey Snyder Collection, The °CCU
CPP-BEL SV8332 $5.00   (S531)

Friend Like You, A
3pt mix cor CPP-BEL SV8813 $.95,
accomp tape available   (S532)

SNYDER, MICHAEL
Sing Out For Freedom
3pt mix cor LEONARD-US 08603683
$.85   (S533)

SO BEN MI CH'A BON TEMPO see Vecchi,
Orazio (Horatio)

SO DA, MEIN LIEBES BRUDERLEIN see
Schein, Johann Hermann

SO FAR UNCHANGED see Wallin, Rolf

SO I LET HIM LEAD ME HOME see
Mulholland, James

SO LONG THROUGH THE NIGHT see Paull

SO SCHON WIE HEUT', SO MUSST' ES
BLEIBEN see Grothe

SO WAHR DIE SONNE SCHEINET see
Schumann, Robert (Alexander)

SOAR LIKE AN EAGLE see Althouse

SOBAJE, MARTHA
Christmas Lullaby
2pt cor CPP-BEL SV8104 $.95 (S534)

One Little Star
2pt treb cor,opt fl CPP-BEL SV8201
$1.10   (S535)

SOBOTENKA IDE
(Plojhar, F.) [Czech/Slovak] TTBB,Bar
solo HARMONIA 3708   (S536)

SOCIAL COMMENTARY see Russavage, Kathy

SODERLIND, RAGNAR (1945-   )
    Folkevise
        [Norw] mix cor,acap NORGE   (S537)

    Landskap Med Sne
        [Norw] mix cor,acap NORGE   (S538)

    Mort Des Pauvres, La *Op.15
        [Fr] men cor,perc,opt 4trom NORGE
                                       (S539)
    Nocturne
        [Norw] mix cor,acap NORGE   (S540)

    Se, Dagen Bryter Frem Med Magt
        [Norw] mix cor,acap NORGE   (S541)

    Varnatt *Op.28,No.1
        [Norw] mix cor,acap NORGE   (S542)

SODOI
    Temps Du Muguet, Le *see Lemarque,
        F.

SOFTEST THINGS IN THE WORLD, THE see
    Coyner, Lou

SOFTLY AS I LEAVE YOU
    (Simon) SATB CPP-BEL SV8346 $1.25
                                       (S543)
    (Simon) SSA CPP-BEL SV8347 $1.25
                                       (S544)
SOFTLY FALL THE SHADES OF EVENING see
    Roberton, Hugh Stevenson

SOFTLY, SOFTLY FELL THE SNOW see
    Anderson

SOIR APPROCHE, LE see Waelrant, Hubert

SOIR D'ETE see Depassel, L.

SOIR D'ETE see Lauber, Emile

SOIR EN MONTAGNE see Huber, F.

SOJO, VINCENTE E.
    Amanecer
        3pt mix cor A COEUR JOIE 1031
                                       (S545)
SOKOLOV, NIKOLAI ALEXANDROVICH
        (1859-1922)
    School Of Choral Singing, A: Vol. 2
        (composed with Popov, V.;
        Abelyan, L.) *CCU
        [Russ] jr cor MEZ KNIGA 482   (S546)

    Sur Les Hautes Cimes (Chant Du Soir)
        TTBB HUGUENIN EB 421   (S547)

SOL see Agnestig, Carl-Bertil

SOL OCH MANE
    (Lonna, Kjell) TTBB PROPRIUS 7950
        contains also: Namnsdagsvisa (S548)

SOLAR see Tate, Phyllis

SOLBERG, LEIF (1914-   )
    Naki Grein, Ei
        mix cor NORSK NMO 9549   (S549)

    Sigrid Slokjedalen
        TTBB NORSK   (S550)

SOLDATENKOOR UIT FAUST see Gounod,
    Charles Francois

SOLDIER, SOLDIER
    (Oxley, Harrison) SATB,acap ROBERTON
        $1.50 contains also: Billy Boy;
        Drummer, The   (S551)

SOLEIL DE JUIN see Lauber, Emile

SOLEIL MIRACULEUX- SONNENKRAFT see
    Mathey, Paul

SOLEILS COUCHANTS see Neumann, Veroslav

SOLFATARA see Zielinska, Lidia

SOLFEGGING see Gould, Morton

SOLFERINO, SOL, FA, RE, UT see Herr,
    Francoise

SOLID
    (Chinn) SATB CPP-BEL 6061SC1X $1.25,
        accomp tape available   (S552)
    (Chinn) SSA CPP-BEL 6061SC2X $1.25,
        accomp tape available   (S553)
    (Chinn) SAB CPP-BEL 6061SC3X $1.25,
        accomp tape available   (S554)

SOLID AS A ROCK see Fry

SOLITUDE see Telfer, Nancy

SOLOMON, ROBERT
    Leaving Mother Russian
        SATB,T solo,kbd TRANSCON. 991251
        $1.80   (S555)

SOLSONG FRA TINN see Kjeldaas, Arnljot

SOM BLOMSTEN see Alterhaug, Bjorn

SOMDALEN, BJORN
    Play Together 2
        cor,gtr,rec,Orff inst NORSK
        NMO 9330   (S556)

SOME ENCHANTED EVENING see Rodgers,
    Richard

SOME FOLKS see Foster, Stephen Collins

SOMEBODY SPECIAL see Poorman, Sonja

SOMEBODY'S CALLING MY NAME
    (Whalum, Wendall) TTBB LAWSON
        LG 51932 $.85   (S557)

SOMEBODY'S KNOCKIN' see Weiss-
    Steinberg, Hans

SOMEONE
    (Chinn) SATB CPP-BEL 6099SC1X $1.25,
        accomp tape available   (S558)
    (Chinn) SAB CPP-BEL 6099SC3X $1.25,
        accomp tape available   (S559)

SOMEONE see Harris, Louis

SOMEONE IN THE DARK (THEME FROM "E.T.
    THE EXTRA-TERRESTRIAL")
    (Snyder) 3pt cor CPP-BEL SV8646
        $1.25, accomp tape available   (S560)
    (Snyder) 2pt cor CPP-BEL SV8644
        $1.25, accomp tape available   (S561)
    (Snyder) SSA CPP-BEL SV8645 $1.25,
        accomp tape available   (S562)

SOMETHING IN YOUR EYES see Carpenter,
    Richard Lynn

SOMETHING SPECIAL see Besig, Don

SOMETIMES I FEEL LIKE A MOTHERLESS
    CHILD
    (Childs, Edwin T.) SATB, woodwind
        solo WOODL A050205 $.95   (S563)
    (Parks, James) SATB LEONARD-US
        08603701 $.85   (S564)

SOMMEIL
    see Quand La Marie

SOMMEIL, BERCEUSE
    (Nahoum, J.) 4 eq voices HEUGEL
        HE 32418   (S565)

SOMMER VERGEHT, DER see Burthel, Jakob

SOMMERDAGEN see Sveinsson, Atli Heimir

SOMMERFELDT, OISTEIN (1919-   )
    Fra Norsk Landskap (Suite No. 2)
        Op.64
        [Norw] mix cor,acap NORGE   (S566)

    Mari's Kulokk Og Bruremarsj
        [Norw] SATB,acap [4'] NORGE   (S567)

    Pyramiden
        jr cor NORSK   (S568)

    Suite No. 2 *see Fra Norsk Landskap

SOMMERFUGL see Brevik, Tor

SOMMERLICHES LIEBESLIED see Distler,
    Hugo

SOMMERMORGENLIED see Schallehn, Hilger

SOMMERS ABSCHIED
    mix cor BRAUN-PER 1078 see from Drei
        Volkslieder   (S569)

SOMMERTRALL see Hartmann, Christian

SON MET HIS FATHER, A see Sviridov,
    Georgy

SONETTO DI TASSO see Kleiberg, Stale

SONEVYTSKY, IHOR (1926-   )
    Love Ukraine
        [Ukranian] mix cor,SBar soli,pno
        DUMA $15.00   (S570)

SONG AND I ARE TRUE FRIENDS, THE: VOL.
    2 *CCU,Eng
    [Russ] jr cor,pno MEZ KNIGA 500
                                       (S571)
SONG AS A SOUVENIR *CCU
    [Russ] jr cor MEZ KNIGA 228   (S572)

SONG COLLECTION FOR YOUNG OCTOBERISTS
    *CCU
    [Russ] jr cor MEZ KNIGA 181   (S573)

SONG COLLECTION FOR YOUNG PIONEERS
    *CCU
    [Russ] jr cor MEZ KNIGA 182   (S574)

SONG FOR AMERICA see Halferty

SONG FOR CANADA see Tilley, Alexander

SONG FOR PARTING, A see Auld Lang Syne

SONG FOR TEXAS, A see Smith, Julia
    Frances

SONG FOR THE CHRISTMAS TREE see Grieg,
    Edvard Hagerup

SONG FROM MR. WILDE see Biggs, John

SONG FROM WAR see Lidl, Vaclav

SONG OF A THOUSAND VOICES see Fradkin,
    Leslie Martin, Neem Mijn Hand

SONG OF CHERUBUM see Penderecki,
    Krzysztof

SONG OF CORNWALL see Matthews, Michael

SONG OF DEGREES see Sheriff, Noam, Shir
    Hama'alot

SONG OF GENA, THE CROCODILE
    [Russ] jr cor MEZ KNIGA 501 see from
        Picture Songs, Vol. 5   (S575)

SONG OF MYSELF see Kistler

SONG OF NOEL, A see Madsen

SONG OF THANKSGIVING see Vaughan
    Williams, Ralph

SONG OF THE AZORES
    (Roff, Joseph) SSA,pno (med) THOMAS
        1C108007 $.90   (S576)

SONG OF THE AZORES see Roff, Joseph

SONG OF THE CALIFORNIA LOW COUNTRY see
    Thorne, Francis Burritt

SONG OF THE DEER (from Chippewa Melody)
    (Bray, Kenneth) SATB/SSA,acap HARRIS
        $.95   (S577)

SONG OF THE FATES see Brahms, Johannes,
    Gesang Der Parzen

SONG OF THE HIGHWAYMEN see Rimsky-
    Korsakov, Nikolai

SONG OF THE HOME, THE see Bachorek,
    Milan

SONG OF THE LITTLEST ANGEL see Artman

SONG OF THE UNIVERSAL see Danner

SONG PANORAMA, VOL. 5 *CCU
    [Russ] cor,gtr MEZ KNIGA 179   (S578)

SONG PATTERNS, VOL. 1 *CCU
    [Russ] jr cor,acap MEZ KNIGA 502
                                       (S579)
SONG PATTERNS, VOL. 2 *CCU
    [Russ] jr cor,acap MEZ KNIGA 533
                                       (S580)
SONG PATTERNS, VOL. 3 *CCU,folk song
    [Russ] jr cor MEZ KNIGA 230   (S581)

SONG TO A DOLL see Baksa, Robert Frank

SONG TO THE MOON see Dvorak, Antonin

SONGEN see Volle, Martin

SONGEN OM KJAERLIGHETA see Lystrup,
    Geirr

SONGS see Sirotkin, Y.

SONGS AND CHORUSES see Mozart, Wolfgang
    Amadeus

SONGS BY SOVIET COMPOSERS *CCU
    [Russ] cor,acap MEZ KNIGA 172   (S582)

SONGS FOR A CHILD see Weigl, [Mrs.]
    Vally

SONGS FOR CHILDREN see Chichkov, Y.

SONGS FOR THE SCHOOL YEAR see Tilley,
    Alexander

SONGS FOR TINY TOTS *CCU
    [Russ] jr cor MEZ KNIGA 180   (S583)

SONGS FOR URI see Zorman, Moshe

SONGS FROM AUSTRALIA *CC3U
    (Roff, Joseph) 2pt cor,pno,opt fl,opt
        perc (med) THOMAS 1C107807 $.90
                                       (S584)
SONGS FROM MATRASZENTIMRE see Ligeti,
    Gyorgy

SONGS FROM SOMERSET HILLS see Weigl,
    [Mrs.] Vally

SONGS FROM THE LAND BETWEEN RIVERS see Bottje, Will Gay

SONGS FROM THE SEA see Sallinen, Aulis

SONGS FROM "TING TANG THE ELEPHANT" see Coombes, Douglas

SONGS OF INNOCENCE see Wienhorst, Richard

SONGS OF NATURE see Dvorak, Antonin

SONGS OF OPHELIA see Brahms, Johannes

SONGS OF PAPUA NEW GUINEA
(Roff, Joseph) 1-2pt cor,pno THOMAS C10-8709 $.95
contains: Cockatoo, The; Father, Father; He Is Looking For Something; My Only Love; My Rooster   (S585)

SONGS OF SUNDRY NATURES see Byrd, William

SONGS OF THE ARTEK   °CCU
[Russ] jr cor,pno MEZ KNIGA 489   (S586)

SONGS OF THE PEOPLES OF THE USSR   °CCU
[Russ] cor,acap MEZ KNIGA 166   (S587)

SONGS OF THE SETTLERS see Crawley, Clifford

SONGS OF THE SETTLERS see Crawley, Clifford

SONGS OUT OF HOSHEN VALLEY see Orgad, Ben-Zion, Shirim Me'emek Hoshen

SONGS TO ENHANCE MOVEMENT VOCABULARY OF YOUNG CHILDREN see Palmer, Hap

SONGSTREAM see Parker, Alice

SONN' IST UNTERGANGEN, DIE see Poos, Heinrich

SONNEN-HYMNE see Mussorgsky, Modest Petrovich

SONNENGESANG see Rotas, Nikiforos

SONNENUNTERGANG see Genzmer, Harald

SONNET 11 BY SHAKESPEARE see Ehrlich, Abel

SONNET 60 BY SHAKESPEARE see Ehrlich, Abel

SONNET 129 BY SHAKESPEARE see Ehrlich, Abel

SONNET: O ENGEL DIE MET SCHOONHEID OVERTOGEN see Smeets, Leo

SONNTAG see Brahms, Johannes

SONNTAG IST HEUTE see Hollfelder, Waldram

SONNTAGSAUSFLUG see Killmayer, Wilhelm

SONNTAGSGEDANKEN see Killmayer, Wilhelm

SONNTAGSGESCHICHTEN see Killmayer, Wilhelm

SONNTAGSNACHMITTAGSKAFFEE see Killmayer, Wilhelm

SONSTEVOLD, GUNNAR (1912-   )
Forhandlinger I Et Magert Land
[Norw] SATB&jr cor,narrator,vln, vcl,perc,gtr,db,2pno [55'] NORGE   (S588)

Fredskjemperens Dod
[Norw] SATB,fl,2clar,sax,trp,trom, pno,db,perc NORGE   (S589)

SONSTEVOLD, MAJ (1917-   )
Kjaerlighetens Vei
[Norw] SMezATBarB,alto fl,harp NORGE   (S590)

Stillhet
SATB,fl,clar,pno,perc,vla,vcl NORGE   (S591)

Var-Von   °Op.6
men cor,T solo,pno NORGE   (S592)

SONTHONAY, F.
Fete Des Ours, La (composed with Mason)
unis jr cor,Orff inst HEUGEL HE 31979 contains also: Banuwa   (S593)

SORROW AND JOY   °folk song,Icelandic
(Vidar, Jorunn) mix cor ICELAND 015-9   (S594)

SORRY-CARDS FOR KEPT-IN PUPILS see Bachorek, Milan

SOSPAN FACH see Arch, Gwyn

SOULIERS, LES see Beart, Guy

SOUND AN ALARM see Handel, George Frideric

SOUND OF THE BELL, THE see Bergman, Erik

SOUND PATTERNS see Oliveros, Pauline

SOUND THE TRUMPET see Kirk, Theron Wilford

SOUND THE TRUMPET see Purcell, Henry

SOUNDS ARE see Tanenbaum, Elias

SOUNDS OF CHRISTMAS, THE see Pierpont, J.

SOURCE, LA see Djian, H.

SOURCE CLAIRE, UNE
(Reichel, B.) jr cor,Orff inst HEUGEL HE 31858 contains also: Danse De Locmine   (S595)

SOUS LES SAULES
(Landry, Fredy) TTBB,Bar solo HUGUENIN CH 1058-2   (S596)

SOUSA, JOHN PHILIP (1854-1932)
Stars And Stripes Forever, The
(Ermey, William) dbl cor,opt kbd oct DEAN HRD 143 $1.95   (S597)

SOUTH OF THE LINE see Joubert, John

SOUVENIR see Chatton, Pierre

SOUVENIRS DU TEMPS PASSE, LES see Bovet, Joseph

SOUVENT AMOUR see Pelletier, R. Octave

SOV, DU VESLE GUTEN MIN see Hartmann, Christian

SOVIET COMPOSERS FOR CHILDREN'S CHORUS, VOL. 4 °CCU
[Russ] jr cor,acap/pno MEZ KNIGA 242   (S598)

SOVIET COMPOSERS FOR CHILDREN'S CHORUSES, VOL. 2 °CCU
[Russ] jr cor MEZ KNIGA 513   (S599)

SOVIET COMPOSERS FOR CHILDREN'S CHORUSES, VOL. 3 °CCU
[Russ] jr cor MEZ KNIGA 545   (S600)

SOWASH
Bromfield Testament, The
SATB MUSIC SEV. M70-500 $.90 (S601)

Country Fair, The (Philosophical Anecdotes)
SATB,acap MUSIC SEV. M70-490 $.95   (S602)

Philosopher, The (Philosophical Anecdotes)
SATB,acap MUSIC SEV. M70-488 $.95   (S603)

Search, The (Philosophical Anecdotes)
SATB,acap MUSIC SEV. M70-489 $.90   (S604)

SOYONS JOYEUX SUR LA PLAISANT VERDURE see Lassus, Roland De (Orlandus)

SPACE BELLS: FIFTH SYMPHONY see Emmert, Frantisek

SPACE SHUTTLE, THE see Bailey

SPANIENREISE see Trapp, Willy

SPANISH CAROL, A see Knox

SPANISH SONG: VESAME Y ABRACAME
(Owen) SSA,acap,opt tamb CPP-BEL SV8703 $1.10   (S605)
(Owen) 3pt mix cor,acap,opt tamb CPP-BEL SV8704 $1.10   (S606)

SPANISH SONGS see Schumann, Robert (Alexander)

SPAT WAR ES SCHON ZU DER ABENDSTUND °Xmas,Span
(Deutschmann, Gerhard) 4-6pt cor BOHM   (S607)

SPATABENDS: BUSCH UND FALTER SCHLAFEN see Jessler, Fritz

SPEAK OUT YOUR WORDS, O LONELY ONE see Ovadia, Tuvia

SPEIGHT, JOHN A. (1945-   )
Shepherd's Carol, A
SATB,acap ICELAND 011-24 see from Two Choruses For Satb   (S608)

Two Choruses For Satb   °see Shepherd's Carol, A; Why?   (S609)

SPEIGHT, JOHN A. (cont'd.)

Why?
SATB,acap ICELAND 011-24 see from Two Choruses For Satb   (S610)

SPELL OF SLEEP see Bennett, Richard Rodney

SPELL OF TIME LONG PAST see Telfer, Nancy

SPENCER, WILLIAMETTA (1932-   )
Among The Apple Trees
SATB NATIONAL NMP-191 $.85   (S611)

As I Rode Out This Enders Night
SATB SCHIRM.G 229420 $.70   (S612)

As I Sat Under A Sycamore Tree
SATB SCHIRM.G 232800 $.70   (S613)

SPENDER
Teacher, Help Me
SSB&camb CAMBIATA ARS980154 $.75   (S614)

SPHARENKLANGE see Strauss, Josef

SPIEGELBILD, DAS see Kratochwil, Heinz

SPIELMANN UND DAS MADCHEN, DER see Backer, Hans

SPIERDIJK, J.
Eenzame Schaatser, De
(Linden, N.V.D.) SSA MOLENAAR 15024505   (S615)

SPIES, LEO (1899-1965)
Wind, Wind, Sause   °CCU
1-3pt jr cor,pno sc BREITKOPF-L 7943   (S616)

SPILLEMAEND see Hvoslef, Ketil

SPIN, EARTH see Armer, Elinor

SPIRIT OF CHRISTMAS, THE see Donnelly

SPIRITS see Stock, David Frederick

SPIRITUAL RHAPSODY see Yoder, Paul V.

SPOHR, LUDWIG (LOUIS) (1784-1859)
An Die Musik   °Op.97
mix cor,pno/org,opt brass BAREN. BA 6908   (S617)

Vierstimmige Lieder Fur Gemischten Chor   °CC8L
BAREN. BA 6385   (S618)

SPOTLIED see Jong, F. de

SPRANGER, JORG (1911-   )
Seufzer Lief Schlittschuh, Ein
4pt wom cor BOHM   (S619)

Winde Wehn, Schiffe Gehn
mix cor BOHM   (S620)

SPRICH, O HERZ see Miller, Franz R.

SPRING see Mathias, William

SPRING AND FALL see Sandler, F.

SPRING CAN REALLY HANG YOU UP THE MOST
(Chinn) SATB CPP-BEL SVJ8701 $1.25, accomp tape available   (S621)

SPRING CAROL, A see Diemer, Emma Lou

SPRING! COME, SPRING, AGAIN! see Rosewall, Richard B.

SPRING FEVER see Mitchell, Bob

SPRING LEADS DEATH TO LIFE see Licht, Myrtha B.

SPRING MOTIFS see Kvech, Otomar

SPRING NECKLACE see Slavicky, Milan

SPRING SONG see Filas, Juraj

SPRING SONGS THAT TICKLE YOUR FUNNY BONE! see Roberts, Ruth

SPRINGDANS FRA BERGEN I
(Rormark, Joar) mix cor MUSIKK MH 2434 see from Fire Slatter For Kor   (S622)

SPRINGDANS FRA BERGEN II
(Rormark, Joar) mix cor MUSIKK MH 2434 see from Fire Slatter For Kor   (S623)

SPRING'S COMING   °CCU
[Russ] jr cor,acap/pno MEZ KNIGA 237   (S624)

SPRING'S RETURN see Weigl, [Mrs.] Vally

SPRINGTIME see Paull

SPRINGTIME IN FUNEN see Nielsen, Carl, Fynsk Forar

SPRINGTIME IS RETURNING see Rollin

SPRINGTIME: MADRIGALVARIATIONEN see Seeger, Peter

SPRUCHE DES KONFUZIUS see Rammo, Peeter

SPRUNGER, DAVID
    Bright New Day Waiting For Me, A
        2pt cor,kbd GENTRY JG2054 $.85,
        accomp tape available   (S625)

    Come Away With Me
        cor ALFRED   (S626)

    Hello, My Brother
        SATB ALFRED 7667 $.95, accomp tape
            available   (S627)
        1-2pt cor ALFRED 7669 $.95, accomp
            tape available   (S628)
        SAB ALFRED 7668 $.95, accomp tape
            available   (S629)

    With One Voice
        SAB ALFRED 7619 $.95, accomp tape
            available   (S630)
        SATB ALFRED 7618 $.95, accomp tape
            available   (S631)

SPUCH see Schumann, Robert (Alexander)

STAINBROOK
    Oh Star
        SSA SHAWNEE 0539 $.95   (S632)

STAND UP AND SING see Davis

STANDCHEN
    (Brahms, Johannes) SSAA HARMONIA 3818
                                     (S633)

STANDCHEN see Brahms, Johannes

STANDCHEN see Melchers, Walter

STANDCHEN see Schubert, Franz (Peter)

STANDCHEN: SELIG DURCH DIE LIEBE see
    Schubert, Franz (Peter)

STANFORD, CHARLES VILLIERS (1852-1924)
    Hush Sweet Lute
        TTBB,acap ROBERTON 53035   (S634)

    Quick! We Have But A Second
        SATB,acap [45"] ROBERTON 63114
                                     (S635)
    Swallow, The
        SATB STAINER 3.3230 $.85   (S636)

STANLEY, JOHN
    For Whom Shall I Weep?
        SATB, pitch pipes NEW MUSIC NMA-121
        $.50   (S637)

STANZAS FOR LOVERS see Gaathaug, Morten

STANZAS FOR MUSIC see Miller

STAR SHONE DOWN, A see Perry

STAR SPANGLED BANNER see Smith, John
    Stafford

STAR SPANGLED BANNER, THE see Smith

STAR THOUGHTS see Burroughs, Bob Lloyd

STARDUST
    SSATB CPP-BEL 64414 f.s.   (S638)
    (Mattson, Phil) mix cor CPP-BEL
        SVJ8502 $26.00   (S639)

STAREN see Kjeldaas, Arnljot

STARLIGHT see Thomas

STARLIGHT NIGHT see Paynter, John P.

STARR, [PAUL] DOUGLAS (1952-   )
    Legend For Spring
        SA,kbd LAWSON 52450 $.90   (S640)

    Words For Kentucky
        SSA,acap LAWSON 52451 $1.00 (S641)

STARRY SKIES see Butler, Eugene Sanders

STARS see Pfautsch, Lloyd Alvin

STARS see Strommen, Carl

STARS AND STRIPES FOREVER, THE see
    Sousa, John Philip

STARS ARE WITH THE VOYAGER, THE see
    Kirk

STARS FELL ON ALABAMA see Perkins,
    Frank

STARS LOOK DOWN, THE see Franco, Johan

STARSONG see Carter

START A NEW LIFE see Huff, Mac

STATEMENT: 1976 see Fisher, Irwin

STAY, TIME, A WHILE THY PASSING see
    Dowland

STEARNS, PETER PINDAR (1931-   )
    Grand Is The Seen
        SATB [4'] (Whitman) AM.COMP.AL.
        $3.10   (S642)

STEEN
    Baker's Dozen, A °see Frazee, J.

STEFFY, THURLOW
    Reach Out (composed with Mallow,
        Monti)
        SAB CPP-BEL SV8319 $.95   (S643)

    You Can Be °see Mallow, Monti

STEHN ZWEI STERN see Trapp, Willy

STEIG, O STEIG HERAB see Schroeder,
    Hermann

STEIGE ZU MIR IN DEN NACHEN see
    Siegler, Winfried

STEIRISCHE MUNDARTLIEDER ZUR MESS see
    Koringer, Franz

STELE FUR BUCHNER see Engelmann, Hans
    Ulrich

STELLDICHEIN
    (Opienski, Henryk) TTBB HUGUENIN
        EB 27   (S644)

STELLT'S ENK Z'SAMM UND HIAZ SING MA
    OANS see Muthspiel, K.

STENKA RAZIN see Davies, Bryan

STENSAAS, JANET
    In Springtime
        SSA oct DEAN HRD 213 $.75   (S645)

STENZ, HERMAN
    Als Donkere Dagen Henengaan °see
        Lenteliedje

    Als Ik Bij Uw Wiegsken Sta °see
        Moederliedje

    Hoor, De Muzikanten.. Spelen In De
        Straat
        4 eq voices,acap ZENGERINK 90
                                     (S646)
        mix cor ZENGERINK 91   (S647)
        unis cor,pno ZENGERINK Z 609 (S648)
        [Dutch] 2 eq voices,acap ZENGERINK
        V 335   (S649)

    Huwelijkslied: Op Het Hoogfeest Van
        Uw Leven
        [Dutch] 3 eq voices,acap ZENGERINK
        V 334   (S650)

    Kop Op: 'T Leven Is Niet Altijd Licht
        SAT ZENGERINK 111   (S651)

    Laat Ons Samen Nu Gaan Zingen
        SAB ZENGERINK 336   (S652)

    Lenteliedje
        "Als Donkere Dagen Henengaan"
        [Dutch] unis cor,kbd ZENGERINK
        Z 610   (S653)

    Moederliedje
        "Als Ik Bij Uw Wiegsken Sta" unis
        cor,kbd ZENGERINK Z 612   (S654)

    Wandellied
        "Wandlen Langs De Wijde Wegen" unis
        cor,kbd ZENGERINK Z 608   (S655)

    Wandlen Langs De Wijde Wegen °see
        Wandellied

    Zingen Is Gezond: Laat Ons Samen Nu
        Gaan Zingen
        SAB ZENGERINK 336   (S656)

    Zingen Is Gezond: Nu Te Saam Een Lied
        Gezongen
        unis cor,kbd ZENGERINK Z 611 (S657)

STEP TO THE REAR see Bernstein, Elmer

STEPHEN FOSTER- IMMORTAL MELODIES see
    Foster, Stephen Collins

STEPHEN FOSTER SET, A see Weinhorst,
    Richard

STEPHEN FOSTER SET, A see Wienhorst,
    Richard

STEPHENS, MICHELE
    Just Make Music!
        SSA DVM 1588-3 f.s., accomp tape
            available   (S658)
        SAB DVM 1588-2 f.s., accomp tape
            available   (S659)
        SA DVM 1588-4 f.s., accomp tape
            available   (S660)

    Love Is The Key
        SSA DVM 1688-3 f.s., accomp tape
            available   (S661)
        SAB DVM 1688-2 f.s., accomp tape
            available   (S662)
        SA DVM 1688-4 f.s., accomp tape
            available   (S663)

    Our Christmas Dream
        SATB DVM 1088-1 f.s., accomp tape
            available   (S664)
        SSA DVM 1088-3 f.s., accomp tape
            available   (S665)
        SAB DVM 1088-2 f.s., accomp tape
            available   (S666)
        SA DVM 1088-4 f.s., accomp tape
            available   (S667)

    Will I See You Again?
        SSA DVM 1488-3 f.s., accomp tape
            available   (S668)
        SATB DVM 1488-1 f.s., accomp tape
            available   (S669)
        SAB DVM 1488-2 f.s., accomp tape
            available   (S670)

STEPPE, ALLEEN MAAR STEPPE! see Bos-
    Maurer, A. Van De

STEPPIN' OUT ON BROADWAY
    (Althouse, Jay) SATB (contains Give
        My Regards To Broadway, Hey! Look
        Me Over, Step To The Rear, and If
        My Friends Could See Me Now) CPP-
        BEL CO145C1X $2.50, accomp tape
        available   (S671)
    (Althouse, Jay) SAB (contains Give My
        Regards To Broadway, Hey! Look Me
        Over, Step To The Rear, and If My
        Friends Could See Me Now) CPP-BEL
        CO145C3X $2.50   (S672)
    (Althouse, Jay) 2pt cor (contains
        Give My Regards To Broadway, Hey!
        Look Me Over, Step To The Rear, and
        If My Friends Could See Me Now)
        CPP-BEL CO145C5X $2.50   (S673)

STEPPING OUT TOGETHER see Ross, Brad

STEPTOE, ROGER
    In Winter's Cold Embraces Dye
        SATB,MezT soli,orch STAINER B671
                                     (S674)
    Sweet Neglect
        SATB,acap STAINER W130   (S675)

    Winter
        SATB,acap STAINER W131   (S676)

STERNLEIN, DAS see Reger, Max

STERRENHEMEL see Stoop, Henk

STEUERLEIN, JOHANN (1546-1613)
    Mit Lieb Bin Ich Umfangen
        see MADRIGALE FUR GEMISCHTEN CHOR A
        CAPPELLA: BLATT VI

STEUERMANN, EDWARD (1892-1964)
    Auf Des Galeries
        SATB,orch sc APNM rent, perf mat
        rent   (S677)

    Three Choruses With Instruments
        SATB,1.1.1.1. 1.0.1.0. pno,harp,
        perc,vcl,db [10'0"] sc APNM
        $4.75, perf mat rent   (S678)

STEUERMANN, LASS DIE WACHT! see Wagner,
    Richard

STEVENS, RAY
    Streak, The: A Medley Of Ray Stevens'
        Hits
        (Gilpin, Greg) SATB CPP-BEL
        CO139C1X $2.25, accomp tape
        available   (S679)
        (Gilpin, Greg) SAB CPP-BEL CO139C3X
        $2.25, accomp tape available (S680)
        (Gilpin, Greg) 2pt cor CPP-BEL
        CO139C5X $2.25, accomp tape
        available   (S681)

STEVENSON
    Wind, The (composed with Snyder)
        SAB CPP-BEL SV8323 $1.10   (S682)

STEWART, ROBERT
    Four Songs °CCU
        SATB AM.COMP.AL. $9.95 text by
        Joyce   (S683)

STILL O HIMMEL
    cor HIEBER MH 5022   (S684)

STILL REMEMBERING NAMES see Harlap,
    Ah'aron

STILL WILL BE see Weigl, [Mrs.] Vally

STILLE see Lyssand, Henrik

STILLHET see Sonstevold, Maj

STILMAN
    America, Which Way Are You Going?
    TTB SOUTHERN $.90   (S685)

STIMMEN DER VOLKER see Kunad, Rainer

STIMMEN FUR DEN FRIEDEN see Hamel,
    Peter Michael

STIMMT AN DEN LOBGESANG see
    Gunsenheimer, Gustav

STINE
    Doorway, The
    SSA CPP-BEL SV8314 $.95   (S686)

STJENKA RASIN see Wolff, H. de

STOCK, DAVID FREDERICK (1939-   )
    Spirits
    SATB,vibra,elec pno,harp,opt perc
    [5'] AM.COMP.AL. $5.40   (S687)

STOCKHAUSEN, KARLHEINZ (1928-   )
    Befruchtung Mit Klavierstuck
    girl cor,pno,orch STOCKHAUS
    57 TWO THIRDS   (S688)

    Botschaft (from Evas Zauber)
    cor,basset horn,alto fl,opt orch
    STOCKHAUS 58 ONE HALF   (S689)

    Evas Erstgeburt (from Montag Aus
    Licht)
    cor&jr cor,SSSTTB soli,orch, actor
    STOCKHAUS 56   (S690)

    Evas Zauber (from Montag Aus Licht)
    cor&jr cor,basset horn,alto fl,pic,
    orch STOCKHAUS 58   (S691)

    Evas Zweitgeburt (from Montag Aus
    Licht)
    cor&girl cor,7 boy soli,basset
    horn,pno,orch STOCKHAUS   (S692)

    Kinderfanger, Der (from Evas Zauber)
    jr cor,alto fl,pic,orch,opt basset
    horn STOCKHAUS 58 TWO THIRDS
                              (S693)
    Madchenprozession
    girl cor&cor,orch STOCKHAUS
    57 ONE HALF   (S694)

    Montags-Abschied (Eva-Abschied)
    jr cor,pic,orch/elec org STOCKHAUS
                              (S695)

STODOLA PUMPA *Czech
    (Roff, Joseph) 2pt cor,pno (med easy)
    THOMAS 1C108408 $.80   (S696)

STOLZ, ROBERT (1880-1975)
    Abend Bei Robert Stolz, Ein
    men cor/mix cor,pno pno-cond sc,cor
    pts LEUCKART f.s.   (S697)

    Adieu, Mein Kleiner Gardeoffizier
    (Waldenmaier) mix cor,acord/gtr
    LEUCKART LSB 502   (S698)

    Auf Der Heide Bluhn Die Letzten Rosen
    (Waldenmaier) mix cor,gtr LEUCKART
    LSB 504   (S699)
    (Waldenmaier) men cor LEUCKART
    LSB 104 f.s.   (S700)

    Es Lebe Die Liebe
    (Waldenmaier) men cor,opt gtr
    LEUCKART LSB 106 f.s.   (S701)
    (Waldenmaier) mix cor,acord
    LEUCKART LSB 506   (S702)

    Ganze Welt Ist Himmelblau, Die
    (Grieshaber) mix cor,pno LEUCKART
    LSB 505   (S703)
    (Grieshaber) men cor,pno LEUCKART
    LSB 105 f.s.   (S704)

    Ich Sing' Mein Lied Heut' Nur Fur
    Dich!
    (Waldenmaier) mix cor LEUCKART
    LSB 513   (S705)

    Im Prater Bluh'n Wieder Die Baume
    (Waldenmaier) men cor,pno LEUCKART
    LSB 103 f.s.   (S706)
    (Waldenmaier) mix cor,pno LEUCKART
    LSB 503   (S707)

    Jung San Ma! Fesch San Ma!
    (Waldenmaier) men cor,pno,db
    LEUCKART LSB 108 f.s.   (S708)

    Leutnant Warst Du Einst Bei Den
    Husaren
    (Grieshaber) mix cor,opt pno
    LEUCKART LSB 508   (S709)

STOLZ, ROBERT (cont'd.)
    Mein Herz Ruft Immer Nur Nach Dir, O
    Marita!
    (Waldenmaier) men cor LEUCKART
    LSB 109 f.s.   (S710)

    Mein Liebeslied Muss Ein Walzer Sein
    (Waldenmaier) mix cor,pno LEUCKART
    LSB 512   (S711)

    Mein Schones Holland *see Mijn
    Dierbaar Holland

    Mijn Dierbaar Holland
    "Mein Schones Holland" SATB,pno
    HARMONIA HU 3804   (S712)

    Ob Blond, Ob Braun, Ich Liebe Alle
    Frau'n
    (Waldenmaier) men cor,pno,opt gtr
    LEUCKART LSB 102 f.s.   (S713)

    Salome
    (Waldenmaier) men cor,pno,opt gtr
    LEUCKART LSB 107 f.s.   (S714)

    Singend, Klingend Ruft Dich Das Gluck
    (Grieshaber) mix cor,pno LEUCKART
    LSB 510   (S715)
    (Grieshaber) men cor,pno LEUCKART
    LSB 110 f.s.   (S716)

    Traume Unterm Christbaum
    men cor,opt pno LEUCKART NWL 102
    f.s.   (S717)
    mix cor,opt pno LEUCKART NWL 502
    f.s.   (S718)

    Von Rudesheim Bis Heidelberg
    (Grieshaber) men cor,opt pno
    LEUCKART LSB 112 f.s.   (S719)

    Wanderlied (Ein Bischen Singsang)
    (Grieshaber) men cor,opt pno
    LEUCKART LSB 111 f.s.   (S720)

    Wanderlied (Ein Bisschen Singsang)
    (Grieshaber) mix cor,opt pno
    LEUCKART LSB 511   (S721)

    Wenn Die Kleinen Veilchen Bluhen...
    (Waldenmaier) mix cor,opt gtr
    LEUCKART LSB 509   (S722)

    Zwei Herzen Im Dreivierteltakt
    (Waldenmaier) mix cor,pno LEUCKART
    LSB 507   (S723)

STOMP, HENK JOHAN
    Wandellied: Wij Trekken Onder 'T Loof
    SSA/TTB ZENGERINK 353   (S724)

STOMPIN' AT THE SAVOY see Goodman,
    Benny (Benjamin David)

STONE, THE see Ragnarsson, Hjalmar H.

STONE PRAYER see Kopelent, Marek

STOOP, HENK (1943-   )
    Sterrenhemel
    TTBB,2.2.2.2. 2.2.2.1. timp,3perc,
    harp,strings [13'] DONEMUS (S725)

STOPPING BY THE WOODS
    (Quaranto) SATB CPP-BEL SV8616 $1.25,
    accomp tape available   (S726)

STOPPING BY WOODS see Manners

STORBEKKEN, EGIL
    Fjelltrallen Og To Andre Sanger
    mix cor,pno NORSK NMO 9500B (S727)

STORCH VON STORKOW, DER see Glockner,
    Gottfried

STORM 'N BLOW
    (Jeffers) TB EARTHSNG EM-8 $.50
                              (S728)

STORY OF GAROO, THE see Aldema, Gil

STORY OF MARY O'NEILL, THE see LeFanu,
    Nicola

STRAESSER, JOEP (1934-   )
    Motetus
    6pt mix cor [11'] DONEMUS (S729)

    Uber Erich M
    SSSSSSSSAAAAAAAATTTTTTBBBBB,T solo,
    2.1.2.1. 2.1.1.0. 2perc,pno,
    strings [10'] DONEMUS   (S730)

    Verzauberte Lieder
    cor,2.2.2.2. 2.2.1.1. perc,pno,
    strings [16'] DONEMUS   (S731)

STRATEGIER, HERMAN (1912-1988)
    Aulo Novis Gaudet
    4pt mix cor,1.1.1.1. 1.0.0.0. perc,
    strings [15'] DONEMUS   (S732)

STRATEGIER, HERMAN (cont'd.)
    Nachtegaal In Echternach, Een
    see Viva La Musica

    O Lied
    see Viva La Musica

    Op Een Kat
    see Viva La Musica

    Op Een Zangkraai
    see Viva La Musica

    Sinte Caecilia
    see Viva La Musica

    Viva La Musica
    HARMONIA HU 3712 f.s.
    contains: Nachtegaal In
    Echternach, Een (TTBB,pno); O
    Lied (SATB,pno); Op Een Kat (jr
    cor,pno); Op Een Zangkraai (jr
    cor,pno); Sinte Caecilia (SSAA,
    pno); Viva La Musica (jr cor&
    SSAA&TTBB&SATB,pno)   (S733)

    Viva La Musica
    see Viva La Musica

STRATING, S.
    Koorfantasie
    SATB MOLENAAR 15006103   (S734)

STRAUSS, JOHANN
    Zepperl-Polka *Op.202
    wom cor&jr cor DOBLINGER 65 922
                              (S735)
STRAUSS, JOHANN, [SR.] (1804-1849)
    Radetzky-Marsch
    (Hlinak, K.) cor,pno cor pts,voc sc
    DOBLINGER 46 826   (S736)

STRAUSS, JOHANN, [JR.] (1825-1899)
    Fledermaus-Walzer
    (Huber, F.) cor,pno cor pts,voc sc
    DOBLINGER 46 831   (S737)

    Kaiser-Walzer
    (Scholtys) cor,pno cor pts,voc sc
    DOBLINGER 46 828   (S738)

    Sangerlust-Polka
    (Korda, V.) cor,pno cor pts,voc sc
    DOBLINGER 46 835   (S739)

    Schatz-Walzer (from Der
    Zigeunerbaron)
    (Huber, F.) cor,pno DOBLINGER
    46 832   (S740)

    Wein, Weib Und Gesang
    (Schemitsch, H.) cor,pno cor pts,
    voc sc DOBLINGER 46 829   (S741)

STRAUSS, JOSEF (1827-1870)
    Spharenklange
    (Lehner, L.) cor,pno cor pts,voc sc
    DOBLINGER 46 830   (S742)

STRAUSS, RICHARD (1864-1949)
    Altdeutsches Schlachtlied *Op.42,
    No.2
    (Herder, G. V.) men cor,acap
    LEUCKART   (S743)

    Hut Du Dich
    men cor,acap LEUCKART   (S744)

    Liebe *Op.42,No.1
    (Herder, G. V.) men cor,acap
    LEUCKART   (S745)

    Schwabische Erbschaft
    (Loewe, F.) men cor,acap LEUCKART
                              (S746)
    Tummel Dich, Guts Weinlein
    men cor,acap LEUCKART   (S747)

STRAUSS-KONIG, RICHARD (1930-   )
    Ach Blumlein Blau
    men cor BOHM   (S748)

    Erntelied: Es Steht Ein Goldnes
    Garbenfeld
    mix cor BOHM   (S749)

    Gaudeamus: Bruder, Lasst Uns Lustig
    Sein
    men cor BOHM   (S750)

STRAVINSKY, IGOR (1882-1971)
    Noces, Les
    [Ger/Eng] SATB,SMezATB soli,orch
    voc sc KALMUS K 06452 $17.25
                              (S751)
    [Fr/Russ] SSAATTBB cor pts KALMUS
    K 06453 $4.75   (S752)

    Renard
    [Fr/Russ] TTBB KALMUS K 06469 $5.75
                              (S753)
    Roi Des Etoiles, Le
    (McAlister) men cor,2+pic.4(English
    horn).3.3(contrabsn). 4.8.3.1.
    timp,cel,2harp,strings [5']

STRAVINSKY, IGOR (cont'd.)

    KALMUS voc sc $3.00, sc $6.00,
      pts $18.00   (S754)

STRAWBERRY FAIR see Brown, Christopher
  (Roland)

STREAK, THE: A MEDLEY OF RAY STEVENS'
  HITS see Stevens, Ray

STREAMLET, THE see Schubert, Franz
  (Peter), Wohin?

STRECKE, GERHARD (1890-1968)
  Bin I Net A Purschle °see Obendrauf,
    Der

  Fein Sein, Beinander Bleiben
    mix cor BOHM   (S755)

  Obendrauf, Der
    "Bin I Net A Purschle" mix cor BOHM
                   (S756)

STRID
  Be Life A Butterfly
    SSA SHAWNEE 0519 $.85   (S757)

  Oh, Susanna! Oh Eliza!
    2pt cor SHAWNEE 0074 $.85 (S758)

STRIKE IT UP, TABOR see Weelkes, Thomas

STRIMER
  Chanteries Du Jeune Age, Les
    unis cor JOBERT   (S759)

STROM
  Under The Stars
    (Krumnach) SAB KJOS C8815 $.80
                   (S760)

STROMAN, SCOTT
  Gentle Rain
    SATB,acap STAINER W167   (S761)

STROMHOLM, FOLKE (1941-)
  Tre Sanger For Mannskor °Op.22, CC3U
    [Norw] men cor,acap NORGE (S762)

STROMMEN, CARL
  Another Bridge To Cross
    SSA ALFRED 7511 $.95, accomp tape
      available   (S763)
    SAB ALFRED 7510 $.95, accomp tape
      available   (S764)
    SATB ALFRED 7509 $.95, accomp tape
      available   (S765)

  Christmas Memories
    cor ALFRED   (S766)

  Here I Am
    SSA ALFRED 7453 f.s., accomp tape
      available   (S767)
    SAB ALFRED 7452 f.s., accomp tape
      available   (S768)
    SATB ALFRED 7451 f.s., accomp tape
      available   (S769)

  High Road Home
    cor ALFRED   (S770)

  I Am A Rock
    cor ALFRED   (S771)

  Just For Today
    cor ALFRED   (S772)

  Light A Candle
    SAB ALFRED 7693 $.95, accomp tape
      available   (S773)
    SATB ALFRED 7656 $.95, accomp tape
      available   (S774)

  Merry Christmas, Once Again
    ALFRED   (S775)

  My Shining Hour
    ALFRED   (S776)

  New Age Dawning
    SSA ALFRED 7364 f.s., accomp tape
      available   (S777)
    SAB ALFRED 7365 $.95, accomp tape
      available   (S778)
    SATB ALFRED 7366 $.95, accomp tape
      available   (S779)

  Old Fashioned Christmas °Xmas
    SAB ALFRED 7455 f.s., accomp tape
      available   (S780)
    SATB ALFRED 7454 f.s., accomp tape
      available   (S781)
    SSA ALFRED 7456 f.s., accomp tape
      available   (S782)

  One More Song
    SSA ALFRED 7514 $.95, accomp tape
      available   (S783)
    SAB ALFRED 7513 $.95, accomp tape
      available   (S784)
    SATB ALFRED 7512 $.95, accomp tape
      available   (S785)

STROMMEN, CARL (cont'd.)
  Peace Be To This House
    ALFRED   (S786)

  Ride The Wind
    ALFRED   (S787)

  Ring Out The Old, Ring In The New
    SATB ALFRED 7635 $.95   (S788)

  Shine On America
    unis cor/2pt cor ALFRED 7601 $.95,
      accomp tape available   (S789)
    SAB ALFRED 7600 $.95, accomp tape
      available   (S790)
    SATB ALFRED 7599 $.95, accomp tape
      available   (S791)

  Simple Gifts
    ALFRED   (S792)

  Stars
    SAB ALFRED 7596 $.95   (S793)
    SATB ALFRED 7595 $.95   (S794)
    SSA ALFRED 7598 $.95   (S795)

  Thank You For Your Kindness
    ALFRED   (S796)

  This House
    SATB ALFRED 7457 f.s., accomp tape
      available   (S797)
    SAB ALFRED 7458 f.s., accomp tape
      available   (S798)
    SSA ALFRED 7459 f.s., accomp tape
      available   (S799)

  Together We Stand
    SATB ALFRED 7460 f.s., accomp tape
      available   (S800)
    SAB ALFRED 7461 f.s., accomp tape
      available   (S801)
    SSA ALFRED 7462 f.s., accomp tape
      available   (S802)

STROUSE, CHARLES LOUIS (1928-)
  Applause
    (Huff) SAB CPP-BEL 5025AC3X $1.25,
      accomp tape available   (S803)

  Applause, Applause (Medley Of
    Broadway Rhythm- Applause)
    (Huff) SATB CPP-BEL C0107C1X $2.25,
      accomp tape available   (S804)

STRUIJK, P.
  Waltzing Matilda
    TTBB MOLENAAR 13016603   (S805)

STRUM
  What! No Women? °see Meskill

STURM, DER see Haydn, [Franz] Joseph

SU, SU, SU, PASTORELLI VEZZOSI see
  Monteverdi, Claudio

SUB OLEA PACIS ET PALMA VIRTUTIS see
  Zelenka, Jan Dismas

SUBEN, JOEL ERIC (1946-)
  Birthday Fragment
    SATB,AT soli,pno [2'0"] sc APNM
      $3.50, perf mat rent   (S806)

SUC, P.
  Gargouille, La
    (Grindel, J.) 4pt mix cor HEUGEL
      HE 31922   (S807)

SUDDENLY
  (Chinn) SAB CPP-BEL 6860SC3X $1.25,
    accomp tape available   (S808)
  (Chinn) SATB CPP-BEL 6860SC1X $1.25,
    accomp tape available   (S809)
  (Chinn) SSA CPP-BEL 6860SC2X $1.25,
    accomp tape available   (S810)

SUE see Adler, Samuel Hans

SUITE DE BOURREES EN RONDO: AUVERGNE
  (Filleul, Jacques) SATB A COEUR JOIE
  285   (S811)

SUITE DE LORCA see Rautavaara,
  Einojuhani

SUITE DE RIGAUDONS EN RONDO: DAUPHINE
  (Filleul, Jacques) SATB A COEUR JOIE
  284   (S812)

SULEJ, MICHAL (1928-)
  My Vistula River, A Little Quail Flew
    Away °see Wislo Moja, Uciekla Mi
    Przepioreczka

  Wislo Moja, Uciekla Mi Przepioreczka
    "My Vistula River, A Little Quail
    Flew Away" [Polish] 3pt jr cor
    POLSKIE NPCH 64   (S813)

SULLA BARCHETTA-DANS MON BATEAU see
  Barblan, Emmanuel

SULLIVAN
  Ah, Leave Me Not To Pine (composed
    with Wilson)
    SATB oct DEAN HRD 197 $.75 (S814)

SULLIVAN, [SIR] ARTHUR SEYMOUR
  (1842-1900)
  Long Day Closes, The
    TTBB,acap [3'] ROBERTON 53127
                   (S815)

SULLIVAN SONGS see Carl, Robert

SUMARNATTA see Tveitt, Geirr

SUMMER see Mathias, William

SUMMER see Paull

SUMMER DAY see Slavicky, Klement

SUMMER FIELDS, THE see Hamilton, Iain

SUMMER FIELDS, THE see Hamilton, Iain

SUMMER HAPPINESS see Hamilton, Iain

SUMMER NIGHT see Forbes, Sebastian

SUMMER VACATION see Braun, Yeheskiel,
  Hahofesh Hagadol

SUMMER'S GOOD FEELIN' see Williams,
  Julius A.

SUMMERTIME BLUES see Cooper, Steve

SUN IS SHINING, THE see Blevins, Patsy
  Ford

SUN ON THE CELADINES, THE see Walker,
  Robert

SUN-WARMED BALK see Hurnik, Ilja

SUNDAY'S CHILD (NURSERY RHYMES, NO.2)
  see Walters, Edmund

SUNDIN, NILS GORAN (1951-)
  Hanryckning
    mix cor STIM   (S816)

SUNNY DAY see McPheeters

SUNNY LAND see Emmert, Frantisek

SUNNY SONGS °CCU
  [Russ] jr cor,pno MEZ KNIGA 234
                   (S817)

SUNRISE, SUNSET see Bock, Jerry

SUNSHINE IN MY SOUL
  (Jackson, Gregory) SATB JACKMAN
    JMC7078   (S818)

SUNSHINE MEDLEY:, A °medley
  (Billingsley, Alan) SATB CPP-BEL
    C0137C1X $2.25, accomp tape
    available   (S819)
  (Billingsley, Alan) SSA CPP-BEL
    C0137C2X $2.25, accomp tape
    available   (S820)
  (Billingsley, Alan) SAB CPP-BEL
    C0137C3X $2.25, accomp tape
    available   (S821)
  (Billingsley, Alan) 2pt cor CPP-BEL
    C0137C5X f.s.   (S822)

SUPERTOAD see Lawson, Peter

SUPPE, FRANZ VON (1819-1895)
  Landliche Konzertprobe, Die (composed
    with Trapp, Willy)
    mix cor BRAUN-PER 1061   (S823)

SUR LA ROUTE DU MOULIN see Bigot,
  Pierre

SUR LA TOMBE D'UNE SAUTERELLE see
  Apotheloz, Jean

SUR L'ALPE see Lauber, Emile

SUR L'ALPE see Lauber, Joseph

SUR L'BORD DE LOIRE
  (Delsarte, Andre) SAB A COEUR JOIE
  1021   (S824)

SUR LE CALVAIRE see Huguenin, Charles

SUR LES HAUTES CIMES (CHANT DU SOIR)
  see Sokolov, Nikolai Alexandrovich

SUR L'HERBE see Ronfort, Jean-
  Christophe

SUR TOUS REGRETS see Gero, Ihan

SURREN LAULELEN see Palmgren, Selim

SURSUM CORDA see Pinos, Alois

SUSANNA see Handel, George Frideric

SUSATO, TIELMAN (? -ca. 1561)
Premier Livre Des Chansons, Le: Vol.1
*CC15U
(Agnel, A.) 2-3pt cor HEUGEL
HE 32053   (S825)

Premier Livre Des Chansons, Le: Vol.2
*CC15U
(Agnel, A. N He 32127) HEUGEL
(S826)

SUTERMEISTER, HEINRICH (1910-   )
Ode Aupres De Roseaux
men cor,acap SCHOTTS C 46375 (S827)

SVANSTANKAR see Werle, Lars-Johan

SVARTERABBEN see Arnestad, Finn

SVEIN SVANE
(Eielsen, Steinar) SATB MUSIKK
MH 2466 see from Tre Folkeviser Fra
Rogaland   (S828)

SVEINSSON, ATLI HEIMIR (1938-   )
Autumn Pictures
mix cor,2vln,vla,acord ICELAND
002-51   (S829)

Death, Be Not Proud
mix cor ICELAND 002-43 see from Two
Choir Pieces (In Memoriam Of
Benjamin Britten)   (S830)

Dried Flower
dbl cor,acap ICELAND 002-41 (S831)

Japanese Poems
mix cor,gtr ICELAND 002-50   (S832)

Sick Rose, The
mix cor ICELAND 002-43 see from Two
Choir Pieces (In Memoriam Of
Benjamin Britten)   (S833)

Sommerdagen
dbl cor, solo voices ICELAND 002-61
(S834)

Two Choir Pieces (In Memoriam Of
Benjamin Britten) *see Death, Be
Not Proud; Sick Rose, The   (S835)

Useless Days
mix cor,acap ICELAND 002-42 (S836)

SVERRE-LUREN see Kjeldaas, Arnljot

SVIRIDOV, GEORGY (1915-   )
Choral Works, Vol. 1 *CCU
[Russ] cor,acap/instrumental
ensemble MEZ KNIGA 165   (S837)

Choral Works, Vol. 2 *CCUL
[Russ] cor,acap/instrumental
ensemble MEZ KNIGA 179   (S838)

Czar Fedor Ivanovitch *see Holy
Love; Prayer Full; Repentance
(S839)
Holy Love
SATB SCHIRM.G 321360 $.70 see from
Czar Fedor Ivanovitch   (S840)

How A Song Was Born
SATB SCHIRM.G 321830 $.75 see from
Three Choruses On Poems Of
Russian Poets   (S841)

Of My Lost Childhood
SATB SCHIRM.G 321810 $.70 see from
Three Choruses On Poems Of
Russian Poets   (S842)

Poem In Memory Of Sergei Yesenin
[Russ] mix cor,T solo,orch voc sc
MEZ KNIGA 474   (S843)

Prayer Full
SATB SCHIRM.G 321350 $.75 see from
Czar Fedor Ivanovitch   (S844)

Repentance
SATB SCHIRM.G 321370 $.70 see from
Czar Fedor Ivanovitch   (S845)

Son Met His Father, A
SATB SCHIRM.G 321820 $.70 see from
Three Choruses On Poems Of
Russian Poets   (S846)

Three Choruses On Poems Of Russian
Poets *see How A Song Was Born;
Of My Lost Childhood; Son Met His
Father, A   (S847)

S'VIVON see Barnett, Steve

SVOGAVA CON LE STELLE see Monteverdi,
Claudio

SWALLOW, THE see Stanford, Charles
Villiers

SWANEE RIVER see Foster, Stephen
Collins

SWANS see Wright, Maurice

SWEARS
Hanukkah's Child
2pt cor SHAWNEE 0110 $.95   (S848)

Let Those Merry Bells Ring!
2pt cor SHAWNEE 0115 $1.25   (S849)

SWEARS, LINDA
Calypso Melody
2pt cor CPP-BEL SV8521 $.95, accomp
tape available   (S850)

SWEELINCK, JAN PIETERSZOON (1562-1621)
Vocal Secular Works *CCU
(Verhoeven-Kooij, A.J.)
VER.NED.MUS. SWE 7   (S851)

SWEET BETSY FROM PIKE *folk song,US
(De Cormier, Robert) SATB LAWSON
LG 52133 $.85   (S852)
(Haugland, Oscar) SATB HOA $1.00
(S853)

SWEET DREAMS
(Lapin) SATB CPP-BEL 7476SC1X $1.25
(S854)

SWEET FREEDOM
(Hanson) SATB CPP-BEL 7530SC1X $1.25,
accomp tape available   (S855)
(Hanson) SSA CPP-BEL 7530SC2X $1.25,
accomp tape available   (S856)
(Hanson) SAB CPP-BEL 7530SC3X $1.25,
accomp tape available   (S857)

SWEET HOME
(Whalum, Wendall) mix cor LAWSON
LG 51869 $.75   (S858)

SWEET LASS OF RICHMOND HILL
(Walters) TTBB,pno [1'30"] ROBERTON
392-00541 $1.25   (S859)

SWEET NEGLECT see Steptoe, Roger

SWEET POWER OF SONG see Beethoven,
Ludwig van

SWEET SHEPHERDESS, ADDIO see Giordano,
Umberto

SWEET SUFFOLK OWL see Edwards

SWIDER, JOZEF (1930-   )
Grande Valse Chorale; Marche *see
Wielki Walc Choralny; Marsz

Quattro Pezzi *CC4U
mix cor POLSKIE   (S860)

Rhymes *see Rymowanki

Rymowanki
"Rhymes" [Polish] jr cor,acap
POLSKIE NPCH 68   (S861)

Samogloski
"Vocali, Le" wom cor POLSKIE (S862)

Vocali, Le *see Samogloski

Wielki Walc Choralny; Marsz
"Grande Valse Chorale; Marche" mix
cor POLSKIE   (S863)

SWIETLICKI
I'm In Favor Of Friendship *see
Hilliard

School
2pt cor BOURNE B240440 $.65 (S864)

SWIM, SAM see Goemanne

SWING, THE see Gallina, Jill C.

SWING LOW
(Penders, J.) SATB MOLENAAR 13033806
(S865)
SWINGIN' see Davidson, Charles Stuart

SWITEZIANKA see Rimsky-Korsakov,
Nikolai

SYLLABES MOUVEMENTEES see Kopelent,
Marek

SYLLABLES ON THE MOVE see Kopelent,
Marek, Syllabes Mouvementees

SYLVESTRE, ANNE
Cathedrales, Les
(Frochot, J.) 4pt mix cor HEUGEL
HE 32191   (S866)

Gregoire Ou Sebastien
(Frochot, J.) 4pt mix cor HEUGEL
HE 32334   (S867)

Il S'appelait Richard
(Passaquet, R.) 3 eq voices HEUGEL
HE 32198   (S868)

Je Pense A Noel
(Passaquet, R.) 2-3pt jr cor&4pt
mix cor HEUGEL HE 32425   (S869)

SYLVESTRE, ANNE (cont'd.)

Mon Mari Est Parti
(Passaquet) 3 eq voices HEUGEL
HE 31925   (S870)

Rose De Decembre, La
(Passaquet, R.) 3 eq voices HEUGEL
HE 32424   (S871)

T'en Souviens-Tu La Seine
(Grindel, J.) 4pt mix cor HEUGEL
HE 31850   (S872)

SYMFONIA PASTORALIS IN E see Salva,
Tadeas

SYNCOPATED CLOCK, THE see Anderson,
Leroy

SZABO
Mother Of Mine, I Still Have You
*see Keys

SZENEN AUS GOETHES "FAUST" see
Schumann, Robert (Alexander)

SZESC PIESNI WESELNYCH LUDOWYCH
POLSKICH W FORMIE SUITY see
Pankiewicz, Eugeniusz

T

'T AVONDT: TENDEN 'S WERELDS PALEN see
   Geraedts, Henri

'T HAESKEN see Schrijvers, Jean

'T IS STILLE ALLENGERHAND see Geraedts,
   Henri

'T WAS NIETS DAN ZONNIG RITME see
   Mengelberg, Karel, Valse De La
   Poupee

TA MERE see Bovet, Joseph

TABOUROT, JEHAN
   see ARBEAU, THOINOT

TAGESKREIS, DER see Kutzer, Ernst

TAHITI NUI see Lund, Eddie

TAILOR AND THE MOUSE, THE
   (LaMance Jr., Edgar) SATB,acap LAWSON
   52276 $.90   (T1)

TAKE A SPIN
   (Davis, Bill) 2pt cor BUGZY BGZ-1013
                                      (T2)

TAKE CARE see Guss

TAKE IN THE SUNSHINE see Loper

TAKE ME OUT TO THE BALL GAME see
   Taylor, Lemoyne

TAKE THE "A" TRAIN
   (Shaw, Kirby) SATB LEONARD-US
   08664371 $.95   (T3)
   (Shaw, Kirby) 3pt mix cor LEONARD-US
   08664372 $.95, ipa   (T4)

TAKE THE TIME see Fitzmartin

TAKEMITSU, TORU (1930-   )
   Cinderella's Misfortune
   6pt men cor SCHOTT SJ 1041 see from
      Handmade Proverbs   (T5)

   Farewell Gift, A
   6pt men cor SCHOTT SJ 1041 see from
      Handmade Proverbs   (T6)

   Handmade Proverbs °see Cinderella's
      Misfortune; Farewell Gift, A;
      Three Bones; Your Eyes   (T7)

   Three Bones
   6pt men cor SCHOTT SJ 1041 see from
      Handmade Proverbs   (T8)

   Your Eyes
   6pt men cor SCHOTT SJ 1041 see from
      Handmade Proverbs   (T9)

TAL, JOSEPH (1910-   )
   Dream Of The Circles °see Halom
      Ha'igulim

   Halom Ha'igulim
      "Dream Of The Circles" [Heb] mix
      cor,Bar solo,4inst [20'] voc sc
      ISR.MUS.INST. 6528B   (T10)

   Laga'at Makom
      "Touch A Place" [Heb] 3pt cor,solo
      voice [6'0"] ISR.MUS.INST. 6583
                                      (T11)
   Touch A Place °see Laga'at Makom

TALE OF MILLINGTON RIVER, THE see
   Lubetkin

TALISMANE see Schumann, Robert
   (Alexander)

TALKIN' 'BOUT AMERICA see Leisy, James
   Franklin

TALL TOM JEFFERSON see Roberts, Ruth

TAM TI DE LAM see Vigneault, Gilles

TAMARIS
   Qui Vient Ce Jour (composed with
      Grimbert, Jacques)
      SSATB HEUGEL HE 32547   (T12)

TANCUJ
   (Plojhar, F.) [Czech/Slovak] TTBB
   HARMONIA 3706   (T13)

TANENBAUM, ELIAS (1924-   )
   Sounds Are
   16pt cor,electronic tape,pno [12']
   AM.COMP.AL.   (T14)

TANEYEV
   Cloister At Kazbek, The
      SATB SCHIRM.G 321200 $.70   (T15)

TANEYEV, SERGEY IVANOVICH (1856-1915)
   Choruses, Vol. 2 °CCUL
   [Russ] cor,acap MEZ KNIGA 174   (T16)

TANT QUE VIVRAY see Sermisy, Claude de
   (Claudin)

TANT QUE VIVRAY EN AGE FLORISSANT see
   Gero, Ihan

TANZ-CHOR see Lully, Jean-Baptiste
   (Lulli)

TANZ, MA MILA see Heinrichs, Wilhelm

TANZ, MADCHEN, TANZ...UND ANDERE
   CHORLIEDER see Koch, Johannes H.E.

TANZ MIR NICHT MIT see Hausmann

TANZ RUBER, TANZ NUBER see Buchner,
   Johann

TANZEN UND SPRINGEN see Hassler, Hans
   Leo

TANZLUSTIGE, DIE: TANZEN WILL DIE
   LIEBSTE see Trapp, Willy

TAPESTRIES see Locklair, Dan Steven

TARENSKEEN, BOUDEWIJN (1952-   )
   Schreber Preview
   4pt mix cor,Bar solo,0.2.2.1.5sax.
      2.2.2.2. perc,strings [13']
      DONEMUS   (T17)

TATE, PHYLLIS (1912-1987)
   All The World's A Stage
   mix cor,2.2.2.2. 4.2.3.1. timp,
      perc,strings OXFORD 338344-6
      $9.50   (T18)

   Choral Scene From "The Bacchae" Of
      Euripides
   dbl cor,opt org OXFORD   (T19)

   Gnat, The
      see To Words By Joseph Beaumont

   House And Home
      see To Words By Joseph Beaumont

   Nocturne For Four Voices
   STBarB,string quar,bass clar,cel,db
      OXFORD   (T20)

   Saint Martha And The Dragon
   SATB&jr cor,ST&narrator,ob,horn,
      pno,harp,harmonium/org,gtr,timp,
      2perc,strings,electronic tape
      OXFORD 338397-7 $18.00   (T21)

   Solar
   1-2pt jr cor,pno/orch [35'] OXFORD
      19 338356X f.s., ipr   (T22)

   To Words By Joseph Beaumont
   SSA,pno OXFORD 338382-9 $6.75
      contains: Gnat, The; House And
      Home; When Love   (T23)

   When Love
      see To Words By Joseph Beaumont

   Witches And Spells °CC4U
   SSAA,pno OXFORD   (T24)

T'AVONT SULLEN WI VROLIC SIJN see
   Appeldoorn, Dina

TAYLOR
   Ballad De Bon Conseyl
   3 eq voices,pno/org LAWSON 52129
                                      (T25)

TAYLOR, CLIFFORD OLIVER (1923-   )
   Masquerade
   mix cor [7'] AM.COMP.AL. $4.60   (T26)

TAYLOR, LEMOYNE
   Blues For Fickle Fools
      SATB BUGZY BGZ-1001   (T27)

   Daisy, Daisy
   (Davis, Bill) SAB BUGZY BGZ-1006
                                      (T28)

   Greenwich Funk Time
      SATB BUGZY BGZ-1003   (T29)

   Nothin' Sweeter
      SATB BUGZY BGZ-1004   (T30)

   Outrageous, That Shortnin' Bread
   (Davis, Bill) SATB BUGZY BGZ-1005 (T31)

   Scat Song, The
      SATB BUGZY BGZ-1002   (T32)

   Sidewalks Of New York
      SAB BUGZY BGZ- 1012   (T33)

TAYLOR, LEMOYNE (cont'd.)

   Take Me Out To The Ball Game
      SAB BUGZY BGZ-1010   (T34)

TCHAIKOVSKY, PIOTR ILYICH (1840-1893)
   Autumn (from The Seasons)
      SCHIRM.G 320960 $.75   (T35)

   Cantata For The Opening Of The Moscow
      Polytechnic Exposition
   [Russ] SATB,T solo KALMUS K 06769
      $5.00   (T36)

   Eleven Part-Songs And Secular
      Choruses °CCU
   [Russ] 2-6pt mix cor KALMUS K 06759
      $7.00   (T37)

   Golden Cloudlet, The
   [Russ] SATB EARTHSNG ER-4 $.75
                                      (T38)

   Moscow
      see Tchaikovsky, Piotr Ilyich, To
      Touch The Heart Of Man

   Ode To Joy
   [Russ] SSAATTBB,SATB soli KALMUS
      K 06768 $6.00   (T39)

   On Coming Sleep
      see Tchaikovsky, Piotr Ilyich, To
      Touch The Heart Of Man

   Three Songs By Peter Ilych
      Tchaikovsky °CCU
   (Ades) SATB SHAWNEE 1797 $1.25;
      SSAA SHAWNEE 0521 $1.25   (T40)

   To Touch The Heart Of Man °cant
   [Russ] SSAATTBB,MezBar soli KALMUS
      K 06770 $5.00 contains also:
      Moscow; On Coming Sleep   (T41)

TCHUM BI-RI CHUM
   (Goldman) SSA LAWSON LG 52099 $.85
                                      (T42)

TCHUM BI-RI TCHUM see Goldman

TE DEUM see Patterson, Paul

TE KIELDRECHT see Kulvers, J.

TEACHER, HELP ME see Spender

TEAR THEM DOWN see Shaw, Kirby

TEARS see Wallach, Joelle

TED E. BEAR AND ME see Lentz

TEDDY BEAR'S PICNIC, THE
   (Carter, Andrew) SATB OXFORD
   19 343131 9   (T43)

TEDDY'S CHRISTMAS see Holdstock, Jan

TEL EN MEDIT see Mittantier

TELEMANN, GEORG PHILIPP (1681-1767)
   Geht Schlafen
   (Bresgen, Cesar) SAB MULLER 1481
                                      (T44)
   Hamburger Admiralitatsmusik 1723
      °ora
   (Maertens, W.) SATB,SATBBB soli,
      3trp,timp,3horn,bass fl,fl,2pic,
      2ob,ob d'amore,2bsn,2vln,vla,cont
      BREITKOPF-L   (T45)

   Jauchze, Jubilier Und Singe
   (Maertens, W.) SATB,SATBB soli,
      2vln,vla,cont BREITKOPF-L   (T46)

   Schulmeister, Der
   2pt boy cor,Bar solo,strings
      without vla,hpsd [18'] KALMUS
      A7126 cor pts f.s., sc f.s., ipa
                                      (T47)
   Serenata Eroica
   (Maertens, W.) SATB,SSTTBB soli,
      6trp,timp,2horn,2fl,pic,2ob,
      2clar,2bsn,2vln,vla,cont
      BREITKOPF-L   (T48)

TELFER, NANCY
   Day Before Christmas, The
   unis cor,pno LESLIE 1140 f.s.   (T49)

   If You Should Meet A Crocodile
   unis cor LESLIE 1145 f.s.   (T50)

   Love Song, A
   SATB HARRIS HC-5017 f.s. see from
      Spell Of Time Long Past   (T51)

   Lullaby
   unis cor LESLIE 1146 f.s.   (T52)

   Noel!
   SATB,fl,harp/pno BEAUDN MJ-1   (T53)

   Noise
   unis cor LESLIE 1147 f.s.   (T54)

TELFER, NANCY (cont'd.)

Sailor's Sweetheart, The
SATB HARRIS HC-5020 f.s. see from
Spell Of Time Long Past   (T55)

Searching For A Gift
unis cor LESLIE 1141 f.s.   (T56)

Seven Fat Fishermen
2pt cor LESLIE 2057 f.s.   (T57)

Sing Me A Song
1-2pt cor LESLIE 2061 f.s.   (T58)

Solitude
SATB HARRIS HC-5018 f.s. see from
Spell Of Time Long Past   (T59)

Spell Of Time Long Past *see Love
Song, A; Sailor's Sweetheart,
The; Solitude; Wind And The
Flower, The   (T60)

Wind And The Flower, The
SATB HARRIS HC-5019 f.s. see from
Spell Of Time Long Past   (T61)

TELL ME TRULY see Cherubini, Luigi

(TELL ME) WHEN WILL I SEE YOU AGAIN see
McPheeters

TELL ME WHERE IS FANCY BRED see Lane,
Philip

TEMPESTA, LA see Haydn, [Franz] Joseph,
Sturm, Der

TEMPETE, LA see Haydn, [Franz] Joseph

TEMPI see Simpson, Robert

TEMPLA, BRAS, ESE PSALTERIO
(Rumery, L.) [Span/Eng] SAB,acap
(med) THOMAS 1C288501 $.75   (T62)

TEMPLE see Woolen, R.

TEMPS A LAISSE SON MANTEAU, LE see
Debussy, Claude

TEMPS DU MUGUET, LE see Lemarque, F.

TEMPS PASSE, LE
(Gevaert, Francois-Auguste) SATB,acap
HUGUENIN EB 299   (T63)
(Piguet, Robert) SATB,acap HUGUENIN
EB 433   (T64)

TEMPS PERDU, LE see Kerstens, Huub

TEMPS QUI COURT, LE
(Agnel, A.) 2 eq voices HEUGEL
HE 32140 contains also: Je Ne Puis
Tenir D'aimer   (T65)

TEN FOLK SONGS see Willcocks, Jonathan

T'EN SOUVIENS-TU LA SEINE see
Sylvestre, Anne

T'EN SOUVIENT-IL ENCORE? see Bally,
Paul

TENDRE ET DANGEREUX VISAGE DE L'AMOUR,
LE see Prevert, J.

TERHUNE, CHARLES
Goodwill To All This Year
3pt mix cor CPP-BEL SV8810 $1.10,
accomp tape available   (T66)

Reach To The Stars
3pt mix cor CPP-BEL SV8911 $1.10,
accomp tape available   (T67)
3pt mix cor CPP-BEL SV8911 $1.10,
accomp tape available   (T68)

There Stood A Man (Martin Luther
King, Jr.)
2pt cor CPP-BEL SV8739 $1.10,
accomp tape available   (T69)

There's A Song That I Sing
2pt cor CPP-BEL SV8726 $.95   (T70)
2pt cor CPP-BEL SV8726 f.s., accomp
tape available   (T71)

TERMOS, PAUL (1942-   )
Fortuna
chamber choir [10'] DONEMUS   (T72)

TERRAIN OF THE KINGS, THE see
Williamson, Malcolm

TERRAL, F.
Cinq Suites Canoniques
3pt cor HEUGEL HE 32145   (T73)

TERRE HAUTE see Lauber, Emile

TERRE PROMISE see Landry, Fredy

TERSEN see Fougstedt, Nils-Eric

TES PETITS SABOTS
(Grimbert, J.) 3 eq voices HEUGEL
HE 31900   (T74)

TESSIER, CHARLES (ca. 1550- ?)
Au Joli Bois
SATB,acap HUGUENIN EB 31A   (T75)

TESTER, WAYNE
Freedom For All
SSA CPP-BEL 5794FC2X $1.40   (T76)
SATB CPP-BEL 5794FC1X $1.40, accomp
tape available   (T77)
SAB CPP-BEL 5794FC3X $1.40   (T78)

TETE DE FAUNE see Andriessen, Hendrik

TETTERODE, L. ADR. VON
Hollands Lied, Een
(Kooij, E.) SATB MOLENAAR 15004202
(T79)

TEURE HEIMAT see Verdi, Giuseppe

TEXAS see Reese, Jan

TEZE, M.
Chagrin D'amour, Un (composed with
Salvador, Henri)
(Frochot, J.) mix cor HEUGEL
HE 32511   (T80)

THANK YOU FOR BEING A FRIEND see Gold

THANK YOU FOR YOUR KINDNESS see
Strommen, Carl

THANK YOU, SANTA see Mancini

THANKS FOR THE MEMORY
(Chinn) SATB CPP-BEL 2661TC1X $1.25,
accomp tape available   (T81)
(Chinn) SAB CPP-BEL 2661TC3X $1.25,
accomp tape available   (T82)

THANKSGIVING see Crawley, Clifford

THANKSGIVING SONGS THAT TICKLE YOUR
FUNNY BONE! see Roberts, Ruth

THAT GIRL PLAYING see Balzonelli,
Alberto, Jugaba La Nina Aquella

THAT OLD HAT AND CANE see Lutz,
Lawrence

THAW see Forbes, Sebastian

THAYER, FRED
Winter Scene
SATB,pno LAWSON 52444 $1.00   (T83)

THEN HE SAID, "SING!"
(Brymer) SATB LEONARD-US 08639271
$.95   (T84)
(Brymer) SAB LEONARD-US 08639272 $.95
(T85)
(Brymer) SSA LEONARD-US 08639273
$.95, ipa, accomp tape available
(T86)

THEODORAKIS, MIKIS (1925-   )
Axion Esti *ora
mix cor,Bar&speaking voice,1.1.1.1.
0.0.0.0. timp,perc,strings,
2balalaika,gtr,pno [70'] voc sc
BREITKOPF-L   (T87)

Fruhlingssinfonie *see Sinfonie Nr.
7

Nur Diese Eine Schwalbe
(Vogel, H.) mix cor, solo voices,
orch sc BREITKOPF-L 7945   (T88)

Sinfonie Nr. 3
mix cor,S solo,3.2.2.3. 4.3.3.1.
timp,4perc,kbd,strings [70'] sc
BREITKOPF-L 1138   (T89)

Sinfonie Nr. 7
"Fruhlingssinfonie" mix cor,SATB
soli,3.2.2.3. 4.4.4.4. timp,
3perc,pno,strings [72'] sc
BREITKOPF-L 1145   (T90)

THERE BENEATH THE HILLS, THE HIGH HILLS
see Zamecnik, Evzen

THERE IS A LADY
(Snyder) SATB CPP-BEL SV8643 $1.10,
accomp tape available   (T91)

THERE IS A LADY see Eddleman, David

THERE IS A LADYE see Collins

THERE IS SWEET MUSIC see Clements, John

THERE IS SWEET MUSIC see Gawthrop

THERE STOOD A MAN (MARTIN LUTHER KING,
JR.) see Terhune, Charles

THERE WILL BE SUN see Asgeirsson, Jon

THERE'LL BE NO NEW TUNES ON THIS OLD
PIANO: A TWENTIES MEDLEY *medley
(Huff) 2pt cor CPP-BEL CO127C5X
$2.25, accomp tape available   (T92)
(Huff) SATB CPP-BEL CO127C1X $2.25,
accomp tape available   (T93)
(Huff) SAB CPP-BEL CO127C3X $2.25,
accomp tape available   (T94)

THERE'S A RAINBOW 'ROUND MY SHOULDER
(Anderson) SSAA (women's barbershop)
BOURNE B239152   (T95)

THERE'S A SONG THAT I SING see Terhune,
Charles

THERE'S ANOTHER CHRISTMAS COMING SOON
see Cobine

THERE'S MAGIC IN THE AIR see Crawley,
Clifford

THERE'S NOTHIN' LIKE SUMMER see Kunz

THESE DREAMS
(Huff, Mac) SATB LEONARD-US 08603781
$.95   (T96)
(Huff, Mac) SAB LEONARD-US 08603782
$.95   (T97)

THIELE, SIEGFRIED (1934-   )
Apokalypse
mix cor,S solo,3trp,3trom,timp
[22'] cor pts BREITKOPF-L 7071
(T98)

THIJSSE, WIM (1916-   )
Merk Toch Hoe Sterk
SSA MOLENAAR 15026503   (T99)

Si La Face Est Pale, La Cause Est
Aimer
4 eq voices,acap ZENGERINK 371
(T100)

THIMAN, ERIC HARDING (1900-1975)
When I Was A Little Boy
2pt cor,pno [1'] ROBERTON 75352
(T101)

You Spotted Snakes
2pt cor,pno [2'30"] ROBERTON 75353
(T102)

THIN SNOW, THE see Simon, Richard

THINGS SHALL NEVER DIE see Burton, Mark

THIRIET, MAURICE (1906-1972)
Place De La Concorde
(Passaquet, R.) 4pt mix cor HEUGEL
HE 32039   (T103)

Tendre Et Dangereux Visage De
L'amour, Le *see Prevert, J.

THIS HAPPY DAY see Thliveris, Elizabeth
Hope (Beth)

THIS HOUSE see Strommen, Carl

THIS IS MY COUNTRY see Jacobs

THIS IS OUR HOMELAND *CCU
[Russ] jr cor,pno MEZ KNIGA 225
(T104)

THIS IS YOUR DAY see Bair

THIS LAND IS YOUR LAND- A PANORAMA
AMERICANA see Guthrie

THIS LAND OF OURS see Sleeth, Natalie
Wakeley

THIS LITTLE LIGHT OF MINE
(Moore, Donald P.) SAB,pno CPP-BEL
SV8839 $1.10   (T105)
(Moore, Donald P.) SA,pno CPP-BEL
SV8840 $1.10   (T106)
(Moore, Donald P.) SATB,pno CPP-BEL
SV8838 $1.10   (T107)

THIS NEARLY WAS MINE see Rodgers,
Richard

THIS TRAIN *folk song
(Siltman) BB&camb CAMBIATA U978114
$.70   (T108)

THIS TRAIN GOES MARCHING IN
(Feldstein) 2pt cor ALFRED 7593 $.95,
accomp tape available   (T109)

THIS WE KNOW see Jeffers

THIS WORLDE'S JOIE see Mathias, William

THLIVERIS, ELIZABETH HOPE (BETH)
(1939-   )
Jamaican Spring
SATB KJOS GC138 $.70   (T110)

Keep Christmas Around
SATB KJOS C8918 $.90   (T111)

THLIVERIS, ELIZABETH HOPE (BETH)
(cont'd.)

Little Boy Blue
2pt cor (med easy) THOMAS 1C127814
$.60   (T112)

This Happy Day
SATB,fl,strings MUSIC SEV. M70-484
$.90   (T113)

Yellow And Red Balloon, A
2pt cor KJOS GC148 $.90   (T114)

THO' I AM YOUNG see Shearer, C.M.

THOMA, A.
In Nacht Und Dunkel
cor HIEBER 5023   (T115)

THOMAS
Starlight
(Mayfield) SATB SHAWNEE 6417 $.85
(T116)

THOMMESSEN, OLAV ANTON (1946-   )
Blasfemi
[Norw] SATB,fl,alto clar in E flat,
bass clar,alto sax,trp,trom,pno,
perc,db NORGE   (T117)

THOMSON, VIRGIL GARNETT (1896-1989)
Fanfare For Peace
(Larson) SATB,pno/org,opt brass,opt
perc oct PEER 60440-122 $.85,
ipa, sc PEER 60439-166 f.s., pts
PEER 60441-167 f.s.   (T118)

THORARINSSON, LEIFUR (1934-   )
Outlaw's Poem
mix cor ICELAND 017-15   (T119)

THORDUR KAKALI °folk song
(Kristinsson, Sigursveinn D.) men cor
ICELAND 021-2   (T120)

THORESEN, LASSE (1949-   )
To Aukrust-Sanger
[Norw] SMezA NORGE   (T121)

THORNE, FRANCIS BURRITT (1922-   )
Song Of The California Low Country
SATB,1+pic1.1+bass clar.1.
2.2.2.0. 3perc,timp,harp,strings
[40'] AM.COMP.AL. f.s.   (T122)

THORNTON
Grasshopper, The
SATB SOUTHERN $1.50   (T123)

THREE ANATOLIAN TURKISH FOLK SONGS
°CC3U
(Roff, Joseph) 2pt cor,pno,opt fl
(med easy) THOMAS 1C107902 $.70
(T124)

THREE ANCIENT SONGS see Braun,
Yeheskiel

THREE ARRANGEMENTS
(Tschaikowsky, Peter Ilyich) [Russ/
Lat/It] cor KALMUS K 04075 $7.00
contains: Gaudeamus Igitur;
Recitatives And Chorus From
Auber's "Le Domino Noir";
Recitatives From "Le Nozze Di
Figaro"   (T125)

THREE BARRELS see Ligeti, Gyorgy

THREE BIRD SONGS see Alexander, Haim

THREE BONES see Takemitsu, Toru

THREE CAROLS see Boni, Giovanni

THREE CHORAL SONGS see Christiansen

THREE CHORAL WORKS see Rimsky-Korsakov,
Nikolai

THREE CHORUSES ON POEMS OF RUSSIAN
POETS see Sviridov, Georgy

THREE CHORUSES WITH INSTRUMENTS see
Steuermann, Edward

THREE CHORUSES see Blake

THREE DISHES AND SIX QUESTIONS see
Laplante, Pierre

THREE EARLY ENGLISH LYRICS see Walker,
Robert

THREE EASY ROUNDS see Weigl, [Mrs.]
Vally

THREE EPITAPHS see Adams

THREE FOLK SONGS
(Southers, Leroy) SATB NATIONAL
NMP-183 $1.00   (T126)

THREE FOLK SONGS FROM SRI LANKA °CC3U
(Roff, Joseph) 2pt cor,pno,opt fl,opt
perc (med) THOMAS 1C108118 $.80
(T127)

THREE FOR THE CHILDREN see Kearns, Ann

THREE FOURTEENTH-CENTURY MOTETS IN
HONOUR OF GASTON FEBUS °CC3U
(Lefferts, Peter) 4pt cor ANTICO AE23
(T128)

THREE GREEK FOLK SONGS °CC3U
(Roff, Joseph) 2pt cor,opt fl,opt
perc (med diff) THOMAS 1C108308
$.80   (T129)

THREE HOLY SONNETS see Brings, Allen
Stephen

THREE HOVDEN-SONGS see Kjeldaas,
Arnljot

THREE HUNDRED YEARS OF ENGLISH
PARTSONGS °CCU
(Hillier) cor FABER 10045 7 f.s.
(T130)

THREE LITTLE COMMENTARIES see Riley,
Dennis

THREE MADRIGALS see Avni, Tzvi

THREE MADRIGALS
(Mckinney, Howard) SAB (contains
works by Weelkes, Bateson, and
East) CPP-BEL FEC 09455 $1.25
(T131)

THREE MEDIEVAL LYRICS see Mathias,
William

THREE O'CLOCK REHEARSAL see Roberts,
Ruth

THREE ORIENTAL PIECES see Saladino,
David

THREE PIECES see Wachtel, Levi

THREE PIECES see Gelbrun, Arthur

THREE POEMS BY JAN ERIK VOLD see
Odegaard, Henrik

THREE POEMS BY OSCAR WILDE see Diemer,
Emma Lou

THREE POEMS (DREI GEDICHTE), OP. 6 see
Weigl, Karl

THREE PROVERBIAL LOVES °CC3U
(Collins) S&camb,SA soli CAMBIATA
ARS980150 $.65   (T132)

THREE RENAISSANCE PIECES FOR TREBLE
VOICES see Harris

THREE RENAISSANCE PIECES FOR TREBLE
VOICES, VOL. 2 see Harris

THREE ROBERT LOUIS STEVENSON SETTINGS
see Gallina, Jill C.

THREE SATIRES see Schoenberg, Arnold

THREE SCORE REFLECTIONS see Bavicchi,
John Alexander

THREE SEA CHORUSES see Ogdon, Wilbur L.

THREE SELF-PORTRAITS OF ODD NERDRUM see
Ronnes, Robert, Trois Images

THREE SHANTIES °CC3U
(Halsey, L.) SATB,Bar solo,acap
NOVELLO 07 0464 04   (T133)

THREE SONGS BY PETER ILYCH TCHAIKOVSKY
see Tchaikovsky, Piotr Ilyich

THREE SONGS FOR FOUR VOICES see Brahms,
Johannes

THREE SONGS FOR MIXED CHOIR see
Karlsen, Kjell Mork

THREE SONGS FOR SATB CHORUS see
Hayvoronsky, Mykhajlo

THREE SONGS OF SERVICE see Procter,
Leland

THREE SONGS OF THE SEA see Skolnik,
Walter

THREE SONGS see Harrison, Lou

THREE SPOOFS IN CLASSICAL STYLE see
Hicken, Ken L.

THREE STATEMENTS see Ogdon, Wilbur L.

THREE TIMES A LADY
(Williams) SATB CPP-BEL 2596TC1X
$1.25   (T134)
(Williams) TTBB CPP-BEL 2596TC4X
$1.25   (T135)

THREE UNACCOMPANIED PART-SONGS see
Elgar, [Sir] Edward (William)

THREE WELSH SONGS see Palsson, Pall P.

THREE WHIMSICAL FANCIES see Butler,
Eugene Sanders

THREE WHITMAN VISIONS see Wallach,
Joelle

THRILLER
(Chinn) SATB CPP-BEL SV8456 $2.25
(T136)

THROUGH THE EYES OF A CHILD see
Blackford, Richard

THROUGH THE FIRE
(Chinn) SSATB CPP-BEL 6427TCWX $1.25,
accomp tape available   (T137)
(Chinn) SATB CPP-BEL 6427TC1X $1.25,
accomp tape available   (T138)
(Chinn) SAB CPP-BEL 6427TC3X $1.25,
accomp tape available   (T139)

THUNDER AND LIGHTNING see Crawley,
Clifford

THURGAU, DER see Zahner, Bruno

THURM, JOACHIM (1927-   )
Ans Fenster Kommt Und Seht °song
cycle
jr cor,pno/chamber orch [15']
BREITKOPF-L 6129   (T140)

THY BODY see Hicken, Ken L.

THY CHERRY-RED LIPS, O MAIDEN MEEK see
Belle, J., O Amoureusich Mondeken
Root

THYGERSON
Christmas Waltz
SAB KJOS C8919 $.80   (T141)

Reach Out °see Hughes

Sing A Christmas Song
2pt cor KJOS C8827 $.80   (T142)

TI ARSTIDER, DE see Lerstad, Terje B.

TIBULLI ELEGIA PACIS see Jung, Helge

TIBUR see Diepenbrock, Alphons

TIC-TAC DU MOULIN, LE see Blanchard

TICINESI
(Ganter, C.) mix cor,acap PELIKAN
PE1187   (T143)

TICK-TOCK see Van Slyck, Nicholas

TIDLEG VARSONG see Killengreen,
Christian

TIDLIG SOMMERMORGEN see Vassdal, Tore

TIEN KINDERLIEDJES see Meima, Herman

TILLEUL, LE see Lauber, Emile

TILLEY, ALEXANDER
In Flanders Fields
SATB HARRIS HC-6011   (T144)
SA HARRIS HC-5028   (T145)

Magic Store
SA HARRIS HC-5026 $1.25   (T146)

O Waly, Waly
"Water Is Wide" SATB HARRIS HC-6014
$.90   (T147)

Song For Canada
unis cor HARRIS HC-5025 $1.25
(T148)
Songs For The School Year
SATB HARRIS HC-6019 $1.50   (T149)

Vagabond Song
SA HARRIS HC-5024 $1.25   (T150)

Water Is Wide °see O Waly, Waly

TILT. DRAMA see Rehnqvist, Karin

TIME AND AGAIN see Eddleman, David

TIME AND WATER see Asgeirsson, Jon

TIME DRAWS NEAR THE BIRTH OF CHRIST,
THE see Getty, Gordon

TIME FOR JOY, A see Besig, Don

TIME OF ROSES, THE see Forbes,
Sebastian

TIME-PIECE, OP. 16 see Patterson, Paul

TIME TO BE GOIN' see Perry

TIME WILL REVEAL see Madsen

TIMOTHY see Adler, Samuel Hans

TINY CANTATA, A see Maros, Rudolf

TINY LITTLE BABY see Blevins, Patsy Ford

TIRITOMBA see Backer, Hans

TIRUKKURAL-SUITE see Karlsen, Kjell Mork

'TIS A PITY SHE'S A WHORE: BALLET see Jahn, Thomas

'TIS THE SEASON TO BE JOLLY see Liebergen, Patrick

'TIS WINTER NOW see Grundahl

TISCH
   Open The Door *see Ross

TO A COUSIN see Haydn, [Franz] Joseph, An Den Vetter

TO A SKYLARK see Liddell, Claire

TO AUKRUST-SANGER see Thoresen, Lasse

TO FIELDS WE DO NOT KNOW see Casken, John

TO FOLKETONEBEARBEIDELSER see Karlsen, Kjell Mork

TO FOLKETONER *see Gjendines Banlat; Inga Litimor   (T151)

TO HAVE AND TO BE see Berkowitz, Sol

TO LIVE TO LOVE see Clarke, Henry Leland

TO LOVE see Rabe, Folke

TO ME
   (Althouse) SATB CPP-BEL 4866TC1X
      $1.25   (T152)
   (Althouse) SAB CPP-BEL 4866TC3X $1.25
                                         (T153)
   (Althouse) 2pt cor CPP-BEL 4866TC5X
      $1.25   (T154)

TO MOTHER: POLISH CRADLE-SONG, AT MY MOTHER'S HOME see Laprus, Lucjan, Do Matki: Kolysanka Polska, U Moji Matusi

TO ORPHEUS see Blaustein, Susan

TO PLANTAR FOR LJOSE ROYSTER see Am, Magnar

TO REYKJAVIK see Palsson, Pall P.

TO SANGER OM BARN see Bottcher, Eberhard

TO SANGER TIL DIKT AV ASLAUG VAA see Brevik, Tor

TO SMA see Brevik, Tor

TO THE HILLS see Leech, Bryan Jeffery

TO THE STARS see Schumann, Robert (Alexander), An Die Sterne

TO TOUCH THE HEART OF MAN see Tchaikovsky, Piotr Ilyich

TO VISER see Lystrup, Geirr

TO WORDS BY JOSEPH BEAUMONT see Tate, Phyllis

TOBOGGAN, LE see Bigot, Pierre

TOCHTER DER HEIDE, DIE see Poos, Heinrich

TOD UND VERKLARUNG: TONDICHTUNG see Vranken, Petrus Johannes Josephus

TOD VON BASEL, DER
   (Barblan, Emmanuel) TTBB HUGUENIN
      EB 68   (T155)

TODAY
   (Simon) SATB CPP-BEL T5440TC1 $.95
                                         (T156)

TODAY IS YOURS AND MINE see Butler

TOEBOSCH, LOUIS (1916-   )
   Huldegedicht Aan Singer *Op.143
      4pt mix cor,2.2.2.2. 4.2.3.0.
      3perc,strings [12'30"] DONEMUS
                                         (T157)

TOGETHER see Robertson

TOGETHER WE STAND see Strommen, Carl

TOGETHER WE'LL MAKE THE... see Beal

TOI QUI M'ES CHERE see Lassus, Roland de (Orlandus)

TOLLING see Gould, Morton

TOM THE PIPER'S SON (NURSERY RHYMES, NO.1) see Walters, Edmund

TOM THE TIDDLER, ALL CLEAR see Hellinck, Lupus, Janne Moye, Al Claer

TOMKINS
   How Great Delight
      SAB STAINER 3.3192   (T158)

TOMORROW
   (Strommen) SATB CPP-BEL SV8342 $.95
                                         (T159)
   (Strommen) SA CPP-BEL SV8341 $.95
                                         (T160)

TONEDIGT see Waldeier, Erik

TONEN see Kleiberg, Stale

TONEN - THE SONG see Lunde, Ivar

TONNELIERS see Bleuse, Marc

TOP OF THE WORLD see Carpenter, Richard Lynn

TORCHE, CH.
   Chanson Du Vent, La
      men cor HUGUENIN CH 2065   (T161)

   Neuchatel
      SATB,acap HUGUENIN CH 2046   (T162)

TORMALA, JOUKO
   Koulukuoro 3, Kuusi Laulua Nuorisokuorolle
      SAB FAZER F 06948-4   (T163)

TORO LITI: FOLK TUNE FROM VALDRES see Nystedt, Knut

TORSTENSSON, KLAS (1951-   )
   Isogloss
      24 solo voices playing 12 pairs of planks, 12 maracas, 12 megaphones [18'] DONEMUS   (T164)

TOSTO CHE L'ALBA see Firenze, Ghirardello da

TOTARI, GEORG
   Karleken Till Livet
      (Eriksson, Gunnar) SATB PROPRIUS 7977   (T165)

TOUATI, RAYMOND
   Ami Que J'avais Au Logis, L'
      (Passaquet, Raphael) mix cor,pno A COEUR JOIE CA 13 see from Trois Chansons De L'auxerrois   (T166)

   J'ai Dans Le Coeur Un Grand Amour
      (Passaquet, Raphael) mix cor,pno A COEUR JOIE CA 15 see from Trois Chansons De L'auxerrois   (T167)

   Ou Va L'eau Qui S'en Va?
      (Daniel, Etienne) SATB A COEUR JOIE 043   (T168)

   Trois Chansons De L'auxerrois *see Ami Que J'avais Au Logis, L'; J'ai Dans Le Coeur Un Grand Amour; Trois Peines Sont Autour De Nous   (T169)

   Trois Peines Sont Autour De Nous
      (Passaquet, Raphael) mix cor,pno A COEUR JOIE CA 14 see from Trois Chansons De L'auxerrois   (T170)

TOUCH A HAND, MAKE A FRIEND
   (Chinn) SAB CPP-BEL 4885TC3X $1.25, accomp tape available   (T171)
   (Chinn) 2pt cor CPP-BEL 4885TC5X $1.25, accomp tape available (T172)

TOUCH A PLACE see Tal, Joseph, Laga'at Makom

TOUCH THEM SOFTLY see Owen, John Warren

TOUR DE CONSTANCE, LA
   1-4pt cor HUGUENIN see from Chansons Pour La Jeunesse, Septieme Cahier   (T173)

TOUR DE CONSTANCE, LA see Huguenin, Charles

TOUR DE CONSTANCE, LE see Huguenin, Charles

TOUR, PRENDS GARDE, LA
   (Brasseur, M.A.; Teniere, C.) 2pt jr cor,Orff inst HEUGEL HE 32364 contains also: Eh Aye Aye Aye
                                         (T174)

TOURNENT LES JOURS see Daniel, Etienne

TOURNESOL, LE see Delanoe

TOUT A L'ENTOUR DE NOS REMPARTS see Lauber, Emile

TOUT AU LONG DU DOUBS see Girod, Vincent

TOUT CE QU'ON PEULT EN ELLE VEOIR see Castro, Jean de

TOUT EST JOIE see Schubert, Franz (Peter)

TOUTES LES NUITS see Janequin, Clement

TOWDY DOWDY
   (Lewis, A.) 2pt cor,pno (med easy) THOMAS 1C258423 $.80   (T175)

TRACK, GERHARD (1934-   )
   Discovery *see Gefunden

   Gefunden
      "Discovery" [Ger/Eng] SATB,fl,vln NEW MUSIC NMA-160 $.70   (T176)

   Ode To Youth
      SATB,opt orch NEW MUSIC NMA-151 $.80   (T177)

TRAIN BOUND FOR GLORY see Althouse

TRAINS see Fitch

TRANSPARENCE see Leeuw, Ton de

TRAPP, WILLY
   Des Mullers Froloches Wandern
      mix cor,opt pno BOHM   (T178)

   Freunde, Vernehmet Die Geschichte
      men cor,opt solo voice,pno BOHM
                                         (T179)

   Freut Euch Des Lebens *cant
      mix cor,pno,combo BOHM   (T180)

   Gesellen, Stimmet All Mit Ein *see Gesellen-Trinklied

   Gesellen-Trinklied
      (Miller, Franz R.) "Gesellen, Stimmet All Mit Ein" men cor, 5winds/pno BOHM   (T181)

   Humoreske
      mix cor,pno/orch BRAUN-PER   (T182)

   Kleine Lachmusik, Eine
      mix cor BRAUN-PER 1074   (T183)

   Landliche Konzertprobe, Die *see Suppe, Franz von

   Lustige Geschichte
      mix cor BRAUN-PER 1034   (T184)
      men cor BRAUN-PER 1033   (T185)
      wom cor/jr cor BRAUN-PER 1035
                                         (T186)

   Sauferballade
      men cor BRAUN-PER 1028   (T187)

   Spanienreise
      mix cor/men cor,pno&opt perc/winds/ string orch BOHM   (T188)

   Stehn Zwei Stern
      mix cor BOHM   (T189)

   Tanzlustige, Die: Tanzen Will Die Liebste
      men cor,pno/combo BOHM   (T190)

   Vergnugte Stunden
      men cor BRAUN-PER 1031   (T191)
      mix cor BRAUN-PER 1032   (T192)

   Volkslieder Im Rhythmus Der Zeit
      2-4pt wom cor,pno,opt combo BOHM
                                         (T193)

   Wohlauf In Gottes Schone Welt! *medley
      4pt mix cor/2pt treb cor,winds BOHM f.s., ipa   (T194)

TRARA: FRISCH AUF ZUM JAGEN see Biebl, Franz

TRAUME, DER see Schumann, Robert (Alexander)

TRAUME UNTERM CHRISTBAUM see Stolz, Robert

TRAUMEREI see Schumann, Robert (Alexander)

TRAURIGE JAGER, DER see Poos, Heinrich

TRAVAILLONS see Lauber, Joseph

TRAVELIN' see Kirk, Theron Wilford

TRAVELIN' MAN see Newbury, Kent Alan

TRAVELLER ON THE WIND see Van Slyck, Nicholas

TRAVELLING MUSIC see Wright, Maurice

TRAV'LER see Wilson, Mark

TRE BARNESANGER AV INGER HAGERUP see Lyssand, Henrik

TRE BEVINGADE ORD see Malmlof-Forssling, Carin

TRE CIECHI SIAMO see Nola, G. Domenico da

TRE DIKT AV EBBA LINDQUIST see Janson, Alfred

TRE DIKTER AV LARS GUSTAF ANDERSSON see Andersson, Magnus F.

TRE ETYDER TILLAGNADA DET PATAFYSISKA KOLLEGIET see Jennefelt, Thomas

TRE FINNMARKSRIM see Vea, Ketil

TRE FOLKEVISER FRA ROGALAND *see Adle Sine Menne; Krakevise; Svein Svane   (T195)

TRE GLADA VISOR FOR MANSKOR see Sjoblom, Heimer

TRE MANNSKORSATSER see Vea, Ketil

TRE SANGER FOR MANNSKOR see Stromholm, Folke

TRE SKJEMTEVISER see Volle, Bjarne

TRE SONGAR TIL DIKT AV IVAR ORGLAND see Grov, Magne

TRE STYCKEN, OP. 19 see Runnstrom, William

TRE VED STRANDEN see Mortensen, Finn

TREIBMANN, KARL OTTOMAR (1936-   )
   Frieden, Der
      mix cor,T&speaking voice,3.0.3.3.
      0.3.3.0. timp,5perc,electronic
      tape [40'] sc BREITKOPF-L 1135
                                         (T196)

TREK ER OP UIT see Dijk, Jan van

TRELAWNY see Miller, Harold

TRENET, CHARLES
   Ame Des Poetes, L'
      (Gauffriau, Jean) 4pt mix cor,pno A
      COEUR JOIE CA 12   (T197)

   Jardin Extraordinaire, Le
      (Gauffriau, Jean) 4pt mix cor,pno A
      COEUR JOIE CA 18   (T198)

TRESORS DE LA CHANSON POPULAIRE, LES see Burdet, Jacques

TRETTEN TROLL-TRILLINGER see Nystedt, Knut

TRI GJETERVISER FRA GUDBRANDSDALEN see Karlsen, Kjell Mork

TRIBUTE TO AIR SUPPLY, A
   (Fry) SSA CPP-BEL 5782TC2X $2.25
                                         (T199)
   (Fry) SAB CPP-BEL 5782TC3X $2.25
                                         (T200)

TRIBUTE TO ANNE MURRAY, A
   (Fry) SATB CPP-BEL C0083C1X $2.25
                                         (T201)
   (Fry) SSA CPP-BEL C0083C2X $2.25
                                         (T202)
   (Fry) SAB CPP-BEL C0083C3X $2.25
                                         (T203)

TRIBUTE TO DOLLY PARTON, A
   (Fry) SAB CPP-BEL 5787TC3X $2.25   (T204)

TRIBUTE TO JUDY GARLAND, A
   (Leavitt) SATB CPP-BEL SV8737 $2.25,
      accomp tape available   (T205)

TRIBUTE TO KENNY ROGERS, A
   (Fry) SATB CPP-BEL C0095C1X $2.25
                                         (T206)
   (Fry) SSA CPP-BEL C0095C2X $2.25
                                         (T207)
   (Fry) SAB CPP-BEL C0095C3X $2.25
                                         (T208)

TRIBUTE TO MR. CURWEN, A see Lissmann, Kurt, Aus Der Traube In Die Tonne

TRIBUTE TO OLIVIA NEWTON-JOHN, A
   (Fry) SAB CPP-BEL C0085C3X $2.25   (T209)
   (Fry) SATB CPP-BEL C0085C1X $2.25   (T210)
   (Fry) SSA CPP-BEL C0085C2X $2.25   (T211)

TRIBUTE TO STEVIE WONDER, A
   (Fry) SATB CPP-BEL C0084C1X $2.25   (T212)
   (Fry) SAB CPP-BEL C0084C3X $2.25

TRIBUTE TO THE CARPENTERS, A   (T213)
   (Fry) SATB CPP-BEL C0091C1X $2.25
                                         (T214)
   (Fry) SSA CPP-BEL C0091C2X $2.25
                                         (T215)
   (Fry) SAB CPP-BEL C0091C3X $2.25
                                         (T216)

TRIBUTE TO THE COMMODORES, A
   (Fry) SAB CPP-BEL 5892TC3X $2.25
                                         (T217)
   (Fry) SATB CPP-BEL 5792TC1X $2.25
                                         (T218)
   (Fry) SSA CPP-BEL 5792TC2X $2.25
                                         (T219)

TRIMAZO
   (Perisson) 5pt mix cor HEUGEL
   HE 32266   (T220)

TRINKLIED
   (Hilfrich) TTBB MULLER 883   (T221)
   (Willisegger, H.R.) mix cor,acap
   PELIKAN PE1188   (T222)

TRIOLETT see Schumann, Robert (Alexander)

TRIPTYCH see Austin, Larry

TRIPTYQUE DE LA VIE see Veysseyre, Henri

TRIST' ET PENSI see Gero, Ihan

TRISTESSE see Schubert, Franz (Peter)

TRISTIS EST ANIMA MEA see Kuhnau, Johann

TROHJARTAT see Lindgren, Olof

TROIS BEAUX OISEAUX DU PARADIS see Ravel, Maurice

TROIS BELLES PRINCESSES see Blanchard

TROIS CANONS A VOIX EGALES
   see C'est La Veille Etrambire

TROIS CHANSONS see Ravel, Maurice

TROIS CHANSONS see Ravel, Maurice

TROIS CHANSONS see Ravel, Maurice

TROIS CHANSONS CAHIER 1 see Bovet, Joseph

TROIS CHANSONS CAHIER 2 see Bovet, Joseph

TROIS CHANSONS CAHIER 3 see Bovet, Joseph

TROIS CHANSONS D'AUTREFOIS *see Au Bon Vieux Temps; Je Possede Un Reduit Obscur; Troubadour, Le   (T223)

TROIS CHANSONS DE L'AUXERROIS see Touati, Raymond

TROIS CHANSONS DE METIERS see Bleuse, Marc

TROIS CHANSONS PARISIENNES see Oosten, Roel van

TROIS CHANSONS POPULAIRES *see A La Claire Fontaine; Il Etait Une Fille, Une Fille D'honneur; Petite Jeanneton, La   (T224)

TROIS CHANSONS RUSSES see Rachmaninoff, Sergey Vassilievich

TROIS CHANTS D'EGLISE see Caplet, Andre

TROIS COMPTINES POUR ANNE see Guyot

TROIS IMAGES see Ronnes, Robert

TROIS MADRIGAUX see Gagliano, Marco da

TROIS MADRIGAUX A 3 VOIX MIXTES see Arcadelt, Jacob

TROIS PASTORALES see Andriessen, Hendrik

TROIS PEINES SONT AUTOUR DE NOUS see Touati, Raymond

TROIS ROSES, LES see Miche, Paul

TROP LOIN see Curti, F.

TROST see Reger, Max

TROSTERIN MUSIK: MUSIK! DU HIMMLISCHES GEBILDE see Bruckner, Anton

TROUBADOUR, LE
   (Barblan, Emmanuel) SATB,acap
   HUGUENIN EB 93 see from Trois
   Chansons D'autrefois   (T225)

TROUBLE IN PARADISE
   (Chinn) SAB CPP-BEL SV8470 $2.25
                                         (T226)

TROUT AS YOU LIKE IT see Schoeggl, F.

TROUW (OUD BALLADE) see Naberman, Mar

TROVATORE, IL see Goorhuis, Rob

TRUE LOVE see Ligeti, Gyorgy

TRUESDALE
   Ted E. Bear And Me *see Lentz

TRULS MED BOGEN *folk song
   (Eielsen, Steinar) SATB MUSIKK
   MH 2485   (T227)

TRUMPET VOLUNTARY see Purcell, Henry

TRUMPETS, THE see Vinter, Gilbert

TRUT AVANT, IL FAUT BOIRE see Richafort, Joannes

TRY see Kaufmann, Dieter

TSCHAIKOWSKY, PJOTR ILJITSCH
   see TCHAIKOVSKY, PIOTR ILYICH

TU AS TOUT SEUL see Janequin, Clement

TUCAPSKY, ANTONIN (1928-   )
   White Goose, The
      SSA,acap [3'30"] ROBERTON 392-00484
      $1.00   (T228)

TUCK ME TO SLEEP
   (Minihane) SSAA (women's barbershop)
   BOURNE B239145 $.50   (T229)

TULE ARMAANI see Bergman, Erik

TUMBALAIKA
   (De Cormier, Robert) men cor LAWSON
   LG 52388 $.85   (T230)

TUMMEL DICH, GUTS WEINLEIN see Strauss, Richard

TUNE, A see Eben, Petr

TURELLIER, JEAN
   Adieu Foulard
      4pt mix cor,opt gtr HEUGEL HE 32217
                                         (T231)

   Aux Marches Du Palais
      4pt mix cor,2rec,opt gtr HEUGEL
      HE 32006   (T232)

   Chanson Norvegienne
      4pt mix cor,opt gtr HEUGEL HE 32149
                                         (T233)

   Filles De Lorient, Les
      SATB,fl/ob/vln HEUGEL HE 31905
      contains also: Quand Je Menais
      Mes Chevaux Boire   (T234)

   Jamaica Farewell
      SAB,gtr,perc HEUGEL HE 32536   (T235)

   Jenin L'avenu
      SATB,opt gtr HEUGEL HE 32537   (T236)

   Quand Ce Beau Printemps Je Voy
      SATB,vln,fl,vcl HEUGEL HE 31912
                                         (T237)

   Quand Je Menais Mes Chevaux Boire
      see Turellier, Jean, Filles De
      Lorient, Les
      SAB,3rec HEUGEL HE 31905   (T238)

   Roy S'en Va-T-En Chasse, Le
      4pt mix cor,opt brass quin HEUGEL
      HE 32469   (T239)

TURKISCHES SCHENKENLIED see Mendelssohn-Bartholdy, Felix

TURN ON THE MUSIC see Palmer, Hap

TURN THAT WATER OFF! see Atkinson, Condit Robert

TURN YE TO ME
   (Goldman) SATB,Bar solo LAWSON
   LG 51907 $.70   (T240)

TURNHOUT, JAN-JACOBVAN
   Ghij Meyskens Die Van Der Comenschap Sijt
      (Lagas, R.) "You Ladies Who Move In
      Circles Of Trade" SATB,acap
      (diff) ZENGERINK G 535   (T241)

   You Ladies Who Move In Circles Of
      Trade *see Ghij Meyskens Die Van
      Der Comenschap Sijt

TURTLE DOVE, THE
   (Strommen) SATB,kbd CORONET 392-41425
   $.85   (T242)

TUTTLE, BILLIE G.
  One Verse At A Time
    2pt cor JACKMAN JMC7094   (T243)

TUTTO LO DI MI DICI see Lassus, Roland
  de (Orlandus)

TUUTULAULU see Kortekangas, Olli

TVA KORPOEM see Sandstrom, Jan

TVEIT, SIGVALD (1945-   )
  Gode Landet, Det
    cor,instrumental ensemble NORSK
                                     (T244)

  Ingen Er Sa Trygg I Fare
    mix cor NORSK NMO 9527   (T245)

  Tvo Kirkelige Shanties
    TTBB NORSK   (T246)

TVEITT, GEIRR (1908-1981)
  God Natt °Op.246,No.3
    [Norw] SMezA NORGE NC 3862   (T247)

  Sanger Til Dikt Av Johan Falkberget
    [Norw] men cor,TB soli,timp,perc,db
    [2'] NORGE   (T248)

  Sumarnatta °Op.246,No.2
    [Norw] SMezA NORGE   (T249)

TVO KIRKELIGE SHANTIES see Tveit,
  Sigvald

'TWAS THE NIGHT BEFORE CHRISTMAS (THE
  NIGHT BIG DADDY DROPPED IN) see
  Grundahl

TWEE AMOUREUZE EN EEN LUSTIGH LIEDEKEN
  see Schrijvers, Jean

TWEE KOREN see Voorn, Joop

TWEE OUDNEDERLANDSE LIEDEREN see
  Schrijvers, Jean

TWELVE CANONS see Braun, Yeheskiel

TWELVE DAYS AFTER CHRISTMAS see
  Silverberg, Frederick Irwin

TWELVE DAYS BEFORE CHRISTMAS see
  Silverberg, Frederick Irwin

TWELVE DAYS OF CHRISTMAS, THE
  (Humphris, Ian) SATB,acap NOVELLO
  $1.30   (T250)

TWELVE INDONESIAN FOLKSONGS °CC12U
  (Nobel, F. De) mix cor BROEKMANS
  BP 1087   (T251)

TWILIGHT IN SUMMER see Hamilton, Iain

TWINKLE, TWINKLE, CHRISTMAS STAR see
  Kupferschmid, Steven

TWINKLE, TWINKLE LITTLE STAR see
  Salerno, Chris Paquin

TWO BY TWO see Reilly

TWO CHOIR PIECES (IN MEMORIAM OF
  BENJAMIN BRITTEN) see Sveinsson,
  Atli Heimir

TWO CHORAL SETTINGS see Harlao, Aharon

TWO CHORAL WORKS see Rimsky-Korsakov,
  Nikolai

TWO CHORUSES FOR CHILDREN'S VOICES see
  Rimsky-Korsakov, Nikolai

TWO CHORUSES FOR MIXED VOICES, OP. 18
  see Rimsky-Korsakov, Nikolai

TWO CHORUSES FOR SATB see Speight, John
  A.

TWO CHRISTMAS PARTNER SONGS see Ashton,
  Bob Bruce

TWO EARLY FIFTEENTH-CENTURY
  CHANSONNIERS FROM THE LOW COUNTRIES
  °CCU
  (Biezen, J. Van; Gumbert, J.P.) cor
  VER.NED.MUS. MMN 15   (T252)

TWO EMILY DICKINSON CHORUSES see
  Barkin, Elaine R.

TWO EVA see Yavelow, Christopher
  Johnson

TWO IRISH SONGS
  (Jeffers) TTBB EARTHSNG EM-2 $.50
    contains: Cobbler, The; Eileen
    Aroon   (T253)

TWO KARELIAN FOLK SONGS see Bergman,
  Erik, Zwei Karelische Volkslieder

TWO LITTLE PIECES FOR CHOIR see
  Eiriksdottir, Karolina

TWO MADRIGALS °see Morley, Thomas, Now
  Is The Month Of Maying; Purcell,
  Henry, In These Delightful Pleasant
  Groves   (T254)

TWO MEDIEVAL LATIN LYRICS, OP.1 see
  Pert, Morris

TWO MEDIEVAL LATIN SONGS see Kohs,
  Ellis Bonoff

TWO MOVEMENTS FOR CHORUS WITH ORCHESTRA
  see Schnabel, Artur

TWO MOVEMENTS FOR CHORUS WITH ORCHESTRA
  see Schnabel, Artur

TWO NEGRO SPIRITUALS
  (Eielsen, Steinar) men cor MUSIKK
                                    (T255)
  (Eielsen, Steinar) mix cor MUSIKK
                                    (T256)

TWO PATHS OF VIRTUE see Schubert, Franz
  (Peter)

TWO PIECES see Gelbrun, Arthur

TWO POEMS BY ROLF JACOBSEN see Wallin,
  Rolf

TWO POEMS (IN ONE SONG) see Bialosky,
  Marshall H.

TWO ROSES, THE see Werner

TWO RUSSIAN FOLK SONGS see Biggs, John

TWO SONGS FROM "FIVE CHILDHOOD LYRICS"
  see Rutter, John

TWO SONGS OF LOVE see Ragnarsson,
  Hjalmar H.

TWO SONNETS see Pisk, Paul Amadeus

TWO SPANISH TRADITIONAL SONGS see
  Neaum, Michael

TWO THE SAME see Lunde, Ivar

TWO TONGUE TWISTERS see Goemanne

TWO TREE-TOADS see Bond, Victoria

TWO WHITE HORSES see Hays

TWO WINGS see Harter

TWO WITCHES, THE see Blank, Allan

TYRLE, TYRLOW see Willan, Healey

TYROLIENNE see Rossini, Gioacchino

TYTTOSET - THE LASSES - THREE FINNISH
  FOLK SONGS see Bergman, Erik

U

U ZIJ DE GLORIE see Oertel, L.

U ZIJ DE GLORIE see Oertel, L., Graf
  Waldersee

UAXUCTUM see Scelsi, Giacinto

UBER DIE HUGEL WUCHERT DER GINSTER see
  Schlunz, Annette

UBER ERICH M see Straesser, Joep

UBERS LOATERL see Deutschmann, Gerhard

UDOW, MICHAEL WILLIAM (1949-   )
  As The Wind Colors
    8 chanters in canoes and 4 gong
    players [45'] AM.COMP.AL. $1.60
                                     (U1)
  Music For Concert Choir And Carillon
    mix cor,carillon [9'] AM.COMP.AL.
    $7.70   (U2)

UGLAND, JOHAN VAREN
  A Dyp Av Rikdom
    wom cor MUSIKK   (U3)

UKRAINE! see Hayvoronsky, Mykhajlo

ULTAN, LLOYD (1929-   )
  Peace Be Multiplied
    SATB [3'] AM.COMP.AL. $3.10   (U4)

ULYSSE 2000 see Volery, Francis

UM LIEBE see Cadow, Paul

UNCLE DEAN see Sand, Cary J.

UNCLE SAM'S FARM see Hutchinson, J.E.

UND ALS DIE SCHNEIDER JAHRSTAG HATT'N
  see Kutzer, Ernst

UND AN EINEN TAG IM FEBRUAR see
  Deutschmann, Gerhard

UND DER HIMMEL HANGT VOLLER GEIGEN see
  Fall

...UND DES FRIEDENS KEIN ENDE see Poos,
  Heinrich

UND IN DEM SCHNEEGEBIRGE see Hensel,
  Walther

UND IN DEM SCHNEEGEBIRGE see Rothschuh,
  F.

UND SCHAU ICH HIN, SO SCHAUST DU HER
  see Reger, Max, Liebesqual

UND WIEDER GEHT EIN SCHONER TAG ZU ENDE
  see Winkler

UNDER HIMMELTEIKNET see Beck, Thomas
  Ludvigsen

UNDER LINDEN see Gaathaug, Morten

UNDER THE EAVES OF SNOW see Wiechowicz,
  Stanislaw, Pod Okapem Sniegu

UNDER THE GREENWOOD TREE see Adams,
  Leslie

UNDER THE GREENWOOD TREE see Schultz,
  Donna Gartman

UNDER THE STARS see Strom

UNGDOMSDROM see Bergman, Erik

UNGEWISSES LICHT see Schumann, Robert
  (Alexander)

UNGEWITTER see Schumann, Robert
  (Alexander)

UNICORNS, THE see Crawley, Clifford

UNSEEN, UNHEARD see Podesva, Jaromir

UNSER DAS LAND UND DIE ZEIT see Kohler,
  Siegfried

UNSERE VATER see Brahms, Johannes

UNTER APFELBLUTEN
  (Fassler, Guido) men cor,acap PELIKAN
  PE 1202   (U5)

UNTER DES LAUBDACHS HUT see Hensel,
  Fanny Mendelssohn

UNTIL WE MEET SOMEWHERE AGAIN see Simms

UNTREUE see Gluck, Fr.

UP! GOOD CHRISTEN FOLK (from Piae
  Cantiones)
  (Coombes, Douglas) unis cor,kbd
  LINDSAY   (U6)

UP ON THE HOUSETOP see Hanby

UP WHERE WE BELONG
  (Strommen) SATB CPP-BEL 5016UC1X
  $1.25   (U7)
  (Strommen) SSA CPP-BEL 5016UC2X $1.25
                                             (U8)
  (Strommen) SAB CPP-BEL 5016UC3X $1.25
                                             (U9)

UPON HER GRAVE see Mendelssohn-
  Bartholdy, Felix

UPPER MEADOWS see Sir, N.

URFER, ALBERT
  Polka Des Dimanches, La
    SATB HUGUENIN CH 2055   (U10)

  Va Petit Gars
    SATB HUGUENIN CH 2056   (U11)
    men cor HUGUENIN CH 2057   (U12)

URSPRUNG see Blomberg, Erik

USELESS DAYS see Sveinsson, Atli Heimir

USK see Paynter, John P.

UT OMNES HOMINES VIRANT HUMANITER see
  Laburda, Jiri

UTENDAL, ALEXANDER (ca. 1530-1581)
  Petite Nymphe Folatre
    SATB,acap HUGUENIN EB 447   (U13)

UTVIKLING? see Bakke, Ruth

V

VA PENSIERO see Verdi, Giuseppe

VA PETIT GARS see Urfer, Albert

VAAL, O. DE
  Lente-Mars
    SATB MOLENAAR 15006303   (V1)

  Lentemars
    (Smeets, L.) SSA MOLENAAR 15027404
                                     (V2)

VAARKJENNING see Baden, Conrad

VACCARO, JEAN-MICHEL
  Pierre, Tenez-Moi Pres De Vous
    3pt mix cor A COEUR JOIE 178   (V3)

VACHE NOIRE, LA see Bakfark, Balint
  (Valentin)

VACILLAT PES MEUS see Kopelent, Marek

VAER HILSET see Kleiberg, Stale

VAER UTALMODIG MENNESKE see Kruse,
  Bjorn Howard

VAGABOND SONG see Tilley, Alexander

VAGEHENS OTETUT NEIDIZET see Jalkanen,
  Pekka

VAGGSONG see Ostern, Per Hroar

VAGORNA see Sjoblom, Heimer

VAGUE EMPORTE AU LOIN, LA see Robin,
  Marie-Therese

VAGUES CHANTENT, LES see Abt, Franz

VAGUES DE LA MER, LES see Lama, S.

VAILLANT, RAYMOND (1935-   )
  Offrande Lyrique
    cor,4contrabsn,4vcl,4trom,perc
    TRANSAT. TRO01789   (V4)

VALCARCEL, EDGAR (1932-   )
  Checan IV
    SATB SEESAW   (V5)

VALCOLLA see Castelnuovo, V.

VALENTIN
  (Lattion, Guy) SATB,acap HUGUENIN
    CH 1194   (V6)

VALENTINE SONG, THE see Lawrence,
  Stephen L.

VALENTINE SONGS THAT TICKLE YOUR FUNNY
  BONE! see Roberts, Ruth

VALERIUS
  Wilt Heden Nu Treden
    SATB MOLENAAR 15021502   (V7)

VALERY
  Comme Un P'it Coqu'licot °see Asso

VALS see Grieg, Edvard Hagerup

VALSE see Chopin, Frederic

VALSE see Schubert, Franz (Peter)

VALSE DE LA POUPEE see Mengelberg,
  Karel

VALSE EN LA MINEUR see Chopin, Frederic

VAMPS °medley
  (Shaw, Kirby) SSA (contains Big
  Spender and Whatever Lola Wants)
  CPP-BEL CO153C2X $1.10, accomp tape
  available   (V8)

VAN BUITEN IJS, VAN BINNEN GLOED see
  Schweinsberg, Franz Joseph

VAN DE VATE, NANCY HAYES (1930-   )
  American Essay, An
    SATB,S solo,pno,perc [30']
    AM.COMP.AL. sc $27.15, pts $59.75
                                   (V9)

  Cantata For Women's Voices
    SSA,pic,fl,clar,harp,cel,2perc
    [19'] AM.COMP.AL. sc $34.30, pts
    $30.10   (V10)

  Pond, The
    (Flores, Angel) SATB [4']
    AM.COMP.AL. $5.40   (V11)

VAN DER MUELEN, SERVAES
  Altijt So Moet Ic Trueren
    (Lagas, R.) "Bowed Down With Grief
    And Pain" SATB,acap (med diff)
    ZENGERINK G 531   (V12)

  Bowed Down With Grief And Pain °see
    Altijt So Moet Ic Trueren

VAN DIJK, JAN
  see DIJK, JAN VAN

VAN IDERSTINE, ARTHUR PRENTICE
  (1920-   )
  Down The River
    SATB SCHIRM.G 320750 $.70   (V13)

VAN PARYS, GEORGES (1902-1971)
  Complainte De La Butte
    (Passaquet, R.) 4pt mix cor HEUGEL
    HE 31845   (V14)

VAN SLYCK, NICHOLAS (1922-   )
  Tick-Tock
    SSA WILLIS 10939 $.75   (V15)

  Traveller On The Wind
    SSA WILLIS 10938 $.75   (V16)

VAN WIJK, JAN
  Boudoir
    SATB,acap HARMONIA HU 3834   (V17)

  Fingers Of The Light, The
    SATB,acap HARMONIA HU 3832   (V18)

VANCE, M.
  April Is In My Mistress' Face
    SATB SCHIRM.G 323040 $.80   (V19)

VANDERLOVE, ANNE
  Ballade En Novembre
    (Frochot, J.) 4pt mix cor HEUGEL
    HE 32194   (V20)

  Chanson De Virginia, La
    (Frochot, J.) 4pt mix cor HEUGEL
    HE 32512   (V21)

  Civilisations Perdues
    (Frochot, J.) 4pt mix cor HEUGEL
    HE 32480   (V22)

  Enfants Tristes, Les
    (Frochot, J.) 4pt mix cor HEUGEL
    HE 32193   (V23)

VAPORS see White, Gary C.

VAR JE OG DET VAR DU, DET: FOLK TUNE
  FROM ELVERUM see Nystedt, Knut

VAR-VON see Sonstevold, Maj

VARDOGER see Rypdal, Terje

VAREN see Grieg, Edvard Hagerup

VARIATIONEN see Scheck, Helmut

VARIETY OF CURSES AND A BLESSING, A see
  Klerkx, Wim

VARIOUS CHORAL WORKS FOR TREBLE VOICES
  see Schumann, Robert (Alexander)

VARNATT see Soderlind, Ragnar

VASIJA DE BARRO, LA
  (Fourcaud, G.) mix cor HEUGEL
  HE 32519   (V24)

VASSDAL, TORE
  Tidlig Sommermorgen
    SATB NORSK   (V25)

VAUGHAN WILLIAMS, RALPH (1872-1958)
  Antiphon (from Five Mystical Songs)
    SATB GALAXY 1.5028 $.75   (V26)

  Bright Is The Ring Of Words
    (Wagner) SSA oct DEAN HRD 232 $.75
                                  (V27)
  Bushes And Briars
    TTBB NOVELLO 16 0202   (V28)

  Epithalamion
    SATB,B solo,fl,pno,strings OXFORD
                                  (V29)
  Infinite Shining Heavens, The
    (Wagner) SSA oct DEAN HRD 224 $.95
                                  (V30)
  Song Of Thanksgiving
    SATB&opt jr cor,S&speaking voice,
    2.2.3.3. 4.3.3.1. timp,perc,harp/
    pno,opt org,strings OXFORD
    339455-3 $3.75   (V31)

  Whither Must I Wander?
    (Wagner) SSA oct DEAN HRD 237 $.95
                                  (V32)

VEA, KETIL (1932-   )
  Morgonstund
    [Norw] mix cor,acap NORGE   (V33)

VEA, KETIL (cont'd.)

Tre Finnmarksrim
[Norw] SSAA NORGE   (V34)

Tre Mannskorsatser *CCU
[Norw] men cor,acap NORGE   (V35)

VECCHI
Imitatione Del Venetiano
(Marvin) TBB OXFORD 385726-X $1.00
(V36)

VECCHI, ORAZIO (HORATIO) (1550-1605)
So Ben Mi Ch'a Bon Tempo
CAILLARD PC 217   (V37)

VED EN MILEPEL see Kjeldaas, Arnljot

VEILLEE DES CONFEDERES, LA see
Schumann, Robert (Alexander)

VEINJE see Am, Magnar

VELDE, H.V.D.
Des Winters Als Het Regent
SATB MOLENAAR 15021603   (V38)

VELSIGNA BAND SOM BIND see Odegaard,
Henrik

VENERID see Bottcher, Eberhard

VENI SPONSA MEA *mot
(Turellier, J.) 5pt mix cor,org
HEUGEL HE 32515   (V39)

VENOSA, CARLO GESUALDO DA
see GESUALDO, [DON] CARLO

VENT D'ORAGE, LE see Schumann, Robert
(Alexander)

VENT ET LA JEUNESSE, LE see Rivat

VENTINOVE LUGLIO, IL
(Frochaux, Jean-Bernard) SATB,acap
HUGUENIN CH 2027   (V40)

VENUS SCHOON, EEN see Clemens, Jacobus
(Clemens non Papa)

VERBESSELT, AUGUSTE (1919-   )
Ares En Irene
cor,orch [25'30"] CBDM f.s.   (V41)

VERBOOM, BERNARD
Bidden Is Niet Enkel Knielen
4 eq voices,acap ZENGERINK 353
(V42)

VERCOE, ELIZABETH (1941-   )
Irreveries From Sappho
SSA,pno [7'] oct ARSIS $2.00 (V43)

VERDELOT, PHILLIPPE (? -ca. 1550)
O Sweetest Nighttime
(Campbell, Robert) SATB,acap (med
diff) FISCHER,C CM8307 $.85 (V44)

One Smiling Summer Morning *see
Vostr' Acuti Dardi, Il

Vostr' Acuti Dardi, Il
(Neuen, Donald) "One Smiling Summer
Morning" [It/Eng] mix cor LAWSON
LG 52059 f.s.   (V45)

VERDI, GIUSEPPE (1813-1901)
Bandietenkoor (from Ernani)
(Elsenaar, E.) TTBB MOLENAAR
15011403   (V46)

Chor Der Gefangenen *see Teure
Heimat

Chorus Of The Hebrew Slaves *see Va
Pensiero

Choruses From Operas *CCU
[Russ/It] cor,pno MEZ KNIGA 171
(V47)

Inno Delle Nazioni
SATB,T solo,2+pic.2.2.2. 4.2.3.1.
timp,perc,2harp,strings [18']
KALMUS A7167 voc sc f.s., sc
f.s., ipa, ipr   (V48)

Monnikenkoor (from La Forza Del
Destino)
(Lemarc, A.) TTBB MOLENAAR 15013002
(V49)

Slavenkoor (from Nabucco)
TTBB MOLENAAR 15014204   (V50)

Teure Heimat (from Nabuccodonosor)
(Korda, V.) "Chor Der Gefangenen"
mix cor,acap DOBLINGER NR 133
(V51)

Va Pensiero (from Nabucco)
(Neuen, Donald) "Chorus Of The
Hebrew Slaves" SATB,pno LAWSON
52493 $1.00   (V52)

VERDONK, JAN
Je L'aime Bien
(Agnel, A.) 2pt mix cor HEUGEL
HE 32072   (V53)

VERGEBENS see Reger, Max

VERGEBLICHE WARNUNG - HANSEL, DEIN
GRETELEIN *Op.38
(Gebhard, L.) men cor BOHM see from
Was Scheren Mich Sorgen: Drei
Heitere Volkslieder   (V54)

VERGISS MICH NICHT! see May, Karl

VERGISSMEINNICHT see Bruckner, Anton

VERGNUGTE STUNDEN see Trapp, Willy

VERHULST, JOHANNES (1816-1891)
Moet Je Varen: Daar Ging Er Een
Meisje
(Regenzki) SSA/TTB ZENGERINK 302
(V55)

VERMACHTNIS see Weiss, Manfred

VERMULST, JAN (1925-   )
Ballade Van De Fiets
SATB MOLENAAR 15014704   (V56)

Ballade Van Het Zout
[Dutch/Ger] SATB,acap HARMONIA 3686
(V57)

Ballade Van Het Zout, De
"Salz-Ballade, Die" SSAA BANK (V58)

Des Winters Als Het Regent
SSA MOLENAAR 15024404   (V59)

Drink Mij Niet Toe *see Drink To Me
Only With Thine Eyes

Drink To Me Only With Thine Eyes
(Kooij, E.J.) "Drink Mij Niet Toe"
SATB MOLENAAR 15002402   (V60)
(Kooij, E.J.) "Drink Mij Niet Toe"
TTBB MOLENAAR 15011802   (V61)
(Kooij, E.J.) "Drink Mij Niet Toe"
MOLENAAR 15015703   (V62)

Golden Slumbers
"Sluimer Zacht" SATB MOLENAAR
15003503   (V63)

Ik Zag Cecilia Komen
SATB MOLENAAR 15027303   (V64)

Lied Van De Droge Haring
SATB MOLENAAR 15015003   (V65)

Reuzegom
TTBB MOLENAAR 15015304   (V66)

Reuzegom (Oud Vlaams Volkslied)
SATB MOLENAAR 15015204   (V67)

Salz-Ballade, Die *see Ballade Van
Het Zout, De

Sluimer Zacht *see Golden Slumbers

VERSTOHLEN GEHT DER MOND AUF see
Brahms, Johannes

VERSTOVSKY, A.
Choruses From Operas *CCU
[Russ] cor,pno MEZ KNIGA 161
includes choruses from Askold's
Tomb, Pan Tvardovsky, and
Homesickness   (V68)

VERTUE see White

VERWUNDBAR SIND WIR, ABER NICHT
BESIEGBAR see Schubert, Manfred

VERY GOLDEN SEASON, A see McPheeters

VERZAUBERTE LIEDER see Straesser, Joep

VESNYANKA (SPRING SONG) *CCU
[Russ] jr cor MEZ KNIGA 510   (V69)

VEYSSEYRE, HENRI
Brumes
4pt mix cor,org A COEUR JOIE CA 17
see from Triptyque De La Vie
(V70)

Eveil
4pt mix cor,org A COEUR JOIE CA 17
see from Triptyque De La Vie
(V71)

Joie
4pt mix cor,org A COEUR JOIE CA 17
see from Triptyque De La Vie
(V72)

Triptyque De La Vie *see Brumes;
Eveil; Joie   (V73)

VEZZOSI AUGELLI see Wert, Giaches de
(Jakob van)

VI TROSTER see Lyssand, Henrik

VI VIL GA UT see Hovland, Egil

VIADANA, LODOVICO GROSSI DA (1560-1627)
Sing, Rejoice, Ye Righteous
(Minton, Larry) SATB (med) GENTRY
JG2101 $1.00   (V74)

VIATIQUE see Cornaz, Emmanuel

VIATONTEN VALSSI see Rautavaara,
Einojuhani

VIC, C.H.
Don Leon
(Vaccaro, J.M.) SATB A COEUR JOIE
819   (V75)

VICK
Mark Well, My Heart
SAB&camb CAMBIATA C117209 $.70
(V76)

VICTOIRE EN CHANTANT, LA see Funck-
Brentano, Fr.

VICTORIA STATION see Price, Beryl

VICTORY
(Chinn) SATB CPP-BEL 2746VC1X $1.25,
accomp tape available   (V77)
(Chinn) SAB CPP-BEL 2746VC3X $1.25,
accomp tape available   (V78)

VIDALIE
Actualites (composed with Goldmann)
(Tritsch, J.) 4 eq voices HEUGEL
HE 32065   (V79)

VIDALIN, M.
Printemps, Le (composed with Fugain,
Michel; Blanes, G.)
(Gentilhomme, M.) SATB/3 eq voices
HEUGEL HE 32550   (V80)

VIDAR, JORUNN (1918-   )
Love Song
mix cor,pno ICELAND 015-7   (V81)

VIE, LA see Girod, Vincent

VIEILLE MAISON VOL. 1, LA see Lauber,
Emile

VIEILLE MAISON VOL. 2, LA see Lauber,
Emile

VIEILLE MERE see Cossetto, Emil

VIEILLES MAISONS, LES see Rochat, Jean

VIENI IMENCO see Monteverdi, Claudio

VIENS, DOUX PRINTEMPS see Haydn,
[Franz] Joseph

VIENS, PRINTEMPS see Schubert, Franz
(Peter)

VIENS SOUS MON MANTEAU
(Fombonne, Jacques) SATB A COEUR JOIE
360   (V82)

VIER CANONS see Schubert, Franz (Peter)

VIER CHORE see Schleiermacher, Steffen

VIER DOPPELCHORIGE GESANGE, OP. 141 see
Schumann, Robert (Alexander)

VIER FRANZOSISCHE LIEBESLIEDER *see
Bergere Et Le Monsieur, La;
Fillette, Une; Je Suis Trop
Jeunette   (V83)

VIER FRUHLINGSLIEDER see Schroeder,
Hermann

VIER GESANGE see Schumann, Robert
(Alexander)

VIER GESANGE see Brahms, Johannes

VIER HEINE-LIEDER see Andriessen,
Jurriaan

VIER HEITERE EUROPAISCHE VOLKSLIEDER
*see Flohe Wimmeln Meinem Weibe;
Junggeselle, Der; Konig Dagobert,
Der; Petruschka   (V84)

VIER MADRIGALE AUS "DIE LEIDEN DES
JUNGEN WERTHERS" see Bose, Hans-
Jurgen Von

VIER MINNELIEDER see Schroeder, Hermann

VIER RUCKERT-LIEDER see Haus, Karl

VIER VERHALTNISSE, DIE see Biebl, Franz

VIER WEVERKENS ZAG MEN TER BOTERMARKT
GAAN
(Schmitz, Jan) [Dutch] 3 eq voices,
acap ZENGERINK V-G 416   (V85)

VIER WEVERKENS ZAG MEN TER BOTERMARKT
GAAN see Anonymous

VIERSTIMMIGE LIEDER FUR GEMISCHTEN CHOR
see Spohr, Ludwig (Louis)

VIERSTIMMIGE VOLKSLIEDER *CCU
(Silcher, Friedrich) SATB,pno BAREN.
6378 piano accomp available: BA
6384; arr. by Hermann Kahlenbach
(V86)

VIGIL OF VENUS, THE see Lloyd, George

VIGL, KARL H.
Haus Steht Jetzt Vollendet, Das
(Miller, Franz R.) men cor,4winds/
kbd BOHM   (V87)

VIGNEAULT, GILLES
Beau Voyageur (composed with Rochon,
G.)
(Passaquet, R.) 3pt mix cor/eq
voices/6pt mix cor HEUGEL
HE 32480   (V88)
(Passaquet, R.) 6pt mix cor HEUGEL
HE 32481   (V89)
(Passaquet, R.) 3-6 eq voices
HEUGEL HE 32481   (V90)

Doux Chagrin, Le
(Holstein) SAB,opt pno CAILLARD
PC 179   (V91)

Mon Pays
(Holstein) SAB,opt pno CAILLARD
PC 180   (V92)

Petit Bonhomme, Le
(Passaquet, R.) 3 eq voices/4pt mix
cor HEUGEL HE 32336   (V93)
(Passaquet, R.) 4pt mix cor/3 eq
voices HEUGEL HE 32336   (V94)

Tam Ti De Lam
(Holstein) SAB,opt pno CAILLARD
PC 181   (V95)

Voyageur Sedentaire, Le
(Ziberlin, F.) 3 eq voices/4pt mix
cor HEUGEL HE 32261   (V96)

VIGNERON, LE
(Passaquet, R.) 4-8pt mix cor HEUGEL
HE 32271   (V97)

VIIHDESOVITUKSIA MIESKUOROLLE see
Hilden, Sakari

VILANCETES, CANTIGAS E ROMANCES
*CC145U,16th cent
1-4pt cor PORT.MUS. PM 47   (V98)

VILLANELLE see Lagger, Oscar

VILLARD, JEAN (GILLES) (1895-   )
A L'enseigne De La Fille Sans Coeur
(Frochaux, J.C.) TTBB HUGUENIN
CH 2051   (V99)

Mannerchor De Steffisbourg, Le
(Tritsch, J.) 4 eq voices HEUGEL
HE 32189   (V100)

VILLE DE SARLAT see Blanchard

VILLEGAGNON see Prado, Jose-Antonio
(Almeida)

VILLIERS, PIERRE DE
Hiver Sera, Et L'ete, Variable, L'
(Agnel, A.) 2 eq voices,opt 2rec
HEUGEL HE 32455   (V101)

VILLOTTE NAPOLITAINE see Donati,
Baldassare (Donato)

VIN VAUDOIS, LE see Pileur, G.

"VINDUER" FOR CHOIR AND MAGNETIC TAPE
see Berge, Hakon

VINETA see Brahms, Johannes

VINGER see Janson, Alfred

VINGESLAG see Killengreen, Christian

VINS DU PAYS ROMAND, LES see Lauber,
Emile

VINSON, HARVEY
Busy Ben By The Sea (composed with
Hewitt-Jones, Tony)
see Great Granny's Seaside Songs

Great Granny's Seaside Songs
(composed with Hewitt-Jones,
Tony)
unis cor,pno,opt strings,opt perc
ROBERTON $1.25
contains: Busy Ben By The Sea;
Paddling; Sandcastle Cake; Sea
Shell Song   (V102)

VINSON, HARVEY (cont'd.)

Paddling (composed with Hewitt-Jones,
Tony)
see Great Granny's Seaside Songs

Sandcastle Cake (composed with
Hewitt-Jones, Tony)
see Great Granny's Seaside Songs

Sea Shell Song (composed with Hewitt-
Jones, Tony)
see Great Granny's Seaside Songs

VINTER, GILBERT (1909-1969)
Trumpets, The *cant
mix cor,B solo,brass,perc,opt org
[40'] WEINBERGER   (V103)

VINTERLAND see Forselv, Randi

VIOLETS ARE FOR PICKING see Emig, Lois
Irene (Myers)

VIOLETTE, ANDREW
Love Is Colder Than Death
SATB,org [7'] AM.COMP.AL. $6.15
(V104)

VIRGINIA see Paynter, John P.

VIRKELIGGJORELSE see Schaathun, Asbjorn

VISA OM RIMFROST OCH VINTERSTRA see
Paulson

VISA TILL EN LITEN MANNISKA see
Blomberg, Erik

VISA VID VINDENS ANGAR see Paulson

VISE OM A VAERA GLAD see Bergh, Sverre

VISIONS see Masson, Askell

VISIT FROM THE SEA, A see Liddell,
Claire

VISOCCHI, MARK
Easy Mix 'N' Match: Instant Part
Singing *see Jenkins, David

VITA SINE PROPOSITO VAGA EST see
Malmlof-Forssling, Carin

VITEJ, MAJI see Berkovec, Jiri

VIVA LA MUSICA see Strategier, Herman

VIVA LA MUSICA see Jochum, Otto

VIVA LA MUSICA see Strategier, Herman

VIVA LA MUSICA: MUSICA, DU SCHONE ZIER
see Mutter, Gerbert

VIVACE (ANDANTINO) see Wijnnobel, P.

VIVAS! see Rinehart, John

VIVAS CRESCAS, FLOREAS see Malmlof-
Forssling, Carin

VIVE HENRI IV see Daniel, Etienne

VIVE L'AMOUR
(Siltman) BB&camb CAMBIATA U980146
$.65   (V105)

VIVISEKTION see Melin, Sten

V'LA L'BON VENT
(Perisson, J.) 4pt mix cor HEUGEL
HE 32265   (V106)

VLA L'BON VENT see Caillard, Philippe

VLEUG'LEN: EEN LIED, EEN LIED, UW LEVEN
LANG see Maassen, Johannes Ant.

VLOED IN KLANK, DE see Franken, Wim

VOCAL SECULAR WORKS see Sweelinck, Jan
Pieterszoon

VOCAL WORKS ON TEXTS BY YAR SLAVUTYCH
*CC14U
cor,pno DUMA $10.00 contains works by
Bilohrud, Borodievych and others
(V107)

VOCALI, LE see Swider, Jozef,
Samogloski

VOCERO DU NIOLO
(Fombonne, Jacques) SMezAB A COEUR
JOIE 352   (V108)

VOCHT, LODEWIJK DE (1887-   )
Fabelen Naar Eeuwenoude Verdichtsels
In Volkstrant: eerste Reeks
*CC6U
unis cor,kbd ZENGERINK Z 621 (V109)

Fabelen Naar Eeuwenoude Verdichtsels
In Volkstrant: tweede Reeks
*CC6U
unis cor,kbd ZENGERINK Z 622 (V110)

VOCHT, LODEWIJK DE (cont'd.)

Fabelen Naar Eeuwenoude Verdichtsels
In Volkstrant: derde Reeks *CC6U
unis cor,kbd ZENGERINK Z 623 (V111)

Joie Printanniere *see Lentevreugd

Jonge Jaar, Het
"Printemps" SSAATTBB ZENGERINK 639
(V112)
Lentevreugd
"Joie Printanniere" SSAATTBB
ZENGERINK 640   (V113)

Merel In De Morgen: Ik Sliep In
Frisschen Druivelaar
unis cor,kbd ZENGERINK Z 616 (V114)

Printemps *see Jonge Jaar, Het

Slaap Kindeke, Slaap *see Wiegezang

Wiegezang
"Slaap Kindeke, Slaap" unis cor
ZENGERINK Z 617   (V115)

VOERMANSLIED see Evertse, J.

VOEU see Piantoni, Louis

VOGEL, ROGER CRAIG (1947-   )
My Secret Love
SSA [2'] AM.COMP.AL. $1.60   (V116)

Nature Of The Cat, The
SSA,pno [5'] AM.COMP.AL. $5.40
(V117)

VOGGEVISE see Killengreen, Christian

VOI MI PONESTI UN FOCO see Arcadelt,
Jacob

VOICE FROM A DREAM, A see Bacak, Joyce
Eilers

VOICES OF SLEEP see Patterson, Paul

VOICI LA PENTECOTE see Blanchard

VOICI LE GAI PRINTEMPS
(Langree, Alain) 2-3 eq voices A
COEUR JOIE 9 016 from Quartre
Chansons Populaires Hongroises
(V118)
(Lauber, Emile) TTBB HUGUENIN SP 7
(V119)
VOICI LE JOLI MOIS DE MAI
(Grimbert, J.) 4 eq voices HEUGEL
31901   (V120)

VOICI LE VERT ET BEAU MAI see Mauduit,
Jacques

VOICI VENIR LE MOIS DE MAI
(Estermann, J.) mix cor,acap PELIKAN
PE1179   (V121)

VOILA L'BEAU TEMPS see Lauber, Emile

VOILA LE PRINTEMPS
see Mare De Deu, La

VOIX DES NAUFRAGES, LES see Blareau,
Ludovic

VOLERY, FRANCIS
Je Vois Neuchatel
SATB,acap HUGUENIN CH 2047   (V122)

Marins Des Etoiles
TTBB HUGUENIN CH 2050   (V123)

Ulysse 2000
mix cor HUGUENIN CH 2066   (V124)

VOLEZ, ZEPHIRS! VOLEZ! see Rameau,
Jean-Philippe

VOLKSLIEDCHEN see Schumann, Robert
(Alexander)

VOLKSLIEDER AUS ALLER WELT *see
Coconut And Banana; Crawdad Song,
The; Down By De Riverside; I Want
To Be Ready; My Lord, What A
Mornin'; Peter Go Ring Dem Bells
(V125)
VOLKSLIEDER IM RHYTHMUS DER ZEIT see
Trapp, Willy

VOLKSLIEDER see Reger, Max

VOLKSLIEDSATZE *see Jetzt Fangt Das
Schone Fruhjahr An; Mai Tritt Ein
Mit Freuden, Der   (V126)

VOLLE, BJARNE
Du Ska Itte Tro I Graset
[Norw] SAB,acap NORGE   (V127)

Du Ska Itte Tro I Graset *CC3U
[Norw] mix cor NORGE   (V128)

VOLLE, BJARNE (cont'd.)

Liten Vise, En °CC3U
[Norw] men cor NORGE   (V129)

Tre Skjemteviser °CC3U
[Norw] SATB NORGE   (V130)

VOLLE, MARTIN
Songen
(Volle, Bjarne) [Norw] SATB,acap
NORGE   (V131)

VOM LEBEN see Gebhard

VON BAUMEN, KNOSPEN UND NACHTIGALLEN
see Kohler, Siegfried

VON DEN SIEBEN SCHWABEN: HORET DIE
GESCHICHTE see Miller, Franz R.

VON DER LIEBE UND DEM SUFF see
Schroeder, Hermann

VON GOLD EIN RINGELEIN see Goller,
Fritz

VON HERZ UND SCHMERZ see Seeger, Peter

VON REH UND FUCHS see Irrgang, Horst

VON RUDESHEIM BIS HEIDELBERG see Stolz,
Robert

VON SCHELMEN UND SPITZBUBEN see
Hollfelder, Waldram

VOOR ALLEN: DE AARDE IS VOOR ALLEN see
Zwager, Piet

VOORJAAR: DE WINTER IS GEWEKEN see
Bruggen, Willem Van

VOORJAAR: DE WINTER IS GEWEKEN see
Smeets, Leo

VOORJAARSNACHT: GIJ ZIJT MIJN LUST see
Schubert, Franz (Peter), Nacht,
Die: Wie Schon Bist Du

VOORN, JOOP (1932-   )
Twee Koren
3pt mix cor [7'] DONEMUS   (V132)

VOR DEM GEWITTER see Kohler, Siegfried

VORSICHT
cor HIEBER MH 5027   (V133)

VOSTR' ACUTI DARDI, IL see Verdelot,
Phillippe

VOSTRAK, ZBYNEK (1920-   )
Kantata Na Text Franze Kafky °Op.34
mix cor,fl,clar,bsn,2trp,tam-tam,
tom-tom [20'0"] SUPRAPHON H 4631
(V134)

VOULZY, LAURENT
Belle-Ile-En-Mer Marie-Galante
(Ott, Norbert) SAB A COEUR JOIE
1029   (V135)

VOUS MARCHEZ DU BOUT DU PIED see
Willaert, Adrian

VOUS ME TUEZ SI DOUCEMENT see Mauduit,
Jacques

VOUS PERDEZ TEMPS see Mittantier

VOUS QUI AIMEZ LES DAMES see Castro,
Jean de

VOYAGE see Roussakis, Nicolas

VOYAGE DE DECOUVERTES see Denereaz,
Alexandre

VOYAGERS see Hoddinott, Alun

VOYAGEUR SEDENTAIRE, LE see Vigneault,
Gilles

VOYANT SOUFFRIR CELLE QUI ME TOURMENTE
see Cosson, A.

VOZ MIA, CANTA, CANTA see Denhoff,
Michael

VRAI DIEU D'AMOUR see Gero, Ihan

VRAI DIEU D'AMOUR see Opienski, Henryk

VRAIMENT, C'EST ETRANGE
(Terral, F.) jr cor,Orff inst HEUGEL
HE 32289   (V136)

VRANKEN, JOSEPH
Fragment Uit Het Lied Der Achttien
Doden: Een Cel Is Maar Twee Meter
Lang
4 eq voices,acap ZENGERINK 208
(V137)
Zonne Straalt, De: Zilver Glanzend
4 eq voices,acap ZENGERINK 26
(V138)

VRANKEN, PETRUS JOHANNES JOSEPHUS
Domine, Salvam Fac Reginam Nostram
4 eq voices,acap ZENGERINK 308
(V139)
Tod Und Verklarung: Tondichtung
4 eq voices,acap ZENGERINK 71
(V140)
Zon, De: Lieve Meid, De Lucht Is
Dronken °Op.76
4 eq voices,acap ZENGERINK 309
(V141)

VREDE (SONG OF OLYMPIA) see Blum,
Herbert

VREDE: VREDE, SPREIDT GIJ UW ZACHTE
VLEUGELS see Zwager, Piet

VREUGDE see Schubert, Franz (Peter)

VRIES, KLAAS DE (1944-   )
Phrases
4pt mix cor,S solo,3.3.3.3.
4.3.3.1. 3perc,xylo/vibra,
marimba,2pno,2harp,strings [16']
DONEMUS   (V142)

VROLIJKE ZANGERS, DE see Bruch, Max,
Frohliche Musicus, Der

VRUECHT EN DUECHT MYN HERT VERHUECHT
see Episcopius, L.

VUATAZ, ROGER (1898-   )
Belle Au Jardin De Mai °Op.10
TTBB HUGUENIN CH 772   (V143)

C'est Un Vrai Bateau, Fantaisie
TTBB HUGUENIN CH 774   (V144)

Chanson De Rosette °Op.3,No.2
TTBB HUGUENIN CH 775   (V145)

Chansons Pour Enfants De Tout Age
°CC8L
eq voices,pno HUGUENIN CH 864
(V146)
Chant Des Serfs, Le
TTBB HUGUENIN CH 770   (V147)

Gugler, Les
TTBB HUGUENIN CH 771   (V148)

Mere Godichon, La
TTBB HUGUENIN CH 773   (V149)

Pauvre Laboureur, Le
TTBB HUGUENIN CH 769   (V150)

VULLY, LE see Bovet, Joseph

W

WABASH CANNONBALL, THE
(Freed) 1-3pt cor CPP-BEL DMC 08118
$.95   (W1)

WACH AUF, MEIN HORT see Kubizek,
Augustin

WACH AUF, WACH AUF MIT HELLER STIMM see
Gebhard, Hans

WACHTEL, LEVI (1920-   )
Three Pieces
speaking cor,perc [11'] perf sc
ISR.MUS.INST. 6375   (W2)

WADE
Christmas Again
SATB KJOS C8723 $.80   (W3)

WADE IN THE WATER
(Howorth) SAB CPP-BEL OCT 02219 $.95
(W4)

WAEBER, MICHEL
J'ai De Toi Une Image
SATB HUGUENIN CH 2080   (W5)

WAELRANT, HUBERT (ca. 1517-1595)
Musiciens Qui Chantez
SATB,acap HUGUENIN EB 318 (W6)

Soir Approche, Le
SATB,acap HUGUENIN EB 280 (W7)

WAGNER
Advent Legend, An °see Lee

Over The Sea To Skye
SSA SHAWNEE 0514 $.85   (W8)

WAGNER, DOUGLAS EDWARD (1952-   )
Pasture, The
SSA SHAWNEE 0513 $.80   (W9)

WAGNER, RICHARD (1813-1883)
Bridal Chorus (from Lohengrin)
mix cor,pno 4-hands sc SCHOTTS
ST07154 $11.95, cor pts SCHOTTS
ST07154-01 $1.95   (W10)

Choeur Des Messagers De Paix (from
Rienzi)
TTBB HUGUENIN CH 461   (W11)

Choeur Des Pelerins (from Tannhauser)
TTBB HUGUENIN EB 440   (W12)

Chor Der Spinnerinnen (from Flying
Dutchman: Spinner's Chorus)
wom cor,pno 4-hands sc SCHOTTS
ST07153 $8.95, cor pts SCHOTTS
ST07153-01 $1.50   (W13)

Choruses From Operas °CCU
[Russ/Ger] cor,pno MEZ KNIGA 170
(W14)
Mit Gewitter Und Sturm (from Flying
Dutchman)
(Poos, Heinrich) "Sailor's Chorus"
men cor,pno 4-hands sc SCHOTTS
ST07151 $6.95, cor pts SCHOTTS
ST07151-01 $1.50   (W15)

Pilgrim's Chorus (from Tannhauser)
men cor,pno 4-hands sc SCHOTTS
ST07155 $12.95, cor pts SCHOTTS
ST07155-01 $1.50   (W16)
(Goldman) SAB LAWSON OC 10251 $.70
(W17)
Roman War Song, A (from Rienzi)
(Fletcher) TTBB,pno ROBERTON $1.00
(W18)
Sailor's Chorus °see Mit Gewitter
Und Sturm

Steuermann, Lass Die Wacht! (from
Flying Dutchman: Norwegian
Sailor's Chorus)
men cor,pno 4-hands sc SCHOTTS
ST07152 $8.95, cor pts SCHOTTS
ST07152-01 $1.50   (W19)

WAHRE FREUNDSCHAFT SOLL NICHT WANKEN
see Backer, Hans

WAHREND DER TRENNUNG see Brahms,
Johannes

WAITIN' FOR THE DAWN OF PEACE
(Jeffers) TTBB EARTHSNG EM-1 $.50
(W20)
WAITIN' FOR THE ROBERT E. LEE see
Madsen

WAKE UP, IT'S SPRINGTIME see
Kupferschmid, Steven

WAKE UP, JACOB °spir
(De Cormier, Robert) SATB,acap LAWSON
52400   (W21)

WALDEIER, ERIK
  Tonedigt
    SATB,vln,vla,vcl,pno NORGE   (W22)

WALDEN - 1974 see Oliver, Harold

WALDEN POND see Kelly, Robert T.

WALDESKLANG see Naegeli, Hans Georg

WALDESNACHT see Brahms, Johannes

WALDHOORN, DE see Silcher, Friedrich

WALDKANTATE see Jochum, Otto

WALDKANTATE see Rudinger, Gottfried

WALK A LITTLE SLOWER, MY FRIEND see
  Price

WALK ALONG BESIDE ME see Bourque

WALK ON BY see Bacharach, Burt F.

WALK SOFTLY IN SPRINGTIME see
  Burroughs, Bob Lloyd

WALKER
  Hand In Hand °see Rogers

WALKER, ROBERT (1946-   )
  Five Summer Madrigals
    SATB,acap NOVELLO   (W23)

  Sun On The Celadines, The
    mix cor NOVELLO   (W24)

  Three Early English Lyrics
    SSAA,acap WEINBERGER   (W25)

WALKING HOME FROM SCHOOL see Barnes

WALL IS DOWN, THE see Nystedt, Knut

WALLACH, JOELLE
  Five American Echoes
    SATB [13'] AM.COMP.AL. $5.40   (W26)

  Look Down Fair Moon
    SATB [3'] AM.COMP.AL. $3.45   (W27)

  Plaint For A Prince And King
    TB,pno/org [7'] AM.COMP.AL. $4.60
                                     (W28)

  Tears
    SATB [5'] AM.COMP.AL. $7.65   (W29)

  Three Whitman Visions
    SATB [15'] AM.COMP.AL. $20.60   (W30)

  Youth's Serenade
    jr cor,fl,bsn,harmonium,harp [14']
    AM.COMP.AL. $9.15   (W31)

WALLEK-WALEWSKI, BOLESLAW (1885-1944)
  Bajeczka O Chorym Kotku
    "Fairy-Tale About A Sick Pussy-Cat,
    A" [Polish] men cor,acap POLSKIE
    NPCH 67   (W32)

  Fairy-Tale About A Sick Pussy-Cat, A
    °see Bajeczka O Chorym Kotku

WALLIN, ROLF (1957-   )
  So Far Unchanged
    SATB,electronic tape manuscript
    NORGE   (W33)

  Two Poems By Rolf Jacobsen
    mix cor NORSK NMO 9606   (W34)

WALTER
  Make A Joyful Noise
    3pt mix cor CPP-BEL SV8642 $1.10,
    accomp tape available   (W35)

  Merry Christmas Waltz
    2pt cor CPP-BEL SV8709 $.95, accomp
    tape available   (W36)

WALTER, FRIED (1907-   )
  Funf Chore Nach Gedichten Von Theodor
    Storm °CC5U
    mix cor ZIMMER. 620   (W37)

WALTER, LANA
  Christmas Bells
    2pt cor,opt bells CPP-BEL SV8708
    $.95, accomp tape available   (W38)

  Music Is Full Of Dreams
    2pt cor CPP-BEL SV8606 f.s.   (W39)

WALTERS, EDMUND
  Andalusian Love Song
    TTBB,pno [3'30"] ROBERTON 392-00546
    $1.25   (W40)

  Lady And The Swine, The (Nursery
    Rhymes, No.3)
    TTBB,pno ROBERTON 392-00506 $1.25
                                     (W41)

  Sunday's Child (Nursery Rhymes, No.2)
    TTBB,acap ROBERTON 392-00512 $1.25
                                     (W42)

WALTERS, EDMUND (cont'd.)

  Tom The Piper's Son (Nursery Rhymes,
    No.1)
    TTBB,pno ROBERTON 392-00509 $1.25
                                     (W43)

WALTZ OF THE INNOCENTS see Rautavaara,
  Einojuhani

WALTZ OF THE INNOCENTS see Rautavaara,
  Einojuhani, Viatonten Valssi

WALTZING MATILDA °Austral
  (Cooper) S&camb,SA soli CAMBIATA f.s.
                                     (W44)

WALTZING MATILDA see Struijk, P.

WALZER FUR DICH UND FUR MICH, EINEN see
  Grothe

WANDELLIED see Stenz, Herman

WANDELLIED: WIJ TREKKEN ONDER 'T LOOF
  see Stomp, Henk Johan

WANDERKANTATE see Hollfelder, Waldram

WANDERLIED DER ZEIT see Kaufmann,
  Dieter

WANDERLIED (EIN BISCHEN SINGSANG) see
  Stolz, Robert

WANDERLIED (EIN BISSCHEN SINGSANG) see
  Stolz, Robert

WANDLEN LANGS DE WIJDE WEGEN see Stenz,
  Herman, Wandellied

WARD, JOHN (1571?-1641)
  Satyr Once, A
    SATB STAINER 3.3205 $.85   (W45)

WARD, NORMAN
  Know Who You Are
    SA (easy) HHP   (W46)

WARD, SAMUEL AUGUSTUS
  America, The Beautiful
    (Althouse) SATB SHAWNEE 1851 $.95
                                     (W47)
    (Barker, Warren) SA/SAB,opt pno/
    band oct ALFRED 7664 $.95, pts
    ALFRED 3448 $40.00   (W48)
    (Berglund) SATB,opt band/orch KJOS
    C8822 $.90, ipa   (W49)
    (Leidzen) SATB CPP-BEL OCT 01961
    $.95   (W50)
    (Ross, Robert) TTBB,kbd THOMAS
    1C668911 $.95   (W51)
    (Vance) SA/TB CPP-BEL OCT 02017
    $.95   (W52)
    (Wilson) SATB&desc CPP-BEL
    SCHCH01116 $1.10   (W53)

WAREN TWEE CONINCKSKINDEREN, HET see
  Schrijvers, Jean

WARFIELD, GERALD ALEXANDER (1940-   )
  Noiseless Patient Spider, A
    SATB/TTBB [4'] (Whitman)
    AM.COMP.AL. $6.15   (W54)
    boy cor,acap [3'] AM.COMP.AL. $6.15
                                     (W55)

WARING, ROB
  Kvar Skal Eg Vel Av?: Variations On A
    Norwegian Folk Tune
    [Norw] SATB manuscript NORGE   (W56)

WARLOCK, PETER
  see HESELTINE, PHILIP

WARMLAND see Martin

WARMTH AND LIGHT see Snyder

WARNAAR, D.J.
  Als Je Bidt
    SATB MOLENAAR 13033304   (W57)

  Dank Voor Uw Komst
    SATB MOLENAAR 13027805   (W58)

  Met Je Handen
    SATB MOLENAAR 13055004   (W59)

WARNOCK, COLIN
  Pied Piper, The
    mix cor NOVELLO   (W60)

WARNUNG: MANNER SUCHEN STETS ZU NASCHEN
  see Mozart, Wolfgang Amadeus

WARREN, B.
  Apple-Tree Madrigals, The
    (Whitman, Ruth) SSAA,2pno WISCAS
                                     (W61)

  Five Songs In 5 Minutes °CC5U
    (McCord, D.) cor WISCAS   (W62)

  Night Watch In The City Of Boston
    cor, solo voices,chamber orch
    WISCAS   (W63)

WARREN, B. (cont'd.)

  Pussy Cat Duets
    2pt cor,pno WISCAS   (W64)

  Six Poems Of Emily Dickinson °CC6U
    SSATBarB,acap WISCAS   (W65)

WARREN, ELINOR REMICK (1905-   )
  On The Echoing Green
    SATB,pno (med diff) LAWSON 52361
    $.90   (W66)

WARREN, HARRY (1893-1981)
  On The Atcheson, Topeka And The Santa
    Fe
    (Behnke, Martin) SATB CPP-BEL
    T58800C1 $1.10, accomp tape
    available   (W67)
    (Behnke, Martin) SAB CPP-BEL
    T58800C3 $1.10   (W68)
    (Behnke, Martin) SSA CPP-BEL
    T58800C2 $1.10   (W69)

WAS SCHEREN MICH SORGEN: DREI HEITERE
  VOLKSLIEDER °see Ei, Wie Geht's Im
  Himmel Zu, Op.38; Jung Bin Ich,
  Op.38; Vergebliche Warnung -
  Hansel, Dein Gretelein, Op.38 (W70)

WAS SOLL ICH IN DER FREMDE TUN see
  Biebl, Franz, In Der Heimat Ist's
  So Schon

WASHBURN, ROBERT BROOKS (1928-   )
  Ode To Freedom
    SATB,band/orch OXFORD 385416-3
    $6.50   (W71)

WASHINGTON, NED (1901-   )
  When You Wish Upon A Star °see
    Harline, Leigh

WASSERMANN, DER see Schumann, Robert
  (Alexander)

WATCHING THE COLORS OF THE WORLD see
  Donner

WATCHMAN'S REPORT, THE see Weigl, Karl

WATER see Shaw, Marshall L.

WATER-GO-ROUND, THE see Franco, Johan

WATER IS WIDE see Tilley, Alexander, O
  Waly, Waly

WATER IS WIDE, THE
  (Bune) SATB CPP-BEL SCHCH 04005 $.95
                                     (W72)
  (Freed, Arnold) SATB,kbd CORONET
    392-41530 F 95   (W73)

WATER, LITTLE WATER see Hurnik, Ilja

WATER ZAL DE STENEN BREKEN, HET see
  Ansink, Caroline

WATKINSON, PERCY GERD (1918-   )
  Frauen Von Ravenna, Die
    4pt mix cor,timp MULLER 2666 see
    from Funf Villanellen   (W74)

  Funf Villanellen °see Frauen Von
    Ravenna, Die; Hier Mocht Ich
    Stunden Vertreiben; Ihr Burschen
    Und Ihr Frauen; In Einem Alten
    Garten; Madonna (Gebet Der
    Fischer)   (W75)

  Hier Mocht Ich Stunden Vertreiben
    4pt mix cor,timp MULLER 2665 see
    from Funf Villanellen   (W76)

  Ich Bin Der Junge Hirtenknab
    3-4pt mix cor BAREN. 174 see from
    GULDNE SONNE, VOLL FREUD UND
    WONNE, DIE   (W77)

  Ihr Burschen Und Ihr Frauen
    4pt mix cor,timp MULLER 2663 see
    from Funf Villanellen   (W78)

  In Einem Alten Garten
    4pt mix cor,timp MULLER 2664 see
    from Funf Villanellen   (W79)

  Madonna (Gebet Der Fischer)
    4pt mix cor,timp MULLER 2667 see
    from Funf Villanellen   (W80)

WAXMAN
  Chantons, Je Vous Prie
    "O Let Us Sing, I Pray You" GALAXY
    1.3025 f.s.   (W81)

  I Hear The Minstrels In Our Street
    °see J'entends Par Notre Rue

  J'entends Par Notre Rue
    "I Hear The Minstrels In Our
    Street" GALAXY 1.3023 $.85   (W82)

WAXMAN (cont'd.)

O Let Us Sing, I Pray You *see
Chantons, Je Vous Prie

WAY HE MAKES ME FEEL, THE
(Strommen) SAB CPP-BEL T0915WC3 $1.25
(W83)

WAY IT IS, THE see Hornsby, G.F.

WAYNE
See You In September *see Edwards

WE ARE CHILDREN OF THE SOVIET LAND
*CCU
[Russ] jr cor,pno MEZ KNIGA 519 (W84)

WE ARE PART OF THE SOVIET POWER *CCU
[Russ] jr cor,pno MEZ KNIGA 498 (W85)

WE ARE THE KOMSOMOL! *CCU
[Russ] cor,pno MEZ KNIGA 159   (W86)

WE ARE THE MUSIC MAKERS see
Porterfield, Sherrie

WE ARE THE YOUNG see Donnelly

WE BE THREE POOR MARINERS
(Cobb, Donald) SA,pno MUSIC SEV.
M70-530 $.85   (W87)

WE BE THREE POOR MARINERS see
Ravenscroft, Thomas

WE BELONG TO YOU, O REVOLUTION! *CCU
[Russ] jr cor MEZ KNIGA 507   (W88)

WE DON'T NEED ANOTHER HERO
(Chinn) SATB CPP-BEL 1566WC1X $1.25,
accomp tape available   (W89)
(Chinn) SSA CPP-BEL 1566WC2X $1.25,
accomp tape available   (W90)
(Chinn) SAB CPP-BEL 1566WC3X $1.25,
accomp tape available   (W91)

WE HOLD THE FUTURE see Ray, Jerry

WE LOVE LENIN *CCU
[Russ] jr cor,pno MEZ KNIGA 485 (W92)

WE LOVE TO SING see Crawley, Clifford

WE LOVE TO SING see Crawley, Clifford

WE MUST SAY GOODBYE see Gilpin, Greg

WE SHALL OVERCOME
see Red River Valley

WE, THE CHILDREN (A PRAYER FOR PEACE)
see Goemanne

WE, THE CHILDREN OF AMERICA see
Feldstein, Saul (Sandy)

WE WILL STAND
(Lojeski) SATB LEONARD-US 08396751
$.95   (W93)
(Lojeski) SAB LEONARD-US 08396752
$.95   (W94)
(Lojeski) SSA LEONARD-US 08396753
$.95, ipa, accomp tape available
(W95)

WE WILL WALK WITH MOTHER AND MORN see
Gilbert

WE WISH YOU A MERRY CHRISTMAS
(Hugo, John) SATB THOMAS 1C418933
$1.25   (W96)

WE WISH YOU A MERRY CHRISTMAS, VOL.1
(Chinn) SATB,acap CPP-BEL SV8624 $.95
(W97)

WEARIN' O' THE GREEN, THE
(Jeffers) TTBB,T solo EARTHSNG EM-3
$.50   (W98)

WEBB, CHICK (WILLIAM) (1902-1939)
Stompin' At The Savoy *see Goodman,
Benny (Benjamin David)

WEBB, EVELYN (1923-   )
Dashing Away With The Smoothing Iron
SATB,acap [2'15"] ROBERTON 63143
(W99)

WEBER
Ruse Petit Jean, Le
eq voices,pno,inst [34'] SALABERT
EAS18330P   (W100)

WEBER, CARL MARIA VON (1786-1826)
Drei Sterne: So Viel Sternlein Als Da
Wallen
mix cor BOHM   (W101)

Ei, Wie Scheint Der Mond So Hell
SSA HARMONIA 3670   (W102)

Sieben Lieder Fur Gemischten Chor
*CC7L
(Schafer, Ewald) SATB LIENAU   (W103)

WEBER, GUSTAV (1845-1887)
Deux Chansons De Mai *see En La
Saison Jolie; Hola Mon Coeur
(W104)
En La Saison Jolie
TTBB HUGUENIN EB 91 see from Deux
Chansons De Mai   (W105)

Hola Mon Coeur
TTBB HUGUENIN EB 91 see from Deux
Chansons De Mai   (W106)

Il Faut Vouloir
TTBB HUGUENIN EB 92   (W107)

Ma Mie
TTBB HUGUENIN EB 199A   (W108)

Rosenglaube
TTBB HUGUENIN EB 361   (W109)

WEBSTER
Love Is A Many- Splendored Thing
(composed with Fain)
(Ringwald) SATB SHAWNEE 1753 $.90
(W110)

WECKERLIN, JEAN-BAPTISTE-THEODORE
(1821-1910)
Fille Du Vigneron, La
TTBB HUGUENIN EB 350   (W111)

WEDDING see Laburda, Jiri

WEED, THE see Hicken, Ken L.

WEEKEND IN NEW ENGLAND
(Strommen) SATB CPP-BEL SV8475 $1.25
(W112)
(Strommen) SSA CPP-BEL SV8476 $1.25
(W113)
(Strommen) SAB CPP-BEL SV8477 $1.25
(W114)

WEELKES, THOMAS (ca. 1575-1623)
Ayeres Or Phantasticke Spirites For
Three Voices *CCU
3pt cor PERF.ED. PF 33 $30.00 sold
in set of three part-books (W115)

Cease Sorrows Now *madrigal
SAB,acap HARMONIA 3805   (W116)
(Rumery, L.) SAB,acap (med) THOMAS
1C288510 $.85   (W117)

Hark All Ye Lovely Saints
(Thoburn, Crawford) SSAB,acap CPP-
BEL SV8913 $1.10   (W118)

In Pride Of May
SSATB STAINER 3.3207 $.95   (W119)

Since Robin Hood
ATB/TTB STAINER 3.3212 $.85   (W120)

Sing We At Pleasure
SSATB NATIONAL CMS-129 $.95   (W121)

Strike It Up, Tabor
3pt mix cor CPP-BEL SV8639 $1.10
(W122)

WEEP, O MINE EYES see Bennet, John

WEEP, WEEP MINE EYES see Wilbye, John

WEICHET NUR see Bach, Johann Sebastian

WEIDBERG, RON (1953-   )
Automobile, The *see Hamechonit

Hamechonit
"Automobile, The" [Heb/Eng] jr cor
[5'] ISR.MUS.INST. 6563   (W123)

WEIGL, KARL (1881-1949)
Folksongs From Many Lands
mix cor [22'] AM.COMP.AL. $9.15
(W124)
Nature *Op.29
SATB [6'] AM.COMP.AL. $5.40   (W125)

Six Children's Songs
2pt jr cor,acap [13'] AM.COMP.AL.
$5.40   (W126)

Three Poems (Drei Gedichte), Op. 6
*CC3U
SATB AM.COMP.AL. f.s.   (W127)

Watchman's Report, The *Op.39
SATB,Bar solo,pno [8'] AM.COMP.AL.
$6.15   (W128)

WEIGL, [MRS.] VALLY (1889-1982)
Along The Way
SSA,pno [3'] (text by American
women poets) AM.COMP.AL. $7.70
(W129)
SSA [3'] AM.COMP.AL. $1.20   (W130)

Ballad Of My Father, The
SATB,pno AM.COMP.AL. $5.40   (W131)

Bold Heart
SSA/SATB [2'] AM.COMP.AL. $1.20
(W132)

WEIGL, [MRS.] VALLY (cont'd.)

Choruses Of Concern
SATB,pno [29'] AM.COMP.AL. $12.10
(W133)

Drums Of War, The
SATB,pno AM.COMP.AL. $.80   (W134)

From The Far Corners
SATB,speaking voice,opt inst,pno,
drums [4'] AM.COMP.AL. sc $2.35,
pts $.80   (W135)

Harbingers Of Spring
SSA,fl,pno [15'] AM.COMP.AL. $9.15
(W136)

Heart's Content
3pt wom cor/SATB [4'] AM.COMP.AL.
$.45   (W137)

Let My Country Awake
SATB,pno AM.COMP.AL. $6.15   (W138)

Madrigal
SSA [3'] AM.COMP.AL. $1.20   (W139)

My God, What Is A Heart?
SSA [3'] AM.COMP.AL. $1.20   (W140)

Night Will Never Stay, The
2pt cor,pno [2'] AM.COMP.AL. $1.20
(W141)

Ode To The Westwind
SATB [5'] (Shelley) AM.COMP.AL.
$1.95   (W142)

Ode: We Are The Music Makers
SATB [4'] AM.COMP.AL. $3.85   (W143)

People Is A Polychrome, The
SATB [3'] (Sandburg) AM.COMP.AL.
$1.20   (W144)

Sea Sunsets
wom cor,pno,fl/clar/vln [5']
AM.COMP.AL. sc $1.95, pts $.80
(W145)

Shepherdess Moon
SSA,pno [3'] AM.COMP.AL. $3.10 (W146)

Songs For A Child
1-2pt cor,rec/fl,pno [60']
AM.COMP.AL. $16.80   (W147)

Songs From Somerset Hills
SATB,pno [9'] AM.COMP.AL. $4.60
(W148)

Spring's Return
SSA,S solo,tamb,castanets [2']
AM.COMP.AL. $1.95   (W149)

Still Will Be
SSA [1'] AM.COMP.AL. $1.20   (W150)

Three Easy Rounds *round
3-4pt cor [5'] AM.COMP.AL. $.80
(W151)

Who Bids Us Sing
SSA,fl/clar,pno [4'] AM.COMP.AL.
$1.95   (W152)

WEIHNACHT see Scherber, M.

WEIHNACHT, WEIHNACHT see Dostal, Nico

WEIHNACHTSFANFARE *Xmas
cor HIEBER MH 5024   (W153)

WEIHNACHTSFRIEDE see Kollo, Rene

WEIHNACHTSUHR, DIE see Lang, Hans

WEILL, KURT (1900-1950)
Ballad Of Magna Carta, The *cant
mix cor,narrator& solo voices,pno
EUR.AM.MUS. EA00585 $3.95   (W154)

WEIN, WEIB UND GESANG see Strauss,
Johann, [Jr.]

WEINHORST, RICHARD
Choral Matins, A
SATB,3perc [17'] AM.COMP.AL. $9.95
(W155)
Intrada For Voices
SA/TB [1'] AM.COMP.AL. $.80   (W156)

Stephen Foster Set, A
SATB [11'] AM.COMP.AL. $5.75 (W157)

WEINLIED see Pappert, Robert

WEINSCHROTERLIED see Fork, Gunter

WEISENBERG, MENACHEM (1950-   )
Imi Menagenet Valz
"My Mother Plays A Waltz" [Heb] 3pt
jr cor,acap [2'] ISR.MUS.INST.
6737   (W158)

My Mother Plays A Waltz *see Imi
Menagenet Valz

WEISS
Music! Music! Music! (composed with Baum)
(Sterling) SATB SHAWNEE 1775 $.95 (W159)
(Sterling) SSA SHAWNEE 0527 $.95 (W160)
(Sterling) SAB SHAWNEE 0365 $.95 (W161)

WEISS, MANFRED (1935-)
Vermachtnis
mix cor sc BREITKOPF-L 7665 (W162)

Weiss Mir Ein Maidlein Hubsch Und Fein
mix cor sc BREITKOPF-L 7692 (W163)

WEISS ICH DEN WEG AUCH NICHT see Weiss-Steinberg, Hans

WEISS MIR EIN BLUMLEIN BLAUE see Kracke, Hans

WEISS MIR EIN MAIDLEIN HUBSCH UND FEIN see Weiss, Manfred

WEISS MIR EIN SCHONES ROSELEIN see Mittelbach, Otto

WEISS-STEINBERG, HANS (1927-)
Auf De Schwabsche Eisebahne
mix cor BRAUN-PER 1006 (W164)

Burden Down
men cor BRAUN-PER 1005 (W165)

Ewiges Wandern
wom cor/jr cor BRAUN-PER 1087 (W166)
mix cor BRAUN-PER 1086 (W167)
men cor BRAUN-PER 1085 (W168)

Fruhling
mix cor BRAUN-PER 1065 (W169)

Philadelphia-Marsch
men cor BRAUN-PER 1007 (W170)

Somebody's Knockin'
mix cor BRAUN-PER 1076 (W171)

Weiss Ich Den Weg Auch Nicht
men cor BRAUN-PER 1019 (W172)
mix cor BRAUN-PER 1020 (W173)

Zu Lauterbach
men cor BRAUN-PER 1084 (W174)
mix cor BRAUN-PER 1088 (W175)

WEITES LAND, WIE STUMM DU BIST *folk song,Norw
(Olpen, Friedrich W.) men cor BOHM (W176)

WELCOME, LIGHT see Zakrzewska-Nikiporczyk, Barbara, Witaj, Jasnosci

WELCOME SPRING see Cutter, Bill

WELIN, KARL-ERIK (1934-)
Avsked
men cor STIM (W177)

I Am Nobody *Op.51
men cor,fl,3perc STIM (W178)

Lamento *Op.41
mix cor STIM (W179)

Maxi-Min
mix cor,acap STIM (W180)

WE'LL BLAZE A TRAIL see Crawley, Clifford

WELTLAUF see Poos, Heinrich

WELTLICHE MADRIGALE *CCU
(Zimmer, Ulrich) mix cor BAREN. 6361 (W181)

WELTLICHES CHORMUSIK DER ROMANTIK *CC24U
(Zimmer, Ulrich) SATB BAREN. 6370 (W182)

WELTREISE IM ZIMMER, DIE see Schwaen, Kurt

WENN ALLE BRUNNLEIN FLIESSEN see Backer, Hans

WENN ALLE BRUNNLEIN FLIESSEN see Hein, H.

WENN ALLE BRUNNLEIN FLIESSEN see Mutter, Gerbert

WENN DIE KLEINEN VEILCHEN BLUHEN... see Stolz, Robert

WENN EIN STARKER GEWAPPNETER see Brahms, Johannes

WENN ICH EIN VOGLEIN WAR see Friemel, G.

WENN ICH EIN VOGLEIN WAR see Lehrndorfer, F.

WENN ICH FRUH IN DEN GARTEN GEH' see Schumann, Robert (Alexander), Volksliedchen

WENN ICH GEDENK DER STUND see Regnart, Jacob

WENN ICH VOM KLAREN WEINE TRINKE (Seckinger) TTBB MULLER 939 see from Zwei Franzosische Volkslieder (W183)

WENN WIR UNTERM FIEDELBOGEN see Hempel, Rolf

WENN ZWEI VON EINANDER SCHEIDEN see Andriessen, Jurriaan

WENN ZWEIE SICH GUT SIND see Hauptmann, Moritz

WER DER MUSIK ERGEBEN see Backer, Hans

WER IMMER ANNEHMLICHE FREUDEN WILL HABEN see Haus, K., Jager Lust Und Freud, Der

WER IST HIER JUNG, WER HAT HIER SCHWUNG see Bochmann

WER SEINE HEIMAT LIEBT see Schmid, A.

WER SICH VERTREIBEN WILL SCHLECHTE LAUNE see Scheck, Helmut

WER WAR ICH DOCH? see Bose, Hans-Jurgen Von

WER WILL MIT UNS NACH ISLAND GEHN? see Deutschmann, Gerhard

WE'RE NUMBER ONE! see Harris, Louis

WE'RE SO COOL! see Pollack

WERLE, LARS-JOHAN (1926-)
Svanstankar
men cor,pno STIM (W184)

WERNER
Two Roses, The
TTBB,acap [3'] ROBERTON 53144 (W185)

WERT, GIACHES DE (JAKOB VAN) (1535-1596)
Chi Salira Per Me
SATB HARMONIA 3652 (W186)

Jour Je M'en Allai, Un
SATB,acap HUGUENIN EB 408 (W187)

Vezzosi Augelli
SSATB NATIONAL NMP-189 $.95 (W188)

WEST-SIDE STORY see Bernstein, Leonard

WEST SUSSEX DRINKING SONG see Cook, Melville

WESTERN WIND SONGBOOK, VOL. 1, THE *CCU
(Bennett) SATB SHAWNEE 5041 $8.95 (W189)

WETZLER
Laughing Song
SATB KJOS C8823 $.80 (W190)

WE'VE COME FROM THE CITY see Haufrecht, Herbert

WE'VE GOT A SHOW FOR YOU see Pollack, Lisa Lauren

WHALE OF A TALE, A
(Artman, Ruth) TBB LEONARD-US 08598248 $.85 (W191)

WHAM! IN CONCERT
(Lojeski) SATB LEONARD-US 08276251 $1.95 (W192)
(Lojeski) SAB LEONARD-US 08276252 $1.95 (W193)
(Lojeski) 2pt cor LEONARD-US 08276253 $1.95, ipa (W194)

WHAT A TEAM! see Brownsey

WHAT ABOUT LOVE
(Chinn) SSA CPP-BEL 6879WC2X $1.25 (W195)
(Chinn) SAB CPP-BEL 6879WC3X $1.25 (W196)

WHAT ABOUT ME
(Riley; Watson) SATB CPP-BEL 6848WC1X $1.25 (W197)

WHAT CAN I DO see Snyder

WHAT CHILD IS THIS?
(North) ALFRED (W198)

WHAT DO ALL OF THESE THINGS see Kirby

WHAT DO I WANT IN MY CHRISTMAS STOCKING? see Albrecht

WHAT DOTH MY DAINTY DARLING? see East, Michael

WHAT IS THE CONSTITUTION see Perry, Janice Kapp

WHAT IS THE KEY TO HAPPINESS see Donahue

WHAT IS YOUR CHOICE see Monroe

WHAT MAKES A DAD? see Allen, David Len

WHAT! NO WOMEN? see Meskill

WHAT SHALL WE DO
(Turellier, J.) 4pt mix cor,2gtr HEUGEL HE 31936 (W199)

WHAT SHALL WE DO FOR A CHRISTMAS PLAY? see Roberts, Ruth

WHAT SHALL WE SING? see Liebergen

WHAT THOUGH THE TIMES BE DOLOROUS see Wintelroy, Johan, Al Is Den Tijt Nu Doloreus

WHAT TIME IS IT? see Anderson, T.J.

WHAT WOULD WE DO WITHOUT MUSIC? see Sleeth, Natalie Wakeley

WHAT'S FOREVER FOR see Madsen

WHAT'S LOVE GOT TO DO WITH IT
(Strommen) SATB CPP-BEL 6821WC1X $1.25 (W200)
(Strommen) SSA CPP-BEL 6821WC2X $1.25 (W201)
(Strommen) SAB CPP-BEL 6821WC3X $1.25 (W202)

WHEELER, JANET
Four Spirituals *medley
SATB OXFORD X298 19 3431009 (W203)

WHEN I FALL IN LOVE
(Shaw, Kirby) SATB LEONARD-US 08665912 $.85 (W204)
(Shaw, Kirby) SAB LEONARD-US 08665913 $.85 (W205)

WHEN I FIRST CAME TO THIS LAND see Brand

WHEN I GO A-CHRISTMAS-ING see Beebe, Hank

WHEN I TAKE MY SUGAR TO TEA
(Craig) SSAA CPP-BEL 6705WC4X $1.25 (W206)

WHEN I THINK OF CHRISTMAS see Jorgensen, Brent

WHEN I WAS A LITTLE BOY see Thiman, Eric Harding

WHEN I WAS BUT A MAIDEN see Kubik

WHEN ICICLES HANG see Rutter, John

WHEN I'M A COMEDIAN see Beebe

WHEN IN THE LANGUOR OF EVENING see Luening, Otto

WHEN IT'S LOVE see Kirk

WHEN JESUS WEPT
see John's Gone To Hilo

WHEN JOHNY COMES MARCHING HOME see Lambert

WHEN LOVE see Tate, Phyllis

WHEN MOMENTS WERE GOLD see Page

WHEN MOONLIGHT FALLS see Read, Gardner

WHEN SMOKEY SINGS: A TRIBUTE TO SMOKEY ROBINSON see Robinson, William (Smokey)

WHEN THE GOING GETS TOUGH, THE TOUGH GET GOING see Brymer, Mark

WHEN THE SWALLOWS HOMEWARD FLY see White, Maude Valerie

WHEN WE SING TOGETHER see Snyder

WHEN WILL I SEE YOU AGAIN see McPheeters, (Tell Me) When Will I See You Again

WHEN YOU WISH UPON A STAR see Harline, Leigh

WHEN YOU'RE SMILING see Fisher

WHENCE COMES MUSIC? see Dubravin, Y.

WHENE'ER YOU THINK OF see Berger

WHERE ARE THE FLOWERS? see Ashton, Bob Bruce

WHERE DO BROKEN HEARTS GO?
    (Ray, Jerry) SATB ALFRED 7193 $1.25,
        accomp tape available   (W207)
    (Ray, Jerry) SAB ALFRED 7192 $1.25,
        accomp tape available   (W208)
    (Ray, Jerry) SSA ALFRED 7176 $1.25,
        accomp tape available   (W209)

WHERE GO THE BOATS see Bacon, Ernst L.

WHERE, O WHERE ARE THE HEBREW CHILDREN?
    see Owen, John Warren

WHERE THE BEE SUCKS see Lane, Philip

WHERE WILD CARNATIONS BLOW see Gideon, Miriam

WHERE'ER YOU WALK see Cram

WHILE I STILL AM see Berger

WHILE STROLLING THROUGH THE PARK ONE DAY
    (Madsen) TTB CPP-BEL SV8494 $.95,
        accomp tape available   (W210)

WHISPER SONG, THE see Paull

WHISPERING HOPE see Winner, Septimus
    ("Alice Hawthorne")

WHISTLE WHISTLE see Rausch, Carlos

WHITE
    Vertue
        unis cor MUSIC SEV. M70-468 $.70
                                     (W211)

WHITE, GARY C. (1937-   )
    Dark, The
        mix cor,acap, small instruments
            used be members of chorus LUDWIG
            L-1208 $1.50 see from Night
            Images   (W212)

    Gems
        mix cor,acap, small instruments
            used by members of chorus LUDWIG
            L-1206 $3.00 see from Night
            Images   (W213)

    Light, The
        mix cor,acap, small instruments
            used by members of chorus LUDWIG
            L-1209 $3.25 see from Night
            Images   (W214)

    Night Images *see Dark, The; Gems;
        Light, The; Orb, The; Vapors
                                     (W215)
    Orb, The
        mix cor,acap, small instruments
            used by members of chorus LUDWIG
            L-1207 $2.50 see from Night
            Images   (W216)

    Vapors
        mix cor,acap, small instruments
            used by members of chorus LUDWIG
            L-1205 $3.50 see from Night
            Images   (W217)

WHITE, MAUDE VALERIE (1855-1937)
    When The Swallows Homeward Fly
        (Roberton, Hugh S.) TTBB,acap
        ROBERTON 53133   (W218)

WHITE GOOSE, THE see Tucapsky, Antonin

WHITE IN THE MOON see Mulholland, James

WHITE ISLAND, THE see Martino, Donald James

WHITE ROADS see Emmert, Frantisek

WHITE STAR A BRIGHT STAR see Larsen, Pat

WHITE WINGS see Quiett

WHITHER MUST I WANDER? see Vaughan Williams, Ralph

WHITMAN CREDO see Jeffers

WHITTAKER, ROGER
    Kijk Naar De Hemel *see Show Me Your Mountain

    Last Farewell, The
        (Karsemeijer) SATB MOLENAAR
        13016505   (W219)

    Show Me Your Mountain
        (Verheijen, J.) "Kijk Naar De
        Hemel" SATB MOLENAAR 13001303
                                     (W220)

WHITWORTH
    More Indispensable Incidentals
        SATB SHAWNEE   (W221)

WHO BIDS US SING see Weigl, [Mrs.] Vally

WHO HAS SEEN THE WIND?
    (Snyder) 2pt cor CPP-BEL SV8727 $1.10
                                     (W222)
    (Snyder) 3pt cor CPP-BEL SV8728 $1.20
                                     (W223)

WHO HAS SEEN THE WIND? see Kreutz

WHO HAS SEEN THE WIND? see Woodward, Ralph, Jr.

WHO IS THE PATRIOT see Clarke, Henry Leland

WHO NEEDS CHRISTMAS? see Harte

WHY? see Speight, John A.

WHY DO SWEET SONGS see Dvorak, Antonin

WICKED WALK ON EVERY SIDE see Gabel, Gerald L.

WIDMANN, ERASMUS (1572-1634)
    Floh, Der
        SATB HARMONIA 3678   (W224)

WIE DIE KRAHE see Eisler, Hanns

WIE GAAT MEE OVER ZEE see Anonymous

WIE KOMMT'S, DASS DU SO TRAURIG BIST
    (Reger, Max) SATB HARMONIA 3645
                                     (W225)

WIE LEUCHTET ES UBER DEM WALDE see Pappert, Robert

WIE MELODIEN ZIEHT ES MIR see Brahms, Johannes

WIE SCHON BIST DU see Schroeder, Hermann

WIE SCHON IST DOCH DIE WEITE WELT see Koester, Werner

WIE SOLL ICH TRAURIG LEBEN see Schto Mnje Shit'

WIECHOWICZ, STANISLAW (1893-1963)
    Choral Songs *see Z Piesni Choralnych

    Koledziolki Beskidzkie (Christmas
        Carols From The Beskid Mountains)
        *see O Sojek Koralowych Oczach,
        "Of The Jay's Coral-Red Eyes"; O
        Zalotach Oczarowanych, "Of
        Enchanted Courtship"; Pod Okapem
        Sniegu, "Under The Eaves Of Snow"
                                     (W226)
    O Sojek Koralowych Oczach
        "Of The Jay's Coral-Red Eyes"
        [Polish] wom cor,acap POLSKIE see
        from Koledziolki Beskidzkie
        (Christmas Carols From The Beskid
        Mountains)   (W227)

    O Zalotach Oczarowanych
        "Of Enchanted Courtship" [Polish]
        wom cor,acap POLSKIE see from
        Koledziolki Beskidzkie (Christmas
        Carols From The Beskid Mountains)
                                     (W228)

    Of Enchanted Courtship *see O
        Zalotach Oczarowanych

    Of The Jay's Coral-Red Eyes *see O
        Sojek Koralowych Oczach

    Pod Okapem Sniegu
        "Under The Eaves Of Snow" [Polish]
        wom cor,acap POLSKIE see from
        Koledziolki Beskidzkie (Christmas
        Carols From The Beskid Mountains)
                                     (W229)
    Under The Eaves Of Snow *see Pod
        Okapem Sniegu

    Z Piesni Choralnych
        "Choral Songs " mix cor POLSKIE
                                     (W230)

WIEGENLIED see Brahms, Johannes

WIEGENLIED see Flies, J. Bernhard

WIEGENLIED see Mozart, Wolfgang Amadeus

WIEGENLIED see Schumann, Robert (Alexander)

WIEGENLIED, EIN see Gorl, Willibald

WIEGENLIED: GUTEN ABEND, GUT NACHT see Brahms, Johannes

WIEGEZANG see Vocht, Lodewijk de

WIELKI WALC CHORALNY; MARSZ see Swider, Jozef

WIENHORST, RICHARD (1920-   )
    Little Woodlark, The
        SSA [3'] AM.COMP.AL. $4.25   (W231)

    Songs Of Innocence
        SA,pno/harp [8'] AM.COMP.AL. $6.80
                                     (W232)

    Stephen Foster Set, A
        SSAA,pno [11'] AM.COMP.AL. $6.15
                                     (W233)

WIERTS, J.P.J.
    Hollands Vlag
        (Loovendaal) SSA MOLENAAR 15023302
                                     (W234)

WIGGLESWORTH, FRANK (1918-   )
    Choral Study
        SATB,Bar solo,pno [10'] AM.COMP.AL.
                                     (W235)

    Police Log Of The Ipswich Chronicle
        SATB,pno [20'] AM.COMP.AL. $23.15
                                     (W236)

WIJ COMEN HIER GHELOOPEN see Anonymous

WIJ COMEN HIER GHELOOPEN see Anonymous,
    Beggar's Song, The: O, Here We Come
    Awandring

WIJ LEVEN VRIJ, WIJ LEVEN BLIJ see
    Wilms, Johann Wilhelm

WIJ ZANGERS: WIJ TREKKEN DE VOREN see
    Anonymous

WIJD IS 'T LAND EN WIJD DE ZEE see
    Appeldoorn, Dina

WIJDE RUST: WIJDE RUST LIGT OVERAL see
    Appeldoorn, Dina

WIJNNOBEL, P.
    Vivace (Andantino)
        (Biersma, P.) SATB MOLENAAR
        15009803   (W237)

WILBUR, SANDY
    She Still Carries The Torch
        (Ray, Jerry) SATB ALFRED 7676
        $1.25, accomp tape available
                                     (W238)
        (Ray, Jerry) SSA ALFRED 7678 $1.25,
            accomp tape available   (W239)
        (Ray, Jerry) SAB ALFRED 7677 $1.25,
            accomp tape available   (W240)
        (Ray, Jerry) 1-2pt cor ALFRED 7679
            $1.25, accomp tape available
                                     (W241)

WILBYE, JOHN (1574-1638)
    Adieu Sweet Amarillis
        SATB,acap HARMONIA HU 3847   (W242)

    Adieu, Sweet Amaryllis
        (Kaplan, Abraham) mix cor LAWSON
        LG 51865 $.70   (W243)

    Come Shepherd Swains
        ATB STAINER 3.3194   (W244)

    Flora Gave Me Fairest Flowers
        (Morgan, Hilda) TTBB,acap [1'15"]
        ROBERTON 53136   (W245)

    Lady, Your Words Do Spite Me
        SSATB STAINER 3.3206 $.95   (W246)

    Weep, Weep Mine Eyes
        SSATB,acap HARMONIA HU 3798 (W247)

WILD MOUNTAIN THYME, THE
    (Scott, Michael) SATB CPP-BEL SV8747
    $1.20   (W248)

WILD SWANS AT COOLE, THE see Rockmaker, Jody

WILDHORN see Landry, Fredy, Cabane, La

WILGEN, DE: DAAR WAREN EENS ZEVEN
    WILGEN see Averkamp, Anton

WILHELMUS VAN NASSAUEN
    [Dutch] 3 eq voices,acap ZENGERINK
    V 406   (W249)

WILHELMUS VAN NASSAUEN: TIEMEN OTTINK
    see Anonymous

WILHOUSKY, PETER J. (1902-1978)
    Carol-Noel
        SATB,acap FISCHER,C CM6520   (W250)

WILL I SEE YOU AGAIN? see Stephens, Michele

WILL YE NO COME BACK AGAIN? see
    Dewhurst, Robin

WILLAERT, ADRIAN (ca. 1490-1562)
    Allons, Allons Gai
        (Agnel, A.) 3pt mix cor HEUGEL
        HE 31886   (W251)

WILLAERT, ADRIAN (cont'd.)

Ceduntur Gladus
(Agnel, A.) 3 eq voices HEUGEL
HE 32500   (W252)

Equalis Eterno
(Agnel, A.) 3 eq voices HEUGEL
HE 32501   (W253)

J'aime Par Amour
(Agnel, A.) 3pt mix cor HEUGEL
HE 31892   (W254)

Jeune Dame S'en Va Au Moulin, La
(Dottin, G.) 3pt mix cor HEUGEL
HE 32137   (W255)

Or Suis-Je Bien Au Pire
(Agnel, A.) 3pt mix cor HEUGEL
HE 32311   (W256)

Rousee Du Mois De Mai, La
(Agnel, A.) 3 eq voices HEUGEL
HE 32313   (W257)

Vous Marchez Du Bout Du Pied
(Agnel, A.) 3pt mix cor HEUGEL
HE 32312   (W258)

WILLAN, HEALEY (1880-1968)
Agincourt Song
TTBB,pno OXFORD 385202-0 $.40
                                (W259)

Tyrle, Tyrlow
SSAA HARRIS HC-3005 $.75   (W260)

WILLCOCKS, DAVID VALENTINE (1919-   )
Barbara Allen (from Five Folk Songs)
see Five Folk Songs
SATB,acap OXFORD 385565-8 $.40
                                (W261)

Bobby Shaftoe
see Five Folk Songs

Drink To Me Only
see Five Folk Songs

Early One Morning
see Five Folk Songs

Five Folk Songs
SATB,acap OXFORD 343836-4 $5.95
contains: Barbara Allen; Bobby
Shaftoe; Drink To Me Only;
Early One Morning; Lass Of
Richmond Hill   (W262)

Lass Of Richmond Hill
see Five Folk Songs

WILLCOCKS, JONATHAN
Riddle Of The World, The
SATB,TBar soli,2.2.2.2. 2.2.0.0.
timp,strings voc sc OXFORD
338737-9 f.s.   (W263)

Ten Songs °CC10U
treb cor,acap NOVELLO   (W264)

WILLEN WIJ 'T HAESKEN JAGEN DOOR DE HEI
see Schrijvers, Jean, 'T Haesken

WILLIAMS
I Will Give My Love An Apple
unis cor NOVELLO 0745 $1.55 (W265)

My Door Is Always Open
SATB CPP-BEL SV8614 $.95, accomp
tape available   (W266)

WILLIAMS, HANK
Hey, Good Lookin'
(Shaw, Kirby) SATB CPP-BEL 1745HC1X
$1.40, accomp tape available
                                (W267)
(Shaw, Kirby) SAB CPP-BEL 1745HC3X
$1.40   (W268)

WILLIAMS, JULIUS A.
Fall, The
SATB,pno LAWSON 52294 $.90 (W269)

Summer's Good Feelin'
SATB,acap LAWSON 52290 $.80 (W270)

WILLIAMS, RALPH VAUGHAN
see VAUGHAN WILLIAMS, [SIR] RALPH

WILLIAMS-WIMBERLY, LOU
Circles Of Silence
SATB CPP-BEL OCT 02509 $1.20 (W271)

Nest Eggs
3-4pt mix cor SOUTHERN f.s. (W272)

Rondeau Of Life, A
SSA,acap SOUTHERN SC-234 $.45
                                (W273)

Wind, The
3-4pt mix cor SOUTHERN f.s. (W274)

WILLIAMSON, MALCOLM (1931-   )
Death Of Cuchulain
AATBarB,perc [22'] WEINBERGER
                                (W275)

God Save The Queen
SATB,2.2.1+bass clar.2. 4.3.0.0.
timp,strings WEINBERGER (W276)

Musicians Of Bremen, The
AATBarBarB,acap WEINBERGER (W277)

Six English Lyrics °CC6U
(Saunders) SATB,pno WEINBERGER
                                (W278)

Terrain Of The Kings, The
cor,2fl/rec,ob/rec,clar/rec,2bsn,
2cornet,2trp,euphonium,4trom,
perc,pno 4-hands,gtr,strings
[20'] WEINBERGER   (W279)

WILLINGHAM, LAWRENCE
Ghost Of Abel, The °Op.8
SATB,narrator,3.2.2.2. 2.1.1.0.
pno,perc,strings [35']
AM.COMP.AL. $40.40   (W280)

WILLOW, THE see Fomenko, Mykola

WILLS, ARTHUR (1926-   )
Light Invisible, The
SATB,perc,harp,org WEINBERGER
                                (W281)

WILLST DU MIT MIR SINGEN see
Rosenstengel, Albrecht

WILMS, JOHANN WILHELM (1772-1847)
Wij Leven Vrij, Wij Leven Blij
mix cor ZENGERINK 301   (W282)
(Hermans, Petra) 4 eq voices,acap
ZENGERINK 301   (W283)

WILSON
Ah, Leave Me Not To Pine °see
Sullivan

Gift, The (composed with Knox)
SSA CPP-BEL SV7935 $.95   (W284)
SSAB CPP-BEL SV7938 $.95 (W285)

I Believe In You And Me °see Riley

WILSON, ALAN (1947-   )
Seasonal Carols Old & New Vols. 1-3
°sac/sec,CCU
cor WEINBERGER   (W286)

Seasonal Carols Vol. 4 °CCU
cor WEINBERGER   (W287)

WILSON, BRIAN
Little Saint Nick
(Althouse, Jay) SAB CPP-BEL
2949LC3X $1.40   (W288)
(Althouse, Jay) SATB CPP-BEL
2949LC1X $1.40, accomp tape
available   (W289)
(Althouse, Jay) TBB CPP-BEL
2949LC4X $1.40   (W290)

WILSON, JOHN FLOYD (1929-   )
Be Smart, Don't Start °see
Hawthorne, Grace

WILSON, MARK
Follow (composed with Knox)
2pt cor CPP-BEL SV7913 $.95 (W291)

Trav'ler (composed with Knumann, Jo)
SAB CPP-BEL SV7920 $1.10   (W292)

WILSON, R.
Elegy
SATB SCHIRM.G 502040 $.80 (W293)

WILT HEDEN NU TREDEN see Schrijvers,
Jean

WILT HEDEN NU TREDEN see Valerius

WIND see Shaw, Marshall L.

WIND, THE see Stevenson

WIND, THE see Williams-Wimberly, Lou

WIND AND THE FLOWER, THE see Telfer,
Nancy

WIND HAS BLOWN, A see Mellnas, Arne

WIND IN THE WEST see Avni, Tzvi

WIND IN THE WILLOWS, THE see Rutter,
John

WIND SONGS see Rhodes, Phillip

WIND, WIND, SAUSE see Spies, Leo

WINDE WEHN, SCHIFFE GEHN see Spranger,
Jorg

WINDS see Pfautsch, Lloyd Alvin

WINDS OF CHANGE see Snyder

WINE FEAST see Schoen, Victor R., Chiu
Yen

WINGED SWINGS °CCU
[Russ] jr cor MEZ KNIGA 495 (W294)

WINKLER
Und Wieder Geht Ein Schoner Tag Zu
Ende
(Hess) mix cor,opt pno LEUCKART
LSB 524   (W295)
(Hess) men cor,opt pno LEUCKART
LSB 124 f.s.   (W296)

WINNER, SEPTIMUS ("ALICE HAWTHORNE")
(1827-1902)
Fluist'rend Verlangen °see
Whispering Hope

Whispering Hope
(Browne, M.) "Fluist'rend
Verlangen" SATB MOLENAAR 15002802
                                (W297)

WINTELROY, JOHAN
Al Is Den Tijt Nu Doloreus
(Lagas, R.) "What Though The Times
Be Dolorous" SATB,acap (diff)
ZENGERINK G 548   (W298)

What Though The Times Be Dolorous
°see Al Is Den Tijt Nu Doloreus

WINTER see Mathias, William

WINTER see Paull

WINTER see Steptoe, Roger

WINTER, DE: DE WINTER HEEFT, HOE GRIJS
VAN KIN see Zwager, Piet

WINTER AFTERNOONS see Hultqvist, Anders

WINTER CANTABILE see Eccard

WINTER CELEBRATION see Snyder

WINTER FANTASY see Gilpin, Greg

WINTER HOLIDAY see Roberts, Ruth

WINTER HOLIDAY SPECTACULAR!, A
(Leavitt, John) SATB CPP-BEL SV8826
$1.40, accomp tape available (W299)
(Leavitt, John) SAB CPP-BEL SV8827
$1.40   (W300)
(Leavitt, John) SATB CPP-BEL SV8826
$1.40, accomp tape available (W301)
(Leavitt, John) SAB CPP-BEL SV8827
$1.40, accomp tape available (W302)

WINTER IS HERE see Eddleman, David

WINTER IS PAST, THE see Carmel, Dov

WINTER IS VERGANGEN, DIE see Anonymous

WINTER IS VERGANGHEN, DIE see Evertse,
J.

WINTER IS VERGANGHEN, DIE see
Schrijvers, Jean

WINTER NIGHTS see Rutter, John

WINTER OF MY SOUL, THE see Wolff

WINTER SCENE see Thayer, Fred

WINTER SNOWFLAKES see Snyder

WINTER WAKENETH ALL MY CARE see Rutter,
John

WINTER WILD see Cooper, Steve

WINTER WIND, THE see Wright, Maurice

WINTERKILL... see Fennelly, Brian

WINTERTIME AGLOW see Snyder

WIR ALLE LEBEN IN GESTUNDETER ZEIT see
Erdmann-Abele, Veit

WIR FAHREN UBERS WEITE MEER see
Deutschmann, Gerhard

WIR KAMEN EINST VON PIEMONT °folk
song,Fr
(Haus, Karl) [Ger] men cor BOHM
                                (W303)

WIR ZIEHEN ZUR MUTTER DER GNADE see
Zwyssig, Alberich

WIR ZWEI see Matthus, Siegfried

WISDOM COMETH WITH THE YEARS see Adler,
Samuel Hans

WISER
  Look Beyond Tomorrow
    (Dunbar) SSA SHAWNEE 0520 $.70
                                        (W304)

WISHES see Crawley, Clifford

WISLO MOJA, UCIEKLA MI PRZEPIORECZKA
  see Sulej, Michal

WISST IHR, WANN MEIN KINDCHEN see
  Brahms, Johannes

WIT AND WISDOM see Krapf, Gerhard

WITAJ, JASNOSCI see Zakrzewska-
  Nikiporczyk, Barbara

WITCHES AND SPELLS see Tate, Phyllis

WITH A RING AND A JINGLE AND A POP see
  Lawrence

WITH JUST ONE LOOK IN YOUR EYES see
  Davis, Stephen

WITH MUSIC STRONG see Rinehart, John

WITH ONE VOICE see Sprunger, David

WITH RUE MY HEART IS LADEN see
  Mulholland, James

WITH WINGS HE'LL TOUCH YOUR EYELIDS see
  Balzonelli, Alberto, Con Alas En
  Los Ojos

WITHOUT A SONG see Youmans, Vincent
  Millie

WITTINGER, ROBERT (1945-   )
  Maldoror-Requiem *Op.42
    mix cor,narrator,orch [60'] MOECK
    5328   (W305)

WITWE PAPAI (WIDOW PAPAI) see Ligeti,
  Gyorgy, Papaine

WIZ, THE: SELECTIONS
  SSA CPP-BEL 1453SC2X $2.25   (W306)

WIZ-OZ MEDLEY see Shaw, Oz-Wiz Medley

WIZARD OF OZ, THE: SELECTIONS
  (Wilson) SATB CPP-BEL T6510WC1 $2.25
                                        (W307)

WO IST EIN SO HERRLICH VOLK see Brahms,
  Johannes

WOHIN? see Schubert, Franz (Peter)

WOHL DEM MENSCHEN, DER WEISHEIT FINDET
  see Jenner, Gustav

WOHL MITT'S I DER NACHT
  (Estermann, J.) mix cor,acap PELIKAN
  PE1192   (W308)

WOHLAUF, DIE LUFT GEHT FRISCH UND REIN
  see Schlerf, L.

WOHLAUF IN GOTTES SCHONE WELT see
  Kracke, Hans

WOHLAUF IN GOTTES SCHONE WELT! see
  Trapp, Willy

WOLF, HUGO (1860-1903)
  Dem Vaterland
    (Jancik, Hans) 4pt men cor,2+
    pic.2.2.2. 4.3.3.1. timp,
    triangle,perc,strings MUSIKWISS.
                                        (W309)
  Elfenlied
    (Jancik, Hans) SSAA,S solo,2+
    pic.2.2.2. 2.0.0.0. strings,harp
    MUSIKWISS. contains also:
    Feuerreiter, Der (SATB,2+
    pic.2.2.3. 4.3.3.1. timp,tam-tam,
    strings)   (W310)

  Feuerreiter, Der
    see Wolf, Hugo, Elfenlied

  Fruhlingschor (from Manuel Venegas)
    see Wolf, Hugo, Morgenhymnus
    (Spitzer, L.) cor,pno cor pts,voc
    sc DOBLINGER 46 789   (W311)

  Geistesgruss *Op.13,No.3
    men cor DOBLINGER 54 016 see from
    Lieder Fur Mannerchor A Cappella
                                        (W312)
  Im Sommer *Op.13,No.3
    men cor DOBLINGER 54 015 see from
    Lieder Fur Mannerchor A Cappella
                                        (W313)
  Lieder Fur Mannerchor A Cappella
    *see Geistesgruss, Op.13,No.3; Im
    Sommer, Op.13,No.3; Mailied,
    Op.13,No.3   (W314)

  Mailied *Op.13,No.3
    men cor DOBLINGER 54 017 see from
    Lieder Fur Mannerchor A Cappella
                                        (W315)

WOLF, HUGO (cont'd.)

  Morgenhymnus
    (Jancik, Hans) SATB,2.2+English
    horn.2.3. 4.3.3.1. timp,perc,
    harp,strings MUSIKWISS. contains
    also: Fruhlingschor (SATB,3.2+
    English horn.3.0. 4.3.3.1. timp,
    triangle,perc,harp,strings)
                                        (W316)

WOLFF
  I Have Not Seen My Love Of Late
    SATB CPP-BEL OCT 02533 $1.10 (W317)

  My Love Has Soft Skin
    SATB,S solo CPP-BEL OCT 02534 $1.20
                                        (W318)

  Winter Of My Soul, The
    SATB CPP-BEL OCT 02532 $1.10 (W319)

WOLFF, H. DE
  Doedelzak
    "Hornpipe" SATB MOLENAAR 15004403
                                        (W320)

  Hornpipe *see Doedelzak

  Ierse Selectie (Van Bekende Ierse
    Liedjes)
    SATB MOLENAAR 15004604   (W321)

  Rode Sarafaan, De
    SATB MOLENAAR 15008602   (W322)

  Stjenka Rasin
    SATB MOLENAAR 15009202   (W323)

WOLSCHINA, REINHARD (1952-   )
  Martial-Epigramme
    (Wolschina, R.) mix cor,T solo,
    2.2.2.1. 2.1.1.1. pno,3perc [15']
    voc sc BREITKOPF-L 6137   (W324)

WOLTERS, KARL-HEINZ (1929-1987)
  Gaa
    men cor,acap [4'] SCHOTTS C 46414
                                        (W325)

WOMAN WITH A TORCH see Hervig, Richard
  B.

WOMAN'S LAMENT, A see Kopelent, Marek

WOMAN'S WORLD, A see Blyton, Carey

WOMEN see Berkeley, Michael

WONDER, STEVIE
  see MORRIS, STEVLAND

WOODCREST CAROL, THE see Beaudrot

WOODS, HARRY MACGREGOR (1896- ?)
  Poor Papa
    (Calvin, Dot) SSAA BOURNE
    B239368-353 $.50   (W326)

WOODWARD, RALPH, JR.
  Day In Spring, A
    SSA,pno WOODWARD 501 f.s.   (W327)
    SATB,pno WOODWARD 501-A f.s. (W328)

  New Shoes (from Two Small Songs)
    unis cor,pno WOODWARD 502 f.s.
                                        (W329)
  Who Has Seen The Wind? (from Two
    Small Songs)
    SSA,pno WOODWARD 502 f.s.   (W330)

WOOLEN, R.
  Temple
    SATB [6'] (Donne) AM.COMP.AL. $4.60
                                        (W331)

WORDS see Chasalow, Eric

WORDS see Fitch

WORDS FOR KENTUCKY see Starr, [Paul]
  Douglas

WORDS GET IN THE WAY
  (Hanson, Mark) SATB CPP-BEL 4824WC1X
    $1.25, accomp tape available (W332)
  (Hanson, Mark) SSA CPP-BEL 4824WC2X
    $1.25, accomp tape available (W333)
  (Hanson, Mark) SAB CPP-BEL 4824WC3X
    $1.25, accomp tape available (W334)

WORDSWORTHIAN DREAM IN BLANK VERSE, A
  see Berl, Christine

WORKS FOR WOMEN'S, MEN'S AND MIXED
  CHORUSES, VOL. 52 *CCU
  [Russ] MEZ KNIGA 175   (W335)

WORKS OF JOSQUIN DES PREZ, THE: SECULAR
  WORKS, VOL. 1 see Des Prez, Josquin

WORKS OF JOSQUIN DES PREZ, THE: SECULAR
  WORKS, VOL. 2 see Des Prez, Josquin

WORKS OF JOSQUIN DES PREZ, THE: SECULAR
  WORKS, VOL. 3 see Des Prez, Josquin

WORKS OF JOSQUIN DES PREZ, THE: SECULAR
  WORKS, VOL. 4 see Des Prez, Josquin

WORKS OF JOSQUIN DES PREZ, THE: SECULAR
  WORKS, VOL. 5 see Des Prez, Josquin

WORLD SINGS CHRISTMAS, THE see
  Mitchell, Bob

WORLD'S END, THE see Burtch, Mervyn

WORP, JOHANNES (1821-1891)
  Bijtje, Het: Zoem-Zoem-Zoem, Daar
    Kwam Een Bijtje Vliegen
    SSA/TTB ZENGERINK 60   (W336)

WOUDCONCERT: MEJUFFROUW LENTE GEEFT
  CONCERT see Abt, Franz

WRIGHT, DON
  Youthful Voices *CCUL
    4pt jr cor CPP-BEL TMF0140 $1.95
                                        (W337)

WRIGHT, MAURICE (1949-   )
  Like An Autumn Sky
    SATB,pno,perc [11'0"] sc APNM
    $7.25, perf mat rent   (W338)

  Loneliness
    SSA,trp,vcl,pno [10'] AM.COMP.AL.
    $7.70   (W339)

  Madrigals
    SATB [12'0"] sc APNM $5.75, perf
    mat rent   (W340)

  Swans
    SATB,vla,vcl,hpsd [8'] AM.COMP.AL.
    sc $9.15, pts $3.10   (W341)

  Travelling Music
    SATB [8'0"] sc APNM $4.00, perf mat
    rent   (W342)

  Winter Wind, The
    SATB,2pic,pno,tuba [8'] AM.COMP.AL.
    $7.70   (W343)

WUILLEUMIER, HENRI
  Pays, Garde Tes Fils!
    TTBB HUGUENIN CH 980   (W344)

WUNDRICH
  Das Ist Kindersache! *CCU
    jr cor AUTOGR   (W345)

WUORINEN, CHARLES (1938-   )
  Be Merry All That Be Present
    SATB,pic,ob,bsn,trp,2vln,vla,vcl
    [4'] AM.COMP.AL.   (W346)

WURTZEL
  Lady In New York Harbor
    (Lojeski) 3pt mix cor LEONARD-US
    08235784 $.85   (W347)
    (Lojeski) SATB LEONARD-US 08235783
    $.85   (W348)
    (Lojeski) SSA LEONARD-US 08235785
    $.85   (W349)

WYATT
  I Have A Song To Sing *CC5UL
    unis jr cor,pno,perc,opt gtr
    LINDSAY   (W350)

  O Music *see Mason

WYRTZEN, DON
  Eeuwig Dankbaar Zijn *see Yesterday,
    Today And Tomorrow

  Leef Vandaag *see Love Is Now

  Love Is Now
    (Zwaan, S.P.) "Leef Vandaag" SATB
    MOLENAAR 13019805   (W351)

  Yesterday, Today And Tomorrow
    (composed with Wyrtzen, J.)
    (Raadsheer, W.) "Eeuwig Dankbaar
    Zijn" SATB MOLENAAR 13020704
                                        (W352)

WYRTZEN, J.
  Yesterday, Today And Tomorrow *see
    Wyrtzen, Don

WYTON
  Indifference
    SATB oct DEAN HRD 241 $.95   (W353)

Y

YA BA BOM
(Goldman) LAWSON LG 51958 $.85 (Y1)

YA TOCAN LOS ATABALES see Brudieu, Joan

YAGER, R. STEWART
Penny Fiddle, The
unis cor,pno STAINER 3.3314 $.85 (Y2)

YANKEE DOODLE *folk song,US
(De Cormier, Robert) SATB LAWSON
LG 52216 $.85 (Y3)

YANOMAMO see Rose, Peter

YANOMANI see Nobre, Marlos

YARROW, PETER (1938-   )
Light One Candle
(De Cormier, Robert) mix cor,pno,
gtr LAWSON LG 52347 $1.25 (Y4)

YAVELOW, CHRISTOPHER JOHNSON
(1950-   )
Auguries Of Innocence
SSA [1'] (Blake) AM.COMP.AL. $1.20 (Y5)

Horse With Violin In Mouth, The
SSAA,pno [3'] AM.COMP.AL. $6.90 (Y6)

SSA,string orch [3'] AM.COMP.AL.
$6.90 (Y7)

Two Eva
SST [1'] AM.COMP.AL. $.80 (Y8)

YDSTIE
Celebration Now!
2 eq voices KJOS C8601 $.70 (Y9)

Every Heart Was Made For Song
2pt cor KJOS C8712 $.80 (Y10)

It's December Once Again (composed
with Ydstie, Arlene)
SA KJOS C8623 $.70 (Y11)

YDSTIE, ARLENE (1928-   )
It's December Once Again *see Ydstie

YE BANKS AND BRAES
(Koning, Leen) STB/SATB,S/T solo
EXC.MH 19.001.001 (Y12)

YE TUNEFUL MUSES see Purcell, Henry

YEGOROV
Choruses To Words By Russian Poets
*CCU
[Russ] cor,acap MEZ KNIGA 166 (Y13)

Drinking Song
SATB SCHIRM.G 232520 $.75 (Y14)

YELLOW AND RED BALLOON, A see
Thliveris, Elizabeth Hope (Beth)

YELLOW SHEEPSKIN see Hoddinott, Alun

YELLOW SUN, THE see Marsh, Mary Val

YESTERDAY ONCE MORE see Carpenter,
Richard Lynn

YESTERDAY, TODAY AND TOMORROW see
Wyrtzen, Don

YEUX, LES see Perrinjaquet, G.

YIKHAV STRILETS see Hayvoronsky,
Mykhajlo

Y'MEI CHANUKAH see Barnett, Steve

YODER, PAUL V. (1908-   )
Spiritual Rhapsody
SATB/TTBB,band MOLENAAR 08118108 (Y15)

YOLLECK, MARY
Once Upon A Christmas (composed with
Garvin, Joyce)
SATB LEONARD-US 08603507 $3.95,
ipa, accomp tape available (Y16)

YOU AND I
(Strommen) SATB CPP-BEL 5022YC1X
$1.25 (Y17)
(Strommen) SSA CPP-BEL 5022YC2X $1.25
(Y18)
(Strommen) SAB CPP-BEL 5022YC3X $1.25
(Y19)

YOU AND I see Poorman, Sonja

YOU AND ME
(Kern) SATB CPP-BEL T1260YC1 $1.25,
accomp tape available (Y20)
(Kern) SSA CPP-BEL T1260YC2 $1.25,
accomp tape available (Y21)
(Kern) SAB CPP-BEL T1260TC3 $1.25,

accomp tape available (Y22)

YOU AND ME see Gregor, Cestmir

YOU ARE MY MUSIC, YOU ARE MY SONG
(Hanson) SATB CPP-BEL 5146YC1X $1.25,
accomp tape available (Y23)
(Hanson) SAB CPP-BEL 5146YC3X $1.25,
accomp tape available (Y24)
(Hanson) 2pt cor CPP-BEL 5146YC5X
$1.25, accomp tape available (Y25)

YOU ARE SO BEAUTIFUL
(Chinn) SATB CPP-BEL SV8647 $1.25 (Y26)

YOU ARE THE ONE
(Hannisian) SATB CPP-BEL SV8512 $.95 (Y27)

YOU CAN BE see Mallow, Monti

YOU CAN STILL BELIEVE IN AMERICA see
Copeland

YOU CAN'T RUN FROM LOVE see Robb

YOU GAVE ME LOVE
(Graham) SAB CPP-BEL 5013YC3X $1.25 (Y28)

YOU GOT IT ALL
(Hanson) SATB CPP-BEL 5187YC1X $1.25,
accomp tape available (Y29)
(Hanson) SAB CPP-BEL 5187YC3X $1.25,
accomp tape available (Y30)

YOU GOT TO REAP JUST WHAT YOU SOW see
Dawson

YOU LADIES WHO MOVE IN CIRCLES OF TRADE
see Turnhout, Jan-Jacobvan, Ghij
Meyskens Die Van Der Comenschap
Sijt

YOU LIGHT UP MY LIFE
(Marzuki) SAB CPP-BEL 4881YC9X $1.25
(Y31)
(Marzuki) SATB CPP-BEL 4881YC7X $1.25
(Y32)
(Marzuki) SA CPP-BEL 4881YC8X $1.25
(Y33)

YOU MADE ME LOVE YOU
(Puerling, Gene) SATB LEONARD-US
07359465 $.95 (Y34)

YOU MADE ME LOVE YOU see Monaco

YOU NEED A FRIEND see Powell

YOU SMILE see Gilpin, Greg

YOU SPOTTED SNAKES see Thiman, Eric
Harding

YOU STOLE MY LOVE see MacFarren

YOU THERE IN THE BACK ROW see Coleman,
Cy

YOU TOUCHED MY LIFE see Madsen

YOULL
In The Merry Month Of May
(Greyson, Norman) SSA BOURNE
B240341 $.75 (Y35)

YOUMANS, VINCENT MILLIE (1898-1946)
Great Day
(Artman) SATB CPP-BEL SV8847 $1.40,
accomp tape available (Y36)
(Artman) 2pt cor CPP-BEL SV8848
$1.40, accomp tape available (Y37)

Without A Song
(Behnke) SATB CPP-BEL SVJ8604
$1.25, accomp tape available (Y38)

YOUNG
Let There Be Music *CCU
SATB SHAWNEE 5039 $4.25 (Y39)

Rock-A-Bye Your Baby With A Dixie
Melody *see Lewis

YOUNG, G.
Now Sing We All Noel
SATB SHAWNEE 6494 $.85 (Y40)

YOUR EYES see Takemitsu, Toru

YOUR IMAGINATION see Donnelly

YOUR LULLABY see Paull

YOUR SHINING EYES AND GOLDEN HAIR see
Bateson, Thomas

YOU'RE A GRAND OLD FLAG see Cohan,
George Michael

YOU'RE DANCING (IN MY SOUL) see Gilpin,
Greg

YOU'RE LOOKING GOOD, AMERICA see
Leavitt, John

YOU'RE MY FRIEND see Norton

YOU'RE THE INSPIRATION
(Althouse) SATB CPP-BEL 5095YC1X
$1.25 (Y41)
(Althouse) SSA CPP-BEL 5095YC2X $1.25
(Y42)
(Althouse) SAB CPP-BEL 5095YC3X $1.25
(Y43)

YOUTH RHYTHMS, VOL. 1 *CCU
[Russ] jr cor MEZ KNIGA 233 (Y44)

YOUTHFUL VOICES see Wright, Don

YOUTH'S SERENADE see Wallach, Joelle

YPEREN, R. VAN (1914-   )
Sijt Nu Verblijt
SATB MOLENAAR 13014604 (Y45)

YSORE, GUILLAUME
Si J'ai Eu Du Mal Ou Du Bien
(Agnel, A.) 2-3 eq voices HEUGEL
HE 32047 (Y46)

YVART, J.
Fils Du Capitaine Achab, Le (composed
with Passaquay, F.)
3 eq voices,opt perc HEUGEL
HE 32374 (Y47)

Z

Z PIESNI CHORALNYCH see Wiechowicz, Stanislaw

ZAAGMANS, JAN
Kindje: Op De Peul Mijns Herten Rust Uw Hoofdeke
SSA/TTB ZENGERINK 80   (Z1)

ZACHT IS UW HAND, O WINDEKE see Geraedts, Henri

ZACHT ZINGT DE ZEE see Naberman, Mar

ZADOK THE PRIEST see Handel, George Frideric

ZAHNER, BRUNO (1919-   )
Ade Zur Guten Nacht
see Zahner, Bruno, Thurgau, Der

Thurgau, Der
mix cor,acap CRON contains also:
Ade Zur Guten Nacht   (Z2)

ZAKRZEWSKA-NIKIPORCZYK, BARBARA
Welcome, Light °see Witaj, Jasnosci

Witaj, Jasnosci
"Welcome, Light" [Polish] men cor,
acap [4'20"] POLSKIE NPCH 65 (Z3)

ZALLMAN, ARLENE (PROCTOR) (1934-   )
And With Ah! Bright Wings
SATB,org [8'0"] sc APNM $5.75, perf
mat rent   (Z4)

Emerson Motets
SATB [12'0"] sc APNM $8.25, perf
mat rent   (Z5)

ZAMECNIK, EVZEN (1939-   )
Around Frydek
mix cor [5'] CESKY HUD.   (Z6)

Beskydy
wom cor [5'] CESKY HUD.   (Z7)

Four Children's Choruses °CC4U
jr cor CESKY HUD.   (Z8)

Games
mix cor,ST soli,fl,vla,brass [15']
CESKY HUD.   (Z9)

How We Are To Behave
mix cor [6'30"] CESKY HUD.   (Z10)

Impromtus I
mix cor,acap [4'] CESKY HUD. (Z11)

Impromtus II
mix cor,trp [8'] CESKY HUD. (Z12)

Indian Summer
mix cor,S solo,2tam-tam [7'] CESKY
HUD.   (Z13)

Let's Create A Land Of Song
jr cor&jr cor [9'] CESKY HUD. (Z14)

Peasant's Prayer °CC3U
mix cor CESKY HUD.   (Z15)

Rivers °CC3U
men cor CESKY HUD.   (Z16)

Sine Amore Nihil
mix cor [8'] CESKY HUD.   (Z17)

There Beneath The Hills, The High Hills
wom cor,Bar&narrator,orch [35']
CESKY HUD.   (Z18)

ZANINELLI
For Spacious Skies
SATB SHAWNEE 1862 $2.50   (Z19)

ZEBRAS see Belyea, H.

ZECHLIN, RUTH (1926-   )
Sieg Von Guernica, Der
mix cor sc BREITKOPF-L 7665 (Z20)

ZEG KWEZELKEN, WILDE GIJ DANSEN
"Geestelijk En Een Geestig Oudnederlands Lied, Een, Nr. 2"
[Dutch] 3 eq voices,acap ZENGERINK
R 635   (Z21)

ZEG KWEZELKEN, WILDE GIJ DANSEN see Schrijvers, Jean

ZEHAVAN see Handelsman, Smadar

ZEHN POETISCHE DUETTE see Eben, Petr

ZEIT UND EWIGKEIT see Miller, Franz R.

ZELENA SE SNITKA see Eben, Petr

ZELENKA, JAN DISMAS (1679-1745)
Sub Olea Pacis Et Palma Virtutis
sc SUPRAPHON   (Z22)

ZELM, JAN VAN (1959-   )
Achter De Schutting Wordt Gebouwd
4pt mix cor,3clar,2trom,pno [60']
DONEMUS   (Z23)

ZELTER, CARL FRIEDRICH (1758-1832)
Johanna Sebus
SATB,fl,strings,hpsd [6'] KALMUS
A7123 cor pts f.s., pno-cond sc
f.s., ipa   (Z24)

ZENDER, HANS (1936-   )
Animula
wom cor,5fl,3perc [11'] BREITKOPF-W
(Z25)

ZEPPERL-POLKA see Strauss, Johann

ZER PRAHIM see Braun, Yeheskiel

ZERREISSET, ZERSPRENGET, ZERTRUMMENT
DIE GRUFT see Bach, Johann Sebastian

ZES BRUILOFTSZANGEN II see Schaik, Johan Ant. Stephanus Van

ZES BRUILOFTZANGEN II see Schaik, Johan Ant. Stephanus Van

ZES GELDERSE GEDICHTEN see Michans, Carlos

ZIEGLER, JOSEF W.
Herbsteszeit, Reiche Zeit
men cor BRAUN-PER 1066   (Z26)

ZIEH, SCHIMMEL, ZIEH! see Biebl, Franz

ZIEH, SCHIMMEL, ZIEH see Ophoven, Hermann

ZIELINSKA, LIDIA
Solfatara
SSAATTBB [3'0"] sc APNM $3.50, perf
mat rent   (Z27)

ZIGEUNERLAGER, DAS see Biebl, Franz

ZIGEUNERLIEDER see Brahms, Johannes

ZIGEUNERLIEDER, OP. 103 see Brahms, Johannes

ZIGEUNERLIEDER, OP. 103 see Brahms, Johannes

ZIGEUNERLIEDER, OP. 103 see Brahms, Johannes

ZIGEUNERLIEDER, OP. 103 see Brahms, Johannes

ZILVERVLOOT, DE see Holman, F.

ZIMMERMANN, UDO (1943-   )
Ode An Das Leben
SATB&SATB&SATB,Mez solo,0.0.0.0.
2.4.2.0. timp,3harp,48strings
[15'] BREITKOPF-L   (Z28)

ZINGARELLA see Biebl, Franz

ZINGEN IS GEZOND: LAAT ONS SAMEN NU GAAN ZINGEN see Stenz, Herman

ZINGEN IS GEZOND: NU TE SAAM EEN LIED GEZONGEN see Stenz, Herman

ZIPP, FRIEDRICH (1914-   )
Den Ackermann Soll Man Loben
mix cor BOHM   (Z29)

Es Wandels Sich Die Reiche
[Ger] men cor,2trp,2trom,opt org,
opt strings SCHOTTS C 46380 see
from Zwei Festspruche   (Z30)

Lied Ist Uber Dem Wort
[Ger] men cor,2trp,2trom,opt org,
opt strings SCHOTTS C 46380 see
from Zwei Festspruche   (Z31)

Lob Des Liedes
SATB,2trp,2trom,strings MULLER 810
(Z32)

Zwei Festspruche °see Es Wandels
Sich Die Reiche; Lied Ist Uber
Dem Wort   (Z33)

ZOLL, PAUL (1907-1978)
Ach, Wenn Es Nun Die Mutter Wusst
SSAA MULLER 309C see from Bange
Liebe   (Z34)

Bange Liebe °see Ach, Wenn Es Nun
Die Mutter Wusst; Im Volkston
(Z35)

ZOLL, PAUL (cont'd.)
Ich Ging An Einem Fruhmorgen
men cor BOHM   (Z36)

Im Volkston
SSAA MULLER 309B see from Bange
Liebe   (Z37)

Madchenlied
SSAATTBB MULLER 309A see from BANGE
LIEBE   (Z38)

Mein Herz, Ich Will Dich Fragen
SSAATTBB MULLER 309D see from BANGE
LIEBE   (Z39)

ZOLLNER, KARL FRIEDRICH (1800-1860)
En Route
TTBB HUGUENIN EB 199   (Z40)

ZOMER see Maes, Jef

ZOMER, DE: DE GROTE ZOMERDAG STAAT OPEN
see Zwager, Piet

ZOMER KWAM, DE: DE ZOMER KWAM MET BLOEMEN see Zwager, Piet

ZOMERAVOND: OP GINDSE STOPPELVELDEN see Appeldoorn, Dina

ZOMMER see Rippen, Piet

ZON, DE: LIEVE MEID, DE LUCHT IS DRONKEN see Vranken, Petrus Johannes Josephus

ZONDER see Janssen, Guus

ZONNE STRAALT, DE: ZILVER GLANZEND see Vranken, Joseph

ZONNELIED, HET see Kersters, Willem

ZONSONDERGANG see Schubert, Franz (Peter)

ZOO PAS HAD GOD UW JA GESCHREVEN see Schaik, Johan Ant. Stephanus Van

ZORMAN, MOSHE (1952-   )
Songs For Uri
jr cor,acap [8'] (texts by A. A.
Milne) ISR.MUS.INST. 6740   (Z41)

ZPEV ZASTUPU see Krejci, Isa

ZU LAUTERBACH see Weiss-Steinberg, Hans

ZU REGENSBURG see Kanetscheider, Artur

ZU REGENSBURG AUF DER KIRCHTURMSPITZ
see Kutzer, Ernst, Und Als Die
Schneider Jahrstag Hatt'n

ZU RUDESHEIM IN DER DROSSELGASS see Krome

ZUM MEER "IN DER KLEINEN STADT AM HAFEN" see Rebscher, Helmut

ZUR FEIER see Gluck, Christoph Willibald, Ritter von

ZUR HOHEN JAGD see Schumann, Robert (Alexander)

ZUR NACHT see Reger, Max

ZUR WASSERFAHRT see Naegeli, Hans Georg

ZUVERSICHT see Schumann, Robert (Alexander)

ZWAAN, J.
Meizang: 'T Is Lente, 'T Is Lente
SSA/TTB ZENGERINK 306   (Z42)

ZWAGER, PIET
Avondrood: Nog Nauwlijks Is Het Groen
Der Boomen
SSA/TTB ZENGERINK 343   (Z43)

Hazegrauwt, Het: Vroeg Avondt Het
mix cor ZENGERINK 491   (Z44)

In De Maand Van Mei
SSA/TTB ZENGERINK 71   (Z45)
SSA/TTB ZENGERINK 71   (Z46)

In 'T Voorjaar: Blijde Dalen Zonnestralen
SSA/TTB ZENGERINK 76   (Z47)

Leeuwerik, De: De Sneeuwklok Bloeit
mix cor ZENGERINK 342   (Z48)

Lentezang: Stil, In Wazig Nevelgrauwen
SSA/TTB ZENGERINK 177   (Z49)

Populier, De: Daar Staat Hij, 'T Edel
Hoofd Omhoog
4 eq voices,acap ZENGERINK 341
(Z50)

ZWAGER, PIET (cont'd.)

Voor Allen: De Aarde Is Voor Allen
    mix cor ZENGERINK 344   (Z51)

Vrede: Vrede, Spreidt Gij Uw Zachte
    Vleugels
    SSA/TTB ZENGERINK 145   (Z52)

Winter, De: De Winter Heeft, Hoe
    Grijs Van Kin
    4 eq voices,acap ZENGERINK 11 (Z53)

Zomer, De: De Grote Zomerdag Staat
    Open
    4 eq voices,acap ZENGERINK 342
                                 (Z54)

Zomer Kwam, De: De Zomer Kwam Met
    Bloemen
    4 eq voices,acap ZENGERINK 25 (Z55)

ZWALUWEN, DE see Naberman, Mar

ZWEI ABENDLIEDER see Kuntz, M.

ZWEI ALTDEUTSCHE LIEBESLIEDER *see Es
    Flog Ein Klein's Waldvogelein; Ich
    Spring In Diesem Ringe   (Z56)

ZWEI FESTSPRUCHE see Zipp, Friedrich

ZWEI FRANZOSISCHE VOLKSLIEDER *see A
    La Claire Fontaine; Wenn Ich Vom
    Klaren Weine Trinke   (Z57)

ZWEI GESANGE see Baumgartl, Michael

ZWEI GESELLIGE LIEDER NACH BAROCKEN
    WEISEN see Seckinger, Konrad

ZWEI HERZEN IM DREIVIERTELTAKT see
    Stolz, Robert

ZWEI JAGERLIEDER see Kanetscheider,
    Artur

ZWEI KARELISCHE VOLKSLIEDER see
    Bergman, Erik

ZWEI LIEDER DES GLUCKS see Schneider,
    W.

ZWEI LIEDER VOM WEIN AUF BAROCKE WEISEN
    see Scheck, Helmut

ZWEI QUARTETTE AUS DEM MINNESPIEL see
    Schumann, Robert (Alexander)

ZWEI VOLKSWEISEN see Deutschmann,
    Gerhard

ZWERVERSLIED: IK HEB GEEN VROUW see
    Appeldoorn, Dina

ZWOLF LIEDER UND ROMANZEN see Brahms,
    Johannes

ZWOLF MONATSKANONS *CC12U
    (Uber, Gerhard) eq voices BOHM works
    by Biebl, Haus, Helmschrott and
    others   (Z58)

ZWYSSIG, ALBERICH (1808-1854)
    Cantique Patriotique
    1-4pt cor HUGUENIN see from
    CHANSONS POUR LA JEUNESSE,
    SEPTIEME CAHIER   (Z59)

Wir Ziehen Zur Mutter Der Gnade
    mix cor,acap CRON   (Z60)

ABRAMSZ, S.; LEMARC, A.
Hollands Liedje

ABSCHATZ, ASSMANN VON
Bose, Hans-Jurgen Von
Ich Leb Ohne Ruh Im Herzen

ADES
Berlin, Irving
Irving Berlin- A Choral Portrait

Ingalls
Gift Of Song, The

Tchaikovsky, Piotr Ilyich
Three Songs By Peter Ilych
Tchaikovsky

ADLER
Atsey Zeytim Omdin

ADLER, JAMES
Joplin, Scott
Ragtime Fantasy

AGNEL
C'est La Veille Etrambire

AGNEL, A
Anonymous
Coeur De Vous, Le
Dale Si Le Das
Du Coeur Le Don
J'ai Mis Mon Coeur
Je Demeure Seule Egaree
M'amie Un Jour
Quand Je Bois Du Vin Claret
Si J'ai Eu Du Mal Ou Du Bien

Arcadelt, Jacob
Dormendo Un Giorno A Baia
Gravi Pene In Amor
Je Ne Me Confesserai Point
Voi Mi Ponesti Un Foco

Byrd, William
Nightingale So Pleasant, The

Castro, Jean de
Bonjour Mon Coeur
Elle S'en Va De Moi La Mieux Aimee
Je L'aime Bien
Mon Coeur Se Recommande A Vous
Quand Mon Mari Vient De Dehors
Tout Ce Qu'on Peult En Elle Veoir
Vous Qui Aimez Les Dames

Certon, Pierre
Amour Voyant L'ennui
Dulcis Amica

Concerts Imaginaires De La
Renaissance

Contentez-Vous

Cosson, A.
Voyant Souffrir Celle Qui Me
Tourmente

Courtois, Jean
Deduc Me Domine

Du Boys, Francoise
J'aime Bien Mon Ami

Festa, Costanzo
Altro Non E'l Mio Amor

Fevin, Antoine de
On A Mal Dit De Mon Ami

Gardane, Antonio
Fini Le Bien
M'amie Un Jour
Quatre Duos A Voix Egles
Si J'ai Du Bien
Six Duos A Voix Mixtes

Gascongne, Mathieu
J'ai Dormi La Matinee

Gero, Ihan
Au Joli Son Du Sansonnet
Incessamment Mon Pauvre Coeur
Lamente
J'ai Mis Mon Coeur
Je L'ai Aimee Bien Sept Ans Et Demi
Je M'y Complains De Mon Ami
La, La, Maitre Pierre
Mort Et Fortune
Ne Sais Pourquoi Votre Grace Ai
Perdu
Pauvre Coeur, Tant Il M'ennoie
Quand Je Bois Du Vin Claret
Quand Je Vois Du Vin Claret
Sur Tous Regrets
Trist' Et Pensi

Gervaise, Claude
Elle Voyant Approcher Son Depart

Hesdin, Nicolle Des Celliers D'
Helas, Madame, Faites-Lui Quelque
Bien
Mon Pere M'a Tant Battu

AGNEL, A (cont'd.)
Jacotin, Jacques
Amour Me Point
Dame D'honneur
Je Suis Desheritee
Qui Veut Aimer

Janequin, Clement
C'est Mon Ami
Or Sus, Or Sus, L'alouette A 3

Je Ne Veux Plus A Mon Mal Consentir

Layolle, Francesco
Bourguignons, Les

Le Blanc, Didier
Elle S'en Va De Moi La Mieux Aimee
Mon Coeur Se Recommande A Vous

Mare De Deu, La

Mittantier
Tel En Medit

Moulu, Pierre
J'ai Par Trop Longuement Aime

Mouton, Jean
Grand Desir D'aimer Me Tient, Le

Pelletier, R. Octave
Si Mon Malheur M'y Continue

Penet, Hilaire
Au Joly Bois

Richafort, Joannes
En Revenant Du Bois
Il Est En Vous

Rore, Cipriano de
Grave Pen'in Amor

Sermisy, Claude de (Claudin)
Ayez Pitie Du Grand Mal Que
J'endure
Changeons Propos
Coeur De Vous, Le
D'amour Je Suis Desheritee
J'aime Le Coeur De M'amie
On En Dira Ce Qu'on Voudra

Susato, Tielman
Premier Livre Des Chansons, Le:
Vol.1

Temps Qui Court, Le

Verdonk, Jan
Je L'aime Bien

Villiers, Pierre de
Hiver Sera, Et L'ete, Variable, L'

Willaert, Adrian
Allons, Allons Gai
Ceduntur Gladus
Equalis Eterno
J'aime Par Amour
Or Suis-Je Bien Au Pire
Rousee Du Mois De Mai, La
Vous Marchez Du Bout Du Pied

Ysore, Guillaume
Si J'ai Eu Du Mal Ou Du Bien

AGNEL, A. N HE 32127
Susato, Tielman
Premier Livre Des Chansons, Le:
Vol.2

ALAIN, MARIE-CLAIRE
Alain, Jehan
Chanson A Bouche Fermee
Fantaisie Pour Choeur A Bouche
Fermee

ALBRECHT
Sing N' Do Songs, Vol II

ALLEN
Dvorak, Antonin
Christmas Tree, The

ALTHOUSE
Barge
School Is Out

Boyce
Pretty Little Angel Eyes

Carpenter, Richard Lynn
Top Of The World

Dancing In The Dark

Davis, Stephen
With Just One Look In Your Eyes

Desert Moon

Donnelly
Your Imagination

ALTHOUSE (cont'd.)
Fisher
When You're Smiling

Gayle, Crystal
Nobody Wants To Be Alone

Grean
Thing, The

Hanby
Up On The Housetop

I Just Called To Say I Love You

Kupferschmid, Steven
Christmas On The Isthmus Of Panama

Murray
Nobody Loves Me Like You Do

Never Surrender

On The Wings Of Love

Rock And Roll Girls

To Me

Ward, Samuel Augustus
America, The Beautiful

You're The Inspiration

ALTHOUSE, JAY
Hey! Baby!

Rothenberg, Irv
Feel The Power

Simon, Carly
Let The River Run (New Jerusalem)

Steppin' Out On Broadway

Wilson, Brian
Little Saint Nick

ALTINK
Mendelssohn-Bartholdy, Felix
Lieblingsplatzchen

AMUNDSEN, LARS
Lystrup, Geirr
Diger Dag
Songen Om Kjaerligheta

ANDERS
Oh! What A Beautiful City

ANDERSON
Lullaby Of The Leaves

There's A Rainbow 'Round My Shoulder

ANDREWS
Dedrick
Kites Are Fun

ANTICO, ANDREA
Motetti Novi E Chanzoni Franciose A
Quatro Sopra Doi

ANTONOWYCZ, M.; ELDERS, W.
Des Prez, Josquin
Works Of Josquin Des Prez, The:
Secular Works, Vol. 4
Works Of Josquin Des Prez, The:
Secular Works, Vol. 5

APPEL, BERNHARD
Schumann, Robert (Alexander)
Glockenturmers Tochterlein
Handschuh, Der

AQUILAR
Berbel, Marcelo
Quimey, Neuquen

ARNOLD, DENIS; HARMAN, ALEC; LEDGER,
PHILIP
Book Of Four-Part Madrigals, A

ARTMAN
O Dear, What Can The Matter Be?

Youmans, Vincent Millie
Great Day

ARTMAN, RUTH
Whale Of A Tale, A

ASGEIRSSON, JON
Fourteen Icelandic Folk Songs

Fransiska

Kalinka

ASHTON
Eveningtime Medley

ASHTON (cont'd.)

  Foster
    Foster Mania

ASTON, PETER
  Jeffreys, G.
    Felice Pastorella

AUFRAY; VLINE
  Bourtayre
    Adieu, Monsieur Le Professeur

AVERRE
  Bach, Johann Sebastian
    Scat Bourree

  Schubert, Franz (Peter)
    Linden Tree, The

AVERRE, DICK
  Chipmunk Song

  Lennon, John
    All You Need Is Love
    Blackbird
    Norwegian Wood

BABICHEV, I.
  Choruses By Soviet Composers

BACKER, H.
  Heute Sing Ich Euch Ein Liedchen

BACON, BOYD
  Please Do Not Go My Love

BAERISWYL, HENRI
  Babylon's Falling

BAGAN
  Barley
    Gull And I, The

BAKER, JONATHAN
  Family (Soar With Eagles)

BARBLAN, E.
  Costeley, Guillaume
    Mignonne, Allons Voir Si La Rose

  Debousset, Jean-Baptiste
    A L'Amour Je Declare La Guerre

BARBLAN, EMMANUEL
  A Chasa!-Rentrons

  As Marider-Le Mariage

  Au Bon Vieux Temps

  Hochzyter, Der

  Je Possede Un Reduit Obscur

  Mort De Bale, La

  Pecheur, Le

  Que Fais-Tu La, Bel Oiseau?

  Tod Von Basel, Der

  Troubadour, Le

BAREZZANI, MARIA TERESA ROSA
  Monteverdi, Claudio
    Madrigali: Libro 3

BARGIEL, WOLDEMAR
  Schumann, Robert (Alexander)
    Szenen Aus Goethes "Faust"

BARKER, WARREN
  Ward, Samuel Augustus
    America, The Beautiful

BARNES
  Coleman, Cy
    Rhythm Of Life, The

BECKER, G.
  Jerakina

  Nun Ist April Und Freudenzeit

BEEKUM, J.V.
  Gluck, Christoph Willibald, Ritter
    von
    Drei Klassische Chore
    Ewig Zurnt Die Gottheit Nicht
    Zur Feier

BEHNKE
  I've Got The World On A String

  Youmans, Vincent Millie
    Without A Song

BEHNKE, MARTIN
  Ellington, Edward Kennedy (Duke)
    Don't Get Around Much Anymore

  Kaper, Bronislaw
    On Green Dolphin Street

BEHNKE, MARTIN (cont'd.)
  McHugh, Jimmy
    I'm In The Mood For Love

  Perkins, Frank
    Stars Fell On Alabama

  Warren, Harry
    On The Atcheson, Topeka And The
    Santa Fe

BENNETT
  Western Wind Songbook, Vol. 1, The

BENTHEM, JAAP VAN; BROWN, HOWARD MAYER
  Des Prez, Josquin
    Secular Works For Three Voices

BEREAU, J.S.
  Brassens, Georges
    Priere, La

  Revil, Rudi
    A La Saint-Medard

BERGLUND
  Ward, Samuel Augustus
    America The Beautiful

BERGMAN
  Jacobs
    This Is My Country

BESIG
  Forever Everly

  Hamlisch, Marvin F.
    Ice Castles: Theme (Through The
    Eyes Of Love)

  Leisy, James Franklin
    Me And You

  Price
    It's Time To Ring Those Christmas
    Bells!

BIEBL
  Alte Lied, Das

  Hausierer, Der

  Sascha

BIEBL, F.
  Bach, Wilhelm Friedemann
    Kein Halmlein Wachst Auf Erden

  Schubert, Franz (Peter)
    An Die Musik: Du Holde Kunst

BIERSMA, P.
  Bernstein, Leonard
    West-Side Story

  Cleber, Joseph
    Postkoets, De

  Laetantius, Br.
    Als In Ons Hart
    Nachtegaal, De

  Wijnnobel, P.
    Vivace (Andantino)

BIEZEN, J. VAN; GUMBERT, J.P.
  Two Early Fifteenth-Century
    Chansonniers From The Low
    Countries

BILLINGSLEY
  Bernstein, Elmer
    Step To The Rear

BILLINGSLEY, ALAN
  Best From Dirty Dancing, The

  Fogerty, J.C.
    Proud Mary

  Gordy, Berry
    Shop Around

  I Wanna Dance With Somebody (Who
    Loves Me)

  1-2-3

  Sunshine Medley:, A

BLAIR, D.
  Colorado Trail, The

  Red River Valley; Trail To Mexico

BLANC, H.
  Ah! Si J'avais Un Sou

BLEUSE, M.
  Petit Mousse, Le

BOCKER, CHRISTINE
  Eccard, Johannes
    Heitere Weltliche Chorsatze

BOGDANOV, Y.
  From The Repertoire Of The USSR
    Ministry Of Culture Chamber
    Chorus

BOGERT, HANS VAN DEN
  Anonymous
    Winter Is Vergangen, Die

BRAHMS, JOHANNES
  German Folk Songs

  Standchen

BRANDON, G.
  Sad Song Of The Sea

BRASSEUR, M.A.; TENIERE, C.
  Autre Jour, J'etais En Route, L'

  Melchior Et Balthazar

  Moi, Gardais Les Chevres

  O Caille, Pauvre Caille

  Pauvre Soldat

  Tour, Prends Garde, La

BRAY, KENNETH
  Song Of The Deer

BRESGEN, CESAR
  Telemann, Georg Philipp
    Geht Schlafen

BRISMAN
  Brahms, Johannes
    Songs Of Ophelia

BRISSET, CH.
  Becaud, Gilbert
    Orange, L'

BRISSLER, F.F.
  Handel, George Frideric
    Halleluja

BRITT
  Monath, Norman
    Magic Of Believing, The

BROWNE, M.
  Winner, Septimus ("Alice Hawthorne")
    Whispering Hope

BRUBAKER
  O Tannenbaum

BRYMER
  Then He Said, "Sing!"

BRYMER, MARK
  Back To The Future: A Medley

  Eighty's Gold: A Medley

  Just One Person

BUCHHOLZ
  All At Once

  Crush On You

  Heaven In Your Eyes

  Laura

  Razzamatazz

  Respect Yourself

BUCHHOLZ, BUCK
  Carpenter, Richard Lynn
    Something In Your Eyes

  Come Into My Life

  Pitchford, Dean
    After All

BULLOCK
  Schubert, Franz (Peter)
    Al Par Del Rustelletto

BUNE
  Water Is Wide, The

BURDET, JACQUES
  Hier Au Soir J'ai Tant Danse

BURGER, DAVE
  All Ye Who Music Love

BURNAND, ALAIN
  Licorne, La

BURROUGHS
  Deck The Halls

BUSH, GEOFFREY; HURD, MICHAEL
  Invitation To The Partsong 4: Glees &
    Madrigals

BUURMAN, H.H.
  Anonymous
    Merk Toch Hoe Sterk

CACAVAS
  Ellington, Edward Kennedy (Duke)
    Portrait Of Duke Ellington

CADOW, P.
  Foster, Stephen Collins
    Alter Joe
    Swanee River

CAILLARD, PHILIPPE
  C'est Dans Le Mois De Mai

CALVIN, DOT
  Smile

  Woods, Harry MacGregor
    Poor Papa

CAMPBELL, ROBERT
  Sermisy, Claude de (Claudin)
    My Dearest Love

  Verdelot, Phillippe
    O Sweetest Nighttime

CARACI, MARIA
  Monteverdi, Claudio
    Madrigali: Libro 5

CARPENTIER
  Milhaud, Darius
    Incantations

CARTER, ANDREW
  Teddy Bear's Picnic, The

CASEY
  Casey, Thomas
    Drill, Ye Tarriers

CASSETTO, E.
  Chopin, Frederic
    Valse En La Mineur

CHAILLEY, JACQUES
  Marseillaise, La: Chant Du Depart

CHILDS, EDWIN T.
  Sometimes I Feel Like A Motherless
    Child

CHINN
  American Heritage Tribute, An

  Boogie Down

  Brooks, Randy
    Grandma Got Run Over By A Reindeer

  Cahn, Sammy
    Let It Snow! Let It Snow! Let It
      Snow!

  Car Tunes: Medley Of Beach Boys' Hits

  Conga

  Didn't We

  For Just A Moment (Love Theme From
    St. Elmo's Fire)

  Ghostbustin': A Medley Of
    Superstition, Thriller And
    Ghostbusters

  Glory Of Love

  Goodman, Benny (Benjamin David)
    Stompin' At The Savoy

  Hands Across America

  Heaven

  I Heard It Through The Grapevine

  I Knew You Were Waiting (For Me)

  If You Say My Eyes Are Beautiful

  Living In America

  Mancini, Henry
    Moon River

  Movie Classics: The Best Of The 80's

  Movie Classics: Through The Eyes Of
    Love

  Nightshift (Commodores)

  Now And Forever (You And Me)

CHINN (cont'd.)

  Our Day Will Come

  Pierpont, J.
    Sounds Of Christmas, The

  Raposo, Joseph G.
    America Is (Official Statue Of
      Liberty Song)

  Rhythm Of The Night

  Simply Meant To Be

  Solid

  Someone

  Spring Can Really Hang You Up The
    Most

  Suddenly

  Thanks For The Memory

  Thriller

  Through The Fire

  Touch A Hand, Make A Friend

  Trouble In Paradise

  Victory

  We Don't Need Another Hero

  We Wish You A Merry Christmas, Vol.1

  What About Love

  You Are So Beautiful

CHINN, TEENA
  Carmichael, Hoagy
    Nearness Of You, The

  Coleman, Cy
    Hey! Look Me Over: A Medley Of Cy
      Coleman Hits

  Didn't We Almost Have It All

  Ellington, Edward Kennedy (Duke)
    Satin Doll

  Honesty

  Hudson, Will
    Moonglow

  (I've Had) The Time Of My Life

  Legrand, Michel
    Little Boy Lost (Pieces Of Dreams)

  Let's Go! Movie Classics On The Move

  Masser, Michael
    Greatest Love Of All, The

  Michael, Row The Boat Ashore

  Montgomery, Lisa
    Dreamin'

  Morris, Stevland (Stevie Wonder)
    Go Home

  Once Upon A Time

  Robinson, William (Smokey)
    When Smokey Sings: A Tribute To
      Smokey Robinson

  Seger, Bob
    Shakedown

CHRISTIANSEN
  Skip To My Lou

CHRISTIANSEN, P.
  Can't You Live Humble?

  Over Yonder

CHURCHILL, STUART
  Keeper Of The Eddystone Light, The

CLARKE, ROSEMARY
  Come, Let Us Light The Menorah

CLAUDIUS
  Hessenberg
    Mond Ist Aufgegangen, Der

COATES
  Robinson
    Harriet Tubman

COBB
  Begone, Dull Care

COBB, DONALD
  We Be Three Poor Mariners

COLLINS
  Pray Tell Me, Oh, Please

  Smith
    Star Spangled Banner, The

  Three Proverbial Loves

COOMBES, DOUGLAS
  Lindsay Folk Book

  Rossini, Gioacchino
    Duetto Buffo Di Due Gatti

  Up! Good Christen Folk

COOPER
  Foster
    Nelly Bly

  Simple Gifts

  Waltzing Matilda

COOPER, GWYNETH
  O Canada

COOPER, KENNETH
  All My Trials

COOPERSMITH
  Davidowitz
    Bar Yohai

  Karachevsky
    Agada

CORNELOUP, MARCEL
  Plaisirs Sont Doux, Les

CORNWALL, J.
  Carey, Henry
    America (My Country, Tis Of Thee)

CORPATAUX, MICHEL
  Anonymous
    Rondo

COSSETTO, E.
  Chopin, Frederic
    Valse

CRAIG
  When I Take My Sugar To Tea

CROCKER
  How Lovely Is The Rose

DAHLE
  Lippman
    God's Christmas Tree

DANIEL, ETIENNE
  Little David

  Naty-Boyer, Jean
    Chemin De La Plage, Le

  Oh! I Want To Go

  Red River Valley

  Robin, Marie-Therese
    Vague Emporte Au Loin, La

  Touati, Raymond
    Ou Va L'eau Qui S'en Va?

DAVIES, BRYAN
  Lissmann, Kurt
    Aus Der Traube In Die Tonne

DAVIS, BILL
  Take A Spin

  Taylor, Lemoyne
    Daisy, Daisy
    Outrageous, That Shortnin' Bread

DAVIS, CRAIG
  Rosebud In June

DE CORMIER, ROBERT
  Brand
    When I First Came To This Land

  Crawford
    Amen

  De Cormier, Robert
    Connecticut Peddler, The
    Legacy

  Erie Canal, The

  Farmer Is The Man, The

  Foster, Stephen Collins
    Fosterama

  Frankie And Johnny

  Great Grandad

DE CORMIER, ROBERT (cont'd.)

Hallelujah

Hays
  Two White Horses

He's The Man For Me

Hutchinson, J.E.
  Uncle Sam's Farm

I Been In The Storm So Long

I'se The B'y

I've Been Working On The Railroad

Jenny Jenkins

John Henry

Miner's Lament

Morris
  If I Had-A My Way

Ol' Dan Tucker

She'll Be Comin' 'Round The Mountain

Sweet Betsy From Pike

Tumbalaika

Wake Up, Jacob

Yankee Doodle

Yarrow, Peter
  Light One Candle

DE PIETTO
  Boito, Arrigo
    Salmodia Finale

DELSARTE, ANDRE
  Sur L'bord De Loire

DEPUE
  Foster, Stephen Collins
    Camptown Races, The

  Sing Dem Herrn

DEPUE, WALLACE
  Haydn, [Franz] Joseph
    Minor Masterpiece, A

DESCH, RUDOLF
  Bei Des Mondes Scheine

DESSEN
  Deep River

DEUTSCHMANN, GERHARD
  Alle Fangt An

  Frohliche Weihnacht Uberall

  Laufet All, Ihr Kinder

  Spat War Es Schon Zu Der Abendstund

DIEPENBEEK, FR.
  Gounod, Charles Francois
    Soldatenkoor Uit Faust

DIJK
  Carpenter, Richard Lynn
    Yesterday Once More

DOBBINS, FRANK
  Oxford Book Of French Chansons, The

DORFF
  Morley, Thomas
    My Bonny Lass She Smileth

DOTTIN, G.
  Anonymous
    Pensez De Faire Garnison

  Douze Canons Du 16 Siecle

  Fevin, Antoine de
    J'ai Vu La Beaute M'amie

  Richafort, Joannes
    Trut Avant, Il Faut Boire

  Willaert, Adrian
    Jeune Dame S'en Va Au Moulin, La

DRAHEIM, J.
  Mendelssohn-Bartholdy, Felix
    Antigone

DRISCOLL
  Me And My Shadow

DUMAS, H.
  Becaud, Gilbert
    Important, C'est La Rose, L'

DUMAS, H. (cont'd.)
  Djian, H.
    Source, La

DUNBAR
  Wiser
    Look Beyond Tomorrow

DUNCAN
  Fink
    Keepin' Good Company

DUPUIS, ALB.
  Schumann, Robert (Alexander)
    Traumerei

DUSING, DAVID
  Riddle Song, The

  Ritchie, Jean
    Courtin' Song, The

EDWARDS
  Anderson, Leroy
    Sleigh Ride

  Danzig, Evelyn
    Scarlet Ribbons

EHRET
  Gay90's Fantasy

  O It's Goodbye Liza Jane

EHRET, WALTER
  Oh Fare You Well, My Own True Love

EIELSEN, STEINAR
  Adle Sine Menne

  Gjendines·Banlat

  Inga Litimor

  Krakevise

  Svein Svane

  Truls Med Bogen

  Two Negro Spirituals

ELSENAAR, E.
  Gastoldi, Giovanni Giacomo
    Amor Nel Battello

  Verdi, Giuseppe
    Bandietenkoor

ERB
  Arcadelt, Jacob
    Margot

  Brahms, Johannes
    Abendstandchen
    Darthulas Grabesgesang
    Vineta

ERIKSSON, GUNNAR
  Totari, Georg
    Karleken Till Livet

ERMEY, WILLIAM
  Sousa, John Philip
    Stars And Stripes Forever, The

ESTERMANN, J.
  E Tempo Di Partire, L'

  Reich Und Arm

  Voici Venir Le Mois De Mai

  Wohl Mitt's I Der Nacht

EVERIST, MARK
  Five Anglo-Norman Motets

EVERTSE
  Mendelssohn-Bartholdy, Felix
    Morgengebed

EVERTSE, J.
  Gretry, Andre Ernest Modeste
    Rossignol, Le

  Hassler, Hans Leo
    Nun Fanget An

  Rossini, Gioacchino
    Tyrolienne

  Silcher, Friedrich
    Loreley, Die

FALQUET, RENE
  Petite Suite Romande

FARROW, LARRY
  Get On Board, Little Children

FASSLER, GUIDO
  Unter Apfelbluten

FAVEZ, DANIEL
  Andreae, Volkmar
    Chasseron, Le

FELDSTEIN
  This Train Goes Marching In

FELLOWES, EDMUND
  Farmer, John
    Fair Phyllis I Saw

FERGUSON, BARRY
  Heseltine, Philip ("Peter Warlock")
    Birds, The

FEUILLIE, J.
  Quatre Chansons Populaires

FILLEUL, JACQUES
  Grandes: Suite De 7 Chants De Labour

  Suite De Bourrees En Rondo: Auvergne

  Suite De Rigaudons En Rondo: Dauphine

FINETTI
  Bacharach, Burt F.
    Walk On By

FLEIG, G.
  Halmchen Kann Am Grossen Halme

  Kuckuck, Der

  Schliesse, Schliesse Dich, Zyklus

FLETCHER
  Wagner, Richard
    Roman War Song, A

FLORES, ANGEL
  Van de Vate, Nancy Hayes
    Pond, The

FOMBONNE, J.
  Naty, Jean
    Au Chateau

FOMBONNE, JACQUES
  Viens Sous Mon Manteau

  Vocero Du Niolo

FORSTER, G.
  Ausbund Schoener Teutscher Liedlein,
    Ein

FOURCAUD, G.
  A Vuestros Pies, Madre

  Cielito Lindo

  Kernoa, J.P.
    Education Sentimentale

  Lancha Nueva Esparta, La

  Vasija De Barro, La

FRACKENPOHL, ARTHUR
  All The Pretty Little Horses

FRANCESCHI
  Old Familiar Faces

FRASER, SHENA
  I Know Where I'm Going

FREED
  Wabash Cannonball, The

FREED, ARNOLD
  Water Is Wide, The

FREY, MAX
  Chor Aktuell, Heft 2: Volkslieder In
    Europa

FRISCHMAN
  Franck
    Do Not Be Amazed

FROCHAUX, J.C.
  Villard, Jean (Gilles)
    A L'enseigne De La Fille Sans Coeur

FROCHAUX, JEAN-BERNARD
  Legende De Saint-Nicolas, Le

  Quel Mazzolin Di Fiori

  Ventinove Luglio, Il

FROCHAUX, JEAN-CHARLES
  Castelnuovo, V.
    Bella Valmaggina
    Malcantonesina
    Poschiavina
    Valcolla

FROCHET, J.
Contet, H.
Complainte Du Corsaire, La

FROCHOT, J.
Delanoe
Tournesol, Le

Je Suis

Lemarque, F.
Marjolaine

Polnareff, M.
Qui A Tue Grand' Maman?

Sylvestre, Anne
Cathedrales, Les
Gregoire Ou Sebastien

Teze, M.
Chagrin D'amour, Un

Vanderlove, Anne
Ballade En Novembre
Chanson De Virginia, La
Civilisations Perdues
Enfants Tristes, Les

FRY
Beach Boys Medley, A

Tribute To Air Supply, A

Tribute To Anne Murray, A

Tribute To Dolly Parton, A

Tribute To Kenny Rogers, A

Tribute To Olivia Newton-John, A

Tribute To Stevie Wonder, A

Tribute To The Carpenters, A

Tribute To The Commodores, A

FYODOROV, V.
Let's Sing, Friends! Vol. 11

GANTER, C.
Cucu, Il

Per Fare L'amore

Ticinesi

GATES, C.
Annie Laurie

Night Song For The Mountains

O No John

GAUDIN, J.Y.
Lemarque, F.
Temps Du Muguet, Le

Marnay
Enfants Qui Pleurent, Les

GAUFFRIAU, JEAN
Trenet, Charles
Jardin Extraordinaire, Le

GAUFFRIAU, JEAN
Trenet, Charles
Ame Des Poetes, L'

GAY, RUTH MORRIS
Leech, Bryan Jeffery
To The Hills

GEBHARD, L.
Ei, Wie Geht's Im Himmel Zu

Jung Bin Ich

Vergebliche Warnung – Hansel, Dein
Gretelein

GENTILHOMME, M.
Vidalin, M.
Printemps, Le

GEOFFRAY, CESAR
Arbre, L'

Distler, Hugo
Berceuse
Danse Des Morts: Motet

Lac Lomond, Le

GERAEDTS, HENRI
Anonymous
Naar Oostland Willen Wij Rijden
Patriotjes, De: Wat Zullen Ons
Patriotjes Eten

GEVAERT, FRANCOIS-AUGUSTE
Abandonnee, L'

Temps Passe, Le

GILPIN, GREG
Stevens, Ray
Streak, The: A Medley Of Ray
Stevens' Hits

GLARUM
Senfl, Ludwig
Bells At Speyer, The

GOEMANNE
Pachelbel, Johann
Canon In D

GOETZE, M.
Cat Came Back, The

GOETZE, MARY
Simply Sung

GOLDMAN
Beethoven, Ludwig van
Ich Liebe Dich

Dvorak, Antonin
Song To The Moon

For Jefferson And Liberty

Giordano, Umberto
Sweet Shepherdess, Addio

Golden Slumbers

Haydn, [Franz] Joseph
O Wondrous Harmony

Hi-Ney Ma Tov

Miller's Tears, The

Monteverdi, Claudio
Lasciatemi Morire

Near The Tiny Hearth

Pfautsch, Lloyd Alvin
Beautiful But Truthful

Pick The Cherries Ripe

Poet's Soliloquy, The

Tchum Bi-Ri Chum

Turn Ye To Me

Wagner, Richard
Pilgrim's Chorus

Ya Ba Bom

GOLDMAN; ERG
Golden Slumbers

GOLDSMITH
Beethoven, Ludwig van
Ich Liebe Dich

GOTTER, F.W.
Flies, J. Bernhard
Wiegenlied

GOUNOD, CHARLES
Le Febvre, Jacques
Aime-Moi, Bergere

GRAHAM
You Gave Me Love

GRASBECK, GOTTFRID
Fougstedt, Nils-Eric
Tersen

Helan

GREYSON
Arcadelt, Jacob
Now Spring In All Her Glory

Bateson, Thomas
Your Shining Eyes And Golden Hair

GREYSON, NORMAN
Youll
In The Merry Month Of May

GRIESHABER
Abraham
Honved Banda

Benatzky
Im "Weissen Rossl" Am Wolfgangsee

Bochmann
Mit Musik Geht Alles Besser
Wer Ist Hier Jung, Wer Hat Hier
Schwung

Dostal
Es Wird In Hundert Jahren Wieder So
Ein Fruhling Sein

Fall
Und Der Himmel Hangt Voller Geigen

GRIESHABER (cont'd.)
Grothe
An Der Donau, Wenn Der Wein Bluht
Mitternachtsblues
So Schon Wie Heut', So Musst' Es
Bleiben

Heymann
Das Muss Ein Stuck Vom Himmel Sein

Kattnigg, Rudolf
Leise Erklingen Glocken Vom
Campanile

Krome
Zu Rudesheim In Der Drosselgass

Raymond
Ich Hab' Mein Herz In Heidelberg
Verloren

Stolz, Robert
Ganze Welt Ist Himmelblau, Die
Leutnant Warst Du Einst Bei Den
Husaren
Singend, Klingend Ruft Dich Das
Gluck
Von Rudesheim Bis Heidelberg
Wanderlied (Ein Bischen Singsang)
Wanderlied (Ein Bisschen Singsang)

GRIMBERT, J.
Berceuse Basque

Berger He La!

Chroietan Buruzagi

Danae, La

Donati, Baldassare (Donato)
Villotte Napolitaine

D'un Vanneur De Ble

Eluard, P.
A Peine Defiguree

Gabrieli, Andrea
Battaglia

Gagliano, Marco da
Trois Madrigaux

Grimbert, Jacques
Doucette, Sucrine

Guantanamera

Guignolot

Isabeau S'y Promene

J'ai Du Chagrin

Kalinka

Laine, La

Lassus, Roland de (Orlandus)
O Doux Parlez

Le Blanc, Didier
Mignonnette

Le Jeune, Claude
Amour, Quand Fus-Tu Ne?

Michael

Monte, Philippe de
Comme La Tourterelle

Monteverdi, Claudio
Madrigali Guerrieri Et Amorosi:
Altri Canti D'amor
Madrigali Guerrieri Et Amorosi:
Altri Canti Di Marte

Pavane

Pendubidu

Prevert, J.
Message, Le

Quand Le Rossignol Chante

Regnard, Francois
Mamie Et Moy
O Voux, Beaux Yeux

Tes Petits Sabots

Voici Le Joli Mois De Mai

GRINDEL, J.
Aragon, L.
Nous Dormirons Ensemble

Bourgeois, Gerard
Amitie, L'

GRINDEL, J. (cont'd.)

Brel, Jacques
Bourree Du Celibataire, La
Colombe, La
Qu'avons-Nous Fait?

Ferrat, Jean
Nuit Et Brouillard

Gainsbourg, S.
Poinconneur Des Lilas, Le

Java Des Hommes Grenouilles, La

Marcy, Robert
Queue Du Chat, La

Suc, P.
Gargouille, La

Sylvestre, Anne
T'en Souviens-Tu La Seine

GRIZEY, G.
Roi Renaud, Le

GROMBERT, J.
Ribon, Ribonbaine

GROTH, KLAUS
Hauptmann, Moritz
An Der Kirche Wohnt Der Priester
Aus "Mirza Schaffy"
Hell Ins Fenster Scheint
Im Holz
Lerchenbaum, Der
Wenn Zweie Sich Gut Sind

GRUNDAHL
Grieg, Edvard Hagerup
Song For The Christmas Tree

Polish Lullaby

Russian Candle Carol

Russian Peace Songs

GUENTNER
Janequin, Clement
Dur Acier Et Diamont
Rossignol, Le: En Coutant
Si Le Coucou En Ce Mois

GUENTNER, FRANCIS J.
Anonymous
C'est Grand Erreur

Janequin, Clement
Il Etait Une Fillette
Il N'est Plaisir

HALFERTY
Erie Canal, The

HALL
Johnny Has Gone For A Soldier

HALLORAN, JACK
Foster, Stephen Collins
Camptown Races

HALSEY, L.
Three Shanties

HAM, J.
Kalinka

HAN, ISAAC
Canadien Errant, Un

Donkey Riding

I'll Give My Love An Apple

Land Of The Silver Birch

Morning Dew

HANDRICKSON
Rore, Cipriano de
Although When I Depart

HANNISIAN
You Are The One

HANSEN
Christmas Is Coming

Keep In The Middle Of The Road

HANSON
Christmas Time

Heart Is Not So Smart, The

Sweet Freedom

You Are My Music, You Are My Song

You Got It All

HANSON, MARK
Astley, Rick
She Wants To Dance With Me

Best Of Miami Sound Machine, The

From The Heart: A Medley Of Love
Songs

Love Will Save The Day

Never Gonna Give You Up

Rhythm Is Gonna Get You

Words Get In The Way

HARRIS
De Sermisy
Amours, Partes

MacFarren
You Stole My Love

HARRIS, JERRY W.
Jeep, Johann
O Music, Thou Most Lovely Art

HARRIS, JERRY WESELEY
Cui, Cesar Antonovich
Cloud Messengers

HARRIS, RON
Foster, Stephen Collins
Beautiful Dreamer
Jeanie With The Light Brown Hair

HARRISON, FRANK L.
Now Make We Merthe, Book 1: 12-14th
Cent. Latin

Now Make We Merthe, Book 2: 14-15th
Cent. English

Now Make We Merthe, Book 3: 15-16th
Cent. Continental

HAUG, HANS
Cucu, Il

Rossignolet Gentil

HAUGLAND, OSCAR
I Laid Me Down To Rest

Lad Up The Hill, The

Sweet Betsy From Pike

HAUS, K.
Lustig, Lustig, Ihr Lieben Bruder:
Sieben Frankische Volkslieder

HAUS, KARL
Jetzt Fangt Das Schone Fruhjahr An

Mai Tritt Ein Mit Freuden, Der

Wir Kamen Einst Von Piemont

HAYES
Berlin, Irving
Alexander's Ragtime Band

Harris
Break Forth Into Singing

HAYES; GOOCH
Pachelbel, Johann
Canon On Alleluia

HEGAR, F.
Brahms, Johannes
Jour S'enfuit, Le

HEILMANN, HARALD
Schubert, Franz (Peter)
Am Brunnen Vor Dem Tore

HELMBACHER, XAVIER
Cycle Du Vin, Le

HEMMERLING, CARLO
J'ai Demande Z'a La Vieille

HERDER, G. V.
Strauss, Richard
Altdeutsches Schlachtlied
Liebe

HERMANS, PETRA
Anonymous
Daer Was E Wuf Die Spon
Den Uyl Die Op Den Peerboom Zat
Des Winters Als Het Regent
Geluckig Is Het Land
Vier Weverkens Zag Men Ter
Botermarkt Gaan

Wilms, Johann Wilhelm
Wij Leven Vrij, Wij Leven Blij

HERR, F.
Belle Est Au Jardin D'amour, La

Dragons De Noailles, Les

Nadal Tindaire

HERR, FRANCOISE
Reveillez-Vous Picards

HESS
Abraham
Reich' Mir Zum Abschied Noch Einmal
Die Hande

Grothe
Fruhling In Wien
Postillion-Lied
Walzer Fur Dich Und Fur Mich, Einen

Heymann
Das Gibt's Nur Einmal

Millocker
Dunkelrote Rosen

Schroder
Ich Tanze Mit Dir In Den Himmel
Hinein

Winkler
Und Wieder Geht Ein Schoner Tag Zu
Ende

HEYWOOD
Foster, Stephen Collins
Oh Susanna

HICKEN, K.
Carol, W.
Deck The Hall

HICKS, VAL
Back In Nineteen Twenty-Nine

HILDEBRAND
Laetantius, Br.
Orgellied, Het

HILFRICH
Echo, Das

Trinklied

HILLIER
Three Hundred Years Of English
Partsongs

HILLIER, PAUL
Catch Book [B], The

English Romantic Partsongs

HINES
Haydn, [Franz] Joseph
Piercing Eyes

HINES, ROBERT S.
Haydn, [Franz] Joseph
Recollection

HLINAK, K.
Strauss, Johann, [Sr.]
Radetzky-Marsch

HOKANSON
Brahms, Johannes
She Walks In Beauty

HOLCOMBE
Mendelssohn-Bartholdy, Felix
Autumn Song

HOLDERLIN, FR.
Bose, Hans-Jurgen Von
Herbst, Der

HOLLFELDER, WALDRAM
Flohe Wimmeln Meinem Weibe

Junggeselle, Der

Konig Dagobert, Der

Petruschka

HOLMAN, F.
Brahms, Johannes
Guten Abend, Gut' Nacht

HOLSTEIN
Brassens, Georges
Chasse Aux Papillons, La
Mauvaise Reputation, La
Sabots D'Helene, Les

Greensleeves

Vigneault, Gilles
Doux Chagrin, Le
Mon Pays
Tam Ti De Lam

HOLSTEIN, J.P.
Nez De Martin, Le

P'tit Quinquin, Le

Reveillez-Vous Picards Et
  Bourguignons

HOLSTEIN, JEAN-PAUL
Le Forestier, Maxime
  Dialogue
  Education Sentimentale
  Fontenay Aux Roses

HOOGERWERF, N.
Hol, Richard
  Draaiersjongen, Een

HOOGEVEEN, G.H.
Kloek, D.
  Raak Mij Niet Kwijt

HOPSON
Handel, George Frideric
  Sing With Songs Of Joy

HOWORTH
Wade In De Water

HOWORTH, WAYNE
Joshua Fit De Battle Ob Jericho

HUBER, F.
Strauss, Johann, [Jr.]
  Fledermaus-Walzer
  Schatz-Walzer

HUBNER, W.
Kunad, Rainer
  Kitschpostille, Die
  Stimmen Der Volker

HUFF
Arthur Murray Taught Me Dancing In A
  Hurry

Chattanooga Choo Choo

Coleman, Cy
  You There In The Back Row

Ellington, Edward Kennedy (Duke)
  It Don't Mean A Thing (If It Ain't
  Got That Swing)

Forever

Get Ready

Hunsecker, Ralph Blane
  Have Yourself A Merry Little
  Christmas

I Go To Rio

Strouse, Charles Louis
  Applause
  Applause, Applause (Medley Of
  Broadway Rhythm- Applause)

There'll Be No New Tunes On This Old
  Piano: A Twenties Medley

HUFF, MAC
More Than You Know

These Dreams

HUGO, JOHN
We Wish You A Merry Christmas

HUGO, JOHN W.
Mozart, Wolfgang Amadeus
  Minuet

HUGUENIN, C
Janequin, Clement
  Ce Moys De Mai

HUGUENIN, CHARLES
Bateliere, La

Beethoven, Ludwig van
  Hymne A La Joie

Chansons Pour La Jeunesse, Cinquieme
  Cahier

Chasseur De Chamois, Le

Filles Du Hameau

HUGUENIN, CHARLES-ANDRE
Passant Par Paris

Salut Vigneron

HUMBERT, G.
Barbara
  Petit Bois De Saint-Amand, Le

HUMPHRIS, IAN
Twelve Days Of Christmas, The

HUNGER
Koschat
  Schneewalzer

HUNTER
Arne, Thomas Augustine
  Hush To Peace

Au Claire De La Lune

HUNTER; SHAW; PARKER
Believe Me, If All Those Endearing
  Young Charms

IERSWOUD, FREDERIK VAN
Cornelius, Peter
  Konige, Die

Last Rose Of Summer, The

Schumann, Robert (Alexander)
  Volksliedchen

JACKMAN, JERRY
Balkin, Alfred
  Little Love Goes A Long Way, A

Mary Had A Little Cat

JACKSON, GREGORY
Sunshine In My Soul

JAMES, S.; MARTIN, V.
Handel, George Frideric
  Allegro, Il Penseroso Ed Il
  Moderato, L'

JAMISON
Are You Lonesome Tonight

JANCIK, HANS
Wolf, Hugo
  Dem Vaterland
  Elfenlied
  Morgenhymnus

JEFFERS
A Rovin'

Johnny Has Gone For A Soldier

Landlord, Fill The Flowing Bowl

Minstrel Boy, The

Storm 'N Blow

Two Irish Songs

Waitin' For The Dawn Of Peace

Wearin' O' The Green, The

JENNINGS
Schumann, Robert (Alexander)
  An Die Sterne

JENNY, ALBERT
Herbst Im Seetal

JOHNSON, DAVID
Scholars' Book Of Glees, The

JOHNSON, DERRIC
Carol Of The Russian Children: The
  Sleigh

JOHNSON, PAUL
Burt, Bates
  Christmas Minuet

JUNG
Kanons, 187

JURGENS, JURGEN
Mozart, Wolfgang Amadeus
  Overture From "Die Zauberflote"

KALININ, S.
Folk Songs Arranged By Alexander
  Sveshnikov

KAPLAN, ABRAHAM
Hassler, Hans Leo
  Herz Tut Mir Aufspringen, Das

Lind
  Hayom Teamtzenu

Wilbye, John
  Adieu, Sweet Amaryllis

KARPOWITSCH
Ach, Dieses Schwarze Augenpaar

Bandura

Buran

Kosaken- Reitermarsch

Kunak

Leb Wohl, Mein Tabor

KARPOWITSCH; IGNATIEFF
Mascha

Schwarze Husaren

KARSEMEIJER
Whittaker, Roger
  Last Farewell, The

KASPERSMA
Purcell, Henry
  Trumpet Voluntary

KELLY, STEPHEN
Perugia, Niccolo da
  Eleven Ballate

KERN
Bacharach, Burt F.
  Back To Bacharach: A Medley

You And Me

KERN, PHILIP
Kander, John
  New York, New York: Theme

Ross, Brad
  Melody Maker

KERPER, WILLEM
Anonymous
  O Nederland, Let Op U Saeck

KERR
Loesser
  I Hear Music

KERR, ANITA
Rodgers, Richard
  King And I, The: A Medley

KEVEREN, PHILLIP
My Heart Can't Tell You No

KICKLIGHTE
English Street Cry

KINGSBURY
Morley, Thomas
  Now Is The Month Of Maying

Purcell, Henry
  In These Delightful Pleasant Groves

KIRK, THERON
Great Day

Little Wheel A-Turnin'

KJELSON
Gute Nacht

I Walk The Unfrequented Road

KJELSON, LEE
I'm Goin' To Sing!

KLEIN
Des Prez, Josquin
  Ecce, Tu Pulchra Es

KLOS, TON
Golowalj Moja

Jechali Bojare

Nje Boitjessia Djewizy

Schto Mnje Shit'

KNOWLES, JULIE
Danny Boy

KOEPKE, ALLEN
Kum Bah Ya

KOESTER, WERNER
Bernstein, Leonard
  Ich Gefall Mir

KOLLER, MARTIN
Bergere Et Le Monsieur, La

Fillette, Une

Je Suis Trop Jeunette

KONING, LEEN
Ye Banks And Braes

KOOIJ, E.
Tetterode, L. Adr. von
  Hollands Lied, Een

KOOIJ, E.J.
Silcher, Friedrich
  Waldhoorn, De

Vermulst, Jan
  Drink To Me Only With Thine Eyes

KOPYLOVA, V.
  Rimsky–Korsakov, Nikolai
    Choruses From Operas, Vol. 4

KORDA, V.
  Strauss, Johann, [Jr.]
    Sangerlust–Polka

  Verdi, Giuseppe
    Teure Heimat

KORT, JACOBUS
  Anonymous
    Blauwe Lucht

KRAL, JOSEPH
  Smith, John Stafford
    Star Spangled Banner

KREMSER, EDOUARD
  Mon Coeur Est Dans La Peine

KRISTINSSON, SIGURSVEINN D.
  Now I Am Happy

  Snow Disappeared, The

  Thordur Kakali

KRONE
  Foster, Stephen Collins
    Some Folks

KRUMNACH
  Hopkins
    Christmas Comes Again

  Strom
    Under The Stars

KUBIK
  Foster, Stephen Collins
    Beautiful Dreamer

KUNZ
  Have You Seen My Man?

KUPRIAN, H.
  Kratochwil, Heinz
    Spiegelbild, Das

KUZMA; HOLCOMBE
  Beethoven, Ludwig van
    Ode To Joy

LAGAS, R.
  Anonymous
    Beggar's Song, The: O, Here We Come
      Awandring

  Belle, J.
    Int Groene Met U Alderliefste
    Laet Ons Nu Al Verblijden
    O Amoureusich Mondeken Root

  Clemens, Jacobus (Clemens non Papa)
    Lustelijcke Mey, De
    Venus Schoon, Een

  Episcopius, L.
    Laet Varen Alle Fantasie
    More Ale, More Ale And Cake
    Vruecht En Duecht Myn Hert
      Verhuecht

  Hellinck, Lupus
    Janne Moye, Al Claer

  Turnhout, Jan–Jacobvan
    Ghij Meyskens Die Van Der
      Comenschap Sijt

  Van Der Muelen, Servaes
    Altijt So Moet Ic Trueren

  Wintelroy, Johan
    Al Is Den Tijt Nu Doloreus

LALLEMENT, B.
  J'ai Vu Le Loup, Le R'nard, Le Lievre

  Mon Pere Tot M'a Mariee

LALLEMENT, BERNARD
  All Through The Night

  Chant D'adieu

  Cui, Cesar Antonovich
    Chant Des Moissonneurs D'ukraine

LAMANCE
  Bells Of Paradise, The

  Lass From The Low Country, The

LAMANCE JR., EDGAR
  Tailor And The Mouse, The

LAMBERT
  Leisy, James Franklin
    Miracles Still Happen At Christmas

LAMPART, R.
  Drei Spirituals

LANDRY, FREDY
  Chanson Du Vigneron, La

  Saisons A La Sagne, Les

  Sous Les Saules

LANGEJANS
  Happy Love (Great Lakes Sea Song)

  Red Iron Ore (Michigan Sea Song)

LANGREE, A.
  Mazurka Souto Li Pins, La

LANGREE, ALAIN
  Au Marche De Yanochida

  Chanson Du Couturier

  Frochaux, Jean–Chs.
    Marche Des Soldats De Turenne

  Mehul
    Chant Du Depart

  Ohe, Meunier

  Patre Des Montagnes

  Voici Le Gai Printemps

LANTZ
  Smith
    Sing Joyfully

LAPIN
  Sweet Dreams

LAPIN, LARRY
  Boy From New York City, The

LARSON
  Thomson, Virgil Garnett
    Fanfare For Peace

LARSON, DAVID
  Muge

LATTION, GUY
  Quatre–Vingts Chasseurs, Les

  Valentin

LAUBER, EMILE
  Calme Du Soir

  Chasse, La

  Je Possede Un Reduit Obscur

  Je Possede Un Reduit Obscur

  Michel Et Christine

  Nonnette, La

  Voici Le Gai Printemps

LAVOISY–DROUOT
  Ronsard
    Chanson Du Printemps Retourne

LAVOISY– DROUOT, CH.
  Aufray, H.
    Pipeau, Le

  Ferrat, Jean
    Hourrah

  Hadjidakis, Manos
    Facteur, Le

LAWRENCE
  Drink To Me Only With Thine Eyes

LAWRENCE, STEPHEN L.
  Dean, Jimmy
    Big Bad John

LE LACHEUR, REX
  O Canada

LEAVITT
  Christmas Cheer!

  Tribute To Judy Garland, A

LEAVITT, JOHN
  Blow Away The Morning Dew

  Coleman, Cy
    Colors Of My Life, The

  Flow Gently Sweet Afton

  Sherman, Joe
    Graduation Day

  Winter Holiday Spectacular!, A

LEBEDEVA, N.
  Antsev, M.
    Selected Choruses

LEEUWEN, A.C.
  Gounod, Charles Francois
    Judex (Mors Et Vita)

LEFFERTS, PETER
  Three Fourteenth–Century Motets In
    Honour Of Gaston Febus

LEHNER, L.
  Strauss, Josef
    Spharenklange

LEIDZEN
  Ward, Samuel Augustus
    America, The Beautiful

LELEU, F.
  Ferre, Leo
    Merde A Vauban

LELEU, FRANCOISE
  Balaio

  Flor De Chaner

  Ollanta, La

LEMARC, A.
  Bruch, Max
    Frohliche Musicus, Der

  Gastoldi, Giovanni Giacomo
    Amor Nel Battello

  Hassler, Hans Leo
    Tanzen Und Springen

  Verdi, Giuseppe
    Monnikenkoor

LENOBLE, J.
  Cuatro Mulieros, Los

  Ferrat, Jean
    Montagne, La

  Mareuil, J.
    Lune Est Morte, La

  Queneau, R.
    Porc, Le

  Qui Peut–Etre

LENZ, J.M.R.
  Bose, Hans–Jurgen Von
    Ich Will Den Nagenden Beschwerden
    Wer War Ich Doch?

LEUTHOLD, H.J.
  Obbirger–Lied

LEVINE
  Ribbon In The Sky

LEWIS, A.
  Run, Rabbit, Run

  Towdy Dowdy

LIEBERGEN, PATRICK
  Blow The Wind Southerly

LIEBERGEN, PATRICK M.
  Auld Lang Syne

LINDEN, N.V.D.
  Schubert, Franz (Peter)
    Litanei

  Spierdijk, J.
    Eenzame Schaatser, De

LOCKE
  Oliver Cromwell

LOEWE, F.
  Strauss, Richard
    Schwabische Erbschaft

LOJESKI
  Big River: A Medley

  Chorus Line, A (The Movie): A Medley

  Mancini
    Thank You, Santa

  Music Of Goodbye, The

  Sara

  Sing, Just Sing

  We Will Stand

  Wham! In Concert

  Wurtzel
    Lady In New York Harbor

LOJESKI, ED
  American Portrait, An

  Gaelic Rhapsody

  He's Gone Away

LONNA, KJELL
  Auld Lang Syne

  Paulson
    Gang Skall Jag Stilla Somna, En
    Lyser En Stjarna, Det
    Visa Om Rimfrost Och Vinterstra
    Visa Vid Vindens Angar

  Sol Och Mane

LOOVENDAAL
  Wierts, J.P.J.
    Hollands Vlag

LUCAS, C.
  Purcell, Henry
    Trumpet Voluntary

LUTOLF, M.
  Campra, Andre
    Festes Venitiennes, Les

LYLE
  Colorado Trail, The

LYSSAND, HENRIK
  Grieg, Edvard Hagerup
    Vals
    Varen

MCALISTER
  Stravinsky, Igor
    Roi Des Etoiles, Le

MCCARTHY
  Albert, Prince Consort of Queen
      Victoria
    Love's Plea, A

MCCULLOUGH
  Brahms, Johannes
    I Have A Wish, Dear Mother

MACMILLAN, ERNEST
  God Save The Queen

MCNEIL, ALBERT
  All My Trials

  Little Wheel A-Turning

MADSEN
  Does Your Chewing Gum Lose Its Flavor
      (On The Bedpost Over Night?)

  Fain, Sammy
    Let A Smile Be Your Umbrella (On A
      Rainy Day)

  Footloose

  For Me And My Gal (A Medley Of Hits
      From The Twenties)

  He Set My Life To Music

  While Strolling Through The Park One
      Day

MAERTENS, W.
  Telemann, Georg Philipp
    Hamburger Admiralitatsmusik 1723
    Jauchze, Jubilier Und Singe
    Serenata Eroica

MAGNE; HILLE
  Marnay
    Cent Mille Chansons

MAHLING, CHRISTOPH- HELLMUTH
  Kling Auf, Mein Lied Und Singe

MAITRE, M.M.
  Anonymous
    C'est Grande Erreur
    Incessamment, Je M'y Tourmente
    J'aurais Grand Tort

  Bruhier, Antoine
    Amoureux, Un

MALEWICKI
  Dream So Fair, A

MALIN
  Calvisius, Seth(us)
    Musiken Klang

  Peuerl
    Frisch Auf Und Lasst Uns Singen

  Schein
    Dame Nightingale
    Fresh Is The Maytime
    Once More The Flowers Bloom

MANN, JOHNNY
  Patriotic Medley

MARAGNO, VIRTU
  Carnavalito Quebradeno

MARSH
  Davis
    Holy Nation

MARVIN
  Brumel, Antoine
    Du Tout Plongiet: Fors Seulement

  Vecchi
    Imitatione Del Venetiano

MARZUKI
  You Light Up My Life

MASLANKA
  Paull
    So Long Through The Night
    Springtime
    Summer
    Whisper Song, The
    Winter
    Your Lullaby

MASON, R.
  Banuwa

MASON, ROGER
  John's Gone To Hilo

MATTSON
  Deep River

  Foster, Stephen Collins
    Jeanie With The Light Brown Hair

  Londonderry Air

MATTSON, PHIL
  Stardust

MAYER, H.
  Lassus, Roland de (Orlandus)
    Bauer Von Eselskirchen, Der

MAYFIELD
  Thomas
    Starlight

MAYOR, CHARLES
  La-Haut Sur La Montagne

MCCORD, D.
  Warren, B.
    Five Songs In 5 Minutes

MCCRAY
  Dowland, John
    Fine Knacks For Ladies

  Purcell, Henry
    How Happy The Lover

  Schubert, Franz (Peter)
    Two Paths Of Virtue

MCKINNEY, HOWARD
  Three Madrigals

MCPHEETERS
  Shelter From The Rain

MEIJ, J. DE
  Ketelbey, Albert William
    In The Mystic Land Of Egypt

MERMOUD, ROBERT
  A La Claire Fontaine

  Il Etait Une Fille, Une Fille
      D'honneur

  Jacques De Courtion

  Petite Jeanneton, La

MEY
  Rodgers, Richard
    Some Enchanted Evening
    This Nearly Was Mine

MEY, J. DE
  Morricone, Ennio
    Moment For Morricone

MEYER, PAUL- PHILIPPE
  Brel, Jacques
    Amsterdam

MIERHOUT, FRANK
  Cantus Romantica

MILLER, FRANZ R.
  Biebl, Franz
    Zieh, Schimmel, Zieh!

  Deutschmann, Gerhard
    Chor Der Nachtlichter

MILLER, FRANZ R. (cont'd.)

  Erdmann-Abele, Veit
    Wir Alle Leben In Gestundeter Zeit

  Hollfelder, Waldram
    Muckenhochzeit
    Musikantenstandchen

  Miller, Franz R.
    Ausserlich Und Innerlich

  Scheck, Helmut
    Seht Doch, Wie Der Rheinwein Tanzt
    Variationen
    Wer Sich Vertreiben Will Schlechte
      Laune

  Schneider, W.
    Gluck Ist Wie Ein Sonnenblick
    Gluckliche Stunde

  Trapp, Willy
    Gesellen-Trinklied

  Vigl, Karl H.
    Haus Steht Jetzt Vollendet, Das

MIMET, A.M.
  Mon Per' M'a Envoyee Au Bois

MINIHANE
  I'm Confessin

  Tuck Me To Sleep

MINTON, LARRY
  Viadana, Lodovico Grossi da
    Sing, Rejoice, Ye Righteous

MOLLER; ZOLLER
  Kolenden: Sechzehn Polnische
      Weihnachtslieder

MONROE, A.
  Simple Gifts

MOORE
  Children, Go Where I Send Thee

  Erie Canal, The

MOORE, DONALD P.
  This Little Light Of Mine

MORGAN
  All Through The Night

MORGAN, HILDA
  Wilbye, John
    Flora Gave Me Fairest Flowers

NAHOUM, J.
  Quand La Marie

  Quand La Mer Rouge

  Sommeil, Berceuse

NEIJENRODE, H.
  Brahms, Johannes
    In Stiller Nacht

NEUEN, DONALD
  Verdelot, Phillippe
    Vostr' Acuti Dardi, Il

  Verdi, Giuseppe
    Va Pensiero

NICHOL
  Shady Grove

NIELAND, H.
  Four Indonesian Folksongs

NOBEL, F. DE
  Twelve Indonesian Folksongs

NOBLE
  Handel, George Frideric
    Sound An Alarm

NORTH
  Here We Come A-Caroling

  What Child Is This?

NORTH, JACK
  Kocher, Konrad
    Holy Was The Night

NOSKE, FRITS
  Padbrue, Cornelis Thymans
    Nederlandse Madrigalen

NOWAK
  All Out Of Love

  Best Of Times, The

  Cohan, George Michael
    You're A Grand Old Flag

  Do They Know It's Christmas?

NOWAK (cont'd.)

  Lewis
    Judy's Turn To Cry

  One That You Love, The

NOWAK, LEOPOLD
  Bruckner, Anton
    Arneth-Kantate
    Entsagen
    Fest-Cantate
    Festgesang (Jodok-Kantate)
    Germanenzug
    Helgoland
    Mayr-Kantate
    Vergissmeinnicht

NOYON, JOSEPH
  Faure, Gabriel-Urbain
    Clair De Lune

NYGARD
  Otey
    Make Believe

OGURA
  Hotaru Koi

OKUN
  De Cormier, Robert
    One And Twenty Pennies

OLPEN, FRIEDRICH W.
  Weites Land, Wie Stumm Du Bist

OPIENSKI, HENRYK
  Liebessehnsucht

OPIENSKI, HENRYK
  Bakfark, Balint (Valentin)
    Vache Noire, La

  Jean P'tit Jean

  Stelldichein

OTT, NORBERT
  Beaucarne, Julos
    Je Chante Pour Vous

  Beausonge, Lucid
    Oiseau, L'

  Duteil, Yves
    Langue De Chez Nous, La

  Ferrat, Jean
    Heureux Celui Qui Meurt D'aimer

  Lavoie, Daniel
    Ils S'aiment

  Lenoir, Jean
    Parlez-Moi D'amour

  Lund, Eddie
    Tahiti Nui

  Schumann, Robert (Alexander)
    Gai Laboureur, Le

  Voulzy, Laurent
    Belle-Ile-En-Mer Marie-Galante

OUVRARD, J.P.
  Certon, Pierre
    Bien Qu'a Grand Tort
    Fortune Helas
    J'espere Et Crains

  Crecquillon, Thomas
    Oncques Amour

  Janequin, Clement
    Nature Ornant La Dame

  Lassus, Roland de (Orlandus)
    Deus Qui Bonum Vinum Creasti
    Lucescit; Nunc Bibamus
    Pronuba Juno

OWEN
  Cornyshe, William (Cornish)
    Blow Thy Horn, Hunter

  I'm Bound Away

  Spanish Song: Vesame Y Abracame

OWEN, HAROLD
  Praetorius, Michael
    Canon

OWENS
  Henry VIII, King of England
    O My Heart

  Ravenscroft, Thomas
    We Be Three Poor Mariners

OXLEY, HARRISON
  Barbra Ellen

  Soldier, Soldier

PAGOT, JEAN
  Couste, Francis
    Chanson A Boire
    Quand Le Guerrier
    Si J'etais

  Galere, La

PALMER, ANTHONY
  Bury Me Beneath The Willow

PANTILLON, GEORGES-LOUIS
  J'ai Cueilli La Belle Rose

  Maman Ne Veut Pas Que J'aille Au Bois

PARKER, ALICE
  Folksong Transformations

PARKS, JAMES
  Sometimes I Feel Like A Motherless
    Child

PASSAQUAY, F.
  Ramoneur, Le

PASSAQUET
  Sylvestre, Anne
    Mon Mari Est Parti

PASSAQUET, R.
  Asso
    Comme Un P'it Coqu'licot

  Beart, Guy
    Souliers, Les

  Becaud, Gilbert
    Nathalie

  Brafford, P.
    Menuet Pour La Joconde

  Brassens, Georges
    Chasse Aux Papillons, La
    Guerre De 14-18, La
    Jeanne
    Pauvre Martin
    Petit Joueur De Fluteau, Le

  Brel, Jacques
    Air De La Betise, L'
    Ne Me Quitte Pas

  Duteil, Yves
    Petit Pont De Bois, Le
    Prendre Un Enfant

  Gerard
    C'est A L'aube

  Glanzberg, N.
    Grands Boulevards

  Lama, S.
    Vagues De La Mer, Les

  Morin, M.
    Alchimiste, L'

  Moustaki, Georges
    Danse
    Il Y Avait Un Jardin
    Requiem Pour N'importe Qui

  Perret, P.
    Mere Noel

  Provins, J.
    Amour En Dix-Neuf Ponts

  Sylvestre, Anne
    Il S'appelait Richard
    Je Pense A Noel
    Rose De Decembre, La

  Thiriet, Maurice
    Place De La Concorde

  Van Parys, Georges
    Complainte De La Butte

  Vigneault, Gilles
    Beau Voyageur
    Petit Bonhomme, Le

  Vigneron, Le

PASSAQUET, RAPHAEL
  Touati, Raymond
    Ami Que J'avais Au Logis, L'
    J'ai Dans Le Coeur Un Grand Amour
    Trois Peines Sont Autour De Nous

PENDERS, J.
  Drie Nationale Liederen

  Hoezee

  Londonderry Air

  Swing Low

PERISSON
  Trimazo

PERISSON, J.
  V'la L'bon Vent

PERISSON, JEAN
  Good Night Ladies

PERRET, F.
  Lassus, Roland de (Orlandus)
    Madrigal

PERRET, FRANCIS
  Laine Des Moutons, La

  O Ma Belle Aurore

PETTI, ANTHONY
  Chester Book Of Madrigals, The, Book
    3: The Seasons

  Chester Book Of Madrigals, The, Book
    4: Desirable Women

  Chester Book Of Madrigals, The, Book
    7: Warfare

  Chester Book Of Madrigals, The, Book
    8: Place Names

PFAUTSCH, LLOYD
  Hello, Girls

  Schumann, Robert (Alexander)
    Minnesingers, The

PHELPS
  Deck The Halls

  Happy Christmas Comes Once More, The

PIGUET, ROBERT
  Temps Passe, Le

PLACEK
  Collins
    Huckleberry Finn

PLANK
  My Pigeon House

PLOJHAR, F.
  Dobru Noc

  Sobotenka Ide

  Tancuj

POMMER
  Reger, Max
    Volkslieder

PONSOT, O.
  Gentil Coquelicot

POOS, HEINRICH
  Brahms, Johannes
    Wiegenlied: Guten Abend, Gut Nacht

  Santa Lucia

  Wagner, Richard
    Mit Gewitter Und Sturm

POPPLEWELL, R
  National Anthem, The

PORTER
  Arkansas Traveler, The

  Harline, Leigh
    When You Wish Upon A Star

  Schein, Johann Hermann
    Die Mit Tranen Saen

POTGIESER, P.
  Prins, J.
    Bruid, De

PTITSA, K.
  Mussorgsky, Modest Petrovich
    Selected Choruses

PUERLING, GENE
  Johnny One Note

  People

  You Made Me Love You

QUARANTO
  Stopping By The Woods

RAADSHEER, W.
  Wyrtzen, Don
    Yesterday, Today And Tomorrow

RASTALL, RICHARD
  Six Songs From The York Mystery Play
    "The Assumption Of The Virgin"

RAY
Folk Song Trilogy

Franklin
I Knew You Were Waiting

Hornsby, G.F.
Way It Is, The

Marx, Richard
Hold On To The Nights

Parnes
Happy Is

Richie, Lionel
Deep River Woman

RAY, JERRY
Armato
I Still Believe

Bellson, Louie
It's The Time Of Year

Hokey Pokey Medley, The

Moments To Remember

Where Do Broken Hearts Go?

Wilbur, Sandy
She Still Carries The Torch

RAYE
Jacobs
This Is My Country

READ
Billings, William
Rosa Of Sharon

READ, VAIL
Read, Gardner
When Moonlight Falls

REED, EVERETT
Mendelssohn-Bartholdy, Felix
Farewell To The Forest

Schubert, Franz (Peter)
Wohin?

REGENZKI
Verhulst, Johannes
Moet Je Varen: Daar Ging Er Een
Meisje

REGENZKI, N.
Abt, Franz
Woudconcert: Mejuffrouw Lente Geeft
Concert

REGER, MAX
Wie Kommt's, Dass Du So Traurig Bist

REHAK, JENO
Chanter L'Europe 2: Musiques Des Pays
De L'Ouest

O Tannenbaum

REHAK, JEON
Chanter L'Europe 1: Musiques Des Pays
De L'Est

REICHEL, B.
Source Claire, Une

RHEIN
Baloo, Baloo

Banks O'Doon, The

De'il's Awa Wi' The Exiseman, The

RICE, MARTIN
Oh, Love Of Mine

RIFFLINGER, DONALD H.
Erie Canal, The

RIJKEN, J.
Oertel, L.
Graf Waldersee
U Zij De Glorie

RILEY; WATSON
What About Me

RILEY; WILSON
Eye In The Sky

Pac-Man Fever

RINGWALD
Allen
Home For The Holidays

Guthrie
This Land Is Your Land- A Panorama
Americana

Kern
I've Told Every Little Star

RINGWALD (cont'd.)
Webster
Love Is A Many- Splendored Thing

RINGWALD, ROY
Berlin, Irving
God Bless America
God Bless America (Festival
Edition)

ROBERT, F.
Perrine Etait Servante

ROBERTON, HUGH S.
White, Maude Valerie
When The Swallows Homeward Fly

ROBERTS, HOWARD
Beulah Land

Hold On

I Want Jesus To Walk With Me

ROBIN, P.
Blanche
Boites A Musique, Les

ROCHAT, J.
Bovet, Joseph
P'tit Vin D'Lavaux, Le

ROCHAT, JEAN
Jeunes Filles De La Rochelle, Les

Petrouchka

ROFF, JOSEPH
Four Folk Songs From China

Four Songs From Easter Island

Four Songs From Indonesia

Hey Anna Mae

Nine Men Slept In A Boardinghouse Bed

Rodby, Walter
Music Alone Shall Live

Sipping Cider Through A Straw

Song Of The Azores

Songs From Australia

Songs Of Papua New Guinea

Stodola Pumpa

Three Anatolian Turkish Folk Songs

Three Folk Songs From Sri Lanka

Three Greek Folk Songs

ROLLIN, J.
A Bordeaux

Lully, Jean-Baptiste (Lulli)
Cadmus Et Hermione

Mozart, Wolfgang Amadeus
Gondelfahrt

ROOSLI, JOSEPH
Andante

RORMARK, JOAR
Brurelat Fra Vaga

Mazurka Fra Lom

Norske Danseviser

Springdans Fra Bergen I

Springdans Fra Bergen II

ROSCOE
Love Always

Shame

ROSCOE, JEFFREY
Party All The Time

ROSS
Belaubre, Louis-Noel
Six Poems Of Rolland Pierre

ROSS, ROBERT
Ward, Samuel Augustus
America The Beautiful

ROSTING, E.
Cottrau, Teodoro
Sancta Lucia

RUMERY, L.
Mundy, John
Of All The Birds That I Have Heard

Templa, Bras, Ese Psalterio

RUMERY, L. (cont'd.)
Weelkes, Thomas
Cease, Sorrows, Now

RUNYAN, MICHAEL
Goodrich, Jeff
I Heard Him Come

RUTTER, JOHN
Folk-Songs For Choirs 1

Folk-Songs For Choirs 2

RYVKINA, E.; MALYAVINA, N.
From The Repertoire Of The Men's
Chorus Of The Moscow Engineering
And Physics Institute

SAND, EDWARD J.
Sand, Cary J.
Uncle Dean

Singin' That Simple Melody

SANDERS, V.
Coffee Grows On White Oak Trees

SANVOISIN, M.
Lambert, Michel
Pour Estre Ayme

Monteverdi, Claudio
Vieni Imenco

SANVOISIN, MICHEL
Gastoldi, Giovanni Giacomo
Balletti A Cinque Voci

SATEREN, LELAND
Gift To Be Simple, The

SAUNDERS
Williamson, Malcolm
Six English Lyrics

SCHAFER, EWALD
Weber, Carl Maria von
Sieben Lieder Fur Gemischten Chor

SCHEIDEGGER, J.
Musikalische Familie, Die

SCHEMITSCH, H.
Strauss, Johann, [Jr.]
Wein, Weib Und Gesang

SCHEREN, FRANS
Anonymous
'K Heb Mijn Wagen Volgeladen

SCHERER
Coconut And Banana

Crawdad Song, The

Down By De Riverside

Gelbes Mondlicht Und Schalmeien

Hora Jerusalem

I Want To Be Ready

My Lord, What A Mornin'

Peter Go Ring Dem Bells

SCHERER, E.
A Dios Mi Chaparita

By An' By

Coconut And Banana

Crawdad Song, The: Come On, Honey

Down By De Riverside: Lay Down

I Want To Be Ready

J'ai Du Bon Tabac

My Lord, What A Mornin'

Peter Go Ring Dem Bells

SCHERER, ERNST
Amour De Moy, L'

SCHILLIO
Bird's Courting Song

SCHMID, REINHOLD
Holla, Mein Bruderlein: Guten Tag!

SCHMITZ, JAN
Anonymous
Daer Was E Wuf Die Spon
Ik Zeg Adieu, Wij Twee Wij Moeten
Scheiden
Komt Vrienden In Het Ronde

Vier Weverkens Zag Men Ter Botermarkt
Gaan

SCHNEIDER, WALTHER
  Es Flog Ein Klein's Waldvogelein

  Ich Spring In Diesem Ringe

SCHOLTYS
  Strauss, Johann, [Jr.]
    Kaiser-Walzer

SCHOLTYS, H.
  Lanner, Josef
    Schonbrunner, Die

SCHREUDER
  Laetantius, Br.
    Holland

SCHREUDER, G.
  Schubert, Franz (Peter)
    Forelle, Die

SCHUBERT, PETER
  Loos, Armin
    Elegy

SCOTT
  Do You Want To Know A Secret?

  Doo-Wah Days

  Jacobs
    This Is My Country

  Overjoyed

SCOTT, K. LEE
  Campian, Thomas (Campion)
    Never Weather-Beaten Sail

SCOTT, MICHAEL
  Carpenter, Richard Lynn
    Merry Christmas, Darling

  Cheers: A Toast To Prime Time

  Cindy

  Colinda: Cajun French Folk Song

  Everybody Loves Saturday Night

  Gillespie
    Santa Claus Is Comin' To Town: A
      Medley

  Wild Mountain Thyme, The

SEALS, KAREN
  Don't Be Weary, Traveler

SECKINGER
  A La Claire Fontaine

  Wenn Ich Vom Klaren Weine Trinke

SEEGER, PETER
  Haydn, [Franz] Joseph
    Deutschlandlied

SELIVANOV, B.
  Repertoire Of Amateur Choruses, Vol.
    10

SEMENOVSKY, D.
  Alexandrov, A.
    Selected Choruses

SHARP; KARPELES
  Eighty English Folksongs

SHAW
  Adler, Richard
    Hernando's Hideaway

  Feller
    Snow, Snow, Beautiful Snow

  Oh Happy Day

  Rogers
    Hand In Hand

  Ross
    Open The Door

SHAW, KIRBY
  Auctioneer, The

  Big Girls Don't Cry

  Carmichael, Hoagy
    Lazy River

  Dixieland Jamboree

  Everybody Loves My Baby

  Hit Me With A Hot Note And Watch Me
    Bounce!

  Jailhouse Rock

  Let Me Dance For You

SHAW, KIRBY (cont'd.)
  Ram, Samuel (Buck)
    Great Pretender, The

  Santa Claus Is Coming To Town

  Take The "A" Train

  Vamps

  When I Fall In Love

  Williams, Hank
    Hey, Good Lookin'

SHAW, P.
  Anonymous
    I Went To The Market
    I've Been To Harlem

SHAW, ROBERT
  Brahms, Johannes
    Five Waltzes

SHAW, ROBERT; HUNTER, RALPH
  Li'l Liza Jane

SHAW, ROBERT; PARKER, ALICE
  A-Roving

  Adios, Catedral De Burgos

  Al Olivo

  Auld Lang Syne

  Billings, William
    Chester

  Bound For The Rio Grande

  Brahms, Johannes
    German Folk Songs

SHIROKOV, A.
  Repertoire Of Russian Folk Choruses,
    Vol. 10

SIEGEL
  Joseph
    Griselda, The Reindeer Nobody Knows

SIEGMUND-SCHULTZE, W.
  Handel, George Frideric
    Caecilien-Ode

SILCHER, FRIEDRICH
  Annchen Von Tharau

  Gluck, Fr.
    Untreue

  Vierstimmige Volkslieder

SILTMAN
  This Train

  Vive L'amour

SIMEONE
  Carpenter, Richard Lynn
    Merry Christmas Darling

  Regney, Noel
    Do You Hear What I Hear?

SIMMS, PATSY FORD
  Have A Good Time Tonight

SIMON
  Singin' In The Rain

  Softly As I Leave You

  Today

SIMON, WILLIAM
  Coleman, Cy
    Colors Of My Life (From Barnum),
      The

SMEETS, L.
  Vaal, O. de
    Lentemars

SMEETS, LEO
  Anonymous
    Bergere Legere
    O Nederland! Let Op U Saeck

  Giordani, Tommaso
    Caro Mio Ben, Credi Mi Almen

SMIJERS, A.
  Des Prez, Josquin
    Petite Camusette
    Works Of Josquin Des Prez, The:
      Secular Works, Vol. 1
    Works Of Josquin Des Prez, The:
      Secular Works, Vol. 2
    Works Of Josquin Des Prez, The:
      Secular Works, Vol. 3

SMITH
  Blow The Candles Out

  If Your Heart Isn't In It

SMITH, DOUGLAS FLOYD
  Dem Dry Bones

SMITH, GREGG
  Gershwin, George
    Sing Of Spring

SNYDER
  Garner, Erroll
    Misty

  Goldsmith, Jerry
    Flying Dreams (From Secret Of Nimh)

  Livingston, Jay Harold
    Silver Bells

  Put A Little Love In Your Heart

  Regnart
    Free I Am Once Again

  Ross, Brad
    One Of A Kind

  Someone In The Dark (Theme From "E.T.
    The Extra-Terrestrial")

  There Is A Lady

  Who Has Seen The Wind?

SNYDER, AUDREY
  Always

  Ashford, Nickolas
    Reach Out And Touch (Somebody's
      Hand)

  I Live For Your Love

  Ross, Brad
    Reach For A Star

SOLBERG, LEIF
  Gronfur, Bjarne
    Kvifor Blinkar Stjernone?

SOMERVELL, ARTHUR
  Handel, George Frideric
    Silent Worship

SOUTHERS, LEROY
  Three Folk Songs

SPETA
  I Feel A Song Comin' On

SPITZER, L.
  Wolf, Hugo
    Fruhlingschor

SPRAGUE, RAYMOND
  Brahms, Johannes
    Gang Zur Liebsten
    Minnelied
    Morgen Muss Ich Fort Von Hier

STALMEIER, P.
  Gluck, Christoph Willibald, Ritter
    von
    Chor Der Selige Geister

STEEN, HENDRIK
  Anonymous
    Ik Zeg Adieu, Wij Moeten Scheiden

STEEN, J.
  Radstake, L.J.
    Ruhe Zum Herzen

STEGEN
  Kollo
    Heimat, Land Der Lieder

STERLING
  Brown
    Oh! You Beautiful Doll

  Garland
    In The Mood

  Weiss
    Music! Music! Music!

STEVENS
  Lassus, Roland de (Orlandus)
    Quel Rossignuol

STOCKER, D.
  Oh Shenandoah

STONE
  Shenandoah

STRAUSS
  Blue Rondo A La Christmas

STRID
  Donnelly
    All Over The World
    Come, Follow The Star
    I'm Proud To Call America My Home
    I've Got Music In My Soul
    Spirit Of Christmas, The
    We Are The Young
STRID, GEORGE
  Donnelly, Mary
    I Have A Dream
STROMMEN
  Against All Odds

  All I Need

  Along Comes A Woman

  Anthony
    Poetry In Motion

  California Girls

  Carmichael, Hoagy
    Georgia On My Mind

  Cheers: Theme (Where Everybody Knows
    Your Name)

  Cherish

  Edwards
    See You In September

  Farewell My Summer Love

  Footloose (Best Of) Medley

  Gold
    Thank You For Being A Friend

  Hard To Say I'm Sorry

  Hold Me (In Your Arms)

  If Ever You're In My Arms Again

  I'll Be Home For Christmas

  Kweller, Lee
    Crystal Voice

  Lewis, Huey
    Naturally
    Perfect World

  Monaco
    You Made Me Love You

  Ross, Brad
    Bright New Day, A

  Self Control

  (Sittin' On) The Dock Of The Bay

  Tomorrow

  Turtle Dove, The

  Up Where We Belong

  Way He Makes Me Feel, The

  Weekend In New England

  What's Love Got To Do With It

  You And I
STROMMEN, CARL
  Kweller, Lee
    Ain't Too Tired To Dance

  Lewis, Huey
    Give Me The Keys

  Richie, Lionel
    Ballerina Girl
STRUVE, G.
  "Pioneria" Chorus Sings, The
SUERTE
  Green Grow The Rushes, Oh
SUMNER
  Miller
    Cat Came Back, The
SUTTNER, KURT
  Chor Aktuell, Heft 1: Swingende
    Chormusik
SWENSON
  Cunningham
    Sea Song, A

  Li'l Liza Jane

  Scarborough Fair

SWIFT
  "I'se The B'y"
SWINGLE
  Bach, Johann Sebastian
    Fugue In D Major (From The Well
      Tempered Clavier)
SWINGLE, WARD
  Bach, Johann Sebastian
    Aria (From Suite In D Major)
    Bouree (From The English Suite,
      No.2)
    Fugue In C Minor
    Sleepers Wake: Chorale-Prelude
TALL, DAVID
  Grainger, Percy Aldridge
    Country Gardens
TAYLOR, DEEMS
  May Day Carol
TERHUNE
  Charlottown
TERHUNE, CHARLES
  Pick A Bale O' Cotton
TERRAL, F.
  Aufray, H.
    Jour Ou Le Bateau Viendra, Le

  Druon, M.
    Galerien, Le

  Vraiment, C'est Etrange
TERRI, SALLI
  Barbara Allen

  Deep River

  Simple Gifts
THAYER, FRED
  Cancion de Cuna
THIJSSE, W.H.
  Janequin, Clement
    Ce Mois De Mai
THIJSSE, WIM HERMAN
  Last Rose Of Summer, The

  Merk Toch Hoe Sterk
THIRAULT, R.
  Lancen, Serge
    Hymne De Fraternite
THLIVERIS, B.
  Old, Old Man, An
THOBURN, CRAWFORD
  Weelkes, Thomas
    Hark All Ye Lovely Saints
THOBURN, CRAWFORD R.
  Dowland, John
    Flow Not So Fast, Ye Fountains
THOMAS; CHEVALLIER
  Rivat
    Vent Et La Jeunesse, Le
THOMAS, MANSEL
  Ireland, John
    Sea Fever
THOMPSON, GLENDA
  Appenzeller, Benedictus
    Chansons
THYGERSON
  Cannon, Hughie
    Bill Bailey, Won't You Please Come
      Home?

  Ross, Brad
    Christmas Is Comin' Along
    Stepping Out Together
TISHMAN
  Here We Come A-Caroling
TRAPP, WILLY
  Elgar, [Sir] Edward (William)
    Klange Der Freude

  Hassler, Hans Leo
    Tanzen Und Springen
TRITSCH, J.
  Brafford, P.
    Petit Atome, Le
    Polka Des Tortues, La

  Brassens, Georges
    Cane De Jeanne, La

  Le Cannu, G.
    Rat, Le

TRITSCH, J. (cont'd.)

  Lemarque, F.
    Quand Un Soldat

  Pottar, O.
    Sirene Et Scaphandrier

  Rey, L.
    Dans La Marine Suisse

  Vidalie
    Actualites

  Villard, Jean (Gilles)
    Mannerchor De Steffisbourg, Le
TSCHAIKOWSKY, PETER ILYICH
  Three Arrangements
TUCKER
  Beard
    I Believe (Quodlibet With Bach-
      Gounod Ave Maria)
TURELLIER, J.
  Barbara
    Aigle Noir, L'

  Charlicou

  Dumont, Henri
    Absent De Vous Je Languis De
      Tristesse
    Je Ne Sais Que C'est D'un Fa Ni
      D'un Sol

  Filles De Lorient, Les

  Miraval, Raymond De
    Sehl Que No Vol

  Monteverdi, Claudio
    Scherzi Musicali

  Moustaki, Georges
    Il Est Trop Tard
    Ma Liberte

  My Old Kentucky Home

  Veni Sponsa Mea

  What Shall We Do
TURELLIER, JEAN
  Anonymous
    Chanson De Goliard

  Berthelot, Rene
    Bergere Aux Champs, La

  Daniel, Etienne
    Ou Vas-Tu?

  Dufay, Guillaume
    Ce Moys De May
    Flos Florum
    Je Ne Vis Oncques La Pareille,
      Rondeau

  Dukas, Paul
    Bon Jour, Bon Mois

  Firenze, Ghirardello da
    Tosto Che L'alba

  Langree, Alain
    Bourree Auvergnate

  Machaut, Guillaume de
    De Tout Suis Si Confortee
    Qui Es Promesse
    Se Je Souspire

  Monteverdi, Claudio
    Su, Su, Su, Pastorelli Vezzosi

  Morin, Jean Baptiste
    Belle Corinne
    Charmant Amour

  Mozart, Wolfgang Amadeus
    Ecoutez La Chanson Bien Douce

  Rossi, Luigi
    Berceuse
UBER, GERHARD
  Zwolf Monatskanons
UGLAND, JOHAN VAREN
  Liten Norsk Korrapsodi
VACCARO, J.M.
  Vic, C.H.
    Don Leon
VACCHELLI, ANNA MARIA MONTEROSSO
  Monteverdi, Claudio
    Madrigali E Canzonette: Libro 9

VALENTINE
All Things Joyful

VAN IDERSTINE, A.P.
Dashing Away With The Smoothing Iron

VAN WELY, MAX PRICK
Brahms, Johannes
Ich Schell Mein Horn
Standchen

VANCE
All The Pretty Little Horses

Ward, Samuel Augustus
America, The Beautiful

VANCE, MARGARET
New River Train

VANCIL
Brahms, Johannes
Wie Melodien Zieht Es Mir

Cherubini, Luigi
Tell Me Truly

Haydn, [Franz] Joseph
An Den Vetter
An Die Frauen

VANTINE, BRUCE
Irish Slumber Song

VELTMAN, B.
Carpenter, Richard Lynn
Top Of The World

VERHEIJEN, J.
Blum, Herbert
Vrede (Song Of Olympia)

Fradkin, Leslie Martin
Neem Mijn Hand

Whittaker, Roger
Show Me Your Mountain

VERHOEVEN-KOOIJ, A.J.
Sweelinck, Jan Pieterszoon
Vocal Secular Works

VERMULST, J.
Bruyns, M.
Ballade Van De Fiets

VERMULST, JAN
Cantus Europa

VIDAR, JORUNN
Sorrow And Joy

VLAK, K.
Scheepmaker, N.
Polderstad

VOGEL, H.
Theodorakis, Mikis
Nur Diese Eine Schwalbe

VOLERY, FRANCIS
Danks, Hart Pease
Silver Threads

VOLLE, BJARNE
Volle, Martin
Songen

VREE
Caccini
Amarilli, Mia Bella

Monteverdi, Claudio
A Che Tormi Il Ben Mio

VUATAZ, ROGER
Message D'Amour

Pauvre Laboureur, Le

WAGNER
Adieux A La Jeunesse

Bach, Johann Sebastian
Give Ear Unto My Words

Vaughan Williams, Ralph
Bright Is The Ring Of Words
Infinite Shining Heavens, The
Whither Must I Wander?

WAGNER, DOUGLAS E.
Berlin, Irving
Alexander's Ragtime Band

Blow The Candles Out

Praetorius, Michael
Jubilate Deo!

WAGNER, ROGER
Goldman
Beside The Golden Door

WALDENMAIER
Stolz, Robert
Adieu, Mein Kleiner Gardeoffizier
Auf Der Heide Bluhn Die Letzten
Rosen
Es Lebe Die Liebe
Ich Sing' Mein Lied Heut' Nur Fur
Dich!
Im Prater Bluh'n Wieder Die Baume
Jung San Ma! Fesch San Ma!
Mein Herz Ruft Immer Nur Nach Dir,
O Marita!
Mein Liebeslied Muss Ein Walzer
Sein
Ob Blond, Ob Braun, Ich Liebe Alle
Frau'n
Salome
Wenn Die Kleinen Veilchen Bluhen...
Zwei Herzen Im Dreivierteltakt

WALKER
Mendelssohn-Bartholdy, Felix
Auf Dem See

WALTERS
Bobby Shafto

Sweet Lass Of Richmond Hill

WATSON, WALTER
Dellasandro, G.
Mrs. Santa Claus

WEAVER, DAVID
Du Fugl Som Flyver

Margit Hjukse

WEBER, BEN
Schnabel, Artur
Two Movements For Chorus With
Orchestra

WEBER, G.
Schumann, Robert (Alexander)
Vent D'orage, Le

WEIR, MICHELLE
C'est Si Bon

WHALUM, WENDALL
James
Roberta Lee

Krapf, Gerhard
Wit And Wisdom

Somebody's Calling My Name

Sweet Home

WHITMAN, RUTH
Warren, B.
Apple-Tree Madrigals, The

WIELAKKER, GERHARD
Last Rose Of Summer, The

WILKINSON, SCOTT
Little David

WILL, M.
Aime-Moi Bergere

En Vain La Severe Raison

Quand Je Vais Au Jardin D'amour

WILLEIEGGER, H.R.
Ash Grove, The

WILLIAMS
Pfeil, Heinrich
Calm Is The Sea

Three Times A Lady

WILLIAMS, WENDY
Johnny Has Gone For A Soldier

Over The River And Through The Wood

WILLIAMSON; HUGUENIN
Chansons De Route Et De Bivouac

WILLIAMSON, MALCOLM
Mowing The Barley

North Country Songs

WILLISEGGER, H.R.
Believe Me If All Those Endearing
Young Charms

Du Fragsch, Was I Mocht Singe

Early One Morning

Es Ist Fur Uns Eine Zeit Angekommen

Greensleeves

Mis Schatzeli, Mis Haarzeli

Roy's Wife Of Aldivalloch

WILLISEGGER, H.R. (cont'd.)

Trinklied

WILSON
Knox
Spanish Carol, A

Ward, Samuel Augustus
America, The Beautiful

Wizard Of Oz, The: Selections

WIND
Boleras Sevillanas

Guten Abend, Gut Nacht

Heidenroslein

WIND, GERHARD
Du, Du Liegst Mir Im Herzen

WOLFF, H.W.D.
Bastiannse, F.
Lied Van De Dorschers, De

WOLFF, H.W.DE
Brahms, Johannes
Goeden Nacht En Wiegenlied

WOLSCHINA, R.
Wolschina, Reinhard
Martial-Epigramme

WULLNER; SCHWICKERATH; STEPHANI
Chorubungen

YABLONEV, E.
Eternal Flame, The

YANNERELLA, CHARLES
Hi Ho, Jerum

YOUNG, P.M.
Dowland, John
In Praise Of Cynthia

ZEGREE, STEVE
Mystery

Ray's Rockhouse

Smile

ZENDER, HANS
Schubert, Franz (Peter)
Gondelfahrer, Der, "Es Tanzen Mond
Und Stern"
Nachthelle, "Die Nacht Ist Heiter"

ZENGERINK, HERMAN
Handel, George Frideric
Chorus Of Virgins: See The Godlike
Youth Advance
Chorus Of Youths: See, The
Conqu'ring Hero Comes

Purcell, Henry
Sound The Trumpet

ZIBERLIN, F.
Darnal, Jean Claude
Dites-Moi, M'sieur

Debronckart, J.
Adelaide

Giraudoux, J.
Chanson De Tessa
Chansons De Tessa

Lefarge, G.
Seine, La

Pingault, Cl.
Marin Et La Rose, Le

Prevert, J.
Tendre Et Dangereux Visage De
L'amour, Le

Vigneault, Gilles
Voyageur Sedentaire, Le

ZIHLMANN, H.
S' Luzarnerbiet

ZIMMER, ULRICH
Singt Im Chor

Weltliche Madrigale

Weltliches Chormusik Der Romantik

ZWAAN, JACOBUS
Anonymous
Geluckig Is Het Land
Wie Gaat Mee Over Zee

ZWAAN, S.P.
Wyrtzen, Don
Love Is Now

ZWAGER, PIET
  Anonymous
    Men Roept Van Groenlands Bergen

ZWART, W.
  Lijnschooten, H.V.
    Choral Figure

Publisher Directory

The list of publishers which follows contains the code assigned for each publisher, the name and address of the publisher, and U.S. agents who distribute the publications. This is the master list for the Music-In-Print series and represents all publishers who have submitted information for inclusion in the series. Therefore, all of the publishers do not necessarily occur in the present volume.

Code	Publisher	U.S. Agent
A COEUR JOIE	Éditions A Coeur Joie Les Passerelles, BP 9151 24 avenue Joannès Masset F-69263 Lyon cédex 09 France	
A MOLL DUR	A Moll Dur Publishing House 7244 D'Evereux Court Alexandria, VA 22301	
A-R ED	A-R Editions, Inc. 315 West Gorham Street Madison, WI 53703	
AAP	Edition Aap Aas-Wangsvei 8 N-1600 Fredrikstad Norway	
ABC	ABC Music Co.	BOURNE
ABER.GRP.	The Aberbach Group 988 Madison Avenue New York, NY 10021	
ABERDEEN	Aberdeen Music, Inc. 170 N.E. 33rd Street Fort Lauderdale, FL 33334	
ABINGDON	Abingdon Press P.O. Box 801 Nashville, TN 37202	
ABRSM	Associated Board of the Royal Schools of Music 14 Bedford Square London WC1B 3JG England	PRESSER
ACADEM	Academia Music Ltd. 16-5, Hongo 3-Chome Bunkyo-ku Tokyo, 113 Japan	KALMUS,A
ACCURA	Accura Music P.O. Box 4260 Athens, OH 45701-4260	
ACORD	Edizioni Accordo	CURCI
ACSB	Antigua Casa Sherry-Brener, Ltd. of Madrid 3145 West 63rd Street Chicago, IL 60629	
ADD.PRESS	Addington Press	ROYAL
ADD.-WESLEY	Addison-Wesley Publishing Co., Inc. 2725 Sand Hill Road Menlo Park, CA 94025	
AEOLUS	Aeolus Publishing Co. 60 Park Terrace West New York, NY 10034	
AGAPE	Agape	HOPE
AHLINS	Ahlins Musikförlag Box 26072 S-100 41 Stockholm Sweden	

Code	Publisher	U.S. Agent
AHN	Ahn & Simrock Sonnenstraße 19 D-8 München Germany	
AKADDV	Akademische Druck- und Verlagsanstalt Graz Austria	
AKADEM	Akademiska Musikförlaget Sirkkalagatan 7 B 41 SF-20500 Abo 50 Finland	
ALBERSEN	Muziekhandel Albersen & Co. Groot Hertoginnelaan 182 NL-2517 EV Den Haag Netherlands	DONEMUS
ALBERT	J. Albert & Son Pty. Ltd. 139 King Street Sydney, N.S.W. Australia 2000	
ALBERT	J. Albert & Son - U.S.A. 1619 Broadway New York, NY 10019	
ALCOVE	Alcove Music	WESTERN
ALEX.HSE.	Alexandria House 468 McNally Drive Nashville, TN 37211	
ALFRED	Alfred Publishing Co. 16380 Roscoe Blvd. P.O. Box 10003 Van Nuys, CA 91410	
ALKOR	Alkor Edition	FOR.MUS.DIST.
ALLANS	Allans Music Australia Ltd. Box 513J, G.P.O. Melbourne 3001 Australia	PRESSER
ALLOWAY	Alloway Publications P.O. Box 25 Santa Monica, CA 90406	
ALMITRA	Almitra	KENDOR
ALMO	Almo Publications	CPP-BEL
ALPEG	Alpeg	PETERS
ALPHENAAR	W. Alphenaar Kruisweg 47-49 NL-2011 LA Haarlem Netherlands	
ALPUERTO	Editorial Alpuerto Caños del Peral 7 28013 Madrid Spain	
ALSBACH	G. Alsbach & Co. P.O. Box 338 NL-1400 AH Bussum Netherlands	
ALSBACH&D	Alsbach & Doyer	

Code	Publisher	U.S. Agent
AM.COMP.ALL.	American Composers Alliance 170 West 74th Street New York, NY 10023	
AM.INST.MUS.	American Institute of Musicology	FOSTER
AM.MUS.ED.	American Music Edition 263 East Seventh Street New York, NY 10009	PRESSER (partial)
AMADEUS	Amadeus Verlag Bernhard Päuler Am Iberghang 16 CH-8405 Winterthur Switzerland	FOR.MUS.DIST
	American Musicological Society 201 South 34th Street Philadelphia, PA 19104	SCHIRM.EC
	American String Teachers Association see ASTA	
AMICI	Gli Amici della Musica da Camera Via Bocca di Leone 25 Roma Italy	
AMP	Associated Music Publishers 225 Park Avenue South New York, NY 10003	LEONARD-US (sales) SCHIRM.G (rental)
AMPHION	Éditions Amphion 12, rue Rougement F-75009 Paris France	
AMS PRESS	AMS Press, Inc. 56 East 13th Street New York, NY 10003	
AMSCO	AMSCO Music Publishing Co.	MUSIC
AMSI	Art Masters Studios, Inc. 2710 Nicollet Avenue Minneapolis, MN 55408	
ANDEL	Edition Andel Madeliefjeslaan, 26 B-8400 Oostende Belgium	ELKAN,H
ANDERSONS	Anderssons Musikförlag Sodra Forstadsgatan 6 Box 17018 S-200 10 Malmö Sweden	
ANDRE	Johann André Musikverlag Frankfurterstraße 28 Postfach 141 D-6050 Offenbach-am-Main Germany	
ANERCA	Anerca Music 35 St. Andrew's Garden Toronto, Ontario M4W 2C9 Canada	
ANFOR	Anfor Music Publishers (Div. of Terminal Music Supply) 1619 East Third Street Brooklyn, NY 11230	MAGNA D
ANTARA	Antara Music Group P.O. Box 210 Alexandria, IN 46001	
ANTICO	Antico Edition North Harton, Lustleigh Newton Abbot Devon TQ13 9SG England	BOSTON EMC
APM	Artist Production & Management	VIERT

Code	Publisher	U.S. Agent
APNM	Association for Promotion of New Music 2002 Central Avenue Ship Bottom, NJ 08008	
APOGEE	Apogee Press	WORLD
APOLLO	Apollo-Verlag Paul Lincke Weihergarten 5 6500 Mainz Germany	
ARCADIA	Arcadia Music Publishing Co., Ltd. P.O. Box 1 Rickmansworth Herts WD3 3AZ England	
ARCO	Arco Music Publishers	WESTERN
ARGM	Editorial Argentina de Musica & Editorial Saraceno	PEER
ARION	Coleccion Arion	MEXICANAS
ARION PUB	Arion Publications, Inc. 4964 Kathleen Avenue Castro Valley, CA 94546	
ARISTA	Arista Music Co. 8370 Wilshire Blvd. Beverly Hills, CA 90211	CPP-BEL
ARNOLD	Edward Arnold Series	NOVELLO
ARS NOVA	Ars Nova Publications 121 Washington San Diego, CA 92103	PRESSER
ARS POLONA	Ars Polona Krakowskie Przedmieście 7 Skrytka pocztowa 1001 PL-00-950 Warszawa Poland	
ARS VIVA	Ars Viva Verlag Weihergarten D-6500 Mainz 1 Germany	EUR.AM.MUS.
ARSIS	Arsis Press 1719 Bay Street SE Washington, DC 20003	PLYMOUTH
ARTHUR	J. Arthur Music The University Music House 4290 North High Street Columbus, OH 43214	
ARTIA	Artia Prag Ve Smečkách 30 Praha 2 Czechoslovakia	FOR.MUS.DIST.
	Artist Production & Management see APM	
ARTRANSA	Artransa Music	WESTERN
ASCHERBERG	Ascherberg, Hopwood & Crew Ltd. 50 New Bond Street London W1A 2BR England	
ASHBOURN	Ashbourne Publications 425 Ashbourne Road Elkins Park, PA 19117	
ASHDOWN	Edwin Ashdown Ltd.	BRODT
ASHLEY	Ashley Publications, Inc. P.O. Box 337 Hasbrouck Heights, NJ 07604	

Code	Publisher	U.S. Agent
ASPEN	Aspen Grove Music P.O. Box 977 North Hollywood, CA 91603	
ASSMANN	Hermann Assmann, Musikverlag Franz-Werfel-Straße 36 D-6000 Frankfurt 50 Germany	
	Associated Board of the Royal Schools of Music see ABRSM	
	Associated Music Publishers see AMP	
	Association for Promotion of New Music see APNM	
ASTA	American String Teachers Association 2740 Spicewood Lane Bloomington, IN 47401	PRESSER
ATV	ATV Music Publications 6255 Sunset Boulevard Hollywood, CA 90028	CHERRY
AUG-FOR	Augsburg Fortress Publishers 426 South Fifth Street P.O. Box 1209 Minneapolis, MN 55440	
AULOS	Aulos Music Publishers P.O. Box 54 Montgomery, NY 12549	
AUTOGR	Autographus Musicus Ardalavägen 158 S-124 32 Bandhagen Sweden	
AUTRY	Gene Autry's Publishing Companies	CPP-BEL
AVANT	Avant Music	WESTERN
BAGGE	Jacob Bagge	STIM
BANK	Annie Bank Musiek P.O. Box 347 1180 AH Amstelveen Netherlands	
BANKS	Banks Music Publications 139 Holgate Road York YO2 4DF England	BRODT
BAREN.	Bärenreiter Verlag Heinrich Schütz Allee 31-37 Postfach 100329 D-3500 Kassel-Wilhelmshöhe Germany	FOR.MUS.DIST.
BARNHS	C.L. Barnhouse 205 Cowan Avenue West P.O. Box 680 Oskaloosa, IA 52577	
BARON,M	M. Baron Co. P.O. Box 149 Oyster Bay, NY 11771	
BARRY-ARG	Barry & Cia Talcahuano 860, Bajo B Buenos Aires 1013-Cap. Federal Argentina	BOOSEY
BARTA	Barta Music Company	JERONA
BASART	Les Éditions Internationales Basart	GENERAL

Code	Publisher	U.S. Agent
BASEL	Musik-Akademie der Stadt Basel Leonhardsstraße 6 CH-4051 Basel Switzerland	
BAUER	Georg Bauer Musikverlag Luisenstraße 47-49 Postfach 1467 D-7500 Karlsruhe Germany	
BAVTON	Bavariaton-Verlag München Germany	ORLANDO
	Mel Bay Publications see MEL BAY	
BEACON HILL	Beacon Hill Music	LILLENAS
BEAUDN	Stuart D. Beaudoin 629 Queen Street Newmarket, Ontario Canada L3Y 2J1	
BECKEN	Beckenhorst Press P.O. Box 14273 Columbus, OH 43214	
BEECHWD	Beechwood Music Corporation 1750 Vine Street Hollywood, CA 90028	WARNER
BEEK	Beekman Music, Inc.	PRESSER
BEIAARD	Beiaardschool Belgium	
BELAIEFF	M.P. Belaieff Kennedyallee 101 D-6000 Frankfurt-am-Main 70 Germany	PETERS
	Centre Belge de Documentation Musicale see CBDM	
BELLA	Bella Roma Music 1442A Walnut Street Suite 197 Berkeley, CA 94709	
BELMONT	Belmont Music Publishers P.O. Box 231 Pacific Palisades, CA 90272	
BELWIN	Belwin-Mills Publishing Corp. 15800 N.W. 48th Avenue P.O. Box 4340 Miami, FL 33014	CPP-BEL PRESSER (rental)
BENJ	Anton J. Benjamin Werderstraße 44 Postfach 2561 D-2000 Hamburg 13 Germany	PRESSER
BENNY	Claude Benny Press 1401½ State Street Emporia, KS 66801	
BENSON	John T. Benson P.O. Box 107 Nashville, TN 37202-0107	
BERANDOL	Berandol Music Ltd. 110A Sackville Street Toronto, Ontario M5A 3E7 Canada	
BERBEN	Edizioni Musicali Berben Via Redipuglia 65 I-60100 Ancona Italy	PRESSER

Code	Publisher	U.S. Agent
BERGMANS	W. Bergmans	BANK
BERKLEE	Berklee Press Publications	LEONARD-US
BERLIN	Irving Berlin Music Corp. 29 W. 46 Street New York, NY 10036	
BERNOUILLI	Ed. Bernouilli	DONEMUS
BESSEL	Éditions Bessel & Cie	BREITKOPF-W
BEUSCH	Éditions Paul Beuscher Arpège 27, Boulevard Beaumarchais F-75004 Paris France	
BEZIGE BIJ	De Bezige Bij	DONEMUS
BIELER	Edmund Bieler Musikverlag Thürmchenswall 72 D-5000 Köln 1 Germany	
BIG BELL	Big Bells, Inc. 33 Hovey Avenue Trenton, NJ 08610	
BIG3	Big Three Music Corp.	CPP-BEL
BILLAUDOT	Éditions Billaudot 14, rue de l'Echiquier F-75010 Paris France	PRESSER
BIRCH	Robert Fairfax Birch	PRESSER
BIRNBACH	Richard Birnbach Musikverlag Aubinger Straße 9 D-8032 Lochheim bei München Germany	
BIZET	Bizet Productions and Publications	PRESSER
BMI	Broadcast Music, Inc. 320 West 57th Street New York, NY 10019	
	Boccaccini and Spada Editori see BSE	
BOCK	Fred Bock Music Co. P.O. Box 333 Tarzana, CA 91356	ANTARA
BODENS	Edition Ernst Fr. W. Bodensohn Dr. Rumpfweg 1 D-7570 Baden-Baden 21 Germany see also ERST	
BOEIJENGA	Boeijenga Muziekhandel Kleinzand 89 NL-8601 BG Sneek Netherlands	
BOELKE-BOM	Boelke-Bomart Music Publications Hillsdale, NY 12529	JERONA
BOETHIUS	Boethius Press Clarabricken, Clifden Co. Kilkenny Ireland	
BOHM	Anton Böhm & Sohn Postfach 110369 Lange Gasse 26 D-8900 Augsburg 11 Germany	
BOIS	Bureau De Musique Mario Bois 17 Rue Richer F-75009 Paris France	
BOMART	Bomart Music Publications	BOELKE-BOM

Code	Publisher	U.S. Agent
BONART	Bonart Publications	CAN.MUS. CENT.
BONGIOVANI	Casa Musicale Francesco Bongiovanni Via Rizzoli 28 E I-40125 Bologna Italy	
BOONIN	Joseph Boonin, Inc.	EUR.AM.MUS.
BOOSEY	Boosey & Hawkes Inc. 24 East 21st Street New York, NY 10010 Boosey & Hawkes Rental Library 52 Cooper Square New York, NY 10003-7102	
BOOSEY-CAN	Boosey & Hawkes Ltd. 279 Yorkland Boulevard Willowdale, Ontario M2J 1S7 Canada	BOOSEY
BOOSEY-ENG	Boosey & Hawkes 295 Regent Street London W1 R 8JH England	BOOSEY
BORNEMANN	Éditions Bornemann 15 rue de Tournon F-75006 Paris France	KING,R PRESSER
BOSSE	Gustav Bosse Verlag Von der Tann Straße 38 Postfach 417 D-8400 Regensburg 1 Germany	EUR.AM.MUS.
BOSTON	Boston Music Co. 9 Airport Drive Hopedale, MA 01747	
BOSTON EMC	Boston Early Music Center P.O. Box 483 Cambridge, MA 02238-0483	
BOSWORTH	Bosworth & Company, Ltd. 14-18 Heddon Street, Regent Street London W1 R 8DP England	BRODT
BOTE	Bote & Bock Hardenbergstraße 9A D-1000 Berlin 12 Germany	LEONARD-US SCHIRM.G (rental)
BOURNE	Bourne Co. 5 W. 37th Street New York, NY 10018-6232	
BOWDOIN	Bowdoin College Music Press Department of Music Bowdoin College Brunswick, ME 04011	
BOWM	Bowmaster Productions 3351 Thornwood Road Sarasota, FL 33581	
BR.CONT.MUS.	British And Continental Music Agencies Ltd.	EMI
BRADLEY	Bradley Publications 80 8th Avenue New York, NY 10011	CPP-BEL
BRANCH	Harold Branch Publishing, Inc. 95 Eads Street West Babylon, NY 11704	

Code	Publisher	U.S. Agent
BRANDEN	Branden Press, Inc. 17 Station Street P.O. Box 843 Brookline Village, MA 02147	
BRASS PRESS	The Brass Press 136 8th Avenue North Nashville, TN 37203-3798	
BRATFISCH	Musikverlag Georg Bratfisch Hans-Herold-Str. 23 D-8650 Kulmbach Germany	
BRAUER	Les Éditions Musicales Herman Brauer 30, rue St. Christophe B-1000 Bruxelles Belgium	
BRAUN-PER	St. A. Braun-Peretti Hahnchenpassage D-53 Bonn Germany	
BRAVE	Brave New Music	SON-KEY
BREITKOPF-L	Breitkopf & Härtel Karlstraße 10 DDR-7010 Leipzig Germany	
BREITKOPF-LN	Breitkopf & Härtel	
BREITKOPF-W	Breitkopf & Härtel Walkmühlstraße 52 Postfach 1707 D-6200 Wiesbaden 1 Germany	SCHIRM.G (rental)
BRENNAN	John Brennan Music Publisher Positif Press Ltd. 130 Southfield Road Oxford OX4 1PA England	ORGAN LIT
BRENT	Michael Brent Publications, Inc. P.O. Box 1186 Port Chester, NY 10573	CHERRY
BRENTWOOD	Brentwood Publishing Group Inc. P.O. Box 19001 Brentwood, TN 37027	
BRIDGE	Bridge Music Publishing Co. 1350 Villa Street Mountain View, CA 94042	
BRIGHT STAR	Bright Star Music Publications	WESTERN
	British and Continental Music Agencies Ltd. see BR.CONT.MUS.	
	Broadcast Music, Inc. see BMI	
BROADMAN	Broadman Press 127 Ninth Avenue, North Nashville, TN 37234	
BRODT	Brodt Music Co. P.O. Box 9345 Charlotte, NC 28299-9345	
BROEKMANS	Broekmans & Van Poppel B.V. van Baerlestraat 92-94 NL-1071 BB Amsterdam Netherlands	
BROGNEAUX	Éditions Musicales Brogneaux 73, Avenue Paul Janson B-1070 Bruxelles Belgium	ELKAN,H

Code	Publisher	U.S. Agent
BROOK	Brook Publishing Co. 3602 Cedarbrook Road Cleveland Heights, OH 44118	
BROUDE,A	Alexander Broude, Inc.	PLYMOUTH
BROUDE BR.	Broude Brothers Ltd. 141 White Oaks Road Williamstown, MA 01267	
	Broude Brothers Ltd.-Rental Dept. 170 Varick St. New York, NY 10013	
BROWN	Brown University Choral Series	BOOSEY
BROWN,R	Rayner Brown 2423 Panorama Terrace Los Angeles, CA 90039	
BROWN,WC	William C. Brown Co. 2460 Kerper Boulevard Dubuque, IA 52001	
BRUCK	Musikverlag M. Bruckbauer "Biblioteca de la Guitarra" Postfach 18 D-7953 Bad Schussenried Germany	
BRUCKNER	Bruckner Verlag Austria	PETERS (rental)
BRUZZI	Aldo Bruzzichelli, Editore Borgo S. Frediano, 8 I-50124 Firenze Italy	MARGUN
BSE	Boccaccini and Spada Editori Via Francesco Duodo, 10 I-00136 Roma Italy	PRESSER
BUBONIC	Bubonic Publishing Co. 706 Lincoln Avenue St. Paul, MN 55105	
BUDAPEST	Editio Musica Budapest (Kultura) P.O.B. 322 H-1370 Budapest Hungary see also EMB	BOOSEY PRESSER (partial)
BUDDE	Rolf Budde Musikverlag Hohenzollerndamm 54A D-1000 Berlin 33 Germany	
BUGZY	Bugzy Bros. Vocal Athletics P.O. Box 900 Orem, UT 84057	MUSICART
BUSCH	Hans Busch Musikförlag Stubbstigen 3 S-18147 Lidingö Sweden	
BUSCH,E	Ernst Busch Verlag Schlossstrasse 43 D-7531 Neulingen-Bauschlott Germany	
BUTZ	Dr. J. Butz Musikverlag Postfach 3008 5205 Sankt Augustin 3 Germany	
CAILLARD	Création & Diffusion Musicale L'Ensemble Vocal Philippe Caillard 60, rue de Brément 93130 Noisy-Le-Sec France	

Code	Publisher	U.S. Agent
CAILLET	Lucien Cailliet	SOUTHERN
CAM	Camerica Music	CPP-BEL
CAMBIATA	Cambiata Press P.O. Box 1151 Conway, AR 72032	
CAMBRIA	Cambria Records & Publishing P.O. Box 374 Lomita, CA 90717	
CAMBRIDGE	Cambridge University Press The Edinburgh Building Shaftesbury Road Cambridge CB2 2RU England	
CAMERICA	Camerica Music 535 Fifth Avenue, Penthouse New York, NY 10017	CPP-BEL
CAMPUS	Campus Publishers 713 Ellsworth Road West Ann Arbor, MI 48104	
CAN.MUS.CENT.	Canadian Music Centre 20 St. Joseph Street Toronto, Ontario M4Y 1J9 Canada	
CAN.MUS.HER.	Canadian Musical Heritage Society Patrimoine Musical Canadien P.O. Box 262, Station A Ottawa, Ontario K1N 8V2 Canada	
CANAAN	Canaanland Publications	WORD
CANT DO	Cantate Domino Editions de musique Mont d'Or 11 CH-1007 Lausanne Switzerland	
CANTANDO	Cantando Forlag Bj. Bjørnsonsgt. 2 D N-4021 Stavanger Norway	
CANTORIS	Cantoris Music P.O. Box 162004 Sacramento, CA 95816	
CANYON	Canyon Press, Inc. P.O. Box 447 Islamorada, FL 33036	KERBY
CAPELLA	Capella Music, Inc.	BOURNE
CAPPR	Capital Press	PODIUM
CARABO	Carabo-Cone Method Foundation 1 Sherbrooke Road Scarsdale, NY 10583	
CARISCH	Carisch S.p.A. See Nuova Carisch	
CARLIN	Carlin Publications P.O. Box 2289 Oakhurst, CA 93644	
CARLTON	Carlton Musikverlag	BREITKOPF-W
CARUS	Carus-Verlag	FOSTER
CATHEDRAL	Cathedral Music School House, The Croft Cocking, Midhurst West Sussex GU29 0HQ England	
	Catholic Conference see U.S.CATH	

Code	Publisher	U.S. Agent
CAVATA	Cavata Music Publishers, Inc.	PRESSER
CAVELIGHT	Cavelight Music P.O. Box 85 Oxford, NJ 07863	
CBC	Cundey Bettoney Co.	FISCHER,C
CBDM	CeBeDeM Centre Belge de Documentation Musicale rue d'Arlon 75-77 B-1040 Bruxelles Belgium	
CCMP	Colorado College Music Press Colorado Springs, CO 80903	
CEL	Celesta Publishing Co. P.O. Box 560603, Kendall Branch Miami, FL 33156	
	Centre Belge de Documentation Musicale see CBDM	
	Éditions du Centre Nationale de la Recherche Scientifique see CNRS	
CENTURY	Century Music Publishing Co. 263 Veterans Boulevard Carlstadt, NJ 07072	ASHLEY
CENTURY PR	Century Press Publishers 412 North Hudson Oklahoma City, OK 73102	
CESKY HUD.	Cesky Hudebni Fond Parizska 13 CS-110 00 Praha 1 Czechoslovakia	BOOSEY (rental)
CHANT	Éditions Le Chant du Monde 23, rue Royale F-75008 Paris France	
CHANTERL	Editions Chanterelle S.A. Postfach 103909 D-69 Heidelberg Germany	BAREN.
CHANTRY	Chantry Music Press, Inc. Wittenberg University P.O. Box 1101 Springfield, OH 45501	
CHAPLET	Chaplet Music Corp.	PARAGON
CHAPPELL	Chappell & Co., Inc. 1290 Avenue of the Americas New York, NY 10019	LEONARD-US
CHAPPELL-CAN	Chappell Music Canada Ltd 85 Scarsdale Road, Unit 101 Don Mills, Ontario M3B 2R2 Canada	LEONARD-US
CHAPPELL-ENG	Chappell & Co., Ltd. Printed Music Division 60-70 Roden Street Ilford, Essex IG1 2AQ England	LEONARD-US
CHAPPELL-FR	Chappell S.A. 25, rue d'Hauteville F-75010 Paris France	LEONARD-US
CHAR CROS	Charing Cross Music, Inc. 1619 Broadway, Suite 500 New York, NY 10019	
CHARTER	Charter Publications, Inc. P.O. Box 850 Valley Forge, PA 19482	PEPPER

Code	Publisher	U.S. Agent
CHENANGO	Chenango Valley Music Press P.O. Box 251 Hamilton, NY 13346	
CHERITH	Cherith Publishing Co.	SON-KEY
CHERRY	Cherry Lane Music Co. 110 Midland Avenue Port Chester, NY 10573	ALFRED
CHESTER	Chester Music 8-9 Frith Street London W1V 5TZ England	SCHIRM.G
CHILTERN	Chiltern Music	CATHEDRAL
CHOIR	Choir Publishing Co. 564 Columbus Street Salt Lake City, UT 84103	
CHORISTERS	Choristers Guild 2834 West Kingsley Road Garland, TX 75041	LORENZ
CHOUDENS	Édition Choudens 38, rue Jean Mermoz F-75008 Paris France	PRESSER PETERS
CHRI	Christopher Music Co. 380 South Main Place Carol Stream, IL 60188	PRESSER
CHRIS	Christophorus-Verlag Herder Hermann-Herder-Straße 4 D-7800 Freiburg Breisgau Germany	
CHURCH	John Church Co.	PRESSER
CJC	Creative Jazz Composers, Inc. 1240 Annapolis Road Odenton, MD 21113	
CLARION	Clarion Call Music	SON-KEY
CLARK	Clark and Cruickshank Music Publishers	BERANDOL
CLIVIS	Clivis Publicacions C-Còrsega, 619 Baixos Barcelona 25 Spain	
CMP	CMP Library Service MENC Historical Center/SCIM Music Library/Hornbake University of Maryland College Park, MD 20742	
CNRS	Éditions du Centre National de la Recherche Scientifique 20-22 rue Saint-Amand F-75015 Paris France	SMPF
CO OP	Co-op Press RD2 Box 150A Wrightsville, PA 17368	
COBURN	Coburn Press	PRESSER
CODERG	Coderg-U.C.P. sàrl 42 bis, rue Boursault F-75017 Paris France	
COLE	M.M. Cole Publishing Co. 919 North Michigan Avenue Chicago, IL 60611	
COLEMAN	Dave Coleman Music, Inc. P.O. Box 230 Montesano, WA 98563	

Code	Publisher	U.S. Agent
COLFRANC	Colfranc Music Publishing Corp.	KERBY
COLIN	Charles Colin 315 West 53rd Street New York, NY 10019	
COLOMBO	Franco Colombo Publications	CPP-BEL PRESSER (rental)
	Colorado College Music Press see CCMP	
COLUM UNIV	Columbia University Music Press 562 West 113th Street New York, NY 10025	SCHIRM.EC
COLUMBIA	Columbia Music Co.	PRESSER
CPP	Columbia Pictures Publications 15800 N.W. 48th Avenue Miami, FL 33014	CPP-BEL
COMBRE	Consortium Musical, Marcel Combre Editeur 24, Boulevard Poissonnière F-75009 Paris France	PRESSER
COMP.FAC.	Composers Facsimile Edition	AM.COMP.AL.
COMP.LIB.	Composer's Library Editions	PRESSER
COMP-PERF	Composer/Performer Edition 2101 22nd Street Sacramento, CA 95818	
COMP.PR.	The Composers Press, Inc.	OPUS
COMPOSER'S GR	Composer's Graphics 5702 North Avenue Carmichael, CA 95608	
CONCERT	Concert Music Publishing Co. c/o Studio P-R, Inc. 16333 N.W. 54th Avenue Hialeah, FL 33014	CPP-BEL
CONCORD	Concord Music Publishing Co.	ELKAN,H
CONCORDIA	Concordia Publishing House 3558 South Jefferson Avenue St. Louis, MO 63118-3968	
CONGRESS	Congress Music Publications 100 Biscayne Boulevard Miami, FL 33132	
CONSOL	Consolidated Music Publishers, Inc. 33 West 60th Street New York, NY 10023	
CONSORT	Consort Music, Inc. (Division of Magnamusic Distributors) Sharon, CT 06069	
CONSORT PR	Consort Press P.O. Box 50413 Santa Barbara, CA 93150-0413	
CONSORTIUM	Consortium Musical	PRESSER
	Consortium Musical, Marcel Combre Editeur see COMBRE	
CONTINUO	Continuo Music Press, Inc.	PLYMOUTH
	Editorial Cooperativa Inter-Americana de Compositores see ECOAM	
COPPENRATH	Musikverlag Alfred Coppenrath Neuottinger Straße 32 D-8262 Altotting-Obb. Germany	

Code	Publisher	U.S. Agent
COR PUB	Cor Publishing Co. 67 Bell Place Massapequa, NY 11758	
CORMORANT	Cormorant Press P.O. Box 169 Hallowell, ME 04347	UNICORN
CORONA	Edition Corona-Rolf Budde Hohenzollerndamm 54A D-1 Berlin 33 Germany	
CORONET	Coronet Press	PRESSER
COROZINE	Vince Corozine Music Publishing Co. 6 Gabriel Drive Peekskill, NY 10566	
COSTALL	Éditions Costallat 60 rue de la Chaussée d'Antin F-75441 Paris Cedex 09 France	PRESSER
COVENANT	Covenant Press 3200 West Foster Avenue Chicago, IL 60625	
COVENANT MUS	Covenant Music 1640 East Big Thompson Avenue Estes Park, CO 80517	
CPP-BEL	CPP-Belwin Music 15800 N.W. 48th Avenue Miami, FL 33014	
CRAMER	J.B. Cramer & Co., Ltd. 23 Garrick Street London WC2E 9AX England	CPP-BEL
CRANZ	Éditions Cranz 30, rue St.-Christophe B-1000 Bruxelles Belgium	ELKAN,H
	Creative Jazz Composers see CJC	
CRES.-NETH	Uitgeverij Crescendo	DONEMUS
CRESCENDO	Crescendo Music Sales Co. P.O. Box 395 Naperville, IL 60540	FEMA
CRESPUB	Crescendo Publications, Inc. 6311 North O'Connor Road #112 Irving, TX 75039-3112	
CRITERION	Criterion Music Corp. P.O. Box 660 Lynbrook, NY 11563	
CROATICA	Croatian Music Institute	DRUS.HRVAT. SKLAD.
CRON	Edition Cron Luzern Zinggentorstraße 5 CH-6006 Luzern Switzerland	
CROWN	Crown Music Press 4119 North Pittsburgh Chicago, IL 60634	BRASS PRESS (partial)
	Cundey Bettoney Co. see CBC	
CURCI	Edizioni Curci Galleria del Corso 4 I-20122 Milano Italy	
CURTIS	Curtis Music Press	KJOS
CURWEN	J. Curwen & Sons	LEONARD-US SCHIRM.G (rental)
CZECH	Czechoslovak Music Information Centre Besední 3 CS-118 00 Praha 1 Czechoslovakia	BOOSEY (rental)
DA CAPO	Da Capo Press, Inc. 233 Spring Street New York, NY 10013	
	Samfundet til udgivelse af Dansk Musik see SAMFUNDET	
DANTALIAN	Dantalian, Inc. Eleven Pembroke Street Newton, MA 02158	
DAVIMAR	Davimar Music M. Productions 159 West 53rd Street New York, NY 10019	
DAYBRK	Daybreak Productions	ALEX.HSE.
DE MONTE	De Monte Music F-82240 Septfonds France	
DE SANTIS	Edizioni de Santis Viale Mazzini, 6 I-00195 Roma Italy	
DEAN	Roger Dean Publishing Co. 345 West Jackson Street, #B Macomb, IL 61455-2112	LORENZ
DEIRO	Pietro Deiro Publications 133 Seventh Avenue South New York, NY 10014	
DELRIEU	Georges Delrieu & Cie Palais Bellecour B 14, rue Trachel F-06000 Nice France	SCHIRM.EC
DENNER	Erster Bayerischer Musikverlag Joh. Dennerlein KG Beethovenstraße 7 D-8032 Lochham Germany	
DESERET	Deseret Music Publishers P.O. Box 900 Orem, UT 84057	MUSICART
DESHON	Deshon Music, Inc.	CPP-BEL PRESSER (rental)
DESSAIN	Éditions Dessain Belgium	
DEUTSCHER	Deutscher Verlag für Musik Postschließfach 147 Karlstraße 10 DDR-7010 Leipzig Germany	FOR.MUS.DIST. (rental)
DEWOLF	DeWolfe Ltd. 80/88 Wardour Street London W1V 3LF England	DONEMUS
DIAPASON	The Diapason Press Dr. Rudolf A. Rasch P.O. Box 2376 NL-3500 GJ Utrecht Netherlands	

Code	Publisher	U.S. Agent
DIESTERWEG	Verlag Moritz Diesterweg Hochstraße 31 D-6000 Frankfurt-am-Main Germany	
	Dilia Prag see DP	
DIP PROV	Diputacion Provincal de Barcelona Servicio de Bibliotecas Carmen 47 Barcelona 1 Spain	
DITSON	Oliver Ditson Co.	PRESSER
DOBER	Les Éditions Doberman-Yppan C.P. 2021 St. Nicholas, Quebec G0S 3L0 Canada	BOOSEY
DOBLINGER	Ludwig Doblinger Verlag Dorotheergasse 10 A-1011 Wien I Austria	FOR.MUS.DIST.
DOMINIS	Dominis Music Ltd. Box 11307, Station H Ottawa Ontario K2H 7V1 Canada	
DONEMUS	Donemus Foundation Paulus Potterstraat 14 NL-1071 CZ Amsterdam Netherlands	PRESSER
DOORWAY	Doorway Music 2509 Buchanan Street Nashville, TN 37208	
DORABET	Dorabet Music Co. 170 N.E. 33rd Street Ft. Lauderdale, FL 33334	PLYMOUTH
DORING	G.F. Döring Musikverlag Hasenplatz 5-6 D-7033 Herrenburg 1 Germany	
DOUBLDAY	Doubleday & Co., Inc. 501 Franklin Avenue Garden City, NY 11530	
DOUGLAS,B	Byron Douglas	CPP-BEL
DOVEHOUSE	Dovehouse Editions 32 Glen Avenue Ottawa, Ontario K1S 2Z7 Canada	
DOVER	Dover Publications, Inc. 31 East 2nd Street Mineola, NY 11501	ALFRED
DOXO	Doxology Music P.O. Box M Aiken, SC 29801	
DP	Dilia Prag	BAREN.
DRAGON	Dragon Music Co. 28908 Grayfox Street Malibu, CA 90265	
DREIK	Dreiklang-Dreimasken Bühnen- und Musikverlag D-8000 München Germany	ORLANDO
DRUS.HRVAT. SKLAD.	Društvo Hrvatskih Skladatelja Berislavićeva 9 Zagreb Yugoslavia	
DRUSTVA	Edicije Drustva Slovenskih Skladateljev Trg Francoske Revolucije 6 YU-61000 Ljubljana Yugoslavia	
DRZAVNA	Drzavna Zalozba Slovenije	DRUSTVA
DUCKWORTH	Gerald Duckworth & Co., Ltd. 43 Gloucester Crescent London, NW1 England	
DUMA	Duma Music Inc. 580 Alden Street Woodbridge, NJ 07095	
DURAND	Durand & Cie 215, rue du Faubourg St.-Honoré F-75008 Paris France	PRESSER
DUTTON	E.P. Dutton & Co., Inc. 201 Park Avenue South New York, NY 10003	
DUX	Edition Dux Arthur Turk Beethovenstraße 7 D-8032 Lochham Germany	DENNER
DVM	DVM Productions P.O. Box 399 Thorofare, NJ 08086	
EAR.MUS.FAC.	Early Music Facsimiles P.O. Box 711 Columbus, OH 43216	
	East West Publications see EWP	
EARTHSNG	Earthsongs 220 N.W. 29th Corvallis, OR 97330	
EASTMAN	Eastman School of Music	FISCHER,C
EBLE	Eble Music Co. P.O. Box 2570 Iowa City, IA 52244	
ECK	Van Eck & Zn.	DONEMUS
ECOAM	Editorial Cooperativa Inter-Americana de Compositores Casilla de Correa No. 540 Montevideo Uruguay	PEER
EDI-PAN	Edi-Pan	DE SANTIS
EDUTAIN	Edu-tainment Publications (Div. of the Evolve Music Group) P.O. Box 20767 New York, NY 10023	
EERSTE	De Eerste Muziekcentrale Flevolaan 41 NL-1411 KC Naarden Netherlands	
EGTVED	Edition EGTVED P.O. Box 20 DK-6040 Egtved Denmark	FOSTER
EHRLING	Thore Ehrling Musik AB Linnegatan 9-11 Box 5268 S-102 45 Stockholm Sweden	
EIGEN UITGAVE	Eigen Uitgave van de Componist (Composer's Own Publication)	DONEMUS

Code	Publisher	U.S. Agent
ELITE	Elite Edition	SCHAUR
ELKAN,H	Henri Elkan Music Publisher P.O. Box 279 Hastings On Hudson, NY 10706	
ELKAN&SCH	Elkan & Schildknecht Vastmannagatan 95 S-113 43 Stockholm Sweden	
ELKAN-V	Elkan-Vogel, Inc. Presser Place Bryn Mawr, PA 19010	
ELKIN	Elkin & Co., Ltd	PRESSER
EMB	Editio Musica Budapest P.O.B. 322 H-1370 Budapest Hungary see also BUDAPEST	BOOSEY PRESSER
EMEC	Editorial de Musica Española Contemporanea Ediciones Quiroga Alcalá, 70 Madrid 9 Spain	
EMERSON	Emerson Edition Windmill Farm Ampleforth York YO6 4HF England	EBLE GROVE KING,R WOODWIND PRESSER
EMI	EMI Music Publishing Ltd. 127 Charing Cross Road London WC2H 0EA England	INTER.MUS.P.
ENGELS	Musikverlag Carl Engels Nachf. Auf dem Brand 3 D-5000 Köln 50 (Rodenkirchen) Germany	
ENGSTROEM	Engstroem & Soedering Palaegade 6 DK-1261 København K Denmark	PETERS
ENOCH	Enoch & Cie 193 Boulevard Pereire F-75017 Paris France	PRESSER SCHIRM.G (rental-partial)
ENSEMB	Ensemble Publications P.O. Box 98, Bidwell Station Buffalo, NY 14222	
ENSEMB PR	Ensemble Music Press	FISCHER,C
EPHROS	Gershon Ephros Cantorial Anthology Foundation, Inc	TRANSCON.
ERDMANN	Rudolf Erdmann, Musikverlag Adolfsallee 34 D-62 Wiesbaden Germany	
ERES	Edition Eres Horst Schubert Hauptstrasse 35 Postfach 1220 D-2804 Lilienthal/Bremen Germany	
ERICKSON	E.J. Erickson Music Co. 606 North Fourth Street P.O. Box 97 St. Peter, MN 56082	
ERIKS	Eriks Musikhandel & Förlag AB Karlavägen 40 S-114 49 Stockholm Sweden	

Code	Publisher	U.S. Agent
ERST	Erstausgaben Bodensohn see also BODENS	
ESCHENB	Eschenbach Editions 28 Dalrymple Crescent Edinburgh, EH9 2NX Scotland	
ESCHIG	Éditions Max Eschig 48 rue de Rome F-75008 Paris France	LEONARD-US SCHIRM.G (rental)
	Editorial de Musica Española Contemporanea see EMEC	
	Union Musical Española see UNION ESP	
ESSEX	Clifford Essex Music	MUSIC-ENG
ESSO	Van Esso & Co.	DONEMUS
ETLING,F	Forest R. Etling see HIGHLAND	
ETOILE	Etoile Music, Inc. Publications Division Shell Lake, WI 54871	MMB
EULENBURG	Edition Eulenburg	FOR.MUS.DIST. EUR.AM. (miniature scores)
EURAM.MUS.	European American Music Corp. P.O. Box 850 Valley Forge, PA 19482	
EWP	East West Publications	MUSIC
EXC.MH	Excellent Music Holland Postbus 347 1180 AH Amstelveen Netherlands	
EXCELSIOR	Excelsior Music Publishing Co.	PRESSER
EXPO PR	Exposition Press 325 Kings Highway Smithtown, NY 11787	
FABER	Faber Music Ltd. 3 Queen Square London WC1N 3AU England	LEONARD-US (sales) SCHIRM.G (rental)
FAIR	Fairfield Publishing, Ltd.	PRESSER
FAITH	Faith Music	LILLENAS
FALLEN LEAF	Fallen Leaf Press P.O. Box 10034-N Berkeley, CA 94709	
FAR WEST	Far West Music	WESTERN
FARRELL	The Wes Farrell Organization	LEONARD-US
FAZER	Musik Fazer P.O. Box 169 SF-02101 Espoo Finland	WALTON (choral)
FEEDBACK	Feedback Studio Verlag Gentner Strasse 23 D-5 Köln 1 Germany	BAREN.
FELDMAN,B	B. Feldman & Co., Ltd	EMI
FEMA	Fema Music Publications P.O. Box 395 Naperville, IL 60566	
FENETTE	Fenette Music Ltd.	BROUDE,A

Code	Publisher	U.S. Agent
FENTONE	Fentone Music Ltd. Fleming Road, Earlstrees Corby, Northants NN17 2SN England	PRESSER
FEREOL	Fereol Publications Route 8, Box 510C Gainesville, GA 30501	
FEUCHT	Feuchtinger & Gleichauf Schwarze Bärenstraße 5 D-8400 Regensburg 11 Germany	
FIDDLE	Fiddle & Bow 7 Landview Drive Dix Hills, NY 11746	HHP
FIDELIO	Fidelio Music Publishing Co. 39 Danbury Avenue Westport, CT 06880	
FIDULA	Fidula-Verlag Johannes Holzmeister Ahornweg, Postfach 250 D-5407 Boppard/Rhein Germany	HARGAIL
FILLMH	Fillmore Music House	FISCHER,C
FINE ARTS	Fine Arts Press 2712 W. 104th Terrace Leawood, KS 66206	ALEX.HSE.
FINN MUS	Finnish Music Information Center Runeberginkatu 15 A SF-00100 Helsinki 10 Finland	
FISCHER,C	Carl Fischer, Inc. 62 Cooper Square New York, NY 10003	
FISCHER, J	J. Fischer & Bro.	BELWIN PRESSER (rental)
FISHER	Fisher Music Co.	PLYMOUTH
FITZSIMONS	H.T. FitzSimons Co., Inc. 18345 Ventura Boulevard P.O. Box 333, Suite 212 Tarzana, CA 91356	ANTARA
FLAMMER	Harold Flammer, Inc.	SHAWNEE
FMA	Florilegium Musicae Antiquae	HANSSLER
FOETISCH	Foetisch Frères Rue de Bourg 6 CH-1002 Lausanne Switzerland	SCHIRM.EC
FOG	Dan Fog Musikforlag Grabrodretorv 7 DK-1154 København K Denmark	
FOLEY,CH	Charles Foley, Inc.	FISCHER,C PRESSER (rental)
FORBERG	Rob. Forberg-P. Jurgenson, Musikverlag Mirbachstraße 9 D-5300 Bonn-Bad Godesberg Germany	PETERS
FOR.MUS.DIST.	Foreign Music Distributors 13 Elkay Drive Chester, NY 10918	
FORLIVESI	A. Forlivesi & C. Via Roma 4 50123 Firenze Italy	

Code	Publisher	U.S. Agent
FORNI	Arnaldo Forni Editore Via Gramsci 164 I-40010 Sala Bolognese Italy	
FORSTER	Forster Music Publisher, Inc. 216 South Wabash Avenue Chicago, IL 60604	
FORTEA	Biblioteca Fortea Fucar 10 Madrid 14 Spain	
FORTISSIMO	Fortissimo Musikverlag Margaretenplatz 4 A-1050 Wien Austria	
	Fortress Press 2900 Queen Lane Philadelphia, PA 19129	AUG-FOR
FOSTER	Mark Foster Music Co. 28 East Springfield Avenue P.O. Box 4012 Champaign, IL 61820-1312	
FOUR ST	Four Star Publishing Co.	CPP-BEL
FOXS	Sam Fox Publishing Co. 5276 Hollister Avenue Suite 251 Santa Barbara, CA 93111	PLYMOUTH (Sales) PRESSER (rental)
FRANCAIS	Éditions Françaises de Musique	PRESSER
FRANCE	France Music	AMP
FRANCIS	Francis, Day & Hunter Ltd.	CPP-BEL
FRANG	Frangipani Press P.O. Box 669 Bloomington, IN 47402	ALFRED
FRANK	Frank Music Corp.	LEONARD-US SCHIRM.G (partial)
FRANTON	Franton Music 4620 Sea Isle Memphis, TN 38117	
FREDONIA	Fredonia Press 3947 Fredonia Drive Hollywood, CA 90068	SIFLER
FREEMAN	H. Freeman & Co., Ltd.	EMI
FROHLICH	Friedrich Wilhelm Fröhlich Musikverlag Ansbacher Straße 52 D-1000 Berlin 30 Germany	
FUJIHARA	Fujihara	BROUDE,A
FURST	Fürstner Ltd.	BOOSEY
GAF	G.A.F. and Associates 1626 E. Williams Street Tempe, AZ 85281	
GAITHER	Gaither Music Company	ALEX.HSE.
GALAXY	Galaxy Music Corp.	SCHIRM.EC
GALLEON	Galleon Press 17 West 60th St. New York, NY 10023	BOSTON
GALLERIA	Galleria Press 170 N.E. 33rd Street Fort Lauderdale, FL 33334	PLYMOUTH

Code	Publisher	U.S. Agent
GALLIARD	Galliard Ltd. Queen Anne's Road Southtown, Gt. Yarmouth Norfolk England	GALAXY
GARLAND	Garland Publishing, Inc. 136 Madison Avenue New York, NY 10016	
GARZON	Éditions J. Garzon 13 rue de l'Échiquier F-75010 Paris France	
GEHRMANS	Carl Gehrmans Musikförlag Odengatan 84 Box 6005 S-102 31 Stockholm Sweden	BOOSEY
GEMINI	Gemini Press Music Div. of the Pilgrim Press Box 390 Otis, MA 01253	PRESSER
GENERAL	General Music Publishing Co., Inc. 145 Palisade Street Dobbs Ferry, NY 10522	BOSTON
GENERAL WDS	General Words and Music Co.	KJOS
GENESIS	Genesis	PLYMOUTH
GENTRY	Gentry Publications	ANTARA
GERIG	Musikverlage Hans Gerig Drususgasse 7-11 (Am Museum) D-5000 Köln 1 Germany	BREITKOPF-W
GIA	GIA Publications 7404 South Mason Avenue Chicago, IL 60638	
GILBERT	Gilbert Publications 4209 Manitou Way Madison, WI 53711	
GILLMAN	Gillman Publications P.O. Box 155 San Clemente, CA 92672	
GLOCKEN	Glocken Verlag Ltd. 12-14 Mortimer Street London W1N 8EL England	EUR.AM.MUS.
GLORY	Glory Sound Delaware Water Gap, PA 18327	SHAWNEE
GLOUCHESTER	Glouchester Press P.O. Box 1044 Fairmont, WV 26554	HEILMAN
GM	G & M International Music Dealers Box 2098 Northbrook, IL 60062	
GOLDEN	Golden Music Publishing Co. P.O. Box 383 Golden, CO 80402-0383	
GOODLIFE	Goodlife Publications	CPP-BEL
GOODMAN	Goodman Group (formerly Regent, Arc & Goodman)	WARNER
GOODWIN	Goodwin & Tabb Publishing, Ltd.	PRESSER
GORDON	Gordon Music Co. Box 2250 Canoga Park, CA 91306	
GORNSTON	David Gornston	FOX,S

Code	Publisher	U.S. Agent
GOSPEL	Gospel Publishing House 1445 Boonville Avenue Springfield, MO 65802	
GRAHL	Grahl & Nicklas Braubachstraße 24 D-6 Frankfurt-am-Main Germany	
GRANCINO	Grancino Editions 15020 Burwood Dr. Lake Mathews, CA 92370 Grancino Editions 2 Bishopswood Road London N6 4PR England Grancino Editions Schirmerweg 12 D-8 München 60 Germany	
GRAS	Éditions Gras 36 rue Pape-Carpentier F-72200 La Flèche (Sarthe) France	SOUTHERN
GRAY	H.W. Gray Co., Inc.	CPP-BEL PRESSER (rental)
GREENE ST.	Greene Street Music 354 Van Duzer Street Stapleton, NY 10304	
GREENWOOD	Greenwood Press, Inc. 88 Post Road West P.O. Box 5007 Westport, CT 06881	WORLD
GREGG	Gregg International Publishers, Ltd. 1 Westmead, Farnborough Hants GU14 7RU England	
GREGGMS	Gregg Music Sources P.O. Box 868 Novato, CA 94947	
	Gregorian Institute of America see GIA	
GROEN	Muziekuitgeverij Saul B. Groen Ferdinand Bolstraat 6 NL-1072 LJ Amsterdam Netherlands	
GROSCH	Edition Grosch Phillip Grosch Bahnhofstrasse 94a D-8032 Gräfelfing Germany	THOMI
GROVEN	Eivind Grovens Institutt for Reinstemming Ekebergveien 59 N-1181 Oslo 11 Norway	
GUARANI	Ediciones Musicals Mundo Guarani Sarmiento 444 Buenos Aires Argentina	
GUILYS	Edition Guilys Case Postale 90 CH-1702 Fribourg 2 Switzerland	
GUNMAR	Gunmar Music, Inc. see Margun/Gunmar Music, Inc.	JERONA
HA MA R	Ha Ma R Percussion Publications, Inc. 333 Spring Road Huntington, NY 11743	BOOSEY

Code	Publisher	U.S. Agent
HAMBLEN	Stuart Hamblen Music Co. 26101 Ravenhill Road Canyon Country, CA 91351	
HAMELLE	Hamelle & Cie 175 rue Saint-Honoré F-75040 Paris Cedex 01 France	KING,R PRESSER SOUTHERN
HAMPE	Adolf Hampe Musikverlag Hohenzollerndamm 54A D-1000 Berlin 33 Germany	BUDDE
HAMPTON	Hampton Edition	MARKS
HANSEN-DEN	Wilhelm Hansen Musikforlag Bornholmsgade 1,1 1266 Copenhagen K Denmark	SCHIRM.G
HANSEN-ENG	Hansen, London see CHESTER	
HANSEN-GER	Edition Wilhelm Hansen, Frankfurt	SCHIRM.G
HANSEN-NY	Edition Wilhelm Hansen- Chester Music New York Inc. New York, NY	SCHIRM.G
HANSEN-SWED	Edition Wilhelm Hansen see NORDISKA	SCHIRM.G
HANSEN-US	Hansen House Publications, Inc. 1824 West Avenue Miami Beach, FL 33139-9913	
HANSSLER	Hänssler-Verlag Röntgenstrasse 15 Postfach 1230 D-7312 Kirchheim/Teck Germany	ANTARA
HARGAIL	Hargail Music Press P.O. Box 118 Saugerties, NY 12477	
HARMONIA	Harmonia-Uitgave P.O. Box 126 NL-1200 AC Hilversum Netherlands	FOR.MUS.DIST.
HARMS,TB	T.B. Harms	WARNER
HARMUSE	Harmuse Publications 529 Speers Road Oakville, Ontario L6K 2G4 Canada	
HARP PUB	Harp Publications 3437-2 Tice Creek Drive Walnut Creek, CA 94595	
HARRIS	Frederick Harris Music Co., Ltd. 529 Speers Road Oakville, Ontario L6K 2G4 Canada	HARRIS-US
HARRIS-US	Frederick Harris Company, Ltd. 340 Nagel Drive Buffalo, NY 14225-4731	
HARRIS,R	Ron Harris Publications 22643 Paul Revere Drive Woodland Hills, CA 91364	
HART	F. Pitman Hart & Co., Ltd.	BRODT
HARTH	Harth Musikverlag Karl-Liebknecht-Straße 12 DDR-701 Leipzig Germany	PRO MUSICA

Code	Publisher	U.S. Agent
HASLINGER	Verlag Carl Haslinger Tuchlauben 11 A-1010 Wien Austria	FOR.MUS.DIST.
HASTINGS	Hastings Music Corp.	CPP-BEL
HATCH	Earl Hatch Publications 5008 Aukland Ave. Hollywood, CA 91601	
HATIKVAH	Hatikvah Publications	TRANSCON.
HAWK	Hawk Music Press 668 Fairmont Avenue Oakland, CA 94611	
HAYMOZ	Haydn-Mozart Presse	EUR.AM.MUS.
	Hebrew Union College Sacred Music Press see SAC.MUS.PR.	
HEER	Joh. de Heer & Zn. B.V. Muziek-Uitgeverij en Groothandel Rozenlaan 113, Postbus 3089 NL-3003 AB Rotterdam Netherlands	
HEIDELBERGER	Heidelberger	BAREN.
HEILMAN	Heilman Music P.O. Box 1044 Fairmont, WV 26554	
HEINRICH.	Heinrichshofen's Verlag Liebigstraße 16 Postfach 620 D-2940 Wilhelmshaven Germany	PETERS
HELBING	Edition Helbling Kaplanstraße 9 A-6021 Neu-Rum b. Innsbruck Austria	
HELBS	Helbling Edition Pffäfikerstraße 6 CH-8604 Volketswil-Zürich Switzerland	
HELICON	Helicon Music Corp.	EUR.AM.MUS.
HELIOS	Editio Helios	FOSTER
HENKLE	Ted Henkle 5415 Reynolds Street Savannah, GA 31405	
HENLE	G. Henle Verlag Forstenrieder Allee 122 Postfach 71 04 66 D-8000 München 71 Germany G. Henle USA, Inc. P.O. Box 1753 2446 Centerline Industrial Drive St. Louis, MO 63043	
HENMAR	Henmar Press	PETERS
HENN	Editions Henn 8 rue de Hesse Genève Switzerland	
HENREES	Henrees Music Ltd.	EMI
HERALD	Herald Press 616 Walnut Avenue Scottdale, PA 15683	
HERITAGE	Heritage Music Press	LORENZ
HERITAGE PUB	Heritage Music Publishing Co.	CENTURY

Code	Publisher	U.S. Agent
HEUGEL	Heugel & Cie 175 rue Saint-Honoré F-75040 Paris Cedex 01 France	KING,R PRESSER SOUTHERN
HEUWEKE.	Edition Heuwekemeijer & Zoon Postbus 289 NL-1740 AG Schagen Netherlands	PRESSER
HHP	Hollow Hills Press 7 Landview Drive Dix Hills, NY 11746	
HIEBER	Musikverlag Max Hieber KG Liebfrauenstrasse 1 D-8000 München 2 Germany	FOR.MUS.DIST.
HIGH GR	Higher Ground Music Publishing	ALEX.HSE.
HIGHGATE	Highgate Press	SCHIRM.EC
HIGHLAND	Highland/Etling Music Co. 1344 Newport Avenue Long Beach, CA 90804	
HINRICHSEN	Hinrichsen Edition, Ltd.	PETERS
HINSHAW	Hinshaw Music, Inc. P.O. Box 470 Chapel Hill, NC 27514	
HINZ	Hinz Fabrik Verlag Lankwitzerstraße 17-18 D-1000 Berlin 42 Germany	
HIRSCHS	Abr. Hirschs Forlag Box 505 S-101 26 Stockholm Sweden	GEHRMANS
HISPAVOX	Ediciones Musicales Hispavox Cuesta Je Santo Domingo 11 Madrid Spain	
HOA	HOA Music Publisher 756 S. Third Street Dekalb, IL 60115	
HOFFMAN,R	Raymond A. Hoffman Co. c/o Fred Bock Music Co. P.O. Box 333 Tarzana, CA 91356	ANTARA
HOFMEISTER	VEB Friedrich Hofmeister, Musikverlag, Leipzig Karlstraße 10 DDR-701 Leipzig East Germany	
HOFMEISTER-W	Friedrich Hofmeister Musikverlag, Taunus Ubierstraße 20 D-6238 Hofheim am Taunus West Germany	
HOHLER	Heinrich Hohler Verlag	SCHNEIDER,H
	Hollow Hills Press see HHP	
HOLLY-PIX	Holly-Pix Music Publishing Co.	WESTERN

Code	Publisher	U.S. Agent
HONG KONG	Hong Kong Music Media Publishing Co., Ltd. Kai It Building, 9th Floor 58 Pak Tai Street Tokwawan, Kowloon Hong Kong	
HONOUR	Honour Publications	WESTERN
HOPE	Hope Publishing Co. 380 South Main Place Carol Stream, IL 60188	
HORNPIPE	Hornpipe Music Publishing Co. 400 Commonwealth Avenue P.O. Box CY577 Boston, MA 02215	
HUEBER	Hueber-Holzmann Pädagogischer Verlag Krausstraße 30 D-8045 Ismaning, München Germany	
HUG	Hug & Co. Flughofstrasse 61 CH-Glattbrugg Switzerland	SOUTHERN
HUGUENIN	Charles Huguenin & Pro-Arte Rue du Sapin 2a CH-2114 Fleurier Switzerland	
HUHN	W. Huhn Musikalien-Verlag Jahnstraße 9 D-5880 Lüdenshied Germany	
HULST	De Hulst Kruisdagenlaan 75 B-1040 Bruxelles Belgium	
HUNTZINGER	R.L. Huntzinger Publications	WILLIS
HURON	Huron Press P.O. Box 2121 London, Ontario N6A 4C5 Canada	
ICELAND	Iślenzk Tónverkamidstöd Iceland Music Information Centre Freyjugata 1 P.O. Box 978 121 Reykjavik Iceland	ELKAN,H
IISM	Istituto Italiano per la Storia della Musica Academia Nazionale di Santa Cecilia Via Vittoria, 6 I-00187 Roma Italy	
IMB	Internationale Musikbibliothek	BAREN.
IMC	Indiana Music Center 322 South Swain P.O. Box 582 Bloomington, IN 47401	
IMPERO	Impero-Verlag Liebigstraße 16 D-2940 Wilhelmshavn Germany	PRESSER (partial)
INDEPENDENT	Independent Publications P.O. Box 162 Park Station Paterson, NJ 07513	

Code	Publisher	U.S. Agent
INDIANA	Indiana University Press Tenth & Morton Streets Bloomington, IN 47405	
INST ANT	Instrumenta Antiqua, Inc. 2530 California Street San Francisco, CA 94115	
INST.CO.	The Instrumentalist 200 Northfield Road Northfield, IL 60093-3390	
	Institute Of Stringed Instruments Guitar & Lute see ISI	
	Editorial Cooperativa Inter-Americana de Compositores see ECOAM	
INTERLOCH	Interlochen Press	CRESCENDO
INTERNAT.	International Music Co. 5 W. 37th Street New York, NY 10018	
INTER.MUS.P.	International Music Publications Woodford Trading Estate Southend Road Woodford Green, Essex IG8 8HN England	
	Internationale Musikbibliothek see IMB	
INTERNAT.S.	International Music Service P.O. Box 66, Ansonia Station New York, NY 10023	
IONA	Iona Music Publishing Service P.O. Box 8131 San Marino, CA 91108	
IONE	Ione Press	SCHIRM.EC
IRIS	Iris Verlag Hernerstraße 64A Postfach 100.851 D-4350 Recklinghausen Germany	
IROQUOIS PR	Iroquois Press P.O. Box 2121 London, Ontario N6A 4C5 Canada	
	Íslenzk Tónverkamidstöd see ICELAND	
ISI	Institute of Stringed Instruments, Guitar & Lute Poststraße 30 4 Düsseldorf Germany	SANDVOSS
	Aux Presses d'Isle-de-France see PRESSES	
ISR.MUS.INST.	Israel Music Institute P.O. Box 3004 61030 Tel Aviv Israel	BOOSEY (rental)
ISR.PUB.AG.	Israel Publishers Agency 7, Arlosoroff Street Tel-Aviv Israel	
ISRAELI	Israeli Music Publications, Ltd. 25 Keren Hayesod Jerusalem 94188 Israel	PRESSER

Code	Publisher	U.S. Agent
	Istituto Italiano per la Storia della Musica see IISM	
J.B.PUB	J.B. Publications 404 Holmes Circle Memphis TN 38111	
J.C.A.	Japan Composers Association 3-7-15, Akasaka Minato-Ku Tokyo Japan	
JACKMAN	Jackman Music Corp. P.O. Box 900 Orem, UT 84057	MUSICART
JAPAN	Japan Federation of Composers Shinanomachi Building 602 33 Shinanomachi Shinjuku-Ku Tokyo Japan	
JAREN	Jaren Music Co. 9691 Brynmar Drive Villa Park, CA 92667	
JASE	Jasemusiikki Ky Box 136 SF-13101 Hämeenlinna 10 Finland	
JAZZ ED	Jazz Education Publications P.O. Box 802 Manhattan, KS 66502	
JEANNETTE	Ed. Jeannette	DONEMUS
JEHLE	Jehle	HANSSLER
JENSON	Jenson Publications, Inc. 7777 W. Bluemound Road Milwaukee, WI 53213	
JERONA	Jerona Music Corp. P.O. Box 5010 Hackensack, NJ 07606-4210	
JOAD	Joad Press 4 Meredyth Road London SW13 0DY England	FISCHER,C (rental- partial)
JOBERT	Editions Jean Jobert 76, rue Quincampoix F-75003 Paris France	PRESSER
JOHNSON	Johnson Reprint Corp. 757 3rd Avenue New York, NY 10017	
JOHNSON,P	Paul Johnson Productions P.O. Box 2001 Irving, TX 75061	
JOSHUA	Joshua Corp.	GENERAL
JRB	JRB Music Education Materials Distributor	PRESSER
JUNNE	Otto Junne GmbH Sendlinger-Tor-Platz 10 D-8000 München Germany	
JUS-AUTOR	Jus-Autor Sofia, Bulgaria	BREITKOPF-W
JUSKO	Jusko Publications	WILLIS

Code	Publisher	U.S. Agent
KAHNT	C.F. Kahnt, Musikverlag Kennedyalle 101 6000 Frankfurt 70 Germany	PETERS
KALMUS	Edwin F. Kalmus P.O. Box 5011 Boca Raton, FL 33431	CPP-BEL (string and miniature scores)
KALMUS,A	Alfred A. Kalmus Ltd. 38 Eldon Way, Paddock Wood Tonbridge, Kent TN12 6BE England	EUR.AM.MUS.
KAMMEN	J. & J. Kammen Music Co.	CENTURY
KAPLAN	Ida R. Kaplan 1308 Olivia Avenue Ann Arbor, MI 48104	
KARTHAUSE	Karthause Verlag Panzermacherstrasse 5 D-5860 Iserlohn Germany	
KAWAI	Kawai Gafuku	JAPAN
KAWE	Edition KaWe Brederodestraat 90 NL-1054 VC Amsterdam 13 Netherlands	KING,R
KAY PR	Kay Press 612 Vicennes Court Cincinnati, OH 45231	
KELTON	Kelton Publications 1343 Amalfi Drive Pacific Palisades, CA 90272	
KENDALE	Kendale Company 6595 S. Dayton Street Englewood, CO 80111	
KENDOR	Kendor Music Inc. Main & Grove Streets P.O. Box 278 Delevan, NY 14042	
KENSING.	Kensington Music Service P.O. Box 471 Tenafly, NJ 07670	
KENYON	Kenyon Publications	LEONARD-US
KERBY	E.C. Kerby Ltd. 198 Davenport Road Toronto, Ontario M5R IJ2 Canada	LEONARD-US BOOSEY (rental)
KINDRED	Kindred Press	HERALD
KING,R	Robert King Sales, Inc. Shovel Shop Square 28 Main Street, Bldg. 15 North Easton, MA 02356	
KISTNER	Fr. Kistner & C.F.W. Siegel & Co. Adrian-Kiels-Straße 2 D-5000 Köln 90 Germany	CONCORDIA
KJOS	Neil A. Kjos Music Co. 4382 Jutland Drive Box 178270 San Diego, CA 92117-0894	
KLIMENT	Musikverlag Johann Kliment Kolingasse 15 A-1090 Wien 9 Austria	
KNEUSSLIN	Edition Kneusslin Amselstraße 43 CH-4059 Basel Switzerland	FOR.MUS.DIST.

Code	Publisher	U.S. Agent
KNOPF	Alfred A. Knopf 201 East 50th Street New York, NY 10022	
KNUF	Frits Knuf Uitgeverij Rodeheldenstraat 13 P.O. Box 720 NL-4116 ZJ Buren Netherlands	PENDRGN
KODALY	Kodaly Center of America, Inc. 1326 Washington Street West Newton, MA 02165	SUPPORT
KON BOND	Kon. Bond van Chr. Zang- en Oratoriumverenigingen	DONEMUS
KONINKLIJK	Koninklijk Nederlands Zangersverbond	DONEMUS
KOPER	Musikverlag Karl-Heinz Köper Schneekoppenweg 12 D-3001 Isernhagen NB/Hannover Germany	
KRENN	Ludwig Krenn Verlag Neulerchenfelderstr. 3-7 A-1160 Wien Austria	
KROMPHOLZ	Krompholz & Co Spitalgasse 28 CH-3001 Bern Switzerland	
KRUSEMAN	Ed. Philip Kruseman	DONEMUS
KUNZEL	Edition Kunzelmann Grutstrasse 28 CH-8134 Adliswil Switzerland	FOR.MUS.DIST.
KYSAR	Michael Kysar 1250 South 211th Place Seattle, WA 98148	
LAKES	Lake State Publishers P.O. Box 1593 Grand Rapids, MI 49501	
LAMP	Latin-American Music Pub. Co. Ltd. 8 Denmark Street London England	
LAND	A. Land & Zn. Muziekuitgevers	DONEMUS
LANDES	Landesverband Evangelischer Kirchenchöre in Bayern	HANSSLER
LANG	Lang Music Publications P.O. Box 11021 Indianapolis, IN 46201	
LANSMAN	Länsmansgarden PL-7012 S-762 00 Rimbo Sweden	
	Latin-American Music Pub. Co. Ltd. see LAMP	
LAUDINELLA	Laudinella Reihe	FOSTER
LAUMANN	Laumann Verlag Alter Gartenweg 14 Postfach 1360 D-4408 Dülmen Germany	
LAUREL	Laurel Press	LORENZ
LAVENDER	Lavender Publications, Ltd. Borough Green Sevenoaks, Kent TN15 8DT England	

Code	Publisher	U.S. Agent	Code	Publisher	U.S. Agent
LAWSON	Lawson-Gould Music Publishers, Inc. 250 W. 57th St., Suite 932 New York, NY 10107	ALFRED	LINDSBORG	Lindsborg Press P.O. Box 737 State Road 9 South Alexandria, VA 46001	ANTARA
LEA	Lea Pocket Scores P.O. Box 138, Audubon Station New York, NY 10032	EUR.AM.MUS.	LINGUA	Lingua Press P.O. Box 3416 Iowa City, IA 52244	
LEAWOOD	Leawood Music Press	ANTARA	LISTER	Mosie Lister	LILLENAS
LEDUC	Alphonse Leduc 175 rue Saint-Honoré F-75040 Paris Cedex 01 France	KING,R SOUTHERN PRESSER (rental)	LITOLFF,H	Henry Litolff's Verlag Kennedy Allee 101 Postfach 700906 D-6000 Frankfurt 70 Germany	PETERS
LEEDS	Leeds Music Ltd. MCA Building 2450 Victoria Park Avenue Willowdale, Ontario M2J 4A2 Canada	MCA	LITURGICAL	Liturgical Music Press St. Johns Abbey Collegeville, MN 56321	
LEMOINE	Henry Lemoine & Cie 17, rue Pigalle F-75009 Paris France	PRESSER	LLUQUET	Guillermo Lluquet Almacen General de Musica Avendida del Oeste 43 Valencia Spain	
LENGNICK	Alfred Lengnick & Co., Ltd. Purley Oaks Studios 421a Brighton Road South Croydon CR2 6YR, Surrey England			London Pro Musica Edition see LPME	
LEONARD-ENG	Leonard, Gould & Bolttler		LONG ISLE	Long Island Music Publishers	BRANCH
LEONARD-US	Hal Leonard Music 7777 West Bluemound Road Milwaukee, WI 53213		LOOP	Loop Music Co.	KJOS
LESLIE	Leslie Music Supply P.O. Box 471 Oakville, Ontario L6J 5A8 Canada	BRODT	LORENZ	Lorenz Corporation 501 East Third Street P.O. Box 802 Dayton, OH 45401-9969	
LEUCKART	F.E.C. Leuckart Nibelungenstraße 48 D-8000 München 19 Germany	LEONARD-US SCHIRM.G (rental)	LPME	The London Pro Musica Edition 15 Rock Street Brighton BN2 1NF England	MAGNA D
LEXICON	Lexicon Music P.O. Box 2222 Newbury Park, CA 91320		LUCKS	Luck's Music Library P.O. Box 71397 Madison Heights, MI 48071	
LIBEN	Liben Music Publications 1191 Eversole Road Cincinnati, OH 45230		LUDWIG	Ludwig Music Publishing Co. 557-67 East 140th Street Cleveland, OH 44110	
LIBER	Svenska Utbildningsförlaget Liber AB Utbildningsförlaget, Centrallagret S-136 01 Handen Stockholm Sweden		LUNDEN	Edition Lundén Bromsvagen 25 S-125 30 Alvsjö Sweden	
LICHTENAUER	W.F. Lichtenauer	DONEMUS	LUNDMARK	Lundmark Publications 811 Bayliss Drive Marietta, GA 30067	SUPPORT
LIED	VEB Lied der Zeit Musikverlag Rosa-Luxemburg-Straße 41 DDR-102 Berlin East Germany		LUNDQUIST	Abr. Lundquist Musikförlag AB Katarina Bangata 17 S-116 25 Stockholm Sweden	
LIENAU	Robert Lienau, Musikverlag Lankwitzerstraße 9 D-1000 Berlin 45 Germany	PETERS	LYCHE	Harald Lyche Postboks 2171 Stromso N-3001 Drammen Norway	WALTON (partial)
LILLENAS	Lillenas Publishing Co. P.O. Box 419527 Kansas City, MO 64141		LYDIAN ORCH	Lydian Orchestrations 31000 Ruth Hill Road Orange Cove, CA 93646	SHAWNEE
LINDSAY	Lindsay Music 23 Hitchin Street Biggleswade, Beds SG18 8AX England	PRESSER	LYRA	Lyra Music Co. 133 West 69th Street New York, NY 10023	
			MACNUTT	Richard Macnutt Ltd. Hamm Farm House Withyham, Hartfield Sussex TN7 4BJ England	

Code	Publisher	U.S. Agent
	Mac Murray Publications see MMP	
MAGNA D	Magnamusic Distributors Route 49 Sharon, CT 06069	
MALCOLM	Malcolm Music Ltd.	SHAWNEE
MANNA	Manna Music, Inc. 22510 Stanford Avenue Suite 101 Valencia, CA 91355	
MANNHEIM	Mannheimer Musikverlag Kunigundestraße 4 D-5300 Bonn 2 Germany	
MANU. PUB	Manuscript Publications 120 Maple Street Wrightsville, PA 17368	
MAPA MUNDI	Mapa Mundi—Music Publishers 72 Brewery Road London N7 9NE England	SCHIRM.EC
MARBOT	Edition Marbot GmbH Mühlenkamp 43 D-2000 Hamburg 60 Germany	PEER
MARCHAND	Marchand, Paap en Strooker	DONEMUS
MARGUN	Margun/Gunmar Music, Inc. 167 Dudley Road Newton Centre, MA 02159	JERONA
MARI	E. & O. Mari, Inc. 38-01 23rd Avenue Long Island City, NY 11105	
MARK	Mark Publications	CRESPUB
MARKS	Edward B. Marks Music Corp. 1619 Broadway New York, NY 10019	LEONARD-US (sales) PRESSER (rental)
MARSEG	Marseg, Ltd. 18 Farmstead Road Willowdale, Ontario M2L 2G2 Canada	
MARTIN	Editions Robert Martin 106, Grande rue de la Coupée F-71009 Charnay-les-Macon France	PRESSER
MASTER	Master Music	CRESPUB
MAURER	J. Maurer Avenue du Verseau 7 B-1020 Brussel Belgium	
MAURRI	Edizioni Musicali Ditta R. Maurri Via del Corso 1 (17 R.) Firenze Italy	
MCA	MCA and Mills/MCA Joint Venture Editions 1755 Broadway, 8th Floor New York, NY 10019	LEONARD-US (sales) PRESSER (rental)
MCAFEE	McAfee Music Corp.	CPP-BEL
MCGIN-MARX	McGinnis & Marx 236 West 26th Street, #11S New York, NY 10001	

Code	Publisher	U.S. Agent
MDV	Mitteldeutscher Verlag Thalmannplatz 2, Postfach 295 DDR-4010 Halle — Saale Germany	PETERS
MEDIA	Media Press P.O. Box 250 Elwyn, PA 19063	
MEDICI	Medici Press 100 W. 24th Street Owensboro, KY 42301	
MEDIT	Mediterranean	GALAXY
MEL BAY	Mel Bay Publications, Inc. P.O. Box 66 Pacific, MO 63069	
MELE LOKE	Mele Loke Publishing Co. Box 7142 Honolulu, Hawaii 96821	HIGHLAND (continental U.S.A.)
MELODI	Casa Editrice Melodi S.A. Galleria Del Corso 4 Milano Italy	
MENC	Music Educators National Conference Publications Division 1902 Association Drive Reston, VA 22091	
MERCATOR	Mercator Verlag & Wohlfahrt (Gert) Verlag Köhnenstraße 5-11 Postfach 100609 D-4100 Duisberg 1 Germany	
MERCURY	Mercury Music Corp.	PRESSER
MERIDIAN	Les Nouvelles Éditions Meridian 5, rue Lincoln F-75008 Paris 8 France	
MERION	Merion Music, Inc.	PRESSER
MERRYMOUNT	Merrymount Music, Inc.	PRESSER
MERSEBURGER	Merseburger Verlag Motzstraße 13 D-3500 Kassel Germany	
METRO	Metro Muziek Uilenweg 38 Postbus 70 NL-6000 AB Weert Netherlands	
METROPOLIS	Editions Metropolis Van Ertbornstraat, 5 B-2018 Antwerpen Belgium	ELKAN,H
MEULEMANS	Arthur Meulemans Fonds Charles de Costerlaan, 6 2050 Antwerpen Belgium	
MEXICANAS	Ediciones Mexicanas de Musica Avenida Juarez 18 Mexico City Mexico	PEER
MEZ KNIGA	Mezhdunarodnaya Kniga 39, Dimitrov St. Moscow 113095 U.S.S.R.	
MIDDLE	Middle Eight Music	CPP-BEL
MILLER	Miller Music Corp.	CPP-BEL

Code	Publisher	U.S. Agent	Code	Publisher	U.S. Agent
MILLS MUSIC	Mills Music Jewish Catalogue	TRANSCON. PRESSER (rental)	MT.SALUS	Mt. Salus Music 709 East Leake Street Clinton, MS 39056	
MINKOFF	Minkoff Reprints 8 rue Eynard CH-1211 Genève 12 Switzerland		MT.TAHO	Mt. Tahoma	BROUDE,A
MIRA	Mira Music Associates 199 Mountain Road Wilton, CT 06897		MULLER	Willy Müller, Süddeutscher Musikverlag Marzgasse 5 D-6900 Heidelberg Germany	
	Mitteldeutscher Verlag see MDV		MUNSTER	Van Munster Editie	DONEMUS
MJQ	M.J.Q. Music, Inc. 1697 Broadway #1100 New York, NY 10019	FOX,S	MURPHY	Spud Murphy Publications	WESTERN
			MUS.ANT.BOH.	Musica Antiqua Bohemica	SUPRAPHON
MMB	MMB Music, Inc. 10370 Page Industrial Boulevard St. Louis, MO 63132		MUS.ART	Music Art Publications P.O. Box 1744 Chula Vista, CA 92010	
MMP	Mac Murray Publications	MUS.SAC.PRO.	MUS.PERC.	Music For Percussion, Inc. 17 West 60th Street New York, NY 10023	
MMS	Monumenta Musica Svecicae	STIM			
MOBART	Mobart Music Publications	JERONA	MUS.RARA	Musica Rara Le Traversier Chemin de la Buire F-84170 Monteux France	
MOD ART	Modern Art Music	SON-KEY			
MODERN	Edition Modern Musikverlag Hans Wewerka Elisabethstraße 38 D-8000 München 40 Germany		MUS.SAC.PRO	Musica Sacra et Profana P.O. Box 7248 Berkeley, CA 94707	
MOECK	Hermann Moeck Verlag Postfach 143 D-3100 Celle 1 Germany	EUR.AM.MUS. MAGNA D	MUS.SUR	Musica del Sur Apartado 5219 Barcelona Spain	
MOLENAAR	Molenaar's Muziekcentrale Industrieweg 23 Postbus 19 NL-1520 AA Wormerveer Netherlands	GM	MUS.VERA	Musica Vera Graphics & Publishers 350 Richmond Terrace 4-M Staten Island, NY 10301	ARISTA
MONDIAL	Mondial-Verlag KG 8 rue de Hesse Genève Switzerland		MUS.VIVA	Musica Viva 262 King's Drive Eastbourne Sussex, BN21 2XD England	
MONTEVERDI	Fondazione Claudio Monteverdi Corso Garibaldi 178 I-26100 Cremona Italy		MUS.VIVA HIST.	Musica Viva Historica	SUPRAPHON
			MUSIA	Musia	PETERS
	Moravian Music Foundation	CPP-BEL BOOSEY BRODT PETERS	MUSIC	Music Sales Corp. Executive Offices 225 Park Avenue South New York, NY 10003 Music Sales Corp. (Rental) 5 Bellvale Road Chester, NY 10918	
MORN.ST.	Morning Star Music Publishers 3303 Meramec, Suites 205-207 St. Louis, MO 63118-4310		MUSIC BOX	Music Box Dancer Publications Ltd.	PRESSER
MOSAIC	Mosaic Music Corporation	BOSTON		Music Educators National Conference see MENC	
MOSELER	Karl Heinrich Möseler Verlag Hoffman-von-Fallersleben-Straße 8-10 Postfach 1460 D-3340 Wolfenbüttel Germany		MUSIC-ENG	Music Sales Ltd. Newmarket Road Bury St. Edmunds Suffolk IP33 3YB England	MUSIC
MOSER	Verlag G. Moser Kirschweg 8 CH-4144 Arlesheim Switzerland		MUSIC INFO	Muzicki Informativni Centar—ZAMP Ulica 8 Maja 37 P.O. Box 959 YU-41001 Zagreb Yugoslavia	BREITKOPF-W
MOWBRAY	Mowbray Music Publications Saint Thomas House Becket Street Oxford OX1 1SJ England	PRESSER	MUSIC SEV.	Music 70, Music Publishers 170 N.E. 33rd Street Fort Lauderdale, FL 33334	PLYMOUTH
MSM	MSM Music Publishers	BRODT		Société d'Éditions Musicales Internationales see SEMI	

Code	Publisher	U.S. Agent
MUSICART	Musicart West P.O. Box 1900 Orem, UT 84059	
MUSICIANS PUB	Musicians Publications P.O. Box 7160 West Trenton, NJ 08628	
MUSICO	Musico Muziekuitgeverij	DONEMUS
MUSICPRINT	Musicprint Corporation P.O. Box 20767 New York, NY 10023	BROUDE,A
MUSICUS	Edition Musicus P.O. Box 1341 Stamford, CT 06904	
MUSIKAL.	Musikaliska Konstföreningen Aarstryck, Sweden	WALTON
MUSIKHOJ	Musikhojskolens Forlag ApS	EUR.AM.MUS.
MUSIKINST	Verlag das Musikinstrument Klüberstraße 9 D-6000 Frankfurt-am-Main Germany	
MUSIKK	Musikk-Huset A-S P.O. Box 822 Sentrum 0104 Oslo 1 Norway	
MUSIKWISS.	Musikwissenschaftlicher Verlag Wien Dorotheergasse 10 A-1010 Wien 1 Austria	FOR.MUS.DIST. PETERS (Bruckner works only)
	Eerste Muziekcentrale see EERSTE	
MYRRH	Myrrh Music	WORD
MYRTLE	Myrtle Monroe Music 2600 Tenth Street Berkeley, CA 94710	
NAGELS	Nagels Verlag	FOR.MUS.DIST.
NATIONAL	National Music Publishers 16605 Townhouse Tustin, CA 91680	ANTARA
NEUE	Verlag Neue Musik Leipziger Straße 26 Postfach 1306 DDR-1080 Berlin Germany	BROUDE,A
NEW HORIZON	New Horizon Publications	TRANSCON.
NEW MUSIC	The New Music Co., Inc. 6595 S. Dayton St. Englewood, CO 80111	SON-KEY
	New Music Edition see NME	
NEW MUSIC WEST	New Music West P.O. Box 7434 Van Nuys, CA 91409	
NEW VALLEY	New Valley Music Press of Smith College Sage Hall 49 Northampton, MA 01063	
NIEUWE	De Nieuwe Muziekhandel	DONEMUS
NIPPON	Nippon Hosu	PRESSER
NME	New Music Edition	PRESSER

Code	Publisher	U.S. Agent
NO.AM.LIT.	North American Liturgy Resources Choral Music Department 10802 North 23rd Avenue Phoenix, AZ 85029	
NOBILE	Nobile Verlag Aixheimer Straße 26 D-7000 Stuttgart 75 Germany	
NOETZEL	Noetzel Musikverlag Liebigstraße 16 Postfach 620 D-2940 Wilhelmshavn Germany	PETERS
NOMOS	Edition Nomos	BREITKOPF-W
NOORDHOFF	P. Noordhoff	DONEMUS
NORDISKA	AB Nordiska Musikförlaget Nybrogatan 3 S-114 34 Stockholm Sweden	
	See also HANSEN-SWEDEN	
NORGE	Norsk Musikkinformasjon Toftesgatan 69 N-0552 Oslo 5 Norway	
NORRUTH	Norruth Music Publishers	MMB
NORSK	Norsk Musikforlag AS Karl Johansgaten 39 P.O. Box 1499 Vika N-0116 Oslo 1 Norway	
NORTHRIDGE	Northridge Music, Inc. 7317 Greenback Lane Citrus Heights, CA 95621	CPP-BEL
NORTON	W.W. Norton & Co., Inc. 500 Fifth Avenue New York, NY 10003	
	Norwegian Music Information Center see NORGE	
NOSKE	A.A. Noske	DONEMUS
NOTERIA	Noteria S-890 30 Borensberg Sweden	STIM
NOVA	Nova Music Ltd. Goldsmid Mews 15a Farm Road Hove Sussex BN3 1FB England	SCHIRM.EC
NOVELLO	Novello & Co., Ltd. 8-10 Lower James Street London W1R 3PL England	PRESSER
NOW VIEW	Now View	PLYMOUTH
	Nuova Carisch s.r.l. Via M.F. Quintiliano, 40 20138 Milano Italy	
NYMPHEN	Edition Nymphenburg Unterföhring, W. Germany	PETERS
OAK	Oak Publications	MUSIC
OCTAVA	Octava Music Co., Ltd.	WEINBERGER
OECUM	Oecumuse 51 Eleanor Road Bounds Green London N11 2QS England	CANTORIS

Code	Publisher	U.S. Agent	Code	Publisher	U.S. Agent
OISEAU	Éditions de L'Oiseau-Lyre Les Remparts Boite Postale 515 MC-98015 Monaco Cedex	MAGNA D	OUVRIERES	Les Éditions Ouvrières 12, Avenue Soeur-Rosalie F-75621 Paris Cedex 13, France	KING,R
OJEDA	Raymond J. Ojeda 98 Briar Road Kentfield, CA 94904		OXFORD	Oxford University Press 7-8 Hatherly Street London SW1P 2QT England	
OKRA	Okra Music Corp.	SEESAW	OXFORD	Oxford University Press 200 Madison Avenue New York, NY 10016	
OLIVIAN	Olivian Press	ARCADIA			
OLMS	G. Olms Verlag Hagentorwall 7 D-3200 Hildesheim Germany		PAGANI	O. Pagani & Bro., Inc. c/o P. Deiro Music 289 Bleecker Street New York, NY 10014	
ONGAKU	Ongaku-No-Tomo Sha Co., Ltd. Kagurazaka 6-30, Shinjuku-ku Tokyo Japan	PRESSER	PAGANINI PUB	Paganiniana Publications, Inc. 1 T.F.H. Plaza 3rd & Union Avenues Neptune City, NJ 07753	
OPUS	Opus Music Publishers, Inc. 1318 Chicago Avenue Evanston, IL 60201		PAIDEIA	Paideia Editrice	BAREN.
			PALLMA	Pallma Music Co.	KJOS
OPUS-CZ	Opus Ceskoslavenske Hudobne Vydaratelstro Dunajska 18 CS-815 04 Bratislava Czechoslovakia	BOOSEY (rental)	PAN	Editions Pan Schaffhauserstraße 280 Postfach 176 CH-8057 Zürich Switzerland	PRESSER
OR-TAV	Or-Tav Music Publications Israel Composers League P.O. Box 3200 Tel-Aviv Israel		PAN AM	Pan American Union	PEER
			PANTON	Panton Ricni 12 CS-118 39 Praha 1 Czechoslovakia	
ORGAN	Organ Music Co.	WESTERN			
ORGAN LIT	Organ Literature Foundation 45 Norfolk Road Braintree, MA 02184		PARACLETE	Paraclete Press P.O. Box 1568 Hilltop Plaza, Route 6A Orleans, MA 02653	
ORGMS	Organmaster Music Series 282 Stepstone Hill Guilford, CT 06437		PARAGON	Paragon Music Publishers	CENTURY
			PARAGON ASS.	Paragon Associates	ALEX.HSE.
ORION MUS	Orion Music Press P.O. Box 145, University Station Berrien Springs, MI 49104	OPUS	PARIS	Uitgeverij H.J. Paris	DONEMUS
			PARKS	Parks Music Corp.	KJOS
ORLANDO	Orlando Musikverlag Kaprunerstraße 11 D-8000 München 21 Germany		PASTORALE	Pastorale Music Company 235 Sharon Drive San Antonio, TX 78216	
ORPHEUM	Orpheum Music 10th & Parker Berkeley, CA 94710		PASTORINI	Musikhaus Pastorini AG Kasinostraße 25 CH-5000 Aarau Switzerland	
OSTARA	Ostara Press, Inc.	WESTERN	PATERSON	Paterson's Publications, Ltd. 8-10 Lower James Street London W1R 3PL England	FISCHER,C
OSTER	Österreichischer Bundesverlag Schwarzenberg Platz 5 A-1010 Wien Austria				
OSTIGUY	Editions Jacques Ostiguy Inc. 12790 Rue Yamaska St. Hyacinthe, Quebec Canada J2T 1B3			Patrimoine Musical Canadien see CAN.MUS.HER.	
			PAXTON	Paxton Publications Sevenoaks, Kent, England	PRESSER
OSTNOR	Østnorsk Musikkforlag Nordre Langgate 1 B N-9950 Vardø Norway		PEER	Peer Southern Concert Music 810 Seventh Avenue New York, NY 10019	PRESSER
OTOS	Otos Edizioni Musicali Via Marsilio Ficino, 10 I-50132 Firenze Italy		PEER MUSIK	Peer Musikverlag GmbH Muhlenkamp 43 Postfach 602129 D-2000 Hamburg Germany	PEER

Code	Publisher	U.S. Agent
PEG	Pegasus Musikverlag Liebig Straße 16 Postfach 620 D-2940 Wilhelmshaven Germany	PETERS
PELIKAN	Musikverlag Pelikan	EUR.AM.MUS.
PEMBROKE	Pembroke Music Co., Inc.	FISCHER,C
PENADES	José Penadés En Sanz 12 Valencia Spain	
PENDRGN	Pendragon Press R.R. 1, Box 159 Stuyvesant, NY 12173-9720	
PENGUIN	Penguin Books 120 Woodbine Street Bergenfield, NJ 07621	
PENN STATE	Pennsylvania State University Press 215 Wagner Building University Park, PA 16802	
PENOLL	Penoll Goteberg, Sweden	STIM
PEPPER	J.W. Pepper And Son, Inc. P.O. Box 850 Valley Forge, PA 19482	
PERF.ED.	Performers' Editions	BROUDE BR.
PERMUS	Permus Publications P.O. Box 02033 Columbus, OH 43202	
PETERER	Edition Melodie Anton Peterer Brunnwiesenstraße 26 Postfach 260 CH-8409 Zürich Switzerland	
PETERS	Edition Peters C.F. Peters Corp. 373 Park Avenue South New York, NY 10016 Edition Peters Postfach 746 DDR-7010 Leipzig East Germany C.F. Peters Musikverlag Postfach 700851 Kennedyallee 101 D-6000 Frankfurt 70 Germany Peters Edition Ltd. Bach House 10-12 Baches Street London N1 6DN England	
PETERS,K	Kermit Peters 1515 90th Street Omaha, NE 68124	
PETERS,M	Mitchell Peters 3231 Benda Place Los Angeles, CA 90068	
PFAUEN	Pfauen Verlag Adolfsallee 34 Postfach 471 D-6200 Wiesbaden Germany	
PHILH	Philharmonia	EUR.AM.MUS.

Code	Publisher	U.S. Agent
PHILIPPO	Editions Philippo	ELKAN-V
PIEDMONT	Piedmont Music Co.	PRESSER (rental)
PILES	Piles Editorial de Musica Apartado 8.012 E-46080 Valencia Spain	
PILLIN	Pillin Music	WESTERN
PILLON	Pillon Press	THOMAS
PIONEER	Pioneer Music Press	MUSICART
PIPER	Piper Music Co. P.O. Box 1713 Cincinnati, OH 45201	LIBEN
PLAINSONG	Plainsong & Medieval Music Society Catherine Harbor, Hon. Sec. c/o Turner 72 Brewery Road London N7 9NE England	
PLAYER	Player Press 139-22 Caney Lane Rosedale, NY 11422	
PLENUM	Plenum Publishing Corp. 233 Spring Street New York, NY 10013	DA CAPO
PLESNICAR	Don Plesnicar P.O. Box 4880 Albuquerque, NM 87106	
PLOUGH	Plough Publishing House Rifton, NY 12471	
PLUCKED ST	Plucked String P.O. Box 11125 Arlington, VA 22210	
PLYMOUTH	Plymouth Music Co., Inc. 170 N.E. 33rd Street P.O. Box 24330 Fort Lauderdale, FL 33334	
PODIUM	Podium Music, Inc. 360 Port Washington Boulevard Port Washington, NY 11050	
POLSKIE	Polskie Wydawnictwo Muzyczne Al. Krasinskiego 11a PL31-111 Krakow Poland	LEONARD-US (partial) PRESSER (rental)
POLYPH MUS	Polyphone Music Co.	ARCADIA
POLYPHON	Polyphon Musikverlag	BREITKOPF-W
PORT.MUS.	Portugaliae Musicae Fundaçao Calouste Gulbenkian Avenida de Berna 45 P-1093 Lisboa Codex Portugal	
	Positif Press Ltd. see BRENNAN	
POWER	Power and Glory Music Co. 6595 S. Dayton St. Englewood, CO 80111	SON-KEY
PRAEGER	Praeger Publications 383 Madison Avenue New York, NY 10017	
PREISSLER	Musikverlag Josef Preissler Postfach 521 Bräuhausstraße 8 D-8000 München 2 Germany	

Code	Publisher	U.S. Agent	Code	Publisher	U.S. Agent
PRELUDE	Prelude Publications 150 Wheeler Street Glouchester, MA 01930		PUSTET	Verlag Friedrich Pustet Gutenbergstraße 8 Postfach 339 D-8400 Regensburg 11 Germany	
PRENTICE	Prentice-Hall, Inc. Englewood Cliffs, NJ 07632		PYRAMINX	Pyraminx Publications	ACCURA
PRESSER	Theodore Presser Co. Presser Place Bryn Mawr, PA 19010		QUIROGA	Ediciones Quiroga Alcalá, 70 28009 Madrid Spain	PRESSER
PRESSES	Aux Presses d'Isle-de-France 12, rue de la Chaise F-75007 Paris France		RAHTER	D. Rahter Werderstraße 44 D-2000 Hamburg 13 Germany	PRESSER
PRICE,P	Paul Price Publications 470 Kipp Street Teaneck, NJ 07666		RAMSEY	Basil Ramsey Publisher of Music	BRODT
PRIMAVERA	Editions Primavera	GENERAL	RARITIES	Rarities For Strings Publications 11300 Juniper Drive University Circle Cleveland, OH 44106	
PRINCE	Prince Publications 1125 Francisco Street San Francisco, CA 94109		RECITAL	Recital Publications, Ltd. P.O. Box 1697 Huntsville, TX 77340	
PRO ART	Pro Art Publications, Inc.	CPP-BEL		Regent, Arc & Goodman see GOODMAN	
PRO MUSICA	Pro Musica Verlag Karl-Liebknecht-Straße 12 Postfach 467 DDR-7010 Leipzig Germany		REGENT	Regent Music Corp. 488 Madison Avenue 5th Floor New York, NY 10022	LEONARD-US
PRO MUSICA INTL	Pro Musica International 130 Bylor P.O. Box 1687 Pueblo, CO 81002		REGINA	Regina Verlag Schumannstraße 35 Postfach 6148 D-6200 Wiesbaden 1 Germany	
PROCLAM	Proclamation Productions, Inc. Orange Square Port Jervis, NY 12771				
PROGRESS	Progress Press P.O. Box 12 Winnetka, IL 60093		REGUS	Regus Publisher 10 Birchwood Lane White Bear Lake, MN 55110	
PROPRIUS	Proprius Musik AB Vartavagen 35 S-115 29 Stockholm Sweden		REIMERS	Edition Reimers AB Box 15030 S-16115 Bromma Sweden	PRESSER
PROSVETNI	Prosvetni Servis	DRUSTVO	REINHARDT	Friedrich Reinhardt Verlag Missionsstraße 36 CH-4055 Basel Switzerland	
PROVIDENCE	Providence Music Press 251 Weybosset St. Providence, RI 02903		REN	Les Editions Renaissantes	EUR.AM.MUS.
PROVINCTWN	Provincetown Bookshop Editions 246 Commercial Street Provincetown, MA 02657		RENK	Musikverlag Renk "Varia Edition" Herzog-Heinrich-Straße 21 D-8000 München 2 Germany	
PROWSE	Keith Prowse Music Publishing Co. 138-140 Charing Cross Road London, WC2H 0LD England	INTER.MUS.P	RESEARCH	Research Publications, Inc. Lunar Drive Woodbridge, CT 06525	
PRUETT	Pruett Publishing Co. 2928 Pearl Boulder, CO 80301-9989		RESTOR	Restoration Press	THOMAS
PSALTERY	Psaltery Music Publications P.O. Box 11325 Dallas, TX 75223	KENDALE	REUTER	Reuter & Reuter Förlags AB Box 26072 S-100 41 Stockholm Sweden	
PSI	PSI Press P.O. Box 2320 Boulder, CO 80306		RHODES,R	Roger Rhodes Music, Ltd. P.O. Box 1550, Radio City Station New York, NY 10101	
PURIFOY	Purifoy Publishing P.O. Box 30157 Knoxville, TN 37930	JENSON	RICHMOND	Richmond Music Press, Inc.	
			RICHMOND ORG.	The Richmond Organization 10 Columbus Circle New York, NY 10019	PLYMOUTH

Code	Publisher	U.S. Agent
	see also TRO	
RICORDI-ARG	Ricordi Americana S.A. Cangallo, 1558 1037 Buenos Aires Argentina	LEONARD-US BOOSEY (rental)
RICORDI-BR	Ricordi Brasileira S.A. R. Conselheiro Nebias 773 1 S-10-12 Sao Paolo Brazil	LEONARD-US BOOSEY (rental)
RICORDI-CAN	G. Ricordi & Co. Toronto Canada	LEONARD-US BOOSEY (rental)
RICORDI-ENG	G. Ricordi & Co., Ltd. The Bury, Church Street Chesham, Bucks HP5 1JG England	LEONARD-US BOOSEY (rental)
RICORDI-FR	Société Anonyme des Éditions Ricordi	LEONARD-US BOOSEY (rental)
RICORDI-GER	G. Ricordi & Co. Gewürzmühlstraße 5 D-8000 München 22 Germany	LEONARD-US BOOSEY (rental)
RICORDI-IT	G. Ricordi & Co. Via Salomone 77 I-20138 Milano Italy	LEONARD-US BOOSEY (rental)
RIDEAU	Les Éditions Rideau Rouge 24, rue de Longchamp F-75116 Paris France	**PRESSER** SCHIRM.G
RIES	Ries & Erler Charlottenbrunner Straße 42 D-1000 Berlin 33 (Grunewald) Germany	
RILEY	Dr. Maurice W. Riley Eastern Michigan University 512 Roosevelt Boulevard Ypsilanti, MI 48197	
ROBBINS	Robbins Music Corp.	CPP-BEL
ROBERTON	Roberton Publications The Windmill, Wendover Aylesbury, Bucks, HP22 6JJ England	PRESSER
ROBERTS,L	Lee Roberts Music Publications, Inc. P.O. Box 225 Katonah, NY 10536	
ROBITSCHEK	Adolf Robitschek Musikverlag Graben 14 (Bräunerstraße 2) Postfach 42 A-1011 Wien Austria	
ROCHESTER	Rochester Music Publishers, Inc. 358 Aldrich Road Fairport, NY 14450	ACCURA
RODEHEAVER	Rodeheaver Publications	WORD
ROLLAND	Rolland String Research Associates 404 E. Oregon Urbana, IL 61801	BOOSEY
RONCORP	Roncorp, Inc. P.O. Box 724 Cherry Hill, NJ 08003	
RONGWEN	Rongwen Music, Inc.	BROUDE BR.
ROSSUM	Wed. J.R. van Rossum	ZENGERINK

Code	Publisher	U.S. Agent
ROUART	Rouart-Lerolle & Cie	SCHIRM.G
ROW	R.D. Row Music Co.	FISCHER,C
ROYAL	Royal School of Church Music Addington Palace Croydon, Surrey CR9 5AD England	HINSHAW (partial) CANTORIS
	Associated Board of the Royal Schools of Music see ABRSM	
ROYAL TAP.	Royal Tapestry 50 Music Square West Suite 500A Nashville, TN 37203	ALEX. HSE.
ROZSAVO.	Rozsavölgi & Co.	BUDAPEST
RUBANK	Rubank, Inc. 16215 N.W. 15th Avenue Miami, FL 33169	LEONARD-US
RUBATO	Rubato Musikverlag Hollandstraße 18 A-1020 Wien Austria	DONEMUS
RUH,E	Emil Ruh Musikverlag Zürichstraße 33 CH-8134 Adliswil - Zürich Switzerland	
RUMAN.COMP.	Uniunea Compozitorilor din R.S. România (Union of Rumanian Composers) Str. C. Escarcu No. 2 Bucureşti, Sector 1 Rumania	
RUTGERS	Rutgers University Editions	JERONA
RYDET	Rydet Music Publishers P.O. Box 477 Purchase, NY 10577	
SAC.MUS.PR.	Sacred Music Press of Hebrew Union College One West Fourth Street New York, NY 10012	TRANSCON.
SACRED	Sacred Music Press	LORENZ
SACRED SNGS	Sacred Songs, Inc.	WORD
SALABERT	Francis Salabert Éditions 22 rue Chauchat F-75009 Paris France	LEONARD-US (sales) SCHIRM.G (rental)
SAMFUNDET	Samfundet til udgivelse af Dansk Musik Valkendorfsgade 3 DK-1151 Kobenhavn Denmark	PETERS
SAN ANDREAS	San Andreas Press 3732 Laguna Avenue Palo Alto, CA 94306	
SANJO	Sanjo Music Co. P.O. Box 7000-104 Palos Verdes Peninsula, CA 90274	
SAUL AVE	Saul Avenue Publishing Co. 4172 Fox Hollow Drive Cincinnati, OH 45241-2939	
SAVGOS	Savgos Music Inc. P.O. Box 279 Elizabeth, NJ 07207	

Code	Publisher	U.S. Agent
SCARECROW	The Scarecrow Press, Inc. 52 Liberty Street P.O. Box 656 Metuchen, NJ 08840	
SCHAUM	Schaum Publications, Inc. 2018 East North Avenue Milwaukee, WI 53202	
SCHAUR	Richard Schauer, Music Publishers 67 Belsize Lane, Hampstead London NW3 5AX England	PRESSER
SCHEIDT	Altonaer Scheidt-Ausgabe	HANSS
SCHERZANDO	Muziekuitgeverij Scherzando Lovelingstraat 20-22 B-2000 Antwerpen Belgium	ELKAN,H
SCHIRM.EC	E.C. Schirmer Music Co. 138 Ipswich Street Boston, MA 02215-3534	
SCHIRM.G	G. Schirmer, Inc. (Executive Offices) 225 Park Avenue South New York, NY 10003	LEONARD-US (sales)
	G. Schirmer Rental Performance Dept. 5 Bellvale Road Chester, NY 10918	
SCHMIDT,H	Musikverlag Hermann Schmidt Berliner Straße 26 D-6000 Frankfurt-am-Main 1 Germany	
SCHMITT	Schmitt Music Editions	CPP-BEL
SCHNEIDER,H	Musikverlag Hans Schneider Mozartstraße 6 D-8132 Tutzing Germany	
SCHOLA	Editions Musicales de la Schola Cantorum Rue du Sapin 2A CH-2114 Fleurier Switzerland	PRESSER
SCHOTT	Schott & Co. Ltd. Brunswick Road Ashford, Kent TN23 1DX England	EUR.AM.MUS.
SCHOTT-FRER	Schott Frères 30 rue Saint-Jean B-1000 Bruxelles Belgium	EUR.AM.MUS.
SCHOTT,J	Schott & Co. #301, 3-4-3 Iidabashi, Chiyoda-ku Tokyo 102 Japan	EUR.AM.MUS.
SCHOTTS	B. Schotts Söhne Weihergarten 5 Postfach 3640 D-6500 Mainz Germany	EUR.AM.MUS.
SCHROTH	Edition Schroth Kommandatenstrasse 5A D-1 Berlin 45 Germany	BAREN.
SCHUBERTH	Edward Schuberth & Co., Inc.	CENTURY
SCHUBERTH,J	J. Schuberth & Co. Rothenbaumchaussee 1 D-2000 Hamburg 13 Germany	
SCHUL	Carl L. Schultheiß Denzenbergstraße 35 D-7400 Tübingen Germany	
SCHULZ,FR	Blasmusikverlag Fritz Schulz Am Märzengraben 6 D-7800 Freiburg-Tiengen Germany	
SCHWANN	Musikverlag Schwann	PETERS
SCHWEIZER.	Schweizerischer Kirchengesangbund Markusstrasse 6 CH-2544 Bettlach Switzerland	FOSTER
SCOTT	G. Scott Music Publishing Co.	WESTERN
SCOTT MUSIC	Scott Music Publications	ALFRED
SCOTUS	Scotus Music Publications, Ltd.	ESCHENB
SCREEN	Screen Gems Columbia Pictures	WARNER
SEESAW	Seesaw Music Corp. 2067 Broadway New York, NY 10023	
SELMER	Selmer Éditions 18, rue de la Fontaine-au-Roi F-75011 Paris France	
SEMI	Société d'Editions Musicales Internationales	PEER
SENART	Ed. Maurice Senart 22 rue Chauchat F-75009 Paris France	SCHIRM.G
SERENUS	Serenus Corp. 145 Palisade Street Dobbs Ferry, NY 10522	
SERVANT	Servant Publications P.O. Box 8617 840 Airport Boulevard Ann Arbor, MI 48107	
SESAC	Sesac, Inc. 10 Columbus Circle New York, NY 10019	
SHALL-U-MO	Shall-U-Mo Publications P.O. Box 2824 Rochester, NY 14626	
SHAPIRO	Shapiro, Bernstein & Co., Inc. 10 East 53 Street New York, NY 10022	PLYMOUTH
SHATTINGER	Shattinger Music Co. 1810 S. Broadway St. Louis, MO 63104	
SHAWNEE	Shawnee Press, Inc. 1 Waring Drive Delaware Water Gap, PA 18327	MUSIC
SHEPPARD	John Sheppard Music Press	EUR.AM.MUS.
	Antigua Casa Sherry-Brener, Ltd. see ACSB	
SIDEMTON	Sidemton Verlag	BREITKOPF-W
SIFLER	Paul J. Sifler 3947 Fredonia Drive Hollywood, CA 90068	
SIGHT & SOUND	Sight & Sound International 3200 South 166th Street Box 27 New Berlin, WI 53151	

Code	Publisher	U.S. Agent
SIJN	D. van Sijn & Zonen Banorstraat 1 Rotterdam Netherlands	
SIKORSKI	Hans Sikorski Verlag Johnsallee 23 Postfach 132001 D-2000 Hamburg 13 Germany	SCHIRM.G (rental)
SIMROCK	Nicholas Simrock Lyra House 37 Belsize Lane London NW3 England	PRESSER
SINGSPIR	Singspiration Music The Zondervan Corp. 1415 Lake Drive S.E. Grand Rapids, MI 49506	
SIRIUS	Sirius-Verlag	PETERS
SKAND.	Skandinavisk Musikforlag Gothersgade 9-11 DK-1123 København K. Denmark	
SLATKINE	Slatkine Reprints 5 rue des Chaudronniers Case 765 CH-1211 Genève 3 Switzerland	
SLOV.AKA.	Slovenska Akademija Znanosti in Umetnosti Trg Francoske Revolucije 6 Ljubljana Yugoslavia	DRUSTVO
SLOV.HUD. FOND.	Slovenský Hudobný Fond Fucikova 29 CS-801 00 Bratislava Czechoslovakia	BOOSEY (rental)
SLOV.MAT.	Slovenska Matica	DRUSTVO
SMITH PUB	Smith Publications-Sonic Art Editions 2617 Gwynndale Avenue Baltimore, MD 21207	
SMPF	SMPF, Inc. 16 E. 34th St., 7th Floor New York, NY 10016	
SOC.FR.MUS.	Société Française de Music	TRANSAT.
SOC.PUB.AM.	Society for the Publication of American Music	PRESSER
	Société d'Éditions Musicales Internationales see SEMI	
	Society of Finnish Composers see SUOMEN	
SOLAR	The Solar Studio 178 Cowles Road Woodbury, CT 06798	
SOLID	Solid Foundation Music	SON-KEY
SOMERSET	Somerset Press	HOPE
SON-KEY	Son-Key, Inc. P.O. Box 31757 Aurora, CO 80041	
SONANTE	Sonante Publications P.O. Box 74, Station F Toronto, Ontario M4Y 2L4 Canada	

Code	Publisher	U.S. Agent
SONOS	Sonos Music Resources, Inc. P.O. Box 1510 Orem, UT 84057	
SONSHINE	Sonshine Productions	LORENZ
SONZOGNO	Casa Musicale Sonzogno Via Bigli 11 I-20121 Milano Italy	PRESSER
SOUTHERN	Southern Music Co. 1100 Broadway P.O. Box 329 San Antonio, TX 78292	
SOUTHERN PUB	Southern Music Publishing Co., Pty. Ltd. Sydney, Australia	PEER
SOUTHWEST	Southwest Music Publications Box 4552 Santa Fe, NM 87501	
SPAN.MUS.CTR.	Spanish Music Center, Inc. 4 Division Street P.O. Box 132 Farmingville NY 11738	
SPIRE	Spire Editions	FISCHER,C WORLD
SPRATT	Spratt Music Publishers 17 West 60th Street, 8th Fl. New York, NY 10023	PLYMOUTH
ST.GREG.	St. Gregory Publishing Co. 64 Pineheath Road High Kelling, Holt Norfolk, NR25 6RH England	ROYAL
ST. MARTIN	St. Martin Music Co., Inc.	ROYAL
STAFF	Staff Music Publishing Co., Inc. 170 N.E. 33rd St. Ft. Lauderdale, FL 33334	PLYMOUTH
STAINER	Stainer & Bell Ltd. 82 High Road East Finchley London N2 9PW England	SCHIRM.EC
STAMON	Nick Stamon Press 4280 Middlesex Drive San Diego, CA 92116	
STAMPS	Stamps-Baxter Music Publications Box 4007 Dallas, TX 75208	SINGSPIR
STANDARD	Standard Music Publishing, Inc.	
STANGLAND	Thomas C. Stangland Co. P.O. Box 19263 Portland, OR 97219	
STEIN	Edition Steingräber Auf der Reiswiese 9 D-6050 Offenbach/M. Germany	
STIM	STIMs Informationcentral för Svensk Musik Sandhamnsgatan 79 Box 27327 S-102 54 Stockholm Sweden	
STOCKHAUS	Stockhausen-Verlag Kettenberg 15 D-5067 Kürten Germany	

Code	Publisher	U.S. Agent
	Stockhausen-Verlag, U.S. 2832 Maple Lane Fairfax, VA 22030	
STOCKTON	Fred Stockton P.O. Box 814 Grass Valley, CA 95945	
STRONG	Stronghold Publications	ALEX.HSE.
STUD	Studio 224	STUDIO
STUDIO	Studio P/R, Inc.	CPP-BEL
STYRIA	Verlag Styria Schönaugasse 64 Postfach 435 A-8011 Graz Austria	
SUECIA	Edition Suecia	STIM
SUISEISHA	Suiseisha Editions	ONGAKU
SUMMIT	Summit Music Ltd. 38 North Row London W1R 1DH England	
SUMMY	Summy-Birchard Co. 265 Secaucus Road Secaucus, NJ 07096-2037	
SUOMEN	Suomen Säveltäjät ry (Society of Finnish Composers) Runeberginkatu 15 A SF-00100 Helsinki 10 Finland	
SUPPORT	Support Services 79 South Street P.O. Box 478 Natick, MA 01760	
SUPRAPHON	Supraphon Pulackeho 1 CS-112 99 Praha Czechoslovakia	FOR.MUS.DIST. (rental)
	Svenska Utbildningsförlaget Liber AB see LIBER	
SWAN	Swan & Co. P.O. Box 1 Rickmansworth, Herts WD3 3AZ England	ARCADIA
SWAND	Swand Publications 120 North Longcross Road Linthicum Heights, MD 21090	
	Swedish Music Information Center see STIM	
SYMPHON	Symphonia Verlag	CPP-BEL
TAUNUS	Taunus	HOFMEIS- TER-W
TECLA	Tecla Editions Preacher's Court, Charterhouse London EC1M 6AS England	
TEESELING	Muziekuitgeverij van Teeseling Buurmansweg 29B NL-6525 RV Nijmegen Netherlands	
TEMPLETN	Templeton Publishing Co., Inc.	SHAWNEE

Code	Publisher	U.S. Agent
TEMPO	Tempo Music Publications 3773 W. 95th Street Leawood, KS 66206	ALEX. HSE.
TEN TIMES	Ten Times A Day P.O. Box 230 Deer Park, L.I., NY 11729	
TENUTO	Tenuto Publications see also TRI-TEN	PRESSER
TETRA	Tetra Music Corp.	PLYMOUTH WESL (rental)
TFS	Things For Strings Publishing Co. P.O. Box 9263 Alexandria, VA 22304	
THOMAS	Thomas House Publications P.O. Box 1423 San Carlos, CA 94070	ANTARA
THOMI	E. Thomi-Berg Musikverlag Bahnhofstraße 94A D-8032 Gräfelfing Germany	
THOMP.	Thompson Music House P.O. Box 12463 Nashville, TN 37212	
THOMP.G	Gordon V. Thompson, Ltd. 29 Birch Avenue Toronto, Ontario M4V 1E2 Canada	OXFORD
TIEROLFF	Tierolff Muziek Centrale Markt 90-92 NL-4700 AA Roosendaal Netherlands	
TISCHER	Tischer und Jagenberg Musikverlag Nibelungenstraße 48 D-8000 München 19 Germany	
TOA	Toa Editions	ONGAKU
TONGER	P.J. Tonger, Musikverlag Auf dem Brand 3 Postfach 501865 D-5000 Köln-Rodenkirchen 50 Germany	
TONOS	Editions Tonos Ahastraße 7 D-6100 Darmstadt Germany	SEESAW
TOORTS	Muziekuitgeverij De Toorts Nijverheidsweg 1 Postbus 576 NL-2003 RN Haarlem Netherlands	
TRANSAT.	Éditions Musicales Transatlantiques 50, rue Joseph-de-Maistre F-75018 Paris France	PRESSER
TRANSCON.	Transcontinental Music Publications 838 Fifth Avenue New York, NY 10021	
TREKEL	Joachim-Trekel-Verlag Postfach 620428 D-2000 Hamburg 62 Germany	
TRI-TEN	Tritone Press and Tenuto Publications P.O. Box 5081, Southern Station Hattiesburg, MS 39401	PRESSER

Code	Publisher	U.S. Agent
TRIGON	Trigon Music Inc.	LORENZ
TRINITY	Trinity House Publishing	CRESPUB
TRIUNE	Triune Music, Inc. Box 23088 Nashville, TN 37202	LORENZ
TRN	TRN Music Publishers 111 Torreon Loop P.O. Box 1076 Ruidoso, NM 88345	
TRO	Tro Songways Service, Inc. 10 Columbus Circle New York, NY 10019	PLYMOUTH
	see also RICHMOND ORG.	
TROY	Troy State University Library Troy, AL 36081	
TUSKEGEE	Tuskegee Institute Music Press	KJOS
U.S.CATH	United States Catholic Conference Publications Office 1312 Massachusetts Avenue N.W. Washington, D.C. 20005	
UBER,D	David Uber Music Department Trenton State College Trenton, NJ 08625	
UFATON	Ufaton-Verlag	ORLANDO
UNICORN	Unicorn Music Company, Inc.	
UNION ESP.	Union Musical Española Carrera de San Jeronimo 26 Madrid 14 Spain	SCHIRM.G
UNISONG	Unisong Publishers	PRESSER
UNITED ART	United Artists Group	CPP-BEL PRESSER (rental)
UNITED MUS.	United Music Publishers Ltd. 42 Rivington Street London EC2A 3BN England	PRESSER
UNIV. ALA	University of Alabama Press Box 870380 Tuscaloosa, AL 35487-0380	
UNIV.CAL	University of California Press 2120 Berkeley Way Berkeley, CA 94720	
UNIV.CH	University of Chicago Press 5801 South Ellis Avenue Chicago, IL 60637	
UNIV.CR.	University College - Cardiff Press P.O. Box 78 Cardiff CF1 1XL, Wales United Kingdom	
UNIV.EVAN	University of Evansville Press P.O. Box 329 Evansville, IN 47702	
UNIV.IOWA	University of Iowa Press Iowa City, IA 52242	
UNIV.MIAMI	University of Miami Music Publications P.O. Box 8163 Coral Gables, FL 33124	PLYMOUTH
UNIV.MICRO	University Microfilms 300 North Zeeb Road Ann Arbor, MI 48106	

Code	Publisher	U.S. Agent
UNIV.MINN	University of Minnesota Press 2037 University Avenue S.E. Minneapolis, MN 55455	
UNIV.MUS.ED.	University Music Editions P.O. Box 192-Ft. George Station New York, NY 10040	
UNIV.NC	University of North Carolina Press P.O. Box 2288 Chapel Hill, NC 27514	
UNIV.OTAGO	University of Otago Press P.O. Box 56 Dunedin New Zealand	
UNIV.TEXAS	University of Texas Press P.O. Box 7819 Austin TX 78712	
UNIV.UTAH	University of Utah Press Salt Lake City, UT 84112	
UNIV.WASH	University of Washington Press Seattle, WA 98105	
UNIVER.	Universal Edition Bösendorfer Straße 12 Postfach 3 A-1015 Wien Austria	EUR.AM.MUS.
	Universal Edition (London) Ltd. 2/3 Fareham Street, Dean Street London W1V 4DU England	EUR.AM.MUS.
UNIVERSE	Universe Publishers 733 East 840 North Circle Orem, UT 84057	PRESSER
UP WITH	Up With People 3103 North Campbell Avenue Tucson, AZ 85719	LORENZ
VALANDO	Valando Music, Inc.	PLYMOUTH
VAMO	Musikverlag Vamö Leebgasse 52-25 Wien 10 Austria	
VAN NESS	Van Ness Press, Inc.	BROADMAN
VANDEN-RUP	Vandenhoeck & Ruprecht Theaterstrasse 13 Postfach 3753 D-3400 Göttingen Germany	
VANDERSALL	Vandersall Editions	EUR.AM.MUS.
VANGUARD	Vanguard Music Corp. 357 W. 55th Street New York, NY 10019	
VER.HUIS.	Vereniging voor Huismuziek Utrechtsestraat 77 Postbus 350 NL-3041 CT IJsselstein Netherlands	
VER.NED.MUS.	Vereniging voor Nederlandse Muziek- geschiedenis Postbus 1514 NL-3500 BM Utrecht Netherlands	
VEST-NORSK	Vest-Norsk Musikkforslag Nye Sandviksvei 7 N-5000 Bergen Norway	

Code	Publisher	U.S. Agent
VIERT	Viertmann Verlag Lübecker Straße 2 D-5000 Köln 1 Germany	
VIEWEG	Chr. Friedrich Vieweg, Musikverlag Nibelungenstraße 48 D-8000 München 19 Germany	LEONARD-US SCHIRM.G (rental)
VIKING	Viking Press, Inc. P.O. Box 4030 Church Street Station New York, NY 10261-4030	
VIOLA	Viola World Publications 14 Fenwood Road Huntington Station, NY 11746	
VOGGEN	Voggenreiter Verlag Viktoriastraße 25 D-5300 Bonn Germany	
VOGT	Musikverlag Vogt & Fritz Friedrich-Stein-Straße 10 D-8720 Schweinfurt Germany	
VOLK	Arno Volk Verlag	BREITKOPF-W
VOLKWEIN	Volkwein Brothers, Inc.	CPP-BEL
WADSWORTH	Wadsworth Publishing Co. 10 Davis Street Belmont, CA 94002	
WAGENAAR	J.A.H. Wagenaar Oude Gracht 109 NL-3511 AG Utrecht Netherlands	ELKAN,H
WAI-TE-ATA	Wai-te-ata Press Dept. of Music Victoria Univ. of Wellington Wellington, New Zealand	CAN.MUS. CENT.
WALKER	Walker Publications P.O. Box 61 Arnold, MD 21012	
WALKER MUS.PRO.	Walker Music Productions 643 Oenoke Ridge New Canaan, CT 06840	
WALTON	Walton Music Corp.	PLYMOUTH
WARNER	Warner Brothers Publications, Inc. 265 Secaucus Road Secaucus, NJ 07096	LEONARD-US SCHIRM.G (rental)
	Warner-Chappell Music 810 Seventh Avenue New York, NY 10019	
WATERLOO	Waterloo Music Co. Ltd. 3 Regina Street North Waterloo, Ontario N2J 4A5 Canada	
WEHMAN BR.	Wehman Brothers, Inc. Ridgedale Avenue Morris County Mall Cedar Knolls, NJ 07927	
WEINBERGER	Josef Weinberger Ltd. 12-14 Mortimer Street London W1 N 7RD England	BOOSEY NORTHRIDGE (partial)
	Josef Wienberger Neulerchenfelderstraße 3-7 A-1160 Wien Austria	
WEINTRAUB	Weintraub Music Co.	MUSIC

Code	Publisher	U.S. Agent
WELT	Welt Musik Josef Hochmuth Verlage Hegergasse 21 A-1160 Wien Austria	
WESL	Wesleyan Music Press P.O. Box 1072 Fort George Station New York, NY 10040	
WESSMAN	Wessmans Musikforlag S-620 30 Slite Sweden	STIM
WESTEND	Westend	PETERS
WESTERN	Western International Music, Inc. 3707 65th Avenue Greeley, CO 80634	
WESTMINSTER	The Westminster Press 925 Chestnut Street Philadelphia, PA 19107	
WESTWOOD	Westwood Press, Inc. 3759 Willow Road Schiller Park, IL 60176	WORLD
WHITE HARV.	White Harvest Music Publications P.O. Box 1144 Independence, MO 64051	
WIDE WORLD	Wide World Music, Inc. Box B Delaware Water Gap, PA 18327	
WIEN BOH.	Wiener Boheme Verlag GmbH Sonnenstraße 19 D-8000 München 2 Germany	
WIENER	Wiener Urtext Edition	EUR.AM.MUS.
WILDER	Wilder	MARGUN
WILHELM	Wilhelmiana Musikverlag see HANSEN-GER	
	Williams School of Church Music see WSCM	
WILLIAMSN	Williamson Music, Inc.	LEONARD-US
WILLIS	Willis Music Co. 7380 Industrial Highway Florence, KY 41042	
WILLSHIRE	Willshire Press Music Foundation, Inc.	WESTERN
WILSHORN	Wilshorn	HOPE
WILSON	Wilson Editions 13 Bank Square Wilmslow SK9 1AN England	
WIMBLEDN	Wimbledon Music Inc. 1888 Century Park East Suite 10 Century City, CA 90067	
WIND MUS	Wind Music, Inc. 153 Highland Parkway Rochester, NY 14620	KALMUS,A
WINGERT	Wingert-Jones Music, Inc. 2026 Broadway P.O. Box 419878 Kansas City, MO 64141	
WISCAS	Wiscasset Music Publishing Company Box 810 Cambridge, MA 02138	

Code	Publisher	U.S. Agent
WOITSCHACH	Paul Woitschach Radio-Musikverlag Grosse Friedberger Strasse 23-27 D-6000 Frankfurt Germany	
WOLF	Wolf-Mills Music	WESTERN
WOLLENWEBER	Verlag Walter Wollenweber Schiffmannstrasse 4 Postfach 1165 D-8032 Gräfelfing vor München Germany	KUNZEL
WOODBURY	Woodbury Music Co. 33 Grassy Hill Road P.O. Box 447 Woodbury, CT 06798	PRESSER (rental- partial)
WOODWARD	Ralph Woodward, Jr. 1033 East 300 South Salt Lake City, UT 84102	
WOODWIND	Woodwind Editions P.O. Box 457, Station K Toronto, Ontario Canada M4P 2G9	
WORD	Word, Incorporated P.O. Box 1790 Waco, TX 76703	
WORD GOD	The Word of God Music	SERVANT
WORLD	World Library Publications, Inc. 3815 Willow Road P.O. Box 2701 Schiller Park, IL 60176	
WORLDWIDE	Worldwide Music Services P.O. Box 995, Ansonia Station New York, NY 10023	RICHMOND ORG.
WSCM	Williams School of Church Music The Bourne Harpenden England	
WYE	WYE Music Publications	EMERSON
WYNN	Wynn/Music Publications P.O. Box 739 Orinda, CA 94563	
XYZ	Muziekuitgeverij XYZ P.O. Box 338 NL-1400 AH Bussum Netherlands	
YAHRES	Yahres Publications 1315 Vance Avenue Coraopolis, PA 15108	

Code	Publisher	U.S. Agent
YBARRA	Ybarra Music P.O. Box 665 Lemon Grove, CA 92045	
YORKE	Yorke Editions 31 Thornhill Square London N1 1BQ England	SCHIRM.EC
YOUNG WORLD	Young World Publications 10485 Glennon Drive Lakewood, CO 80226	
	Yugoslavian Music Information Center see MUSIC INFO	
ZALO	Zalo Publications & Services P.O. Box 913 Bloomington, IN 47402	FRANG
ZANIBON	G. Zanibon Edition Piazza dei Signori, 44 I-35100 Padova Italy	
ZEN-ON	Zen-On Music Co., Ltd. 3-14 Higashi Gokencho Shinjuku-ku Tokyo 162 Japan	EUR.AM.MUS MAGNA D
ZENEM.	Zenemukiado Vallalat	BOOSEY GENERAL
ZENGERINK	Herman Zengerink, Urlusstraat 24 NL-3533 SN Utrecht Netherlands	
ZERBONI	Edizioni Suvini Zerboni Via Quintiliano 40 I-20138 Milano Italy	BOOSEY (rental)
ZIMMER.	Musikverlag Zimmermann Gaugrafenstraße 19-23 Postfach 940183 D-6000 Frankfurt-am-Main Germany	
ZIMMER.PUBS.	Oscar Zimmerman Publications 4671 State Park Highway Interlochen, MI 49643-9527	
	The Zondervan Corp. see SINGSPIR	
ZURFLUH	Editions Zurfluh 73, Boulevard Raspail F-75006 Paris France	PRESSER

Advertisements

Index to Advertisers

The Diapason 187

Duke University Press—Opera Quarterly................................. 184

Leslie Music Supply Inc 183

Music Library Association—NOTES 188

Musicdata, Inc... 183

University of California Press—19th Century Music.................... 186

University of California Press—Journal of Musicology................. 179

University of California Press—Music Perception 181

University of California Press—Writing About Music.................. 185

University of Illinois Press—American Music 180

University of Texas Press—Latin American Music Review................ 182

If you are interested in any or all of the following —

Broadway show tunes, the origins of black spirituals, bluegrass sound tracks, white gospel music, jazz and the concert halls, the reed organ and Mark Twain, Scott Joplin, John Cage, Leopold Stokowski, Art Tatum —

American Music

is for you. "This first-class quarterly [covers] everything from early jazz to new compositions by John Cage. A section of record reviews provides long, signed reviews of Indian songs, brass music, and string quartets — in short, the whole scope of US musical heritage. The book reviews are equally extensive. Destined to be a core journal in all collections." — *Choice*

Individuals, $28.00 ($31.00 foreign) and institutions, $38.00 ($41.00 foreign). Quarterly. Published by the Sonneck Society and the University of Illinois Press. Complete sets of volumes still available.

Address subscriptions to

 UNIVERSITY OF ILLINOIS PRESS
54 E. Gregory Drive, Champaign, IL 61820

Revista de Música Latino Americana

Latin American Music Review

Editor: Gerard Béhague, University of Texas at Austin

LAMR is devoted exclusively to Latin America's diverse oral and written musical traditions. The journal features scholarly work from many countries and explores the music of many cultural groups including Puerto Ricans, Mexican Americans, Cubans and Portugese in the United States. This journal enhances the understanding of the music-making process as one of our most highly structured expressive behaviors.

In addition to noteworthy articles, **LAMR** makes a significant contribution to the musicological community with its *Book and Record Review* section. *Communications and Announcements* informs readers of key performances and organizational activities.

Volume 11, Number 2, Fall/Winter 1990

Gerhard Kubik, Drum Patterns in the *Batuque* of Benedito Caxias
James Robbins, The Cuban *Son* as Form, Genre, and Symbol
Steven Loza, Contemporary Ethnomusicology in Mexico
Alfonso Arrivillaga Cortés, La Música Trádicional Garifuna de Guatemala
Ricardo Miranda-Pérez, Muros Verdes and the Creation of a New Musical Space

Rates (one year): Individual/$16; Institution/$27
            Foreign add $2.50/subscription for postage
            Individual single copy rate/$9
            Institution single copy rate/$14
            Foreign add $1.50/copy for postage

University of Texas Press Journals, Box 7819, Austin, Texas 78713

WRITING ABOUT MUSIC

A Style Sheet from
the Editors of *19th-Century Music*
D. KERN HOLOMAN

How do you spell Rachmaninov? Where do you place the hyphen in Hofmannsthal if it breaks across two lines? Is it *premiere* or *première*? The answers and much more can be found in this new, essential resource for authors, students, editors, concert producers — anyone who deals with music in print. An expanded version of the style sheet for the well-known journal *19th-Century Music*, this small volume covers some of the thorniest issues of musical discourse: how to go about describing musical works and procedures in prose, the rules for citations in notes and bibliography, and proper preparation of such materials as musical examples, tables, and illustrations. One section discusses program notes, another explains the requirements of submitting manuscripts written on a word-processor. An appendix lists common problem words.

$7.50 per copy
University of California Press
2120 Berkeley Way
Berkeley, California 94720

For Visa or Mastercard charge orders,
use our Toll Free Number: 800-822-6657

THE DIAPASON

An International Monthly
Devoted to the Organ,
Harpsichord and Church Music

Official Journal of the
International Society for Organ History and Preservation

- *Feature articles by noted contributors*
- *Reviews of organ, choral and handbell music, books and recordings*
- *Stoplists and photos of organ installations*
- *Monthly calendar of events*
- *Extensive classified advertising section*

THE DIAPASON
380 Northwest Highway
Des Plaines, IL 60016
(708) 298-6622